Lecture Notes in Computer Science

Commenced Publication in 1973
Founding and Former Series Editors:
Gerhard Goos, Juris Hartmanis, and Jan van Leeuwen

John Derrick   Jüri Vain (Eds.)

Formal Techniques for Networked and Distributed Systems – FORTE 2007

27th IFIP WG 6.1 International Conference
Tallinn, Estonia, June 27-29, 2007
Proceedings

 Springer

Volume Editors

John Derrick
University of Sheffield
Department of Computer Science
Regent Court, 211 Portobello Street, Sheffield, S1 4DP, UK
E-mail: J.Derrick@dcs.shef.ac.uk

Jüri Vain
Tallinn University of Technology
Department of Computer Science
Ehitajate tee 5, 19086 Tallinn, Estonia
E-mail: vain@ioc.ee

Library of Congress Control Number: 2007928737

CR Subject Classification (1998): C.2.4, D.2.2, C.2, D.2.4-5, D.2, F.3, D.4

LNCS Sublibrary: SL 2 – Programming and Software Engineering

ISSN   0302-9743
ISBN-10   3-540-73195-4 Springer Berlin Heidelberg New York
ISBN-13   978-3-540-73195-5 Springer Berlin Heidelberg New York

Springer is a part of Springer Science+Business Media

springer.com

© IFIP International Federation for Information Processing 2007

Typesetting: Camera-ready by author, data conversion by Scientific Publishing Services, Chennai, India
Printed on acid-free paper   SPIN: 12079162   06/3180   5 4 3 2 1 0

Preface

These proceedings contain papers from the 27th FORTE conference. FORTE (Formal Techniques for Networked and Distributed Systems) is the joint international annual conference combining the former PSTV (Protocol Specification Testing and Verification) and former FORTE (Formal Description Techniques for Distributed Systems and Communication Protocols) conferences. The first PSTV conference took place in 1981, and the first FORTE took place in 1988. They were merged into one larger conference in 1996 and have run under the name of FORTE from 2001. The conference is a forum for presentation and discussion of the state of the art in theory, application, tools, and industrialization of formal methods. Over the years, FORTE has been held in numerous locations, and this is reflected by its recent history, with meetings in Pisa (Italy), Cheju Island (Korea), Houston (USA), Berlin (Germany), Madrid (Spain), Paris (France), Taiwan and now Tallinn, Estonia.

FORTE was sponsored by Working Group 6.1 of Technical Committee 6 (TC6) of the InternationalFederation for Information Processing (IFIP). Indeed FORTE is one of the flagship conferences of Working Group 6.1 (Architectures and Protocols for Distributed Systems), and covers many aspects of the main themes of WG6.1, namely, formal description techniques, open distributed systems, and quality of service. WG6.1 provided a Best Paper Award as well as funds to help student participation, and we are particularly grateful for this.

The 27th FORTE conference was held during June 26–29, 2007, in Tallinn (Estonia), in the historical building of the Brotherhood of the Black Heads. The focus of FORTE 2007 was on service-oriented computing and architectures using formalized and verified approaches. In addition to the classical protocol specification and verification problems, FORTE 2007 addressed the issues of composition of protocol functions and of algorithms for distributed systems.

We had a large number of submissions, and finally selected 22 papers from 67 submissions These papers covered a variety of topics, and the program was divided into eight sessions: Message Sequence Charts and SDL; Concurrency; Model Programs; Theory; Verification; Model Checking; Requirements and QoS; and Components. Our invited speaker this year was Susanne Graf, and it was a pleasure to welcome her to Tallinn and FORTE.

In a new departure for FORTE, this year's conference was co-located with TESTCOM/FATES.TESTCOM/FATES is itself a merger of two conferences: the 19th edition of the IFIP-sponsored International Conference on Testing of Communicating Systems and the seventh edition of the International Workshop on Formal Approaches to Testing of Software. TESTCOM is a series of international conferences addressing the problems of testing communicating systems, including communication protocols, services, distributed platforms, and middleware. FATES is an international series of workshops discussing the challenges of using rigorous and formal methods for testing software systems, such as communication-, control-, embedded-, administrative-, and Web-based software. The aim of the combined TESTCOM/FATES 2007 conference was to produce a forum for researchers, developers, testers, vendors, and users to review, discuss, and learn about new approaches, concepts, theories, methodologies, tools, and experiences in the field of testing of software and communicating systems. Testing is, of course, a subject which has had a strong presence in FORTE, and, in particular, in PSTV. It was a pleasure to welcome our colleagues in TESTCOM and FATES, and we ensured that testing-related papers were dealt with in TESTCOM/FATES rather than FORTE. We shared invited speakers, and Antti Huima of Conformiq Software gave the TESTCOM/FATES invited talk on "Implementing Conformiq Qtronic," which appears in the TEST-COM/FATES LNCS volume.

FORTE 2007 was organized jointly by the Department of Computer Science and the Institute ofCybernetics at Tallinn University of Technology. We owe special thanks to the local organization team, who provided a very smooth organization and excellent set of facilities. Juhan Ernits acted as Local Arrangements Chair, Monika Perkmann as Registrations Chair, and they were assisted by Jaagup Irve, Ando Saabas, Kristi Uustalu, and Tarmo Uustalu. Kirill Bogdanov (University of Sheffield, UK) acted as Publicity Chair. The proceedings are published by Springer in the *Lecture Notes in Computer Sciences* series, and we are grateful to all those at Springer for their help in producing the proceedings. Submissions were made through EasyChair. Finally, we would like to thank members of the FORTE Steering Committee, the Chair of WG6.1 Elie Najm, and the Chair of TC6 Guy Leduc for their support in preparing the event. Of course, special thanks go to all members of the Program Committee and additional reviewers for their efforts in compiling rigorous reviews.

June 2007   John Derrick
                                                                                                    Jüri Vain

Organization

FORTE is one of the flagship conferences of Working Group 6.1 (Architectures andProtocols for Distributed Systems) of IFIP.

Steering Committee

Gregor v. Bochmann (Canada) Tommaso Bolognesi (Italy)
John Derrick (UK) Ken Turner (UK)

Program Chairs

John Derrick (UK) Jüri Vain (Estonia)

Local Organization

Juhan Ernits Jaagup Irve
Monika Perkmann Ando Saabas
Kristi Uustalu Tarmo Uustalu
Kirill Bogdanov

Program Committee

G. V. Bochmann (Canada) K. Bogdanov (UK)
T. Bolognesi (Italy) M. Bravetti (Italy)
A. Cavalli (France) J. Colom (Spain)
J. Derrick (UK) L. Duchien (France)
C. Fidge (Australia) D. de Frutos-Escrig (Spain)
H. Garavel (France) R. Gotzhein (Germany)
S. Haddad (France) T. Higashino (Japan)
D. Hogrefe (Germany) G. J. Holzmann (USA)
P. Inverardi (Italy) C. Jard (France)
M. Kim (Korea) H. Koenig (Germany)
L. Logrippo (Canada) J. Magee (UK)
E. Najm (France) M. Nunez (Spain)
O. Owe (Norway) D. A. Peled (UK)
A. Petrenko (Canada) F. Plasil (Czech Republic)
J.-F. Pradat-Peyre (France) W. Reisig (Germany)
J.B. Stefani (France) K. Suzuki (Japan)
P. Traverso (Italy) K. Turner (UK)
H. Ural (Canada) J. Vain (Estonia)
F. Wang (Taiwan)

Additional Reviewers

Omar Alfandi
Marco Beccuti
Sergiy Boroday
Henrik Brosenne
Tomas Bures
Patryk Chamuczynski
Fida Dankar
Sami Evangelista
Johan Fabry
Dirk Fahland
Blaise Genest
Andreas Glausch
Nicolas Gorse
Hesham Hallal
Irfan Hamid
May Haydar
Seng-Phil Hong
Akira Idoue
Baik Jongmoon

Sungwon Kang
In-Young Ko
Fang-Chun Kuo
Marcel Kyas
Ivan Lanese
Frédéric Lang
Luis Llana
Niels Lohmann
Natalia Lopez
Stephane Maag
Wissam Mallouli
Radu Mateescu
Mercedes G. Merayo
Yutaka Miyake
Satoshi Nishiyama
Tomohiko Ogishi
Yolanda Ortega-Mallén
Patrizio Pelliccione
Isabel Pita

Tomas Poch
Olivier Ponsini
Cristian Prisacariu
Fernando Rosa-Velardo
Gerardo Schneider
Soonuk Seol
Wendelin Serwe
Ondrej Sery
Carron Shankland
Christian Stahl
Martin Steffen
Massimo Tivoli
Miguel Valero
Bachar Wehbi
Gianluigi Zavattaro
Marcel Kyas

Supporting Institutions

Institute of Cybernetics at Tallinn University of Technology

Department of Computer Science, Tallinn University of Technology

Table of Contents

Invited Talk

Contracts for BIP: Hierarchical Interaction Models for Compositional
Verification 1
Susanne Graf and Sophie Quinton

Technical Session 1. Message Sequence Charts and SDL

Thread–Based Analysis of Sequence Diagrams 19
Haitao Dan, Robert M. Hierons, and Steve Counsell

Recovering Repetitive Sub-functions from Observations 35
Guy-Vincent Jourdan, Hasan Ural, Shen Wang, and Hüsnü Yenigün

Specification of Timed EFSM Fault Models in SDL.................. 50
S.S. Batth, E.R. Vieira, A. Cavalli, and M.Ü. Uyar

Technical Session 2. Concurrency

Coordination Via Types in an Event-Based Framework 66
*Gianluigi Ferrari, Roberto Guanciale, Daniele Strollo, and
Emilio Tuosto*

Exploring the Connection of Choreography and Orchestration with
Exception Handling and Finalization/Compensation 81
Yang Hongli, Zhao Xiangpeng, Cai Chao, and Qiu Zongyan

Towards Modal Logic Formalization of Role-Based Access Control with
Object Classes 97
Junghwa Chae

Technical Session 3. Model Programs

State Isomorphism in Model Programs with Abstract Data
Structures 112
Margus Veanes, Juhan Ernits, and Colin Campbell

Composition of Model Programs 128
Margus Veanes, Colin Campbell, and Wolfram Schulte

Technical Session 4. Theory

New Bisimulation Semantics for Distributed Systems 143
David de Frutos-Escrig, Fernando Rosa-Velardo, and
Carlos Gregorio-Rodríguez

Event Correlation with Boxed Pomsets 160
Thomas Gazagnaire and Loïc Hélouët

A Simple Positive Flows Computation Algorithm for a Large Subclass
of Colored Nets 177
S. Evangelista, C. Pajault, and J.F. Pradat-Peyre

Technical Session 5. Verification

Improvements for the Symbolic Verification of Timed Automata 196
Rongjie Yan, Guangyuan Li, Wenliang Zhang, and Yunquan Peng

The DHCP Failover Protocol: A Formal Perspective 211
Rui Fan, Ralph Droms, Nancy Griffeth, and Nancy Lynch

Verifying Erlang/OTP Components in μCRL 227
Qiang Guo

Technical Session 6. Model Checking

Formal Analysis of Publish-Subscribe Systems by Probabilistic Timed
Automata 247
Fei He, Luciano Baresi, Carlo Ghezzi, and Paola Spoletini

Testing Distributed Systems Through Symbolic Model Checking 263
Gabriel Kalyon, Thierry Massart, Cédric Meuter, and
Laurent Van Begin

An Incremental and Modular Technique for Checking LTL\X Properties
of Petri Nets 280
Kais Klai, Laure Petrucci, and Michel Reniers

Technical Session 7. Requirements and QoS

Identifying Acceptable Common Proposals for Handling Inconsistent
Software Requirements 296
Kedian Mu and Zhi Jin

Formalization of Network Quality-of-Service Requirements 309
Christian Webel and Reinhard Gotzhein

Technical Session 8. Components

Robustness in Interaction Systems 325
Mila Majster-Cederbaum and Moritz Martens

Transactional Reduction of Component Compositions 341
Serge Haddad and Pascal Poizat

Specifying and Composing Interaction Protocols for Service-Oriented
System Modelling 358
João Abreu, Laura Bocchi, José Luiz Fiadeiro, and Antónia Lopes

Author Index 375

Contracts for BIP: Hierarchical Interaction Models for Compositional Verification*

Susanne Graf and Sophie Quinton

Verimag/CNRS and Verimag/ENS Cachan

Abstract. This paper presents an extension of the BIP component framework to hierarchical components by considering also port sets of atomic components to be structured (ports may be in conflict or ordered, where a larger port represents an interaction set with larger interactions). A composed component consisting of a set of components connected through BIP connectors and a set of ports representing a subset of the internal connectors and ports, has two semantics: one in terms if interactions as defined by the BIP semantics, and one in terms of the actions represented by external ports where the structure of the port set of the component is derived from the internal structure of the component.

A second extension consists in the addition of implicit interactions which is done through an explicit distinction of conflicting and concurrent ports: interactions involving only non conflicting ports can be executed concurrently without the existence of an explicit connector.

Finally, we define contract-based reasoning for component hierarchies.

1 Introduction

We aim at contract-based verification. We consider a framework where a system is a hierarchically structured set of *components*. For this purpose, we extend the component framework BIP [GS05,BBS06] and in particular its instance based on hierarchical connectors [BS07] to a framework for hierarchical components enriched with contracts as defined in the SPEEDS project [BC07+].

In the BIP framework, components interact through ports typed by *trig* or *sync* and are connected via hierarchical n-ary connectors which are typed in the same way as ports. In BIP, only connectors are hierarchical and we consider here also a hierarchical organisation of the components. Only leaf components represent models with behaviour explicitly defined by a transition system labelled by interactions. Originally, in BIP, atomic components have a sequential behaviour, but here they are not different from hierarchical components, at least from outside. We represent behaviours by an asynchronous transition system, and we may choose other, more efficient, representations in the future.

The behaviour of a hierarchical component is obtained as a composition of the behaviours of its leaf components depending on its internal connectors.

A hierarchical rich component (HRC) K has includes contracts, in the form of an assumption A and a guarantee G, represented both by transition systems. A

---

* This work has been partially financed by the project SPEEDS and the NoE Artist.

defines a property of the environment of K, and G a property of K that should hold if K runs in an environment guaranteeing A. We define a framework for verifying that components satisfy their contracts compositionally, by showing that the contracts associated with each component dominate the contracts of its inner components, and leaf components satisfy their contracts.

In Section 2, we define the syntactic framework of hierarchical components and connectors. We define the semantics in two steps. First, we say how to obtain a transition system defining the behaviour of a hierarchical component from the transition systems of its subcomponents and the connectors between them.

The BIP framework allows expressing synchronous and asynchronous interaction and execution, including blocking rendez-vous. Here, we only represent the abstract setting without taking into account data flow.

A main issue in embedded systems is absence of interference between transactions, possibly executed concurrently. Using BIP interactions, we can guarantee interference freedom by construction, as only non interfering transactions are executed concurrently. As a counterpart, it must be verified that interlock situations and violations of non functional requirements cannot occur; such bad situations can be reduced a deadlock in a modified system.

In Section 3, we describe how we intend to verify the consistency of a contract hierarchy. We adapt classical assume guarantee reasoning (see [RB+01] for a good overview) to our framework. To prove that a contract (A, G) of K dominates a composition of contracts $\{(A_i, G_i)\}$ — those of the subcomponents of K — it is sufficient to show that

- $A\|G_1\|....\|G_n \models G$; that is, if every K_i ensures its guarantee, then the composition ensures G, as long as the environment behaves according to A
- $A\|G_1\|...\|G_n \models A_i$ for all i; that is, each assumption A_i can be derived from A and the guarantees G_j of the peer components.

This proof rule is sound as A and G constrain different components. Notice that this proof rule is global at a given level of hierarchy, the gain comes from a hierachical structure with several layers.

In Section 4 we give a first idea on how we intend to achieve a more efficient and scalable handling of contracts. In particular, proving verification conditions is reduced to showing deadlock freedom of a transformed system, and we are presently developing efficient methods for such checks.

2   Specifications and Their Semantics

Definition 1 (Interaction set). *Let Σ be a set, and $<, \# \subseteq \Sigma \times \Sigma$ binary relations. Then $(\Sigma, <, \#)$, sometimes simply denoted Σ, is an interaction set if the following conditions hold:*

- *$<$ is a partial order relation;*
- *$\#$ is a non reflexive and symmetric conflict relation such that $a\#b$ and $a < c$ implies $c\#b$.*

For $a \in \Sigma$, we denote by $\uparrow a = \{b \in \Sigma \,|\, a < b\}$ the upwards closure of a in Σ and by $\downarrow a = \{b \in \Sigma \,|\, b < a\}$ the downwards closure of a in Σ and we extend these notions pointwise to sets and sequences.

Denote by $a \sqcup b$ the $c \in \Sigma$ representing the least upper bound of a and b, if it exists. Define the closure of Σ, $cl(\Sigma)$, the interaction set obtained by recursively adding elements $a \sqcup b$, whenever $a, b \in \Sigma$, not $a\#b$ and there exists no $c = a \sqcup b$ in the set.

Note that $a\#b$ may hold even if $a \sqcup b$ exists. Interactions for which $a \sqcup b$ exists can be connected, and only interactions for which not $a\#b$ can be executed concurrently.

Definition 2 (Interaction model). *An interaction set* $(\Sigma, <, \#)$ *is an interaction model if whenever a and b are not in conflict, that is not $a\#b$, then there exists an action $c \in \Sigma$ that is a least upper bound of a and b.*

Property 1. For an interaction set Σ, $cl(\Sigma)$ is an interaction model.

Here, we consider interaction models that are defined as closures of an interaction set Σ. And, we refer to $a \sqcup b \subseteq cl(\Sigma) \setminus \Sigma$ as an *implicit* interaction.

In particular, a union of interaction (sets) models is an interaction set. The product of interaction models, denoted $\Sigma_1 \cdot \Sigma_2 \ni a_1 \cdot a_2$ or $\Pi_i \Sigma_i \ni (a_1, ..., a_n)$, is already an interaction model.

In interaction models of [GS05], $a\#b$ holds (implicitly) whenever $a \cdot b = a \sqcup b$ is not explicitly defined. Here, we can avoid the definition of an explicit interaction $a \cdot b$ when a and b are independent; such interactions are implicitly captured by $a \sqcup b$ in $cl(\Sigma)$.

Definition 3 (Ports and component interfaces). *A* port *is defined as in [BS07] by a name and a type trig or sync, where $\{sync, trig\}$ form a boolean algebra with* sync $<$ trig.

For $\mathcal{P}$ a set of (typed) ports, an (external) interface Int *is the interaction model* $(cl(\mathcal{P}), <, \#)$ *defined by the interaction set* $(\mathcal{P}, <, \#)$.

The type of implicit ports $p \sqcup r \in (cl(Sigma) \setminus \Sigma)$ is the $\vee$ of the types of p and r.

Interactions on ports of type *sync* need to realise an interaction on a connector, the collaboration of peer components, whereas those of type *trig* can go alone for realising an interaction on a connector connecting this port to others. But they need not to be system wide *complete* interactions. We might explicitly distinguish complete ports as well.

Definition 4 (Component). *A component K is defined by $K = ((\mathcal{P}, <, \#), TS)$ where $TS = (Q, q_0, cl(\mathcal{P}), \rightarrow)$ is a transition system on $cl(\mathcal{P})$, such that*

- Q *is a set of states and $q_0 \subseteq Q$ an initial state.*
- $\rightarrow \subseteq Q \times cl(\mathcal{P}) \times Q$ *is a transition relation. For $a \in \mathcal{P}$, $en(a)$ is the set of states in which a is enabled $(\exists q' \in Q \,.\, q \xrightarrow{a} q')$. We use $\rightarrow$ also to represent a sequences of transitions, where $a; b; c : ...$ is used to denote a sequence of interactions. $\rightarrow$ must satisfy the following constraints: for $a, b \in cl(\mathcal{P})$,*

- *if not $a\#b$ and not $(a < b$ or $b < a)$, then $q \in en(a) \cap en(b)$ implies $(q \xrightarrow{a;b} q''$ implies $q \xrightarrow{b;a} q'')$ and $q \xrightarrow{a;b} q''$ implies $q \in en(a) \cap en(b)$*
- *$c = a \sqcup b \in \mathcal{P}$ implies $en(a) \cap en(b) = en(c)$ and $a < b$, implies $en(b) \subseteq en(a)$.*

We call $(\mathcal{P}, <, \#) = Int(K)$ the (external) interface of K and $TS = beh(K)$ the (external) behaviour of K.

That is transitions of independent interactions commute, and the transition sequence $\xrightarrow{a;b}$ is semantically equivalent to $\xrightarrow{b;a}$ and also to $\xrightarrow{a \sqcup b}$, where the latter may or may not exist as an explicit transition in TS. In the semantics, we will explicitly add transitions for $a \sqcup b$. That means, TS represents an asynchronous transition as defined in [WN95].

We now define hierarchical components as compositions of components, and we define two views for them:

- an *external view*, which represents a hierarchical component to the environment exactly as an atomic component, as just defined.
- an *internal view* which makes visible the internal *structure* composition structure, consisting of a set of components K_i and a composition model CM defined by a set of hierarchical connectors as in [BS07].
- the internal and external *interfaces* are linked via a relation $\dashv$ associating subsets of ports and connectors of CM with external ports in $\mathcal{P}$ such that $\dashv$ is a structure preserving relation between the interaction set Σ defined by CM and $(cl(\mathcal{P}), <, \#)$.
  The internal view of the *behaviour* is defined by transitions with labels Σ, whereas the external one has transitions labels in $cl(\mathcal{P})$.

We now define the internal view of a hierarchical component.

Definition 5 (Connector and hierarchical connector). *Let $(\mathcal{P} = \bigcup \mathcal{P}_i, <, \#)$ be the union interaction set induced by the set $\{Int_i = (\mathcal{P}_i, <_i, \#_i)\}$ of (external) component interfaces. A typed connector con on $\{Int_i\}$ consists of:*

- *a subset of $\mathcal{P}$ (also denoted con) such that $\forall p_m, p_n \in con$, the least upper bound $p_m \sqcup p_n$ is defined in the union interaction model but $p_m \sqcup p_n \notin \mathcal{P}$.[1]*
- *a type* sync *or* trig.

A connector $con = \bigcup_{l=1..n} p_i$ defines an interaction set $\Sigma = \mathcal{P} \cup act(con)$ where $act(con)$ contains:

- *if all $p_l \in con$ are of type* sync *(that is, all ports must synchronise), then, $p_1 \cdot ... \cdot p_n$ is the only element of $act(con)$*
- *if con contains also ports of type* trig, *then $act(con)$ contains all $p_1 \cdot ... \cdot p_m$ such that $\bigcup_{l=1..m} p_i \subseteq con$ and $\exists l \in \{1..n\}$ such that p_l of type* trig.

---

[1] We will see that this means that either interactions of p_n and p_m are independent, or $p_m \# p_n$, and then $p_m \sqcup p_n$ is a port defined somewhere "inside" one of the components K_i, but the connector $p_m \sqcup_i p_n$ is not in the interface of K_i.

The preorder relation $<'$ on Σ is derived from $<$ and $p <' p \cdot q$. The conflict relation $\#'$ contains $\#$ and $\sigma \# \sigma'$ if their definitions involve conflicting ports or ports related via $<$.

Extend act to all $p \in Ports$ by $act(p) = \{p\}$ and represent Σ by $\bigcup_{p \in \mathcal{P}} act(p) \cup act(con)$. Now, define an extended port set $\mathcal{P}_{con} = \mathcal{P} \cup \{'con'\}$, that is the set of original ports extended by a port con representing the connector con.

Now we can define hierarchical connectors. Let be $(Ports, <', \#')$ an interaction set and $(Ports \cup CON, <, \#)$ a port set extended by a set of connector ports CON. A hierarchical connector on $\mathcal{P}$ is a connector con on $Ports \cup CON$ that may connect both ports and connector ports. The definition of con must respect exactly the constraints imposed on a connector. But the interaction set $act(con)$ for $con = \bigcup_{i=1..n} p_i$ is defined by recursively instantiating connector ports by their interaction sets:

- if all $p \in con$ are of type sync, then $a_1 \cdot ... \cdot a_n$ such that $a_i \in act(p_i)$
- if con contains ports of type trig then, $a_1 \cdot ... \cdot a_m$ such that $\bigcup_{i=1..m} p_i \subseteq con$, $\exists l \in [1..m]$ s.th. p_l of type trig, and, as before $a_i \in act(p_i)$

The preorder and the conflict relations are defined exactly in the same way as for a connector. Now, the connector set can be extended by adding the hierarchical connector con as a new port for the definition of new hierarchical connectors.

We denote by $CM = (Int_i, (\Sigma, <, \#), \mathcal{P} \cup CON)$, the composition model defined by the set of (hierarchical) connectors CON, where Σ is the derived interaction set.

Property 2. Let $CM = (Int_i, (\Sigma, <, \#), \mathcal{P} \cup CON)$, be a composition model. Then, for all ports, including connectors con, $act(con)$ is an upwards-closed interaction set with maximal element $p_1 \cdot ... \cdot p_k$, such that $\{p_1, ..., p_k\}$ is the set of ports in $\mathcal{P}$ involved in con, obtained by recursively replacing connector ports by the set of ports in $act(p)$. Furthermore, $\forall p, r \in Ports \cup CON$:

- $p < r$ iff $act(p) \subseteq act(r)$
- $p \# r$ iff $\exists a \in act(p) \exists b \in act(r)$ such that $a \# b$

Thus, a connector defines in turn a port, and a hierarchical connector is a connector connecting ports and connectors. A port p defines an interaction set that is the singleton containing just p, and a connector has a recursively defined interaction set containing composed interactions.

Now, we want to turn a composition of a set of components defined by a composition model CM into a (hierarchical) component. For this purpose, we introduce a new (external) interface that makes available for further connection a subset of ports and connectors as new external ports. The internal view of such a component is defined by CM with interactions in Σ, whereas the external view defines interactions in terms of the new external ports.

In a constructive approach, one may keep all ports and connectors available for further composition. Here, we suppose given some global system architecture, such that it is enough to expose those ports which are used in some connection at some level of hierarchy.

We define a relation between ports and connectors and an external interface.

Definition 6 (Mapping an interaction set on a set of ports). *Let $CM = (Int_i, (\Sigma, <, \#), \mathcal{P} \cup CON)$ be a composition model for a set of components, and $\mathcal{P}'$ a set of new ports.*

A relation $\dashv \subseteq \Sigma \cup CON \times \mathcal{P}'$ defines an interaction-port association if

- *for each $p' \in \mathcal{P}'$ there is a $p \in \mathcal{P} \cup CON$ of the same type as p such that $a \dashv p'$ iff $a \in act(p)$*
- *for each $p \in \mathcal{P} \cup CON$, either there exists $p' \in \mathcal{P}'$ with $type(p) < type(p')$ and $act(p) \dashv p'$ (exported port) or $p \in CON$ is of type trig (internal port) or $p \in CON$ is the least upper bound of ports p_i mapped to $\mathcal{P}'$ where $\vee types(p_i) < type(p)$ (implicit $\sqcup$-port)*

Definition 7 (Hierarchical component). *Let K_i be a set of components with (external) interfaces $Int_i = (\mathcal{P}_i, <_i, \#_i)$ and $CM = (\{Int_i\}, (\Sigma, <, \#), \mathcal{P} = \bigcup \mathcal{P}_i \cup CON)$ a composition model, and $\mathcal{P}'$ a set of new ports and $\dashv$ a interaction-port association between Σ and $\mathcal{P}$.*

Then, a hierarchical component K is defined as $K = (\{K_i\}, CM, \dashv, Int)$. Where,

- *we call K_i its subcomponents.*
- *The composition model CM is sometimes referred to as the internal structure of K*
- *We call $(CM, \dashv, \mathcal{P}')$ the internal interface.*
- *$Int = (Ports', <', \#')$ which is derived from CM and $\dashv$ in a straightforward way is the external interface of K.*
- *The behaviour of K, $beh(K)$ is defined from the $beh(K_i)$ by composing them according to CM. The behaviour expressed in terms of interactions in Σ is the internal view, and the one obtained by replacing labels in Σ by labels in $\mathcal{P}'$ the external view of the behaviour of K. We define next how the behaviour of K is defined as a composition of behaviours of K_i.*
- *$(Int, beh(K))$ is the component K as seen from outside K.*

We do not require that K provides an explicit transition system expressing its behaviour. It is implicitly defined by the transition systems of its subcomponents.

We can show that the interaction model of a hierarchical component K does not depend on how atomic components are grouped into subcomponents; this is done by showing that a hierarchical component interface is equivalent to composition of all its atomic components obtained by hierarchically flattening K.

2.1 Semantics of Components

Now, we define the semantic transition system representing the behaviour of a component. First, we transform a transition system defining the behaviour of K into a semantic transition system, that will be interpreted as a set of traces and refusals. and then we compose semantic transition systems to behaviours of hierarchical components.

Definition 8 (Component Semantics). *Let K be a component with an external interface $Int = (Ports', <', \#')$, and if it is a hierarchical component, an internal interface $(CM, \dashv, \mathcal{P}')$ with $CM = (\{Int_i\}, (\Sigma', <, \#), \mathcal{P}')$.*

Suppose that for K, an asynchronous transition system $TS = (Q, q_0, \Sigma, \rightarrow)$ as in Definition 4 is given, where Σ may be either $cl(\Sigma)$ for the internal view of the behaviour and $cl(\mathcal{P}')$ for the external view of the behaviour.

The (internal or external) view of the semantics of K defined by TS, is $TS' = (Q, q_0, \Sigma, \rightarrow_*)$, where $\rightarrow_*$ is like $\rightarrow$, except that:

- *for $a, b \in \Sigma$, $a < b$ and such that $\forall p \in \mathcal{P}' . a \dashv p$ implies $b \dashv p$, then $q \xrightarrow{a} q'$ and $q \xrightarrow{a} q''$ implies $q \xrightarrow{a}_* q''$ but $q \not\xrightarrow{a}_*$.*
- *for $a, b \in \Sigma$, $a \sqcup b \in cl(\Sigma) \setminus \Sigma$, whenever $q \in en(a) \cap en(b)$ and $q \xrightarrow{a;b} q'$, then there is a new transition $q \xrightarrow{a \sqcup b}_* q'$*

If TS' defines the internal view of the semantics on $cl(\Sigma')$, then the external view is defined by $TS'' = (Q, q_0, cl(\mathcal{P}), \Rightarrow)$ obtained from TS' by

- *renaming internal interactions in $\sigma \in \Sigma'$ to external interactions $p \in \mathcal{P}'$: transitions $q \xrightarrow{\sigma}_* q'$ of TS' are replaced by a set of transitions $q \xrightarrow{p}_x q'$ for each p such that $\sigma \dashv p$. If σ is an internal interaction not related to a port in $\mathcal{P}$, then $q \xrightarrow{\sigma}_* q'$ is replaced by $q \xrightarrow{\tau}_x q'$.*
- *then by eliminating internal τ transitions: $\Rightarrow$ is the least transition relation such that $q \xRightarrow{p} q'$ if $\exists q''$ such that $q \xrightarrow{\tau^*;p;\tau^*}_x q''$.*

The maximal progress rule giving priority to larger interactions is as in BIP: In a global system, when $a < b$, then a b-transition has priority over an a-transition. We can apply the maximal progress rule partly in the semantics of a subsystem K, because the external ports define exactly the set of interactions that can be extended to larger connectors in the environment of K and our rule never eliminates all transitions corresponding to a given port, and the executability of an interaction in the global system does not depend on the particular interaction that is executed, only on the port.

The external view of the semantics of K forgets about the actual interactions due to the composition model defined on the subcomponents of K, and replaces interaction σ by port names p defined by $\dashv$.

Property 3. Due constraints on the selection of external ports, τ-transitions may always be executed independently of the environment of K, that is they are complete interactions in the sense of BIP.

We now define the behaviour of a hierarchical component.

Definition 9 (Semantics of a hierarchical component). *Consider a hierarchical component K defined by $K = (\{K_i\}, CM, \dashv, Int)$ with $Int(K_i) = (\mathcal{P}_i, <_i, \#_i)$, composition model $CM = (\{Int_i\}, (\Sigma, <, \#), \mathcal{P})$ and external interface $Int = (Ports', <', \#')$.*

Suppose that the external view of the behaviour of the components K_i is given by a transition system $TS_i = (Q_i, q_{i0}, cl(Ports_i), \rightarrow_i)$ satisfying the requirements of the relation $\rightarrow_*$ of Definition 8 (using the semantic transition relations simplifies the definition, but is not strictly required).

Then, the internal view of the behaviour of K can be defined through the transition system $TS = (Q, q_0, cl(\Sigma), \rightarrow)$, where

- *$Q = \Pi_{i=1..n}Q_i$ where we write $q = (q_1, ...q_n)$ for $q \in Q$; $q_0 = (q_{10}, ...q_{n0})$;*
- *$\rightarrow$ is the smallest transition relation such that:*
  - *if $\sigma = (x_{i_1}..x_{i_J}) \in \Sigma$ such that $\forall j, k \in J$, $x_{i_j} \in Ports_j$, and $\mathcal{P}_j \neq \mathcal{P}_k$, if $q_{i_j} \xrightarrow{x_{i_j}}_j q'_{i_j}$ for $j \in J$, then $(q_1, ...q_n) \xrightarrow{\sigma} (q''_1, ...q''_n)$ where $q''_i = q'_i$ for $i \in J$ and $q''_i = q_i$ for $i \notin J$.*
  - *if $q_i \xrightarrow{\tau}_i q'_i$ and internal transition of TS_i then $(q_1, ..q_i..q_n) \xrightarrow{\tau} (q_1, ..q'_i..q_n)$*

TS may then be transformed in turn into the two different semantic transition systems as in Definition 8.

In the following, we denote the resulting semantic transition system by $\|_{CM}TS_i$, respectively by $\|_{(CM,\mathcal{P})}TS_i$. If the parameters are clear from the context, we may omit them.

Notice that for $\sigma = p_1 \cdot ... \cdot p_k$ and $p_j, p_l \in \sigma \cap \mathcal{P}_i$, $p_j \sqcup p_l$ is always defined. In the definition above, we use the fact that the semantic transition relation of Definition 8 contains explicit transitions for such elements in $cl(\Sigma)$ which simplifies the definition of the product. Nevertheless, we could also directly compose the original asynchronous transition systems in which, for $a \sqcup b \in cl(\Sigma)$, the sequence $a; b$ is enabled implies both a and b are enabled.

Property 4. The transition system $TS'' = (Q, q_0, \Sigma, \Rightarrow)$ defining the external view of the behaviour of K is a again an asynchronous transition system as required by Definition 4. Moreover, TS'' and the transition system TS' defining the internal behaviour are bisimilar.

We derive now the set of traces and refusals used for the definition of the comparison of component behaviours and of the satisfaction relation.

Definition 10 (Traces and refusals). *Let K be hierarchical component $K = (\{K_i\}, CM, \dashv, Int)$ with $Int(K_i) = (\mathcal{P}_i, <_i, \#_i)$, composition model $CM = (\{Int_i\}, (\Sigma', <, \#), \mathcal{P})$ and external interface $Int = (Ports', <', \#')$.*

Let $TS = (Q, q_0, \Sigma, \rightarrow)$ represent either the internal or the the external view of the behaviour of K, depending on the choice of Σ.

- *$traces_\Sigma(K) \subseteq \Sigma^* :\downarrow \{w \in \Sigma^* \mid q_0 \xrightarrow{w}\}$ the downwards closure of the possible traces of K in terms of interactions in Σ, where we use the extension of $<$ on Σ to traces.*
- *$acc_\Sigma(K) \subseteq traces(K) \times 2^\Sigma : \{(w, \downarrow B) \in \Sigma^* \times 2^{\Sigma^*} \mid \exists q' \in Q \exists w'. w < w' \wedge q_0 \xrightarrow{w'} q' \wedge B = \{\sigma \mid q' \xrightarrow{\sigma}\}\}$. For each trace w, this defines the set of maximal downwards closed sets of interactions that may be enabled in K*

after some execution of an observable trace w. This is because internal transitions are under the control of the component and cannot be forbidden by a non cooperative environment.

- $\text{ref}_\Sigma(K) = \{(w, B') \setminus B) \mid B' \subseteq \Sigma, (w, B) \in \text{acc} \wedge B' \subseteq \Sigma \setminus B\}$ *is set defining all interaction sets that may be refused by K in some state after w; it is upwards closed with respect to $<$ and with respect to set inclusion.*
  $\text{REF}_\Sigma(K)$ *is the derived set of refused traces of the form $w; b$, where w is a trace of K and $b \in B$ where (w, B) is a refusal of K.*
- $\text{dead}_\Sigma(K) \subseteq \text{traces}_\Sigma(K) : \{w \mid (w, \emptyset) \subseteq \text{acc}(K)$. *These are deadlocks of K which can only be avoided by environments that avoid w.*

When TS on Σ defines the behaviour of K, we sometimes write $\text{traces}_\Sigma(TS)$ instead of $\text{traces}_\Sigma(K)$, etc.

We define traces to be downwards closed set and thus eliminate the effect of the application of the maximal progress rules. The maximal progress rule is useful for effective execution, whereas traces and refusals are used to define the satisfaction relation. Downwards closing traces normalises the behaviours, but does not change the properties satisfied by a component as *all* sequences must satisfy the property and smaller traces don't add inconsistencies.

For each trace w, exists a refusal set B if there exist in TS an execution for w', $w < w'$ to a state q in which a subset of B is refused. We consider traces, acceptance/refusal sets corresponding to an open semantics. E.g. $\text{acc}_\Sigma(K)$ contains any action that is accepted in K after w and that *may be accepted* in a system containing K. This open semantics is sufficient, as we want to verify contracts defining an assumption on the context of K, such that we always verify a closed system in which the open and the closed semantics coincide.

Definition 11 (Deadlock freedom of a specification). *Let K be a component. Then, K is (locally) deadlock free if $\text{dead}(K) = \emptyset$ that is, if there are no deadlocks in TS.*

Property 5. Let K be a component as above. Then, we have:

- $\overline{\text{traces}_\Sigma(K)}; \Sigma \cap \overline{\text{traces}_\Sigma(K)} \subseteq REF_\Sigma(K)$
- $\overline{\text{traces}_\Sigma(K)}; \Sigma \subseteq \text{traces}_\Sigma(K)$
- the traces, acceptance, refusals of the internal and the external semantics are the same up to the relabelling (and the abstraction) defined by $\dashv$.

2.2 Comparison and Satisfaction Relations

We define first a comparison relation between behaviours, adequate for the intended property verification, in the sense that smaller models satisfy more properties and larger properties are satisfied by more models.

More precisely, define a preorder that only compares transition systems with respect to some given interface. This, because we are interested in the comparison between components that only differ by their behaviour. Comparing components by comparing their interfaces is an equally interesting problem but not addressed in this paper.

Definition 12 (Preorder and equivalence on behaviours). *Let K be a component and $(\Sigma, <, \#)$ its internal or external interaction set. Let TS, TS' be transition systems on Σ.*

We define the preorder relation $\preceq$ on transition systems with respect to Σ:

- *$TS \preceq_\Sigma TS'$, iff*
  1. $\text{traces}_\Sigma(TS) \subseteq \text{traces}_\Sigma(TS')$ *and*
  2. $\text{ref}_\Sigma(TS) \supseteq \text{ref}_\Sigma(TS')_{|\text{traces}_\Sigma(TS)}$ *where*
     $\text{ref}_\Sigma(TS')_{|\text{traces}(TS)} = \{(w, B) \in \text{ref}_\Sigma(TS') \mid w \in \text{traces}_\Sigma(TS)\}$
- *$TS \approx_\Sigma TS'$ iff $TS \preceq_\Sigma TS'$ and $TS' \preceq_\Sigma TS$*
- *The preorder and equivalence on components K and K' with interaction set Σ and behaviour defined by TS, respectively TS' is straightforward:*
  $K \preceq K'$ *iff $TS \preceq_\Sigma TS'$ and $K \approx K'$ iff $TS \approx_\Sigma TS'$.*

Property 6 (Minimal and Maximal behaviours for an interface). Under the same conditions as previously, That is the interaction set $(\Sigma, <, \#)$ for one of the interfaces of a component

- the smallest component, called *dead$_\Sigma$* is defined by any transition system TS which has $\{\epsilon\}$ as its set of traces and refuses everything after ϵ. This means *dead* is locally deadlocking
- the largest component, called *true$_\Sigma$* is defined by any transition system TS which has Σ^* as its set of traces and an epty refusal set. Thus, *true* has no local deadlock but if no interaction in Σ is complete, then *true* may deadlock in a non cooperative environment
- For K defined by any behaviour TS
  - *dead$_\Sigma$* $\preceq K$
  - $K \preceq$ *true$_\Sigma$*

The satisfaction relation expresses that a component K with behaviour TS_K has a property expressed by a transition system TS where TS_K is defined on $(\Sigma, <, \#)$ and TS on $\Sigma' \subseteq \Sigma$.

Definition 13 (Property for an interaction model). *Let $(\Sigma, <, \#)$ be an interaction set and let TS be a transition system on Σ', a subset of Σ that is downwards closed in Σ. That is $(\Sigma', <, \#)$ is a sub interaction set of $(\Sigma, <, \#)$. Then, TS represents a property for Σ, respectively for a component with an interface having $(\Sigma, <, \#)$ as its interaction set.*

We compare now a behaviour TS defined on Σ with a property for Σ, TS' on Σ'. In order to do so, we simply project the traces and refusals of TS on Σ'.

Definition 14 (Projection). *Let be $(\Sigma, <, \#)$ an interaction set and $(\Sigma', <', \#')$ a sub interaction set. We define the projection $proj(TS, \Sigma')$ of TS to Σ', by*

- $\text{traces}_{\Sigma'}(TS) = \text{traces}_\Sigma(TS)_{|\Sigma'}$
- $\text{ref}_{\Sigma'}(TS) = \text{ref}_\Sigma(TS)_{|\Sigma'}$

We do not redefine the other semantic sets as they are derived from the set of traces and refusals.

Definition 15 (Satisfaction relation). *Let TS on $(\Sigma, <, \#)$ be the behaviour of a component K and TS_P on $(\Sigma', <, \#)$ a property P for Σ. Then,*

$$K \models P \quad iff \quad traces_{\Sigma'}(TS)) \cap \mathrm{REF}_{\Sigma'}(TS_P) = \emptyset$$

That is $K \models P$ if no trace w of K projected to Σ' may be refused by P.

Definition 16 (Composition of properties). *Let TS_i be transition systems on $(\Sigma'_i, <, \#)$ defining properties for $(\Sigma_i, <, \#)$.*

- *the product $TS_1 \|_{CM} TS_2$ obtained by a composition model yielding synchronisation on related actions and interleaving on others ($a \in \Sigma_1$ such that exists $b \in \Sigma_2$ and $a < b$ or $b < a$ typed* sync *and a and b are connected by a connector), where for $a < b$, the interaction $a \cdot b$ is then mapped by $\dashv$ to a in the external view, such that the product is a transition system on $\Sigma_1 \cup \Sigma_2$ which is a subinteraction set of Σ. We denote the product $TS_1 \wedge TS_2$.*
- *If TS_i are deterministic the product $TS_1 \|_{CM'} TS_2$ obtained by a composition model connecting as for $\wedge$ all related actions by a connector, but where all individual interactions are considered of type* trig, *and where $a < b$, the interaction $a \cdot b$ is then mapped by $\dashv$ to b in the external view. We denote the product $TS_1 \vee TS_2$.*

Notice that constructing $TS_1 \vee TS_2$ yields exactly the external choice $TS_1 \uplus TS_2$ of CSP [Hoa84] in the case that Σ_i are unstructured. Here we componentise properties for composition of properties. For effectively verifying properties we will also represent the satisfaction relation as a composition with a particular composition model.

Property 7. Let TS, TS' be transition systems on $(\Sigma, <, \#)$ defining components K, K' and $TS_P, TS_{P'}$ on $(\Sigma', <, \#)$ defining properties P and P' for Σ. Then,

- $K \models P$ implies $traces_{\Sigma'}(TS) \subseteq traces_{\Sigma'}(P)$ and $ref_{\Sigma'}(P) \subseteq ref_{\Sigma'}(TS)$, more precisely, every trace that may be refused by P must be refused by K.
- Call a component K deterministic if for each $w \in traces_{\Sigma}(K)$, $w \notin REF_{\Sigma}(K)$, which means that K has a deterministic transition relation.
  If TS_P is deterministic, then $K \models P$ if and only if $traces_{\Sigma'}(TS) \subseteq traces_{\Sigma'}(P)$.
- if $P \preceq P'$ and $K \models P$, then $K \models P'$, that is, larger properties are satisfied by more components.
- if $K' \preceq K$ and $K \models P$, then $K' \models P'$, that is, smaller components satisfy more properties, in particular, more deterministic components satisfy more properties.
- $K \models P$ implies $K \preceq P$

That is, the satisfaction relation implies trace inclusion in all cases and is identical to trace inclusion for deterministic specifications and the preorder $<$ on specifications is adequate for the satisfaction relation.

Now, let TS_i, TS_i' on $(\Sigma_i, <_i, \#_i)$ define the behaviour of components K_i, K_i' with interfaces $Int_i = (\mathcal{P}_i, <_i, \#_i)$, TS_P^i on $(\Sigma_1^i, <, \#)$ define properties P^i for Σ_1. Let CM be a composition model on Int_i and P a property on the interaction set Σ defined by CM. Then,

- if $K_1 \preceq K_1'$ then $K_1 \|_{CM} K_2 \preceq K_1' \|_{CM} K_2$, that is, $\preceq$ is preserved by composition.
- $K_1 \models P$, then $K_1 \|_{CM} K_2 \models P$ where $K_1 \|_{CM} K_2$ represents the internal view of the behaviour. On the external view of $K_1 \|_{CM} K_2$ holds the property P' obtained by mapping interactions in Σ onto external ports which is more abstract.
- $K_1 \models P^1$ and $K_1 \models P^2$ iff $K_1 \models P^1 \wedge P^2$, that is $\wedge$ represents indead conjunction on properties (for a common trace of P^1 and P^2, $P^1 \wedge P^2$ may refuse exactly those traces that may be refused by at least one of P^1 or P^2)
- $K_1 \models P^1$ or $K_1 \models P^2$ iff $K_1 \models P^1 \vee P^2$, that is, $\vee$ represents indead disjunction on properties

2.3   Decomposition and Recomposition of Components

A composition model is not a unique representation for an interaction set. As it is shown in [BS07], there are generally alternative ways of defining connectors on a set of ports for obtaining a given product interaction set Σ.

We have defined in addition the ports and connectors also the notion of interaction model of BIP, as it is simple and contains enough information for deriving several useful properties (it defines the semantics). A components may be defined by providing just an interaction model and a behaviour. The ports are only used for defining the way in which component may be composed.

[BS07] provides the following useful theorem allowing for a component K which is a composition of components K_i to construct the composition models allowing to represent K as a composition of one of the components K_i with a component K' grouping all the other subcomponents.

Consequently, this allows us obtaining for any component the composition model relating K_i to its environment.

Theorem 1 (Decomposition of a connector). *Given an arbitrary connector x and a port p it is always possible to construct a connector $\tilde{x}$ such that x defines the same interaction model as $\tilde{x}$ and $\tilde{x}$ is of the form $(p, con_1, ...con_k)$ and p does not appear in $con_2, ...con_n$.*

The same transformation can be done for any set of ports

This allows the decomposition of a global interaction model on an interaction model of on each of its parts. It yields then a composition model for each part and a global composition models composing the parts. This is enough for defining in a closed system the interaction model between any component in the component hierarchy and "the rest of the system".

Definition 17 (A component and its environment). *Let $Int(K) = (\mathcal{P}, <, \#)$ be the external interface of a component K.*

Then suppose that the environment is given in the form of a component K_E with interface $Int(K_E) = (\mathcal{P}_E, <_E, \#_E)$ and no internal structure such that each port in $\mathcal{P}_E$ is connected to system ports in $\mathcal{P}$ via a set of connectors Con on $\mathcal{P} \cup \mathcal{P}_E$, defining the the composition model between K and its environment K_E.

Then, the internal structure of the component S_K obtained simply by composing K with its environment K_E according to definition 7 as $CM_{EK} = (\{K, E_K\}, (\Sigma, <, \#), Ports \cup \mathcal{P}_E \cup Con)$.

We can now also define a composition model relating any subcomponent K_i of K to its environment K_i^E which is defined by the peer K_j and K_E and the given composition models.

As the internal structure of K is of the form $(\{K_i\}, CM, \dashv, \mathcal{P})$, where the internal composition model is $CM = (\{Int_i\}, (\Sigma, <, \#), \bigcup_i \mathcal{P}_i \cup \mathcal{P}_{CON})$.

Then, due to the theorem above, for any given $i \in I$ one can define a composition model CM' of the form $CM' = (\{K_i, i \in I\} \cup \{K_E\}, (\Sigma', <, \#), \mathcal{P}_{CM'})$ where

- *the set of ports $\mathcal{P}_{CM'}$ is a set of ports defined by a union of 3 sets of connectors: $\mathcal{P}_i$, $CON_{Ei} \subseteq \bigcup_{j \neq i} \mathcal{P}_j \cup \mathcal{P}_E$ a hierarchical set of connectors connecting only ports not in $\mathcal{P}_i$, and finally a hierarchical set of connectors CON_{i-Ei} connecting ports in $Ports_i$ with ports in CON_{Ei}*
- *the interaction set Σ' is obtained according to definition 7 is IS*
- *the definitions of $<'$, $\#'$ and $\dashv$ are straightforward*

We define then an external interface of a component K_{Ei}, $Int(K_{Ei}) = (\mathcal{P}_{Ei}, <, \#)$ representing the elements of CON_{Ei} used by some connector of CON_{i-Ei} and $<$ and $\#$ are again straightforward.

Then, the component S_K can also be defined by composing K_i with its environment K_{Ei} and the corresponding composition model is defined as $CM_{K_i} = (\{K_i, K_{Ei}\}, (\Sigma_{Ei}, <_{Ei}, \#_{Ei}), Ports_i \cup \mathcal{P}_{Ei} \cup CON_{i-Ei})$ such that Σ_{Ei} is obtained by renaming interactions of Σ in terms of $Ports_{Ei}$.

3 Components Enriched with Contracts and Compositional Verification

3.1 HRC: Hierarchical Components Enriched with Contracts

First, we introduce the notion of Rich Component (HRC), similar to the one introduced in [BC07+,BB+07] but adapted to our hierarchical BIP components: the structure of an HRC K is the structure of a component, enriched with a composition model with its environment K_E as defined in Definition 17 and a set of contracts.

A contract is a pair of transition systems (A, G), defined on $\mathcal{P}_K$, respectively $\mathcal{P}_E$. A expresses an assumption of the behaviour of the environment and G

defines a property that K must — or is assumed to — satisfy under the condition that the environment behaves according to A.

A rich component has, exactly as a component, a behaviour that is either explicitly given for a leaf component or implicitly defined by the set of leaf components. In the context of contract based reasoning, we want to be able to do some reasoning without having already defined all the leaf components and/or their behaviour.

Definition 18 (Assumption, Guarantee, Contract). *Let be $Int = (\mathcal{P}, <, \#)$ an interface. A contract for K is given by a pair (A, G) where A and G are transition systems with labels in $\mathcal{P}$; A is called the* assumption *and G is called the* guarantee.

Definition 19 (Rich component (HRC)). *A rich component is of the form* $((\{K_i\}, CM, \dashv, \mathcal{P}_K), (\mathcal{P}_E, CM_{EK}), CONTR)$ *or* $((\mathcal{P}_K, <, \#), (\mathcal{P}_E, CM_{EK}), CONTR)$ *where*

- $(\mathcal{P}_E, CM_{EK})$ *is a set of ports representing the environment and the composition model connecting K to its environment as defined in Definition 17; if K is defined as a part of a larger system then the second construction of this definition is used, whereas if K is a unique outermost component described, then CM_{EK} is given.*
- $\{K_i\}$ *are HRC and $(\{Int_i\}, CM, \dashv, \mathcal{P})$ is defined like an internal interface of a hierarchical component or alternatively, $((\mathcal{P}, <, \#), TS)$ defines an atomic component without a defined substructure.*
- $CONTR$ *is a set of contracts of the form (A_i, G_i) where A_i is defined on $\mathcal{P}_E$ and G_i is defined on $\mathcal{P}$.*

A rich component K is defined by a structure $str(K)$ and by $beh(K)$ defining a transition system on the external interface $(\mathcal{P}_K, <, \#)$ of K.

Notice that for assume/guarantee reasoning, we are mainly interested in the structure of the component K, whereas the behaviour of K may not always be given explicitly.

Given the structure of an HRC K we can now consider the environment K_E of K like any other component. How a valid K_E can be constructed is defined in Section 2.3.

3.2 Compositional Verification of HRC

We need to define a satisfaction relation, defining what it means for a contract (A, G) to be satisfied by K, and a dominance relation such that (A, G) dominates (A', G') if all components satisfying (A', G') satisfy also (A, G). We use the dominance relation for showing that a contract (A, G) associated with a hierarchical component dominates the implicitly defined contract defined by a set of contracts (A_i, G_i) associated with the subcomponents of K.

Intuitively, K satisfies a contract (A, G) if in the system defined by the environment of E_K and K, where the environment behaves like A, this guarantees that K satisfies the property G.

We consider here the case of the satisfaction of a single contract. Multiple contracts can be validated independently of each other.

Definition 20 (Satisfaction of contracts). *Let K be a rich component with an external interface $Int_K = (\mathcal{P}, <, \#)$ and K_E an environment with $Int_E = (\mathcal{P}_E, <, \#)$ and composition model CM_{EK} between K and E and a behaviour representing a transition system TS on $\mathcal{P}$. Then, K satisfies its contract (A, G), denoted $K \models (A, G)$ if*

$$S_K \models G$$

For S_K defined as the composition via CM_{EK} of the components K and K_E defined by the behaviour A.

According to the satisfaction relation of definition 15, as G is defined as a property on the interaction set of K, and the behaviour of S_K is of the form $A\|_{CON}TS$ on the composition of the interaction set of K and E_K, $A\|_{CON}TS \models G$ means that the projection of $A\|_{CON}TS$ onto the interaction set of K satisfies G.

Theorem 2. *Let K be a rich component with an external interface $Int_K = (\mathcal{P}, <, \#)$ and K_E an environment with $Int_E = (\mathcal{P}_E, <, \#)$ and composition model CM_{EK} between K and E. Suppose that the transition system TS on $\mathcal{P}$ represents the implementation of K.*

If K satisfies its contract (A, G), then

$$A\|_{CM_{EK}}TS \preceq_{\mathcal{P}} A\|_{CM_{EK}}G$$

In the particular case that G is deterministic, we have for $TS = G$ that $K \models (A, G)$

proof sketch: *Noting that the behaviour of S_K is equal $A\|_{CM_{EK}}TS$, we can conclude that if the system defined by $A\|_{CM_{EK}}TS$ satisfies property G then $A\|_{CM_{EK}}TS \preceq_{Int_K} G$ by property 7; together with $S_K \preceq_{Int_E} A$ which is due to monotonicity, this allows to derive $A\|_{CM_{EK}}TS \preceq A\|_{CM_{EK}}G$. Using the property saying that $G \models G$ for deterministic G and the fact that $A\|TS \preceq_{Int_K} G$ one obtains the second assertion.*

This important property expresses the fact that G defines an upper bound on all components that satisfy G in any environment satisfying A; and it allows the use of a simple proof rule for verifying contract dominance.

Definition 21. *Let K be a hierarchical rich component with a structure of the form $((str(K_i), (CM, \dashv \mathcal{P}_K), (\mathcal{P}_E, CM_{EK}), (A, G))$ such that each $str(K_i)$ defines a contract (A_i, G_i). Then (A, G) dominates the set of contracts $\{(A_i, G_i)\}$ in the context of K iff*

$$\forall i \,. \, beh(K_i) \models (A_i, G_i) \quad implies \quad beh(K) \models (A, G)$$

Remember that the behaviour of K is defined as the composition of the transition systems defining the behaviour of the K_i according to the composition model CM and renaming the resulting interactions to port names in $\mathcal{P}$ according to $\dashv$.

In [BB+07] an explicit contract (A', G') is associated with the set $\{(A_i, G_i)\}$ and dominance is then defined as a relationship between the contracts (A', G') and (A, G) which are defined on the same alphabets. There, the semantics is defined in terms of sets of traces and the contract (A', G') is defined using negations (complements of trace sets); here, we show the soundness of a similar proof rule, without using negation.

Theorem 3. *Let K be a hierarchical rich component with a structure of the form $((str(K_i), (CM, \dashv \mathcal{P}_K), (\mathcal{P}_E, CM_{EK}), (A, G))$ such that $str(K_i)$ has a contract (A_i, G_i).*

Then (A, G) dominates the set of contracts $\{(A_i, G_i)\}$ in the context of K if the following conditions hold:

- *for the component K obtained by choosing $beh(K_i) = G_i$, we have $K \models (A, G)$*
- *for all i, the component S_K defined as a composition of K_i with K_{Ei} obtained from $\mathcal{P}_{Ei}$ and Definition 17, and by choosing A for the behaviour of E_K and G_j for the behaviours of the K_j, for $j \neq i$, we have*

$$S_K \models A_i$$

meaning that the assumption A_i is not more restrictive than the one defined by the environment of K_i as defined by the guarantees of the pairs and the assumption A of K.

Proof sketch: *The fact that the K_i satisfying (A_i, G_i) are smaller than G_i in an environment granting A_i (Theorem 2), guarantees by the first verification condition that that for K_i having as behaviour the projection of $A_i \| G_i$ as previously defined, one has $K \models (A, G)$.*

The second condition guarantees that the restriction to environments satisfying A_i can be eliminated as A_i is already guaranteed by A and by G_j; indeed, the second item implies that $A \| (A_1 \| G_1)_p \| ... \| (A_n \| G_n)_p$ is equivalent to $A \| G_1 \| ... \| G_n$, where the parallel composition is the one respecting the interaction model and $(A_i \| G_i)_p$ represents the interpretation of the result in the interface of K_i.

4   Handling Verification Conditions Contructively

We have defined a framework for architecture and system modelling based on the BIP framework and we have adapted it for the use in the context of compositional verification, where components are annotated with contracts specifying assumptions on the environment and derived a set of verification conditions for showing the correctness of a contract hierarchy.

Contracts state properties on a specific component under some condition on its environment. We have defined verification conditions which are small if each component has only a small number of subcomponents. In general, this is unlikel to happen as component must on the other hand be units which are not too tightly coupled with their environment in order to make compositional verification feasible.

The verification conditions involve the verification of properties on compositions of component behaviours. $K \models P$ holds if the traces of K cannot be refused by P which means that $K \not\models P$ if for an appropriate composition model, the composition $K \| P$ can reach a deadlock state.

Together with the fact that we want to guarantee deadlock freedom of individual components and globally of the system, this means that methods for showing absence of deadlock are an important issue.

In [GS03,GG$^+$07] we have started to study specific methods for showing deadlock freedom without building products for the BIP framework which are currently being implemented and experimented.

Even if these methods avoid the exploration of the global state graph, they are global and they compute approximative results. Combining such methods or slightly more costly and more precise methods with a compositional approach will hopefully lead to interesting results.

We have defined components which have in their interface not only the possible interactions and a set of contracts, but we define a notion of conflict and dependence on the set of ports of the components themselves defining corresponding properties of the transition system which can be exploited for obtaining efficient means to explore asynchronous transition systems by using either partial order reduction or maximal progress rules. We also envisage to use a Petrinet like representation of asynchronous transition systems, for example UML activity diagrams to represent concurrency in a more explicit manner.

The abstraction defined by the use of typed connectors is particularly intersting if we succeed to construct on-the-fly reductions of composed behaviours. But we envisage also an approach based on incremantal contruction and abstraction as in [GLS96].

References

BB$^+$07. Badouel, E., Benveniste, A., Bozga, M., Caillaud, B., Constant, O., Josko, B., Ma, Q., Passerone, R., Skipper, M.: SPEEDS meta-model syntax and draft semantics. Deliverable D2.1c (February 2007)

BBS06. Basu, A., Bozga, M., Sifakis, J.: Modeling heterogeneous real-time systems in BIP. In: 4th IEEE International Conference on Software Engineering and Formal Methods (SEFM06), Invited talk, September 11-15, 2006, Pune, pp. 3–12 (2006)

BC07$^+$. Bozga, M., Constant, O., Skipper, M., Ma, Q.: SPEEDS meta-model syntax and static semantics. Deliverable D2.1b (January 2007)

BS07. Bliudze, S., Sifakis, J.: The algebra of connectors structuring interaction in BIP. Techreport, Verimag (February 2007)

RB$^+$01. de Roever, W.P., de Boer, F., Hannemann, U., Hooman, J., Lakhnech, Y., Poel, M., Zwiers, J.: Concurrency Verification: Introduction to Compositional and Noncompositional Methods. In: Nr 54 in Cambridge Tracts in Theoretical Computer Science, Cambridge University Press, Cambridge (2001)

GG+07. Gößler, G., Graf, S., Majster-Cederbaum, M., Martens, M., Sifakis, J.: An approach to modeling and verification of component based systems. In: van Leeuwen, J., Italiano, G.F., van der Hoek, W., Meinel, C., Sack, H., Plášil, F. (eds.) SOFSEM 2007. LNCS, vol. 4362, Springer, Heidelberg (2007)

GS03.   Gößler, G., Sifakis, J.: Component-based construction of deadlock-free systems. In: Pandya, P.K., Radhakrishnan, J. (eds.) FST TCS 2003: Foundations of Software Technology and Theoretical Computer Science. LNCS, vol. 2914, Springer, Heidelberg (2003)

GS05.   Goessler, G., Sifakis, J.: Composition for component-based modeling. Science of Computer Programming, pp. 161–183 (March 2005)

GLS96. Graf, S., Lüttgen, G., Steffen, B.: Compositional Minimisation of Finite State Systems using Interface Specifications. In: Formal Aspects of Computation, vol. 8, Appeared as Passauer Informatik Bericht MIP-9505 (1996)

Hoa84. Hoare, C.A.R.: Communicating Sequential Processes. Prentice-Hall, Englewood Cliffs (1984)

WN95.   Winskel, G., Nielsen, M.: Models for concurrency, vol. 4. Oxford Univ. Press, Oxford (1995)

Thread–Based Analysis of Sequence Diagrams

Haitao Dan, Robert M. Hierons, and Steve Counsell

School of Information Systems, Computing & Mathematics,
Brunel University,
Uxbridge, Middlesex UB8 3PH, UK
{hai.dan,rob.hierons,steve.counsell}@brunel.ac.uk

Abstract. Sequence Diagrams (SDs) offer an intuitive and visual way of describing expected behaviour of Object Oriented (OO) software. They focus on modelling the method calls among participants of a software system at runtime. This is an essential difference from its ancestor, basic Message Sequence Charts (bMSCs), which are mainly used to model the exchange of asynchronous messages. Since method calls are regarded as synchronous messages in the Unified Modelling Language (UML) Version 2.0, synchronous messages play a significantly more important role in SDs than in bMSCs. However, the effect of this difference has not been fully explored in previous work on the semantics of SDs. One important aim of this paper is to identify the differences between SDs and bMSCs. We observe that using traditional semantics to interpret SDs may not interpret SDs correct under certain circumstances. Consequently, we propose a new method to interpret SDs which uses thread tags to deal with identified problems.

Keywords: Sequence Diagram, Semantics, Partial Orders, Concurrency, Object Oriented, Thread tags.

1 Introduction

In the Unified Modelling Language (UML) Version 2.0, a Sequence Diagram (SD) is a type of Interaction Diagram (ID), as are Communication Diagrams, Interaction Overview Diagrams and Timing Diagrams [OMG05]. Although an SD is a second-level modelling language in UML 2.0, it is the most commonly used type of notation in ID and is regarded as the most popular UML behaviour modelling language.

In Object Oriented (OO) software, SD-based specifications are usually used to capture system requirements, model function logic or as automatic test models. An SD is a versatile tool that can be used in many parts of the OO software development process; its ancestor, the basic Message Sequence Chart (bMSC), developed in the early 1990s, was designed for modelling communication systems. As a consequence of the difference between application domains, minor changes were introduced into the first version of UML.

Due to their similarity, the semantics developed for bMSC have been naturally inherited by SD. In particular, those based on partial order theory have been

J. Derrick and J. Vain (Eds.): FORTE 2007, LNCS 4574, pp. 19–34, 2007.
© IFIP International Federation for Information Processing 2007

widely adopted in both research and industry, because they are conceptually straightforward when compared with counterparts such as process algebra based semantics [MR94]. Henceforth, we use the term 'traditional semantics' to refer to partial order based semantics.

Although the syntax of SDs and bMSCs are almost identical, we argue that small differences between them may cause significant semantic variations between the two. That is, traditional semantics may not interpret SDs correctly. More specifically, SDs are often used to model OO software systems in which communication is synchronous; bMSCs are normally used in asynchronous message based communication systems. To model communication systems, bMSCs assume that all participants are running concurrently and the messages between them are always asynchronous. On the other hand, the messages between lifelines of SDs are likely to be synchronous and there is no longer a one-to-one correspondence between lifelines and threads of control. The differences described above imply that when traditional semantics are applied on some SDs, it can result in unintentional semantics. To solve this problem, we propose a new method for interpreting sequence diagrams.

To find a proper method of interpreting SDs, we first attempt to solve the problem using only the meta-classes from UML 2.0. We argue that existing UML meta-classes cannot be used because, unlike bMSCs, lifelines are generally orthogonal to threads. This implies that a thread may involve multiple lifelines and a lifeline may involve multiple threads. We thus introduce *thread tags* into SDs and provide an informal semantics for interpreting SDs.

In order to simplify the inference process, we only consider the most important parts of SDs and bMSCs related to our proposed semantics. We assume that a complete semantics based on our work can then be induced.

1.1   Related Work

When discussing the semantics of SDs, it is worth reviewing previous research into bMSCs. Mauw and Reniers [MR94] used a process algebra to interpret the semantics of bMSC and this approach has been adopted as the standard semantics for bMSC [IT98]; Grabowski et al. [GGR93] proposed petri-net based semantics for bMSC; Ladkin and Leue [LL93] used Büchi Automata to capture the meaning of bMSC; Jonsson and Padilla [JP01] used Abstract Execution Machines to describe bMSC semantics and at the same time, considered inline expressions and data in bMSCs; Alur et al. [AHP96] were the first to use labelled partially-ordered structures to formalize bMSCs.

The increased popularity of the UML has led to the semantics of SDs receiving more attention. In UML 2.0, SDs were significantly revised to allow adequate modelling of complex software system based on the new version of bMSC [OMG05]. Although UML 2.0 tried to provide semantics for every modelling language using a meta-model [Sel04], SDs have only been assigned a behaviour informal semantics according to traditional bMSC semantics. In [Sto03, HHRS05, CK04], formal trace based semantics for SDs were provided and [LS06] solved the semantic problem using an automata-theoretic approach. In [GS05], safety and liveness properties were used for distinguishing valid behaviours from invalid. Finally, Harel and Maoz [HM06] proposed Modal UML Sequence Diagrams (MUSD), an extension of SDs based on the approach used in Live Sequence Charts (LSCs) to extend bMSCs [DH01]. These newly developed SD semantics were based on different kinds of bMSC semantics. The bMSC semantics were revised to conform to the intended semantics of UML 2.0 with added semantics for the new meta-classes of UML 2.0 (eg., for CombinedFramgment and InteractionOperator).

Previous work has been largely based on bMSC semantics, the core ideas of which are commonly derived from corresponding bMSC semantics directly. Although the notation used to describe SDs and bMSCs are almost identical, the differences between them do affect how the diagrams are interpreted. For instance, a lifeline in UML 2.0 no longer represents a process. If we still interpret it as bMSC's instance, the correct concurrency information will not be deduced from an SD in certain circumstances. This observation is the motivation for the work described in this paper.

An interesting variation on mainstream bMSCs are LSCs which use a two-layer approach to distinguish mandatory and provisional behaviour in scenarios. Similar to our approach, the semantics of LSCs consider the problem caused by synchronous method calls. It assumes that a synchronous message is received before the next event on the instance which sent the message. This simple solution addressing the additional orders induced by synchronous messages is sufficient for LSCs, but it may be problematic when applied to SDs, because lifelines of SDs no longer contain a thread of control.

The remainder of this paper is structured as follows. A comparison between the SD and bMSC standards is presented and the traditional semantics are introduced informally in Section 2. In Section 3, some possible problems that can arise when using the traditional semantics to interpret SD are described. In Section 4, two unsuccessful solutions that use UML 2.0 meta-classes are analysed. We argue that there are no meta-classes in UML 2.0 that can achieve correct semantics for SDs. After the analysis, inference rules for interpreting SD based on thread tags are proposed in Section 5. Finally, in Section 6, our work is concluded and potential future directions described.

2   Preliminary

This paper is motivated by the observation that the existing semantics of SDs have problems when interpreting SDs with synchronous messages. To illustrate the problems, SD and bMSC standards are first compared to reveal their differences; second, the traditional semantics of SD are introduced based on bMSC partial order semantics.

2.1   The Difference Between SD and bMSC

Both SD and bMSC are complicated modelling languages and both standards use meta-methods to define themselves as hierarchies of meta-classes. We compare the two languages according to the selected constructs of *Lifeline* (*instance* in bMSC), *Message, MessageOccurrenceSpecification* (*event* in bMSC) and *ExecutionSpecification* (*method* and *suspension* in bMSC)[1].

In UML 2.0 meta-models, an SD is decomposed into *Lifelines* and *Messages*. A *Lifeline* commonly represents an instance of a class or component in an OO program and it contains different kinds of *OccurrenceSpecifications. OccurrenceSpecification* is an equivalent concept to *event* in bMSC. Two main kinds of *OccurrenceSpecification* are *MessageOccurrenceSpecification* and *ExecutionSpecification. MessageOccurrenceSpecifications* are used to represent sending or receiving of messages. *ExecutionSpecifications* are specifications of the execution of units of behaviours or actions within the *Lifeline* and always triggered by *Messages*.

The sturctures of *msc* are similar to the structures in an SD meta-model, although *msc* is defined using a meta-language. An *msc body* includes multiple *instances*. Each *instance* has its own thread of control, and each *instance* has a list of *events* which appear along it. *message event* and *method call event* are the two main types of *event*. A pair of *message events* or a pair of *method call events* are used to represent a message between two *instances*. A *method* is a named unit of behaviour inside an *instance*. A *suspension* occurs when a synchronous *method call* is sent and lasts until the reply of the call returns.

Although both modelling languages have similar core constructs and each construct has similar graphical presentations, three underlying differences need to be addressed.

The first difference is that *Lifeline* and *instance* generally represent different things. *instance* of bMSC usually represents a process, a network device or a system. *Lifelines* in SDs always represent objects or instances of a component. *instance* always has its own thread of control (thread)[2], but a *Lifeline* does not.

The second difference is that SD and bMSC's messages are categorised differently. In SD, there are three message types: *synchCall, asynchCall* and *asynchSignal*. Generally speaking, *synchCall* is the more commonly used type of message modelling synchronous method call between objects. For bMSCs, *message* only refers to asynchronous communication between two *instances* and is the most often used type of message in bMSC. In general, the difference is due to the fact that SDs are used to model communication between objects, while bMSCs are designed to model message exchange between processes.

The third difference is that SDs and bMSCs use different ways to model the activity of a *Lifeline* or an *instance*. This difference is also due to the fact that an *instance* has a thread but *Lifeline* does not. Since an *instance* has its thread of control, if there is a synchronous *method call* from an *instance*, the caller will enter a *suspension* region where no events occur until the reply of the call returns. However, SDs do not restrict a *Lifeline* to map to only one thread of

---

[1] The emphasized words are definitions from the standard. A detailed explanation of them can be found in UML 2.0 and MSC standards [OMG05, IT98].

[2] Here, thread of control represents an abstract notion of control unlike *thread* or *process* in operation system (OS). More specifically, an independent task which is executed sequentially should be regarded as owning its own thread of control.

control. It is possible for *ExecutionSpecifications* of multiple threads to overlap in one *Lifeline*. An example of this is given in *Example 9* (Figure 6).

2.2   Traditional Partial Order Semantics

In the UML 2.0, the sequences of *MessageOccurrenceSpecification* are regarded as the meanings of SDs. Thus, traditional semantics can be described by two ordering rules when only considering the meta-classes: *Lifeline*, *Message* and *MessageOccurrenceSpecification*.

1. *MessageOccurrenceSpecifications* that appear on the same *Lifeline* are ordered from top to bottom.
2. Sending *MessageOccurrenceSpecification* always occurs before the corresponding receiving *MessageOccurrenceSpecification*.

Based on the rules, an informal partial order semantics of SDs can be defined. It is the transitive closure of the union of the following two orders:

- the union of total orders of *MessageOccurrenceSpecifications* in each *Lifeline*;
- the ordering relations between the *MessageOccurrenceSpecification* pairs of sending and receiving of the same message;

3   The Effect of Changing from bMSC to SD

In Section 2, we introduced the differences between SD and bMSC and the traditional semantics for SD. In order to illustrate the effects of the changes, five simple SD examples are presented. *Example 1* in Figure 1 shows that synchronous messages convey the events[3] of one thread to multiple lifelines. *Examples 2* and *3* in Figure 2 demonstrate that it is not enough to simply apply traditional semantics for interpreting two kinds of SDs. *Examples 4* and *5* in Figure 3 show what can happen when multiple threads enter the same lifeline in one SD.

Example 1 is an example of an SD where a synchronous message is represented by a solid line with a filled arrowhead (*c1* and *c2*); an open arrowhead is used to represent asynchronous messages (*m1*). The reply to a synchronous message is represented as a dashed line with an open arrowhead pointing back to the caller (*rc1* and *rc2*). Each thin rectangle on a lifeline represents an *ExecutionSpecification* defined as "*a specification of the execution of a unit of behavior or action within the Lifeline*" and denotes that the lifeline is active. In an OO program, when the synchronous message is a call to a method of the object represented by the lifeline, the thin rectangle signifies that the method is on the stack.

According to the UML 2.0 standard, we can interpret *Example 1* as a running method of *a:A* calling the method *c1* in object *b:B* and *b:B* sending an asynchronous message *m1* to object *d:D*. Method *c1* returns after *m1* has been

---

[3] For the sake of simplicity, we use *event* to replace the lengthy *MessageOccurrenceSpecification*.

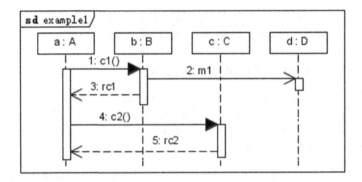

Fig. 1. An SD with synchronous messages

sent. Finally, the method in object *a:A* calls the *c2* method in object *c:C* and *c2* returns.

This scenario means that methods *c1* and *c2* are successively executed in one thread, so the events !c1, ?c1, !m1, !rc1, ?rc2, !c2, ?c2, !rc2 and ?rc2 all belong to one thread but are expanded to three lifelines. Here, the shriek symbol, !, represents sending and the ? symbol represents receiving (of a call or message).

Example 1 illustrates how synchronous messages expand events of one thread into different lifelines. As a consequence, a normal lifeline no longer represents a thread of control.

Applying traditional semantics to this example, the orders of the events are: !c1 <?c1 <!m1 <!rc1 <?rc1 <!c2 <?c2 <!rc2 <?rc2 and !m1 <?m1 which is equivalent to our intuitive understanding.

Now we assume that the orders in *Example 1* define the traces that we want to model and give two other examples (*Examples 2* and *3*) which try to model the same traces.

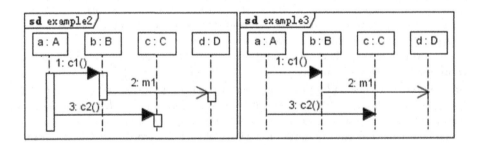

Fig. 2. SDs with *synchCalls*

Example 2 is also a common SD, but the returns of the synchronous calls are not included. Applying traditional semantics, we get following orders: !c1 < ?c1 <!m1, !c1 <!c2 <?c2 and !m1 <?m1. The relations ?c1 <!c2 and !m1 < !c2 are missing. However, according to the meaning of execution specification and synchronous call, the two calls from the same execution specification ($!c1$ and $!c2$) are still in the same thread, so the missing orders should exist. The partial order should be $!c1 <?c1 <!m1 <!c2 <?c2$ and $!m1 <?m1$ which is the partial order of *Example 1* except with reply events removed. This example shows that traditional semantics of SD are not enough to interpret SDs if synchronous messages are included and replies of synchronous calls omitted.

In *Example 3*, a simplified SD is given. Since execution specification is optional in SD, software engineers may draw SDs as shown in *Example 3* to reflect the traces in *Example 1*. Here, it is not easy to induce the desired partial order from *Example 3*. Calls $c1$ and $c2$ may belong to two different threads, so the events of $c1$ and $c2$ may interleave. As a result, the intended orders may be $!c1 < ?c1 <!m1 <?m1$ and $!c1 <!c2 <?c2$, the order produced by applying traditional semantics. Compared with the partial order of *Example 1*, it does not include relations like $?c1 <!c2$ and $!m1 <!c2$.

This example shows that users may draw a diagram based on their own assumption that all the calls are in one thread and are synchronized; the assumed orders can not subsequently be retrieved from the diagram when it is formally analyzed.

The first three examples explain how synchronous messages bring the events of one thread to multiple lifelines, and the problems that may result from this. In fact, in many cases it can also happen that multiple threads enter one lifeline in an SD.

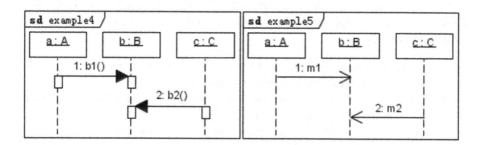

Fig. 3. SDs of multiple thread enter one lifeline

An intuitive interpretation of *Example 4* shown in Figure 3 is that methods $b1$ and $b2$ in object *b:B* are called by *a:A* and *b:B* sequentially from different threads. This example illustrates that sometimes it is impossible to determine whether the events on the same lifeline belong to the same thread. Another version of *Example 4* is shown in *Example 5* (same figure). It is a similar scenario to *Example 4* except that synchronous calls $b1$ and $b2$ are replaced by asynchronous messages $m1$ and $m2$. If *Example 5* is a bMSC, it induces a canonical race condition [AHP96, Mit05]. According to traditional semantics, $m1$, and $m2$ can be sent in either order. There is no way to enforce $m1$ arriving before $m2$ without additional information. If $?m1$ and $?m2$ belong to one thread and the system is implemented following *Example 5*, then a race condition may be introduced into the system. However, when checking this diagram in the context of OO software development, we can not decide whether a race condition applies since $?m1$ and $?m2$ might not belong to the same thread.

According to these examples, we find that the most problematic issue of interpreting an SD with synchronous messages is how to retain thread information in SDs when a lifeline does not correspond to a thread of control.

4   Mapping Events to Threads

To correctly interpret an SD, it is necessary to find a way of mapping different events to existing threads in the SD; we call this *Thread Mapping*.

To achieve this, two related meta-classes in UML 2.0 are selected. First is *execution specification* which can be used for grouping events. The second is *active object* which contains information regarding concurrency. The feasibility of using these meta-classes to do the thread mapping is now analysed.

4.1   Using Execution Specification

Example 2 in Figure 2 shows that using the information contained in execution specifications may help to handle the thread mapping problem. The events triggered by synchronous messages can be grouped together by analysing the connective relations of the execution specifications.

Thread mapping is relatively straightforward for simple diagrams like *Example 1* and *Example 2*. With execution specifications, we can group events inductively as follows:

1. Events that appear on the same lifeline are ordered from top to bottom.[4]
2. A message is always sent before it is received.
3. If there are synchronous messages between two execution specifications a and b, then a and b are connected.
4. If execution specifications a and b are connected, and b and c are connected, then a and c are connected.
5. All events on connected execution specifications are grouped into the same thread.
6. Let us suppose that in an event group, a synchronous message m is sent from execution specification a to execution specification b, then the events on b should always be before the next event on a.

Now consider applying the above inference rules to interpret *Example 2*. From the diagram, the observed orders are $!c1 <?c1 <!m1 <!c2 <?c2$ and $!m1 <?m1$ which is what we want.

Example 6 shown in Figure 4 illustrates a scenario in which $a{:}A$ is a window object that can accept inputs from an actor. When an asynchronous message

---

[4] This rule introduces forced orders between events of different threads on the same *Lifeline*.

arrives, one of the *a:A* methods is activated. The activated method handles the message by calling methods of the connected participants. In this case, the GUI libraries of most programming languages will put the two events on lifeline *a:A* in the same thread[5] and the desired orders of this diagram are $!c1 <?c1 <!m1 <!c3 <?c3 <!m2 <?m2$ and $?m1 <?m2$. However, correct thread information cannot be produced by the rules above and the desired orders cannot be generated. This is due to the fact that, when applying inference rules 3, 4 and 5 to this diagram, the events will be separated into two event groups. The orders obtained by applying the inference rules will be $!c1 <?c1 <!m1 <?m1$, $!c3 <?c3 <!m2 <?m2$, $!c1 <!c3$ and $?m1 <?m2$. In this case, desired relations such as $?c1 <?c3$ and $?c1 <!c3$ are lost.

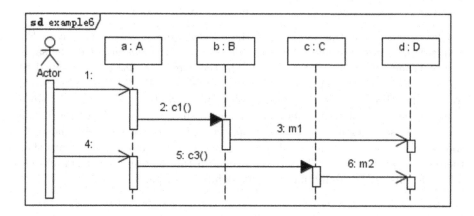

Fig. 4. SDs thread mapping problem

Although execution specifications do not always provide enough information for thread mapping in complicated SDs, these inference rules are still useful because grouped events belong to the same thread.

To apply these inference rules, one issue has to be clarified. According to UML 2.0, overlapping execution specifications on the same lifeline should always be represented by overlapping rectangles. However, a number of UML modelling tools do not follow this definition and this introduces problems in our inference rules.

There are two circumstances in which overlapping execution specifications will occur. Firstly, in the case of callback methods and secondly, for concurrent re-entering methods in the same lifeline.

According to UML 2.0 standard, callback methods should be shown as *Example 7* in Figure 5. Some UML tools depict the callback method as *Example 8* in the same figure and although these tools violate the standard definition, our inference rules still apply because all events of a callback method belong to the same thread.

---

[5] For example, two Java GUI libraries, Swing and SWT and Visual C++'s MFC.

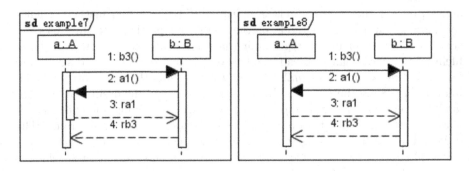

Fig. 5. Callback method

Concurrent re-entering methods of the same lifeline should be shown as *Example 9* in Figure 6. Some UML tools depict it as in *Example 10* in the same figure. When inference rules 3, 4 and 5 in the previous section are applied to *Example 10*, all execution specifications and events in the diagram are grouped to the same thread. This deduction conflicts with what actually happens, since $b1$ and $b2$ should belong to different threads in such scenarios. If inference rule 6 is applied subsequently to *Example 10*, the next event of $!b2$ on lifeline $c : C$ should follow all events on $b : B$ belonging to the same thread. This means that there exists an order $!4 <!3$, thus the events in the diagram may form a circle following this order, conflicting with the definition of partial order.

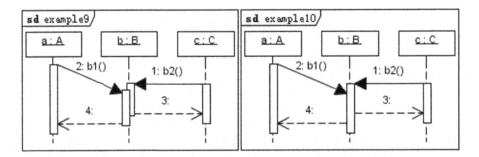

Fig. 6. Re-entering methods of the same lifeline

The semantics of execution specification will therefore be damaged if overlapping execution specifications are not depicted strictly according to the UML 2.0 standard; our inference rules do not work in this instance.

4.2   Using Active Object

In the UML standard related to SD, the only concept related to concurrency is that of active object.

A class may be designated as active (i.e., each of its instances having its own thread of control) or passive (i.e., each of its instances executing within the context of some other object). [OMG05, p423]

   An active object is an object that, as a direct consequence of its creation, commences to execute its classifier behavior, and does not cease until either the complete behavior is executed or the object is terminated by some external object. (This is sometimes referred to as "the object having its own thread of control.") [OMG05, p424]

When an instance of a class with *isActive* property is set to be *true*, it is an active object, otherwise it is a passive object.

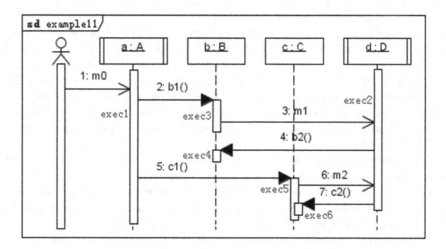

Fig. 7. An SD with active objects

Let us assume that active objects are represented by some lifelines, and execution specifications are fully specified; we could then claim that events can be mapped to threads using the inference rules in Section 4.1. To explain, *Example 11* is provided in Figure 7. Active objects are represented by rectangles, each with an additional vertical bar on either side (eg. *a:A* and *d:D* in *Example 11*). Since active objects are active from creation to termination, the execution specifications of active objects persist from top to bottom of the lifelines in this diagram. We assume that each active object in the diagram contains a thread. In addition, to simplify the discussion, some terms representing the execution specifications are added to the diagram, for example *exec1* refers to the execution specification on lifeline *a:A*. The detailed inference steps are:

- By applying rule 1, orders $?m0 <!b1 <!c1$, $?b1 <!m1 <?b2$, $?c1 <!m2 <?c2$ and $?m1 <!b2 <?m2 <!c2$ are obtained.
- By applying rule 2, orders $!b1 <?b1$, $!m1 <?m1$, $!b2 <?b2$, $!c1 <?c1$, $!m2 < ?m2$ and $!c2 <?c2$ are obtained.

- By applying inference rule 3, the pairs $exec1$ and $exec3$, $exec1$ and $exec5$, $exec2$ and $exec4$, $exec2$ and $exec6$ are connected respectively.
- By applying rules 4 and 5, $exec1$, $exec3$ and $exec5$ are connected; events $?m0$, $!b1$, $?b1$, $!m1$, $!c1$, $?c1$ and $!m2$ belong to the thread containing active object $a : A$. Similarly, $exec2$, $exec4$ and $exec6$ are connected; events $?m1$, $!b2$, $?b2$, $?m2$, $!c2$ and $?c2$ belong to the thread containing active object $d : D$.
- By applying rule 6, orders $?b1 <!c1$, $!m1 <!c1$ and $?b2 <?m2$ are obtained.

After applying these inference steps, the union of all obtained orders are: $?m0 <!b1 <?b1 <!m1 <!c1 <?c1 <!m2$, $?m1 <!b2 <?b2 <?m2 <!c2 <?c2$, $!m1 <?b2$ and $!m2 <?c2$, as expected.

But in OO software, it is hard to judge whether a lifeline represents an active object or not, since active object is defined more specifically than lifeline and, in most situations, they are not equivalent.

The concept of active object originates from research into Concurrent Object Oriented Programming Language (COOPL) [KL89, Nie93]. Active objects of COOPL keep both concurrency and OO features, such as encapsulation and inheritance, together. Consequently, the structure of active objects is generally more complex than common objects in Object Oriented Programing Language (OOPL). Mainstream OOPLs such as Java and C++ use a different approach to realize concurrent computing. They utilize special entities in the language itself or OS to implement concurrent computing, such as *Thread* class in Java and *process* or *thread* in Windows OS. Other research has shown how to implement active objects using normal OOPLs to benefit concurrent programming [CKV98, LS96]. In [LS96], active object is a behavioral pattern with multiple participants, such as Proxy, Scheduler, Servant etc. As a result, using a single lifeline to represent an active object for common OO software is unreasonable.

To summarise, these thread mapping approaches are impossible because the concurrent information kept by UML 2.0 meta-classes is not sufficient for doing so.

5   Inference for SDs with Thread Tags

Since there appears to be no canonical way to map events to threads with UML 2.0 meta-classes, we propose a new approach that extends the notation of UML 2.0. The extension should have two functions: firstly, to group all events in one SD to different threads; secondly, to maintain the temporal order of the events belonging to one thread. A straightforward solution is provided by using thread tags to retain the concurrent information of the systems being modelled. *Example 12* in Figure 8 shows an SD with extended thread tags. In this approach, an *id* is given to every thread in an SD. Each message is tagged with two thread *ids*, one for the source thread and one for the target thread. However, when sending and receiving of a message belong to the same thread, only one thread *id* is tagged in the middle of the message instead of two. The *ids* are then used to classify events into different threads while the temporal order of the grouped events is kept by the positions where the events occur.

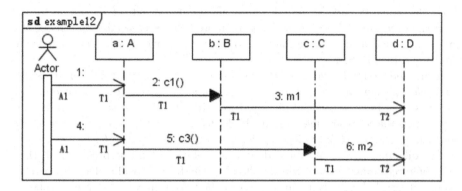

Fig. 8. An SD with thread tags

With a tagged SD, if we only consider the events of synchronous messages, then the orders of events of a *single thread* can be easily obtained using the following inference rules:

1. A message is always sent before it is received.
2. The events should be ordered linearly along the SD.

In the following text, we use $<_T$ to represent the orders obtained from thread tags[6] and $<_L$ to represent the orders obtained from lifelines[7]. We observe that there are differences between $<_T$ and $<_L$. Intuitively, $<_T \setminus <_L$ represents those sound orders that are missing when applying traditional partial order semantics. But it is also worth considering what $<_L \setminus <_T$ means.

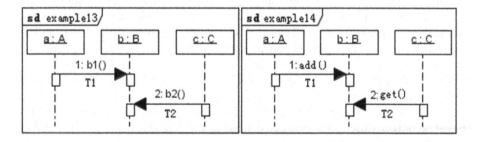

Fig. 9. What does $<_L \setminus <_T$ mean?

Recall *Example 4* in Figure 3; if we tag *Example 4* with thread *id*, we get *Example 13* as shown in Figure 9. Applying the rules for ordering events in one thread, only $!b1 <?b1$ and $!b2 <?b2$ are observed. Applying the first inference rule for inferencing traditional partial order set, we can get one more order relation

---

[6] Orders are obtained by applying the above inference rules to every thread in the SD.
[7] Orders are obtained by applying the first inference rule in Subsection 2.2 to the SD.

$?b1 <?b2$. Since threads $T1$ and $T2$ run concurrently, events of $T1$ can interleave with the events of $T2$, so $?b1 <?b2$ is redundant. It is reasonable to remove the orders obtained using lifeline information from the partial order set while there are thread tags in SDs.

Sometimes, forced orders need to be added to the events of different threads. *Example 14* shows a similar scenario to *Example 13*. The only difference is that the messages have two different signatures. Intuitively, the traditional semantics of this diagram are meaningful. It describes a scenario that $c : C$ can get something from $b : B$ only after $a : A$ has added something to $b : B$.

The dilemma is whether the orders from lifelines should be preserved. If they are, some redundant orders will be added to the final partial order set when we represent parallel executions in one SD. If they are removed, extra meta-classes are needed to maintain the forced orders in the SDs. In fact, there is a meta-class, *GeneralOrdering*, used to express the forced order relation between two events [OMG05, p466]. The notation of *GeneralOrdering* is shown by a dotted line connecting the two events and the direction of the relation is given by an arrowhead placed in the middle of the dotted line. When compared with the first case which may introduce errors into SDs, we believe that using *GeneralOrdering* to maintain the forced orders in the second case is a credible solution.

Moreover, since forced orders are ignored in traditional semantics, we adopted in the Section 2.2, we will also ignore forced orders in SDs here when interpreting thread tagged SDs. The inference rules for interpreting tagged SDs can be revised as follows:

1. A synchronous message is always sent before it is received.
2. The events tagged with the same thread *id* should be ordered linearly along the SD even if the events are on different lifelines.

The traditional inference rules only need positional information about events on each lifeline, but the proposed rules need all event positional information in one thread. Using the proposed rules, it is easy to infer the exact orders from the tagged SD even without the execution specifications. For instance, for *Example 12* shown in Figure 8, because $!c1$, $?c1$, $!m1$, $!c3$, $?c3$, $!m2$ all belong to thread $T1$, the orders are $!c1 <?c1 <!m1 <!c3 <?c3 <!m2$, $?m1 <?m2$, $!m1 <?m1$ and $!m2 <?m2$ as desired.

Finally, without considering the forced orders, an informal semantics for SDs based on partial order theory can be defined as the transitive closure of the union of the following two orders:

- the union of orders of events belonging to the same thread;
- the ordering relation between the event pairs of sending and receiving of a message.

6   Conclusion and Future Work

In this paper, some primary differences between SDs and bMSCs were analysed. Based on these differences, we argued that traditional semantics for SDs had drawbacks when interpreting SDs. Two meta-classes of UML 2.0 were used to resolve the problems within traditional semantics. However, these meta-classes cannot maintain concurrency information needed in order to interpret SDs. As a consequence, an informal semantics for SD with thread tags was proposed. We believe that intended event sequences can be generated by applying this semantics to SDs.

An important area of future work is the development of a formal semantics for SDs with thread tags and then extend it to the Interaction Diagrams (IDs) of UML 2.0. In addition to developing the semantics of IDs, it would also be interesting to conduct a formal analysis of IDs based on the developed semantics, for example, identifying the pathologies of IDs and ID model checking. One of the problems considered in this paper is caused by the absence of return messages. An alternative solution may be to infer these missing return messages but the use of such an approach is a topic for future work.

References

[AHP96]   Alur, R., Holzmann, G., Peled, D.: An analyzer for message sequence charts. Software Concepts and Tools 17(2), 70–77 (1996)

[CK04]   Cengarle, M.V., Knapp, A.: UML 2.0 interactions: Semantics and refinement. In: Proceedings of the 3rd Intl. Workshop on Critical Systems Development with UML, pp. 85–99, Lisbon, Portugal, Technische Universität München (2004)

[CKV98]   Caromel, D., Klauser, W., Vayssiere, J.: Towards seamless computing and metacomputing in Java. Concurrency Practice and Experience 10(11-13), 1043–1061 (1998)

[DH01]   Damm, W., Harel, D.: LSCs: breathing life into message sequence charts. Formal Methods in System Design 19(1), 45–80 (7, 2001)

[GGR93]   Grabowski, J., Graubmann, P., Rudolph, E.: Towards a petri net based semantics definition for message sequence charts. In: Proceedings of SDL'93 - Using Objects, pp. 179–190, Darmstadt, Germany, North-Holland (1993)

[GS05]   Grosu, R., Smolka, S.A.: Safety-liveness semantics for UML 2.0 sequence diagrams. In: Proceedings of the Fifth International Conference on Application of Concurrency to System Design, pp. 6–14. IEEE Computer Society Press, Los Alamitos, CA, USA (2005)

[HHRS05]   Haugen, Ø., Husa, K.E., Runde, R.K., Stølen, K.: STAIRS towards formal design with sequence diagrams. Software and Systems Modeling 4(4), 355–357 (2005)

[HM06]   Harel, D., Maoz, S.: Assert and negate revisited: modal semantics for UML sequence diagrams. In: Proceedings of the 2006 International Workshop on Scenarios and State Machines: Models, Algorithms, and Tools, pp. 13–20, Shanghai, China (2006)

[IT98]   ITU-T. ITU-T Recommendation Z.120 Annex B: Formal semantics of message sequence charts (4, 1998)

[JP01]   Jonsson, B., Padilla, G.: An execution semantics for MSC-2000. In: Reed, R., Reed, J. (eds.) SDL 2001. LNCS, vol. 2078, pp. 365–378. Springer, Heidelberg (2001)

[KL89]   Kafura, D.G., Lee, K.H.: Inheritance in actor based concurrent object-oriented languages. The. Computer Journal 32(4), 297–304 (1989)

[LL93]   Ladkin, P.B., Leue, S.: What do message sequence charts mean. In: Proceedings of the IFIP TC6/WG6.1 Sixth International Conference on Formal Description Techniques, pp. 301–316, Boston, MA, USA, North-Holland (1993)

[LS96]   Lavender, R.G., Schmidt, D.C.: Active object: an object behavioral pattern for concurrent programming. Pattern Languages of Program Design, pp. 483–499 (1996)

[LS06]   Lund, M.S., Stølen, K.: A fully general operational semantics for UML 2.0 sequence diagrams with potential and mandatory choice. In: Misra, J., Nipkow, T., Sekerinski, E. (eds.) FM 2006. LNCS, vol. 4085, pp. 380–395. Springer, Heidelberg (2006)

[Mit05]   Mitchell, B.: Resolving race conditions in asynchronous partial order scenarios. IEEE Transactions on Software Engineering 31(9), 767–784 (2005)

[MR94]   Mauw, S., Reniers, M.A.: An algebraic semantics of basic message sequence charts. The. Computer Journal 37(4), 269–277 (1994)

[Nie93]   Nierstrasz, O.: Regular types for active objects. In: Proceedings of the Eighth Annual Conference on Object-oriented Programming Systems, Languages, and Applications, pp. 1–15, Washington, DC, USA (1993)

[OMG05]   OMG. Unified Modeling Language: Superstructure (8, 2005)

[Sel04]   Selic, B.V.: On the semantic foundations of standard UML 2.0. In: Bernardo, M., Corradini, F. (eds.) Formal Methods for the Design of Real-Time Systems. LNCS, vol. 3185, pp. 181–199. Springer, Heidelberg (2004)

[Sto03]   Storrle, H.: Semantics of interactions in UML 2.0. In: Proceedings of the 2003 IEEE Symposium on Human Centric Computing Languages and Environments, pp. 129–136, Los Alamitos, CA, USA (2003)

Recovering Repetitive Sub-functions from Observations

Guy-Vincent Jourdan[1], Hasan Ural[1], Shen Wang[1], and Hüsnü Yenigün[2]

[1] School of Information Technology and Engineering (SITE)
University of Ottawa
800 King Edward Avenue
Ottawa, Ontario, Canada, K1N 6N5
{gvj,ural,swang010}@site.uottawa.ca
[2] Faculty of Engineering and Natural Sciences
Sabancı University
Tuzla, Istanbul, Turkey 34956
yenigun@sabanciuniv.edu

Abstract. This paper proposes an algorithm which, given a set of observations of an existing concurrent system that has repetitive sub-functions, constructs a Message Sequence Charts (MSC) graph where repetitive sub-functions of the concurrent system are identified. This algorithm makes fewer assumptions than previously published work, and thus requires fewer and easier to generate observations to construct the MSC-graph. The constructed MSC-graph may then be used as input to existing synthesis algorithms to recover the design of the existing concurrent system.

1 Introduction

A concurrent system is a system with two or more processes that are communicating among themselves using message exchanges. Message Sequence Charts (MSCs) [1,2] provide a visual description of a series of message exchanges among communicating processes in a concurrent system. MSCs are often used by designers to depict individual intended behaviors of the concurrent system. However, a collection of such MSCs can only be viewed as providing information on a representative sample of the intended behavior rather than a design representation of the system giving a complete description of the system functionality to be provided [3]. A design representation is useful not only for implementing the system, but also for maintaining it, for example to detect and eliminate errors, to adapt it to a different environment, or simply to better understand the system. It also helps reusing parts of the system in new developments. Unfortunately, complete, up-to-date designs of evolving existing systems are seldom available.

Consequently, one of the aims of reverse engineering [4,5,6] is to recover the design of an existing concurrent system through an analysis of its runtime behavior. Such an analysis requires a finite set of *observations* of the running system. Each observation is a serialization of the events occurring possibly concurrently

J. Derrick and J. Vain (Eds.): FORTE 2007, LNCS 4574, pp. 35–49, 2007.

during a system run. Due to the possible interleavings of these concurrent events, there are other serializations for the same run, all of which can be derived from the given serialization [4]. Each such observation can be seen as a word, which is made of the events being observed, belonging to the language of the system. From one word (observation), it is possible to derive other words corresponding to all remaining interleavings of the concurrent events in that word. If we are given a set of observations, we can thus infer a set of words as a union of the subsets of words where each subset corresponds to all possible interleavings of the events in each of these observations. However, this set is only a representative subset of the complete language of the system. Our aim is to derive, under some assumptions, an MSC-graph [7] that represents the complete language of the system from which a design of the system can be constructed using adaptations of existing synthesis algorithms [4].

Since many concurrent systems have repetitive sub-functionality, some evidence for such sub-functions should at least be implicitly given in the set of observations. For a complete and accurate recovery of the design of a concurrent system, the given set of observations must provide evidence for each repetitive sub-function and must imply its relative position among other repetitive sub-functions of the system. This places some constraints on the nature of the observations which need to be taken into consideration when the set of observations are formed.

Existing methods to infer repetitive sub-functions require several restrictive assumptions on the set of observations. For example, the method presented in [8] requires (among others) the following assumptions:

i. Repetitive sub-functions must be iterated the same number of times in each observation,
ii. Repetitive sub-functions need to be introduced in a specific order,
iii. The ordering of the sub-functions must be unambiguous,
iv. Each sub-function must be "introduced" individually by an observation that contains only "known" sub-functions and this new sub-function.

In [9], the authors introduce a new concept, the *lattice of repetitive sub-functions*, a structure that provides all possible selections of n repetitive sub-functions. Using that lattice, they are able to infer the set of repetitive sub-functions of an application from a set of observations waiving several of the assumptions made in [8]. In particular, the first three assumptions listed above are waived. However, the fourth and the strongest assumption is still required by the approach taken in [9].

In this paper, we eliminate that assumption and provide an algorithm that is capable of recovering several repetitive sub-functions at once under a new assumption that repetitive sub-functions have a single initiator. We believe this to be a significant practical improvement over both previous methods [8,9] since it relieves the user from the requirement of isolating each repetitive sub-function within its own observation, which could be fairly difficult in practice, and sometimes simply impossible if two or more repetitive sub-functions are tied together in the design of the system. The new assumption regarding the unique initiator to repetitive sub-functions does not seem too constraining, since a repetitive sub-function is primarily a function and thus is usually initiated by a single process. In addition, the assumption is introduced for efficiency only and can be waived at the cost of increased complexity.

The paper is organized as follows: in Section 2, we introduce the concepts and definitions required. In Section 3, we review and discuss the assumptions that are made about the system and the observations. The proposed algorithms are described and analyzed in section 5, and in Section 6 we illustrate our approach on an example. We conclude in Section 7, where an implementation of the solution is also described.

2 Preliminaries

In this section, we give the definitions of the concepts and notations required. To do so, we reuse the notions and notations of [9], adapting them as needed.

Figure 1, left, shows an MSC of three processes exchanging a total of five messages. The message m_1 is sent by the process P_2 and received by the process P_3, which is represented by an arrow from P_2 to P_3 and labeled m_1. Each message exchange is represented by a pair of *send* and *receive* events. The local view of the message exchanges of a process (send and receive events of a process) is a total order, but the global view is a partial order. A tuple consisting of a local view for each process of the message exchanges depicted in an MSC uniquely determines that MSC. Thus, an MSC represents a partial order execution of a concurrent system which stands for a set of linearizations (total order executions of the system) determined by considering all possible interleavings of concurrent message exchanges implied by the partial order. Any of the linearizations of an MSC uniquely determines the MSC. These two statements above are consequence of two conditions, the CC1 condition and the non-degeneracy condition given in [4].

To describe a functionality that is composed of several sub-functionalities, an MSC-graph (a graph with a source and a sink node where edges are labeled by MSCs) can be used. An MSC corresponding to the concatenation of MSCs along a path from the source node to the sink node in an MSC-graph is said to be in the language of the MSC-graph. In the following, M^k means that M is repeated k times, and M^* means any number of repetitions of M. Figure 1, right, shows an MSC-graph where the MSC M_p is followed by an arbitrary number of iterations of the MSC M, followed by the MSC M_s, which defines the language $M_p.M^*.M_s$. In this paper we assume that an MSC in the language of an MSC-graph represents a system functionality from the initial state to the final state, without going through the initial state again during the execution.

Formal semantics associated with MSCs provides a basis for their analysis such as detecting timing conflicts and race conditions [10], non–local choices [11], model checking [12], and checking safe realizability [13,4].

In this paper, we consider the reverse engineering of designs of existing concurrent systems from given sets of observations of their implementations. We

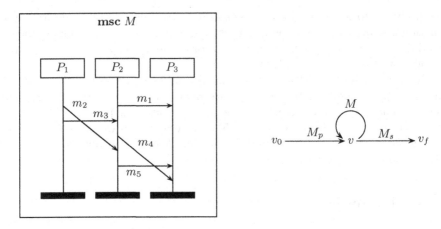

Fig. 1. An MSC of three processes (left) and an example MSC-graph (right)

assume that we are given a set Ω of observations, each observation $O \in \Omega$ being an arbitrary linearization of an MSC m from a set of MSCs that is not given. We use $m(O)$ to denote the MSC m uniquely determined by an observation O. Some of the sub-functions of the system can be *repetitive*, in which case they can be called consecutively a different number of times in different runs of the system. As in [8,9], we assume that a repetitive sub-function does not start (resp. end) at the initial (resp. final) state, and that every repetitive sub-function of the system (if any) is represented in the given set of observations at least twice: once with no occurrence, and once with two or more consecutive occurrences.

A sub-function that is repeated in an observation will create a repeated pattern in the MSC corresponding to that observation. However, a simple pattern repetition is not enough. In order to deduce the existence of a repetitive sub-function, we need to have an evidence such as different number of iterations of the pattern within the same context.

Definition 1. *[9] An MSC M is* the basic repetitive MSC *of MSC M' if $M' = M^k$ for some $k \geq 2$ and there does not exist a basic repetitive MSC of M.*

Consider the visual representation of an MSC M and imagine that we draw a line through M by crossing each process line exactly once, and without crossing any message arrows. Such a line divides M into two parts M_p (the part above the cutting line) and M_s (the part below the cutting line). M_p and M_s can be shown to be MSCs again. M_p and M_s are what we call a prefix of M and a suffix of M, respectively. If an MSC M' is the concatenation of three non empty MSCs M_p, M_m and M_s (i.e. $M' = M_p.M_m.M_s$), we say that M_m occurs *within the context M_p–M_s*, that is, M_m occurs after M_p and is followed by M_s.

Definition 2. *[9] Two MSCs M_1 and M_2 are said to* infer M *to be repetitive within the context M_p–M_s if all the following are satisfied:*

1. M does not have a basic repetitive MSC,

2. $M_1 = M_p.M^k.M_s$ *for some* $k \geq 2$, *with* M_p *and* M_s *non-empty and* $M_2 = M_p.M_s$,
3. M *is not a suffix of* M_p *and* M *is not a prefix of* M_s.

Definition 3. *[9] A common prefix (resp. suffix) of two MSCs M_1 and M_2, is an MSC M, such that M is a prefix (resp. suffix) of both M_1 and M_2. The maximal common prefix (resp. suffix) of M_1 and M_2 is a common prefix (resp. suffix) M of M_1 and M_2 with the largest number of events.*

The set of send and receive events in an MSC can be partially ordered according to *causality*. We define the causal relationship as follows: two events e_1 and e_2 of an MSC M are *causally related*, which we note $e_1 < e_2$ if and only if

1. e_1 is a *send* event and e_2 is the corresponding *receive* event, or
2. e_1 and e_2 are events of the same process and e_1 happens before e_2 on that process, or
3. there exists an event e_3 in M such that $e_1 < e_3 < e_2$.

For any *send* event e, we will define the set *Previous(e)* of elements, one per process, that do not happen *after* e and that are maximal on their process with that property. More formally:

Definition 4. *Let M be an MSC with k processes $\{p_1, p_2, \ldots, p_k\}$, and let e be a send event of M. Previous(e) is a set of up to k events such that $\forall j \in \{1, \ldots, k\}$, for all events e' of $p_j, e' \in Previous(e)$ if and only if $e \not< e'$ and for all events $e'' \neq e'$ of $p_j, e \not< e'' \Rightarrow e'' < e'$.*

A *linear extension* of the events of an MSC is a *total ordering* of the events that respects the (partial) causal ordering:

Definition 5. *Let M be an MSC with n events $\{e_1, e_2, \ldots, e_n\}$. A linear extension of the causal order $<$ of the events of M is a total order $<_L$ on the events of M such that $\forall i, j \leq n, e_i < e_j \Rightarrow e_i <_L e_j$.*

3   Assumptions

As mentioned earlier, previous work [8,9] have been published on the same problem, [9] making fewer assumptions than [8] about the system being reverse engineered. In this paper, we are waiving one of the strongest assumptions made in [9], namely assumption 8 below. We in turn make a couple of less restrictive assumptions for efficiency reasons.

To recap, the most important assumptions made in [8] were the following:

1. There is one observation without any repetitive sub-functions. This observation is called the *initial* observation; it will be the shortest of all the provided observations and every other observation will be made of that initial observation plus a number of iterations of a number of repetitive sub-functions.

2. The initial observation, and each repetitive sub-function having nested repetitive sub-functions, have a non empty, repetitive sub-function free prefix and a non empty, repetitive sub-function free suffix.
3. Repetitive sub-functions have no common prefix with the part of the MSC that starts just after them and no common suffix with the part of the MSC that leads to them.
4. Repetitive sub-functions starting at the same point do not alternate.
5. Repetitive sub-functions must be iterated the same number of times in each observation,
6. Repetitive sub-functions need to be introduced in a specific order,
7. The ordering of the sub-functions must be totally unambiguous,
8. Each sub-function must be "introduced" individually with an observation that contains only "known" sub-functions and this new sub-function.

In [9], the assumptions 5, 6, and 7 are waived, but the strong assumption 8 is kept. In this paper, we waive assumption 8. However, we do introduce the following two new assumptions:

9. Sub-function have a single initiator. That is, there is always a unique *send* event at the beginning of a repetitive sub-function (and this send event is thus repeated at the beginning of each iteration of the sub-function).
10. Repetitive sub-functions repeat at least twice.

We will see that assumption 9 speeds up our algorithm. This assumption seems fairly reasonable, since functions have a single starting point.

Assumption 10 is there to avoid a particular case, where a set of repetitive sub functions "hide" each other, for example an initial observation $P.S$, and two other observation $P.A.B^{k_1}.S$ and $P.A^{k_2}.B.S$ for $k_1 > 1$ and $k_2 > 1$. The single occurrence of A in the second observation prevents B to be recognized as repetitive while the single occurrence of B in the third observation prevents A to be recognized as repetitive. Note that if a fourth observation allows A or B to be recognized then the problem disappears, so this assumption can be weakened to prevent only the problematic pattern. We have used a larger assumption for the sake of readability.

4   Main Algorithm

The main idea behind our algorithm is the following: at any given time, we have already built a particular "knowledge" of the system, the initial knowledge being the initial observation. We gradually enhance this knowledge by uncovering information about repetitive sub-functions. Given the current knowledge (the MSC-Graph obtained so far), say *current*, and an observation, say O, we attempt to "enhance" our knowledge by identifying in $m(O)$ portions that are coherent with *current* (that is, portions that are compliant with what *current* describes of the system), while the parts of $m(O)$ that do not match *current* are made exclusively of repetitive sub-functions.

We can sketch the first algorithm as follows: we first identify the longest common prefix of *current* and $m(O)$. After that common prefix, if O is not entirely recognized yet then we must be looking at the beginning of a repetitive sub-function. That sub-function will iterate a certain number of times, after which $m(O)$ will either "reconnect" with *current* where it left off to go into the repetitive sub-function, or will enter into a second repetitive sub-function. In any case, it will eventually "reconnect" with *current* (that is, reach M_s of definition refdef-infer-loop). The strategy is thus to first look for a possible "reconnection" point between $m(O)$ and *current*. When such a point is found, we check if the portion of $m(O)$ that has been skipped is made of one or more repetitive sub-functions. If that is not the case, we keep looking for another reconnection point further down in time within $m(O)$. If, on the other hand, what we have are repetitive sub-functions, then we have to see if we can complete the comparison starting from that reconnection point (and possibly find a number of additional repetitive sub-functions along the way). The simplest way to achieve this is to make a recursive call to the same algorithm, starting from that reconnection point. If the recursive call succeeds in finishing the comparison of *current* and $m(O)$, then we are done. If not, then we have to look for another reconnection point that would be further down in $m(O)$.

The above sketch achieves the expected result, but can be very inefficient when trying to find the next connection point. Indeed, after identifying the maximum common prefix of $m(O)$ and *current*, we know that the next connection point in $m(O)$ will have to match the next events on each process of *current*. If these events are not causally related (that is, these are independent events) then any combination of matching events on O can potentially be a connection point. If there are k processes involved and O has p matching events on each process, each combination of these p matching events is a possible reconnection point, thus we will have to try up to p^k possible connections.

In order to avoid this combinatorial explosion, we can use Assumption 9 stating that repetitive sub-functions have a single initiator. The algorithm as described cannot benefit from such an assumption, since the connection point is searched at the end of the repetitive sub-function, on which no assumption is made. It is however possible to reverse the algorithm and go through *current* and O from the end to the beginning instead of from the beginning to the end. When going backward, the very same approach can be followed (find the longest *suffix*, then find the *previous* connection point, make sure that what was skipped on $m(O)$ is made of basic repetitive sub-functions and recursively call the same algorithm on the remaining part of *current* and O), except that with this strategy we know that the next connection point will be in $m(O)$ just *before* the beginning of a repetitive sub-function. Since each repetitive sub function has a single send event as initiator, it means that the only possible connection points correspond to the set *Previous*(e) of a send event e, which is the initiator. We thus simply have to try a number of candidates for connection points which are bounded by the number of send events in O.

Algorithm 1 performs the initialization and the loop that will "consume" the provided observations. The variable *current* holds the current knowledge of the system, initialized with the *initial* observation. The first loop is a phase of pre-computation on the set of observations: we calculate an ordering of the events which is compatible with the causal relation, and we pre-compute *Previous(e)* for each send event *e*. Both calculations will be used later in the main algorithm. Then, the observations are compared with *current* one after the other, until they are successfully matched to *current* by Algorithm 4. It may be necessary to compare a given observation to *current* more than once, if the observation includes nested repetitive sub-functions, since *current* might not have inferred the sub-function containing the nested sub-function the first time around.

Algorithm 1. Initialization and Main Loop

1: *current* = the MSC of the shortest observation (assumption refsec-assumptions)
2: Q = a queue of all other observations
3: *KeepGoing=true*
    {Precomputation on the set of observations}
4: **for all** observations $O \in Q$ **do**
5:    Compute *linearExtension(m(O))*, a linear extension of the events of the MSC $m(O)$ induced by O
6:    **for** all *send* event e in O **do**
7:        Compute *Previous(e)*
8:    **end for**
9: **end for**
    {Main loop through the observations}
10: **while** $Q \neq \emptyset$ AND *KeepGoing==true* **do**
11:    *KeepGoing = false;*
12:    **for all** observations $O \in Q$ **do**
13:        **if** InferRepetitive(*current, O*) **then**
14:            remove O from Q
15:            *KeepGoing=true*
16:        **end if**
17:    **end for**
18: **end while**
    {If $Q \neq \emptyset$, some observations were not handled}
19: **if** $Q \neq \emptyset$ **then**
20:    ERROR: some observations were not processed
21: **else**
22:    SUCCESS: the system has been reversed engineered as *current*
23: **end if**

---

5   Repetitive Sub-function Inference Algorithm

Algorithm 2 given below attempts to *trace O* in *current* and to infer new repetitive sub-functions. The call to *FindMaximumSuffix* traces the maximum possible suffix common to *current* and $m(O)$. The location (starting) of this suffix is returned in *cutCurrent* and *cutO*.

Algorithm 2. BOOLEAN InferRepetitive(IN-OUT *current*, IN *O*)

1: FindMaximumSuffix(*current, O, cutCurrent, cutO*)
2: **if** both *cutCurrent* and *cutO* are at the beginning of their MSC **then**
3:    **return** true
4: **else if** one of *cutCurrent* or *cutO* is at the beginning of its MSC **then**
5:    **return** false
6: **end if**
   {A repetitive sub-function might end at *cutO*}
7: startingCut = cutO
8: **while** true **do**
9:    FindNextConnectionPoint(*cutCurrent, O, startingCut, connectionPoint*)
10:    **if** *connectionPoint*== ∅ **then**
11:       **return** false
12:    **end if**
13:    **if** IsMadeOfBasicRepetitives (*O, connectionPoint , cutO*) **then**
14:       **if**   InferRepetitive(*current[0,cutCurrent], O[Previous(connectionPoint)]*) **then**
15:         modify *current* to include the newly discovered repetitive sub-function(s)
16:         **return** true
17:       **end if**
18:    **end if**
   {What we have found wasn't good, either because it wasn't basic repetitive or because it did not allow us to finish trace O inside current. We keep looping.}
19:    startingCut = *Previous(connectionPoint)*
20: **end while**

Algorithm 3 implements *FindNextConnectionPoint*. Due to the assumption of having a single initiator, we simply have to search backward on *linearExtension(m(O))* for a *send* event e so that *Previous(e)* matches *cutCurrent* since all the events in a repeated MSC are causally dependent on the initiator of this MSC.

5.1   Finding Basic Repetitive Sub-functions

In Algorithm 2, we extract a segment S of O which is not present in *current*. We must now see if this segment is made of one or more repetitive sub-functions. In [8], *BasicRepetitiveMSC()*, a linear time algorithm is provided. This algorithm is used to decide whether or not a given MSC is the concatenation of two or more basic MSCs. This algorithm is based on the fact that if an MSC is basic repetitive, then the sequence of labels on each of its processes are also repetitive. Such a sequence of labels forms a word w, and finding the shortest word w' such that $w = (w')^k$ for some $k > 0$ is a well studied problem for which there are linear time algorithms [14].

Algorithm 3. FindNextConnectionPoint(IN *cutCurrent, O, startingCut,*OUT *connectionPoint*)

1: **for all** send event $e \in O$ before *startingCut*, shifting the current position on *linearExtension(m(O))* towards its beginning **do**
2:   **if** *Previous(e)* $==$ *cutCurrent* **then**
3:     *connectionPoint = e*
4:     **return**
5:   **end if**
6: **end for**
   {Connection point not found}
7: *connectionPoint*$== \emptyset$

Under the present assumptions, the segment S of $m(O)$ can be a concatenation of more than one basic repetitive MSCs, that is, S could be of the form $M_1^{k_1} M_2^{k_2} \ldots M_p^{k_p}$, for $p \geq 1$ and $k_1 \geq 2, k_2 \geq 2, \ldots k_p \geq 2$. Therefore, the algorithm *BasicRepetitiveMSC()* must be adapted to the multiple basic repetitive case.

Our approach to address this problem is the following: starting from S, we try to find a *single* basic repetitive MSC on the longest possible prefix of this segment. If we do find such a basic repetitive MSC on a prefix P of S, we recursively call our algorithm on $S \setminus P$ to find more basic repetitive MSCs in S. Here again, we use Assumption 9 stating that repetitive sub-functions have a single initiator, which allows to speed up the search quite dramatically, since it allows one to look only at the prefixes of S that end at *Previous(e)* for some *send* event e.

Algorithm 4. BOOLEAN IsMadeOfBasicRepetitives (IN *O, connectionPoint , cutO*)

1: **if** BasicRepetitiveMSC(*O[connectionPoint, cutO]*) **then**
2:   **return** true
3: **end if**
4: **for all** send event $e \in O$ between *connectionPoint* and *cutO*, moving backward on *linearExtension(m(O))* **do**
5:   **if** BasicRepetitiveMSC(*O[connectionPoint, Previous(e)]*) **then**
6:     **if** IsMadeOfBasicRepetitives(*O, e, cutO*) **then**
7:       **return** true
8:     **end if**
9:   **end if**
10: **end for**
11: **return** false

5.2   Complexity of the Solution

In this section, we evaluate the complexity of the proposed solution in the worst case. We must first evaluate Algorithm 4, *IsMadeOfBasicRepetitives*, which is called by Algorithm 2, *InferRepetitive*.

In the following, we assume that the system being reverse-engineered involves k independent processes, and that the observations that are provided contain up to n events. There are up to p observations, and the size of the reconstructed system is m events. Clearly, $m \in O(p.n)$.

Proposition 1. *Algorithm IsMadeOfBasicRepetitives can be implemented to run in $O(n^3)$.*

Proof. As pointed out in [8], Algorithm *BasicRepetitiveMSC* can be made to run in $O(n)$, and this algorithm is called up to n times in the *for* loop. In addition, one should note that it is not necessary to recursively call *IsMadeOfBasicRepetitives* with the same $e - cut$ argument twice, since it would always return the same result (and actually return false if it was about to be called a second time, since the algorithm terminates as soon as one such call returns true). It is thus possible to record the fact that a particular $e - cut$ was already used and avoid a recursive call when this is the case. This can be checked in $O(n)$ and will limit the number of recursive calls to a maximum of n.

We can now evaluate the complexity of Algorithm 2.

Proposition 2. *Algorithm InferRepetitive can be implemented to run in $O(n^5.m^k + k.n^2.m^{k+1})$.*

Proof. Clearly, the algorithm *FindNextConnectionPoint* can be implemented to run in $O(n)$. Moreover, the algorithm will exit from the *while true* loop after at most n iterations. Proposition 1 tells us that *IsMadeOfBasicRepetitives* runs in $O(n^3)$, so the only missing information is the number of recursive calls to *Infer-Repetitive*. To do so, one should notice that it is not necessary to call *InferRepetitive* twice with the same pair of parameters. The first parameter corresponds to *Previous(e)* for some *send* event e, so the number of possibilities in bounded by n. The second parameter of *InferRepetitive* is a cut of *current*. To represent the worst case, say that we have m events in each of the k processes in *current* and that there are no causal relationships between events belonging to different processes. In this case, any set of k events, one per process, is a cut, giving m^k choices for the second parameter. Thus there are $O(n.m^k)$ possible pairs of parameters for *InferRepetitive*. Finding out if a given pair has already been used can be done in $O(n + k.m)$, so each complete run of one call of *InferRepetitive* (excluding recursive calls) can be completed in $O(n^4 + k.n.m)$.

Theorem 1. *The method proposed in this paper can be made to run in $O(p^2.n^5.m^k + p^2.k.n^2.m^{k+1})$.*

Proof. Immediate from propositions 1 and 2.

6   An Example

Let us illustrate our solution on a simple example. Assume that we are observing a system with three process p_1, p_2 and p_3. We note $s.m_{x,i,j}$ the sending of message

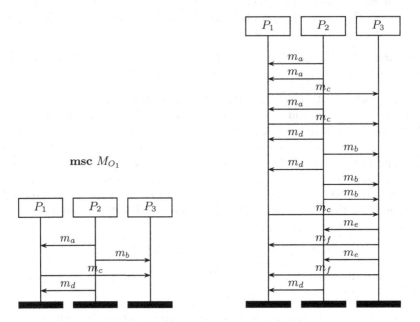

Fig. 2. MSCs infered by O_1 and O_2

m_x by p_i to p_j and $r.m_{x,i,j}$ the reception of message m_x by p_j from p_i. We are provided with the following two observations (omitting on-process ordering information, which is assumed to be preserved in the provided lists, that is, events of the same process are listed in the order they occur on that process):

$O_1 = s.m_{a,2,1}, s.m_{b,2,3}, s.m_{d,2,1}, r.m_{a,2,1}, s.m_{c,1,3}, r.m_{d,2,1}, r.m_{b,2,3}, r.m_{c,1,3}$
and
$O_2 = s.m_{a,2,1}, s.m_{a,2,1}, s.m_{a,2,1}, r.m_{a,2,1}, r.m_{a,2,1}, s.m_{c,1,3}, r.m_{a,2,1}, r.m_{c,1,3},$
$s.m_{c,1,3}, r.m_{c,1,3}, s.m_{d,2,1}, s.m_{b,2,3}, s.m_{d,2,1}, s.m_{b,2,3}, s.m_{b,2,3}, r.m_{d,2,1}, r.m_{b,2,3},$
$r.m_{d,2,1}, r.m_{b,2,3}, r.m_{b,2,3}, s.m_{c,1,3}, r.m_{c,1,3}, s.m_{e,3,2}, s.m_{f,3,1}, s.m_{e,3,2}, s.m_{f,3,1},$
$r.m_{e,3,2}, r.m_{f,3,1}, r.m_{e,3,2}, s.m_{d,2,1}, r.m_{f,3,1}, r.m_{d,2,1}.$

These two observations induce the MSCs M_{O_1} and M_{O_2} respectively, as depicted in Figure 2. The shortest observation, and thus the initial one, is O_1. The algorithm $InferRepetitive(O_1, O_2)$ is thus invoked.

The longest common suffix is the single-message MSC $M_1 = (m_{d,2,1})$. The reconnection point on O_1 is thus the reception of m_c on p_3, the sending of m_c on p_1 and the sending of m_b on p_2, which can be found in O_2 as $Previous(s.m_{e,3,2})$. The call to $IsMadeOfBasicRepetitives$ is then made on the segment $m_{e,3,2}, m_{f,3,1}$, $m_{e,3,2}, m_{f,3,1}$, which infer the two-message MSC $M_2 = (m_{e,3,2}, m_{f,3,1})$ to be basic repetitive.

A recursive call to $InferRepetitive$ is thus made on the MSCs leading up to the last occurrence of $m_{c,1,3}$ on both O_1 and O_2. This time, the maximum common

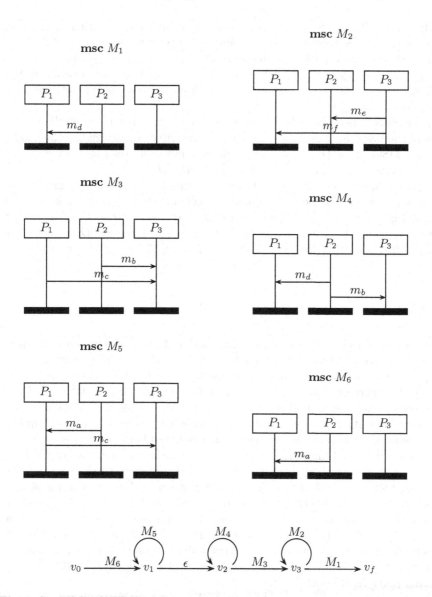

Fig. 3. Six MSCs obtained when processing M_{O_1} and M_{O_2}, and the final MSC-graph of the system as reverse engineered

suffix is the two-message MSC $M_3 = (m_{b,2,3}, m_{c,1,3})$, and the reconnection point is simply $s.m_{a,2,1}$. It is first found on O_2 as $Previous(s.m_{c,1,3})$, and $IsMadeOfBa\text{-}$ $sicRepetitives$ is then called on the segment $m_{c,1,3}, m_{a,2,1}, m_{c,1,3}, m_{d,2,1}, m_{b,2,3}$, $m_{d,2,1}, m_{b,2,3}$.

This call will fail identifying basic repetitive, and thus another connection point on O_2 will be searched for. It is found as $Previous(s.m_{a,2,1})$, and $IsMadeOfBasicRepetitives$ is called on the segment $m_{a,2,1}, m_{c,1,3}, m_{a,2,1}, m_{c,1,3}, m_{d,2,1}, m_{b,2,3}, m_{d,2,1}, m_{b,2,3}$, which this time is recognized as the concatenation of the basic repetitive MSC $M_5 = (m_{a,2,1}, m_{c,1,3})$ followed by the basic repetitive MSC $M_4 = (m_{d,2,1}, m_{b,2,3})$.

A recursive call to $InferRepetitive$ is thus made on what is left of the traces, namely the first message $m_{a,2,1}$, which is immediately recognized as the single-message MSC $M_6 = \{m_{a,2,1}\}$ and the algorithm finishes on a success, with the system reverse engineered as $M_6.M_5^k.M_4^k.M_3.M_2^k.M_1$.

Figure 3 shows the six MSCs obtained as well as the final MSC-graph (the graph as an ϵ transition between v_1 and v_2, meaning that nothing happens when moving from v_1 to v_2). As expected, both O_1 and O_2 can be obtained from that graph: O_1 comes from $v_0.(M_6).v_1.(\epsilon).v_2.(M_3).v_3.(M_1).v_f$, and O_2 comes from $v_0.(M_6).v_1.(M_5).v_1.(M_5).v_1.(\epsilon).v_2.(M_4).v_2. (M_4) .v_2.(M_3) .v_3.(M_2) .v_3. (M_2). v_3. (M_1).v_f$.

7   Conclusion

We have introduced a reverse-engineering method to infer the presence of repetitive sub-functions in an application from which only a set of execution traces are provided. The method is much less restrictive than the previously published ones and is therefore much more practical. Our algorithm is capable of identifying repetitive patterns and repetitive sub-patterns (without limitations in the number of nested levels) that are appearing when comparing different executions of the same application being reverse-engineered, and build an MSC-graph from these patterns that "summarize" the knowledge of the design of the application.

The method described in this paper has been implemented in C++. The resulting tool is a 2000 lines program that takes an arbitrary number of execution traces and builds the corresponding MSCs and infer the MSC-graph in accordance to Algorithm 1. In our tests, the application was able to analyze 100 execution traces totaling over 40,000 message exchanges and infer the corresponding MSC-graph, uncovering 130 repetitive subfunctions in less than 10 seconds on a MS Windows^TM based computer with 1 Gigabyte of RAM and a 3.4 GigaHertz Intel Pentium processor.

Details, documentation and source-code download are available at http://www.site.uottawa.ca/~ural/findloop.

Acknowledgments

This work is supported in part by the Natural Science and Engineering Research Council of Canada under grants RGPIN 976 and RGPIN 312018, CITO/OCE of the Government of Ontario, and a grant by Sabancı University. The authors thank the anonymous referees for their valuable comments.

References

1. ITU Telecommunication Standardization Sector: ITU-T Recommendation Z.120. Message Sequence Charts (MSC96) (1996)
2. Rudolph, E., Graubmann, P., Gabowski, J.: Tutorial on message sequence charts. Computer Networks and ISDN Systems–SDL and MSC, vol. 28 (1996)
3. Uchitel, S., Kramer, J., Magee, J.: Detecting implied scenarios in message sequence chart specifications. In: 9th European Software Engineering Conferece and 9th ACM SIGSOFT International Symposium on the Foundations of Software Engineering (ESEC/FSE'01) (2001)
4. Alur, R., Etessami, K., Yannakakis, M.: Inference of message sequence charts. IEEE Transactions on Software Engineering 29, 623–633 (2003)
5. Chikofsky, E., Cross, J.: Reverse engineering and design recovery. IEEE Software 7, 13–17 (1990)
6. Lee, D., Sabnani, K.: Reverse engineering of communication protocols. In: IEEE ICNP'93, pp. 208–216 (1993)
7. Braberman, V., Oliveto, F., Blaunstein, S.: Scenario-based validation and verification for real-time software: On run conformance and coverage for msc-graphs. In: 2nd International Workshop on Scenarios and State Machines: Models, Algorithms, and Tools, ICSE 2003 (2003)
8. Ural, H., Yenigun, H.: Towards design recovery from observations. In: de Frutos-Escrig, D., Núñez, M. (eds.) FORTE 2004. LNCS, vol. 3235, pp. 133–149. Springer, Heidelberg (2004)
9. Jourdan, G.V., Ural, H., Yenigun, H.: Recovering the lattice of repetitive sub-functions. In: Yolum, p., Güngör, T., Gürgen, F., Özturan, C. (eds.) ISCIS 2005. LNCS, vol. 3733, pp. 956–965. Springer, Heidelberg (2005)
10. Alur, R., Holzmann, G.J., Peled, D.: An analyzer for message sequence charts. Software Concepts and Tools 17, 70–77 (1996)
11. Ben-Abdallah, H., Leue, S.: Syntactic detection of progress divergence and non–local choice in message sequence charts. In: 2nd TACAS, pp. 259–274 (1997)
12. Alur, R., Yannakakis, M.: Model checking of message sequence charts. In: 10th International Conference on Concurrency Theory, pp. 114–129. Springer Verlag, Heidelberg (1999)
13. Alur, R., Etessami, K., Yannakakis, M.: Inference of message sequence charts. In: 22nd International Conference on Software Engineering, pp. 304–313 (2000)
14. Crochemore, M., Rytter, W.: Text Algorithms. Oxford University Press, Oxford (1994)

Specification of Timed EFSM
Fault Models in SDL

S.S. Batth, E.R. Vieira, A. Cavalli, and M.Ü. Uyar

The City College and Graduate Center of the City University of New York,
New York, NY 10016, USA
{batth,umit}@ee-mail.engr.ccny.cuny.edu
Laboratoire SAMOVAR (CNRS) and GET/INT Evry Cedex, France
{elisangela.rodrigues,ana.cavalli}@int-evry.fr

Abstract. In this paper, we apply our timing fault modeling strategy
to writing formal specifications for communication protocols. Using the
formal language of Specification and Description Language (SDL), we
specify the `Controller` process of *rail-road crossing system*, a popular benchmark for real-time systems. Our extended finite state machine
(EFSM) model has the capability of representing a class of timing faults,
which otherwise may not be detected in an IUT. *Hit-or-Jump* algorithm
is applied to the SDL specification based on our EFSM model to generate
a test sequence that can detect these timing faults. This application of
fault modeling into SDL specification ensures the synchronization among
the timing constraints of different processes, and enables generation of
portable test sequences since they can be easily represented in other formal notations such as TTCN or MSC.

Keywords: Extended Finite State Machines, Timing Fault Models,
SDL, Hit-or-Jump.

1 Introduction

If the inherent timing constraints are not properly specified in a formal specification of a communication protocol, start and expiration of concurrent timers
may lead to infeasible test sequences, which can generate false results by failing
correct implementations, or worse, passing the faulty ones.

In this paper, we first introduce an extended finite-state machine (EFSM)
model with timer variables based on our earlier work [FUDA03, UWBWF05,
UBWF06a] for the `Controller` process of the so-called *rail-road crossing system* [ALUR98]. This system has been studied as a benchmark in many real-time
systems [HJL93, HL96, AKLN99, XEN04, CRV05a] . We then augment this timed
EFSM model such that the test sequences generated from the augmented model,
when applied by a tester to an implementation under test (IUT), will detect the
presence of a class of timing faults. In this augmentation, a set of new edges and
states are created in the system model (i.e., the edge conditions and actions use
timing variables as well as the external inputs) such that the resulting model is a

J. Derrick and J. Vain (Eds.): FORTE 2007, LNCS 4574, pp. 50–65, 2007.
© IFIP International Federation for Information Processing 2007

timed EFSM. In addition, a set of special purpose tester timers are implemented inside the testing system (not in the IUT since the implementation is assumed to be a black box). Only a small number of new states and edges are introduced by our augmentation, and hence the overall length of the test sequences generated from the augmented model, compared to the original system model, does not increase significantly.

We focus on the *incorrect timer setting faults* [EDK02, EDKE98, EKD99], which represent the timers that are incorrectly implemented either too short or too long in `Controller`. We then provide a formal specification for this system in Specification and Description Language (SDL) [ITUZ1], which represents the fault detection capabilities of the augmented EFSM model. In this SDL specification of `Controller`, a transition of the EFSM fault model that can be triggered when its time constraint is satisfied is represented by one or more continuous signal operators. We specify these EFSM timing constraints by using two variable types in SDL, namely `time` and `duration`, which are also used to define the test purposes. To achieve the synchronization among the timing constraints of different processes, we introduce a process, called `Clock`, to represent the discrete passage of time and use the variable `now` to verify the global instantiation of the time. The SDL specification can also handle the cases where multiple trains try to cross at the same time.

A test sequence is generated for this SDL specification using the *Hit-or-Jump* [CLRZ99] algorithm. Using the test purposes (also called *stop conditions*), which represent the timing constraints of the EFSM timing fault model, *Hit-or-Jump* algorithm constructs efficient test sequences while avoiding the state explosion. In [CRV05a], *Hit-or-Jump* has been applied to *railroad crossing system* without any fault detection capabilities of our EFSM model. In this paper, we generate the test sequences that are capable of detecting *incorrect timer setting faults*.

Section 2 of this paper presents an English specification of *railroad crossing system*. Section 3 introduces the definitions, graph augmentation algorithms `GA-A`, `GA-B` and `GA-C`, and fault modeling for `Controller`. The SDL specification with timing constraints and test sequence generation using *Hit-or-Jump* algorithm are in Section 4. The concluding remarks are presented in Section 5.

2   English Specification for Railroad Crossing System

The railroad crossing system is one of the popular examples for studying timing constraints in timed FSMs [HJL93, HL94, HL96, AKLN99, ALUR98, XEN04]. It consists of three main processes: `Train,` `Gate` and `Controller`, all of which must communicate with one another within certain time constraints. `Train` process communicates with `Controller` by sending the messages called *approach, in, out* and *exit*. The output signal *approach* must be sent to `Controller` at least two minutes before a train is crossing the railroad. When a train is inside (or outside) the gate, the corresponding output signal *in* (or *out*) is generated. Between the signals *approach* and *exit*, there must be a delay of maximum five minutes. When

`Controller` receives the input signal *approach*, it must send the output signal *lower* to `Gate` at most one minute after the receipt of *approach*. If `Controller` receives *exit*, it must send the output signal *raise* to `Gate` with a maximum delay of one minute.

Gate and `Controller` communicate through the signals *lower, raise, up* and *down*. The signals *lower* and *raise* are inputs to `Gate` process. If *lower* is received, `Gate` must respond with *down* output signal, indicating that the gate is closed and the crossing is safe. The interval between the reception of *lower* and the sending of *down* must be at most one minute. If the input signal *raise* is received by `Gate`, it must send the output signal *up* at least one minute and at most two minutes after the receipt of *raise*.

3   Modeling Timed Extended Finite State Machines

A communication protocol modeled as a finite state machine (FSM) can be represented by a directed graph $G(V, E)$. Vertex set V represents the nodes and edge set E represents the edges triggered by events of a system. A protocol specification may include timing variables and operations based their values. To represent these timing related variables, we extend FSMs with timing variables. Our model is complimentary to those presented in timed automata [ALUR98], and has the advantage that it is specifically designed for test generation without state explosion [FUDA03].

3.1   Definitions and Notations

Let $\mathbf{R}$ denote the set of real, $\mathbf{R}^{\circ+}$ the set of the non-negative real, and $\mathbf{R}^{\infty} = \mathbf{R}^{\circ+} \cup \{-\infty, +\infty\}$ is the set of non-negative real with elements $-\infty$ and $+\infty$. Let $\mathbf{Z}$ denote the set of integers and $\mathbf{Z}^{+}$ is the set of positive integers. Interval $[\alpha, \beta]$ is a subset of $\mathbf{R}^{\circ+}$, $[\alpha, \beta] \subset \mathbf{R}^{\circ+}$, and δ is an instant of $[\alpha, \beta]$, $\delta \in [\alpha, \beta]$. α is the lower bound of δ, $Inf(\delta) = \alpha$; β is the upper bound of δ , $Sup(\delta) = \beta$.

Definition 1. *A timed FSM is an FSM augmented to form an Extended Finite State Machine (EFSM), represented by directed graph G, denoted by $M = (V, A, O, \mathcal{T}, E, v_0)$ where V is a finite set of nodes, $v_0 \in V$ is the initial node, A is a finite set of inputs, O is a finite set of outputs, $\mathcal{T}$ is a finite set of variables, and E is a set of edges $V \times A \times \mathcal{T} \longrightarrow V \times O \times \mathcal{T}$. Edge $e_i \in E$ can be represented by a tuple $e_i = (v_p, v_q, a_i, o_i, P_t(\mathcal{T}) = \langle e_i \rangle, Act_t(\mathcal{T}) = \{e_i\})$, where $v_p \in V$ is a current node, $v_q \in V$ is a next node, $a_i \in I$ is the input that triggers the transition represented by $v_p \xrightarrow{e_i} v_q$, $o_i \in O$ is the output from current transition $v_p \xrightarrow{e_i} v_q$, $P_t(\mathcal{T}) = \langle e_i \rangle$ is the set of possible conditions of timing variables. $Act_t(\mathcal{T}) = \{e_i\}$ is the set of possible actions on timing variables.*

Definition 2. *A timer $tm_j \in TM$ can be defined with timing variables of $(T_j, D_j, f_j) \subseteq \mathcal{T}$, where $TM = \{tm_1, \cdots, tm_j, \cdots\}$ is a set of N timers,*

$T_j \in \{0, 1\}$ is a timer running status variable, $D_j \in \mathbf{R}^{\circ+}$ is a time-characteristic variable, and $f_j \in \mathbf{R}^{\infty}$ is a time-keeping variable.

- Time Keeping Variables (D_j and f_j), where D_j indicates the length of timer tm_j, and f_j indicates the time elapsed since tm_j started. If tm_j has just started, $f_j := 0$; if tm_j is inactive, $f_j := -\infty$. Over an edge e_i, the value of f_j is increased by the amount of time $c_i \in \mathbf{R}^{\circ+}$ required to completely traverse the current transition e_i, $f_j := f_j + c_i$. The difference of $(D_j - f_j)$ represents the remaining time until tm_j's expiry.
- Timer Status Variable (T_j) is a boolean variable, where $T_j == 1$ (T_j) denotes timer tm_j is active and $T_j == 0$ ($\neg T_j$) denotes timer tm_j is passive (i.e., stopped, expired or not started yet).

Definition 3. $TM_{active} \subseteq TM$ and $TM_{passive} \subseteq TM$ are sets of timers which are active and passive, respectively, such that $TM = TM_{active} \bigcup TM_{passive}$.

- For a transition $e_i = (v_p, v_q, a_i, o_i, \langle e_i \rangle, \{e_i\})$, a set of passive timers $tm_j \in TM_{passive}$, $\forall j \in [1, N]$, can be activated by setting $T_j := 1$ and $f_j := 0$ in its edge actions. For all the other active timers $tm_k \in TM_{active}$, $\forall k \in [1, N], k \neq j$, f_k is updated by e_i's traversal time. Formally: $\langle e_i \rangle : \langle \neg T_j \wedge T_k \wedge (f_k < D_k) \rangle$ and $\{e_i\} : \{T_j := 1; f_j := 0; T_k := T_k; f_k := f_k + c_i\} \ \forall k \in [1, N], \forall j \in [1, N], k \neq j$.
- For a transition $e_i = (v_p, v_q, a_i, o_i, \langle e_i \rangle, \{e_i\})$, an active timer $tm_j \in TM_{active}$, $j \in [1, N]$, can be stopped by setting $T_j := 0$ and $f_j := -\infty$ in its edge actions. For all the other active timers $tm_k \in TM_{active}$, $\forall k \in [1, N], k \neq j$, f_k is updated by e_i's traversal time. Formally: $\langle e_i \rangle : \langle T_j \wedge (f_j < D_j) \wedge T_k \wedge (f_k < D_k) \rangle$ and $\{e_i\} : \{T_j := 0; f_j := -\infty; T_k := T_k; f_k := f_k + c_i\} \ \forall k \in [1, N], j \in [1, N], \forall k \neq j$.
- An active timer $tm_j \in TM_{active}$ is defined as expired or timed out iff f_j is equal or greater than the timer length D_j. Formally: $\langle T_j \wedge (f_j \geq D_j) \rangle$ and $\{T_j := 0; f_j := -\infty\}$.

Definition 4. A transition which becomes feasible when one of the active timers, with the least remaining time, expires is defined as a timeout transition. In other words, $tm_j \in TM_{active}$ ($j \in [1, N]$), $tm_k \in TM_{active}$ ($\forall k \in [1, N], \forall k \neq j$), and tm_j's remaining time was the least, then it was tm_j that expired and triggers the timeout edge e_i. The edge actions set $T_j = 0$, $f_j = -\infty$, and f_k is updated by e_i's traversal time. Formally: $\langle e_i \rangle : \langle T_j \wedge (f_j \geqslant D_j) \wedge T_k \wedge (D_j - f_j < D_k - f_k) \rangle$ and $\{e_i\} : \{T_j := 0; f_j := -\infty; T_k := T_k; f_k := f_k + c_i\} \ \forall k \in [1, N], \forall k \neq j$.

Definition 5. A non-timeout transition becomes feasible iff none of the active timers have expired, or all of the timers are passive. In other words, $tm_j \in TM_{active}$, $\forall j \in [1, N]$, and none of these active tm_j's have expired. f_j is updated by e_i's traversal time. Formally: $\langle e_i \rangle : \langle T_j \wedge (f_j < D_j) \rangle$ and $\{e_i\} : \{T_j := T_j; f_j := f_j + c_i\} \ \forall j \in [1, N]$.

Definition 6. *Flow Enforcing Variable (L_p) is an exit condition to leave a state v_p. It is denoted by a boolean variable $L_p \in \{0,1\}\ \forall v_p \in V$, where $L_p == 0$ means none of the transitions is allowed to leave v_p, and $L_p == 1$ means transitions are allowed to leave v_p.*

Definition 7. *A transition whose action updates L_p from 0 to 1 is defined as an observer edge. Formally: $\langle e_{p,obs} \rangle : \langle L_p == 0 \rangle$ and $\{e_{p,obs}\} : \{L_p := 1\}\ \forall v_p \in V$.*

Definition 8. *For an active timer, a transition which consumes the pending timeout is defined as a wait edge. In other words, $tm_j \in TM_{active}\ (j \in [1,N])$, $tm_k \in TM_{active}\ (\forall k \in [1,N], \forall k \neq j)$ and tm_j's remaining time is the least, then the wait edge updates f_j by tm_j's remaining time $D_j - f_j$. Formally: $\langle e_{p,wait} \rangle :$ $\langle T_j \wedge (f_j < D_j) \wedge T_k \wedge (f_k < D_k) \wedge (D_j - f_j < D_k - f_k) \rangle$ and $\{e_{p,wait}\} : \{f_j :=$ $f_j + (D_j - f_j); f_k := f_k + (D_j - f_j)\}\ \forall k \neq j, k \in [1,N], \forall v_p \in V$.*

Definition 9. *A return edge is an edge with no time constraints and actions: $\langle e_p^{ret} \rangle : \langle 1 \rangle$ and $\{e_p^{ret}\} : \{\ \}\ \forall v_p \in V$.*

Definition 10. *During testing an edge $e_i = (v_p, v_q, a_i, o_i, \langle e_i \rangle, \{e_i\})$, after input a_i is applied to an IUT, the expected output o_i should be generated no later than a certain θ time units, $\theta \in \mathbf{R}^{\circ+}$, measured by a timer which is a part of the test harness rather than the IUT.*

3.2   Graph Augmentation Algorithm GA-A

To model the original system along with its timed behavior, we introduce a graph augmentation algorithm, called GA-A [UBWF06a], which is specifically designed for generating tests for the systems whose timer related variables are linear and their values implicitly increase with time. To ensure that the timing conditions and actions of the specification are correctly incorporated into the timed EFSM model, GA-A generates $G'(V', E')$ by converting self-loops in G to node-to-node edges, defining an exit condition for all the nodes, and creating a set of new nodes and edges:

Step (i): If there exists a self loop for $v_p \in V$ in G, an additional node called v_p' is created in G', to which all self-loops $e_{p,k} \in E$ defined in v_p are directed;

Step (ii): All self-loops $e_{p,k} \in E$ in G are converted to node-to-node edges in G' as $e_{p,k} = (v_p, v_p')$.

Step (iii): For $v_p' \in V'$ in G', a return edge e_p^{ret} from v_p' to v_p is created in G' as $e_p^{ret} = (v_p', v_p)$.

Step (iv): An *observer node* is created in G', namely $v_{p,wait}$, which is connected to v_p via newly created an observer edge as $e_{p,obs} = (v_p, v_{p,wait})$, a wait edge as $e_{p,wait} = (v_p, v_{p,wait})$, and a return edge from observer node as $e_{p,obs}^{ret} = (v_{p,wait}, v_p)$. The role of the observer node $v_{p,wait}$ is to *consume* pending timeouts on $e_{p,wait}$ and enable outgoing edges by setting the flow enforcing variable L_p to 1 on $e_{p,obs}$. Fig. 1 shows, for node v_p, the conversion of self-loops to node-to-node edges, the creation of the observer node, wait and observer edges.

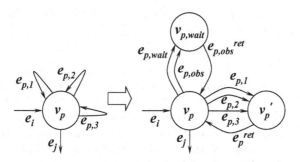

Fig. 1. Modeling self-loops for v_p in G into v_p, v'_p and $v_{p,wait}$ in G'

The time condition and the action for the wait edge $e_{p,wait}$ are formulated as $\langle L_p == 0 \rangle$ and $\{f_j := f_j + (D_j - f_j)\}$, where $D_j - f_j$ is the remaining time of timer $tm_j \in TM_{active}$ to timeout. For the observer edge $e_{p,obs}$ from the original node v_p to the observer node $v_{p,wait}$ in G', the time condition and the action are formulated as $\langle L_p == 0 \rangle$ and $\{L_p := 1\}$, respectively. The return edges of e_p^{ret} and $e_{p,obs}^{ret}$ are added by GA-A to G' are no-cost edges with time condition as: $\langle 1 \rangle$ (i.e., always true with no time constraints imposed) with no actions: $\{\ \}$.

Step (v): The conditions and actions for a *timeout* edge in G' are:

- The condition for a timeout self-loop edge in G becomes: $\langle T_j \wedge (f_j \geqslant D_j) \wedge T_k \wedge (f_k < D_k) \wedge (D_j - f_j < D_k - f_k) \wedge (L_p == 0) \rangle \; \forall T_k \neq T_j$, where the remaining time for $tm_j \in TM_{active}$ is less than that of $tm_k \in TM_{active}$ (i.e., $D_j - f_j < D_k - f_k$) and the flow enforcing variable L_p is zero.
- The condition for a timeout node-to-node edge in G becomes: $\langle T_j \wedge (f_j \geqslant D_j) \wedge T_k \wedge (f_k < D_k) \wedge (D_j - f_j < D_k - f_k) \wedge (L_p == 1) \rangle \; \forall T_k \neq T_j$, where the remaining time for $tm_j \in TM_{active}$ is less than that of $tm_k \in TM_{active}$ (i.e., $D_j - f_j < D_k - f_k$) and L_p is 1.
- The actions for a timeout edge in G become: $\{T_j := 0; f_j := -\infty; T_k := T_k; f_k := f_k + c_i; L_p := 0\} \; \forall \, tm_k \neq tm_j$, where timer $tm_j \in TM_{passive}$ becomes passive and the time keeping variable for $tm_k \in TM_{active}$ is incremented by the edge cost of c_i.

These equations imply that before a timeout edge, tm_j should be still running, remaining time should be the least among all other running timers and the flow-enforcing variable is appropriately set for either a converted (i.e., self-loop edge in G) or an original (i.e., node to node edge in G) edge in G'.

Step (vi): The conditions and actions for a non-timeout edge in G' is formalized as follows:

- A non-timeout self-loop edge in G becomes: $\langle ((\neg T_j \vee (T_j \wedge (f_j < D_j))) \wedge (L_p == 0)) \rangle \; \forall \, tm_j \in TM_{active}$
- A non-timeout node-to-node edge in G becomes: $\langle ((\neg T_j \vee (T_j \wedge (f_j < D_j))) \wedge (L_p == 1)) \rangle \; \forall \, tm_j \in TM_{active}$
- The action for a non-timeout edge in G becomes:

- $\{f_j := f_j + c_i; f_k := f_k + c_i; L_p := 0\} \ \forall \ tm_k \neq tm_j, tm_j \in TM_{active}, tm_k \in TM_{active}$ if edge starts no timers;
- $\{T_j := 1; f_j := 0; T_k := T_k; f_k := f_k + c_i; L_p := 0\} \ \forall \ tm_k \neq tm_j$ if edge starts timer tm_j.

Since both timeout and non-timeout edges disable outgoing edges by setting $L_p := 0$ in Steps (v) and (vi) of GA-A, the only edges whose actions will enable the outgoing edges in G' are the artificially-created observer edges.

It is proven [UBWF06a] that GA-A terminates with a running time of $\mathbb{O}(E)$, and that the total number of the nodes and edges in $G'(V', E')$ and $G(V, E)$ have the same order of magnitude.

3.3 Classification of Timing Faults

A class of timing faults in an implementation of a timed system have been defined in [EDK02, EDKE98, EKD99] as 1-*clock timing faults* (including 1-*clock corner point* and 1-*clock interval faults*) and *incorrect timer length setting faults*.

Incorrect Timer Setting Faults occur in an IUT when a timer length is incorrectly implemented as either too short or too long (i.e., the timer expires either too early or too late). The definition of incorrect timer setting faults is based on the following timing requirement:

- ***Timing Requirement:*** In a test sequence, edge h_k starts timer tm_j and is traversed before e_i. Timeout transition $e_i = (v_p, v_q, timeout\_tm_j, o_i, \langle t_j \rangle, \{t_j\})$ triggers exactly in D_j time units, where D_j is the timer length.
- ***Timing Fault B*** (TF_B): Timeout transition e_i triggers in D'_j time units and output o_i is observed and node v_q is verified in shorter than the expected time (i.e., $D'_j < D_j$).
- ***Timing Fault C*** (TF_C): Timeout transition e_i triggers in D'_j time units and output o_i is observed and node v_q is verified in longer than the expected time (i.e., $D'_j > D_j$).

In a specification, suppose a timer tm_j is defined to be of length D_j to be started by the actions of edge h_k and to expire at edge e_i (reachable from h_k). A special purpose timer tm_s with length $D_s = D_j$ is created in the test harness by GA-2.B to detect if tm_j is set too short as $D'_j < D_j$:

Step (B.i): Edge conditions and actions for h_k are modified such that it starts a *special purpose timer* tm_s.

Step (B.ii): e_i's condition is modified such that it traverses only when both tm_s and tm_j have expired.

Step (B.iii): All self-loops in v_p are represented as node-to-node edges by the creation of an additional node, called v'_p, to which they are directed. A return edge e_p^{ret} (with zero cost) is also created for their return to v_p.

Step (B.iv): An observer node $v_{p,wait}$ is appended to node v_p via a new observer edge $e_{p,obs}$, wait edge $e_{p,wait}$ (with cost $c_{p,wait}$) and return edge e_p^{ret} (with cost $c_p^{ret} := 0$). The edge condition of e_i is modified such that it triggers only when $f_s \geqslant D_s$ and tm_j expires.

As proven in [UBWF06a], GA-2.B terminates with a running time of $\mathbb{O}(E)$, and the order of magnitude of the nodes and edges in G' and G'' are the same. A test sequence generated from G'' will contain $\cdots, h_k, \cdots, e_{i-1}, e_{p,wait}, e_p^{ret}, e_{p,obs}, e_p^{ret}, e_i$ which will not be feasible to traverse if timer tm_j expires earlier than expected. The condition for $e_{p,wait}$ requires that both the timers tm_j from the IUT and tm_s from the test harness are still running. If tm_j times out before tm_s, it will create a deadlock at v_p (i.e., none of the conditions leaving v_p is valid), which in turn will flag the tester that a timing fault TF_B has occurred.

Algorithm GA-2.C [UBWF06a] for TF_C, is similar to GA-2.B, with the same run time complexity and the augmented graph size of G'.

3.4   Timed EFSM Model for Railroad Crossing System

Due to space constraints, we only consider timing fault TF_B in the edges of e_2 and e_4 in Controller, whose FSM model is given in Fig. 2. The steps for generating graph G'' is follows:

Step 1: Obtain graph G from the specification of Controller process. The directed graph representing Controller is in Fig. 2 with its actions and conditions given in Table 1. Timer tm_z can be started either in edge e_1 or in e_3 with the timer length of 1 min (i.e., $D_z = 1$ min).

Step 2: Generate G' for Controller by applying the graph augmentation algorithm GA-A to G. The new observer nodes and edges (i.e., $s_{0,wait}$, $e_{0,wait}$, $e_{0,obs}$, $e_{0,obs}^{ret}$, $s_{1,wait}$, $e_{1,wait}$, $e_{1,obs}$, $e_{1,obs}^{ret}$, $s_{2,wait}$, $e_{2,wait}$, $e_{2,obs}$, $e_{2,obs}^{ret}$, $s_{3,wait}$, $e_{3,wait}$, $e_{3,obs}$, $e_{3,obs}^{ret}$) are added to the original nodes of G. The self-loop edge of e_0 is converted to a node-to-node edge by introducing s_0' and e_0^{ret} in G'.

Step 3: Apply the graph augmentation algorithm GA-B to G' to generate G'' for Controller. A special purpose timer, namely tm_s (with $D_s = 1$), is introduced in the tester (not in the IUT) to model the timing constraints over the edges of e_2 and e_4. Note that, in G'', e_1 starts both the special purpose timer tm_s in the tester and the timer tm_z in the IUT; similarly, e_3 starts the same two timers in the tester and the IUT. Graph G'' is shown in Fig. 3 with its respective edge conditions and actions given in Table 2.

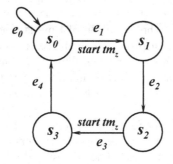

Fig. 2. Finite state machine for Controller

Table 1. Original specification of `Controller` (Fig. 2) and its graph G

Edges	English Specification	Our EFSM Model G	
		Timing Conditions	Timing Actions
e_0	Idle	$\langle 1 \rangle$	$\{\ \}$
e_1	Input *approach* is received	$\langle (a_1 == approach) \rangle$	$\{T_z := 1; f_z := 0\}$
e_2	Output *lower* is generated at maximum delay of 1 mins after input *approach* is received	$\langle T_z \wedge (f_z \geq D_z) \rangle$	$\{o_2 := lower;$ $T_z := 0; f_z := -\infty\}$
e_3	Input *exit* is received	$\langle (a_3 == exit) \rangle$	$\{T_z := 1; f_z := 0\}$
e_4	Output *raise* is generated maximum delay of 1 mins after input *exit* is received	$\langle T_z \wedge (f_z \geq D_z) \rangle$	$\{o_4 := raise;$ $T_z := 0; f_z := -\infty\}$

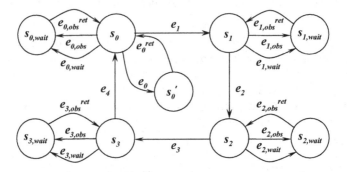

Fig. 3. Augmented Graph G'' for `Controller` (Fig. 2) after applying `GA-A` and `GA-B`

4   SDL Specification Based on Timed EFSM Model

To specify a set of timed EFSM models in SDL one may either *(i)* define each component (e.g., `Train`, `Gate` and `Controller`) as an independent system, where each exchange messages with the environment, or *(ii)* define each component as a process of the same system. Although both approaches are equivalent, in this paper we follow the latter approach. Our SDL specification is designed for testing purposes, where the evolution of time is modeled by the expiration of the clocks. We introduce a process, called `Clock`, as a part of the `Railroad` system to represent the passage of time. Therefore, our SDL specification for the *railroad crossing system* consists of a main `Railroad` system, which includes a `Railroad_Control` block (Fig. 4) with four processes, namely `Train`, `Gate`, `Controller` and `Clock`.

In our EFSM model, each edge e_i is associated with a timing cost c_i, representing the expected time that is required to traverse (or, realize) the edge in an implementation (see Section 3). The corresponding state transition in SDL

Table 2. Augmented edge conditions and actions of graph G'' (Fig. 3) of `Controller`

Edges	$\langle$ **Edge Conditions** $\rangle$	$\{$ **Edge Actions** $\}$
e_0	$\langle \neg approach \rangle$	$\{\,\}$
e_0^{ret}	$\langle 1 \rangle$	$\{\,\}$
$e_{0,obs}$	$\langle L_p == 0 \rangle$	$\{L_p := 1\}$
$e_{0,wait}$	$\langle \neg approach \wedge L_p == 0 \rangle$	$\{f_i := f_i + c_{0,wait}\}$
$e_{0,obs}^{ret}$	$\langle 1 \rangle$	$\{\,\}$
e_1	$\langle approach \wedge L_p == 1 \rangle$	$\{T_s := 1; f_s := 0; L_p := 0\}$
$e_{1,wait}$	$\langle L_p == 0 \rangle$	$\{f_i := f_i + c_{1,wait}\}$
$e_{1,obs}$	$\langle L_p == 0 \rangle$	$\{L_p := 1\}$
$e_{1,obs}^{ret}$	$\langle 1 \rangle$	$\{\,\}$
e_2	$\langle T_s \wedge (f_s \geq D_s) \wedge (T_z \text{timeout}) \wedge L_p == 1 \rangle$	$\{lower; T_s := 0; f_s := -\infty; L_p := 0\}$
$e_{2,wait}$	$\langle \neg exit \wedge L_p == 0 \rangle$	$\{f_i := f_i + c_{2,wait}\}$
$e_{2,obs}$	$\langle L_p == 0 \rangle$	$\{L_p := 1\}$
$e_{2,obs}^{ret}$	$\langle 1 \rangle$	$\{\,\}$
e_3	$\langle exit \wedge L_p == 1 \rangle$	$T_s := 1; f_s := 0; L_p := 0\}$
$e_{3,wait}$	$\langle L_p == 0 \rangle$	$\{f_i := f_i + c_{3,wait}\}$
$e_{3,obs}$	$\langle L_p == 0 \rangle$	$\{L_p := 1\}$
$e_{3,obs}^{ret}$	$\langle 1 \rangle$	$\{\,\}$
e_4	$\langle T_s \wedge (f_s \geq D_s) \wedge (T_z \text{timeout}) \wedge L_p == 1 \rangle$	$\{raise; T_s := 0; f_s := -\infty; L_p := 0\}$

specification can be represented as the difference between two internal variables that are set at the instances of the beginning and end of the transition. This way, these two variables, one with the clock value at the beginning and the other one at the end, can be used to approximate the edge traversal time in SDL, Similarly, the following assumptions are considered to specify a real-time system in SDL [AKLN99, TMCB03]:

- All un-timed events will take a negligible time to realize;
- Time advances through the expiration of local clocks; if two clocks expire at the same moment, only one of them is taken into account first;
- As time progresses, time dependent transitions may trigger only if their conditions are satisfied;
- The global clock called `now` is the only clock which gives the current time.

In this approach, time constraints are represented as continuous signal operators. This construct allows to represent a transition that does not need an input signal to be fired, but is triggered when the time constraint is satisfied. In our SDL specification, two variable types are used: a `time` variable to register the moment when an event occurs, and a `duration` variable to represent the difference between two `time` variables. For example, in the timing condition of $(f_1 - f_2 > D_2)$, variables f_1 and f_2 are of type `time`, whereas D_2 is a `duration` variable. Both `time` and `duration` variables are also defined in our EFSM model in Section 3. For example, for the special purpose timer tm_s in G'' (Section 3.3), time keeping variable f_s and the timer length D_s are represented as the `time` and `duration` types of variables in our SDL specification, respectively.

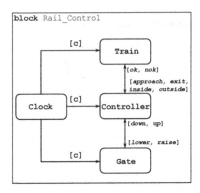

Fig. 4. Rail_Control block of SDL specification

Although we did not utilize the local timer construct in SDL to represent the timer tm_s, we have instead used the variable now and the process Clock to model the evolution of time in our SDL specification. Therefore, for Controller, f_s is represented by four time type variables, namely $zapproach$, $zexit$, $zlower$ and $zraise$. The moment when $approach$ and $exit$ signals are received is represented by $zapproach$ and $zexit$, respectively. Similarly, $zlower$ and $zraise$ are used to capture the moment when $lower$ and $raise$ are sent, respectively. Timer length D_s is modeled by two duration type variables, namely $sent\_lower\_delay$ and $sent\_raise\_delay$, both equal to 1 min. Table 3 illustrates the relationship between our SDL specification and the EFSM model based on G''.

Our SDL specification also allows representation of more than one train trying to cross at the same time. To model multiple trains, additional variables such as ($ntrains$ and max_trains), and signals (ok and nok) are introduced (in the SDL specification given in this paper, $max\_trains = 1$). Since there are a limited number of tracks available, variable $ntrains$ counts the number of trains which have sent $approach$ to Controller. Each $approach$ received from a different train can be distinguished by Controller because an internal identifier with a distinct channel is created for each instantiation of the Train process. Therefore, if the condition of ($ntrains <= max\_trains$) is true, Controller sends ok; otherwise it sends nok. If Train receives ok from Controller, the train continues its approach to the railroad crossing. Similarly, if nok is received by Controller, the train waits until it receives a signal of ok. When one of the Train processes sends $exit$, Controller decrements the value of $ntrains$ by one. If the updated value of $ntrains$ is still greater than zero, Controller sends another ok to one of the Train processes waiting to approach the railroad crossing; otherwise, Controller sends $raise$ signal to Gate.

4.1   Application of *Hit-or-Jump* Algorithm

Hit-or-Jump [CLRZ99] algorithm can be used for embedded testing of complex communication systems which are modeled as communicating EFSMs. It is a generalization and unification of exhaustive search and random walks; both of which

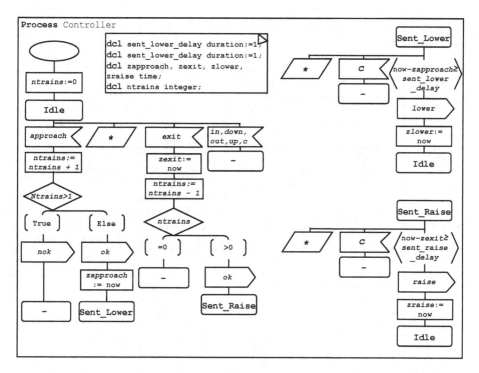

Fig. 5. SDL specification of `Controller`

are special cases of *Hit-or-Jump*. It efficiently constructs testing sequences with a high fault coverage, does not suffer from the drawback of state space explosion as encountered in exhaustive search, and quickly covers the system components under test without being *trapped*, as experienced by random walks. Furthermore, it has also been applied to embedded testing of telephone services [CLRZ99], conformance and interoperability testing of web services [CMZ04] and in the domain of real-time systems [CRV05a, CRV05b]. The strategy used to generate a partial accessibility graph in *Hit-or-Jump* is that if a visited node satisfies the test purposes, it is said that a *hit* is done; otherwise, the algorithm randomly choses another node from the neighborhood graph, and moves (*jump*) to it. Then from this new node, it continues its search. Parameters required to execute the *Hit-or-Jump* are:

(i) **SDL specification** of the IUT (Fig. 5);
(ii) **Test purposes** described in several *stop conditions*, which are the properties to be verified at each node. Each property can be defined in input signals, output signals, **time**, and **duration** variable type. In our case study, the test purposes are defined according to the timing fault models of G'' graph. These are then modeled for SDL specification and used as stop conditions. Table 4 gives the details of test purposes for all the processes of the *railroad crossing system*;

Table 3. Relationship between SDL Specification (Fig 5) and EFSM Model (Fig 3) for `Controller`

Current State		Next State		Edge	Constraint	Action
SDL Spec.	EFSM Model	SDL Spec.	EFSM Model	Name		
Start		Idle	s_0			ntrains:= 0
Idle	s_0	Idle	s_0		$(approach?)$ and $(ntrains > 1)$	$(nok!)$ and (zapproach:= now)
Idle	s_0	Sent_Lower	s_1	e_1	$(approach?)$ and $(ntrains \leqslant 1)$	$(ok!)$ and (zapproach:= now)
Sent_Lower	s_1	Sent_Lower	$s_{1,wait}$	$e_{1,wait}$	$(*?)$ or $(\text{now} - zapproach \leqslant \text{sent\_lower\_delay})$	
Sent_Lower	s_1	Idle	s_2	e_2	$(\text{now} - zapproach \geqslant \text{sent\_lower\_delay})$	$(lower!)$ and (zlower := now)
Idle	s_2	Idle	s_2		$(exit?)$ and $(ntrains \geqslant 0)$	$(ok!)$ and (zexit := now)
Idle	s_2	Sent_Raise	s_3	e_3	$(exit?)$ and $(ntrains \leqslant 0)$	(zexit := now)
Sent_Raise	s_3	Sent_Raise	s_3	$e_{3,wait}$	$(*?)$ or $(\text{now} - zexit \leqslant \text{sent\_raise\_delay})$	
Sent_Raise	s_3	Idle	s_0	e_4	$(\text{now} - zexit \geq 1)$	$(raise!)$ and (zraise := now)

Legend: Input = ?, Output = !, **now** = Global Clock, * = Any other signal;
Time type variables = zapproach, zexit, zraise, zlower;
Duration type variables = sent_lower_delay, sent_raise_delay

Table 4. Test purposes for SDL specification and EFSM model

Process Name	Test Purposes for EFSM Model	Test Purposes for SDL Specification
`Train`	Output *in* is generated in less than 2 minutes after *approach*	$xinside - xapproach < 2$
	Output *exit* is generated in more than 5 minutes after *approach*	$xexit - xapproach > 5$
`Controller`	Output *lower* is generated in less than 1 minutes after *approach*	$zlower - zapproach < 1$
	Output *raise* is generated in more than 1 minutes after *exit*	$zraise - zexit > 1$
`Gate`	Output *down* is generated in more than 1 minutes after *lower*	$ydown - ylower > 1$
	Output *up* is generated in more than 2 minutes after *raise*	$yup - yraise > 2$

(iii) **A preamble scenario** (optional) may be furnished in order to guide the algorithm to easily and quickly find a sequence which satisfies the stop conditions (test purposes). If no preamble scenario is given, the search starts from the initial state of all processes;

(iv) The **strategy of the search**, which can either be a breadth or a depth search, in order to generate an internal accessibility graph;

(v) A **local search parameter** (an integer), which defines the space required for the search before a *jump*.

The test sequence generated from SDL specification of `Controller` by applying *Hit-or-Jump* is given in Table 5. Note that all un-timed transitions have zero cost because of the assumption in SDL that these transitions take insignificant time to run. The cost of the wait edges is expressed in minutes.

Using our SDL specification, *Hit-or-Jump* generates test sequences with timing fault detection capabilities. Although, in our case study only timing fault TF_B is considered for `Controller`, other types of timing faults can also be modeled for `Controller`, `Train` and `Gate` processes [FUDA03, UWBWF05, UBWF06a]. *Hit-or-Jump* can then be used to generate a test sequence which takes into account all of the timing fault models for three processes. Therefore, the test sequences can be used both for unit testing of each process, and for verifying the communication among processes during the integration phase. Another advantage is the flexibility of representing the test sequences in Tree and Tabular Combined Notation (TTCN) [ETSI] or Message Sequence Chart (MSC) [ITUZ2] notation, facilitating the portability of the tests.

Table 5. Test sequence generated from SDL specification of `Controller`

Step No.	Current State	Next State	Cost (Mins.)	Inputs	Outputs
1	Idle	Sent_Lower	0	*approach*	
2	Sent_Lower	Sent_Lower	2		
3	Sent_Lower	Sent_Lower	0		
4	Sent_Lower	Idle	0		*lower*
5	Idle	Sent_Raise	0	*exit*	
6	Sent_Raise	Sent_Raise	2		
7	Sent_Raise	Sent_Raise	0		
8	Sent_Raise	Idle	0		*raise*

5   Conclusions and Future Work

In this paper, we apply our timing fault modeling strategy to writing formal specifications for communication protocols. As part of this approach, using the formal language of SDL, we specify the `Controller` process of *rail-road crossing system*, a popular benchmark for real-time systems. The EFSM model has the capability of representing a class of timing faults, which otherwise may not be detected in an IUT. We then apply *Hit-or-Jump* algorithm to the SDL specification based on our EFSM model to generate a test sequence that can detect these timing faults. In addition, including fault modeling into SDL specification ensures the synchronization among the timing constraints of different processes, and enables generation of portable test sequences since they can be easily represented in other formal languages such as TTCN or MSC.

As an extension of this work, we will consider the EFSM models with fault detection capabilities for other classes of timing faults, and multiple occurrences of these faults. This approach of modeling the timing faults of communicating processes into formal specifications will also applied to generate integration tests.

References

[AKLN99]   Ashour, M., Khendek, F., Le-Ngoc, T.: Formal description of real-time systems using SDL. In: Proc. of the Sixth Int'l. Conf. on Real-Time Comp. Sys. and Appl (RTCSA'99), Hong-Kong (December 1999)

[ALUR98]   Alur, R., Dill, D.: A theory of timed automata. Theoretical Comput. Sci. 126, 183–235 (1994)

[CLRZ99]   Cavalli, A., Lee, D., Rinderknecht, C., Zaidi, F.: Hit-or-jump an algorithm for embedded testing with applications to in services. In: Proc. of IFIP Int'l. Conf. FORTE/PSTV'99, (October 1999)

[CMZ04]   Cavalli, A., Mederreg, A., Zaidi, F.: Application of a Formal Testing Methodology to Wireless Telephony Networks. Journal of the Brazilian Comp. Soc. 10(2), 56–68 (2004)

[CRV05a]   Cavalli, A., Rodrigues, E.: Vieira. Test Case Generation based on Timed Constraints. In: IEEE ICESS 2005, Xian, China (December 2005)

[CRV05b]   Cavalli, A., Rodrigues, E.: Vieira. A Formal Approach of Interoperability Test Cases Generation Applied to Real Time Domain. In: IEEE I2TS 05, Florianpolis, SC, Brazil (December 2005)

[DU04]   Duale, A.Y., Uyar, M.U.: A method enabling feasible conformance test sequence generation for EFSM models. IEEE Trans. Commun. 53(5), 614–627 (2004)

[EDK02]   En-Nouaary, A., Dssouli, R., Khendek, F.: Timed Wp-method: Testing real-time systems. IEEE Trans. Softw. Eng. 28(11), 1023–1038 (2002)

[EDKE98]   En-Nouaary, A., Dssouli, R., Khendek, F., Elqortobi, A.: Timed test cases generation based on state characterization technique. In: Proc. IEEE Real-Time Syst. Symp. (RTSS), pp. 220–229, Madrid, Spain (1998)

[EKD99]   En-Nouaary, A., Khendek, F., Dssouli, R.: Fault coverage in testing real-time systems. In: Proc. IEEE Int'l Conf. Real-Time Comput. Syst. Appl. (RTCSA), Hong Kong, China (1999)

[ETSI]   ETSI. Methods for Testing and Specification (MTS), The Testing and Test Control Notation version 3, Part 1: TTCN-3 Core Language

[FAUD00]   Fecko, M.A., Amer, P.D., Uyar, M.U., Duale, A.Y.: Test generation in the presence of conflicting timers. In: Proc. IFIP Int'l Conf. Test. Commun. Syst. (TestCom), pp. 301–320, Ottawa, Canada (2000)

[FUDA03]   Fecko, M.A., Uyar, M.U., Duale, A.Y., Amer, P.D.: A technique to generate feasible tests for communications systems with multiple timers. IEEE/ACM Trans. Netw. 11(5), 796–809 (2003)

[HJL93]   Heitmeyer, C.L., Jeffords, R.D., Labaw, B.G., Benchmark, A.: for Comparing Different Approaches for Specifying and Verifying Real-Time Systems. In: Proc. Tenth Int'l. Workshop on Real-Time Operating Sys. and Software (May 1993)

[HL94]   Heitmeyer, C., Lynch, N.: The Generalized Railroad Crossing: A Case
              Study in Formal Verification of Real-Time System. In: Proc. of the 15th
              IEEE Real-Time Sys. Symp., Puerto Rico (December 1994)
[HL96]   Heitmeyer, C., Lynch, N.: Formal Verification of Real-time Systems
              Using Timed Automata. In: Heitmeyer, C., Lynch, N. (eds.) Trends in
              Formal Methods for Real-Time Computing, pp. 83–106. John Wiley
              and Sons, Ltd, Chichester (1996)
[ITUZ1]   ITU-T. Rec. Z.100 Specification and Description Language (1980)
[ITUZ2]   ITU-T. Rec. Z. 120 Message Sequence Charts, Geneva (1996)
[LRS98]   Lanphier, R., Rao, A., Schulzrinne, H.: Real time streaming protocol
              (RTSP). RFC 2326, IETF (1998)
[SCFJ96]   Schulzrinne, H., Casner, S., Frederick, R., Jacobson, V.: RTP: A trans-
              port protocol for real-time applications. RFC 1889, IETF (1996)
[TMCB03]   Teyssie, C., Mmammeri, Z., Carcenac, F., Buniol, F.: Etude Compar-
              ative de SDL et UML pour la Modelisation de Systemes Temps Reel.
              In: 11th Conf. on Real-Time and Embedded Systems, pp. 75–97, Paris,
              Teknea (April 2003)
[UWBWF05]   Uyar, M.U., Wang, Y., Batth, S.S., Wise, A., Fecko, M.A.: Timing Fault
              Models for Systems with Multiple Timers, IFIP Int'l. Conf. on Testing
              of Comm. Systems (TESTCOM), Concordia, Canada (2005)
[UBWF06a]   Uyar, M.U., Batth, S.S., Wang, Y., Fecko, M.A.: EFSM graph aug-
              mentation algorithms for modeling a class of single timing faults. IEEE
              Trans. Comput. (In review 2006)
[UFDA01]   Uyar, M.U., Fecko, M.A., Duale, A.Y., Amer, P.D., Sethi, A.S.: A for-
              mal approach to development of network protocols: Theory and appli-
              cation to a wireless standard. In: Proc. Concordia Prestigious Wksp
              Commun. Softw. Eng. (CPWCSE), Montreal, Canada (invited paper)
              (2001)
[UZ93]   Ural, H., Zhu, K.: Optimal length test sequence generation using dis-
              tinguishing sequences. IEEE/ACM Trans. Netw. 1(3), 358–371 (1993)
[XEN04]   Xiang, Z., En-Nouaary, A.: Test cases generation for embedded real-
              time systems based on test purposes. In: NOTERE'2004, Saidia, Maroc
              (Juin 2004)

Coordination Via Types in an Event-Based Framework[*]

Gianluigi Ferrari[1], Roberto Guanciale[2], Daniele Strollo[1,2], and Emilio Tuosto[3]

[1] Dipartimento di Informatica,
Università degli Studi di Pisa, Italy
{giangi,strollo}@di.unipi.it
[2] Istituto Alti Studi IMT Lucca, Italy
{roberto.guanciale,daniele.strollo}@imtlucca.it
[3] Computer Science Department, University of Leicester
et52@mcs.le.ac.uk

Abstract. We propose a novel approach to service choreography through a typed process calculus that features an event notification paradigm for coordinating distributed components (e.g., services). Basically, the type system expresses coordination policies for handling the events spawn in a network so that distributed components react to events when the type of their public interface is "compatible" with (the policies expressed by) the types of signals.

Remarkably, the type system can naturally handle *multi-party sessions*, as shown in the formalisation of the OpenID protocol which requires multi-party sessions for handling user identities.

1 Introduction

A well known paradigm for programming/modeling distributed systems is *event notification* (EN, for short), where distributed computational components can act as *publishers* and/or *subscribers*. When a component intends to send data to or requests a service from other components, it issues an *event* that eventually shall trigger a reaction from *subscribers* that previously *subscribed* for such kind of events. An important characteristic that discriminates EN systems lays in how the middleware dispatches events. Two main approaches are possible: *topic-based* and *content-based* mechanisms [5,16].

The dispatching mechanism in topic-based (also known as *subject-based*) EN systems is simpler than in content-based systems. In topic-based EN systems, events are categorized into topics which subscribers register to. When an event belonging to a topic τ is emitted, all the components subscribed for τ will eventually react to the event. Notice that publishers and subscribers have to know the topics at hand. In content-based EN, component decoupling is enforced by allowing subscribers to register for events satisfying a given *property*. When an event is emitted the middleware has to dispatch it to *all* the subscribers whose property holds on that event (an example of content-based is SIENA [4]). Notoriously, content-based dispatching mechanisms must be efficient because notification sets, i.e. the set of subscribers that must be notified for the event, can be order of magnitude larger than in topic-based EN [6,18]. A main advantage of

---

[*] Research supported by the EU FET-GC2 IST-2004-16004 Integrated Project SENSORIA and by the Italian FIRB Project TOCAI.IT.

content-based EN is that publishers and subscribers do not have to share any *a priori* knowledge about the topics. Subscribers use, instead, a language for expressing properties on events that publishers must simply accomplish with when emitting their events.A more abstract content-based model is the so called *type-based* EN [9] where topics are replaced by types (in a suitable type language). Typed events are also used in commercial middlewares (see [9] and the references therein).

This paper considers the Signal Calculus (SC) [11], a topic-based EN process calculus, and recasts it into a type-based framework, the eXtended Signal Calculus (XSC). The XSC calculus is a "typed version" of SC where events are emitted with types that coordinate publishers/subscribers interactions. For instance, an XSC publisher can emit an event with type $\tau \times \tau'$ that should be received by subscribers that can react to events of type τ *and* τ'. XSC types have a twofold role. First, typing allows subscribers to filter their events of interest (as usual in type-based EN). Second, publishers exploit type information to specify which (kind of) subscribers should react to events. For instance, in the previous example, a subscriber that is able to react only to events of type τ will not be capable of reacting to an event $\tau \times \tau'$. The way types are used is indeed the main original contribution of XSC with respect to standard type-based EN systems.

A further advantage of XSC is that types allow us to handle *sessions* so that a sort of "virtual communication link" among publishers and subscribers can be established despite they do not need to know each other's names. Intuitively, a session identifies the scope within which an event is significant: partners that are not in this scope cannot react to events of the session. Furthermore, the session handling mechanisms provided by XSC can deal with multi-party sessions in a natural way. At the best of our knowledge, multi-party sessions are ruled out from other approaches. For instance, in [13,3,2] only two-party sessions are tackled. Indeed, these proposals aim to model the basic use of sessions as done in many protocols of e.g. the IP-stack (TCP, HTTP, etc.). We argue that XSC complements these approaches by providing higher-level constructs on sessions that allow a closer formalization of more abstract protocols where multi-party sessions are relevant.

To demonstrate the adequacy of our approach, we apply XSC to specify the OpenID protocol [17], a complex protocol for managing distributed identities whose behavior requires many parties to participate to the same session. XSC mechanisms have allowed us to identify and formally specify *all the assumptions* underlying the definition of the OpenID protocol. We argue that our approach will make easier to reason and verify properties of protocols requiring multi-party sessions.

The main effort of this paper is on the formal definition of XSC showing its adequacy to handle complex coordination policies via typing information. This is part of an ongoing work on the design, implementation and experimental evaluation of a middleware, called JSCL [11], supporting coordination policies for service-oriented applications. The distinguished feature of our approach resides in the close interplay between formal definition and implementation: the implementation of the JSCL middleware is driven by the formal definition of the (X)SC calculus.

Structure of the paper. Section 2 reviews the basic features of the SC calculus. Section 3 introduces the concept of multi-party sessions on events and shows how it yields a synchronization mechanism. Section 4 introduces XSC types. The operational semantics of XSC is presented in Section 5. In Section 6 we specify the OpenID protocol. Finally, Section 7 gives some concluding remarks.

2 Preliminaries: Signal Calculus

The *Signal Calculus* (SC) is a process calculus introduced in [11] as a foundational model of the JSCL (after Java Signal Core Layer) programming middleware, for coordinating distributed components (e.g., web services). SC relies on the EN paradigm where *components*, the basic building blocks of SC, interact by issuing/reacting to *events*. A component represents a 'simple' service interacting via asynchronous signal passing. Each component is identified by a unique name, which, intuitively, can be thought of as the URI of the published service. The signals exchanged among components are messages containing information regarding the managed resources and the events raised during internal computations. Signals are classified by *topics*; specifically, each component specifies (i) the reaction to activate on reception of signals of a certain topic and (ii) the set of event flows, namely the collection of component names the emitted signals will be delivered. Hence, while reactions define the interacting behavior of the component, flows define the component view of the coordination policies. The SC primitives allow one to *dynamically* modify the topology of the coordination policies by adding new flows and reactions to components.

Standard EN paradigms rely on brokered communication; SC, instead, adopts a non-brokered notification mechanism where subscription and emission are *explicitly* tagged with naming information, e.g. the name of the target components. This avoids any centralization point by distributing the connection managing to each involved participant. Brokered EN paradigms are more appropriate when coordination is handled by an orchestrator, while non-brokered approaches fit much better when choreography is adopted. For a detailed comparison among brokered and non-brokered EN see [14].

The adoption of the EN paradigm, for managing coordination policies has two main advantages. On the one hand, it is a well known programming model and, on the other hand, it permits the distribution of coordination activities and of the underlying computational infrastructure. This distribution is obtained by decoupling publishers and subscribers. The intuitive idea is that publishers and subscribers do not rely on any 'a priori' knowledge.

The dynamic flavor of the SC calculus permits modeling a wide range of coordination policies for service-oriented applications (e.g. in [10] the primitives have been used to deal with dynamic and heterogeneous networks). However, other primitives providing high-level abstractions for programming are desirable. In particular, in the current formulation, information associated to signals is not structured and topics cannot be created dynamically. Furthermore, the notion of session abstraction is missing: components cannot keep track of concurrent event notifications.

3 Extended Signal Calculus

In this section, we present an extension of the SC calculus, called XSC, that permits managing of sessions and is also capable of handling structured topics via suitable types.

3.1 Managing Sessions

The calculus is centered around the notion of *component*. A component $a[B]_F^R$ is a service identified by a unique name a: the public address of the service. The expression B describes service internal behavior. Expressions R and F, called *reactions* and *flows*, respectively, have to be thought of as the service interface. We assume a set of *topic names* Λ (ranged over by τ), a set of signal variables (ranged over by x) and a set of signal names (ranged over by $s, s_1, s_2...$). Signal names represent data exchanged among components and should carry additional information even if this feature is not explicitly modeled. Finally, we assume a set of component names $a, b, ...$ Hereafter, we adopt the notation a to denote a set of component names.

The syntax of behaviors is given by the following grammar,

$$B ::= 0 \mid B \mid B' \mid !B \mid$$

$$\mid \quad \overline{s} : \tau \copyright \tau'.B' \qquad\qquad (Signal\ emission)$$
$$\mid \quad \nu\tau.B' \qquad\qquad\qquad (Topic\ creation)$$
$$\mid \quad +\lceil x : \tau \copyright \lambda\tau' \rightarrow B\rceil.B' \qquad (Lambda\ reaction)$$
$$\mid \quad +\lceil x : \tau \copyright \tau' \rightarrow B\rceil.B' \qquad (Check\ reaction)$$
$$\mid \quad +\lfloor \tau \rightsquigarrow a\rfloor.B' \qquad\qquad (Flow\ update)$$

where the productions in the first row have the usual process algebraic meaning. A *signal emission* $\overline{s} : \tau \copyright \tau'.B'$ describes the emission of the signal s of topic τ over the session identified by the topic τ'. Topics can be freshly generated using the *topic creation* primitive. A *lambda reaction* $+\lceil x : \tau \copyright \lambda\tau' \rightarrow B\rceil.B'$ installs a "generic reaction" for the topic τ in the component interface; this reaction handles all signals with topic τ, regardless of their session. In the reaction behavior B, τ' and x are bound by the lambda reaction[1]. After the installation of a reaction the continuation B' is executed. Conversely, *check reaction* installs a reaction that can handle only signals having the topic τ issued for the session τ' and, in this case, only x is bound in the reaction behavior B. A *flow update* $+\lfloor \tau \rightsquigarrow a\rfloor.B$ extends the flow of a component, specifying the set of component names a to which deliver signals having topic τ. After the installation of a flow, the behavior B' is executed.

Reactions and flows syntax have the following syntax:

$$R ::= 0 \mid R\mid R \qquad\qquad\qquad\qquad F ::= 0 \mid F\mid F$$
$$\mid \quad x : \tau\copyright\lambda\tau' \rightarrow B \quad (Lambda\ reaction) \qquad\qquad \mid \quad \tau \rightsquigarrow a \quad (single\ flow)$$
$$\mid \quad x : \tau\copyright\tau' \rightarrow B \quad (Check\ reaction)$$

where the *empty reaction (resp. flow)* 0 cannot respond to any signal (resp. cannot emit a signal for any receiver) and *reaction (resp. flow) composition* $R\mid R$ allows a component to react to (resp. to emit) different kinds of signal. Reactions R_1 and R_2 are called *subreactions* of the reaction composition $R_1\mid R_2$.

Reactions describe how a component reacts upon the reception of a signal. As pointed out before, a lambda reaction is triggered by signals independently from their session,

---

[1] See Appendix A for a formal definition of free and bound names of the binders of XSC.

while a check reaction reacts only to signals in the session τ'. Once a reaction to a signal takes place, the behavior B will be executed in the component in parallel with the existing behaviors. Flows describe the component view of the choreography: a component with a single flow $\tau \rightsquigarrow a$ can deliver signals of topic τ to components specified in a.

Networks describe component distribution and carry signals exchanged among components. Network syntax is defined as follows:

$$N ::= \emptyset \mid a[B]_F^R \mid N\|N \mid \langle s : t©\tau@a \rangle \mid \nu\tau.N$$

A network can be empty $\emptyset$, a single component $a[B]_F^R$, or the parallel composition of networks $N\|N'$. Networks carry signals exchanged among components. The signal emission spawns into the network, for each target component, an "envelope" $\langle s : t©\tau@a \rangle$ containing the signal and the name a of the target component. Finally, the last production allows to extend the scope of freshly generated topics over networks.

The structural congruence over reactions, flows and behaviors is the smallest congruence relation that satisfies the commutative monoidal laws for $(R, |, 0)$, $(F, |, 0)$ and $(B, \mid, 0)$. Also, for the structural congruence over behaviors, the following laws hold:

$$\nu\tau.0 \equiv 0, \qquad (\nu\tau.B) \mid B' \equiv \nu\tau.(B \mid B'), \text{ if } \tau \notin fn(B')$$

and, whenever $B \equiv B'$:

$$+\lceil x : \tau©\lambda\tau' \rightarrow B \rceil.B'' \equiv +\lceil x : \tau©\lambda\tau' \rightarrow B' \rceil.B''$$
$$+\lceil x : \tau©\tau' \rightarrow B \rceil.B'' \equiv +\lceil x : \tau©\tau' \rightarrow B' \rceil.B''$$

If $B \equiv B'$, the following rules hold for structural congruence over reactions:

$$x : \tau©\lambda\tau' \rightarrow B \equiv x : \tau©\lambda\tau' \rightarrow B'$$
$$x : \tau©\tau' \rightarrow B \equiv x : \tau©\tau' \rightarrow B'$$

Similarly, $\equiv$ is the smallest equivalence relation that respects the commutative monoidal laws for $(N, \|, \emptyset)$ and the following ones:

$$a[0]_F^0 \equiv \emptyset, \qquad \nu\tau.\emptyset \equiv \emptyset, \qquad (\nu\tau.N)\|N' \equiv \nu\tau.(N\|N'), \text{ if } \tau \notin fn(N')$$

$$\frac{F_1 \equiv F_2 \quad B_1 \equiv B_2 \quad R_1 \equiv R_2}{a[B_1]_{F_1}^{R_1} \equiv a[B_2]_{F_2}^{R_2}}, \qquad \frac{\tau \notin fn(R) \cup fn(F) \cup \{a\}}{a[\nu\tau.B]_F^R \equiv \nu\tau.a[B]_F^R}.$$

To give an intuition of the features and the facilities of XSC, we consider a simple scenario. The operational semantics will be presented in Section 4.

3.2 Joining Events

Since XSC components are autonomous entities communicating through asynchronous primitives, it could be useful to introduce a lightweight synchronization mechanism that allows us to express that a task can be executed whenever other concurrent tasks have been completed. In this scenario we show how to encode a form of join synchronization among concurrent tasks.

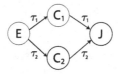

Fig. 1. An example of synchronization between two components

Figure 1 shows an emitter E, two intermediate components C_1 and C_2, and the join service J. The emitter E starts the communications raising two events of different topics toward C_1 and C_2 that perform an internal computation and then notify their termination by issuing an event to the join service. The component J waits that both the intermediate services have completed their tasks and then executes its internal behavior B. The signals sent to C_1 and C_2 are both related to the same session τ that is later used by J to apply the synchronization on the same workflow. Clearly, the two intermediate services C_1 and C_2 can concurrently perform their tasks, while the execution of the service J can be triggered only after the completion of their execution.

This example can be modeled by the XSC network $E \| C_1 \| C_2 \| J$, where:

$$E \triangleq e[\nu\tau.\overline{s} : \tau_1 \textcircled{c}\tau.\overline{s} : \tau_2 \textcircled{c}\tau.0]^0_{\tau_1 \rightsquigarrow c_1 | \tau_2 \rightsquigarrow c_2}$$

$$C_i \triangleq c_i[0]^{x:\tau_i \textcircled{c}\lambda\tau \rightarrow \overline{x}:\tau_i \textcircled{c}\tau.0}_{\tau_i \rightsquigarrow j}, \qquad\qquad i = 1, 2$$

$$J \triangleq j[0]^{x:\tau_1 \textcircled{c}\lambda\tau \rightarrow + \lceil x':\tau_2 \textcircled{c}\tau \rightarrow B \rceil.0}_0$$

The join component has only one active reaction installed for signals having topic τ_1. When the two intermediary services forward their signals, the envelope containing the τ_2 event cannot be consumed by the join, and remains pending over the network. The reception of the τ_1 envelope triggers the activation of the join generic reaction. The reaction *reads* the session of the signal τ_1 and creates a new specialized reaction for the signal topic τ_2. This reaction can be triggered only by signals that refer to the session received by the τ_1 signal. When such kind of signal is received, the proper behavior B is executed. Notice that the creation of the specialized reaction for the τ_2 implies that a possible pendent envelope is consumed.

4   Structured Topics

We have described how the session mechanism permits to specify complex coordination policies by constraining the ways components may react to notification of events. The basic idea is to control the coordination workflow by exploiting information about topics and sessions to trigger the execution of the suitable reactions. In this section, we further develop this idea by introducing some operators on topics that induce an algebraic structure on events. We then show how the algebraic structure on events can be used to have a finer control over the coordination activities of components.

We define the signal topic t as follows:

$$t ::= \varepsilon \mid \star \mid \tau \mid t \times t \mid t + t$$

$$t' \times t'' \equiv t'' \times t'$$
$$t \times t \equiv t$$
$$t' \times (t'' \times t''') \equiv (t' \times t'') \times t'''$$
$$t \times \star \equiv t$$
$$t \times \varepsilon \equiv \varepsilon$$
$$t \times (t' + t'') \equiv (t \times t') + (t \times t'')$$

$$t' + t'' \equiv t'' + t'$$
$$t + t \equiv t$$
$$t' + (t'' + t''') \equiv (t' + t'') + t'''$$
$$t + \varepsilon \equiv t$$
$$t + \star \equiv \star$$

Fig. 2. Structural congruence over topics

The constant topics ε and $\star$ are used to define the *empty* and the *global* event kinds, respectively. Intuitively, a signal having an empty topic can be consumed by a reaction having an empty behavior. A signal having a global topic can be handled by any component, activating any reaction. Signal topics can be composed using the constructors $\times$ and $+$. A signal having topic $t \times t'$ can be consumed only by components that can handle both event kinds t and t'. Moreover a signal having topic $t + t'$ can be consumed by any component that can handle event kinds t or t'. The constructors $+$ and $\times$ can be informally interpreted as logical *disjunction* and *conjunction*.

The formal definition of the meaning of structured topics is given algebraically by introducing a structural congruence over them (see Figure 2). Notice that the $\times$ and $+$ are associative, commutative and idempotent. Also, $\times$ distributes over $+$, moreover, $\star$ and ε are their respective neutral elements. For instance, $t \times \star \equiv t$ and $t + \varepsilon \equiv t$ states that a signal of topic $t \times \star$ or $t + \varepsilon$ activates the same reactions activated by signals having topic t; similarly $t \times \varepsilon \equiv \varepsilon$ states that a signal of topic $t \times \varepsilon$ cannot activate any reaction, while $t + \star \equiv \star$ states that a signal of topic $t + \star$ activates any reaction. Formally, the algebraic structure over topic takes the form of a C-Semiring [1].

Preorder relation. *The binary relation $\sqsubseteq$ over topics is the least preorder satisfying the following axioms:*

$$t \sqsubseteq \varepsilon, \qquad \star \sqsubseteq t, \qquad t \sqsubseteq t, \qquad t \sqsubseteq t \times t', \qquad t + t' \sqsubseteq t$$

Intuitively the preorder $t_1 \sqsubseteq t_2$ formalizes the idea that the topic t_1 is less restrictive than the topic t_2. For example, a signal having topic $\tau_1 + \tau_2$ triggers either a reaction for τ_1 or one for τ_2. Hence, the coordination policy expressed by $\tau_1 + \tau_2$ is less restrictive than the one expressed by τ_1.

The algebraic structure over topics allows us to define the policies to aggregate events. The XSC syntax of behaviors can be extended to deal with the structure of topics by simply refining the signal emission primitive as $\overline{s} : t \copyright \tau'.B'$, where t represents the signal topic. We have now to specify the way a component may react upon the reception of a signal of a certain topic. In other words, a main question, here, is to understand which reactions a component may dynamically activate to match the policy specified by the topics of events. In this paper, we will answer this question by introducing a suitable type system over component reactions. The type system allows us to precisely identify the set of reactions matching a given event topic.

Conversation types (ranged over by T) classify signals by their topic structures (policies) and sessions. Their syntax is defined below:

$$T ::= t©\tau \mid \qquad \textit{(Session conversation type)}$$
$$t©\star \qquad \textit{(Generic conversation type)}$$

A *session conversation type* $t©\tau$ characterizes signals (of a topic t) *within* a session τ. A *generic conversation type* $t©\star$ captures the notion of signals (of a topic t) not belonging to a specific session.

Conversation types are equivalent if the structures of their topics and their sessions are equivalent. Formally, equations in Figure 2 are extended with the following rules:

$$\frac{t \equiv t'}{t©\tau \equiv t'©\tau} \qquad\qquad \frac{t \equiv t'}{t©\star \equiv t'©\star}$$

Conversation types can be equipped with a subtype relation which will be used to formalize how signals are consumed by reactions. Namely, if $T \sqsubseteq T'$ then reactions able to consume signals with conversation type T' can consume signals with conversation type T as well.

Subtype relation. *The subtype relation $T \sqsubseteq T'$ over conversation types is defined as the smallest preorder relation that satisfies the following inference rules:*

$$\frac{t \sqsubseteq t'}{t©\tau \sqsubseteq t'©\tau} \ (1) \qquad \frac{t \sqsubseteq t'}{t©\tau \sqsubseteq t'©\star} \ (2) \qquad \frac{t \sqsubseteq t'}{t©\star \sqsubseteq t'©\star} \ (3)$$

Rules (1) and (3) have a clear interpretation in terms of the preorder over topics. Rule (2) is controvariant wrt the session part of the conversation type and formalizes the idea that a lambda reaction can be activated by signals independently by their session.

A *reaction type* is a (possibly empty) set of conversation types and describes the set of signals that can be consumed by a reaction.

Reaction typing. *A reaction R has reaction type $\mathbb{T}$ when $\vdash R : \mathbb{T}$ can be inferred from the following rules:*

$$\frac{}{\vdash 0 : \emptyset} \ (1) \qquad\qquad \frac{}{\vdash x : \tau©\tau' \to B : \{\tau©\tau'\}} \ (2)$$

$$\frac{}{\vdash x : \tau©\lambda\tau' \to B : \{\tau©\star\}} \ (3) \qquad \frac{\vdash R_1 : \mathbb{T}_1 \qquad \vdash R_2 : \mathbb{T}_2}{\vdash R_1 | R_2 : \mathbb{T}_1 \cup \mathbb{T}_2} \ (4)$$

Rules $(1 \div 4)$ are quite natural; for instance, rule (3) states that the type of a lambda reaction $x : \tau©\lambda\tau' \to B$ is the singleton $\{\tau©\star\}$. Reaction types have a natural subtype relation given by the subset inclusion ($\mathbb{T} \subseteq \mathbb{T}'$).

Given a non-empty reaction type $\mathbb{T} = \{\tau_1©r_1, \ldots, \tau_n©r_n : r_i \in \Lambda \cup \{\star\}$ for $i = 1, \ldots, n\}$, we let

$$^\times\mathbb{T} = \tau_1 \times \ldots \times \tau_n, \quad \mathbb{T}^\times = r_1 \times \ldots \times r_n, \quad {}^+\mathbb{T} = \tau_1 + \ldots + \tau_n, \quad \mathbb{T}^+ = r_1 + \ldots + r_n$$

while $^\times\mathbb{T} = \star = \mathbb{T}^\times$ and $^+\mathbb{T} = \varepsilon = \mathbb{T}^+$ if $\mathbb{T} = \emptyset$. The following properties trivially hold.

$$^\times\mathbb{T} = \star \Leftrightarrow \mathbb{T} = \emptyset \qquad\qquad \mathbb{T}^\times = \tau \Rightarrow (\mathbb{T} \neq \emptyset \wedge \forall r_i.r_i \in \{\tau, \star\})$$
$$\mathbb{T}^+ = \varepsilon \Leftrightarrow \mathbb{T} = \emptyset \qquad\qquad \mathbb{T}^\times = \star \Leftrightarrow (\mathbb{T} = \emptyset \vee \forall r_i.r_i = \star)$$
$$\mathbb{T}^+ = \star \Leftrightarrow (\mathbb{T} \neq \emptyset \wedge \exists r_i.r_i = \star) \qquad \mathbb{T}^+ = \tau \Leftrightarrow (\mathbb{T} \neq \emptyset \wedge \forall r_i.r_i = \tau)$$

After having defined the preorder on topics and the subtype relation for conversation types, we define a formal mechanism that establishes when a reaction is *enabled* to handle a signal reception. This definition is the basic tool that will be exploited at run-time to activate the reaction matching an event notification.

Reaction enabling. *Let $T \equiv t\,\text{\textcircled{c}}\,\tau$ be a conversation type and $\mathbb{T}$ a non empty reaction type. We say that reactions with type $\mathbb{T}$ can be activated by signals with conversation type T, and we write $T \approx \mathbb{T}$, if the following conditions hold:*

1. $t \sqsubseteq {}^{\times}\mathbb{T}$ *and* $\mathbb{T}^{\times} \sqsubseteq \tau$
2. $\forall \mathbb{T}' \subset \mathbb{T}.\mathbb{T}' \not\equiv \emptyset \implies \mathbb{T}'$ *does not enjoy the Condition 1*

Condition 1 expresses that the topic of the signals is less restrictive than the conjunction of the topics of the reactions ($t \sqsubseteq^{\times} \mathbb{T}$) and, since $\mathbb{T}$ is not empty then it is of the form $\{\tau_1\text{\textcircled{c}}r_1, \ldots, \tau_n\text{\textcircled{c}}r_n : r_i \in \Lambda \cup \{\star\}$ for $i = 1, \ldots, n\}$, reactions waiting for a session topic different from τ cannot be activated because $\forall i.r_i \equiv \tau \lor r_i \equiv \star$. Condition 2 ensures that enabled reactions are *minimal*, namely, that each subreaction ($\forall \mathbb{T}' \subset \mathbb{T}$) cannot be activated by signals having signal type T. The following table gives examples where conditions 1 and 2 hold or not.

Conversation Type $t\,\text{\textcircled{c}}\,\tau$	Reaction Type $\mathbb{T}$	$t \sqsubseteq^{\times}\mathbb{T}$	$\mathbb{T}^{\times} \sqsubseteq \tau$	Cond. 2
$\tau_1 + \tau_2\,\text{\textcircled{c}}\,\tau$	$\{\tau_1\text{\textcircled{c}}\tau\}$	$\checkmark$	$\checkmark$	$\checkmark$
$\tau_1 \times \tau_2\,\text{\textcircled{c}}\,\tau$	$\{\tau_1\text{\textcircled{c}}\tau, \tau_2\text{\textcircled{c}}\star\}$	$\checkmark$	$\checkmark$	$\checkmark$
$\tau_1 \times \tau_2\,\text{\textcircled{c}}\,\tau$	$\{\tau_1\text{\textcircled{c}}\tau\}$	$\times$	$\checkmark$	$\checkmark$
$\tau_1\,\text{\textcircled{c}}\,\tau$	$\{\tau_1\text{\textcircled{c}}\tau'\}$	$\checkmark$	$\times$	$\checkmark$
$\tau_1 + \tau_2\,\text{\textcircled{c}}\,\tau$	$\{\tau_1\text{\textcircled{c}}\tau, \tau_2\text{\textcircled{c}}\star\}$	$\checkmark$	$\checkmark$	$\times$
$\tau_1 \times \tau_2\,\text{\textcircled{c}}\,\tau$	$\{\tau_1\text{\textcircled{c}}\tau, \tau_2\text{\textcircled{c}}\star, \tau_3\text{\textcircled{c}}\star\}$	$\checkmark$	$\checkmark$	$\times$

Enabled reaction set. *Given a reaction R, the* set of enabled subreactions by a conversation type $t\,\text{\textcircled{c}}\,\tau$ *is defined as* $R_{t\text{\textcircled{c}}\tau} = \{R'.R \equiv R'|R'' \land \vdash R' : \mathbb{T} \land t\,\text{\textcircled{c}}\,\tau \approx \mathbb{T}\}$.

Let R_1 be $x : \tau_1\,\text{\textcircled{c}}\,\tau \to B_1$ and R_2 be $x : \tau_2\,\text{\textcircled{c}}\,\lambda\tau' \to B_2$, examples exploiting the enabled reaction set are given in Table 1. Notice that in the second row of Table 1 only one

Table 1. Enabled reaction set example

Conversation Type $t\,\text{\textcircled{c}}\,\tau$	Reaction R	$R_{t\text{\textcircled{c}}\tau}$
$\tau_1 + \tau_2\,\text{\textcircled{c}}\,\tau$	R_1	$\{R_1\}$
$\tau_1 \times \tau_2\,\text{\textcircled{c}}\,\tau$	$R_1|R_2$	$\{R_1|R_2\}$
$\tau_1 \times \tau_2\,\text{\textcircled{c}}\,\tau$	R_1	$\emptyset$
$\tau_1 + \tau_2\,\text{\textcircled{c}}\,\tau$	$R_1|R_2$	$\{R_1, R_2\}$

reaction ($R_1|R_2$) is enabled. Upon reception of a signal having conversation type T, both subreactions R_1 and R_2 will be concurrently activated. Also, in the fourth row of Table 1 two different reactions (R_1 and R_2) are enabled. Upon the reception of a signal having conversation type T, only one of them will be activated nondeterministically.

Preferred reactions. *Let R be a reaction and $t\textcircled{c}\tau$ be a session conversation type. The set of preferred reactions in R wrt $t\textcircled{c}\tau$ is defined as:*

$$R_{t\textcircled{c}\tau\downarrow} = \left\{ R_1 \in R_{t\textcircled{c}\tau}.\vdash R_1 : \mathbb{T}_1 \Rightarrow \forall R_2 \in R_{t\textcircled{c}\tau}.\vdash R_2 : \mathbb{T}_2 \Rightarrow \begin{pmatrix} \mathbb{T}_1^+ \equiv \tau \\ \vee \\ \mathbb{T}_2^\times \sqsubseteq \mathbb{T}_1^\times \end{pmatrix} \right\}$$

Basically, each reaction $R_1 \in R_{t\textcircled{c}\tau\downarrow}$ is composed only by check reactions for the τ session or, if it is composed only by lambda reactions, then it cannot exists another subreaction composed by check reactions for τ.

The topic structures can be adopted to model the example described in Section 3.2, refining the emitter component as $E \triangleq e[\nu\tau.\bar{s} : \tau_1 + \tau_2\textcircled{c}\tau.0]^0_{\tau_1 \leadsto c_1 | \tau_2 \leadsto c_2}$.

5 Operational Semantics

The operational semantics of XSC is given in the classical reduction style and exploits the structural congruences defined in Section 3.1. Some auxiliary functions on flows and reactions are introduced for simplifying the definition of the reduction relation on networks.

The *flow projection*, $(F)\downarrow_t$, defined as

$$(\tau \leadsto a)\downarrow_\tau = a \qquad\qquad (\tau \leadsto a)\downarrow_{\tau'} = (\tau \leadsto a)\downarrow_\varepsilon = (0)\downarrow_t = \emptyset$$
$$(\tau \leadsto a)\downarrow_* = a \qquad\qquad (F_1|F_2)\downarrow_t = (F_1)\downarrow_t \cup (F_2)\downarrow_t$$
$$(F)\downarrow_{t_1+t_2} = (F)\downarrow_{t_1} \cup (F)\downarrow_{t_2} \qquad (F)\downarrow_{t_1 \times t_2} = (F)\downarrow_{t_1} \cap (F)\downarrow_{t_2}$$

takes a flow and a topic and yields the set of target component names for the topic t.

The *reaction projection*, $(R)\downarrow_{s:T}$, defined as

$$(0)\downarrow_{s:*} = (0,0)$$
$$(x : \tau'\textcircled{c}\tau'' \to B)\downarrow_{s:t\textcircled{c}\tau} = (\{s/x\}B, 0)$$
$$(x : \tau'\textcircled{c}\lambda\tau'' \to B)\downarrow_{s:t\textcircled{c}\tau} = (\{s/x, \tau/\tau''\}B, x : \tau'\textcircled{c}\lambda\tau'' \to B)$$
$$(R_1|R_2)\downarrow_{s:t\textcircled{c}\tau} = (B' \mid B'', R'|R''), \quad \text{if } (R_1)\downarrow_{s:t\textcircled{c}\tau} = (B', R') \text{ and } (R_2)\downarrow_{s:t\textcircled{c}\tau} = (B'', R'')$$

takes a reaction R and a signal s typed by T and returns a pair (B, R') such that B is the behavior of R instantiated with s and R' is the reaction to be installed. Notice that reaction projection permits to consume check reactions and to maintain lambda reactions installed. Also, reaction projection is applied, by construction, to reactions that can consume the signal s. This assumption is guaranteed by the reduction rules using the type system.

The reduction relation $\to$ over networks is defined in Figure 3. Reactions can be added to a component by executing the behavioral primitives RLambaUpd and RCheck-Upd. These primitives change the interface of a by appending to the set of installed reactions the new one. The only difference between the two primitives regards the kind of reaction installed. Analogously the FlowUpd updates the flow interface of a component by appending new target component names. The Emit and RActivation rules define notification dispatching: at emission time, component a spawns into the network a signal targeted to all the components ($c_i \in b$) subscribed for the signal type (according to the

$$\frac{}{a[+\lceil x:\tau\textcircled{c}\lambda\tau'\to B\rceil.B'\mid B'']^R_F\to a[B'\mid B'']^{R|x:\tau\textcircled{c}\lambda\tau'\to B}_F}\text{(RLambaUpd)}$$

$$\frac{}{a[+\lceil x:\tau\textcircled{c}\tau'\to B\rceil.B'\mid B'']^R_F\to a[B'\mid B'']^{R|x:\tau\textcircled{c}\tau'\to B}_F}\text{(RCheckUpd)}$$

$$\frac{}{a[+\lfloor\tau\rightsquigarrow b\rfloor.B\mid B']^R_F\to a[B\mid B']^R_{F|\tau\rightsquigarrow b}}\text{(FlowUpd)}$$

$$\frac{(F){\downarrow}_{t\textcircled{c}\tau}=b}{a[\bar{s}:t\textcircled{c}\tau.B]^R_F\to a[B]^R_F\|\Sigma_{c_i\in b}\langle s:t\textcircled{c}\tau@c_i\rangle}\text{(Emit)}$$

$$\frac{R\equiv R'|R_0 \quad R'\in R_{t\textcircled{c}\tau\downarrow} \quad (R'){\downarrow}_{s:t\textcircled{c}\tau}=(B',R'')}{\langle s:t\textcircled{c}\tau@a\rangle\|a[B]^R_F\to a[B|B']^{R_0|R''}_F}\text{(RActivation)} \qquad \frac{N\to N'}{N\|N_1\to N'\|N_1}\text{(NStep)}$$

Fig. 3. Operational semantics

$(F){\downarrow}_t$ projection). Once a signal envelop has been spawn into the network the RActivation rule can be applied to the target component; the application of this rule activates, non deterministically, a reaction among the ones in the reaction projection $R'\in R_{t\textcircled{c}\tau\downarrow}$. Then, the activated reaction is replaced in the interface of a by R'' reaction obtained by applying the reaction projection.

6 Federated Identity Example

In order to illustrate the main facilities made available by the XSC calculus, in this section we show an example involving multi-party sessions. A typical scenario in which several agents are involved into the same session is represented by user-centric digital identity systems. We consider an application of the OpenID protocol, an open framework for distributed identity management. The solution presented can be easy adapted for similar systems e.g., i-Name [15] and Microsoft CardSpace [7].

The main advantage of the identity management systems is the unique identification of the user agent on the network in the same manner an URI uniquely identifies a website. To reach this goal, these systems define a special kind of services, called *identity providers*, that act as intermediate agents among service consumers and providers. Another key feature offered by OpenID is the decentralization of the authentication protocol decoupling the service from a particular identity provider.

Hereafter, we denote a service consumer as C, an identity provider as IP and a service provider as SP. The protocol consists of two phases. In the first phase, C accesses its IP to be authenticated and to establish a private session. In the second phase C accesses a service SP specifying its identity and the IP that certifies her/his credentials. Notice that the actual authentication mechanism is not part of the specification of OpenID, and so it will not be treated: here we only deal with the message exchanges among the involved parties.

We start by giving the informal description of the OpenID protocol:

1. C initiates authentication with IP by presenting its credentials.
2. IP verifies user credentials and generates a new session shared with C. The session will be used to identify C.
3. C initiates authentication by presenting a User-Supplied Identifier to the SP via its User-Agent.
4. SP establishes an Endpoint URL used by C for authentication.
5. SP redirects the User-Agent of C to IP with an authentication request.
6. IP establishes whether C is authorized to perform authentication and wishes to do so. The way C authenticates to IP and any authentication policy are out of scope for OpenID.
7. IP redirects the User-Agent of C back to SP with either an assertion stating that the authentication is approved or a message that the authentication failed.
8. SP verifies the information received from the IP.

The OpenID protocol can be formally specified as the XSC network $C\|IP\|SP$ where C, IP and SP are the components defined in Figure 4. Notice that we omit to model the data exchanged among components, because we focus on the session exchanges and message sequences.

$$C \triangleq c[B_c]^0_{Auth \rightsquigarrow i|Claim \rightsquigarrow s|Delegate \rightsquigarrow i}$$

$$B_c \triangleq \mathsf{vr}. + \lceil x : AuthOK \copyright \lambda s_{ip} \rightarrow B_{AuthOK}(s_{ip}) \rceil$$
$$.\overline{credentials} : Auth \copyright r.0$$

$$B_{AuthOK}(s_{ip}) \triangleq \mathsf{vr}. + \lceil x : Redirect_{sp} \copyright \lambda s_{sp} \rightarrow B_{Redirect_{si}}(s_{ip}, s_{sp}) \rceil$$
$$.\overline{identifier} : Claim \copyright r.0$$

$$B_{Redirect_{si}}(s_{ip}, s_{sp}) \triangleq + \lceil x : Redirect_{si} \copyright \lambda s_3 \rightarrow B_{Redirect_{is}}(s_{ip}, s_{sp}, s_3) \rceil .$$
$$\overline{x} : Delegate \copyright s_{ip}.0$$

$$B_{Redirect_{is}}(s_{ip}, s_{sp}, s_3) \triangleq + \lfloor s_{sp} \rightsquigarrow s \rfloor.\overline{p} : s_{sp} \copyright s_3.0$$

$$IP \triangleq i[0]^{R_{ip}}_{AuthOK \rightsquigarrow c|Redirect_{ip} \rightsquigarrow c|Verified \rightsquigarrow s}$$
$$R_{ip} \triangleq x : Auth \copyright \lambda r \rightarrow B_{Auth}(r)$$
$$B_{Auth}(r) \triangleq \mathsf{v}s_{ip}. + \lceil x : Delegate \copyright s_{ip} \rightarrow B_{Delegate}(s_{ip}) \rceil .$$
$$\overline{x} : AuthOK \copyright s_{ip}.0$$
$$B_{Delegate}(s_{ip}) \triangleq \mathsf{v}s_3. + \lceil x : Verify \copyright s_3 \rightarrow B_{Verify} \rceil .\overline{x} : Redirect_{ip} \copyright s_3.0$$
$$B_{Verify} \triangleq \overline{x} : Verified \copyright s_3.0$$

$$SP \triangleq s[0]^{R_{sp}}_{Redirect_{si} \rightsquigarrow c|Verify \rightsquigarrow i}$$
$$R_{sp} \triangleq x : Claim \copyright \lambda r \rightarrow B_{Claim}(r)$$
$$B_{Claim}(r) \triangleq \mathsf{v}s_{sp}. + \lceil x : s_{sp} \copyright \lambda s_3 \rightarrow B_{Check}(s_3) \rceil .\overline{x} : Redirect_{si} \copyright s_{sp}.0$$
$$B_{Check}(s_3) \triangleq + \lceil x : Verified \copyright s_3 \rightarrow B_{Verified} \rceil .\overline{x} : Verify \copyright s_3.0$$

Fig. 4. XSC specification of the OpenID protocol

The user sends its credentials to the Identity Provider, rising an *Auth* event (via the B_c behavior). Notice that the client creates a new reaction to receive an event corresponding to the successful authentication (*AuthOK*) from the identity provider.

When the identity provider receives an authentication request (*Auth* event), it generates a new session (s_{ip}). This will be used later to identify the user agent without an explicit communication of the user credentials. The service provider raises a successful authentication event (*AuthOK*), communicating the generated session. Notice that we assume that the user authentication is always successful, therefore we do not model the implementation verification of the user credentials. Finally, the identity provider creates a new reaction to receive a delegation event. This reaction can be activated only for the generated session. Only the authenticated user owning this session can generate a signal that can be consumed by this reaction.

When the user has been notified about the successful authentication, by receiving the session shared with the identity provider ($B_{AuthOK}(s_{ip})$), it can access to a federated service. The user communicates the claimed identity (*identifier*) (and not the whole credentials) to the service provider rising a *Claim* event.

When a service provider receives a *Claim* event, it delegates the authentication of the identity to the identity provider. This is performed redirecting the client to the identity provider. Observe that the service provider generates a new session s_{sp} that is communicated via the redirect request ($\bar{x} : Redirect_{si}©s_{sp}.0$). The generated session is used as a new event, the service provider waits this event to perform the authentication. In OpenID this is implemented through the generation of a user-specific URL.

When the user receives the *Claim* response and the session shared with the service provider s_{sp}, it forwards the request to the identity provider, delegating the authentication to it.

Finally, on reception of a delegate event for the authenticated user ($Delegate©s_{ip}$), the identity provider generates a three-party session s_3 and requests the user to forward it to the service provider. The identity provider and the service provider use this session to verify the user claim. If the verification is successful, the service provider continues according to $B_{Verified}$ after the reception of the consumer parameter p, i.e., the behavior representing the service supplied by *SP* which depends on the provided service and therefore it is not specified.

7 Concluding Remarks

We introduced a process calculus to handle multi-party sessions and coordination policies in an event-notification (EN) framework. Our approach is based on type information that naturally support and extend typed-based EN systems. We demonstrated the adequacy of the approach by specifying the OpenID protocol.

As future work we plan to investigate which properties the XSC type system enjoys. We are also studying different interpretation for the algebraic structure of topics. For instance, by relaxing the idempotency of $\_ \times \_$ we get a theory which allows one to *count* the number of topics, thus leading to a notion of linear types. Finally, the type system described in this paper yields a *constraint semiring* structure [1] that has been successfully exploited to model QoS aspects of distributed systems [8,12]. We argue that this will allow us to express QoS driven coordination policy within our type system.

We also plan to validate and assess our approach on a variety of languages for programming service coordination policies. A step toward this goal would be to encode the Global Calculus [3] in XSC.

At the implementation level, the JSCL middleware (see Section 2) has already been extended with some of the new concepts of XSC (e.g., logical ports and signal sessions), while topic creation and structured topic composition are under development.

References

1. Bistarelli, S., Montanari, U., Rossi, F.: Semiring-based constraint satisfaction and optimization. Journal of the ACM 44(2), 201–236 (1997)
2. Boreale, M., Bruni, R., Caires, L., De Nicola, R., Lanese, I., Loreti, M., Martins, F., Montanari, U., Ravara, A., Sangiorgi, D., Vasconcelos, V.T., Zavattaro, G.: SCC: A service centered calculus. In: Bravetti, M., Núñez, M., Zavattaro, G. (eds.) WS-FM. LNCS, vol. 4184, pp. 38–57. Springer-Verlag, Heidelberg (2006)
3. Carbone, M., Honda, K., Yoshida, N.: Structured communication-centred programming for web services. In: De Nicola, R. (ed.) Programming Languages and Systems. LNCS, vol. 4421, pp. 2–17. Springer-Verlag, Heidelberg (2007)
4. Carzaniga, A., Rosenblum, D.S., Wolf, A.L.: Achieving scalability and expressiveness in an internet-scale event notification service. In: Annual Symposium on Principles of Distributed Computing PODC, pp. 219–227 (2000)
5. Carzaniga, A., Wolf, A.L.: Content-based networking: A new communication infrastructure. In: König-Ries, B., Makki, K., Makki, S.A.M., Pissinou, N., Scheuermann, P. (eds.) IMWS 2001. LNCS, vol. 2538, pp. 59–68. Springer, Heidelberg (2002)
6. Carzaniga, A., Wolf, A.L.: Forwarding in a content-based network. In: Proceedings of the ACM SIGCOMM 2003 Conference on Applications, Technologies, Architectures, and Protocols for Computer Communication, Karlsruhe, Germany, August 25-29, 2003, pp. 163–174. ACM Press, New York (2003)
7. Chappell, D.: Introducing windows cardspace. MSDN Library. Available, at http://msdn2.microsoft.com/en-us/library/aa480189.aspx
8. De Nicola, R., Ferrari, G., Montanari, U., Pugliese, R., Tuosto, E.: A Basic Calculus for Modelling Service Level Agreements. In: Jacquet, J.-M., Picco, G.P. (eds.) COORDINATION 2005. LNCS, vol. 3454, pp. 33–48. Springer, Heidelberg (2005)
9. Eugster, P.T., Guerraoui, R.: Distributed programming with typed events. IEEE Software 21(2), 56–64 (2004)
10. Ferrari, G., Guanciale, R., Strollo, D.: Event based service coordination over dynamic and heterogeneous networks. In: Dan, A., Lamersdorf, W. (eds.) ICSOC 2006. LNCS, vol. 4294, pp. 453–458. Springer, Heidelberg (2006)
11. Ferrari, G., Guanciale, R., Strollo, D.: Jscl: A middleware for service coordination. In: Najm, E., Pradat-Peyre, J.F., Donzeau-Gouge, V.V. (eds.) FORTE 2006. LNCS, vol. 4229, pp. 46–60. Springer, Heidelberg (2006)
12. Hirsch, D., Tuosto, E.: SHReQ: A Framework for Coordinating Application Level QoS. In: Bernhard, K.A., Bernhard, B. (eds.) 3rd IEEE International Conference on Software Engineering and Formal Methods, pp. 425–434. IEEE Computer Society, Los Alamitos (2005)
13. Honda, K., Vasconcelos, V.T., Kubo, M.: Language primitives and type discipline for structured communication-based programming. In: Hankin, C. (ed.) ESOP 1998 and ETAPS 1998. LNCS, vol. 1381, pp. 122–141. Springer, Heidelberg (1998)

14. Huang, Y., Gannon, D.: A comparative study of web services-based event notification speci-
    fications. In: ICPP Workshops, pp. 7–14. IEEE Computer Society, Los Alamitos (2006)
15. i-name specifications. Available, at http://www.inames.net/developers.html
16. Liu, Y., Plale, B.: Survey of publish subscribe event systems. Technical Report TR574, Com-
    puter Science Department, Indiana University (2003)
17. Recordon, D., Fitzpatrick, B.: OpenID Authentication 1.1. Available at
    http://openid.net/specs/openid-authentication-1_1.html
18. Tam, D., Azimi, R., Jacobsen, H.-A.: Building content-based publish/subscribe systems with
    distributed hash tables. In: Aberer, K., Koubarakis, M., Kalogeraki, V. (eds.) Databases, In-
    formation Systems, and Peer-to-Peer Computing. LNCS, vol. 2944, pp. 138–152. Springer,
    Heidelberg (2003)

A   Free names

We define the free names of our syntactic categories in the usual way:

$$
\begin{aligned}
fn(0) &= \emptyset \\
fn(!B) &= fn(B) \\
fn(+\lfloor \tau \rightsquigarrow a \rfloor.B') &= \{\tau,a\} \cup fn(B') \\
fn(B_1 \mid B_2) &= fn(B_1) \cup fn(B_2) \\
fn(+\lceil x:\tau\copyright\tau' \rightarrow B\rceil.B') &= fn(B) \setminus \{x\} \cup \{\tau,\tau'\} \cup fn(B') \\
fn(+\lceil x:\tau\copyright\lambda\tau' \rightarrow B\rceil.B') &= fn(B) \setminus \{x,\tau'\} \cup \{\tau\} \cup fn(B') \\
fn(\bar{s}:t\copyright\tau.B') &= fn(B') \cup \{s,\tau\} \cup fn(t) \\
fn(\nu\tau.B') &= fn(B') \setminus \{\tau\}
\end{aligned}
$$

$$
\begin{aligned}
fn(0) &= \emptyset \\
fn(R_1 \mid R_2) &= fn(R_1) \cup fn(R_2) \\
fn(x:\tau\copyright\tau' \rightarrow B) &= fn(B) \setminus \{x\} \cup \{\tau,\tau'\} \\
fn(x:\tau\copyright\lambda\tau' \rightarrow B) &= fn(B) \setminus \{x,\tau'\} \cup \{\tau\} \\
fn(0) &= \emptyset \\
fn(F_1 \mid F_2) &= fn(F_1) \cup fn(F_2) \\
fn(\tau \rightsquigarrow b) &= \{\tau,b\}
\end{aligned}
$$

$$
\begin{aligned}
fn(\emptyset) &= \emptyset \\
fn(\nu\tau.N) &= fn(N) \setminus \{\tau\} \\
fn(\langle s:t\copyright\tau@a\rangle) &= \{s,a,\tau\} \cup fn(t) \\
fn(N_1 \| N_2) &= fn(N_1) \cup fn(N_2) \\
fn(a[B]_F^R) &= fn(B) \cup fn(F) \cup fn(R) \cup \{a\}
\end{aligned}
$$

$$
\begin{aligned}
fn(\tau) &= \{\tau\} \\
fn(\varepsilon) = fn(\star) &= \emptyset \\
fn(t_1\copyright\tau) &= fn(t_1) \cup \{\tau\} \\
fn(t_1\copyright\star) &= fn(t_1) \\
fn(t_1 \times t_2) = fn(t_1 + t_2) &= fn(t_1) \cup fn(t_2)
\end{aligned}
$$

Exploring the Connection of Choreography and Orchestration with Exception Handling and Finalization/Compensation*

Yang Hongli, Zhao Xiangpeng, Cai Chao, and Qiu Zongyan

LMAM and Department of Informatics, School of Math.,
Peking University, Beijing 100871, China
{yhl,zxp,caic,qzy}@math.pku.edu.cn

Abstract. Web service choreography describes protocols for multiparty collaboration, whereas orchestration focuses on single peers. One key requirement of choreography is to support transactions, which makes exceptional handling and finalization very important features in modelling choreography. A *projection* is a procedure which takes a choreography and generates a set of processes in the orchestration level. Given a choreography, how to project exceptional handling and finalization constructs is still an open problem. This paper aims to study exception handling and transactionality in choreographies from a projection view. We propose formal languages for both choreography and orchestration with trace semantics, and a projection based on the relationship between *choreography* and *scope* rooted in WS-CDL and WS-BPEL respectively.

Keywords: Choreography, Orchestration, Projection, Exception Handling, Finalization, Compensation.

1 Introduction

Web services promise the interoperability of various applications running on heterogeneous platforms over the Internet. Web service composition refers to the process of combining web services to provide value-added services, which has received much interest to support enterprise application integration.

Two levels of view to the composition of web services exist, namely orchestration and choreography. The description of the single services, possibly with cooperation of other services, is called an orchestration. The *de facto* standard for orchestration is WS-BPEL [3] (Web Services Business Process Execution Language) developed by a consortium comprising BEA, IBM, Microsoft etc. The global view of the interactions are described by the so-called choreography. WS-CDL(Web Service Choreography Description Language) [2] is a W3C candidate recommendation, designed for describing the common and collaborative observable behavior of multiple services that interact with each other. Another

---

* Supported by National Natural Science Foundation of China (No. 60573081).

J. Derrick and J. Vain (Eds.): FORTE 2007, LNCS 4574, pp. 81–96, 2007.

notation, SSDL [1], also allows the description of protocols for multiparty collaboration using message-oriented programming abstractions. In short, choreography describes the system in a global-view manner whereas orchestration focuses on the peers separately.

Using WS-CDL, a contract contains a "global" definition of the common flow ordering conditions and constraints of a task, which should be in turn realized by combination of the several local systems [2]. Once the contract is clearly defined and jointly agreed to, participants can be built and tested according to it independently. However, two challenges exist: (1) how to automatically generate correct local requirements for the roles from the global contract; (2) how to verify whether a given process can play as a participant whose observable behavior conforms to the requirement of a given choreography.

Much work has been carried out, while much is still going on in the projection and conformance validation between choreography and orchestration. Carbone et al. [11] studied a two-level paradigm for the description of communication behaviors, on the global message flows and end-point behavior levels respectively. Three principles for well-structured global description and a theory for projection are developed. In [7,8], Busi et al. formalized choreography and orchestration by using process algebra, where conformance takes the form of a bisimulation-like relation. By means of automaton, Schifanella et al. [4] defined a conformance notion which tests whether interoperability is guaranteed. Fu et al. [12] specified a conversation protocol by a realizable Büchi automaton, and the peer implementations are synthesized from the protocol via projection. Zhao et al. [17] proposed a small language as a formal model of the simplified WS-CDL and projected a given choreography to orchestration views.

One key aspect in composing web services is to support transactions of process executions. Exception handling and transactionality are important features in both choreography and orchestration levels. WS-CDL provides finalizer actions to confirm, cancel or modify the effects of its completed actions. In orchestration level, if a long-running transaction fails, appropriate compensations are executed for the completed parts of the transaction, which is supported by WS-BPEL with its scope-based compensation. Butler et al. integrated the compensation feature into CSP, and provided both operational semantics and denotational (trace) semantics [9,10]. Bruni et al. presented a hierarchy of transactional calculi with increasing expressiveness in [6]. Qiu et al. [15] and Pu et al. [14] studied the semantics of WS-BPEL fault and compensation handling. Li et al. [13] proposed a language with operational semantics to model exception handling and finalization of WS-CDL. To the best of our knowledge, no work is done about modelling exception handling and transactionality from a projection view, which resolves how exception handling and finalization in a choreography can be implemented in orchestration level.

In our previous work [16], we have presented a simplified language for choreography, and a simple process language for participant roles, both with formal syntax and semantics. We discussed the concept of projections, which map a given choreography to a set of role processes. We defined the concept of *restricted natural choreography* which is easily implementable, and proposed two structural conditions as a criterion to distinguish the restricted natural choreography. Although useful as a formal investigation of the relationship between choreography and orchestration, the framework is not powerful enough to specify real case studies. The main weak point for the expressiveness is the shortage of mechanism for describing exception handling and transactionality.

This paper aims at extending our framework for both choreography and orchestration with structures related to exception handling and transactionality. The choreography language *Chor* and orchestration language *Role*, which are inspired by WS-CDL and WS-BPEL respectively, are developed with formal syntax and trace semantics. We present a projection from *Chor* to *Role* which focuses on the relationship between *choreography* in *Chor* and *scope* in *Role* rooted in WS-CDL and WS-BPEL respectively. Both the two structures have actions, exception block, finalizer or compensation action. Because of their similarities, our projection will map a *choreography* in *Chor* to a *scope* at each role process in *Role*. In the work, we develop a technique for define trace semantics of the role process language that introduces a stuck notation.

The rest of the paper is organized as follows. We first introduce the syntax and semantics of *Chor* with exception handling in Section 2. Then we add the finalization feature into *Chor* language in Section 3. Section 4 defines a *Role* language with formal syntax and semantics. Section 5 presents the projection rules with some discussion about the related issue, and Section 6 concludes.

2   The *Chor* Language with Exception Handling

In this section we develop the language *Chor* with syntax and trace semantics.

2.1   Syntax

In the definitions below, A and B range over activity declarations; E ranges over exception blocks; e ranges over exceptions; and n ranges over names. We use $\overline{X}$ as a shorthand for list, similarly, for $\overline{e : A}$. Given a list l, $\mathsf{hd}(l)$ returns the first element of l, and $\mathsf{tl}(l)$ returns the same list with the first element removed.

A choreography is participated by a finite number of roles $R^1, \cdots, R^n$. A choreography specification comprises some choreography declarations $\overline{CDecl}$ and a root choreography RC.

$$CS \ ::= \ \overline{CDecl}, RC$$

The root choreography is enabled by default, whereas other choreography are enabled only when they are performed. The root choreography is a tuple, including an activity A, and an exception block E.

$$RC \ ::= \ [A, E]$$

A declaration of a non-root choreography with name n takes the form:

$$CDecl \ ::= \ n[A, E]$$

Here is the syntax for the activities in *Chor*.

$$
\begin{aligned}
A ::= \ & \textsf{skip} & \text{(no action)} & \quad | \ a^i & \text{(activity)} \\
| \ & c^{[i,j]} & \text{(communication)} & \quad | \ \textsf{throw } e & \text{(throw exception)} \\
| \ & \textsf{perf } n & \text{(perform)} & \quad | \ A; A & \text{(sequence)} \\
| \ & A \stackrel{i}{\sqcap} A & \text{(choice)} & \quad | \ A \parallel A & \text{(parallel)}
\end{aligned}
$$

Activity $\textsf{skip}$ does nothing. Meta-variable a^i denotes a basic activity of role R^i. The communication from R^i to R^j takes the form of $c^{[i,j]}$, where c is a channel name. Activity $\textsf{throw } e$ causes an exception e at each role. Activity $\textsf{perf } n$ performs the declared choreography with name n. The composite activities considered here include sequential composition, choice, and parallel composition.

Here $A \stackrel{i}{\sqcap} A$ means that role R^i is the *dominant role* of the choice. It is used as a directive in projection to specify that R^i is the "decision maker", and all other roles should follow R^i's decision on which branch to take in this choice. A more detailed study about the dominant role can be found in [16].

The exception block E is defined as a sequence of $e : A$, where e is an exception name, and the activity A is the exception handler for e. We allow $* : A$ as a special case to define a universal handler in an exception block.

$$
E ::= \overline{e : A}
$$

A choreography specification is well-formed if all the following conditions hold:

- All non-root choreography names are different from each other.
- In each perform activity $\textsf{perf } n$, the name n ranges over non-root choreography names in the choreography specification.
- All exception names in each exception block are different from each other.

2.2   Semantics

An environment Γ is a map from non-root choreography names to their definitions with the form $[A, E]$, which can be constructed by parsing the text of declarations $\overline{CDecl}$. We will assume that the execution of a choreography is always under the corresponding Γ. For convenience, notation $n.1, n.2$ will be used to obtain the activity and the exception block of choreography n.

We define the semantics of an activity as a set of traces, and will use r, s, and t to denote traces. A trace may have a terminal mark at its end, indicating whether the execution of the activities terminates successfully or not. Mark $\checkmark$ represents a successful termination, and $\mathsf{\Gamma}_e$ represents a termination with exception e. Concatenation of traces is denoted by juxtaposition. For example, $t\langle\checkmark\rangle$ represents a concatenated trace which terminates successfully. In our semantics, we always give maximal traces, i.e. each trace has a terminal mark at its end.

Activity $\textsf{skip}$ does nothing and always terminates successfully. Activity $\textsf{throw } e$ causes exception e. Activity a^i always terminates successfully, so does $c^{[i,j]}$.

$$
\begin{aligned}
[\![\textsf{skip}]\!]_\Gamma &\triangleq \{\langle\checkmark\rangle\} & [\![a^i]\!]_\Gamma &\triangleq \{\langle a^i, \checkmark\rangle\} \\
[\![\textsf{throw } e]\!]_\Gamma &\triangleq \{\langle\mathsf{\Gamma}_e\rangle\} & [\![c^{[i,j]}]\!]_\Gamma &\triangleq \{\langle c^{[i,j]}, \checkmark\rangle\}
\end{aligned}
$$

To define the semantics of the perform activity perf n, we need to define the semantics of executing an exception block under some exception e. We introduce function $hdl(E, e)_\Gamma$, which returns a set of traces after handling exception e in exception block E under environment Γ. If a handler for e, which may take the form of $e : A$ or $* : A$, is found in E, then the traces of A are returned. Otherwise, the exception will be propagated to the immediate enclosing choreography.

$$hdl(E, e)_\Gamma \;\hat{=}\; \begin{cases} [\![A]\!]_\Gamma & \text{if } \mathsf{hd}(E) = e : A \vee \mathsf{hd}(E) = * : A \\ hdl(\mathsf{tl}(E), e)_\Gamma & \text{if } \mathsf{hd}(E) = e' : A \wedge e' \neq e \\ \{\langle \ulcorner_e \rangle\} & \text{if } E \text{ is empty} \end{cases}$$

Now we define the semantics of the perform activity as:

$$[\![\mathsf{perf}\ n]\!]_\Gamma \;\hat{=}\; \{s\langle\checkmark\rangle \mid s\langle\checkmark\rangle \in [\![n.1]\!]_\Gamma\} \ \cup\ \{st \mid s\langle\ulcorner_e\rangle \in [\![n.1]\!]_\Gamma \wedge t \in hdl(n.2, e)_\Gamma\}$$

If activity $n.1$ terminates successfully, so is the perform activity. Otherwise, if $n.1$ throws an exception e, the exception handler in $n.2$ for e is executed, and the trace t produced by this execution is appended to trace s.

The semantics of choice is defined by set union. Although i does not appear in the semantics, it is critical in the projection discussed in Section 5.

$$[\![A \stackrel{i}{\sqcap} B]\!]_\Gamma \;\hat{=}\; [\![A]\!]_\Gamma \cup [\![B]\!]_\Gamma$$

We introduce the sequential and parallel composition of traces, and lift them to sets of traces, then give semantics of sequential and parallel composition.

$$s\langle\checkmark\rangle; t \;\hat{=}\; st \qquad s\langle\ulcorner_e\rangle; t \;\hat{=}\; s\langle\ulcorner_e\rangle$$
$$[\![A; B]\!]_\Gamma \;\hat{=}\; \{s; t \mid s \in [\![A]\!]_\Gamma \wedge t \in [\![B]\!]_\Gamma\}$$
$$s\langle\tau\rangle \parallel t\langle\tau'\rangle \;\hat{=}\; \{r\langle\tau \oplus \tau'\rangle \mid r \in interl(s, t)\}$$
$$[\![A \parallel B]\!]_\Gamma \;\hat{=}\; \{r \mid r \in (s \parallel t) \wedge s \in [\![A]\!]_\Gamma \wedge t \in [\![B]\!]_\Gamma\}$$

Here τ and τ' are meta variables over terminal marks $\{\checkmark, \ulcorner_e\}$. The function $interl(s, t)$ denotes the set of all interleaving traces of s and t. The definition is routine and is omitted here. The terminal mark of parallel composition is defined by operator $\oplus$, as shown in the table below.

$\oplus$	$\checkmark$	$\ulcorner_{e_1}$
$\checkmark$	$\checkmark$	$\ulcorner_{e_1}$
$\ulcorner_{e_2}$	$\ulcorner_{e_2}$	$\ulcorner_{e_1 \uplus e_2}$

If both branches terminate successfully, so is their parallel composition. When both branches terminate with some exception(s), then we need to handle the parallel exceptions by operator $\uplus$. There are many possible ways to define $\uplus$. For example, we can define different priorities for exceptions and return the highest one; or define a hierarchy of exceptions and return the least upper bound. The details of handling parallel exceptions are omitted here. If only one branch fails, we have the exception for the parallel composition. We do not consider the forced termination problem [3] in this paper.

Provided the semantics of activities, we can define the semantics of the root choreography as follows, which is similar with the perform activity:

$$[\![A, E]\!]_\Gamma \mathrel{\hat{=}} \{s\langle\checkmark\rangle \mid s\langle\checkmark\rangle \in [\![A]\!]_\Gamma\} \ \cup \ \{st \mid s\langle \ulcorner_e\rangle \in [\![A]\!]_\Gamma \wedge t \in hdl(E, e)_\Gamma\}$$

Many laws for structural congruence, e.g., associativity and symmetry, hold for choice and parallel composition. Also, skip is the unit element of the sequential operator, and throw e the left zero, i.e. throw $e; A =$ throw e. Besides, we can easily prove that any choreography will always terminate, either successes or fails with an exception, i.e. any choreography is deadlock-free.

Now we present an example to illustrate the semantics.

Example 1. In the following declaration, notation a_l^1, a_m^1 and a_n^1 denote basic activities at role R^1.

$$m[(a_l^1; \mathsf{throw}\ e_n), e_m : a_m^1], \quad [\mathsf{perf}\ m, e_n : a_n^1]$$

Here environment Γ consists of a map from choreography name m to its body, i.e. $\Gamma = \{m \mapsto [(a_l^1; \mathsf{throw}\ e_n), e_m : a_m^1]\}$. When the root choreography [perf $m, e_n : a_n^1$] executes under Γ, choreography m is performed. The activity a_l^1 is executed first, and then exception e_n is thrown. Since e_n cannot be handled in m, it is re-thrown to the root choreography, where e_n is handled by the exception block. When activity a_n^1 terminates successfully, the root choreography terminates. Thus, we derive the following semantics:

$$[\![\mathsf{perf}\ m]\!]_\Gamma = \{\langle a_l^1, \ulcorner_{e_n}\rangle\} \qquad [\![\mathsf{perf}\ m, e_n : a_n^1]\!]_\Gamma = \{\langle a_l^1, a_n^1, \checkmark\rangle\}$$

3   Adding Finalization

In this section, we extend *Chor* language with constructs for finalization.

The non-root choreography declaration is extended to include a finalizer F, with the form:

$$CDecl \ ::= \ n[A, E, F] \qquad F \ ::= \ A$$

Unlike the case for exceptions, we do not consider named finalizers, and F is simply defined as an activity for finalization. However, there is no substantial difficulty to extend the model to support named finalization.

The syntax of activities is extended with the finalize activity fin n, which performs the finalizer of the successfully terminated choreography n.

$$A \ ::= \ \cdots \ \mid \ \mathsf{fin}\ n \ \mid \ \cdots$$

After introducing finalization structures, we need to extend the semantics, since finalizers are dynamically installed during the execution of choreographies. If the performing of a choreography n terminates successfully, the finalizer of n will be installed.

In the definitions below, meta-variable φ, ψ, χ range over finalization contexts. A finalization context is a (possibly empty) sequence of finalization closures of the form $(n : F : \psi)$, where n is a choreography name, F the finalizer of n, and ψ the finalization context accumulated during performing choreography n, as n might perform some other choreographies in its course. Here is an example of a finalization context: $\langle (n_1 : F_1 : \langle \rangle), (n_2 : F_2 : \langle (n_3 : F_3 : \langle \rangle) \rangle) \rangle$.

We express the semantics of an activity as a set of pairs with the form (s, φ'), where s represents a trace of the activity, and φ' represents the new finalization context after executing the activity. We always assume that the execution of activity is under some finalization context φ and environment Γ (now with elements of the form $n \mapsto [A, E, F]$). Initially, φ is empty.

The basic activities skip, a^i, $c^{[i,j]}$ and throw e have no effect on the finalization context, so the extension is trivial.

$$[\![\text{skip}]\!]_\Gamma^\varphi \triangleq \{(\langle \checkmark \rangle, \varphi)\} \qquad [\![\text{throw } e]\!]_\Gamma^\varphi \triangleq \{(\langle \ulcorner_e \rangle, \varphi)\}$$
$$[\![a^i]\!]_\Gamma^\varphi \triangleq \{(\langle a^i, \checkmark \rangle, \varphi)\} \qquad [\![c^{[i,j]}]\!]_\Gamma^\varphi \triangleq \{(\langle c^{[i,j]}, \checkmark \rangle, \varphi)\}$$

For the perform activity perf n, if activity $n.1$ completes successfully, closure $(n : n.3 : \psi)$ is inserted in front of φ, where $n.3$ is the finalizer of choreography n, and ψ is the accumulated finalization context during performing choreography n. If $n.1$ throws an exception, φ remains the same. Symbol "$-$" means something that we do not care about.

$$[\![\text{perf } n]\!]_\Gamma^\varphi \triangleq \{(s\langle \checkmark \rangle, (n : n.3 : \psi) ^\frown \varphi) \mid (s\langle \checkmark \rangle, \psi) \in [\![n.1]\!]_\Gamma^{\langle \rangle}\} \cup$$
$$\{(st, \varphi) \mid (s\langle \ulcorner_e \rangle, \psi) \in [\![n.1]\!]_\Gamma^{\langle \rangle} \wedge (t, -) \in hdl(n.2, e)_\Gamma^\psi\}$$

Here $hdl(E, e)_\Gamma^\varphi$ is an extension of $hdl(E, e)_\Gamma$. When E is empty, the exception is rethrown to the performer of current choreography.

$$hdl(E, e)_\Gamma^\varphi \triangleq \begin{cases} [\![A]\!]_\Gamma^\varphi & \text{if } \mathsf{hd}(E) = e : A \vee \mathsf{hd}(E) = * : A \\ hdl(\mathsf{tl}(E), e)_\Gamma^\varphi & \text{if } \mathsf{hd}(E) = e' : A \wedge e' \neq e \\ \{(\langle \ulcorner_e \rangle, -)\} & \text{if } E \text{ is empty} \end{cases}$$

The semantics of fin n is defined as follows. We assume the execution of a finalizer does not modify the current finalization context. Function $getf(n, \varphi)$ gets the finalizer F of choreography n from φ by searching through the context. Similar to the specification of WS-CDL, if no corresponding finalizer found, nothing happens. If closure $(n : F : \psi)$ is found, we execute F under ψ.

$$[\![\text{fin } n]\!]_\Gamma^\varphi \triangleq \{(s, \varphi) \mid (s, -) \in getf(n, \varphi)_\Gamma\}$$
$$getf(n, \varphi)_\Gamma \triangleq \begin{cases} [\![\text{skip}]\!]_\Gamma^\varphi & \text{if } \varphi = \langle \rangle \\ [\![F]\!]_\Gamma^\psi & \text{if } \mathsf{hd}(\varphi) = (n : F : \psi) \\ getf(n, \mathsf{tl}(\varphi))_\Gamma & \text{if } \mathsf{hd}(\varphi) = (n' : F : \psi) \wedge n \neq n' \end{cases}$$

For sequential composition, we first execute A under context φ. Suppose the context becomes ψ after the execution; we then execute B under ψ, which results in context χ. If A ends with an exception execution, then B does not execute.

$$[\![A; B]\!]_\Gamma^\varphi \triangleq \{(st, \chi) \mid (s\langle \checkmark \rangle, \psi) \in [\![A]\!]_\Gamma^\varphi \wedge (t, \chi) \in [\![B]\!]_\Gamma^\psi\} \cup$$
$$\{(s\langle \ulcorner_e \rangle, \psi) \mid (s\langle \ulcorner_e \rangle, \psi) \in [\![A]\!]_\Gamma^\varphi\}$$

For parallel composition, we execute both branches under context φ and environment Γ, and then combine the traces and accumulated finalization closures interleavingly. Here $s \parallel t$ and *interl* have the same meaning as in Section 2.2.

$$[\![A \parallel B]\!]_\Gamma^\varphi \; \hat{=} \; \{(r, \chi) \mid r \in (s \parallel t) \; \wedge \chi \in (interl(\varphi', \varphi'') ^\frown \varphi) \; \wedge$$
$$(s, \varphi' ^\frown \varphi) \in [\![A]\!]_\Gamma^\varphi \; \wedge (t, \varphi'' ^\frown \varphi) \in [\![B]\!]_\Gamma^\varphi\}$$

The semantics of choice activity is simple: $[\![A \stackrel{i}{\sqcap} B]\!]_\Gamma^\varphi \; \hat{=} \; [\![A]\!]_\Gamma^\varphi \cup [\![B]\!]_\Gamma^\varphi$.

The semantics for the root choreography is similar to the semantics of the perform activity:

$$[\![[A, E]]\!]_\Gamma \; \hat{=} \; \{s\langle \checkmark \rangle \mid (s\langle \checkmark \rangle, -) \in [\![A]\!]_\Gamma^{\langle \rangle}\} \; \cup$$
$$\{st \mid (s\langle \ulcorner_e \rangle), \psi) \in [\![A]\!]_\Gamma^{\langle \rangle} \wedge (t, -) \in hdl(E, e)_\Gamma^\psi\}$$

We show the use of the finalizer construct with the following example.

Example 2. This example includes three non-root choreographies m, n and p. Here a_m^1 and a_f^1 denote basic activities at role R^1; a_p^2 and a_f^2 denote basic activities at role R^2. The notation ϵ denotes that the exception block is empty.

$$m[a_m^1, \epsilon, a_f^1] \qquad n[\text{perf } m, \epsilon, \text{fin } m] \qquad p[a_p^2, \epsilon, a_f^2]$$

In the root choreography, choreographies n and p are performed in parallel. Afterwards, exception e is thrown and handled by the root choreography.

$$[((\text{perf } n \parallel \text{perf } p); \text{throw } e), e : (\text{fin } n)]$$

Initially, choreographies n and p run in parallel with empty finalization context and environment Γ, which maps the choreography names to bodies of three non-root choreographies. Before fin n, the finalization context is $\langle (n : \text{fin } m : \langle (m : a_f^1 : \langle \rangle) \rangle), (p : a_f^2 : \langle \rangle) \rangle$, or in the reverse order. Then fin n executes fin m, which turns to execute activity a_f^1. Afterwards, the root choreography terminates successfully. The two perform activities yield the following traces:

$$[\![\text{perf } p]\!]_\Gamma^{\langle \rangle} \; = \; \{(\langle a_p^2, \checkmark \rangle, \langle (p : a_f^2 : \langle \rangle) \rangle)\}$$
$$[\![\text{perf } n]\!]_\Gamma^{\langle \rangle} \; = \; \{(\langle a_m^1, \checkmark \rangle, \langle (n : \text{fin } m : \langle (m : a_f^1 : \langle \rangle) \rangle) \rangle)\}$$

The trace set of the root choreography is $\{\langle a_m^1, a_p^2, a_f^1, \checkmark \rangle, \langle a_p^2, a_m^1, a_f^1, \checkmark \rangle\}$. $\qquad \square$

4   The *Role* Language

A choreography describes the interaction among roles from a global view. It is intended to be implemented by coordination of a set of independent processes. In order to study the relationship between the globally described choreography and the coordinative activities of each role, we define a simple *Role* language here. The syntax and the trace semantics are defined as follows.

4.1 Syntax

In the definitions below, P ranges over processes. The syntax of *Role* is:

$$
\begin{array}{llll}
P ::= & \mathsf{skip} & \text{(no action)} & \mid\; a & \text{(local action)} \\
\mid & c! & \text{(send)} & \mid\; c? & \text{(receive)} \\
\mid & \mathsf{throw}\; e & \text{(throw)} & \mid\; \mathsf{fin}\; n & \text{(compensation)} \\
\mid & P; P & \text{(sequence)} & \mid\; P \sqcap P & \text{(choice)} \\
\mid & P \parallel P & \text{(parallel)} & \mid\; n[P, E, F] & \text{(scope)} \\
\mid & c_1? {\rightarrow} P_1 \,\|\, c_2? {\rightarrow} P_2 & \text{(guarded choice)} & &
\end{array}
$$

$$
E ::= \overline{e : P} \qquad F ::= P \qquad RP ::= [P, E]
$$

The major difference from *Chor* is that it takes a local view on communications, where sending and receiving actions represent roles' local view of interactions. We would use the term "communication action" to denote either a sending or a receiving action. A sending action and a receiving action engage in a handshake when they have the same channel name and both roles involved are ready to perform them. Besides, here we use the normal non-deterministic choice, and introduce the guarded choice.

Another important difference from *Chor* is that we have scopes embedded in the processes, with its exception block E, and rename the "finalizer" to "compensation". These terms follow the WS-BPEL specification. Also, we have role process RP, which is used to represent independent roles.

The top structure in *Role* is the task S which is the parallel composition of a set of role processes on the set of local channels $\mathcal{CH}$.

$$
S ::= \mathcal{CH} \bullet (\|_i [P_i, E_i])
$$

4.2 Semantics

The trace semantics for *Role* language can be similarly defined as in Section 3. We introduce compensation context φ, which is a (possibly empty) sequence of compensation closures of the form $(n : F : \psi)$, where n is a scope name, F is the compensation block of n, and ψ is a compensation context that accumulates during performing process $n.1$.

We express the semantics of a process under some compensation context φ as a set of pairs with the form (s, φ'), where s represents a trace of the process, and φ' represents the new compensation context after executing the process under φ. Initially, φ is empty.

The basic processes skip, a and $\mathsf{throw}\; e$ have no effect to the compensation context, so the semantics is trivial.

$$
[\![\mathsf{skip}]\!]^\varphi \mathrel{\widehat{=}} \{(\langle \checkmark \rangle, \varphi)\} \qquad [\![a]\!]^\varphi \mathrel{\widehat{=}} \{(\langle a, \checkmark \rangle, \varphi)\} \qquad [\![\mathsf{throw}\; e]\!]^\varphi \mathrel{\widehat{=}} \{(\langle \ulcorner e \rangle, \varphi)\}
$$

For the scope activity $n[P, E, F]$, if process P completes successfully, $\langle n : F : \psi \rangle$ will be inserted to the front of φ. Here ψ is the accumulated compensation closures during performing P. If P throws an exception, φ remains the same.

$$[\![n[P,E,F]\!]^\varphi \triangleq \{(s\langle\checkmark\rangle, \langle n : F : \psi\rangle ^\frown \varphi) \mid (s\langle\checkmark\rangle, \psi) \in [\![P]\!]^{\langle\rangle}\} \cup$$
$$\{(st, \varphi) \mid (s\langle\ulcorner_e\rangle, \psi) \in [\![P]\!]^{\langle\rangle} \wedge (t, -) \in hdl(E, e)^\psi\}$$

The function $hdl(E, e)^\varphi$ can be defined similarly as in Section 3.

$$hdl(E, e)^\varphi \triangleq \begin{cases} [\![P]\!]^\varphi & \text{if } \mathsf{hd}(E) = e : P \vee \mathsf{hd}(E) = * : P \\ hdl(\mathsf{tl}(E), e)^\varphi & \text{if } \mathsf{hd}(E) = e' : P \wedge e' \neq e \\ \{(\langle\ulcorner_e\rangle, -)\} & \text{if } E \text{ is empty} \end{cases}$$

The semantics of fin n is also similar:

$$[\![\text{fin } n]\!]^\varphi \triangleq \{(s\langle\checkmark\rangle, \varphi) \mid (s\langle\checkmark\rangle, -) \in getf(n, \varphi)\}$$

The semantics of choice is simple: $[\![P_1 \sqcap P_2]\!]^\varphi \triangleq [\![P_1]\!]^\varphi \cup [\![P_2]\!]^\varphi$.

The semantic rules given above do not have much difference from what for *Chor*. Now we discuss the more interesting parts related to the communication and parallel structures. The technique used here is inspired by [5] to define the traces of parallel processes. Furthermore, the semantics for sequential composition is redefined, too.

In the forthcoming discussion, α ranges over the local actions and communications (e.g. $c!$ and $c?$). The trace terminal marks $\checkmark$ and $\ulcorner_e$ are still used. Additionally, we introduce a new terminal mark δ_X to represent that the process gets stuck and waits to communicate along channels in X, where X is a power set of communication actions. In general, δ_X represents the interleaving of waiting to communicate. For instance, $\delta_{\{\{a?,b?\},\{c!\}\}}$ waits for either $a?$ or $b?$, or waits for $c!$ interleavingly. For simplification, we will write $\delta_{\{a?,b?\}}$ to represent $\delta_{\{\{a?,b?\}\}}$, and write $\delta_{a!}$ instead of $\delta_{\{\{a!\}\}}$. We use ϵ for the empty trace, and write st for the concatenation of t onto s, which is equal to s if s ends with δ_X.

For the sequential composition of P_1 and P_2, if P_1 ends with either $\ulcorner_e$ or δ_X (raising exception or getting stuck), then P_2 does not execute.

$$[\![P_1; P_2]\!]^\varphi \triangleq \{(st, \chi) \mid (s\langle\checkmark\rangle, \psi) \in [\![P_1]\!]^\varphi \wedge (t, \chi) \in [\![P_2]\!]^\psi\} \cup$$
$$\{(s\langle\tau\rangle, \psi) \mid (s\langle\tau\rangle, \psi) \in [\![P_1]\!]^\varphi \wedge \tau \in \{\ulcorner_e, \delta_X\} \text{ for some } X\}$$

A sending action $c!$ or receiving action $c?$ represents the potential for a process to perform communication. Action $c!$ may eventually succeed with trace $\langle c!, \checkmark\rangle$, which can be reduced to c with a parallel receiving action $c?$; or fail with trace $\langle\delta_{c!}\rangle$, which means that the sending will never succeed in the future (thus the process gets stuck). We have similar explanation to the receiving action.

$$[\![c!]\!]^\varphi \triangleq \{(\langle c!, \checkmark\rangle, \varphi), (\langle\delta_{c!}\rangle, \varphi)\} \quad [\![c?]\!]^\varphi \triangleq \{(\langle c?, \checkmark\rangle, \varphi), (\langle\delta_{c?}\rangle, \varphi)\}$$

The semantics of guarded choice is defined as follows, where $\langle c_1?\rangle s$ denotes a trace composed by concatenation of action $c_1?$ and trace s.

$$[\![c_1? \rightarrow P \mid c_2? \rightarrow Q]\!]^\varphi \triangleq \{(\langle\delta_{\{c_1?,c_2?\}}\rangle, \varphi)\} \cup \{(\langle c_1?\rangle s, \varphi) \mid s \in [\![P]\!]^\varphi\} \cup$$
$$\{(\langle c_2?\rangle s, \varphi) \mid s \in [\![Q]\!]^\varphi\}$$

For the semantics of parallel composition of processes, we introduce some auxiliary definitions in the first. The predicate $match(\alpha_1, \alpha_2, c)$ indicates whether α_1 and α_2 are a pair of matching communication actions on channel c, i.e.

$$match(\alpha_1, \alpha_2, c) \triangleq \begin{cases} true & \text{if } \{\alpha_1, \alpha_2\} = \{c?, c!\} \\ false & \text{otherwise} \end{cases}$$

For the parallel composition of traces, we distinguish two different cases: (1) at most one trace ends with δ_X; (2) both traces end with δ_X.
For the first case, we define:

$$s\langle\tau\rangle \parallel t\langle\tau'\rangle \triangleq \{r\langle\tau \oplus \tau'\rangle \mid r \in merge(s,t)\}$$

where τ and τ' are meta variables over terminal marks $\{\checkmark, \ulcorner_e, \delta_X\}$. The terminal mark of parallel composition is shown in the table below.

$\oplus$	$\checkmark$	$\ulcorner_{e_1}$	δ_X
$\checkmark$	$\checkmark$	$\ulcorner_{e_1}$	δ_X
$\ulcorner_{e_2}$	$\ulcorner_{e_2}$	$\ulcorner_{e_1 \uplus e_2}$	$\ulcorner_{e_2}$

Function $merge(s,t)$ returns the set of all traces formed by merging s and t fairly, allowing synchronization of matching communications. We let $merge(s, \epsilon) = merge(\epsilon, s) = \{s\}$. When s and t are nonempty, their fair merge is defined inductively, where c in the trace denotes a handshake of $c!$ and $c?$

$$merge(\langle\alpha_1\rangle s_1, \langle\alpha_2\rangle t_1) \triangleq \{\langle\alpha_1\rangle r \mid r \in merge(s_1, \langle\alpha_2\rangle t_1)\} \cup$$
$$\{\langle\alpha_2\rangle r \mid r \in merge(\langle\alpha_1\rangle s_1, t_1)\} \cup$$
$$\{\langle c\rangle r \mid match(\alpha_1, \alpha_2, c) \wedge r \in merge(s_1, t_1)\}$$

Thus we have $\langle c!, \checkmark\rangle \parallel \langle c?, \checkmark\rangle = \{\langle c, \checkmark\rangle, \langle c!, c?, \checkmark\rangle, \langle c?, c!, \checkmark\rangle\}$, and $\langle c!, \checkmark\rangle \parallel \langle\delta_{c?}\rangle = \{\langle c!, \delta_{c?}\rangle\}$.
For the second case, we define:

$$s\langle\delta_X\rangle \parallel t\langle\delta_Y\rangle \triangleq \begin{cases} \{\} & \text{if } \exists \alpha \in \bigcup X, \beta \in \bigcup Y, c \bullet \\ & match(\alpha, \beta, c) \\ \{r\langle\delta_{X \cup Y}\rangle \mid r \in merge(s,t)\} & \text{otherwise} \end{cases}$$

If there exists any matching stuck marks (e.g., $\delta_{\{\{a!\}, \{b?, c?\}\}}$ and $\delta_{\{\{c!\}, \{d?\}\}}$ are matched on channel c), then the set of traces of $s \parallel t$ is empty. This is because the merge should be fair: if one process has an action $c!$, another process has a $c?$, and neither of them communicate with other processes, then their parallel composition should not deadlock. In other words, a trace should never end with $\delta_{\{\{c!\}, \{c?\}\}}$. We simply discard such "unfair" traces.

Otherwise, we wait for communication along channels in $X \cup Y$. Thus, we have $\langle\delta_{a!}\rangle \parallel \langle\delta_{a?}\rangle = \{\}$, and $\langle\delta_{a!}\rangle \parallel \langle\delta_{b?}\rangle = \{\langle\delta_{\{\{a!\}, \{b?\}\}}\rangle\}$, which denotes the process waits to communication along the actions $a!$ and $b?$ forever.

The rule for parallel composition of processes is the same as in Section 2.2.

$$[\![P_1 \parallel P_2]\!]^\varphi \triangleq \{(r, \chi) \mid r \in (s \parallel t) \wedge \chi \in (interl(\varphi', \varphi'') ^\frown \varphi) \wedge$$
$$(s, \varphi' ^\frown \varphi) \in [\![P_1]\!]^\varphi \wedge (t, \varphi'' ^\frown \varphi) \in [\![P_2]\!]^\varphi\}$$

As an example, we have $[\![c! \parallel c?]\!]^{\varphi} = \{(\langle c, \checkmark\rangle, \varphi), (\langle c?, c!, \checkmark\rangle, \varphi), (\langle c!, c?, \checkmark\rangle, \varphi),$ $(\langle c!, \delta_{c?}\rangle, \varphi), (\langle c?, \delta_{c!}\rangle, \varphi)\}$. The trace $\langle c, \checkmark\rangle$ denotes that the two actions communicate with each other. The trace $\langle c!, \delta_{c?}\rangle$ denotes that the sending action appearing on the left side of the parallel construct will eventually communicate with some other receiving action (but not the one on the right side), while the receiving action on the right side has to stuck because it cannot find a matching action. We define the semantics in this way so that compositionality is achieved – as an example, please simply consider the semantics of $c? \parallel c! \parallel c?$

The semantics for a role process is similar to a root choreography:

$$[\![P, E]\!] \;\widehat{=}\; \{s\langle\checkmark\rangle \mid (s\langle\checkmark\rangle, -) \in [\![P]\!]^{\langle\rangle}\} \;\cup$$
$$\{st \mid (s\langle\ulcorner e\rangle, \varphi) \in [\![P]\!]^{\langle\rangle} \wedge (t, -) \in hdl(E, e)^{\varphi}\}$$

It is easy to prove that the parallel composition and both forms of choice satisfies commutativity and associativity in the semantics above.

Finally we define the semantics of a task. We introduce $close_{\mathcal{CH}}(T)$ that "closes" all channels of $\mathcal{CH}$ in trace set T, in the sense that the channels in $\mathcal{CH}$ will not used for communication with outside. To achieve this, we take two steps: first, we exclude all the traces that include either $c!$ or $c?$, with them the result of the filter is empty. Then, we modify the stuck mark of the remaining traces by removing communications along channels in $\mathcal{CH}$.

$$close_{\mathcal{CH}}(T) \;\widehat{=}\; \{close_1(t, \mathcal{CH}) \mid t \in T \wedge \forall c \in \mathcal{CH} \bullet t \downarrow \{c!, c?\} = \langle\rangle\}$$
$$close_1(t, \mathcal{CH}) \;\widehat{=}\; \begin{cases} t & \text{if } t = t'\langle\checkmark\rangle \vee t = t'\langle\ulcorner e\rangle \\ t'\langle\delta_{X|\mathcal{CH}}\rangle & \text{if } t = t'\langle\delta_X\rangle \end{cases}$$

Here we define $X \mid \mathcal{CH} \;\widehat{=}\; \{A \mid \exists B \in X \bullet A = (B \setminus \mathcal{CH}) \wedge A \neq \emptyset\}$, where $B \setminus \mathcal{CH}$ removes all communications along channels in $\mathcal{CH}$ from B. For example, $\{\{c!\}\} | \{c\} = \{\}$, and $\{\{a?, b?\}, \{c!\}\} | \{b, c\} = \{\{a?\}\}$.

Thus, we have $close_{\{c\}}([\![c!, \epsilon]\!] \parallel [\![c?, \epsilon]\!]) = \{\langle c, \checkmark\rangle\}$ and $close_{\{c\}}([\![c!, \epsilon]\!] \parallel [\![\mathsf{skip}, \epsilon]\!]) = \{\langle\delta_{\{\}}\rangle\}$, which denotes an internal deadlock.

The semantics of a task is simply defined as follows:

$$[\![\mathcal{CH} \bullet (\parallel_i [P_i, E_i])]\!] \;\widehat{=}\; close_{\mathcal{CH}}([\![\parallel_i [P_i, E_i]]\!])$$

Although the semantics seems complicated, we would point out that the complexity is rooted from the basic communication activities that any process algebra has, as discussed in Brookes's paper [5], rather than the exception handling and finalization constructs.

5 Projection

A projection is a procedure which takes a choreography specification in *Chor* and generates a set of processes in *Role*, where each process corresponds to a role in the choreography. No standard projection is defined in WS-CDL. In this section we give our projection rules, and discuss some issues related.

$$
\begin{aligned}
\pi(\text{skip}, i) &\triangleq \text{skip} \\
\pi(a^i, i) &\triangleq a \\
\pi(a^i, j) &\triangleq \text{skip} && \text{when } j \neq i \\
\pi(c^{[i,j]}, i) &\triangleq c^{[i,j]}! \\
\pi(c^{[i,j]}, j) &\triangleq c^{[i,j]}? \\
\pi(c^{[i,j]}, k) &\triangleq \text{skip} && \text{when } k \neq i \wedge k \neq j \\
\pi(\text{throw } e, i) &\triangleq \text{throw } e \\
\pi(\text{perf } n, i) &\triangleq n[\pi(n.1, i), \pi(n.2, i), \pi(n.3, i)] \\
\pi(\text{fin } n, i) &\triangleq \text{fin } n \\[4pt]
\pi(\overline{e : A}, i) &\triangleq \overline{e : \pi(A, i)} \\
\pi(A_1; A_2, i) &\triangleq \pi(A_1, i); \pi(A_2, i) \\
\pi(A_1 \parallel A_2, i) &\triangleq \pi(A_1, i) \parallel \pi(A_2, i) \\
\pi(A_1 \overset{i}{\sqcap} A_2, i) &\triangleq \gamma_1; \pi(A_1, i) \sqcap \gamma_2; \pi(A_2, i) && \text{where } \begin{cases} \gamma_1 = \|_{j \in 1..n \wedge j \neq i} \; c_j'! \\ \gamma_2 = \|_{j \in 1..n \wedge j \neq i} \; c_j''! \end{cases} \\
\pi(A_1 \overset{i}{\sqcap} A_2, j) &\triangleq c_j'? \to \pi(A_1, j) \,[\!]\, c_j''? \to \pi(A_2, j) && \text{when } j \neq i
\end{aligned}
$$

Fig. 1. Endpoint Projection Rules

Firstly, we give a projection rule for the root choreography $[A, E]$, where A and E are projected to the process and exception block at each role process i.

$$
\pi([A, E], i) \triangleq [\pi(A, i), \pi(E, i)]
$$

The project rules for each form of activity is given in Fig. 1. The basic activity a^i generates action a at role R^i, or skip at other roles. The interactive activity $c^{[i,j]}$ generates sending action $c!$ and receiving action $c?$ at role R^i and R^j respectively. The rule for throw activity throw e is based on an assumption that each exception occurred in a choreography is global, which causes the same exception at every role. The activity perf n is projected to each role as a scope with name n, process $\pi(n.1, i)$, exception block $\pi(n.2, i)$, and compensation block $\pi(n.3, i)$, where $n.1$, $n.2$, and $n.3$ are the activity, exception block and finalizer of choreography n respectively. Note that this rule depends on the corresponding context Γ. Finalizing fin n generates the same action fin n at each role. Exception block $\overline{e : A}$ is simply projected to an exception block $\overline{e : \pi(A, i)}$ at role i. The rules for sequential and parallel compositions are trivial.

The most interesting rules are those for choice structure $A_1 \overset{i}{\sqcap} A_2$. For each role R^j ($j \neq i$), we should introduce two fresh channels, namely c_j' and c_j''. The projection of $A_1 \overset{i}{\sqcap} A_2$ on a role other than R^i takes the form of a guarded choice. On the other hand, the projection on role R^i is an ordinary choice with each branch beginning at a set of sending actions. As a result, when the execution of the roles arrives at their versions of the choice structure, role R^i makes the real choice, and notifies all the other roles on which branch it selects. Thus, all the roles will take the same branch in their versions of the choice consistently.

We illustrate a simple example of projection here.

Example 3. The choreography below involves two roles. After R^2 receives a message from R^1, it may either acknowledge R^1 and proceeds, or throw an exception so that the choreography is interrupted.

$$C = [c^{[1,2]}; (c^{[2,1]} \overset{2}{\sqcap} \text{throw } e), \epsilon]$$

After projection, we get the following processes (we omit the scope here since the exception handler is empty):

$$P_1 = c^{[1,2]}!; (c'? \rightarrow c^{[2,1]}? \| c''? \rightarrow \text{throw } e) \quad P_2 = c^{[1,2]}?; ((c'!; c^{[2,1]}!) \sqcap (c''!; \text{throw } e))$$

where c' and c'' are the fresh channels introduced in projection. It is not difficult to verify that $[\![\mathcal{CH} \bullet ([P_1, \epsilon] \| [P_2, \epsilon])]\!] \downarrow acts(C) = [\![C]\!]$, where $\mathcal{CH} = \{c^{[1,2]}, c^{[2,1]}, c', c''\}$.   □

In the equation above, we use the filter operation $\downarrow$ to restrict a trace (or a trace set) to mention only actions from a given action set. The notation $acts(C)$ denotes the set of all activities appearing in choreography C. This extra step removes the handshake actions of the fresh channels.

Example 4. The choreography C below illustrates concurrent exception:

$$C = [(a_1^1 \overset{1}{\sqcap} \text{throw } e_1) \| (a_2^2 \overset{2}{\sqcap} \text{throw } e_2), \epsilon]$$

After projection, we get the following processes:

$$P_1 = ((c_1'!; a_1^1) \sqcap (c_1''!; \text{throw } e_1)) \| (c_2'? \rightarrow \text{skip} \| c_2''? \rightarrow \text{throw } e_2)$$
$$P_2 = (c_1'? \rightarrow \text{skip} \| c_1''? \rightarrow \text{throw } e_1) \| ((c_2'!; a_2^2) \sqcap (c_2''!; \text{throw } e_2))$$

where c_1', c_1'', c_2' and c_2'' are four fresh channels.

Let $\mathcal{CH}$ include all the channel names, we can also verify that $[\![\mathcal{CH} \bullet ([P_1, \epsilon] \| [P_2, \epsilon])]\!] \downarrow acts(C) = [\![C]\!]$, with the trace set:

$$\{\langle a_1^1, a_2^2, \checkmark \rangle, \langle a_2^2, a_1^1, \checkmark \rangle, \langle a_2^2, \ulcorner_{e_1} \rangle, \langle a_1^1, \ulcorner_{e_2} \rangle, \langle \ulcorner_{e_1 \uplus e_2} \rangle\}$$

Please notice that $\langle \ulcorner_{e_1} \rangle$ and $\langle \ulcorner_{e_2} \rangle$ are not in the trace set, since we do not have forced termination.

We hope that the combination of processes can realize the behavior of the choreography. That is, for projection π and choreography C, we hope to prove the following equation:

$$[\![\mathcal{CH} \bullet (\pi(C, 1) \| \cdots \| \pi(C, n))]\!] \downarrow acts(C) = [\![C]\!] \tag{1}$$

where $\mathcal{CH}$ includes all the communication channels defined in the choreography and the fresh channels added by projection. In the previous examples, we already see this equation holds.

This equation says that if we "close" the set of traces generated by the parallel composition of all the role processes wrt the inter-role channels defined in C, and restrict the activities in each trace to the activity set of C, then the result should be equal to the set of traces of the choreography from which the role processes are projected. A formal proof of Equation (1) is an important future work.

6   Conclusion and Future Work

Web service choreography describes a global-view protocol for collaboration among multiple roles, while a set of suitable orchestrations can form a implementation of the protocol. Formal models of choreography and orchestration are important and useful in exploring the subtle features in languages such as WS-CDL and WS-BPEL, and the connection between them. In this paper, we continue the research initiated in [16], with special focus on exception handling and transactionality. Two languages *Chor* and *Role* for choreography and orchestration respectively are introduced, together with formal semantics. Corresponding projection rules are provided, too.

The main contributions of this paper are:

1. We present a denotational (trace) semantics for exception handling and finalization for the choreography language *Chor*. To the best of our knowledge, no work has been done in this area.
2. We also present a trace semantics for the role process language *Role*, where we introduce a "stuck" notation.
3. We provide a set of projection rules that form a map from the choreography language to the role process language. The projection is based on the similarity of *choreography* and *scope* constructs, and naturally projects a *choreography* to a *scope* at each role process. The concept *dominant role* is also vital in defining the projection.

The correctness of the projection should be investigated further, in the sense to ensures that the combination of the set of processes produced does realize the behavior described by the choreography. For this, we need to formally prove Equation (1). Additionally, we want also to extend the model to support variables, states, and contents of exchanged messages.

Acknowledgements. We would like to thank Shengchao Qin for many helpful comments.

References

1. SOAP service description language. `http://ssdl.org`
2. Web services choreography description language version 1.0 (2005) `http://www.w3.org/TR/2005/CR-ws-cdl-10-20051109/`
3. Business process execution language for web services, version 1.1 (May 2003) `http://www-106.ibm.com/developerworks/webservices/library/ws-bpel`
4. Baldoni, M., Badoglio, C., Martelli, A., Patti, V., Schifanella, C.: Verifying the conformance of web services to global interaction protocols: a first step. In: Bravetti, M., Kloul, L., Zavattaro, G. (eds.) Formal Techniques for Computer Systems and Business Processes. LNCS, vol. 3670, Springer, Heidelberg (2005)
5. Brookes, S.: Traces, pomsets, fairness and full abstraction for communicating processes. In: Brim, L., Jančar, P., Křetínský, M., Kucera, A. (eds.) CONCUR 2002. LNCS, vol. 2421, Springer, Heidelberg (2002)

6. Bruni, R., Melgratti, H., Montanari, U.: Theoretical foundations for compensations in flow composition languages. In: Proc. of POPL'05, ACM Press, New York (2005)

7. Busi, N., Gorrieri, R., Guidi, C., Lucchi, R., Zavattaro, G.: Choreography and orchestration: A synergic approach for system design. In: Benatallah, B., Casati, F., Traverso, P. (eds.) ICSOC 2005. LNCS, vol. 3826, Springer, Heidelberg (2005)

8. Busi, N., Gorrieri, R., Guidi, C., Lucchi, R., Zavattaro, G.: Choreography and orchestration conformance for system design. In: Ciancarini, P., Wiklicky, H. (eds.) COORDINATION 2006. LNCS, vol. 4038, Springer, Heidelberg (2006)

9. Butler, M., Hoare, T., Ferreira, C.: A trace semantics for long-running transactions. In: Abdallah, A.E., Jones, C.B., Sanders, J.W. (eds.) Communicating Sequential Processes. LNCS, vol. 3525, Springer, Heidelberg (2005)

10. Butler, M., Ripon, S.: Executable semantics for compensating CSP. In: Bravetti, M., Kloul, L., Zavattaro, G. (eds.) Formal Techniques for Computer Systems and Business Processes. LNCS, vol. 3670, Springer, Heidelberg (2005)

11. Carbone, M., Honda, K., Yoshida, N., Milner, R., Brown, G., Ross-Talbot, S.: A theoretical basis of communication-centred concurrent programming (2006) http://www.w3.org/2002/ws/chor/edcopies/theory/note.pdf

12. Fu, X., Bultan, T., Su, J.: Conversation protocols: A formalism for specification and verification of reactive electronic services. In: Ibarra, O.H., Dang, Z. (eds.) CIAA 2003. LNCS, vol. 2759, Springer, Heidelberg (2003)

13. Li, J., He, J., Pu, G., Zhu, H.: Towards the semantics for web services choreography description language. In: Liu, Z., He, J. (eds.) ICFEM 2006. LNCS, vol. 4260, Springer, Heidelberg (2006)

14. Pu, G., Zhu, H., Qiu, Z., Wang, S., Zhao, X., He, J.: Theoretical foundations of scope-based compensation flow language for web service. In: Ning, P., Qing, S., Li, N. (eds.) ICICS 2006. LNCS, vol. 4307, Springer, Heidelberg (2006)

15. Qiu, Z., Wang, S., Pu, G., Zhao, X.: Semantics of BPEL4WS-like fault and compensation handling. In: Fitzgerald, J.A., Hayes, I.J., Tarlecki, A. (eds.) FM 2005. LNCS, vol. 3582, Springer, Heidelberg (2005)

16. Qiu, Z., Zhao, X., Chao, C., Yang, H.: Towards the theoretical foundation of choreography. Accepted by WWW'07. Available as a tech. report at http://www.is.pku.edu.cn/~fmows/

17. Zhao, X., Yang, H., Qiu, Z.: Towards the formal model and verification of web services choreography description language. In: Bravetti, M., Núñez, M., Zavattaro, G. (eds.) WS-FM 2006. LNCS, vol. 4184, Springer, Heidelberg (2006)

Towards Modal Logic Formalization of Role-Based Access Control with Object Classes

Junghwa Chae

École Polytechnique de Montréal
Montréal, Québec, Canada
chae@cse.concordia.ca

Abstract. This paper addresses a variation of the role-based access control (RBAC) model with a classification mechanism for objects and a notion of class hierarchies. In the proposed model, the authorization tasks are performed based on the classes instead of the individual objects. This results in more flexibility in terms of security administrative tasks such as downgrading or upgrading individual objects and permission assignments. A formalization for this model is presented using $K45$ modal logic. The prefixed tableaux method is used to reason about the access control. The required rules for the reasoning process are also presented. The proposed model is applied, via an example to protect the secrecy of the information in a typical organization.

Keywords: Role-based access control, object classes, object class hierarchy, modal logic, tableaux method.

1 Introduction

Role-based access control (RBAC) provides the abstraction mechanism for categorizing users in roles based on the organizational responsibilities of users [2,6,8,13]. The role is the association between a set of users and a set of permissions. The role simplifies security management tasks to grant and revoke authorizations to an entire group of subjects at the same time. The defined roles can also have hierarchical structures for more convenient authority managements.

In our analysis of security, we provide the RBAC model with a classification mechanism for objects accessed in information systems. Our thesis is that objects are classified into groups called object classes, and classes can constitute a systematic structure, known as a hierarchy. Once objects are categorized into groups, authorization tasks can be executed based on the classes instead of the individual objects. Semantically or functionally related object classes associate with each other via inheritance relationships, and objects can be involved in these hierarchical relationships through the classes in which they are categorized. Object class hierarchy is a method to achieve further simplification in the reduction of security management tasks and administrative costs. It also provides a way to control the propagation of authorizations and to define boundaries for the

J. Derrick and J. Vain (Eds.): FORTE 2007, LNCS 4574, pp. 97–111, 2007.

validity of authorization rules. This modification of the RBAC model provides greater control and flexibility for the security administrative tasks.

Formal methods and reasoning techniques are useful tools for the representation and decision of access control. In this paper, we present a logical approach based on a modal logic formalism [1, 5, 9]. There already exists a well understood theory of how modalities interact with propositional logic connectives. This framework provides a language for expressing properties and relationships of security policies without considering the specific mechanisms for implementing such policies. The semantics of the policy definitions for security is provided using Kripke structures [5]. In developing a formalism for the proposed model, our main contribution is the incorporation of the notion of object classes into the work done by Abadi [1] and Massacci [9].

There has been much research done on logical frameworks for the reasoning of access control models. Woo and Lam [15] proposed a language to model authorization and control rules. A major issue in their approach was the trade-off between expressiveness and efficiency. For the logical formalism approach, Jajodia et al. [7] proposed a logic-based language for specifying authorization rules. Massacci [9] introduced a logic for reasoning about RBAC, by extending Abadi et al.'s access control calculus [1]. They used modal logic to model concepts such as users, roles, and delegation. Rabitti et al. [11] presented a model of authorization for next-generation database systems using the notion of implicit authorization. They developed an authorization model by including the properties of a class, class hierarchy, and composite objects. Bertino et al. [3] proposed a formal framework for reasoning about access control models. They introduced the concepts that subjects, objects, and privileges can be composed together in hierarchical structures and authorization can be derived along the hierarchies. Most existing work on RBAC concentrated on key points such as role hierarchies, user and privilege attributions. There has been little work that studied the role-object relationships and the hierarchy for object classes in RBAC. The idea of object classification for role-based policies was first introduced by Sandhu and Samarati [14]. An RBAC model that includes the concept of object classes was presented by Chae et al. [4] where the formalization was provided by description logics. In this paper, we use this model together with the calculus developed and extended by Abadi et al. [1] and Massacci [9] for the formalization. The existing formalization, which is based on the modal logics, is modified to include the notions of classification of objects and class hierarchy.

The rest of this paper is organized as follows: We begin with describing the proposed RBAC model with object classification in Section 2. The language developed by Abadi and extended by Massacci is reviewed in Section 3. The syntax required to support the notion of object classes and their hierarchy is given in the same section. The semantics for the existing and proposed operators will be discussed in Section 4. Rules for the reasoning process are presented in Section 5. The application of the proposed model and its formalization is illustrated within an example in Section 6. We summarize our results in Section 7 and conclude with suggestions for future work.

2   Role-Based Access Control

RBAC provides the abstraction of subjects based on the inherent properties of accesses. The abstraction of subjects organizes users with roles reflecting their real job functions or their responsibilities. This approach simplifies security management by breaking user authorizations into two parts: one which assigns users to roles and one which associates access rights to objects for those roles (see Fig. 1).

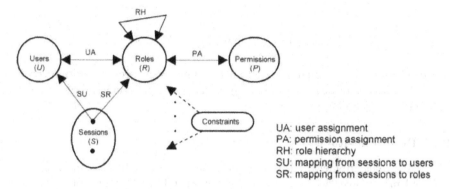

Fig. 1. RBAC model

Analogously, one might expect to achieve further simplification in the security management if some abstraction is provided for objects. Objects could be classified according to their type or to their application area. Grouping objects into classes closely resembles the mapping of users to roles. Fig. 2 shows the proposed model, which consists of five entities including a set of objects and a set of classes. We also added a set of object assignments (OA) that relates each object to a set of classes. Access authorizations of roles should then be defined based on the object classes. A role can be given the authorization to access all objects in a class, instead of giving explicit authorization for each individual object. Objects that are in the same class can be accessible for users with roles that have access right to that class. Ultimately, users exercise permissions on objects via roles to which they are assigned and classes to which the roles have access. We consider roles and object classes as mediators that let users exercise permission. The modified model decomposes each permission into an operation and an object. Therefore, the Permissions entity as depicted in Fig. 1 is removed and two new components Objects and Classes are added in Fig. 2.

This modification of the RBAC model provides greater control and flexibility for security administrative tasks. In particular, this approach simplifies and eases the authorization management ; e.g., in order to add a new object to the system, the corresponding object assignment assertion should only be included, whereas in the RBAC model, permission assignment should be explicitly given for each single role that has the privilege of accessing the new object. Compared to roles,

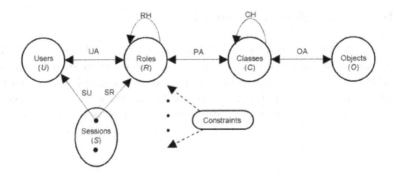

Fig. 2. Proposed modified RBAC model

object classes have a greater potential for simplifying security administration since the number of objects in many systems is generally much larger than the number of subjects.

2.1 Role Inheritance

In RBAC, roles are hierarchically organized into a role-subrole relationship that is called *role inheritance*. The hierarchy is interpreted using a graph where each node represents a role and a directed edge between two roles defines the implication of the authorization. Authorizations are implied along the edges of the role hierarchy. When role R_1 inherits from role R_2, denoted by R_1 isa R_2, every user U explicitly assigned to R_1 is also implicitly associated with R_2; likewise, every permission explicitly associated with role R_2 is implicitly associated with role R_1.

The role hierarchy is a partial order relation, which is reflexive, transitive, and antisymmetric. Inheritance is reflexive because a role inherits its own permissions; transitivity is a natural requirement in this context, and antisymmetry rules out cycles in the role hierarchy; i.e., roles that inherit from one another are disallowed.

2.2 Class Inheritance

In the proposed model, a set of objects are grouped together for security purposes. Each group is, in general, a set of individual objects, and is referred to as a class. Objects are associated with certain properties that can be used to construct groups for the authorization process. Examples of object properties are security levels, ownerships, classes (as in the object-oriented terminology), memberships, etc. Once the objects are categorized into finite sets of groups, authorization tasks can be executed based on the classes instead of individual objects.

Object classes are also organized into a hierarchical structure, called *class inheritance* (note that the word class here is not used in the sense of object-oriented programming but represents any named group of objects). The hierarchy can be based on different criteria such as security levels, generalization and specialization associations, as in object-oriented systems, and so on.

In the role inheritance, the concept of implied authorization is applied. The idea is to propagate the validity of the authorization rule at some level in a hierarchy to its descendants [11]. Similarly, the same idea can be applied to object classes through a hierarchy. Class hierarchies coupled with role hierarchies are implemented in the reasoning process. The definition of object classes and its hierarchical structure provides more reasoning power compared to the conventional RBAC approach.

We propose the following authorization policies:

- Access to a class implies access to the objects explicitly assigned to that class;
- The class hierarchy is defined as follows: the relation $C_1 \preceq_p C_2$ means that all roles given an access privilege p on class C_1 have the same access privilege on class C_2. Therefore, a user U who has a certain access to class C_1 is allowed to exercise the same access on class C_2. In general, the direction of the above inequality relation depends on the type of the operation; e.g., there may exist another operation denoted by p' for which the class inheritance relation between C_1 and C_2 would change to $C_2 \preceq_{p'} C_1$; for example, read and write operations in mandatory policies where classes are formed based on the security level (access classes). In this situation we can replicate each classes by the number of operations that have different hierarchical relations; e.g., C_1^p and $C_1^{p'}$.

3   Language for Access Control

In this paper, we adopted the calculus developed by Abadi [1] et al. to model access control in distributed systems. We equipped the calculus with proper notations to describe the proposed concept of object classes and their hierarchy in the context of modal logic.

The main syntactical components of this logic [1,9,10] are principals, requests and a set of modal and propositional connectives and operators. Users and roles are examples of atomic principals. Atomic users are denoted by A and B and roles by R. Composite principals denoted by P and Q are built by the use of different connectives such as the conjunction of principals (A & B), users in a certain role (A as B) and principal on behalf of another principal (A for B). A complete list of principals in typical distributed information systems is given by Abadi [1].

The common practice in RBAC is to represent the combination of an operation over an object as an atomic request or a statement; e.g., *read_file1*. In this approach, neither the operation nor the object by itself is considered as part of the model; whereas the combination or the request is considered as a proposition that can be true or false depending on the state of the system. Composite requests are then built using propositional logic connectives $\land$, $\neg$, and $\Rightarrow$. Since our main objective is to categorize individual objects into object classes and to use the class hierarchy for a reasoning process, following this common practice would be inappropriate. In the operation-object approach, two statements such as *read_file1* and *write_file1* are considered as two independent propositions ϕ and ψ. However, our goal is to be able to separate these propositions into an operation part plus an object part. This distinction makes it possible to use the hierarchy associated with objects for reasoning about access control.

Atomic objects and classes are denoted by O and C, respectively. Object classification is made using the statement O belong C, which closely resembles Massacci's user assignments to roles, A has R [9]. belong and has are both modal operators. The operation over objects, read O or write O, is considered as an atomic request which is a proposition in the model and can take different truth values depending on the state of the system. These propositions are constructed as a combination of an operator (write or read) and an object or a class (O or C). User assignment statements as well as object classification statements are also simple propositions. Composite propositions are formed by combining the simple ones using propositional logic connectives.

In order to access objects in the system or to perform operations, users and roles (users in roles) make the corresponding requests. The main purpose of the access control policies is to determine whether these requests should be granted or not. The requests are made using the modal operator req [9]; e.g., A req ϕ where ϕ is a proposition such as read O. The statement A req ϕ is considered as a request or proposition by itself.

Privileges are given to users and roles using the control statement [1]. The proposition R control ϕ gives the permission on ϕ to role R; i.e.,

$$(R \text{ control } \phi) \wedge (R \text{ req } \phi) \Rightarrow \phi. \tag{1}$$

Role hierarchies are defined using the isa modal operator; e.g., the statement R_1 isa R_2 means that role R_1 has at least all of the privileges that are assigned to R_2. Operator $\sqsubseteq$ is used to define class hierarchies. The similar statement $C_1 \sqsubseteq C_2$ means that all users or roles that are given certain privileges on class C_1 have at least the same privileges on class C_2 (permissions given on class C_1 are valid for class C_2). The role or object class hierarchy statements are also considered as requests or propositions.

Our objective is to benefit from role and class hierarchies to reason about access control; e.g., to be able to perform the following operations,

$$R_2 \text{ control } \phi \wedge R_1 \text{ req } \phi \wedge R_1 \text{isa } R_2 \Rightarrow \phi,$$
$$R \text{ control } (\text{read } C_1) \wedge R \text{ req } (\text{read } O) \wedge O \text{ belongs } C_2 \wedge C_1 \sqsubseteq C_2 \Rightarrow \text{read } O.$$

4   Semantics

The semantics are defined using Kripke structures [5]. The syntax of the language described in the previous section consists of a set of agents (atomic principals), objects and classes, a set of primitive propositions Φ, atomic requests mainly of the form read O, and modal as well as propositional connectives and operators to construct primitive propositions from objects and classes or build composite agents and propositions. A Kripke structure denoted by $\mathcal{M}$ for a set of agents over Φ is a pair $(W, \mathcal{I})$ where W is a set of possible worlds (states) for a typical information system and $\mathcal{I}$ is the interpretation function. What makes each world distinct from the other is its specific truth values for the set of primitive propositions. Each agent (principal) A is interpreted as a set of pairs such that each pair consists of elements of W, i.e., $A^{\mathcal{I}} \subseteq W \times W$. Pair $(w_i, w_j) \in A^{\mathcal{I}}$ indicates that state w_j is one of the compatible states with state w_i for agent A. The interpretation of a proposition (request) is a set of states where the proposition (request) is true (granted), i.e., $\phi^{\mathcal{I}} \subseteq W$. Classes are interpreted as set of worlds in which they are accessible. Objects are uninterpreted entities within the structure.

4.1 Principals and Hierarchies

The interpretations of a user or a role is given by a set of pairs that define the compatible worlds (states) for the corresponding role or user; e.g.,

$$A^{\mathcal{I}} = \{(w_i, w_j), (w_i, w_k), (w_i, w_m), (w_j, w_n), (w_j, w_m), (w_j, w_p), \ldots\}, \quad (2)$$

where w_j, w_k, w_m are among the compatible states with state w_i for user A; i.e., the state of the system will change from w_i into one of the compatible states according to the requests made by user A in state w_i.

For the role hierarchy given by R_1 isa R_2, since R_1 can also act as R_2, all compatible worlds of R_2 should also be among the compatible worlds of R_1; i.e.,

$$R_2^{\mathcal{I}} \subseteq R_1^{\mathcal{I}}. \quad (3)$$

As mentioned in Section 3, role hierarchy statements are considered as requests or propositions in the system, hence R_1 isa R_2 will be interpreted as a set of worlds where Relation (3) is valid:

$$(R_1 \text{ isa } R_2)^{\mathcal{I}} = \{w | \forall w' \text{ if } (w, w') \in R_2^{\mathcal{I}} \text{ then } (w, w') \in R_1^{\mathcal{I}}\}. \quad (4)$$

4.2 Object Classes and Hierarchies

Each object class is interpreted as a set of states where it is accessible. As explained in Section 2, when there are different types of operations in the information system, we replicate each class by the number of operations, e.g., C^r and C^w. In this case the interpretation of C^r or C^w indicates the set of worlds where the class can be read or written, respectively,

$$C^{r[w]^{\mathcal{I}}} = \{w_i, w_j, w_k, \ldots\}. \quad (5)$$

The state w_i exists in the interpretation of the object class $C^{r[w]}$ iff the statement read[write] $C^{r[w]}$ is valid in this state.

As seen in Section 3, the statement $C_1 \sqsubseteq C_2$ indicates that all permissions given on class C_1 are also valid for class C_2. In all states where class C_1 is accessible, class C_2 is accessible too. From Relation (5), it follows that all states in the interpretation of class C_1 should exist in the interpretation of class C_2; i.e.,

$$C_1^{\mathcal{I}} \subseteq C_2^{\mathcal{I}}. \tag{6}$$

The class hierarchy statement can then be interpreted as,

$$(C_1 \sqsubseteq C_2)^{\mathcal{I}} = \left\{ w \middle| \text{ if } w \in C_1^{\mathcal{I}} \text{ then } w \in C_2^{\mathcal{I}} \right\}. \tag{7}$$

4.3   Request Operator and Properties

The definition of the request operator req is similar to Fagin et al.'s knowledge operator [5]. It has two arguments: a principal that makes the request and a proposition that is requested. A request statement made in state w by principal A is valid when its propositional argument is true in all compatible states with w,

$$(\mathcal{M}, w) \models A \text{ req } \phi \text{ iff } (\mathcal{M}, w') \models \phi \text{ for all } w' \text{ such that } (w, w') \in A^{\mathcal{I}}. \tag{8}$$

Compatible states with state w for principal A are defined as a set of states where all of the requests made by A in w will be granted.

The truth of A req ϕ does not imply that ϕ is granted. In fact, the access control system has the responsibility of verifying whether ϕ should be granted whenever A req ϕ is valid, i.e., the process of verifying if ϕ is true (granted) starts after it is proven that the A req ϕ is true. The distinction between granting a request and the truth of a request statement is crucial. According to the definition (8), if ϕ is invalid in any of the compatible states with w for principal A, then A is unable to make a valid request in w, i.e., $(\mathcal{M}, w) \not\models A$ req ϕ. Whereas, when ϕ is true (granted) in all compatible states with w, then the request statement A req ϕ is valid in w and the reasoner starts the process of verifying whether the propositional argument of the request statement should be granted.

The binary relations formed by the interpretation of users or roles exhibit certain properties. Relations satisfying $K45$ properties; i.e., transitive and Euclidean, fit best with the characteristics of access control in information systems. The Euclidean property requires that for all $w_1, w_2, w_3 \in W$ if $(w_1, w_2) \in A^{\mathcal{I}}$ and $(w_1, w_3) \in A^{\mathcal{I}}$, then $(w_2, w_3) \in A^{\mathcal{I}}$. The interpretation relations for principals should not be reflexive as the reflexivity necessitates that all valid requests made in state w should be granted in the same state. The transitivity is required since successive requests can be combined into one composite request. Similarly, a composite request made in state w can be considered as subsequent individual requests that necessitates Euclidean property for the binary relations. Given the definition (8) as well as the transitive and Euclidean binary relations for users and roles, the request operator holds the following properties in the Kripke structure $\mathcal{M}$:

K $\vdash (A \text{ req } \phi \wedge A \text{ req } (\phi \Rightarrow \psi)) \Rightarrow \vdash A \text{ req } \psi$;
KG if $\vdash \phi$ then $\vdash A \text{ req } \phi$;
4 $\vdash A \text{ req } \phi \Rightarrow \vdash A \text{ req } (A \text{ req } \phi)$;
5 $\vdash \neg A \text{ req } \phi \Rightarrow \vdash A \text{ req } \neg (A \text{ req } \phi)$;
Id $\vdash A \text{ req } (A \text{ req } \phi) \Rightarrow \vdash A \text{ req } \phi$.

K property is the direct consequence of the definition of the request operator. It is valid whether or not binary relations exhibit transitive or Euclidean property. **K** rule indicates that when a user makes a request, it also includes all the logical consequences of her original request. In knowledge representation, properties **4** and **5** are called positive and negative introspection axioms, respectively. The former follows from the transitive property of the binary relations and the latter is the result of both transitive and Euclidean properties. **KG** is the knowledge generalization rule that says if ϕ is granted in all states of structure $\mathcal{M}$, then $A \text{ req } \phi$ is true everywhere. **Id** is the result of Euclidean property. Properties **Id** and **4** show the idempotence of the req operator, i.e., the following equivalence relation is valid,

$$A \text{ req } (A \text{ req } \phi) \equiv A \text{ req } \phi. \tag{9}$$

4.4 User Assignment and Object Classification

The interpretation of user assignment statements has operator is given by,

$$(A \text{ has } R)^{\mathcal{I}} = \left\{ w \middle| \forall w' \text{ if } (w, w') \in R^{\mathcal{I}} \text{ then } (w, w') \in A^{\mathcal{I}} \right\}. \tag{10}$$

The object classification statement $O \text{ belong } C$ is interpreted as follows:

$$O \text{ belong } C^{r[w]} \Rightarrow \text{read[write] } O \equiv \text{read[write] } C^{r[w]}. \tag{11}$$

4.5 Read and Write Statements

In Section 3, the read and write operations on objects and classes are constructed with read and write operators, respectively. From the interpretation of object classes given in Section 4.2, it follows that the statement read C^r is true in world w iff $w \in (C^r)^{\mathcal{I}}$. Hence read and write statements, only for object classes, are interpreted below,

$$\left(\text{read[write] } C^{r[w]} \right)^{\mathcal{I}} = \left\{ w \middle| w \in C^{r[w]}{}^{\mathcal{I}} \right\}. \tag{12}$$

Object interpretation is the similar to the class interpretation, i.e., it is given by a set of individual states. However, the interpretation of objects do not remain constant even within a single state. Depending on the requests made by principals to read or write an object in state w, its interpretation changes to either $C^r{}^{\mathcal{I}}$ or $C^w{}^{\mathcal{I}}$, respectively. Relation (11) is used to convert read and write operations on objects to the read and write operations on classes to which they belong upon the corresponding requests that are made.

5   Rules and Reasoning

Although the semantic is given by the Kripke structure, reasoning at the level of the structure would be inconvenient in access control systems. A set of inference rules are then introduced. These rules together with the axioms form an axiom system. Axioms are mainly given by the access control security policy as the ACL (Access Control List), which consists of the following statements:

- Role hierarchies (RH), $\bigwedge_{i,j} (R_i \text{ isa } R_j)$;
- Object class hierarchies (CH), $\bigwedge_{i,j} (C_i \sqsubseteq C_j)$;
- User assignments (UA), $\bigwedge_{i,j} (A_i \text{ has } R_j)$;
- Object classifications (OC), $\bigwedge_{i,j} (O_i \text{ belong } C_j)$;
- Permission assignments (PA), $\bigwedge_{i,j,k} (P_i \text{ control } \mathsf{Op}_j\, C_k)$;
  $$\mathsf{Op}_j \in \{\mathsf{read}, \mathsf{write}, \ldots\}.$$

The proof method is based on Massacci's prefixed tableaux algorithm [10]. This method is used to test the satisfiability of a proposition. The tableaux method builds a tree-like model $\mathcal{M}$ based on the input proposition and the global axioms. In tree $\mathcal{T}$, each node is labeled with a proposition and has a prefix that indicates the current state of the system. Tableaux rules are then repeatedly applied to nodes in an arbitrary order for as long as possible. A branch $\mathcal{B}$ of tree $\mathcal{T}$ is fully expanded when all rules have been applied to the nodes in $\mathcal{B}$. There exists a clash in $\mathcal{B}$ if a proposition and its negation exist in $\mathcal{B}$ with the same prefix. The proposition ϕ is valid in an axiom system built based on a set of global axioms G, if all branches of tree $\mathcal{T}$ that start with $\neg\phi$ lead to clashes. This indicates that $\neg\phi$ is not satisfiable.

The rules for $K45$ modal logic, users in roles and role hierarchies are due to Massacci [9] and are shown in Fig. 3. Here, σ is the current state of the system. $\sigma.A.n$ and $\sigma.A.m$ are present and new compatible states with σ according to the requests of principal A, respectively. Fig. 4 shows the required rules for object class hierarchies where $\mathsf{Op}_j \in \{\mathsf{read}, \mathsf{write}, \ldots\}$.

$$\alpha: \frac{\sigma: \varphi \wedge \psi}{\sigma: \varphi \quad \sigma: \psi} \qquad \beta: \frac{\sigma: \neg(\varphi \wedge \psi)}{\sigma: \neg\varphi \mid \sigma: \neg\psi} \qquad dn: \frac{\sigma: \neg\neg\varphi}{\sigma: \varphi} \qquad K: \frac{\sigma: A \text{ req } \varphi}{\sigma.A.n: \varphi}$$

$$4: \frac{\sigma: A \text{ req } \varphi}{\sigma.A.n: A \text{ req } \varphi} \qquad 5: \frac{\sigma.A.n: A \text{ req } \varphi}{\sigma: A \text{ req } \varphi} \qquad \pi: \frac{\sigma: \neg(A \text{ req } \varphi)}{\sigma.A.m: \neg(\varphi)}$$

$$ur1: \frac{\sigma: \neg(U \text{ as } R) \text{ req } \varphi}{\sigma: \neg(U \text{ req } (R \text{ req } \varphi))} \qquad ur2: \frac{\sigma: (U \text{ as } R) \text{ req } \varphi}{\sigma: U \text{ req } (R \text{ req } \varphi)}$$

$$IK: \frac{\sigma: R_1 \text{ isa } R_2 \quad \sigma: R_1 \text{ req } \varphi}{\sigma: R_2 \text{ req } \varphi} \qquad I\pi: \frac{\sigma: \neg(R_1 \text{ isa } R_2)}{\sigma: R_1 \text{ req } x_i \quad \sigma: \neg(R_2 \text{ req } x_i)}$$

Fig. 3. Tableaux rules based on $K45$ properties, users in roles, and role hierarchy

$$C_i : \frac{\sigma : \mathsf{Op}_j\ C_1^j \quad \sigma : C_1^j \sqsubseteq C_2^j}{\sigma : \mathsf{Op}_j\ C_2^j} \qquad\qquad C_{ii} : \frac{\sigma : \neg\mathsf{Op}_j\ C_2^j \quad \sigma : C_1^j \sqsubseteq C_2^j}{\sigma : \neg\mathsf{Op}_j\ C_1^j}$$

$$C_k : \frac{\sigma : A\ \mathsf{req}\ (\mathsf{Op}_j\ O) \quad \sigma : O\ \mathsf{belong}\ C^j}{\sigma : A\ \mathsf{req}\ (\mathsf{Op}_j\ C^j)} \quad C_t : \frac{\sigma : A\ \mathsf{control}\ (\mathsf{Op}_j\ C_1^j) \quad \sigma : C_1^j \sqsubseteq C_2^j}{\sigma : A\ \mathsf{control}\ (\mathsf{Op}_j\ C_2^j)}$$

$$C_o : \frac{\sigma : \mathsf{Op}_j\ C^j \quad \sigma : O\ \mathsf{belong} C^j}{\sigma : \mathsf{Op}_j\ O} \qquad\qquad C_n : \frac{\sigma : \neg\mathsf{Op}_j\ C^j \quad \sigma : O\ \mathsf{belong} C^j}{\sigma : \neg\mathsf{Op}_j\ O}$$

Fig. 4. Rules for object classes and hierarchies

6   Example: RBAC Policies with Object Class Hierarchies

In this section, we illustrate a simplified model of a company with marketing and R&D departments. The model includes six different roles: Administrator, R&D-manager, R&D-staff, Marketing-manager, Marketing-staff, Customer. The role hierarchy shown in Fig. 6 is derived based on the lattice $\mathcal{L}$ of the access classes depicted in Fig. 5. Access classes are composed of a set of category and a security level [12]. In this example the set of categories are subsets of {Marketing, R&D} and security levels are defined by C (classified) and U (unclassified). We use the following abbreviation to represent the concept of roles: Admin, RDMag, RDStf, MktMag, MktStf, Cust. The role hierarchy (RH) is modeled using the following inclusion axioms:

Admin isa RDMag, Admin isa MktMag, RDMag isa RDStf,
MktMag isa MktStf, RDStf isa Cust, MktStf isa Cust.

Objects are classified into six categories: Company-agenda, Patent, Technical-report, Contract, Marketing-survey, and General-information. Two object classes are defined for each category; one for read and the other for write operation. Object class concepts are defined as: Agenda^r, Patent^r, TechRep^r, Contract^r,

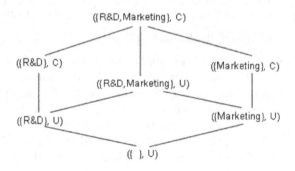

Fig. 5. Security lattice $\mathcal{L}$

MktSur^r, Geninfo^r, Agenda^w, Patent^w, TechRep^w, Contract^w, MktSur^w, Geninfo^w. The classes for read and write are distinguished by superscripts r and w, respectively. The class hierarchy is shown in Fig. 7. This hierarchy is also derived from access classes in Fig. 5. The inheritance relations among classes are given by the following class hierarchy axioms (CH):

Agenda^r ⊑ Patent^r, Agenda^r ⊑ Contract^r, Patent^r ⊑ TechRep^r,
TechRep^r ⊑ Geninfo^r, Contract^r ⊑ MktSur^r, MktSur^r ⊑ Geninfo^r,
Geninfo^w ⊑ TechRep^w, TechRep^w ⊑ Patent^w, Patent^w ⊑ Agenda^w,
Geninfo^w ⊑ MktSur^w, MktSur^w ⊑ Contract^w, Contract^w ⊑ Agenda^w.

Permissions are assigned such that they relate roles and object classes that are

Fig. 6. Role hierarchy   **Fig. 7.** Class hierarchy

located at the same level in the hierarchy; e.g., RDMag can read and write Patent^r and Patent^w, respectively. Permission assignment axioms (PA) for all roles that exist in the model are shown below.

Admin control (read Agenda^r), Admin control (write Agenda^w),
RDMag control (read Contract^r), RDMag control (write Contract^w),
RDStf control (read TechRep^r), RDStf control (write TechRep^w),
MktMag control (read Contract^r), MktMag control (write Contract^w),
MktStf control (read MktSur^r), MktMag control (write MktSur^w),
Cust control (read Geninfo^r), Cust control (write Geninfo^w).

The class hierarchy reduces the number of permission assignment axioms; e.g., for Admin, it is sufficient to specify the read permission only over the class Agenda^r. All read permissions over other classes for Admin can be implied using the class hierarchy. A similar inference capability based on the role hierarchy already exists in the RBAC model, e.g., the specification of permissions for RDStf implicitly gives the same permissions to RDMag. However, the class hierarchy provides additional axioms that can be used together with the role hierarchy to enhance the reasoning power.

Suppose user Bob who is assigned to role Marketing-manager wishes to read file $f1$ that is classified under Marketing-survey, $MktSur^r$. This request is equivalent to the following relation:

$$Bob \ \mathsf{req} \ \mathsf{read} \ f1.$$

We prove that the negation of the propositional argument of the above request, $\neg \mathsf{read} \ f1$, is not satisfiable in any model that is built based on the global axioms RH, CH, UA, OC, and PA. The reasoning process (shown in Fig. 8) starts with the negation statement. The global axioms used in the process of reasoning are indicated with an italicized font. All branches that are shown here lead to clashes. Since the negation is not satisfiable; i.e., the relation itself is valid and Bob's request should be granted.

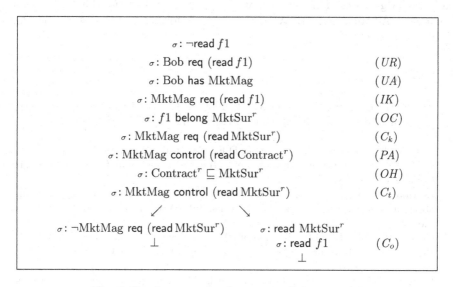

Fig. 8. Proving steps for the request $Bob \ \mathsf{req} \ \mathsf{read} \ f1$

7   Conclusion and Future Work

The notion of object classes is appended to RBAC. A method is introduced, based on the modal logic, to formalize RBAC policies with object classes and to use object class hierarchies for reasoning about access control.

In our approach, we replicated classes by the number of operations (C^r and C^w), and interpreted each of them as a set of individual states, Relation (5). This approach closely resembles the original operation-object ($read\_file1$) definition of permissions in RBAC. Whereas, using the proposed method, one only needs to replicate object classes rather than all individual objects. This results in a great simplification for typical information systems where the number of objects is usually quite large, however they can be categorized into few classes.

Not all axioms in the ACL have the same level of importance in an information system. While user assignment (UA) and object classification (OC) statements can be specified by local managers, role and object class hierarchies as well as permission assignments can be considered as the signature of the access control policies and should be determined by high authority administrators. In the proposed method, object classification and class hierarchies are specified via different operators belong and $\sqsubseteq$. Operator belong provides a mechanism to easily downgrade (sanitize) or upgrade a specific object into the appropriate class, while $\sqsubseteq$ provides the hierarchies between classes determined by the security administrator.

The use of an expressive logic, such as modal logic, simplifies the application of different constraints that will be investigated in future work.

Acknowledgments. This research was supported by Institute for Information Technology Advancement (IITA) & Ministry of Information and Communication (MIC), Republic of Korea.

References

1. Abadi, M., Burrows, M., Lampson, B., Plotkin, G.: A calculus for access control in distributed systems. ACM Trans. Program. Lang. Syst (USA) 15(4), 706–734 (1993)
2. Barkely, J.F., Cincotta, V., Ferraiolo, D.F., Garrvrilla, S., Kuhn, D.R.: Role based access control for the world wide web. NIST 20th National Computer Security Conference, pp. 331–340 (1997)
3. Bertino, E., Catania, B., Ferrari, E., Perlasca, P.: A logical framework for reasoning about access control models. ACM Trans. Inf. Syst. Secur (USA) 6(1), 71–127 (2003)
4. Chae, J.H., Shiri, N.: Formalization of RBAC policy with object class hierarchy. In: Proc. of the 3rd Information Security Practice and Experience Conference (ISPEC) (2007)
5. Fagin, R., Halpern, J.Y., Moses, Y., Vardi, M.Y.: Reasoning about Knowledge. MIT Press, Cambridge, Massachusetts (1995)
6. Ferraiolo, D.F., Barkely, J.F., Kuhn, D.R.: A role based access control model and reference implementation within a corporate Intranet. ACM Trans. Inf. Syst. Secur (USA) 1(2), 34–64 (1999)
7. Jajodia, S., Samarati, P., Sapino, M.L., Subrahmanian, V.S.: Flexible support for multiple access control policies. ACM Trans. Database Syst (USA) 26(2), 214–260 (2001)
8. Koch, M., Mancini, L.V., Parisi-Presicce, F.: A graph-based formalism for RBAC. ACM Trans. Inf. Syst. Secur (USA) 5(3), 332–365 (2002)
9. Massacci, F.: Reasoning about security: A logic and a decision method for role-based access control. In: Nonnengart, A., Kruse, R., Ohlbach, H.J., Gabbay, D.M. (eds.) FAPR 1997 and ECSQARU 1997. LNCS(LNAI), vol. 1244, pp. 421–435. Springer, Heidelberg (1997)
10. Massacci, F.: Tableaux methods for access control in distributed systems. In: Galmiche, D. (ed.) TABLEAUX 1997. LNCS, vol. 1227, p. 246. Springer, Heidelberg (1997)

11. Rabitti, F., Bertino, E.: A model of authorization for next-generation database systems. ACM Trans. Database Syst (USA) 16(1), 88–131 (1991)
12. Samarati, P., Vimercati, S.C.: Foundations of Security Analysis and Design: Tutorial Lectures. In: Access Control: Policies, Models, and Mechanisms, pp. 137–196. Springer, Heidelberg (2001)
13. Sandhu, R.S., Coyne, E.J., Feinstein, H.L., Youman, C.E.: Role-based access control models. IEEE Computer 29(2), 38–47 (1996)
14. Sandhu, R.S., Samarati, P.: Access control: Principles and practice. IEEE Communications Magazine 32(9), 40–48 (1994)
15. Woo, T.Y.C., Lam, S.S.: Authorization in distributed systems: a new approach. J. Comput. Secur (Netherlands) 2(2-3), 107–136 (1993)

State Isomorphism in Model Programs with Abstract Data Structures

Margus Veanes[1], Juhan Ernits[2,*], and Colin Campbell[3,**]

[1] Microsoft Research, Redmond, WA, USA
margus@microsoft.com
[2] Inst. of Cybernetics / Dept. of Comp. Sci.,
Tallinn University of Technology, Tallinn, Estonia
juhan@cc.ioc.ee
[3] Modeled Computation LLC, Seattle, WA, USA
colin@modeled-computation.com

Abstract. Modeling software features with model programs in C# is a way of formalizing software requirements that lends itself to automated analysis such as model-based testing. Unordered structures like sets and maps provide a useful abstract view of system state within a model program and greatly reduce the number of states that must be considered during analysis. Similarly, a technique called linearization reduces the number of states that must be considered by identifying isomorphic states, or states that are identical except for reserve element choice (such as the choice of object IDs for instances of classes). Unfortunately, linearization does not work on unordered structures such as sets. The problem turns into graph isomorphism, for which no polynomial time solution is known. In this paper we discuss the issue of state isomorphism in the presence of unordered structures and give a practical approach that overcomes some of the algorithmic limitations.

1 Introduction

Model programs are a useful formalism for software modeling and design analysis and are used as the foundation of industrial tools such as Spec Explorer [24]. The expressive power of model programs is due largely to two characteristics. First, one can use complex data structures, such as sequences, sets, maps and bags, which is sometimes referred to as having a *rich background universe*. Second, one can use instances of classes or elements from user-defined abstract types; we use the word *object* to mean either case.

The lack of symmetry checking when program states include both unordered structures and objects is a serious practical concern for users of tools like Spec Explorer. If symmetric states are not pruned, the number of states that must be considered during exploration will often become infeasibly large. This problem is known as *state space explosion*. Symmetry reduction is not a universal solution for the state explosion problem but helps to relieve it in many cases. In this paper we present a symmetry reduction

---

* This work was done during an internship at Microsoft Research, Redmond, WA, USA.
** This work was done at Microsoft Research, Redmond, WA, USA.

J. Derrick and J. Vain (Eds.): FORTE 2007, LNCS 4574, pp. 112–127, 2007.
© IFIP International Federation for Information Processing 2007

based on state isomorphism for programs that contain both complex data structures and objects.

Taking into account practical experience with Spec Explorer and user feedback, we can characterize a typical usage scenario of model programs as a three step process: *describe, analyze* and *test* [14].

Describe: A *contract model program* is written to capture the intended behavior of a system or subsystem under consideration. Complex data structures and abstract elements are utilized to produce a contract, or trace oracle, at the desired level of abstraction.

Analyze: Zero or more *scenario model programs* are written to restrict the contract to relevant or interesting cases. The scenarios are composed with the contract and the resulting model program is *explored* to validate the contract. The possible traces of a composition of model programs is the intersection of possible traces of the constituent model programs.

Test: The model program, that is, the contract possibly composed with additional scenarios, is used to generate test cases or used as a test oracle.

The expressive power of combining abstract, unordered data types with objects is useful when describing a model but complicates analysis. The core problem is to efficiently identify "relevant" states during exploration. By a state we mean a collection of all state variables and their values at a given point along the exploration path. It is often the case that two states that are isomorphic should be treated as being equivalent. Isomorphism between states with a rich background universe is well defined. It exists when there is a one-to-one mapping of objects (within each abstract type) that induces a structure-preserving mapping between the states [1].[1] Informally, two states are isomorphic if they differ in choice of object IDs (or elements of the reserve) but are otherwise structurally identical.

Consider for example a state signature containing two state variables V and E. (States are introduced in the next section.) The type of V is a set of vertices (distinct values of an abstract type *Vertex*) and the type of E is a set of vertex sets. Let v_1, v_2, v_3, v_4 be vertices and let S_1 be a state where,

$$V = \{v_1, v_2, v_3, v_4\},$$
$$E_1 = \{\{v_1, v_2\}, \{v_2, v_3\}, \{v_3, v_4\}, \{v_4, v_1\}\}.$$

Intuitively, the state S_1 is an undirected graph that is a circle of four vertices. Let S_2 be a state where V has the same value as in S_1 and,

$$E_2 = \{\{v_1, v_3\}, \{v_3, v_2\}, \{v_2, v_4\}, \{v_4, v_1\}\}.$$

States S_1 and S_2 are isomorphic because structure is preserved if the reserve element v_2 is swapped with v_3. This is an isomorphism that maps v_3 to v_2, v_2 to v_3 and every other vertex to itself. Let S_3 be a state where V has the same value as in S_1 and,

$$E_3 = \{\{v_1, v_2\}, \{v_2, v_3\}, \{v_3, v_1\}, \{v_4, v_1\}\}.$$

---

[1] In ASM theory, what we call *objects* are called *reserve elements*.

State S_3 is not isomorphic to S_1, because all vertices in S_1 are connected to two vertices but v_4 is only connected to one vertex in S_3, i.e., there exists no structure-preserving mapping from S_1 to S_3.

The example illustrates the point that state isomorphism is as hard as graph isomorphism, when objects and unordered data structures are combined. A customer survey of Spec Explorer users within Microsoft has shown that this combination occurs often in practice. It occurs in the standard Spec Explorer example included in the distribution [21] known as the chat model [24,23], where chat clients are objects and the state has a state variable that maps receiving clients to sets of sending clients with pending messages. The state isomorphism problem for reserve elements in unordered structures was not solved in Spec Explorer and to the best of our knowledge has not been addressed in other tools used for model based testing or model checking that support unordered data structures. There are model checkers that support *scalar sets* [13], which are basically ranges of integers, but we do not know of instances where such sets can contain objects with abstract object IDs.

In practical terms this means that users must either use various pruning techniques that only partially address the problem or extend the model program with custom scenario control that tries to work around the problem by restricting the scope of exploration. The results are not always satisfactory.

The pruning techniques that have been partially helpful in this context are state grouping [9] and multiple state grouping [4,24]. The grouping techniques have an orthogonal usage that is similar to abstraction in model checking, but state isomorphism is a clearly defined symmetry reduction that is closely related to state symmetry reduction in explicit state model checking [18]. In general, it is not possible to write a grouping expression that maps two states into the same value if and only if the states are isomorphic; the "only if" part is the problem.

If objects are not used, then state isomorphism reduces to state equality. State equality can be checked in linear time. This is possible because the internal representation of all (unordered) data structures can then be ordered in a canonical way. The same argument is true if objects are used but no unordered data structures are used. Then state isomorphism reduces to what is called heap canonicalization in the context of model checking and can be implemented in linear time [12,19].

In this paper we describe a solution for the state isomorphism problem for model programs with states that have both unordered structures and objects. We do so by providing a mapping from model program states to rooted labeled directed graphs and use a graph isomorphism algorithm to solve the state isomorphism problem. The graph construction and the labeling scheme use techniques from graph partitioning algorithms and strong hashing algorithms to reduce the need to check isomorphism for states that are known not to be isomorphic. We also outline a graph isomorphism algorithm that is customized to the particularities of state graphs. Our algorithm extends a linearization based symmetry-checking algorithm as in [16,27] with backtracking and is, arguably, better suited for this application than existing graph isomorphism algorithms.

Before we continue with the main body of the paper, we illustrate why state isomorphism checking is useful on a small example, shown in Figure 1, that we use also in the later sections. Th example is small but typical for similar situations that arise for

```
namespace Triangle
{
  [Abstract]
  enum Side { S1, S2, S3 }

  [Abstract]
  enum Color { RED, BLUE }

  static class Contract
  {
    static Map<Side, Color> colorAssignments = Map<Side, Color>.EmptyMap;

    static bool AssignColorEnabled(Side s)
    {   return !colorAssignments.ContainsKey(s); }

    [Action]
    static void AssignColor(Side s, Color c)
    {   colorAssignments = colorAssignments.Add(s, c); }
  }
}
```

Fig. 1. A model program where a color, either RED or BLUE, is assigned to the sides of a triangle

example in the chat model [23] or when modeling multithreaded applications where threads are treated as objects [26]. The example is written in C# and uses a modeling library and a toolkit called *NModel*. The formal definition of a model program is given in Section 2, where it is also explained how the C# code maps to a model program. NModel is going to be an open source project that supports the forthcoming text book [14] that discusses the use of model programs as a practical modeling technique. All algorithms described in this paper have been implemented in NModel.

Example

Let us look at a simple model program that describes ways to assign colors to the sides of a triangle. The model program is given in Figure 1. The triangle in the program has three sides, S1, S2, and S3 and each side can be associated with the color RED or BLUE. The model program has a single action that assigns a color to one side at a time. There are $(|Color| + 1)^{|Side|} = 27$ possible combinations of such assignments, including intermediate steps where some sides have not been colored yet. There are three sides; each side has three possible values if you count "no color" as a value.

The state transition graph visualizing all possible transitions and all distinct states of the triangle program is given in Figure 2. In this case the [Abstract] attributes of Side and Color have not been taken into account and each combination of Side $\mapsto$ Color is considered distinct.

2 Definitions

A formal treatment of model programs builds on the ASM theory [11] and can for example be found in [25]. Here we provide some basic terminology and intuition and illustrate the main concepts with examples. A *state* here is a full first-order state, that is intuitively a mapping from a fixed set of *state variables* to a fixed universe of *values*.

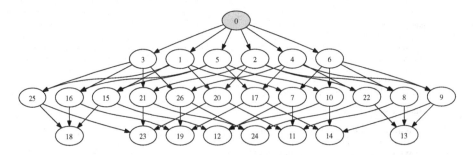

Fig. 2. The result of exhaustive exploration of the triangle example in Figure 1. Each combination of Side ↦ Color is considered distinct and thus the blowup of the state space. The numbers denote exploration sequence of the state space.

States also have a rich *background* [1] that contains sequences, sets, maps, sets of sets, maps of sets, etc. We assume here that all state variables are nullary.[2] For example, the model program in Figure 1 has one state variable colorAssignments.

Since states have a rich background universe they are infinite. However, for representation, we are only interested in the *foreground* part of a state that is the interpretation of the state variables. All values have a *term* representation. Terms that do not include state variables are called *value terms* and are defined inductively over a signature of function symbols. This signature includes constructors for the background elements.[3] We identify a state with a conjunction of equalities of the form $x = t$, where x is a state variable and t a value term.

The interpretation of a value term is the same in all states. Value terms are not unique representations of the corresponding values, i.e., value terms that are syntactically distinct may have the same interpretation. We say value for a value term when it is clear from the context that the particular term representation is irrelevant.

For example, a set of integers, containing the values 1, 2, and 3 is represented by the term Set<int>(1,2,3). The term Set<int>(2,1,3) has the same interpretation. We use a relaxed notation where the arity of function symbols is omitted but is implicitly part of the symbol. For example Set<int>(1,2) represents a set containing 1 and 2, so the constructor Set<int> is binary here and ternary in the previous case. Function symbols are typed. For example, a set containing two sets of strings Set<string>("a") and Set<string>("b") is represented by the term

Set<Set<string>>(Set<string>("a"),Set<string>("b"))

Model programs typically also have user-defined types that are part of the background. For example the model program in Figure 1 has the user-defined type Color. This type has two elements Color.RED and Color.BLUE, respectively. The initial state of this model program is (represented by the equality)

---

[2] In ASM theory, state variables are called *dynamic functions* and may have arbitrary arities. Dynamic functions with positive arities can be encoded as state variables whose values are maps.

[3] In ASM theory, these function symbols are called *static*, their interpretation is the same in all states.

```
colorAssignments = Map<Side,Color>.EmptyMap.⁴
```

A user-defined type may be annotated as being *abstract*, e.g., Color in Figure 1 is abstract. Elements of an abstract type are treated as typed *reserve* elements in the sense of [11]. Intuitively this means that they are interchangeable elements so that a particular choice must not affect the behavior of the model program. A valid model program must not explicitly reference any elements of an abstract type. For example, even though the Color enumeration type provides an operation to return the string name of a color value, the model program must not use that operation if color is to be considered abstract. Abstract types are similar to objects[5] that are treated the same way.

An *update rule* is a collection of (possibly conditional) assignments to state variables. An update rule p that has formal input parameters $\bar{x}$ is denoted by $p[\bar{x}]$. The instantiation of $p[\bar{x}]$ with concrete input values $\bar{v}$ of appropriate type, is denoted by $p[\bar{v}]$. An update rule p denotes a function $[\![p]\!] : State \times Value^n \rightarrow State$. Update rules in model programs are called *actions*.

A *guard* φ is a state dependent Boolean formula that may contain free logic variables $\bar{x} = x_1, \ldots, x_n$, denoted by $\varphi[\bar{x}]$; φ is *closed* if it contains no free variables. Given values $\bar{v} = v_1 \ldots, v_n$ we write $\varphi[\bar{v}]$ for the replacement of x_i in φ by v_i for $1 \leq i \leq n$. A closed formula φ has the standard truth interpretation $s \models \varphi$ in a state s. A *guarded update rule* is a pair (φ, p) containing a guard $\varphi[\bar{x}]$ and an update rule $p[\bar{x}]$; intuitively (φ, p) limits the execution of p to those states and arguments $\bar{v}$ where $\varphi[\bar{v}]$ holds. The guard restricts firing the update rule based on but the update rule itself may contain conditionals to update the state appropriately.

We use a simplified definition a model program here, by omitting control modes. The state isomorphism problem is independent of the presence of explicit control modes. Thus, this simplification does not affect the main topic of this paper.

Definition 1. A *model program* P has the following components:

- A finite vocabulary $X_<$ of *state variables*
- A finite vocabulary Σ of *action symbols*
- An *initial state* s_0 given by a conjunction $\bigwedge_{x \in X} x = t_x$ where t_x is a value term.
- A *reset* action symbol $Reset \in \Sigma$.
- A family $(\varphi_f, p_f)_{f \in \Sigma}$ of guarded update rules.
  - The *arity* of f is the number of input parameters of p_f.
  - The arity of *Reset* is 0 and $[\![p_{Reset}]\!](s) = s_0$ for all $s \models \varphi_{Reset}$.

An *action* has the form $f(v_1, \ldots, v_n)$ where f is an n-ary action symbol and each v_i is a value term that matches the required type of the corresponding input parameter of p_f. We say that an action $f(\bar{v})$ is *enabled* in a state s if $s \models \varphi_f[\bar{v}]$. An action $f(\bar{v})$ that is enabled in a state s can be *executed* or *invoked* in s and yields the state $[\![p_f]\!](s, \bar{v})$.

The model program in Figure 1 has a single action symbol AssignColor. The guard of AssignColor is given by the Boolean function AssignColorEnabled which is

---

[4] The namespace Triangle.Contract is implicit here.

[5] By "objects" we mean object IDs. Instance fields associated with objects are considered to be state variables in their own right and not part of any nested structure. In this way, we can consider only global variables without loss of generality.

associated with `AssignColor` by naming. The action a =`AssignColor(Side.S1, Color.RED)` is enabled in the initial state s_0 as `AssignColorEnabled(Side.S1)` returns true in s_0. The execution of a in s_0 yields the state

$$\text{colorAssignments = Map<Side,Color>(Side.S1} \mapsto \text{Color.RED)}.$$

The unwinding of a model program from its initial state gives rise to a labeled transition system (LTS). The LTS has the states generated by the unwinding of the model program as its states and the actions as its labels.

Definition 2. A *rooted directed labeled graph*, G, is a graph that has a fixed root, has directed edges, and contains labels of vertices and edges. Such graph can be formally represented as a triple $G = (v_r, V, E)$ where $v_r \in V$ is the root vertex, V is a set of vertices v that are pairs $v = (id, l_v)$, where id is an identifier uniquely determining a vertex in a graph and l_v is the label of the vertex. E is the set of triples $(v_1.id, l_e, v_2.id)$ where v_1 is the start vertex, v_2 is the end vertex and l_e is the edge label.

3   States as Graphs

In this section we present a graph representation of the state of a model program.

The states of a model program can contain object instances and other complex data structures, thus we do not deal only with primitive types, such as integers and Boolean values, but also with instances of objects that can be dynamically instantiated and refer to other instances of objects. The state space of a model program may be infinite, but concrete states are finite first order structures. We look at the configuration of values and object instances that have been assigned to the fields of objects and data structures contained in the program.

A state is defined by an assignment of term representations of values to fields, $s = \bigwedge_{x \in X_<} x = t_x$. There are two kinds of fields in a model program: global fields, like `colorAssignments` in the program on Figure 1 and fields of dynamically instantiated objects. For the sake of brevity, we will look only at states containing global fields. Assignments to global fields are simple equations $x = t$. It is important to note that it is possible to establish a binary relation of total ordering, $<$, of field names. This can be achieved by, for example, ordering the field names alphabetically.

Figure 3 outlines the procedure of creating a graph from a state. In general the procedure is straightforward: the function `CreateGraph` creates the graph by analyzing the terms corresponding to each state variable x. The analysis of a term, `TermToGraph`, adds a field index to value mapping to the label of the parent node, if t denotes a value, and adds a new node to the graph, if t is an object. A specialized procedure is used for creating nodes corresponding to built-in abstract data types. In fact, each ADT is handled in a slightly different way.

A `Set` becomes a node that has the count of its elements in the label of the incoming edge. All outgoing edges of a set are given a label with a function symbol 0, denoting membership in a set. It is possible that the label is extended with more arguments as the set may contain other sets.

The representation of a bag (or multiset) has a sorted list of element multiplicities on the incoming label. The label of the edge pointing to each element of a `Bag` is labeled

```
class State {
  Sequence<Pair> X;
}

class G {
  Vertex v_r = new Vertex();
  Set<Vertex> vertices = Set<Vertex>.EmptySet.Add(v_r);
  Set<Edge> eds = Set<Edge>.EmptySet ;
}

G CreateGraph(State s) {
  g=new G();
  foreach (x in s.X) g = TermToGraph(t,g.v_r, g.SequenceNumber(x), g);
  return g;
}

G TermToGraph(Term t, Vertex parent, int fieldIdx, G g) {
  if (!isObject(t))
    parent.label.Add(new Lbl(fieldIdx,t));
  switch(t.functionSymbol) {
    case Set :
      Vertex setv=g.NewVertex();
      g.eds=g.eds.Add(new Edge(parent,new Lbl(fieldIdx,t.argCount),setv));
      forall (Term elem in t.arguments)
        TermToGraph(elem,setv,0,g);
      break;
    case Bag:
      Vertex bagv=g.NewVertex();
      Bag<Pair> bagCounts = Bag<Pair>.EmptyBag;
      forall (Pair<Term,Term> (elem,count) in t.GetArgumentsByPair()) {
        TermToGraph(elem,setv,count,g);
        bagCounts.Add(count);
      }
      g.eds=g.eds.Add(new Edge(parent,new Lbl(fieldIdx,bagCounts.Sort()),setv));
      break;
    case Map:
      forall (Pair<Term,Term> (key,val) in t.GetArgumentsByPair()) {
        Vertex maplet=g.NewVertex();
        TermToGraph(key,maplet,0,g);
        TermToGraph(val,maplet,1,g);
        g.eds=g.eds.Add(new Edge(parent,new Lbl(fieldIdx,t.PairCount()),maplet));
      }
      break;
    default:
      if (isObject(t)) {
        Vertex newVertex=new Vertex();
        g.eds=g.eds.Add(new Edge(parent, new Lbl(fieldIdx),newVertex));
        if (arity(t)>0)
          forall (Term arg in t.arguments)
            TermToGraph(arg,newVertex,sequenceNumber(arg),g);
      }
  }
  return g;
}
```

Fig. 3. Code for generating a rooted labeled directed graph from a state of a model program

by the corresponding multiplicity. In fact, a Bag is a set of pairs, and using a specialized representation is an optimization that helps to reduce the number of nodes in the state graph. A Map is also a Set of pairs but can be converted to a reduced fragment of the graph.

The labelings of outgoing edges may be unique, as in the case of different field indices of a structure, or unordered, as in the case of a set.

Thus, it is possible to classify the outgoing edges of a node into *ordered* and *un-ordered* edges. The graph representations of the abstract data structures Set, Bag, and Map are summarized in Figure 4.

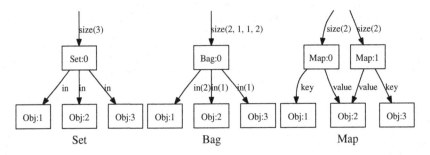

Fig. 4. Graph representations of abstract data types used by model programs. The corresponding term representations are Set(Obj.O1,Obj.O2,Obj.O3), Bag(Obj.O1,2, Obj.O2,1,Obj.O3,1) and Map(Obj.O1,Obj.O2,Obj.O3,Obj.O2).

There are some graphs representing the states of the triangle example in Figure 5. The state graphs have been generated using the procedure outlined in Figure 3.

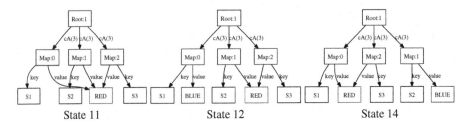

Fig. 5. State graphs of states 11, 12, and 14 of the triangle example on Fig. 2 and Fig. 6. State 14 is isomorphic to state 12 but neither 12 nor 14 is isomorphic to 11. The abbreviation cA stands for colorAssignments and (3) denotes that there are 3 key-value pairs in the map.

State graphs of states of the triangle example denoted by numbers 11, 12, and 14 on Figure 2 and Figure 6 are given in Figure 5. State 14 is isomorphic to state 12 but neither 12 nor 14 is isomorphic to 11. The abbreviation cA stands for colorAssignments and (3) denotes that there are 3 key-value pairs in the map.

Figure 6 illustrates the effects of isomorphism-based symmetry reduction applied to the triangle example studied previously. The state graph on the left shows at which stages of the search isomorphic states were encountered. The dashed arrows point to states that are isomorphic to the state the arrow starts from. The graph on the right is obtained by showing a representative example of a family of isomorphic states.

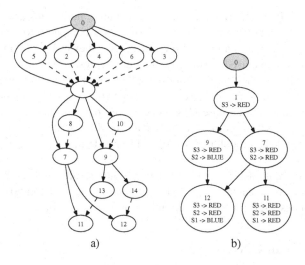

Fig. 6. State space of the Triangle example from Fig. 1, where exploration of isomorphic states has been pruned. The dashed lines on *(a)* exhibit encounters of isomorphic states during exploration. *(b)* exhibits the structure of the state graph when isomorphic states are collapsed.

```
namespace Triangle
{
    [Abstract]
    enum Color { RED, BLUE }

    class Side : LabeledInstance<Side> { public Color color; }

    static class Contract
    {
        static Set<Side> sides = Set<Side>.EmptySet;

        [Action]
        static void AssignColor([New] Side s, Color c)
        {
            s.color = c;
            sides = sides.Add(s);
        }

        static void AssignColorEnabled(Side s)
        { return sides.Count < 3; }
    }
}
```

Fig. 7. A version of the triangle model where sides are objects. The `AssignColor` action is enabled if not all sides have been colored. The `New` keyword indicates that the side is a new object (reserve element).

Field Maps

As mentioned earlier, *objects* are just abstract ids or reserve elements. So how do we deal with *fields* of objects? Fields of objects are represented by state variables, called *field maps*, whose values are finite maps from objects of the given type to values of the given field type.[6] From the point of view of this paper, field maps are handled in the same way as map-valued state variables. A difference compared to map-valued state variables is that field maps can not be referenced as values inside of a model program, which can sometimes be used to simplify the graph representation of a state.

In order to illustrate field maps, consider a version of the triangle example, shown in Figure 7, where sides are instances of a class *Side*. The fact that sides are reserve elements is indicated by the base class. This model program has two state variables, sides and color, where color is a field map. In the initial state, both color and sides are empty. When a color c is assigned to a side s, the color map gets a new entry s ↦ c.

The presented approach is also extended to states resulting in the composition of model programs, as presented in [25]. The root of a state of a composition of model programs becomes a set of two rooted graphs that may share objects.

4   Isomorphism Checking

Unlike arbitrary graphs, state graphs are rooted and encode state information in a way that partially reflects the underlying static structure of a program. For example, all objects of a given type have a fixed set of fields that are ordered alphabetically. Several built-in ordered data types, such as sequences and pairs, also have an order of the elements contained in them according to their position. Moreover, user-defined types, other than abstract types, have a fixed alphabetical order of fields. A typical model program uses both ordered and unordered data structures. As explained above, the resulting state graph includes both ordered and unordered edges.

Our intent was to devise an algorithm for graph isomorphism that takes advantage of the ordered edges as much as possible while handling the unordered cases as a last resort through backtracking. The starting point is that all vertices of the graph have been given strong labels through object ID-independent hashing[7] that already reduces the possible pairings of vertices dramatically. In the case when all edges are ordered the algorithm should not do any backtracking at all. The basic idea of the algorithm is an extension of the linearization algorithm used in Symstra [27] with *backtracking*. The algorithm reduces to linearization when the graphs that are being compared are fully ordered, i.e. have no unordered edges. A small difference compared to Symstra is that the linearizations are computed and compared simultaneously for the two graphs as depth first walks, rather than independently and then compared.

Linearization with Backtracking

The following is an abstract description of the algorithm. Given are two state graphs G_1 and G_2. The algorithm either fails to produce an isomorphism or returns an isomorphism from G_1 to G_2. The abstract description of the algorithm is non-deterministic. In the concrete realization of the algorithm the **choose** operation is implemented through

---

[6] The name of a field map is uniquely determined from the fully qualified name of the class and the name of the field.

[7] The hashing part of the algorithm is outside the scope of this paper.

backtracking to the previous backtrack point where more choices were possible. The details of the particular backtracking mechanism are omitted here.

We say that an edge with label l is an l-edge. The edge labels that originate from ordered background data structures are called *functional*. It is known that for all functional edge labels l and for all nodes x, there can be at most one outgoing l-edge from x. Other edge labels are called *relational*.

Bucketing: Compute a "bucket map" B_i for all nodes in G_i, for $i = 1, 2$. Each node n in G_i with label l is placed in the bucket $B_i(l)$. If either B_1 and B_2 do not have the same labels and the sames sizes of corresponding buckets for all labels then **fail**. Otherwise execute **Extend**$(\emptyset, r_1, r_2)$, where r_i is the root of G_i, for $i = 1, 2$.

Extend(ρ, x_1, x_2)**:** Given is a partial isomorphism ρ and isomorphism candidates x_1 and x_2. If x_1 and x_2 have distinct labels then **fail**, else if x_1 is already mapped to x_2 in ρ the return ρ, else if either x_1 is in the domain of ρ or x_2 is in the range of ρ then **fail**, else let $\rho_0 = \rho \cup \{x_1 \mapsto x_2\}$ and proceed as follows.

Let $l_1, \ldots, l_k$ be the outgoing edge labels from x_1 ordered according to a fixed label-order.[8] For $j = 1, \ldots, k$,

  – For $i = 1, 2$, **choose** l_j-edges (x_i, y_i) in G_i for some y_i.
  If **Extend**(ρ_{j-1}, y_1, y_2) fails then **fail**, else let $\rho_j = $ **Extend**(ρ_{j-1}, y_1, y_2).
  Return ρ_k.

Notice that the algorithm is deterministic and reduces to linearization when all choices are made from singleton sets. A sufficient (but not necessary) condition for this to be true is when all edge labels are functional. A heuristic we are using in the implementation of this algorithm is that all *functional* edge labels appear before all *relational* edge labels in the label-order that is used in the algorithm.

The implementation of the algorithm has also some optimizations when backtrack points can be skipped, that have been omitted in the above abstract description. One particular optimization is the following. When there are multiple l-edges outgoing from a node x for some fixed relational edge label l, but all of the target nodes of those edges have the same label and degree 1, then an arbitrary *but fixed* order of the edges can be chosen that uses the order of the node labels and choice points can be cut. The algorithm bears certain similarities to the practical graph isomorphism algorithm in [16], by using a partitioning scheme of nodes that eliminates a lot of the backtracking. The algorithm has been implemented in NModel.

5   Related Work

Two program states, in the presence of pointers or objects, can be considered equivalent if the structure of the logical links between data objects is equivalent while the concrete physical addresses the pointers point to differ, i.e. when the actual arrangement of objects in memory is different due to the effects of memory allocation and garbage collection. This is known as one form of symmetry reduction and has been used in software model checking. The principles of such symmetry reductions have been outlined

---

[8] At this point we know that x_2 must have the same outgoing edge labels in G_2 as x_1 has in G_1 or else x_2 would have a different label than x_1.

by Iosif in [12]. One of the key ideas in [12] is to canonicalize the representation of program heap by ordering the heap graph during a depth first walk. The order of outgoing edges (pointers) from a node (for example an object) is given by a deterministic ordering by edge labels (field name and order number, for example position in the array, in the parent data structure). Lack of such ordering would render state comparison to an instance of the graph isomorphism problem, which requires exponential time in the number of nodes in the general case [17]. In [19] Musuvathi and Dill elaborate on Iosif's algorithm to allow incremental heap canonicalization, i.e. take into account that state changes are often small and modify only a small part of the heap, thus it should not be necessary to traverse the whole heap after each state change.

In addition to dSpin [6] where the above mentioned principles were initially implemented, there are several analysis tools specifically targeted for object-oriented software that utilize the approach, for example, *XRT* [10] and *Bogor* [20].

XRT is a software checker for common intermediate language, CIL. It processes .Net managed assemblies and provides means for analyzing the processed programs.

Bogor is a customizable software model checking engine that supports constructs that are characteristic to object-oriented software. Although there is support for using abstract data types, like sets, the underlying state enumeration and comparison engine performs heap canonicalization based on an ordering of object IDs based on the previously mentioned work by Iosif [12].

Korat [3] is a tool for automated test generation based on Java specifications. It also uses the concept of heap isomorphism to generate heaps that are non-isomorphic.

We have layered ASM semantics on top of the underlying programming environment and thus the concrete memory locations have been abstracted by interpreting the program state in the ASM semantics. But in addition to using the concrete data structures, we can declare some types to represent instances of abstract objects and there are some data structures, such as the Set, Map and Bag, that are designed to accommodate such objects, among others.

Symstra [27] uses a technique that linearizes heaps into integer sequences to reduce checking heap isomorphism to just comparing the integer sequence equality. It starts from the root and traverses the heap depth first. It assigns a unique identifier to each object, keeps this mapping in memory and reuses it for objects that appear in cycles. It extends the previously mentioned approaches [12,19] in that it also assigns a unique identifier to each symbolic variable, keeps this mapping in memory and reuses it for variables that appear several times in the heap.

In [5] a glass box approach of analyzing data structures is presented. The reductions described therein involve isomorphism-based reductions, but encoding the task requires manual attribution of the data structures to be analyzed. The approach does not present a general way how to handle object-oriented programs containing abstract data types.

Spec Explorer [24,21] is a tool for the analysis of model programs written in AsmL and Spec#. It is possible in some cases to specify symmetry reductions in Spec Explorer using state groupings but the tool does not have a built-in isomorphic state checking mechanisms.

Graph isomorphism is a topic that has received scientific attention for decades. Ullmann's (sub)graph isomorphism algorithm [22] is a well known backtracking algorithm which combines a forward looking technique. As the algorithm is relatively straightforward to implement, we used it as an oracle for testing purposes.

The algorithm described in Section 4 builds on another well known approach also known as the *Nauty* algorithm, which uses node labelings and partitioning based on such labelings [16].

It is known that there exist certain classes of graphs for which there is a polynomial time algorithm for deciding graph isomorphism. In [15] a method for deciding isomorphism of graphs with bounded valence in polynomial time is presented. The reason why such algorithms are not directly usable in practice is that the polynomial complexity result contains large constants [8].

There are model checkers, such as for example *Murφ* [7] and *Symmetric Spin* [2], that allow modeling using scalar sets [13]. These sets are similar to the sets described in the current paper but they do not have support for abstract object IDs. A survey of symmetry reductions in temporal logic model checking is given in [18].

6   Conclusion

In this paper we showed how state isomorphism for states with both unordered structures and objects may be understood in the context of model programs. We reviewed how the concept of background structures and reserve elements can formalize the meaning of isomorphism for program states. We then described how to represent state as a rooted directed labeled graph so that existing isomorphism algorithms could be applied. Finally, we showed an isomorphism-checking algorithm that takes advantage of the information contained in states with elements drawn from a rich background universe.

The techniques in this paper can be applied in a variety of industrially relevant modeling and testing contexts and are motivated by practical concerns that arose from the industrial use of the Spec Explorer tool in Microsoft.

While this current paper gives a solid notion how program states of object-oriented programs can be viewed as graphs, it also leads to a number of interesting open problems. For example, how can one speed up isomorphism checking for the particular graphs of program states? Would it be useful to describe graph isomorphism as a SAT problem? How could this be accomplished?

As future work, we plan on showing how hashing techniques can be used to improve the performance of isomorphism checks for larger numbers of states.

Acknowledgements

We thank Wolfram Schulte for referring us to the Symstra work and Jonathan Jacky for insightful discussions related to the topics of this paper. Additionally we thank the anonymous referees, in particular one of them, for very detailed, insightful, and helpful comments. Juhan Ernits thanks the Estonian Information Technology Foundation and the Estonian Doctoral School in Information and Communication Technology for general support to his PhD studies.

References

1. Blass, A., Gurevich, Y.: Background, reserve, and gandy machines. In: Proceedings of the 14th Annual Conference of the EACSL on Computer Science Logic, London, UK, pp. 1–17. Springer-Verlag, Heidelberg (2000)
2. Bosnacki, D., Dams, D., Holenderski, L.: Symmetric spin. In: Havelund, K., Penix, J., Visser, W. (eds.) SPIN Model Checking and Software Verification. LNCS, vol. 1885, pp. 1–19. Springer, Heidelberg (2000)
3. Boyapati, C., Khurshid, S., Marinov, D.: Korat: automated testing based on java predicates. SIGSOFT Softw. Eng. Notes 27(4), 123–133 (2002)
4. Campbell, C., Veanes, M.: State exploration with multiple state groupings. In: D. Beauquier, E. Börger, and A. Slissenko, editors, 12th International Workshop on Abstract State Machines, ASM'05, pp. 119–130. Laboratory of Algorithms, Complexity and Logic, Créteil, France (March 2005)
5. Darga, P.T., Boyapati, C.: Efficient software model checking of data structure properties. In: OOPSLA '06: Proceedings of the 21st annual ACM SIGPLAN conference on Object-oriented programming systems, languages, and applications, pp. 363–382. ACM Press, New York, NY, USA (2006)
6. Demartini, C., Iosif, R., Sisto, R.: dSPIN: A dynamic extension of SPIN. In: Dams, D.R., Gerth, R., Leue, S., Massink, M. (eds.) Theoretical and Practical Aspects of SPIN Model Checking. LNCS, vol. 1680, pp. 261–276. Springer, Heidelberg (1999)
7. Dill, D.L.: The Murphi verification system. In: Alur, R., Henzinger, T.A. (eds.) CAV 1996. LNCS, vol. 1102, pp. 390–393. Springer, Heidelberg (1996)
8. Fortin, S.: The graph isomorphism problem (1996)
9. Grieskamp, W., Gurevich, Y., Schulte, W., Veanes, M.: Generating finite state machines from abstract state machines. In: ISSTA'02. Software Engineering Notes, vol. 27, pp. 112–122. ACM Press, New York (2002)
10. Grieskamp, W., Tillmann, N., Schulte, W.: XRT — exploring runtime for.Net architecture and applications. Electr. Notes Theor. Comput. Sci. 144(3), 3–26 (2006)
11. Gurevich, Y.: Specification and Validation Methods. In: Evolving Algebras 1993: Lipari Guide (chapter), pp. 9–36. Oxford University Press, Oxford (1995)
12. Iosif, R.: Symmetry reductions for model checking of concurrent dynamic software. STTT 6(4), 302–319 (2004)
13. Ip, C.N., Dil, D.L.: Better verification through symmetry. Form. Methods Syst. Des. 9(1-2), 41–75 (1996)
14. Jacky, J., Veanes, M., Campbell, C., Schulte, W.: Model-based Software Testing and Analysis with C#. Cambridge University Press (Forthcoming 2007)
15. Luks, E.M.: Isomorphism of graphs of bounded valence can be tested in polynomial time. J. Comput. Syst. Sci. 25(1), 42–65 (1982)
16. McKay, B.D.: Practical graph isomorphism. Congressus Numerantium 30, 45–87 (1981)
17. Messmer, B.T.: Efficient graph matching algorithms (1995)
18. Miller, A., Donaldson, A., Calder, M.: Symmetry in temporal logic model checking. ACM Comput. Surv. 38(3), 8 (2006)
19. Musuvathi, M., Dill, D.L.: An incremental heap canonicalization algorithm. In: Godefroid, P. (ed.) Model Checking Software. LNCS, vol. 3639, Springer, Heidelberg (2005)
20. Robby, M., Dwyer, B., Hatcliff, J.: Domain-specific model checking using the bogor framework. In: ASE '06: Proceedings of the 21st IEEE International Conference on Automated Software Engineering (ASE'06), pp. 369–370. IEEE Computer Society, Washington, DC, USA (2006)
21. SpecExplorer (2006) http://research.microsoft.com/SpecExplorer

22. Ullmann, J.R.: An algorithm for subgraph isomorphism. J. ACM 23(1), 31–42 (1976)
23. Utting, M., Legeard, B.: Practical Model-Based Testing - A tools approach. Elsevier Science (2006)
24. Veanes, M., Campbell, C., Grieskamp, W., Nachmanson, L., Schulte, W., Tillmann, N.: Model-based testing of object-oriented reactive systems with Spec Explorer, Tech. Rep. MSR-TR-2005-59, Microsoft Research. Preliminary version of a book chapter in the forthcoming text book Formal Methods and Testing (2005)
25. Veanes, M., Campbell, C., Schulte, W.: Composition of model programs. In the current proceedings (2007)
26. Veanes, M., Campbell, C., Schulte, W., Tillmann, N.: Online testing with model programs. In: ESEC/FSE-13: Proceedings of the 10th European software engineering conference held jointly with 13th ACM SIGSOFT international symposium on Foundations of software engineering, pp. 273–282. ACM Press, New York, NY, USA (2005)
27. Xie, T., Marinov, D., Schulte, W., Notkin, D.: Symstra: A framework for generating object-oriented unit tests using symbolic execution. In: Halbwachs, N., Zuck, L.D. (eds.) TACAS 2005. LNCS, vol. 3440, pp. 365–381. Springer, Heidelberg (2005)

Composition of Model Programs

Margus Veanes[1], Colin Campbell[2,*], and Wolfram Schulte[1]

[1] Microsoft Research, Redmond, WA
{margus,schulte}@microsoft.com
[2] Modeled Computation LLC, Seattle, WA
colin@modeled-computation.com

Abstract. Model programs are a useful formalism for software testing and design analysis. They are used in industrial tools, such as SpecExplorer, as a compact, expressive and precise way to specify complex behavior. One of the challenges with model programs has been the difficulty to separate contract modeling from scenario modeling. It has not been clear how to separate those concerns in a clean way. In this paper we introduce composition of model programs, motivate why it is useful to be able to compose model programs, and what composition of model programs formally means.

1 Introduction

Model programs are a useful formalism for software testing and design analysis. They are used in industrial tools like SpecExplorer [1] as a compact, expressive and precise way to specify complex behavior. Model programs are unwound into transition systems that can be used in model-based testing, for runtime conformance checking of a system under test, and for design validation [4,15,16,17].

In practice we have observed two distinct uses of model programs. The first use is as a *software contract* that encodes the expected behavior of the system under test. Here, the model program acts as an oracle that predicts system behavior in each possible context. The unwinding of such a contract model is typically infinite, since for many systems, such as those that allocate new objects at runtime, there are infinitely many possible states.

The second use is to define the *scenarios* to be tested or analyzed. Here, the purpose of the model program is to produce (when unwound) states and transitions of interest for a particular test or type of analysis. For example, one might want to direct a test to consider only certain interleavings of actions instead of all possible interleavings. Another example would be a model that specifies a finite set of input data to be used as system inputs.

Current practice tends to combine these two roles within a single model program, even though it is recognized that cleanly separating these concerns would be much better engineering practice. In addition, we have observed that as contract models grow, it would be helpful if they could be divided into submodels of manageable size. Up to now we have lacked the formal machinery to accomplish this.

---

* The work in this paper was done at Microsoft Research.

J. Derrick and J. Vain (Eds.): FORTE 2007, LNCS 4574, pp. 128–142, 2007.
© IFIP International Federation for Information Processing 2007

At issue is the separation of design aspects into distinct but related model programs. If model programs are related exclusively by common action labels, then the desired system behavior is the intersection of possible traces for each aspect. In classical automata theory, the technique of achieving intersection of traces is product composition. We extend this technique here to define *parallel composition* of model programs.

Not all composition is parallel; sometimes it is useful to think in terms of phases of system operation. A typical example occurs when there is an initialization phase, followed by an operational phase with many possible behaviors, followed by a shutdown phase. We define the *serial composition* of model programs, which is analogous to serial composition of finite automata for language concatenation.

The main contribution of the paper is the formalization of the parallel composition of model programs in a way that builds on the classical theory of LTSs [12]. Our goal is therefore *not* to define yet another notion of composition but to show how the composition of model programs can be defined in a way that preserves the underlying LTS semantics.

It is important to note here that the composition of model programs is *syntactic*. It is effectively a program transformation that is most interesting when it is formally grounded in an existing semantics and has useful algebraic properties. This fills an important semantic gap and makes compositional modeling more practical in tools like Spec Explorer.

Achieving this goal required us to "rethink" the way actions are treated. Spec Explorer uses a mixture of a Mealy view and an LTS view that causes a complication in the definition of conformance. In this paper we adopt a consistent LTS-based view of action traces. This enables a direct application of the formal LTS based teory of testing using ioco [3] when the direction (input or output) of actions is specified. A key aspect of the composition of model programs is that actions are represented by terms that may include variables and values, and the notion of an action vocabulary is defined using only the function symbol part of the action. When actions are synchonized, values are shared through *unification* and may transfer data from one model program to another.

Model program composition is the cornerstone of the *NModel* framework that provides a modeling library for model programs written in C#. NModel is in the process of becoming an open source project and is the software support for the forthcoming textbook [11] that discusses the use of model programs as a practical modeling technique. While this paper provides the foundations of model program composition, the textbook shows practical techniques and applications, with an emphasis on composition as a method of layering system behavior into independent features.

The techniques for parallel and serial composition of model programs, as we will see below, have characteristics that make them appealing for use in the domain of software testing and design validation. We begin with an example. Then in sections 3 and 4 we give a formalization.

1.1   Example

Consider three model programs M_1, M_2 and M_3 that specify, respectively, a GUI-based application, a dialog box used in that application and a test scenario. The state spaces of the model programs are disjoint but their action signatures have nonempty intersections.

In the presentation that follows we unwind control state but not data state to produce control graphs in the spirit of Extended Finite State Machines (EFSMs) [13]. Figures 1-3 show M_1, M_2 and M_3 using this view.

The model program of the GUI-based application is shown in Figure 1. It has three control states, p_1, p_2 and p_3. Control state p_1 is both the initial state (indicated by the incoming arrow) and an accepting state (indicated by the double circle). The arcs between control states are labeled by guarded update rules called actions. These actions contain enabling conditions (prefixed by requires) and updates in curly braces. The actions include parameters which are substituted by ground values during unwinding.

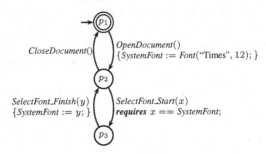

Fig. 1. Application model M_1

The data state of M_1 contains one state variable, *SystemFont*.

Runs of a model program begin in the initial control state and end in an accepting control state. Every step of the run must satisfy the enabling condition of the action that produced it.

Note that this model program uses an *LTS view* instead of a *Mealy view* for the action that sets the system font. In an LTS view, inputs and outputs appear as separate transitions, possibly breaking a single logical action into two parts. *SelectFont_Start* takes an input, namely the current system font given by the data state variable *SystemFont*. The parameter of *SelectFont_Finish* denotes the output. Since the *SelectFont_Finish* action has no enabling condition, any font value could be selected.

Model program M_2 that describes a font-choosing dialog box is shown in Figure 2.

The action signature of M_2 consists of *SelectFont_Start*, *SelectFont_Finish*, *OK*, *Cancel*, *SetFontName* and *SetFontSize*. Notice that this vocabulary has two actions in common with M_1, the application model, as well as four actions that are not shared.

Once started, the dialog box allows the user to set the font size and the font name in any order and as many times as desired. Depending on whether the user presses *OK* or *Cancel* either the newly selected font or the prior font is included in the exit label.

Model program M_3 gives a scenario of interest for testing. It is shown as Figure 3.

The scenario model shows two use cases for the font dialog. There are only two possible traces for this machine.

As is typical with scenario models, M_3 contains no updates to data state. We also use *SetFontSize*(10) as a shorthand for *SetFontSize*(x) **requires** $x == 10$. We use the underscore symbol ("_") to indicate an unconstrained parameter that is not used in any precondition or update.

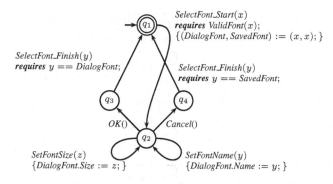

Fig. 2. Font chooser dialog model M_2

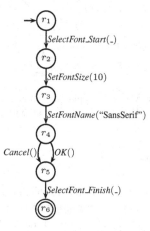

Fig. 3. Scenario model M_3 showing two ways to use the font dialog

Figure 4 shows the parallel composition of M_1, M_2 and M_3. The diagram omits the state update rules for brevity.

Under parallel composition, model programs will synchronize steps for shared actions and interleave actions not found in their common signature. The control states of the composed model program are a subset of the cross product of the control states of the component models.

The enabling conditions of the transitions are the conjunction of the enabling conditions of the component models. The data updates are the union of the data updates of the component programs. There can be no conflicting updates because the data signatures must be disjoint.

An accepting state under parallel composition occurs when all of component control states are accepting states. This accounts for the fact that the font may only be selected exactly one time in the composed model program– the scenario model M_3 does not loop, and its initial state is not an accepting state.

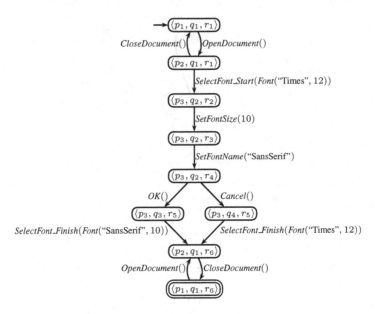

Fig. 4. Parallel composition M_4 of the application model M_1, the font chooser dialog model M_2, and the scenario model M_3. Update rules associated with labels are not shown.

2   Basic Definitions

Let Σ be a fixed signature of function symbols. Some function symbols in Σ, denoted by Σ^{dynamic}, may change their interpretation and are called *state variables*. The remaining set of symbols, denoted by Σ^{static}, have a fixed interpretation with respect to a given *background theory* $\mathcal{B}$. $\mathcal{B}$ is identified with its models that are called *states*. It is assumed that all states share the same universe $\mathcal{V}$ of values. Without loss of generality one may identify a state with a particular interpretation (value assignment) to all the state variables. Note that *logic variables* are distinct from state variables. Logic variables are needed below to be able to construct nonground action terms.

Example 1. Consider the application model M_1 in Figure 1. *SystemFont* is a nullary state variable here. $\mathcal{V}$ is fixed and includes at least strings, integers, and fonts. A font can be constructed using the static binary function *Font*. M_1 has a single nullary state variable *SystemFont*.

Terms are defined inductively over Σ and a set of logic variables disjoint from Σ. An *equation* is an atomic formula $t_1 == t_2$ where t_1 and t_2 are terms and '$==$' is the formal equality symbol. Formulas are built up inductively from atomic formulas using logical connectives and quantifiers.[1] A term or a formula e may contain free logic variables $FV(e)$; e is *ground* or *closed* if $FV(e)$ is empty. A *substitution* is a finite (possibly

---

[1] In general we may also have relation symbols, or Boolean functions, in Σ and form atomic formulas other than equations.

empty) map from logic variables to terms. Given a substitution θ and an expression e, $e\theta$ denotes the replacement of x in e by $\theta(x)$ for each x in $FV(e)$. We say that θ is *grounding for* e if $e\theta$ is ground. Given a closed formula φ and a state S, $S \models \varphi$ is used to denote that S *satisfies* φ, or φ *holds* or *is true* in S.[2] A closed formula is *consistent* if it is true in some state. We write t^S for the interpretation of a ground term t in S. When an n-ary function symbol f is *self-interpreting* or a *free constructor* it means that $f(t_1, \ldots, t_n)^S = g(u_1, \ldots, u_m)^S$ if and only if f and g are the same function symbol (and thus $n = m$) and $t_i^S = u_i^S$ for all i.

Example 2. Consider the signature of M_1 again and let $t = Font(x, y)$; t is a term with $FV(t) = \{x, y\}$. The substitution $\theta = \{x \mapsto \text{"Times"}, y \mapsto 10\}$ is grounding for t and $t\theta$ is the ground term $Font(\text{"Times"}, 10)$ denoting the corresponding font, where *Font* is a free constructor. Let S be a state where the value of *SystemFont* is the Times font of size 12. Then $S \models \neg SystemFont == Font(\text{"Times"}, 10)$ because *Font* is self-interpreting and $10 \neq 12$.

A *location* is a pair $\langle f, (v_1, \ldots, v_n) \rangle$ where f is an n-ary function symbol in Σ^{dynamic} and $(v_1, \ldots, v_n)$ is a sequence of values. An *update* is an ordered pair denoted by $l \mapsto v$, where l is a location and v a value. A set U of updates is *consistent* if there are no two distinct updates $l \mapsto v_1$ and $l \mapsto v_2$ in U. Given a state S and a consistent set U of updates, $S \uplus U$ is the state where, for all $f \in \Sigma^{\text{dynamic}}$ of arity $n \geq 0$ and values $v_1, \ldots, v_n$,

$$ f^{S \uplus U}(v_1, \ldots, v_n) = \begin{cases} w, & \text{if } \langle f, (v_1, \ldots, v_n) \rangle \mapsto w \in U; \\ f^S(v_1, \ldots, v_n), & \text{otherwise.} \end{cases} $$

In other words, $S \uplus U$ is the state after applying the updates U to S.

For the purposes of this paper it is enough to assume that all state variables are nullary, in which case the notions of locations and state variables can be unified.

A *program* P over Σ when applied to (or executed in) a state S, produces a set of updates. Often P also depends on formal parameters $FV(P) = x_1, \ldots, x_n$ for some $n \geq 0$. Thus, P denotes a function $[\![P]\!] : State \times \mathcal{V}^n \to UpdateSet$. It is convenient to extend the notion of expressions to include programs so that we can talk about free variables in programs and apply substitutions to them. Given a grounding substitution θ for P and a data state S, we write $[\![P\theta]\!](S)$ or $[\![P]\!](S, \theta)$ for $[\![P]\!](S, x_1\theta^S, \ldots, x_n\theta^S)$.

Example 3. Returning to M_1 in Figure 1, we have that the transition from p_3 to p_2 is associated with the assignment (i.e. a basic program) *SystemFont* $:= y$, say P, with a single formal parameter y. Given a substitution $\theta = \{y \mapsto t\}$ where t is ground, and any state S, $[\![P\theta]\!](S) = \{SystemFont \mapsto t^S\}$.

We also use the notion of a *labeled transition system* or *LTS* $(\mathcal{S}, \mathcal{S}_0, \mathcal{L}, \mathcal{T})$ that has a nonempty set $\mathcal{S}$ of *states*, a nonempty subset $\mathcal{S}_0 \subseteq \mathcal{S}$ of *initial states*, a nonempty set $\mathcal{L}$ of *labels* and a transition relation $\mathcal{T} \subseteq \mathcal{S} \times \mathcal{L} \times \mathcal{S}$. Here states and labels are abstract elements but in our use of LTSs the notion of LTS states and first-order states as introduced above will coincide. A *run* is a transition sequence $(S_i, L_i, S_{i+1})_{i<k}$, of

---

[2] We have in mind standard Tarski semantics for first order logic.

some (possibly infinite) length k, and if $k > 0$ then $S_0 \in \mathcal{S}_0$; if k is finite and nonzero then S_k is called the *end-state* of the run. An *S-run* for a given initial state S is a nonempty run as above where $S_0 = S$. An *S-trace* of an *S*-run as above is the label sequence $(L_i)_{i<k}$ of length k. Intuitively, a trace is the sequence of labels of a run; the states are not part of a trace. A *finite* run or trace has finite length.

3   Model Programs

A *guarded program* (over Σ) is a pair $[\varphi]/P$ where φ is a formula and P is a program. Let G be a guarded program $[\varphi]/P$. Intuitively, G denotes the restriction of $[\![P]\!]$ to those states and input parameters where φ holds. Let $FV(G) \overset{\text{def}}{=} FV(\varphi) \cup FV(P)$.

Definition 1. Σ^{action} *denotes a fixed subset of the free constructors of* Σ^{static} *called action symbols. An* action term *is a term* $f(t_1, \ldots, t_n)$ *where* f *is an* n-*ary action symbol for some* $n \geq 0$, *and each* t_i *is either a distinct logic variable or a ground term over* $\Sigma^{\text{static}} - \Sigma^{\text{action}}$. *Given* $\Gamma \subseteq \Sigma^{\text{action}}$ *we write* $\mathcal{A}(\Gamma)$ *for the set of all action terms with action symbols in* Γ. *By an* action *we mean the interpretation of a ground action term.*

Notice that the interpretation of a ground action term is the same in all data states. Notice also that there is essentially no difference between a nullary action symbol and the corresponding action (term).

Example 4. Consider M_1 in Figure 1. There are two nullary action symbols *Close-Document* and *OpenDocument*, and two unary action symbols *SelectFont_Start* and *SelectFont_Finish*. *Font* is a free constructor, it is not an action symbol. The terms *SelectFont_Start(Font("Times", 10))* and *SelectFont_Start(x)* are action terms; the terms *SelectFont_Start(SystemFont)* and *SelectFont_Start(Font("Times", y))* on the other hand are *not* action terms, because in the former *SystemFont* is not in Σ^{static} and in the latter the action parameter *Font("Times", y)* is not a logic variable and not a ground term.

Definition 2. *A* model program with explicit control graph M *has the following components.*

1. *A* signature Σ.
2. *An* action signature $\Gamma \subseteq \Sigma^{\text{action}}$.
3. *A finite nonempty set* Q *of* control points.
4. *An* initial control point $q^{\text{init}} \in Q$.
5. *A set of* accepting control points $Q^{\text{acc}} \subseteq Q$.
6. *A finite* control graph $\delta \subseteq Q \times \mathcal{A}(\Gamma) \times Q$. *The elements of* δ *are called* control transitions.
7. *A family* $R = \{r_\rho\}_{\rho \in \delta}$ *of* guarded programs, *where, for all* $\rho = (q, a, p) \in \delta$, $FV(r_\rho) \subseteq FV(a)$; r_ρ *is called the* guarded program for ρ.
8. *A closed formula* φ^{entry} *over* Σ *called an* entry condition.

The guard of the guarded program for a control transition ρ is denoted by φ_ρ and the program is denoted by P_ρ. We denote M by the tuple $(\Sigma, \Gamma, Q, q^{\text{init}}, Q^{\text{acc}}, \delta, R, \varphi^{\text{entry}})$.

By a *model program* in this paper we mean a model program with explicit control graph.

A model program can be thought of as a control-flow graph whose edges are annotated by action terms and program segments similar to an EFSM [13].[3]

We use the special program *skip* that produces no updates.

Example 5. The model program M_1 in Figure 1 has the following components. The signature is described in Example 1. The action signature is described in Example 4. The control points are p_1, p_2 and p_3, where p_1 is both the initial control point and the only accepting control point. There are four control transitions in M_1. The guard of a control transition is indicated with the *requires* keyword or omitted if *true*. The program of a control transition is written within braces or omitted if *skip*. This is the Spec# [16] syntax of model programs.

A *state* of M as above is a pair $\langle S, q \rangle$ where S is a Σ-state and $q \in Q$. S is called the *data component* of S or a *data state*, whereas q is called the *control component* of S or a *control state*.[4] An *initial* state is a state whose control component is an initial control point and whose data component satisfies the entry condition. An *accepting* state is a state whose control component is an accepting control point.

Definition 3. The *labeled transition system underlying M LTS(M)* has the actions of M as its labels. The (initial) states of *LTS(M)* are the (initial) states for M. There is a transition $(\langle S, q \rangle, b, \langle S', q' \rangle)$ in *LTS(M)*, if there is a control transition $\rho = (q, a, q')$ in M and a substitution θ such that:

- $b = a\theta^S$,
- $S \models \varphi_\rho \theta$,
- $[\![P_\rho \theta]\!](S)$ is consistent and $S' = S \uplus [\![P_\rho \theta]\!](S)$.

A transition of *LTS(M)* is called a *step* of M. Given a state S and an action a, we write $\delta(S, a)$ for the set of all states X such that (S, a, X) is a transition of *LTS(M)*. Given a state S and a finite sequence $(a_i)_{i<k}$ of actions, we let

$$\hat{\delta}(S, (a_i)_{i<k}) = \bigcup \{\delta(X, a_{k-1}) : X \in \hat{\delta}(S, (a_i)_{i<k-1})\},$$
$$\hat{\delta}(S, ()) = \{S\}.$$

Thus, $\hat{\delta}(S, \alpha)$ is the set of all end-states of all S-runs whose trace is α. An action sequence α is an *accepting* S-trace if $\hat{\delta}(S, \alpha)$ contains an accepting state.

Definition 4. Let M be a model program with initial control state q_0. An *S-run* of M is an $\langle S, q_0 \rangle$-run of *LTS(M)*. An *S-trace* of M is an $\langle S, q_0 \rangle$-trace of *LTS(M)*. The set of all S-traces of M is denoted by *Traces(S, M)*. An *S-trace* α of M is accepting if it is finite and $\hat{\delta}(\langle S, q_0 \rangle, \alpha)$ contains an accepting state.

---

[3] In general, the control graph of a model program may itself be a control program and the set of generated control states may be infinite. We do not use this generalization in this paper.

[4] Formally, let pc be a fixed nullary function symbol not in Σ and let $\Sigma' = \Sigma \cup \{pc\}$. Then $\langle S, q \rangle$ stands for a Σ'-state where $pc^{\langle S,q \rangle} = q$ and $f^{\langle S,q \rangle} = f^S$ for all $f \in \Sigma$.

Example 6. The example shows how traces can depend on the data component of states. A possible accepting trace of M_1 from any initial state is:

> *OpenDocument,*
>
> *SelectFont_Start(Font("Times", 12)),*
>
> *SelectFont_Finish(Font("SansSerif", 10)),*
>
> *SelectFont_Start(Font("SansSerif", 10)),*
>
> *SelectFont_Finish(Font("Times", 10)),*
>
> *CloseDocument*

The argument to *SelectFont_Start* is the current system font recorded in the data state of M_1. When font selection finishes the new font is recorded in the state, i.e., in the action *SelectFont_Start(font)*, the *font* argument acts like an input argument and in *SelectFont_Finish(font)* the *font* argument acts like an output argument of a font selection procedure.

4   Composition of Model Programs

The main operator underlying parallel composition of model programs is the product of two model programs. We will also use the following action signature extension operation over model programs.

Definition 5. Let M be a model program as above with action signature Γ. Let Γ' be a set of action symbols. We write $M^{+\Gamma'}$ for the model program whose action signature is extended with Γ' and $M^{+\Gamma'}$ has the following additional extensions for each action symbol $f \in \Gamma' - \Gamma$, let a_f denote a fixed action term $f(\_, \ldots, \_)$ where each occurrence of $\_$ stands for a fresh logic variable,

- for all control states q, δ is extended with the control transition, (q, a_f, q),
- for each new control transition (q, a_f, q), $r_{(q, a_f, q)} = [true]/skip$.

The intuition is that for each new action symbol any corresponding action is enabled in every state and produces a self-loop in that state. This is also easily seen in the LTS semantics of $M^{+\Gamma'}$. This construct is used mainly to interleave actions that are not shared between two model programs being composed in a product. Notice that an action does not belong to a model program (or the underlying LTS) if its function symbol is not in the action signature of the model program.

Example 7. Consider M_1 in Figure 1 and let Γ_2 be the action signature of the font chooser dialog model M_2 in Figure 2. The only action symbols that M_1 and M_2 have in common are *SelectFont_Start* and *SelectFont_Finish*. Thus $M_1^{+\Gamma_2}$ has for example the new control transitions $(p_i, SetFontSize(\_), p_i)$ for $1 \le i \le 3$ that are enabled in all states.

4.1   Product Composition

We first define the product of two model programs that share the same signature and the same action signature. We then define parallel composition of model programs by using signature extension and product composition.

Due to the restricted form of action terms, two action terms a_1 and a_2 unify if and only if they have the same action symbol of some arity $n \geq 0$, and for all i, $1 \leq i \leq n$, the i'th argument of a_1 and the i'th argument of a_2 either denote the same value or at least one of them is a logic variable. If a_1 and a_2 unify there is trivially a most general unifier $\theta = mgu(a_1, a_2)$, i.e., any action that is both an instance of a_1 and an instance of a_2 is an instance of $a_1\theta$ (or $a_2\theta$).

We assume that logic variables used in two model programs are distinct so that we do not need to worry about variable renaming. Given two guarded programs $r_1 = [\varphi_1]/P_1$ and $r_2 = [\varphi_2]/P_2$ we write $r_1 \parallel r_2$ for the guarded program $[\varphi_1 \wedge \varphi_2]/P_1 \parallel P_2$, where the parallel composition $P_1 \parallel P_2$ produces the union of the updates of P_1 and P_2, i.e. $[\![P_1 \parallel P_2]\!](S, \theta) = [\![P_1]\!](S, \theta) \cup [\![P_2]\!](S, \theta)$.

Definition 6. Let $M_i = (\Sigma, \Gamma, Q_i, q_i^{\text{init}}, Q_i^{\text{acc}}, \delta_i, \{r_\rho^i\}_{\rho \in \delta_i}, \varphi_i^{\text{entry}})$, for $i = 1, 2$, be two model programs. The *product* of M_1 and M_2, denoted by $M_1 \times M_2$, is the model program

$$(\Sigma, \Gamma, Q_1 \times Q_2, \langle q_1^{\text{init}}, q_2^{\text{init}} \rangle, Q_1^{\text{acc}} \times Q_2^{\text{acc}}, \delta, \{r_\rho\}_{\rho \in \delta}), \varphi_1^{\text{entry}} \wedge \varphi_2^{\text{entry}}),$$

where δ and $\{r_\rho\}_{\rho \in \delta}$ are constructed as follows. For all $\rho_1 = (q_1, a_1, p_1) \in \delta_1$ and $\rho_2 = (q_2, a_2, p_2) \in \delta_2$ such that $\theta = mgu(a_1, a_2)$ exists,

- $\rho = (\langle q_1, q_2 \rangle, a_1\theta, \langle p_1, p_2 \rangle) \in \delta$, and
- $r_\rho = r_{\rho_1}\theta \parallel r_{\rho_2}\theta$.

If M_1 and M_2 are model programs with different action signatures Γ_1 and Γ_2 then $M_1 \times M_2 \stackrel{\text{def}}{=} M_1^{+\Gamma_2} \times M_2^{+\Gamma_1}$.

One can show that the product operator is commutative and associative as far as trace semantics of the final model program is concerned. This is made explicit in the following statement.

Proposition 1. *Let M_1, M_2 and M_3 be model programs with the same signature and action signature, and let S be a data state. Then $Traces(S, M_1 \times M_2) = Traces(S, M_2 \times M_1)$ and $Traces(S, M_1 \times (M_2 \times M_3)) = Traces(S, (M_1 \times M_2) \times M_3)$.*

Example 8. The model program M_4 in Figure 4 shows the product $M_1 \times M_2 \times M_3$. Let Γ_i denote the action signature of M_i. In this case $\Gamma_2 = \Gamma_3$ but Γ_1 has the additional actions for opening and closing a document, and does not include the action for changing the font name/size and the *OK* and *Cancel* actions. If we first construct the product $M_2 \times M_3$, we get a specialization M_{23} of the font chooser dialog model M_2 where we first set the font size to be 10 and then set the font name to be SansSerif. The product $M_1 \times M_{23}$, i.e. M_4, corresponds intuitively to a hierarchical refinement of M_1 with a particular use of the font dialog model as described by M_{23}. The actions that are specific to the font selection model are considered as self-loops in M_1, and conversely, closing and opening of a document are considered as self-loops in M_{23}. The final product M_4 is therefore $M_1^{+\Gamma_2} \times M_{23}^{+\Gamma_1}$. As an example of a guarded update program of M_4 consider the control transition

$$\rho = (\langle p_2, q_1, r_1 \rangle, SelectFont\_Start(Font(\text{``Times''}, 12)), \langle p_3, q_2, r_2 \rangle)$$

If we follow the definitions exactly and do not simplify the formulas and the programs then the guard associated with ρ is

requires $Font(\text{``Times''}, 12) == SystemFont$
$\qquad \wedge\ true$
$\qquad \wedge\ ValidFont(Font(\text{``Times''}, 12)),$

and the program associated with ρ is

$skip \parallel ((DialogFont, SavedFont) := (Font(\text{``Times''}, 12), Font(\text{``Times''}, 12)) \parallel skip)\,.$

4.2 Parallel Composition

When the product composition is used in an unrestricted manner the end result is a new model program, which from the point of view of trace semantics might be unrelated to the original model programs. Essentially, this problem occurs if two model programs can read each others state variables.

Let $SV(e)$ denote the set of all *state variables* that occur in e, where e is either an expression, a program or a model program. Given a Σ_1-state S and a signature $\Sigma_2 \subseteq \Sigma_1$, we write $S{\restriction}\Sigma_2$ for the *reduct* of S to Σ_2. An ASM program is "honest" about its state dependencies in the sense that state variables that are not explicitly mentioned in the program do not influence its behavior and cannot be updated (e.g. there is no implicit stack and the programs cannot change the control state). Formally, we use the following fact:

Lemma 1. *Let S be a data state over Σ, let $SV \subseteq \Sigma^{\text{dynamic}}$, and let P be a program such that $SV(P) \subseteq SV$. Let $\Sigma' = \Sigma^{\text{static}} \cup SV$. Then $[\![P]\!](S) = [\![P]\!](S{\restriction}\Sigma')$.*

Definition 7. *Let M_1 and M_2 be model programs with action signatures Γ_1 and Γ_2, respectively. M_1 and M_2 are composable in parallel if they have the same signature but disjoint state variables, in which case the parallel composition of M_1 and M_2, denoted by $M_1 \parallel M_2$, is defined as the product $M_1 \times M_2$.*

The following theorem shows that parallel composition of model programs corresponds to parallel composition of the underlying LTSs. Such composition has the desired language-theoretic property that the traces produced by the composite model program are the intersection of the traces produced independently by the composed model programs.

Theorem 1. *Let M_1 and M_2 be model programs that are composable in parallel and have the same action signature. Then*

$$Traces(S, M_1 \parallel M_2) = Traces(S, M_1) \cap Traces(S, M_2).$$

Proof. Let $M_i = (\Sigma, \Gamma, Q_i, q_i^{\text{init}}, Q_i^{\text{acc}}, \delta_i, \{r_\rho^i\}_{\rho \in \delta_i}, \varphi_i^{\text{entry}})$, for $i = 1, 2$, be two model programs such that $SV(M_1) \cap SV(M_2) = \emptyset$. Let S be a data state. Let $M = M_1 \times M_2$. We only show that $Traces(S, M_1 \times M_2) \subseteq Traces(S, M_1) \cap Traces(S, M_2)$. The other direction is similar by using the same definitions in the opposite direction. Consider a trace $(a_i)_{i<k} \in Traces(S, M_1 \times M_2)$. There is a corresponding S-run

$$(\langle S_i, \langle q_i, p_i \rangle\rangle, a_i, \langle S_{i+1}, \langle q_{i+1}, p_{i+1}\rangle\rangle)_{i<k}$$

where $\langle q_0, p_0 \rangle$ is the initial control state of the product model program and $S = S_0$. Fix an arbitrary step i in the run. The following holds by Definition 3: there is a control transition $\rho_i = (\langle q_i, p_i \rangle, t_i, \langle q_{i+1}, p_{i+1} \rangle)$ in M and a substitution θ such that

- $a_i = t_i \theta^{S_i}$,
- $S_i \models \varphi_{\rho_i} \theta$, and
- $[\![P_{\rho_i} \theta]\!](S_i)$ is consistent and $S_{i+1} = S_i \uplus [\![P_{\rho_i} \theta]\!](S_i)$.

By Defininition 6, there are control transitions $\rho_i^1 = (q_i, t_i^1, q_{i+1})$ in M_1 and $\rho_i^2 = (p_i, t_i^2, p_{i+1})$ in M_2 such that

- $\sigma = mgu(t_i^1, t_i^2)$ exists and $t_i = t_i^1 \sigma$,
- $\varphi_{\rho_i} = \varphi_{\rho_i^1} \sigma \wedge \varphi_{\rho_i^2} \sigma$, and
- $P_{\rho_i} = P_{\rho_i^1} \sigma \parallel P_{\rho_i^2} \sigma$.

Let $\Sigma_1 = \Sigma - SV(M_2)$ and $\Sigma_2 = \Sigma - SV(M_1)$. Since $SV(M_1)$ and $SV(M_2)$ are disjoint and the guards in M_j may only contain state variables from $SV(M_j)$, it follows that $S_i \restriction \Sigma_1 \models \varphi_{\rho_i^1} \sigma \theta$ and $S_i \restriction \Sigma_2 \models \varphi_{\rho_i^2} \sigma \theta$. Also, since $[\![P_{\rho_i} \theta]\!](S_i) = U_1 \cup U_2$ is consistent, so are U_1 and U_2, where $U_1 = [\![P_{\rho_i^1} \sigma \theta]\!](S_i)$ and $U_2 = [\![P_{\rho_i^2} \sigma \theta]\!](S_i)$. By using Lemma 1 and the disjointness of $SV(M_1)$ and $SV(M_2)$ we know that $U_1 = [\![P_{\rho_i^1} \sigma \theta]\!](S_i \restriction \Sigma_1)$ and $U_2 = [\![P_{\rho_i^2} \sigma \theta]\!](S_i \restriction \Sigma_2)$. By using $S_{i+1} = S_i \uplus U_1 \cup U_2$, we get that $S_{i+1} \restriction \Sigma_1 = S_i \restriction \Sigma_1 \uplus U_1$ and $S_{i+1} \restriction \Sigma_2 = S_i \restriction \Sigma_2 \uplus U_2$.

Since i was chosen freely, we can construct the run

$$(\langle S_i \restriction \Sigma_1, q_i \rangle, a_i, \langle S_{i+1} \restriction \Sigma_1, q_{i+1} \rangle)_{i<k}$$

for M_1 and then expand all states in the run to Σ in such a way that the first state is S. We know also that $S \models \varphi_1^{\text{entry}}$ because $S \models \varphi_1^{\text{entry}} \wedge \varphi_2^{\text{entry}}$. It follows that $(a_i)_{i<k} \in Traces(S, M_1)$. Symmetrical argument applies to M_2. □

Example 9. Consider M_1, M_2, M_3 from above. The state variables of each M_i are clearly disjoint; M_1 has the single state variable *SystemFont*, M_2 has the state variables *DialogFont* and *SavedFont*, and M_3 has no state variables. Thus M_4 is a parallel composition of $M_1^{+\Gamma_2}$, $M_2^{+\Gamma_1}$ and $M_3^{+\Gamma_1}$, where Γ_1 and Γ_2 are as in Example 8.

4.3 Serial Composition

In scenario control it is often useful to compose two model programs serially (i.e. in a sequence). Intuitively, a serial composition of two model programs M_1 and M_2 means that the control flow may transition from an accepting control point of M_1 to the initial control point of M_2. Serial composition is therefore not well-defined for model programs that share control points. Note that, unlike the parallel case, state variable signatures need not be disjoint in serial composition.

Definition 8. Two model programs M_1 and M_2 are *serially composable* if they have the same action signature and disjoint sets of control points.

The formal definition of serial composition uses a new nullary action symbol τ for the transition from M_1 to M_2. The τ transition corresponds to an internal control transition from any accepting control point of M_1 to the initial control point of M_2 whose guard is the entry condition of M_2.

Definition 9. Let $M_i = (\Sigma, \Gamma, Q_i, q_i^{\text{init}}, Q_i^{\text{acc}}, \delta_i, \{r_\rho^i\}_{\rho \in \delta_i}, \varphi_i^{\text{entry}})$, for $i = 1, 2$, be two serially composable model programs and let τ be a fresh action symbol not in Γ. M_1 *followed by* M_2 *using* τ, denoted by $M_1;_\tau M_2$, is the model program

$$(\Sigma, \{\tau\} \cup \Gamma, Q_1 \cup Q_2, q_1^{\text{init}}, Q_2^{\text{acc}}, \underbrace{\delta_1 \cup \delta_2 \cup \{(q, \tau, q_2^{\text{init}}) : q \in Q_1^{\text{acc}}\}}_{\delta}, \{r_\rho\}_{\rho \in \delta}, \varphi_1^{\text{entry}}),$$

where $r_\rho = r_\rho^1$, if $\rho \in \delta_1$; $r_\rho = r_\rho^2$, if $\rho \in \delta_2$; $r_\rho = [\varphi_2^{\text{entry}}]/\textit{skip}$, otherwise.

It is easy to see that an S-trace of $M_1;_\tau M_2$ has the form $\alpha\tau\beta$ where α is an accepting S-trace of M_1 and β is an S'-trace of M_2 for some $S' \in \hat{\delta}_{M_1}(S, \alpha)$. Elimination of τ can be done at the expense of introducing nondeterminism. For parallel composition of two model programs, τ-actions in each one are always considered as distinct actions and are interleaved. One could also introduce τ as a special action that is always interleaved in a parallel composition as is done for example in the definition of LTSs [14].

5   Conclusions and Related Work

There is a tradeoff between how much of the global state should be encoded as control state and how much should be encoded as data state. In pure abstract state machines, states are completely encoded as data states, and there is no separate notion of control state [2,9]. Model programs defined in [16] adopt this view. While this view is more concise and sufficient for many purposes it forces one to encode the control state as data state, and this may not be natural from the point of view of control flow as understood in traditional programming. Not having the distinction between control and data state makes also the definition of certain forms of composition, such as serial composition, harder to formalize because data states are shared whereas control states are disjoint in serial composition.

The approach that we have taken is similar to extended finite state machines (EFSMs) where a finite part of the state is separated as control state. In general, the control part does not need to be finite in model programs, but may encorporate the local stack of a program. Model programs are similar to parameterized EFSMs [13], except that EFSMs are a generalization of Mealy machines, whereas model programs do not distinguish a priori between inputs and outputs and incorporate the notion of accepting states like classical automata. The distinction between inputs and outputs becomes relevant for defining conformance, but is not relevant for the composition operators discussed in this paper that are used for scenario control and for composing aspects of a system model.

An important change from our prior approach of using model programs as a mixed Mealy and LTS view, taken in SpecExplorer, is the introduction of intermediate control states between the input part and the output part of an action. In other words, the underlying semantics is given by an LTS. This separation is also used with FSM based approaches where it is sometimes more convenient to formulate composition using IOTSs [6]. One of the key reasons for us to separate the inputs from the outputs as separate actions, rather than using a Mealy view, was to be able to have a simple definition of conformance relation that allows output nondeterminism when dealing with reactive systems. This is important for using ioco [3] or refinement of interface automata [5] for formalizing the confomance relation.

Further differences from EFSMs are that accepting states in model programs are used for serial composition and for defining validity of traces, and labels are not abstract elements but structured terms that allow sharing of arbitrary data values through unification. The trace semantics of model programs is based on the unwinding of model programs as labeled transition systems [14] where states are considered to be abstract points.

The separation of control state from data state, while allowing communication with terms that can incorporate data values, is important in the model-based testing applications of model programs, e.g. for scenario control and visualization of model programs. The definitions of parallel and serial composition of model programs are related to similar operations on classical automata (see e.g. [10]). There is a large body of work using FSMs and variations of LTSs that use the classical parallel composition of automata where shared actions are synchronized and other actions are interleaved asynchronously. It is important therefore that the semantics of composed model programs is based on the same notion of composition.

Model programs are also related to symbolic transition systems that have an explicit notion of data and data-dependent control flow [7]. Model program composition as defined in this paper is independent of the mechanism of exploration used. Various approaches, including explicit state exploration as well as exploration with symbolic labels and states, may be applied. For example, *action machines* [8] rely on symbolic techniques. The main difference compared to composition of action machines is that composition of model programs is syntactic, whereas composition of action machines is defined in the style of natural semantics using inference rules and symbolic computation that incorporates the notion of computable approximations of subsumption checking between symbolic states. The computable approximations reflect the power of the underlying decision procedures that are being used.

More about model-based testing applications and further motivation for the composition of model programs can be found in [4,8,17,16]. The most recent work related to model programs where composition is discussed from a practical perspective is the forthcoming textbook [11].

References

1. Spec Explorer. released (January 2005) URL:
   `http://research.microsoft.com/specexplorer`
2. Börger, E., Stärk, R.: Abstract State Machines: A Method for High-Level System Design and Analysis. Springer (2003)

3. Brinksma, E., Tretmans, J.: Testing Transition Systems: An Annotated Bibliography. In: Summer School MOVEP'2k – Modelling and Verification of Parallel Processes. LNCS, vol. 2067, pp. 187–193. Springer, Heidelberg (2001)

4. Campbell, C., Grieskamp, W., Nachmanson, L., Schulte, W., Tillmann, N., Veanes, M.: Testing concurrent object-oriented systems with Spec Explorer (extended abstract). In: Fitzgerald, J.A., Hayes, I.J., Tarlecki, A. (eds.) FM 2005. LNCS, vol. 3582, pp. 542–547. Springer, Heidelberg (2005)

5. de Alfaro, L.: Game models for open systems. In: Dershowitz, N. (ed.) Verification: Theory and Practice. LNCS, vol. 2772, pp. 269–289. Springer, Heidelberg (2004)

6. El-Fakih, K., Petrenko, A., Yevtushenko, N.: Fsm test translation through context. In: Uyar, M.Ü., Duale, A.Y., Fecko, M.A. (eds.) TestCom 2006. LNCS, vol. 3964, Springer, Heidelberg (2006)

7. Frantzen, L., Tretmans, J., Willemse, T.: A symbolic framework for model-based testing. In: Havelund, K., Núñez, M., Roşu, G., Wolff, B. (eds.) Formal Approaches to Software Testing and Runtime Verification. LNCS, vol. 4262, pp. 40–54. Springer, Heidelberg (2006)

8. Grieskamp, W., Kicillof, N., Tillmann, N.: Action machines: a framework for encoding and composing partial behaviors. International Journal on Software and Knowledge Engineering 16(5), 705–726 (2006)

9. Gurevich, Y.: Evolving Algebras 1993: Lipari Guide. In: Börger, E. (ed.) Specification and Validation Methods, pp. 9–36. Oxford University Press, Oxford (1995)

10. Hopcroft, J.E., Ullman, J.D.: Introduction to Automata Theory, Languages, and Computation. Addison-Wesley, Reading (1979)

11. Jacky, J., Veanes, M., Campbell, C., Schulte, W.: Model-based Software Testing and Analysis with C#. Cambridge University Press (Submitted to publisher) (2007)

12. Keller, R.: Formal verification of parallel programs. Communications of the ACM, pp. 371–384 (July 1976)

13. Lee, D., Yannakakis, M.: Principles and methods of testing finite state machines – a survey. Proceedings of the IEEE 84(8), 1090–1123 (1996)

14. Lynch, N., Tuttle, M.: Hierarchical correctness proofs for distributed algorithms. In: Proceedings of the sixth annual ACM Symposium on Principles of distributed computing, pp. 137–151. ACM Press, New York (1987)

15. Tretmans, J., Brinksma, E.: TorX: Automated model based testing. In: 1st European Conference on Model Driven Software Engineering, pp. 31–43, Nuremberg, Germany (December 2003)

16. Veanes, M., Campbell, C., Grieskamp, W., Nachmanson, L., Schulte, W., Tillmann, N.: Model-based testing of object-oriented reactive systems with Spec Explorer, Tech. Rep. MSR-TR-2005-59, Microsoft Research. (To appear as a book chapter in Formal Methods and Testing) (2005)

17. Veanes, M., Campbell, C., Schulte, W., Tillmann, N.: Online testing with model programs. In: ESEC/FSE-13: Proceedings of the 10th European software engineering conference held jointly with 13th ACM SIGSOFT international symposium on Foundations of software engineering, pp. 273–282. ACM, New York (2005)

New Bisimulation Semantics for Distributed Systems[*]

David de Frutos-Escrig, Fernando Rosa-Velardo, and
Carlos Gregorio-Rodríguez

Dpto. de Sistemas Informáticos y Computación
Universidad Complutense de Madrid
{defrutos,fernandorosa,cgr}@sip.ucm.es

Abstract. Bisimulation semantics are a very pleasant way to define the
semantics of systems, mainly because the simplicity of their definitions
and their nice coalgebraic properties. However, they also have some dis-
advantages: they are based on a sequential operational semantics defined
by means of an ordinary transition system, and in order to be bisimilar
two systems have to be "too similar". In this work we will present several
natural proposals to define weaker bisimulation semantics that we think
properly capture the desired behaviour of distributed systems. The main
virtue of all these semantics is that they are real bisimulation semantics,
thus inheriting most of the good properties of bisimulation semantics.
This is so because they can be defined as particular instances of Jacobs
and Hughes' categorical definition of simulation, which they have already
proved to satisfy all those properties.

1 Introduction

Bisimulation is a usual way to define the semantics of systems. It is defined
starting from an operational semantics that defines the (low level) behaviour
of the system as a labelled transition system (lts) whose states correspond to
the possible internal states of the systems, while the transitions represent the
change of state, observable by means of labels. Bisimulations have many pleasant
theoretical and practical properties that justify its use to define the semantics of
systems. At the theoretical level, bisimulations are the adequate way to define
the behaviour of a system defined by a coalgebra $s : X \rightarrow \mathcal{P}(A \times X)$. They
capture the idea that in order to be equivalent, two states must have two sets of
labelled successors that have to be related in both directions: $\forall s \xrightarrow{a} s' \ \exists t \xrightarrow{a} t'$
with $(s', t') \in R$ and $\forall t \xrightarrow{a} t' \ \exists s \xrightarrow{a} s'$ with $(s', t') \in R$.

This only slightly generalizes the isomorphism of transition systems, mainly
by taking into account the idempotent law. This means that the correspondence
relating the a-successors of two related states do not need to be bijective. For instance, the relation $R = \{(x, y), (x_1, y_1), (x_2, y_1), (x_3, y_2), (x_3, y_3)\}$ is the smallest
bisimulation relating the two states x and y of the two systems in Fig. 1.

---

[*] Work partially supported by the Spanish projects DESAFIOS TIN2006-15660-C02-
02, WEST TIN2006-15578-C02-01 and PROMESAS-CAM S-0505/TIC/0407.

J. Derrick and J. Vain (Eds.): FORTE 2007, LNCS 4574, pp. 143–159, 2007.

Fig. 1. Two bisimilar systems

Besides the simple and easy to manipulate way in which they are defined, bisimulations and the equivalence relation they induce, bisimilarity, satisfy many pleasant properties that have been thoroughly studied since they were introduced by Park [20]. For instance, we can prove that whenever the operational semantics of a language is defined by a SOS-system [21] of several quite large syntactical classes, such as the De Simone class [6], then bisimulation equivalence is a congruence with respect to all the syntactical constructors of the language.

At the practical level, bisimilarity is an interesting way to define the equivalence of two systems, since it can be checked by efficient algorithms [8]. When, instead, we prefer to use symbolic proofs to prove the equivalence between two systems described by two syntactical terms of a language, we can construct the corresponding bisimulation relating them by using quite powerful techniques such as bisimulation up-to [18].

The most important disadvantage of using bisimulation semantics is that bisimulation equivalence is a too coarse relation: all the extensional semantics that have been proposed to define the semantics of systems by adding some information to the quite simple trace semantics, such as the failure semantics or the readiness semantics, have less discriminatory power than the bisimulation equivalence, as we can see in the famous Van Glabbeek's spectrum [27].

Bisimulation is also too powerful with respect to the testing framework. This is also seen in [27]: copy and "parallel" testing are needed in order to characterize bisimulation equivalence as a testing equivalence. Besides, in [3] Bloom et al. have proved that ready simulation equivalence, that is also weaker than bisimilarity, is the strongest equivalence relation that is preserved by any operator defined by means of GSOS rules. We can sum up this discussion by saying that bisimulation equivalence is too fine because it forces the two compared transition systems to be "too similar". Our aim in this paper will be to present other bisimulation-like semantics that generalize the definition of plain bisimulations, by allowing us to get other equivalences between systems that we will naturally justify when comparing distributed systems.

Simulations are one of the first natural ways to relax the definition of bisimulation. In the one hand, because its definition is obtained by retaining just one half of the two symmetric parts of the definition of bisimulation. In this way, we obtain an order relation, similarity, that also has a coalgebraic definition. However, mutual simulation, that is again an equivalence relation, is not as powerful as bisimulation equivalence. We can try to enforce the simulation semantics by adding some additional constraints, getting for instance the ready simulations and the ready simulation equivalence. However, there is not any non-trivial order relation whose kernel is bisimilarity. Even so, simulations are a reasonable and useful way to compare two given systems, and also a powerful tool to define interesting equivalence relations, as ready similarity.

Another way to generalize the concept of bisimulation is by means of its categorical definition, by allowing any functor F in the definition of the coalgebras $a : X \rightarrow F(X)$ and $b : Y \rightarrow F(Y)$ to be related. Besides the seminal work on the subject [1], you can look at the wonderful monography [16] to find a thorough study of the subject. Even if it would be interesting to know all the technical details, in this paper we mainly pretend to motivate the use of several bisimulation-like equivalence relations, which can in fact be supported by all that abstract machinery. Therefore, we are both saying that those semantics can be formally defined, and have all the pleasant properties of bisimulation semantics; and we are proving that those general abstract studies have indeed a practical use, since these new interesting semantics can be obtained as particular instances of the bisimulation semantics they allow to define.

For instance, we will present "commutative bisimulation", that checks "from time to time", by means of some introduced "checkpoints" that the compared systems have executed the same actions, but possibly in a different order; and "action sets bisimulation", where we also introduce a simple definition of "distributed transition system". We also discuss "approximated bisimulation", where the compared systems need not to execute exactly the same actions but some "similar" ones; this includes the notion of amortized bisimulation, where the costs of the executed actions need to be only similar. All these bisimulation-like equivalences are weaker than strong bisimulation, so that they diminish the proof obligations imposed by the ordinary definition of bisimulation.

Although we will recall that categorical definition, and we will show how can be indeed used to define some of the semantics we propose, in this paper we will mainly focus on the presentation of these new semantics, leaving the details of their categorical definition to other more appropriate forum.

It is important to point out that although there were several proposals for bisimulations for distributed systems in the past, they were in the opposite direction to our approach, since they tried to capture the differences between systems induced by facts such as the location where the actions were executed, and therefore produce semantic equivalences finer than ordinary bisimilarity; instead, as said before, we are looking for coarser equivalences, which therefore are more easily accomplished.

The rest of the paper is structured as follows. Section 2 defines the new bisimulation-like semantics that we propose. Section 3 is a brief survey of abstract results on categorical bisimulations that can be applied to justify the coalgebraic character of all the new bisimulation notions that we have introduced. As an illustration of how this can be done we present the details for one of the semantics. Section 4 discusses some related work, and finally Sect. 5 briefly presents our conclusions and directions for future work.

2   Bisimulations for Distributed Systems

We have looked for several directions in which we could relax the definition of plain bisimulations getting nice weaker semantics which could be still rigorously presented as coalgebraic semantics, thus preserving their good properties. Next we present those simplest proposals that, at the same time, seem to be more promising in practice.

2.1   Commutative Bisimulations

There are several scenarios in which we are not interested in the order in which the actions are executed, but in the set of actions that is finally executed. If we only have finite sequential systems to compare, then we could define the trace semantics as a starting point, by applying the seq-to-multiset operator that transforms the sequence of executed actions into the corresponding multiset of actions. However, if we are considering reactive systems that possibly run forever, we need to consider adequate bisimulation-like versions of that intended semantics.

As a first proposal in this direction, we present *checkpoint commutative bisimulations*, that are defined by incorporating into the transition systems that define the operational semantics of our distributed systems a boolean attribute *checkpoint* that signals the times where we have to check for the equality of the multiset of actions that the systems have executed from their previous checkpoints.

We can describe the desired bisimulation equivalence using plain, but accurate words, as follows: in order to check if two states of two systems are equivalent, we will play the ordinary bisimulation game, but now we are not forced to replicate the execution of any action a by executing the same action in the other process; instead, we remember the multiset of actions executed through the paired computations until we arrive to a checkpoint. Then, the other process has to arrive to another checkpoint and the two remembered multisets of actions should be the same.

To formalize this new class of bisimulations we need to introduce those sets of remembered actions. This is done by defining our bisimulations not just as relations on states, but as relations on pairs $(s, m) \in S \times \mathcal{MS}(A)$, where s is a state and m a multiset of actions. This takes us to the following formal definitions.

Definition 1. $(S, A, \rightarrow, chk)$ *is an* lts *with checkpoints if* $(S, A, \rightarrow)$ *is an ordinary* lts *and* $chk : S \rightarrow \{0, 1\}$ *is the characteristic function of a set of so called checkpoints of the system.*

Definition 2. *A commutative checkpoint bisimulation* relating states of an lts *with checkpoints* $(S, A, \rightarrow, chk)$ *is a relation* $R \subseteq (S \times \mathcal{MS}(A)) \times (S \times \mathcal{MS}(A))$ *that satisfies:*

- $(s_1, m_1)R(s_2, m_2) \wedge (chk(s_1) \vee chk(s_2)) \Rightarrow chk(s_1) \wedge chk(s_2) \wedge m_1 = m_2,$
- $(s_1, m_1)R(s_2, m_2) \wedge s_1 \xrightarrow{a} s_1' \Rightarrow \exists s_2 \xrightarrow{b} s_2' \wedge (s_1', m_1 + \{a\})R(s_2', m_2 + \{b\}),$

Fig. 2. Checkpoint bisimilar states

- $(s_1, m_1)R(s_2, m_2) \wedge s_2 \xrightarrow{b} s_2' \Rightarrow \exists s_1 \xrightarrow{a} s_1' \wedge (s_1', m_1 + \{a\})R(s_2', m_2 + \{b\})$,

where + represents the union of multisets.

As usual, we say that (s_1, m_1) and (s_2, m_2) are *checkpoint bisimilar*, and we write $(s_1, m_1) \sim_{chk} (s_2, m_2)$, if and only if there exists a commutative checkpoint bisimulation R such that $(s_1, m_1)R(s_2, m_2)$. We simply say that s_1 and s_2 are checkpoint bisimilar, and we also write $s_1 \sim_{chk} s_2$, if and only if $(s_1, \emptyset) \sim_{chk} (s_2, \emptyset)$.

First notice that in order to simplify the definition above, we are remembering the complete multiset of executed actions from the very beginning, and not only from the last checkpoint. If we prefer to faithfully capture that more local memory constraint, it is easy to check that changing the second condition in Def. 2 by the following one

$$(s_1, m_2)R(s_2, m_2) \wedge s_1 \xrightarrow{a} s_2' \Rightarrow \exists s_2 \xrightarrow{b} s_2' \wedge \begin{cases} chk(s_1) \Rightarrow (s_1', \{a\})R(s_2', \{b\}) \\ \neg\, chk(s_1) \Rightarrow (s_1', m_1 + \{a\})R(s_2', m_2 + \{b\}) \end{cases}$$

and similarly for the third condition, we obtain an equivalent definition.

As a first and trivial example, let us consider the lts with checkpoints in Fig. 2. In it, we denote by c's the states which are checkpoints. Then, trivially the states c_1 and c_2 are checkpoint bisimilar. Indeed, the relation $R = \{\langle (c_0, \emptyset), (c_1, \emptyset)\rangle, \langle (s_1, \{a\}), (s_2, \{b\})\rangle, \langle (c_1', \{a, b\}), (c_2', \{a, b\})\rangle\}$ is a checkpoint bisimulation.

As it has been done many other times in the past, once we have a bisimulation-like definition of an equivalence relation, we could prove one by one all the properties of such a relation. However, what we advocate here is the use of the general results that have been recently developed in a general framework, so that those properties are obtained just for free, as particular cases of those general results. We will recall in Sect. 3 some of those general results and the way in which they can be used to prove that all the bisimulation-like semantics proposed in this paper have, indeed, a pure coalgebraic flavour.

2.2 Amortized Commutative Bisimulation

One could argue that the use of checkpoints is not very natural, although we could give some examples where they can be introduced in a quite simple way. For instance, we could consider the comparison between two search engines that collect information in the web in two different ways. In this case, the checkpoints correspond to the points in which they have completed a search: it is at that time that we have to compare the results of the search.

However, we could prefer a more "continuous" equivalence where the comparison is done after each step of the bisimulation game, although allowing multiple steps in order to allow the interleaving of other actions whenever we need to replicate the execution of a given action. In order to make easier the presentation of this semantics, we prefer to start in this case by the formal definitions.

Definition 3. *Given a transition system* $(S, A, \rightarrow)$, *we define the* step transition system *induced by it as* $(S, A^*, \Rightarrow)$, *where* $s \overset{\alpha}{\Rightarrow} s'$ *with* $\alpha = a_1 \ldots a_n$ *if and only if*

$$s = s_0 \overset{a_1}{\rightarrow} s_1 \ldots s_i \overset{a_{i+1}}{\rightarrow} s_{i+1} \ldots s_{n-1} \overset{a_n}{\rightarrow} s_n = s'$$

Definition 4. *An* amortized commutative bisimulation *relating states of an lts* $(S, A, \rightarrow)$ *is a relation* $R \subseteq (S \times \mathcal{MS}(A)) \times (S \times \mathcal{MS}(A))$ *that satisfies*

- $(s_1, m_1)R(s_2, m_2) \wedge s_1 \overset{a}{\rightarrow} s_1' \Rightarrow \exists s_2 \overset{\alpha}{\Rightarrow} s_2' \quad m_1 + \{a\} \subseteq m_2 + \{\alpha\}$ *and* $(s_1', \emptyset)R(s_2', m)$ *with* $m + m_1 + \{a\} = m_2 + \{\alpha\}$,
- $(s_1, m_1)R(s_2, m_2) \wedge s_2 \overset{a}{\rightarrow} s_2' \Rightarrow \exists s_1 \overset{\alpha}{\Rightarrow} s_1' \quad m_2 + \{a\} \subseteq m_1 + \{\alpha\}$ *and* $(s_1', m)R(s_2', \emptyset)$ *with* $m + m_2 + \{a\} = m_1 + \{\alpha\}$,

where by abuse of notation we take $\{\alpha\} = \{a_1, \ldots, a_n\}$ *if* $\alpha = a_1 \ldots a_n$.

In this case we could start by considering only the pairs $\langle (s_0, m_0), (s_1, m_1) \rangle$ with $m_0 = \emptyset \vee m_1 = \emptyset$. Then we could see the corresponding set $m_i \neq \emptyset$ as the stock accumulated by s_i when comparing it with s_{1-i}.

We could also consider a restricted variant where the size of this stock is somehow bounded. For instance, given a size bound B we could impose to the sets $m_i = \emptyset$, $m_{1-i} \neq \emptyset$ that $|m_{1-i}| \leq B$, in order to define the corresponding bisimilarity $\sim^B_{acb}$. The idea is that we cannot execute too many other actions in advance when simulating the execution of an action a.

If we disregard checkpoints in Fig.2 then states c_1 and c_2 are amortized bisimilar, since the following relation is an amortized bisimulation.

$$R = \{\langle (c_1, \emptyset), (c_2, \emptyset) \rangle, \langle (s_1, \emptyset), (c_2', \{b\}) \rangle, \langle (c_1', \{a\}), (s_2, \emptyset) \rangle, \langle (c_1', \emptyset), (c_2', \emptyset) \rangle\}$$

2.3   Idempotent Bisimulations

If we assume that the execution of actions should be not only commutative, but also idempotent, so that after executing once an action a the repeated execution of that action is of no use but has no negative consequence either, then we are in a scenario where we should use the powerset constructor $\mathcal{P}$ instead of using multisets. Then we can define an exact ic-bisimulation as follows:

Definition 5. *An* exact ic-bisimulation *relating states of* $(S, A, \rightarrow)$ *is a relation* $R \subseteq S \times S \times \mathcal{P}(A)$ *that satisfies*

- $(s_1, s_2, P) \in R$, $s_1 \xrightarrow{a} s_1' \Rightarrow \exists s_2 \xRightarrow{\alpha} s_2'$ such that $P \cup \{a\} = P \cup \{\alpha\}$ and $(s_1', s_2', P \cup \{a\}) \in R$
- $(s_1, s_2, P) \in R$, $s_2 \xrightarrow{a} s_2' \Rightarrow \exists s_1 \xRightarrow{\alpha} s_1'$ such that $P \cup \{a\} = P \cup \{\alpha\}$ and $(s_1', s_2', P \cup \{a\}) \in R$.

We define as usual the corresponding bisimilarity notion $\sim_{eic}$.

Note that in this case we do not need two sets of remembered actions because the related states have to correspond to the common set of executed actions P. Instead, we need a perpetuous memory, since we consider that the repeated execution of an action, from the very beginning, does not have any consequence, so that it can be replicated by executing any sequence of actions in P^*. We could also imagine that once an action has been executed, and therefore included in the set of executed actions P, from then on the repeated execution of actions in P behaves as if they had become internal actions, so that we could also say that our ic-bisimulations is a kind of dynamic weak bisimulation.

Besides, we could define the corresponding amortized ic-bisimulations and bounded versions of these new bisimilarity notions, where we can also limit the length of the replicating sequences α. This would be related with efficiency issues, in which we want to impose the condition that the number of actions executed by comparable computations of two bisimilar processes will be somehow similar.

Obviously, we can also define checkpoint idempotent bisimulations, although in this case we should also allow replicating steps $\xRightarrow{\alpha}$ in the right-hand side of the defining conditions, since due to the idempotence of actions we could need to repeat the execution of some actions in order to reach the adequate bisimilar state, so that the lengths of two equivalent computations could be different.

2.4 Amortized Quantitative Bisimulation

There have recently been two approaches to amortized bisimulation [15, 30], where the authors had to develop by hand the corresponding theories, in order to proof the good properties of the new bisimulation notions they introduce. These amortized notions, besides the replication of the execution of an action, impose that the total costs of the actions executed by two comparable computations are somehow similar. Next we present our simple proposal for a symmetric notion of amortized bisimulation.

Definition 6. *A weighted lts is a tuple* $(S, A, \rightarrow, w)$ *where* $(S, A, \rightarrow)$ *is an lts and* $w : \{s \xrightarrow{a} s' \in \rightarrow\} \rightarrow \mathcal{P}(\mathbb{R}^+)$.

The function w represents the cost of the execution of a transition. It returns a set of possible costs, because once we have represented the set of transitions as a set, and not as a multiset, this is the way we can represent the possibility of having several ways, with different costs, to execute the same transition.

From now on, we write just $s \xrightarrow[c]{a} s'$ whenever $c \in w(s \xrightarrow{a} s')$.

Definition 7. *An amortized bisimulation relating states of* $(S, A, \rightarrow, w)$ *for the absolute bound* $B \in \mathbb{R}^+$ *is a relation* $R \subseteq S \times S \times [-B, B]$ *that satisfies*

$$- (s_1, s_2, d) \in R \wedge s_1 \xrightarrow[c_1]{a} s_1' \Rightarrow \exists s_2 \xrightarrow[c_2]{a} s_2' \text{ and } (s_1', s_2', d - c_1 + c_2) \in R,$$

$$- (s_1, s_2, d) \in R \wedge s_2 \xrightarrow[c_1]{a} s_2' \Rightarrow \exists s_1 \xrightarrow[c_2]{a} s_1' \text{ and } (s_1', s_2', d - c_1 + c_2) \in R.$$

We write $\sim_{ab}^B$ for the amortized bisimilarity relation. As for any other relation expressing an inexact or approximated equivalence, these amortized bisimilarity relations are not equivalence relations, because we can have $P_1 \sim_{ab}^B P_2 \sim_{ab}^B P_3$ but not $P_1 \sim_{ab}^B P_3$. Instead, they behave as a distance measure, so that we have $P_1 \sim_{ab}^{B_1} P_2 \sim_{ab}^{B_2} P_3 \Rightarrow P_1 \sim_{ab}^{B_1+B_2} P_3$. Oppositely to what was done in [15], we have defined a symmetric relation that can be read as "similarly fast on the large", and not an order relation "amortized faster". We could get an equivalence relation related to the amortized costs by taking $\sim_{ab} = \bigcup \sim_{ab}^B$. Obviously, this would be the full relation if we just considered finite processes, but it becomes interesting for infinite behaviours where this coalgebraic notion accurately reflects the notion of "equal amortized cost".

We can also define an exact distance relation between processes by taking $d_{ab}(P, Q) = min\{B \mid P \sim_{ab}^B Q\}$, which has all the properties imposed to a topological distance relation.

Instead of a pure absolute amortized character that imposes the common bound B, that does not take into account the length of computations, we could also define a relativized amortized bisimilarity as follows

Definition 8. *A relativized amortized bisimulation relating states of $(S, A, \rightarrow, w)$ for the margin $B \in \mathbb{R}^+$ is a relation $R \subseteq (S, S, \mathbb{R}, \mathbb{N})$ that satisfies:*

$$- (s_1, s_2, r, n) \in R \Rightarrow |r| \leq B \cdot n,$$

$$- (s_1, s_2, r, n) \in R \wedge s_1 \xrightarrow[c_1]{a} s_1' \Rightarrow \exists s_2 \xrightarrow[c_2]{a} s_2' \ (s_1', s_2', r - c_1 + c_2, n + 1) \in R,$$

$$- (s_1, s_2, r, n) \in R \wedge s_2 \xrightarrow[c_2]{a} s_2' \Rightarrow \exists s_1 \xrightarrow[c_1]{a} s_1' \ (s_1', s_2', r - c_1 + c_2, n + 1) \in R.$$

We write $\sim_{ra}^B$ for the relativized amortized bisimilarity relation.

It is clear that this relativized notion is closer to the simple approximated cost bisimilarity that just imposed the simulation of the execution of an action with a given cost by executing the same action with a similar cost.

2.5   Bisimulations with Non-atomic Actions

In order to prepare the field for other more interesting examples, here we discuss the case in which the transitions are labelled not with a single action but with a multiset of actions. Then we can replicate the executions of $\xrightarrow{C}$ with $C \subseteq A$ by executing $\xrightarrow{\overline{C}}$ with $\overline{C} = C_1 \cdot \ldots \cdot C_k$ and $C = \bigcup_{i=1}^{k} C_i$, to get a plain non-atomic actions bisimulation, whose induced bisimilarity relation we denote by $\sim_{naa}$. It is immediate to define the corresponding non-atomic actions versions of our checkpoint, idempotent or amortized quantitative bisimulations.

2.6   Distributed Bisimulations

Let us now consider the case in which we have distributed systems composed by agents that execute their actions in parallel. A first simple proposal corresponds to the case in which any agent is just a state of a common ordinary lts.

Definition 9. *A* plain distributed bisimulation *relating multisets of states of* $(S, A, \rightarrow)$ *is a relation* $R \subseteq \mathcal{MS}(S) \times \mathcal{MS}(S)$, *that satisfies:*

- $(M_1, M_2) \in R$, $\{s_1^1, \ldots, s_k^1\} = N_1 \subseteq M_1 \wedge \forall i \in \{1, \ldots, k\}$ $s_i^1 \xrightarrow{a_i} s_i'^1 \Rightarrow$
  $\exists N_2 = \{s_1^2, \ldots, s_k^2\} \subseteq M_2, \forall i \in \{1, \ldots, k\}$ $s_i^2 \xrightarrow{a_i} s_i'^2 \wedge (M_1', M_2') \in R$, *where*
  $M_j' = M_j - N_j + \{s_1'^j, \ldots, s_k'^j\}$, $\forall j \in \{1, 2\}$,
- $(M_1, M_2) \in R$, $\{s_1^2, \ldots, s_k^2\} = N_2 \subseteq M_2 \wedge \forall i \in \{1, \ldots, k\}$ $s_i^2 \xrightarrow{a_i} s_i'^2 \Rightarrow$
  $\exists N_1 = \{s_1^1, \ldots, s_k^1\} \subseteq M_1, \forall i \in \{1, \ldots, k\}$ $s_i^1 \xrightarrow{a_i} s_i'^1 \wedge (M_1', M_2') \in R$, *where*
  $M_j' = M_j - N_j + \{s_1'^j, \ldots, s_k'^j\}$, $\forall j \in \{1, 2\}$.

We say that two systems given by two multisets of actions M_1 and M_2 are distributely bisimilar, and we write $M_1 \sim_d M_2$, if there exists a distributed bisimulation that contains the pair (M_1, M_2).

Under this simple definition, it is clear that in order to be distributely bisimilar, two systems must have the same set of non-completed agents, where we say that s is a completed agent if there is no transition $s \xrightarrow{a} s'$. Instead, the defined equivalence already has an interesting parallel character, so that it does not coincide with the plain bisimulation equivalence that would be obtained by considering the corresponding interleaving semantics.

There are many ways in which we can get more realistic distributed bisimulation notions by extending or modifying the definition above, either by modifying the conditions imposed to the bisimulations, or by defining an adequate notion of distributed transition system.

The first proposal in the first direction is just the combination of the definitions of both distributed and non-atomic actions bisimulation, thus making possible to replicate the simultaneous execution of $s_i^1 \xrightarrow{C_i^1} s_i'^1$ with $N_1 = \{s_1^1, \ldots, s_k^1\} \subseteq$ M_1, by means of $N_2 = \{s_1^2, \ldots, s_l^2\} \subseteq M_2$ with $s_j^2 \xrightarrow{C_j^2} s_j'^2$ and $\bigcup_{i=1}^{k} C_i^1 = \bigcup_{j=1}^{l} C_j^2$.

We could also remove the partial synchronous character of this definition by allowing the sequential firing of transitions in the replicating system, thus getting $s_j^2 \xRightarrow{\overline{C_j^2}} s_j'^2$ with $\bigcup_{i=1}^{k} C_i^1 = \bigcup_{j=1}^{l} \overline{C_j^2}$, where by abuse of notation we are identifying the sequences of multisets $\overline{C_j^2}$ with the multiset composed of its elements.

Obviously, starting from these asynchronous, non-atomic actions, distributed semantics, we could easily define the corresponding checkpoint idempotent or amortized quantitative bisimulation.

In the opposite direction, we could define specific notions of distributed lts's by incorporating special transitions for the creation of agents, or mechanisms to synchronize the firing of transitions when needed. We do not need a special mechanism for the removal of agents since that can be easily represented by means of completed states of the system. Just to give a concrete proposal, which is at the same time flexible and simple, we present the following:

Definition 10. *A distributed transition system is a tuple* $(S, A, \mapsto)$ *where* S *is a set of states,* A *is a set of actions (possibly somehow structured) and* $\mapsto$ *is a distributed transition relation, which means* $\mapsto \subseteq S \times A \times \mathcal{P}(S)$. *A concrete distributed system based on* $(S, A, \mapsto)$ *is just a multiset* $M \in \mathcal{MS}(S)$. *We call each state in* M *an agent of the system.*

In order to impose the adequate synchronization conditions we introduce the following firing rule for distributed transitions:

Definition 11. *We define a synchronized distributed system as a pair* $\langle (S, A, \mapsto), \mathcal{Z} \rangle$, *where* $(S, A, \mapsto)$ *is a plain distributed transition system and* $\mathcal{Z} \subseteq \mathcal{MS}(A)$ *defines the allowed steps of the computations of the system: given a concrete system for it* $M \in \mathcal{MS}(S)$, *we say that* $M \overset{Z}{\Rightarrow} M'$ *is a computation step of the system if* $Z = \{a_1, \ldots, a_n\} \in \mathcal{Z}$ *and there exists* $N = \{s_1, \ldots, s_k\} \subseteq M$ *with* $s_i \overset{a_i}{\mapsto} S'_i$ *for all* $i \in \{1, \ldots, k\}$ *and* $M' = M - N + \sum_{i=1}^{k} S'_i$.

This is indeed quite a general synchronization framework that allows the consideration of autonomous actions that can be executed by a single agent without having to synchronize ($\{a\} \in \mathcal{Z}$), pairs of synchronizing actions in the CCS style ($\{a, \bar{a}\} \in \mathcal{Z}$), and general synchronizing steps ($Z \in \mathcal{Z}$) as they were introduced in E-LOTOS [13]. The framework even considers broadcasting scenarios: if a represents the communication of an action, and $\bar{a}_1, \ldots, \bar{a}_k$ represent the reception of that information by all the "participants" of the system, so that at least one agent of each participant receives the information, then we can represent this scenario by having ($\{a\} + \sum_{i=1}^{k} k_i \cdot \bar{a}_i) \in \mathcal{Z}$ if and only if for all $i \in \{1, \ldots, k\}$ $k_i \geq 1$. We have used an instance of this synchronization model in our ubiquitous nets [10], where we have both autonomous transitions and synchronization transitions that represent the offering and request of services to providers.

3   A Quick Survey on Useful Abstract Bisimulation Results

As we said in the introduction, one of the main objectives of this introductory paper is to establish a bridge between the existing theoretical results that could support our Formal Methods and the concrete application of these results. Whenever the need for new formal methods is detected in one field, we always start by developing ad-hoc theories that are as simple as possible, but close enough to the concrete application that has motivated its introduction. Certainly, these first steps are usually only partially satisfactory from both points of view: the theories are not too general, and at the same time they use to be unnecessarily involved and even clumsy; on the other side, they are only adequate to solve simple cases, or cover partial aspects of what we want to cope in our applications.

When a successful, or at least quite promising new theory attracts the attention of both theoreticians and practitioners we hopefully get quite a heap of nice theoretical results and suggestions for interesting applications. But the problem appears when both communities separate each other because the theoretical studies need quite complicate foundations that produce involved theories that practitioners cannot understand in detail. In many cases this produces a negative attitude which, at the end, even considers those theoretical studies as useless, since they seem unapplicable in practice. On the other side, those nice theories become even more difficult to be understood because nobody looks for interesting and simple examples which, besides illustrating them, constitute a concrete case in which many useful results can be obtained for free, once it is presented as an instance of the general theory first produced.

The formal theory whose great interest we want to illustrate by the long collection of complex notions of bisimulations for distributed systems presented in the previous section, is that of categorical bisimulations [1, 23, 16], that provide a general notion of bisimulation; and categorical simulations [14], that more than a general notion of simulation provide a relaxation of the notion of bisimulation that preserves most of its coalgebraic framework, thus maintaining most of its nice (co)algebraic properties. By lack of space, we cannot give here even their formal definitions in full detail. You could check (and hopefully read in detail) the beautiful studies cited above to look for the details.

We can see a functor $F : Sets \rightarrow Sets$ as a constructor of the "set of successors" of the states of a class of systems. Besides, we need a natural translation of the functions relating two sets of states, that preserves composition and identity functions, that is, $\forall f : X \rightarrow Y,\ g : Y \rightarrow Z,\ F(g \circ f) = F(g) \circ F(f)$ and $F(Id_X) = Id_{F(X)}$.

For instance, for the notion of commutative checkpoint bisimulation in Sect. 2.1 we would need a functor $F_{chk}(\overline{X}) = \{0,1\} \times MS(A) \times \mathcal{P}(A \times \overline{X})$, where roughly the elements of $\overline{X}$ correspond to the tuples in $\{0,1\} \times S \times MS(A)$, so that they keep memory of the multiset of executed actions since the last checkpoint, and indicate us if that state is a checkpoint or not.

F-coalgebras are just functions $\alpha : X \longrightarrow FX$. Then F-bisimulations can be characterized by means of spans, using the general categorical definition by Aczel and Mendler [1]:

$$
\begin{array}{ccccc}
X & \xleftarrow{\ r_1\ } & R & \xrightarrow{\ r_1\ } & Y \\
{\scriptstyle c}\downarrow & & {\scriptstyle e}\downarrow & & \downarrow{\scriptstyle d} \\
FX & \xleftarrow{\ Fr_1\ } & FR & \xrightarrow{\ Fr_2\ } & FY
\end{array}
$$

R is a bisimulation iff it is the carrier of some coalgebra e making the above diagram commute, where the r_i are the projections of R into X and Y.

We can also define them by relation lifting: given $R \subseteq X \times Y$, we take

$$Rel(F)(R) = \{(u,v) \in FX \times FY \mid \exists w \in F(R)\ \ u = Fr_1(w) \wedge v = Fr_2(w)\}$$

Then, F-bisimulations are just the support of any $Rel(F)$-coalgebra.

We will also need the general concept of simulation introduced by Hughes and Jacobs [14] using orders on functors. Let $F : Sets \rightarrow Sets$ be a functor. An order on F is defined by means of a functorial collection of preorders $\sqsubseteq_X \subseteq FX \times FX$ that must be preserved by renaming: for every $f : X \longrightarrow Y$, if $u \sqsubseteq_X u'$ then $Ff(u) \sqsubseteq_Y Ff(u')$.

Given an order $\sqsubseteq$ on F, a $\sqsubseteq$-simulation for coalgebras $c : X \longrightarrow FX$ and $d : Y \longrightarrow FY$ is a relation $R \subseteq X \times Y$ such that

$$\text{if } (x, y) \in R \text{ then } (c(x), d(y)) \in Rel(F)_{\sqsubseteq}(R),$$

where $Rel(F)_{\sqsubseteq}(R)$ is $\sqsubseteq \circ Rel(F)(R) \circ \sqsubseteq$, which can be expanded to

$$Rel(F)_{\sqsubseteq}(R) = \{(u, v) \mid \exists w \in F(\mathcal{R}). \ u \sqsubseteq Fr_1(w) \wedge Fr_2(w) \sqsubseteq v\}.$$

As we discuss in [12], it could be argued that the class of simulations obtained in this way is perhaps too broad. For example, we would expect simulations to be asymmetric order relations. However, equivalence (functorial) relations, represented by $\equiv$, are a particular class of orders on F, thus generating the corresponding class of $\equiv$-simulations. As it is the case for ordinary bisimulations, $\equiv$-simulations themselves need not be equivalence relations, but the induced notion of $\equiv$-similarity clearly is.

Let us briefly explain what is the idea behind this quite nice relaxation of the notion of F-bisimulation: any F-bisimulation has to satisfy a local coherency condition which roughly says that the successors of two related states $(s_1, s_2) \in R$ can be paired each other getting the same attributes when comparing information not in X, and states also related by R, when we compare elements in X. The introduction of the order $\sqsubseteq$ allows us to change these sets of successors according to it, before comparing them as indicated above. Obviously, the possibility of modifying those sets makes it easier to get the needed correspondence and, therefore, for any order $\sqsubseteq$ on F, the corresponding $\sqsubseteq$-similarity relation is weaker than F-bisimulation. In particular, by means of the adequate orderings, we will be able to relax the condition imposed by bisimulations: any information in the successors of two related states not corresponding to the "reached sets" must be exactly the same.

As a consequence, we cannot define any of our bisimulation notions that need the use of any kind of memory as plain F-bisimulations. Instead, we can capture those notions of memory and the necessary comparisons between them by means of the adequate notion of order on F. Next, we will illustrate all this by means of our first notion of commutative checkpoint bisimulation. For the functor F_{chk} we define the equivalence $\equiv_{chk}$ as follows:

- $(0, M, T) \equiv_{chk} (0, M', T') \ \forall M, M', T, T'$ with

$$T = \{(a_i, s_i) \mid i \in \{1, \ldots, k\}\} \Leftrightarrow T' = \{(a'_i, s_i) \mid i \in \{1, \ldots, k\}\},$$

- $(1, M, T) \equiv_{chk} (1, M, T') \ \forall M, T, T'$ with

$$T = \{(a_i, s_i) \mid i \in \{1, \ldots, k\}\} \Leftrightarrow T' = \{(a'_i, s_i) \mid i \in \{1, \ldots, k\}\}.$$

The idea is that whenever we are in a checkpoint the remembered multiset of executed actions must be the same, so that $\equiv_{chk}$ does not allow to change them. However, if we are not in a checkpoint, we do not need to compare the remembered multisets at all. This is why $\equiv_{chk}$ allows to change any of the compared values, thus making it equal to the other in order to satisfy the equality imposed "in the middle of the condition" defining $\equiv_{chk}$-simulations. Note also that the actions executed in the transitions need not to be compared, so that we can always change an action a_i by any other a_i'.

In many of the bisimulation notions that we have defined in this paper, we need to consider transition sequences instead of plain transitions, for instance when defining our amortized commutative bisimulations. Certainly, all these equivalence notions could be studied by means of the derived step transition system $\overset{\alpha}{\Rightarrow}$, as it is done when characterizing the ordinary weak bisimulation as a strong bisimulation on the expanded system $\Rightarrow$. However, we do not want to explicitly construct such a tremendous system which, in fact, presents any computation of the original system as a single transition of the derived step transition system, thus completely losing the ability of reasoning on the full behaviour of a system in a local way. In other words, by expanding the original transition system and then defining bisimulation relations we are apparently still using a coalgebraic language, but the spirit of coinduction that means getting global properties by local reasonings has completely disappeared in practice.

There are a few recent works on the categorical definition of weak bisimulation and step semantics. In particular, a part of the results and techniques used in [26] can be used to formalize several of the new bisimulation notions introduced in this paper, following the general ideas sketched in [25]. Another more technical approach to the subject is that in [22], which needs a more careful study and more developments in order to find the way of using their ideas easily.

4   (Not so Much) Related Work

Since its official introduction in [18], although we can find some related concepts in several older works devoted to different subjects, as explained in [24], quite a number of generalizations of the bisimulation equivalence have been proposed. However, these generalizations tend to preserve more of the structure of processes, thus obtaining even finer equivalences than bisimulation. For instance, in [5] Castellani et al. define a so called distributed bisimulation that deals with the distributed nature of processes, by distinguishing between concurrent processes and nondeterministic but sequential processes. As a consequence, the processes $a|b$ and $ab + ba$ are not identified by this semantics.

In [4], Boudol et al. follow the same intention, that of defining a notion of bisimulation that distinguishes between concurrency and sequential nondeterminism. However, unlike in [5], where the authors focus on the distributed nature of processes, here the authors focus on the atomicity of actions by adding extra structure in the labels of transitions, which become partially ordered sets.

Fig. 3. Bisimilar but not FC-bisimilar nets

Again, the resulting bisimulation semantics is stronger than strong bisimulation. For instance, processes $a|b$, $ab+ba$ and $ab+(a|b)+ba$ are all distinct with respect to that semantics.

Another interesting collection of works, that in this case also introduce a general categorical approach based on so called open maps, is [17, 9, 19], where again a stronger semantics based on event structures that capture the causal relation between actions is studied. History-preserving bisimulation studied by W.Vogler [28] and Maximality preserving bisimulation [7] are other bisimulation semantics for Petri Nets and related models that are based on the so called process semantics for them. This kind of semantics became very popular in the first nineties when action refinement was studied in depth looking for a modular semantics that would be preserved by the implementation of complex actions by means of the corresponding processes (see for instance [29]). In the same direction we can find [2], that presents FC-bisimulation (standing for Fully Concurrent), based on the process semantics of Petri nets, also preserving the level of concurrency. For instance, the two simple nets in Fig. 3 are strong bisimilar, but not FC-bisimilar.

However, when we tried to find previous work on weaker bisimulation semantics we have found nearly nothing, out of, of course, anything related with the classical weak bisimulation. Probably, there is a formal reason why that is the case: any classical bisimulation equivalence imposes the equality of all the compared information, out of the consideration of the compared states themselves, and besides, it has to be defined in a local way. Both conditions produce rather strong equivalences as discussed above.

In order to get weaker equivalences one possibility is to consider adequate bisimulation up-to relations, as we have successfully done in [11], getting coalgebraic characterizations of any semantics in Van Glabbeek's spectrum [27]. The other possibility is to consider categorical simulations, as we have explored in this paper. As a matter of fact, there are some connections between these two approaches, since both relax the proof obligations imposed by the clauses defining bisimulations, by introducing up-to mechanisms. However, an important difference is that orders on functors can only be based in local information in the successors of the compared states, and thus categorial simulations have many pleasant coalgebraic properties. Instead, in [11] we had to renounce to these pure local definitions, since we wanted to characterize all the classical extensional semantics, such as failures or trace semantics, that cannot be captured by local conditions.

5   Conclusions and Future Work

By means of the new coalgebraic semantics for distributed systems presented in this paper, we have tried to narrow the gap between theoretical developments on categorical bisimulations and the applications of coalgebraic techniques to define and study new interesting semantics for distributed systems. Certainly, this is just an introductory paper that, however, already shows the applicability of some recent general results on categorical simulations and categorical weak bisimulations. These results allow us to guarantee that our new bisimulation-like semantics are indeed coalgebraically based, so that they have all the good properties of this kind of semantics, without the need to prove them again, because they were established and proved once and forever.

There are two directions for further work on the subject: we have to present in detail the reformulations of our new semantics in the categorical framework. We have already done it for most of the semantics presented in the paper, either by directly presenting them as instances of the categorical definition of simulation or by using a step semantics defined by hand, for the cases in which we need to consider sequences of transitions in the definitions. As mentioned above, there is not a general theory for categorical step semantics available yet, and therefore in this case we need either to wait for those general results or to apply the particular cases that have already been solved, which fortunately correspond in particular to the functors defining the kind of transition systems in which we are interested.

Concerning the applications, we hope to motivate the people working in the field to consider the new semantics introduced in this paper, looking for those that could be more useful in practice. Practitioners have always considered bisim-ulation semantics not so useful because the equivalence it defines is too strong. By relaxing the conditions to become equivalent, but maintaining the good prop-erties of coalgebraic semantics, we could obtain new promising semantics, and then develop for them all the machinery that makes applicable in practice the bisimulation semantics.

References

[1] Aczel, P., Mendler, N.P.: A final coalgebra theorem. In: Dybjer, P., Pitts, A.M., Pitt, D.H., Poigné, A., Rydeheard, D.E. (eds.) Category Theory and Computer Science. LNCS, vol. 389, pp. 357–365. Springer, Heidelberg (1989)
[2] Best, E., Devillers, R., Kiehn, A., Pomello, L.: Concurrent bisimulation in Petri nets. In: Acta Informatica, vol. 28, pp. 231–264. Springer, Heidelberg (1991)
[3] Bloom, B., Istrail, S., Meyer, A.R.: Bisimulation can't be traced. Journal of ACM 42(1), 232–268 (1995)
[4] Boudol, G., Castellani, I.: Concurrency and atomicity. In: Theoretical Computer Science, vol. 59, pp. 25–84. Elsevier, North-Holland (1988)
[5] Castellani, I., Hennessy, M.: Distributed bisimulations. Journal of the ACM 36(4), 887–911 (1989)
[6] de Simone, R.: Higher-Level Synchronising Devices in Meije-SCCS. In: Theoretical Computer Science, vol. 37, pp. 245–267. Elsevier, North-Holland (1985)

[7] Devillers, R.R.: Maximality Preserving Bisimulation. In: Theor. Comput. Sci., vol. 102(1), pp. 165–183. Elsevier, North-Holland (1992)

[8] Dovier, A., Piazza, C., Policriti, A.: An efficient algorithm for computing bisimulation equivalence. In: Theoretical Computer Science, vol. 311, pp. 221–256. Elsevier, North-Holland (2004)

[9] Fiore, M.P., Cattani, G.L., Winskel, G.: Weak Bisimulation and Open Maps. In: Logic in Computer Science, LICS 1999, pp. 67–76. IEEE Computer Society, Los Alamitos (1999)

[10] Frutos-Escrig, D., Marroquín-Alonso, O., Rosa-Velardo, F.: Ubiquitous Systems and Petri Nets. In: Ubiquitous Web Systems and Intelligence. LNCS, vol. 3841, Springer, Heidelberg (2005)

[11] Frutos-Escrig, D., Gregorio-Rodríguez, C.: Bisimulations Up-to for the Linear Time Branching Time Spectrum. In: Abadi, M., de Alfaro, L. (eds.) CONCUR 2005. LNCS, vol. 3653, pp. 278–292. Springer, Heidelberg (2005)

[12] Frutos-Escrig, D., Palomino, M., Fábregas, I.: Searching for a canonical notion of simulation (In preparation)

[13] Lucero, G.F., Quemada, J.: Specifying the ODP Trader: An Introduction to E-LOTOS. In: 10th Int.Conf. on Formal Description Techniques and Protocol Specification, Testing and Verification, FORTE'97. IFIP Conference Proceedings, vol. 107, pp. 127–142. Chapman & Hall, Sydney (1998)

[14] Hughes, J., Jacobs, B.: Simulations in coalgebra. Theoretical Computer Science 327(1-2), 71–108 (2004)

[15] Kiehn, A., Arun-Kumar, S.: Amortized bisimulations. In: Wang, F. (ed.) FORTE 2005. LNCS, vol. 3731, pp. 320–334. Springer, Heidelberg (2005)

[16] Jacobs, B.: Introduction to coalgebra. Towards mathematics of states and observations. Book in preparation. Available, at
http://www.cs.ru.nl/B.Jacobs/CLG/JacobsCoalgebraIntro.pdf

[17] Joyal, A., Nielsen, M., Winskel, G.: Bisimulation and open maps. In: Logic in Computer Science, LICS'93, IEEE Computer Society, Los Alamitos (1993)

[18] Milner, R.: A Calculus of Communicating Systems. LNCS, vol. 92. Springer, Heidelberg (1980)

[19] Nielsen, M., Winskel, G.: Petri Nets and Bisimulation. Theor. Comput. Sci. 153(1&2), 211–244 (1996)

[20] Park, D.: Concurrency and automata on infinite sequences. In: 5th GI-Conference on Theoretical Computer Science, pp. 167–183. Springer, Heidelberg (1981)

[21] Plotkin, G.D.: A structural approach to operational semantics. TR DAIMI FN-19, Computer Science Dept., Aarhus Univ. (1981)

[22] Rothe, J., Mašulović,D.: A syntactical approach to weak (bi)-simulation for coalgebras. In: Coalgebraic Methods in Computer Science, CMCS'02. ENTCS, vol. 65(1) Elsevier (2002)

[23] Rutten, J.J.M.M.: Universal coalgebra: a theory of systems. Theoretical Computer Science 249(1), 3–80 (2000)

[24] Sangiorgi, D.: Bisimulation and Co-induction: Some Problems. In: Electr. Notes Theor. Comput. Sci., vol. 162, pp. 311–315. Elsevier, North-Holland (2006)

[25] Sokolova, A.: On compositions and paths for coalgebras. Technical report CSR-05-26, TU Eindhoven (2005)

[26] Sokolova, A., de Vink, E.P., Woracek, H.: Weak Bisimulation for Action-Type Coalgebras. In: Category Theory and Computer Science, CTCS'04. ENTCS, vol. 112, pp. 211–228. Elsevier, North-Holland (2005)

[27] van Glabbeek, R.: The linear time - branching time spectrum I; the semantics of concrete, sequential processes. In: Handbook of Process Algebra Chapter 1, pp. 3–99. Elsevier, North-Holland (2001)

[28] Vogler, W.: Deciding History Preserving Bisimilarity. In: Leach Albert, J., Monien, B., Rodríguez-Artalejo, M. (eds.) Automata, Languages and Programming. LNCS, vol. 510, pp. 495–505. Springer, Heidelberg (1991)

[29] Vogler, W.: Bisimulation and Action Refinement. Theor. Comput. Sci. 114(1), 173–200 (1993)

[30] Lüttgen, G., Vogler, W.: Bisimulation on speed: A unified approach. Theor. Comput. Sci. 360(1-3), 209–227 (2006)

Event Correlation with Boxed Pomsets

Thomas Gazagnaire[1] and Loïc Hélouët[2]

[1] IRISA/ENS Cachan, Campus de Beaulieu, 35042 Rennes Cedex, France
[2] IRISA/INRIA, Campus de Beaulieu, 35042 Rennes Cedex, France

Abstract. This paper proposes a diagnosis framework for distributed systems based on pomset languages. Diagnosis is performed by projecting these models on a collection of observable labels and then synchronization with an observation. This paper first proposes a new model called boxed pomset languages, which extends classical pomset-based languages as so called High-level Message Sequence Charts. It can describe infinite scenarios, and has good properties with respect to projections. We then give a solution for the event correlation problem (knowing whether two observed alarms are causally related) for pomset languages.

1 Introduction

Communication systems have become more and more complex over the recent years. Usually, several telecommunication operators share the same physical network to provide services to their clients. In this context, when a breakdown occurs, finding what really happened and who is responsible for it is becoming a major challenge.

Such kind of telecommunication breakdown happened in France in November 2004. In several towns, the whole telecommunication network was unavailable, and worse, even emergency numbers were disabled. It took a full day to restore normal communication. The cause for this trouble was made public much later: a software error in a voice over IP application had forced several equipments to switch off, and as a result, the whole network collapsed.

Similarly, the spreading of DSL (still with several operators sharing a common network) now cause some reliability problems. When a breakdown occurs the problem may be due to the physical network (at the level of the local hook-up or at upper levels), to the service provider, or even worse it may be a consequence of bad interactions between services from several providers. In this situation, finding the cause of the failure is difficult, and the time to get an explanation may be several weeks. According to France Telecom,[1] several providers did not develop sufficient tools needed to detect faults in networks. Beyond technical concerns (repairing the incriminated hardware or replacing software), there are also economical reasons for diagnosis techniques: one wants to find *who* is responsible for a failure of the system - or equivalently *what is the root cause* of the failure. In such a situation, the origin of a breakdown becomes as important as the fault itself.

---

[1] Le monde, 01/08/2007.

J. Derrick and J. Vain (Eds.): FORTE 2007, LNCS 4574, pp. 160–176, 2007.
© IFIP International Federation for Information Processing 2007

In order to quickly fix problems, almost every part of a modern network provides data about what it is doing: operating systems log systems and security events, servers keep records of what they do, applications log errors, warnings and failures, firewalls and VPN gateways record suspicious traffic, routers and switches watch packets between network segments,... In a protocol such as Simple Network Management Protocol (SNMP) [7], these equipments forward alerts to a central management console. Besides monitoring their own behavior, all these agents receive and relay messages from other network components, and may in turn generate new alerts, leading to a propagation of an alarm over the whole network. A single problem can hence generate overabundant alarms, that are collected in huge log files. After a breakdown, these logs have to be searched, but they are often so big that data provided by the network can not be exploited without dedicated tools. Moreover, monitoring everything in a system is not possible because sensors cannot be placed everywhere, and thus only a subset of what occurs in the network is reported in logs. Hence to understand completely what happened during the failure, one needs to rely on partial observations, but also on his knowledge of the systems.

In practice, logs are often analyzed and simplified with the help of some simple rules such as *compression* (takes multiple occurrences of the same event, examines them for duplicate information, removes redundancies and reports them as a single event), *counting* (reports a specified number of similar events as a single one), *suppression* (associates priorities with alarms and suppresses an alarm with low priority if an event with higher-priority has occurred), *generalization* (generates a log of higher-level events from the initial log) [3], *correlation* which establishes "cause and effect" relation between events [12]. All these rules are implemented in expert systems, that read complete logs and output simplified log files. These summaries are then read by a specialist who tries to find a scenario for the failure and its root causes.

Additionally, several model-based formal techniques have been proposed recently to diagnose systems. Sampath et al [14] propose a fault detection technique from finite state machines (FSM), that distinguish safe and faulty states. Lafortune et al also propose a notion of diagnosability for their model. A system, described as a FSM, is diagnosable if for a given sequence of observable transitions, one cannot find two compatible runs of the system such that one that leads to a safe state, and the other to a faulty state. Jeron et al [10] describe a similar approach with enhanced fault models. Benveniste et al [2] propose Petri Nets based diagnosis techniques. They recover complete explanations from an incomplete observation using a Petri Net model of the monitored system. Hélouët et al [8] show how to recover explanations of a fault from a partial observation of a distributed system using High-Level Message Sequence Charts (HMSC) [9].

This paper investigates a model-based diagnosis technique using pomset languages, that are more powerful than FSM and HMSCs. Roughly speaking, such languages are automata labeled by partial orders. The major difference with HMSCs resides in the kind of pomset labeling the automata and in the sequential composition rule that can be parametrized. Using this model, we provide techniques to retrieve explanations (from a given partial observation o, provide all explanations; i.e. runs of the model, that are compatible with o) and to perform event correlation (infer from a partial ordering of events in an observation o whether two events should be causally related). More precisely, we show that deciding whether two observed events are ordered in all runs of a model is CoNP-complete. When the collection of possible labels is fixed and the observation has no auto-concurrency, the problem is in NLOGSPACE and we give an effective algorithm to compute the reconstructed causal order explaining the observation.

This document is organized as follows: Section 2 introduces the basic definitions of pomset languages and boxed pomset languages that will be used as models of monitored systems. Section 3 establishes the main properties of these languages. Section 4 uses these results to solve the event correlation problem. Section 5 concludes this work and gives some perspectives.

2   Pomsets, Boxed Pomsets, and Pomset Languages

Pomsets are a very natural representation to describe runs of distributed systems. Furthermore, they avoid the well known state-space explosion problem due to interleaving. Popular languages based on partial orders such as HMSCs [9] are now standardized. This section introduces a new pomset language called *boxed pomsets*, that has nice properties with respect to projection and embeds the expressive power of HMSCs. The following definitions are mainly due to Gischer [6] and were reused later by Pratt [13].

Pomsets. A *labeled partial order* (or *lpo*) over a set E with labels Σ is a structure $(E, \leq, \lambda, \Sigma)$ where $\leq$ partially orders E and $\lambda : E \rightarrow \Sigma$ assigns an element of Σ to each element of E. When needed, we will denote by $(E_p, \leq_p, \lambda_p, \Sigma_p)$ the components of lpo p. Labels in Σ should be considered as types of actions that can be performed by a system, E as instances of these actions representing *events* in a run of a distributed system. The set of all events is denoted by $\mathbb{E}$. A lpo is *auto-concurrent* iff one can find two incomparable events $e, e' \in E$ (i.e. $e \not\leq e'$ and $e' \not\leq e$) such that $\lambda(e) = \lambda(e')$.

A *map* of lpos $(f, t) : (E_1, \leq_1, \lambda_1, \Sigma_1) \rightarrow (E_2, \leq_2, \lambda_2, \Sigma_2)$ consists of a monotone map $f : (E_1, \leq_1) \rightarrow (E_2, \leq_2)$ of partially ordered sets and an alphabet map $t : \Sigma_1 \rightarrow \Sigma_2$ such that for all e in E, $\lambda_2(f(e)) = t(\lambda_1(e))$. An *isomorphism* of lpos is a map (f, t) where f is an isomorphism of partially ordered sets and t is the identity function.

A *pomset* is the isomorphism class $[E, \leq, \lambda, \Sigma]$ of a lpo $(E, \leq, \lambda, \Sigma)$. More intuitively, pomsets pay attention to cardinality , labeling and ordering of events, but not to their identity. ¿From now on, we consider that the set of events $\mathbb{E}$ and its labeling function $\lambda : \mathbb{E} \rightarrow \Sigma$ are fixed. Thus we will denote a pomset p by $[E_p, \leq_p]$ instead of $[E_p, \leq_p, \lambda_p, \Sigma_p]$, because Σ_p is a subset of Σ and λ_p is the restriction of λ to the domain E_p. We will also denote by $\mathbb{P}$ the set of all possible pomsets.

A *projection* of a pomset p on an observable alphabet Σ_o is a function $\pi_{\Sigma_o} : \mathbb{P} \rightarrow \mathbb{P}$ which restricts p to observable labels, i.e. $\pi_{\Sigma_o}(p) = [E_p \cap E_{\Sigma_o}, \leq_p \cap E_{\Sigma_o}^2]$ with $E_{\Sigma_o} = \lambda^{-1}(\Sigma_o)$.

Given a predicate ψ which associates a boolean to each pair of Σ^2, we can define the *composition* of pomsets p_1 and p_2, denoted by $p_1 \odot_\psi p_2$, or simply $p_1 \odot p_2$, as an operator that computes the disjoint union of two pomsets and then adds an ordering between all pairs of events $(e, e') \in E_{p_1} \times E_{p_2}$ such that $\psi(\lambda(e), \lambda(e'))$. More formally, we have $p_1 \odot_\psi p_2 = (E_{p_1} \uplus E_{p_2}, (\leq_1 \uplus \leq_2 \uplus \leq_\psi)^*)$ where $\leq_\psi = \{(e, e') \in E_{p_1} \times E_{p_2} \mid \psi(\lambda(e), \lambda(e'))\}$. This composition is similar to the local composition of pomsets defined by Pratt [13]. The parameterization of ψ makes the composition law able to express several classical operators such as the parallel composition when $\psi(a, b)$ is *false* for all $a, b \in \Sigma$, the strong concatenation, that is sometimes used to compose MSC's, when $\psi(a, b)$ is *true* for all $a, b \in \Sigma$, and the weak sequential concatenation when Σ is decomposed into p disjoint sets $\Sigma_1, \ldots, \Sigma_p$ representing respectively all actions that can be executed by processes $1, \ldots, p$ and $\psi(a, b)$ holds when $\exists i \in 1 \ldots p$ such that $a, b \in \Sigma_i$. From now on, when ψ is clear from the context, we will only write $p_1 \odot p_2$ instead of $p_1 \odot_\psi p_2$. Figure 1 gives an example of pomset composition and projection. Each event e is represented by a circle labeled by $\lambda(e)$. As we do not pay attention to events themselves, they are unnamed. For clarity, we only show the transitive reduction of the partial orders. Let ψ hold only for pairs in $\{(a, a); (c, c); (c, b); (c, d)\}$. The composition of pomsets p_1 and p_2 is shown on Figure 1-a. Added causalities, corresponding to $\leq_\psi$ are depicted by dotted lines. Figure 1-b shows that projections of pomsets composition is, in general, not equal to composition of pomsets projections. Indeed, for $\Sigma_o = \{a, b\}$, $p_4 = \pi_{\Sigma_o}(p_1) \odot \pi_{\Sigma_o}(p_2)$ is not isomorphic to $p_5 = \pi_{\Sigma_o}(p_1 \odot p_2)$.

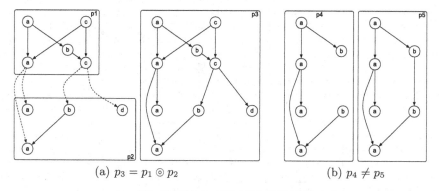

(a) $p_3 = p_1 \odot p_2$ (b) $p_4 \neq p_5$

Fig. 1. Composition of pomsets

Boxed pomsets. In order to manipulate pomsets with projection and composition more easily, we introduce a new model called *boxed pomsets*. A *port* is the isomorphism class of a subset E of $\mathbb{E}$ where each label appears at most once, i.e for every letter a of Σ, $|\lambda^{-1}(a) \cap E| \leq 1$.

A partial order $\leq$ *plugs* a set of events E_1 to another set of events E_2 when, for every label a in Σ, every event of E_1 labeled by a precedes any event in E_2 labeled by a. More formally, we note $\leq_{E_1 \leadsto E_2} = \{(e_1, e_2) \in E_1 \times E_2 \mid \lambda(e_1) = \lambda(e_2)\}$ and we say that $\leq$ plugs E_1 to E_2 iff $\leq_{E_1 \leadsto E_2} \subseteq \leq$.

Definition 1. *A* boxed pomset *is the isomorphism class* $[E^- \uplus E \uplus E^+, \leq]$ *of structures* $(E^- \uplus E \uplus E^+, \leq)$, *where* E^- *and* E^+ *are isomorphic ports called respectively* input port *and* output port, *E is a set of events called* inside box, *and* $\leq \subseteq (E^- \uplus E) \times (E \uplus E^+)$ *is a partial order relation. Moreover,* $\leq$ *plugs* E^- *to* $(E \uplus E^+)$ *and* $(E^- \uplus E)$ *to* E^+.

A boxed pomset b can be seen as an encapsulated pomset, with an access, for each label, to its maximal and minimal events, through respectively output and input ports. Events which occur before b will only interact with its input port, events which occur after b will only interact with its output port. When needed we will detail the components of boxed pomset b as $[E_b^- \uplus E_b \uplus E_b^+, \leq_b]$. The set of all boxed pomsets is denoted by $\mathbb{B}$. Figure 2 show three examples of boxed pomsets called b_1, b_2 and b_3. They are represented as pomsets in which separate rectangles distinguish clearly input ports, inside boxes and output ports. Input ports will always be located above inside boxes, and output ports below. Note that ports are not real executable events but rather pointers to minimal and maximal events of a pomset. Hence boxed pomset b_3 of Figure 2 and pomset p_3 of Figure 1-a have the same meaning.

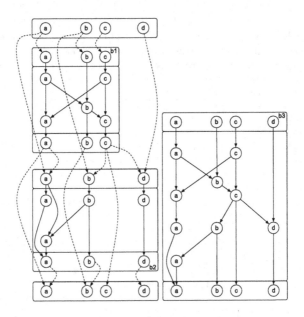

Fig. 2. Boxed pomsets, where $b_1 \boxdot b_2 = b_3$

Definition 2. *A* projection *of a boxed pomset b on an observable alphabet Σ_o is a function* $\bar{\pi}_{\Sigma_o} : \mathbb{B} \to \mathbb{B}$ *which restricts the inside box of b to events which are labeled by Σ_o, with no modification of the input and output ports, i.e.* $\bar{\pi}_{\Sigma_o}(b) = [E_b^- \uplus (E_b \cap E_{\Sigma_o}) \uplus E_b^+, \leq_b \cap (E'_{\Sigma_o})^2]$ *where* $E_{\Sigma_o} = \lambda^{-1}(\Sigma_o)$ *and* $E'_{\Sigma_o} = E_b^- \uplus E_{\Sigma_o} \uplus E_b^+$.

Ports show their usefulness with projections: they are not only labels, but are also used to memorize causal relations with events that may have occurred before or after a given pomset, that disappear during projection. We extend composition over pomsets to composition over boxed pomsets. This composition does not change the global structure of boxed pomsets: an input port, an inside box, and an output port. Intuitively, the composition of boxed pomsets b_1 and b_2, denoted by $b_1 \boxdot_\psi b_2$ (or simply $b_1 \boxdot b_2$ when ψ is clear from the context), performs the composition of intermediate ports (output port of b_1 and input port of b_2) and keeps the resulting partial order over elements of inside boxes. Input and output ports are used to compute new ports that are respectively the minimal and maximal events of the new object. More formally:

Definition 3. *Let* $b_i = [E_i^- \uplus E_i \uplus E_i^+, \leq_i]$ *for* $i \in \{1, 2\}$ *be two boxed pomsets, and* ψ *be a predicate on* Σ^2. *We define the* composition *of* b_1 *and* b_2 *as* $b_1 \boxdot_\psi b_2 = [E_{1\boxdot 2}^- \uplus E_{1\boxdot 2} \uplus E_{1\boxdot 2}^+, \leq_{1\boxdot 2}]$, *where:*

- $E_{1\boxdot 2}^-$ *is a port such that* $\lambda(E_{1\boxdot 2}^-) = \lambda(E_1^-) \cup \lambda(E_2^-)$;
- $E_{1\boxdot 2}$ *is isomorphic to* $E_1 \uplus E_2$;
- $E_{1\boxdot 2}^+$ *is a port such that* $\lambda(E_{1\boxdot 2}^+) = \lambda(E_1^+) \cup \lambda(E_2^+)$;
- $\leq_{1\boxdot 2} = (\leq_1 \cup \leq_2 \cup \leq_\psi \cup \leq_{E_{1\boxdot 2}^- \rightsquigarrow (E_1^- \uplus E_2^-)} \cup \leq_{(E_1^+ \uplus E_2^+) \rightsquigarrow E_{1\boxdot 2}^+})^* \cap E^2$ *where* $E = (E_{1\boxdot 2}^- \uplus E_{1\boxdot 2} \uplus E_{1\boxdot 2}^+)$, *and* $\leq_\psi = \{(e, e') \in E_1^+ \times E_2^- \mid \psi(\lambda(e), \lambda(e'))\}$.

Input and output ports of $b_1 \boxdot_\psi b_2$ contain labels of input and output ports of b_1 and b_2, inside box of $b_1 \boxdot b_2$ is isomorphic to the union of insides boxes of E_1 and E_2, and causality relation of $b_1 \boxdot b_2$ is the union of causality relations

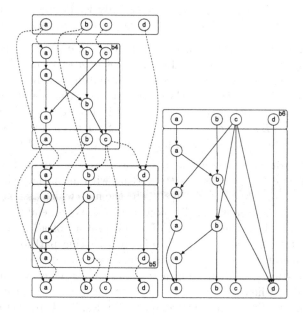

Fig. 3. Projection of boxed pomsets, where $b_4 \odot b_5 = b_6$

of b_1 and b_2, augmented with the composition of output port of b_1 with input port of b_2, projected on events of $E_{1 \square 2}^- \uplus E_{1 \square 2} \uplus E_{1 \square 2}^+$. Moreover, we also ensure that $\leq_{1 \square 2}$ plugs correctly $E_{1 \square 2}^-$, $E_{1 \square 2}$ and $E_{1 \square 2}^+$. Consider again Figure 2, and let ψ hold only for $\{(a,a); (c,c); (c,b); (c,d)\}$. Then, boxed pomset b_3 is the composition of boxed pomsets b_1 and b_2. Added causalities, corresponding to $\leq_\psi \cup \leq_{E_{1 \square 2}^- \rightsquigarrow (E_1^- \uplus E_2^-)} \cup \leq_{(E_1^+ \uplus E_2^+) \rightsquigarrow E_{1 \square 2}^+}$ are symbolized by dotted lines, and the created ports are symbolized by rectangles located respectively above and below b_4 and b_5.

Let us consider the boxed pomsets b_4, b_5 and b_6 of Figure 3 and the examples of Figure 2. In this figure, $b_4 = \bar{\pi}_{\Sigma_o}(b_1)$, $b_5 = \bar{\pi}_{\Sigma_o}(b_2)$ and if we let ψ hold for $\{(a,a), (c,c), (c,b), (c,d)\}$, then we have $b_6 = b_4 \square b_5$. Moreover, we can remark that $b_6 = \bar{\pi}_{\Sigma_o}(b_3)$. Section 3 explains more in detail the relations between pomsets and boxed pomsets, and shows that boxed pomsets have good properties with respect to projections. Hence, it will be easier to manipulate boxed pomsets than pomsets. Thus, we define morphisms to translate problems occurring in pomsets monoid $(\mathbb{P}, \circledcirc)$ to problems in boxed pomsets monoid $(\mathbb{B}, \square)$, which should be solved more easily.

The *boxing operator* $B : \mathbb{P} \to \mathbb{B}$ is used to build a boxed pomset $B(p)$ from a pomset p. The boxed pomset built has an inside box, which corresponds exactly to p, and input and output ports plugged adequately, i.e. input port is plugged to inside box and output port, and inside box is plugged to output port. Thus, $B(p)$ is defined as $B(p) = [E^- \uplus E_p \uplus E^+, (\leq_p \cup \leq_{E^- \rightsquigarrow E_p} \cup \leq_{E_p \rightsquigarrow E^+})^*]$ where E^- and E^+ are ports such that $\lambda(E^-) = \lambda(E_p) = \lambda(E^+)$.

The *unboxing operator* $U : \mathbb{B} \to \mathbb{P}$ is used to extract the inside box from a boxed pomset: $U(b) = [E_b, \leq_b \cap E_b^2]$. Let us consider pomset p_1 from Figure 1, and boxed pomset b_1 from Figure 2. We have $B(p_1) = b_1$, and $U(b_1) = p_1$.

Automata and languages. Single finite pomsets are not sufficient to provide a model for systems that may produce runs of arbitrary size. A good way to design unbounded behaviors is to use an automaton to compose an arbitrary number of pomsets, as in HMSCs. We introduce now classical definitions about automata. For a given set L, a L-*automaton* $\mathcal{A}$ is a tuple $(S, \to, L, S_0, S_f)$ where S is a set of states, L a collection of labels, $\to \subseteq S \times L \times S$ a transition relation, S_0 a set of initial states and S_f a set of final states. A *path* ρ of $\mathcal{A}$ is a succession of consecutive transitions of $\mathcal{A}$ such that $\rho = n_0 \xrightarrow{l_1} n_1 \ldots \xrightarrow{l_k} n_k$ and (n_i, l_{i+1}, n_{i+1}) are in $\to$. An *accepting path* is a path starting with an initial state and ending with a final one. We define $\alpha_*(\rho) = l_1 * \ldots * l_k$, the map which assigns to each path of a L-automaton an element of the monoid $(L, *)$. We extend this definition to L-automaton: $\mathcal{L}_*(\mathcal{A})$ is the language of $\mathcal{A}$, i.e. the set of all elements of $(L, *)$ that $\mathcal{A}$ generates : $\mathcal{L}_*(\mathcal{A}) = \{\alpha_*(\rho) \mid \rho$ is an accepting path of $\mathcal{A}\}$. When the composition operator used is not ambiguous, we write α and $\mathcal{L}$ instead of α_* and $\mathcal{L}_*$. For instance, it shall be clear that we use $\circledcirc$ when we manipulate $\mathbb{P}$-automata, and $\square$ when we manipulate $\mathbb{B}$-automata. Figure 4 gives an example of two L-automata. States are represented by circles, labels by rectangles. Initial states have an incoming arrow without source and final states have an outgoing

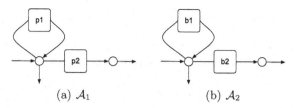

(a) $\mathcal{A}_1$ (b) $\mathcal{A}_2$

Fig. 4. Examples of L-automata

arrow without destination. $\mathcal{A}_1$ is a $\mathbb{P}$-automaton, as p_1 and p_2 (from Figure 1-a) belong to $\mathbb{P}$. $\mathcal{A}_2$ is a $\mathbb{B}$-automaton, as b_1 and b_2 (from Figure 2) belong to $\mathbb{B}$.

We extend operators over $\mathbb{P}$ and $\mathbb{B}$ to operators over $\mathbb{P}$-automata and $\mathbb{B}$-automata. From a map $f : L_1 \rightarrow L_2$, we build a new mapping operator $\mathcal{M}_f$: L_1-automata $\rightarrow L_2$-automata, such that, given $\mathcal{A}$ a L_1-automaton, $\mathcal{M}_f(\mathcal{A})$ is the L_2-automaton where each transition $(s, l, s') \in \rightarrow$ is replaced by a transition $(s, f(l), s')$. In this paper, we will mainly consider $\mathcal{M}_B$, $\mathcal{M}_U$, $\mathcal{M}_{\pi_{\Sigma_o}}$ and $\mathcal{M}_{\bar{\pi}_{\Sigma_o}}$ which are, respectively, the conversion of $\mathbb{P}$-automata to their corresponding $\mathbb{B}$-automata that replaces pomsets by boxed pomsets in transitions, the conversion of $\mathbb{B}$-automata to their corresponding $\mathbb{P}$-automata that replaces boxed pomsets in transitions by unboxed ones, the projection of $\mathbb{P}$-automata, that replaces labels of transitions by projected ones, and the projection of $\mathbb{B}$-automata, that replaces labels of transitions by projected boxed pomsets. For the examples of Figure 4 as $B(p_1) = b_1$ and $B(p_2) = b_2$, we have $\mathcal{M}_B(\mathcal{A}_1) = \mathcal{A}_2$, and conversely $\mathcal{A}_1 = \mathcal{M}_U(\mathcal{A}_2)$. Moreover, we can remark that for any automaton and a pair of mappings f and g, we have $\mathcal{M}_f(\mathcal{M}_g(\mathcal{A})) = \mathcal{M}_{fg}(\mathcal{A})$. $\mathbb{P}$-automata and $\mathbb{B}$-automata can not be considered as new models (they are just standard automata over peculiar alphabets). However, the composition laws on pomsets and boxed pomsets gives them more expressive power than simple HMSCs.

Finally, we naturally extend operators over $\mathbb{P}$ and $\mathbb{B}$ to sets of $\mathbb{P}$ and set of $\mathbb{B}$. For instance, we will write $\pi_{\Sigma_o}(\mathcal{L})$ instead of $\{\pi_{\Sigma_o}(p) \mid p \in \mathcal{L}\}$.

3 Properties of Boxed Pomsets

This section introduces the main properties of boxed pomsets. First, we introduce basic properties of the operators defined in Section 2. Then we show several results on pomset languages and their projections. The nice properties of boxed pomsets with respect to projection motivate the use of this new model to answer diagnosis problems, as a natural way to consider partial observation is to work with projected runs of a model. More especially, Theorem 2, gives an automaton construction for the projection of any pomset automaton.

Let us first consider basic properties of B and U operators with respect to projection and composition. We will focus essentially on pomset and boxed pomsets objects, i.e. we will not consider pomset and boxed pomset languages. Proposition 1 below states that the boxing operation is the inverse relation of the unboxing one. Note that as the unboxing operation is not injective, the converse property does not hold.

Proposition 1. *Let p be a pomset. Then $UB(p) = p$.*

The following proposition shows that boxed pomset projection is a kind of dual operation of pomset projection, used with unboxing operator.

Proposition 2. *Let b be a boxed pomset labeled by Σ, and Σ_o be a subset of Σ. Then, $\pi_{\Sigma_o} U(b) = U \bar{\pi}_{\Sigma_o}(b)$.*

Proposition 3 shows that pomset composition and boxed pomset composition are also strongly related. Unlike projections, compositions are not compatible with unboxing operator as in general $U(b_1) \odot U(b_2)$ is not equal to $U(b_1 \boxdot b_2)$. Fortunately boxing operation and compositions work well together:

Proposition 3. *Let p_1 and p_2 be two pomsets. Then $B(p_1 \odot p_2) = B(p_1) \boxdot B(p_2)$.*

The above propositions give us some basic tools to manipulate pomsets and boxed pomsets together with projections. Let us now focus on pomset and boxed pomset languages. It is well known (see for instance Genest et al's paper [5]) that pomset languages generated by automata are not stable under projection: given a $\mathbb{P}$-automaton $\mathcal{A}$, there is, in general, no $\mathbb{P}$-automaton $\mathcal{A}'$ such that $\mathcal{L}(\mathcal{A}') = \pi_{\Sigma_o}(\mathcal{L}(\mathcal{A}))$.

Let us now consider the case of boxed pomsets languages. Proposition 4 shows that the boxed pomset projection is distributive over boxed composition law $\boxdot$, i.e. the projection of the composition of two boxed pomsets is exactly the composition of the projection of these boxed pomsets.

Proposition 4. *Let b_1 and b_2 be two boxed pomsets labeled by Σ, and Σ_o be a subset of Σ. Then $\bar{\pi}_{\Sigma_o}(b_1 \boxdot b_2) = (\bar{\pi}_{\Sigma_o}(b_1)) \boxdot (\bar{\pi}_{\Sigma_o}(b_2))$*

This result naturally extends to boxed pomset languages: given a $\mathbb{B}$-automaton $\mathcal{A}$, one can easily find another $\mathbb{B}$-automaton $\mathcal{A}'$ such that the projection of the boxed pomset language generated by $\mathcal{A}$ is exactly the boxed pomset language generated by $\mathcal{A}'$. Theorem 1 below shows that it is sufficient to take $\mathcal{A}' = \mathcal{M}_{\bar{\pi}_{\Sigma_o}} \mathcal{A}$. Hence, computing $\mathcal{A}'$ can be performed in linear time.

Theorem 1. *Let $\mathcal{A}$ be a $\mathbb{B}$-automaton whose events are labeled by Σ, and Σ_o be a subset of Σ. Then $\bar{\pi}_{\Sigma_o}(\mathcal{L}(\mathcal{A})) = \mathcal{L}(\mathcal{M}_{\bar{\pi}_{\Sigma_o}}(\mathcal{A}))$.*

Proof. First, let us take a path ρ in $\mathcal{A}$. Then, we have $\alpha(\rho) = b_1 \boxdot \ldots \boxdot b_n$ where b_i are labels of transition of $\mathcal{A}$. Thus, using Proposition 4, we have $\bar{\pi}_{\Sigma_o}(\alpha(\rho)) = \bar{\pi}_{\Sigma_o}(b_1) \boxdot \ldots \boxdot \bar{\pi}_{\Sigma_o}(b_n)$. Moreover, $\bar{\pi}_{\Sigma_o}(b_1), \ldots, \bar{\pi}_{\Sigma_o}(b_n)$ can be found along a path of $\mathcal{M}_{\bar{\pi}_{\Sigma_o}}(\mathcal{A})$. It means that $\bar{\pi}_{\Sigma_o}(\mathcal{L}(\mathcal{A})) \subseteq \mathcal{L}(\mathcal{M}_{\bar{\pi}_{\Sigma_o}}(\mathcal{A}))$.

Second, let us take a path ρ in $\mathcal{M}_{\bar{\pi}_{\Sigma_o}}(\mathcal{A})$. Then, we have $\alpha(\rho) = b_1 \boxdot \ldots \boxdot b_k$, where b_i are labels of transition of $\bar{\pi}_{\Sigma_o}(\mathcal{A})$, i.e. $b_i = \bar{\pi}_{\Sigma_o}(b'_i)$. Thus, using Proposition 4, we have $\alpha(\rho) = \bar{\pi}_{\Sigma_o}(b'_1 \boxdot \ldots \boxdot b'_k)$. Moreover, $b'_1, \ldots, b'_k$ can be found along a path of $\mathcal{A}$. It means that $\mathcal{L}(\mathcal{M}_{\bar{\pi}_{\Sigma_o}}(\mathcal{A})) \subseteq \bar{\pi}_{\Sigma_o}(\mathcal{L}(\mathcal{A}))$. This concludes the proof of Theorem 1.   □

Proposition 5 extends the result of Proposition 3 to languages. More precisely, it shows that the boxing operator can be applied equivalently to each label of the initial automaton, or to the resulting language of this automaton.

Proposition 5. *Let $\mathcal{A}$ be a $\mathbb{P}$-automaton whose events are labeled by Σ, and Σ_o a subset of Σ. Then $\mathcal{L}(\mathcal{M}_B(\mathcal{A})) = B(\mathcal{L}(\mathcal{A}))$.*

The following theorem shows that it is possible to keep an automaton-like representation of $\mathbb{P}$-automata projections. The main idea is to consider the dual boxed pomset automaton projection to do so. Roughly speaking, Theorem 2 says that the projection of a $\mathbb{P}$-automaton language is the unboxing of the language of the corresponding $\mathbb{B}$-automaton projection.

Theorem 2. *Let $\mathcal{A}$ be a $\mathbb{P}$-automaton whose events are labeled by Σ, and Σ_o be a subset of Σ. Then $\pi_{\Sigma_o}(\mathcal{L}(\mathcal{A})) = U(\mathcal{L}(\mathcal{M}_{\bar{\pi}_{\Sigma_o}B}(\mathcal{A})))$*

Proof. We will use the above propositions to demonstrate this main result :
$$\pi_{\Sigma_o}(\mathcal{L}(\mathcal{A})) = \pi_{\Sigma_o}UB(\mathcal{L}(\mathcal{A})) \quad \text{(Prop. 1)} = U\bar{\pi}_{\Sigma_o}(B(\mathcal{L}(\mathcal{A}))) \quad \text{(Prop. 2)}$$
$$= U\bar{\pi}_{\Sigma_o}(\mathcal{L}(\mathcal{M}_B(\mathcal{A}))) \text{ (Prop. 5)} = U(\mathcal{L}(\mathcal{M}_{\bar{\pi}_{\Sigma_o}B}(\mathcal{A}))) \quad \text{(Th. 1)} \qquad \square$$

This theorem shows the interest of $\mathbb{B}$-automata, and boxed pomsets. Indeed, for any $\mathbb{P}$-automaton $\mathcal{A}$, there is in general no $\mathbb{P}$-automaton that can generate $\pi_{\Sigma_o}(\mathcal{L}(\mathcal{A}))$, but the trivial $\mathbb{B}$-automaton $\mathcal{M}_{\bar{\pi}_{\Sigma_o}B}(\mathcal{A})$ generates a language equivalent to $\pi_{\Sigma_o}(\mathcal{A})$. It seems more convenient for a designer to define the behaviors of a system with $\mathbb{P}$-automata, as one does not have to care for ports. On the other hand, $\mathbb{B}$-automata is a kind of model closed under projection. As trivial transformations allow to switch from one model to another, the framework for diagnosis seems rather clear: models of our systems will be $\mathbb{P}$-automata, and formal manipulations will be performed on $\mathbb{B}$-automata.

4   Event Correlation

$\mathbb{P}$-automata can be used to model distributed system or multi-threaded system, distributed robotics system, business work-flows,... In this paper, we will focus on telecommunication networks. These systems are composed of concurrent agents that react to their environment according to their programmed behavior, and report a part of the events occurring in their neighborhood. These events correspond to a finite subset of all the possible actions that may happen and form the finite collection Σ of event labels. Figure 5 shows a typical architecture for a monitored system. It is very similar to the SNMP architecture: each agent is equipped with a sensor (represented by a diamond), which sends observable events it monitors to the centralized log system (represented by a cylinder). Connection between agents are represented by dotted lines. The log system receives observations and records them in a log file that contains few information about causalities between recorded events.

Note that monitoring systems can not record everything that occurs in a network. The first obvious reason is that the size of log files on disk is necessarily

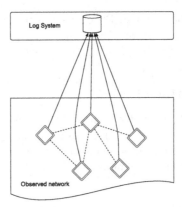

Fig. 5. A monitored system

limited, and hence designers have to choose what to record. The second reason is that some actions that one would like to record are performed by hardware, or in a part of the network that is not owned by the company which monitors the network. Hence, only a subset Σ_o of Σ is observable. Furthermore, one can not record all causal relations among events: this needs very intrusive tools, usually based on vector clocks instrumentation [4,11] which impose a time penalty on communications and again can not be implemented in unobservable places of the network. Hence, most of the time logs contain incomplete information about causal relations between recorded events. The log file can then be defined as a lpo $o = (E_o, \leq_o)$, where $\lambda(E_o) \subseteq \Sigma_o$. However, we show in this section how the lost ordering between events can be reconstructed with a model-based approach.

Within this context, the problems we are interested in are *event correlation*, i.e. infer causalities lost by the observation process, and *root causes* elicitation for faulty behavior, i.e. exhibit the minimal observed events with respect to the inferred causal ordering. Note that the log file is in general not sufficient to infer all lost causal relations among observed events. We propose to use some additional information on the behavior of the monitored system. This information is provided by a model given in terms of a $\mathbb{P}$-automaton $\mathcal{A}$. $\mathcal{A}$ represents all the knowledge of experts about the system behaviors, hence $\mathcal{L}(\mathcal{A})$ is supposed to model a significant part of possible runs of the system.

Definition 4 (Explanations). *An* explanation *of an observation given as a lpo $o = (E_o, \leq_o)$ is a lpo $o' = (E_o, \leq)$ such that $\leq_o \subseteq \leq$. The set of all explanations of o is denoted by $[\![o]\!]$. Moreover, given a $\mathbb{P}$-automaton $\mathcal{A}$ the model-based explanation of o by $\mathcal{A}$ with observation labels Σ_o, is denoted by $[\![o]\!]_{\Sigma_o, \mathcal{A}}$. $[\![o]\!]_{\Sigma_o, \mathcal{A}}$ is the set of explanations whose isomorphism class belong to the projection of the language generated by $\mathcal{A}$ on Σ_o. More formally, $l \in [\![o]\!]_{\Sigma_o, \mathcal{A}}$ if and only if l is an instance of an element of $\pi_{\Sigma_o}(\mathcal{L}(\mathcal{A}))$ and $l \in [\![o]\!]$.*

Note that o and its explanations partially orders the same sets of observed events E_o. Using definition 4, we can formalize the correlation problem as follows:

Definition 5 (Event Correlation Problem). *Let $\mathcal{A}$ be a $\mathbb{P}$-automaton whose events are labeled by Σ, $o = (E_o, \leq_o)$ be an observation labeled by $\Sigma_o \subseteq \Sigma$, and (e_1, e_2) be a pair of events in E_o^2. The Event Correlation Problem for the pair (e_1, e_2), is denoted by $ECP(\Sigma_o, \mathcal{A}, o, e_1, e_2)$ and can be stated as follows: decide whether $e_1 \leq e_2$ for every $p = (E_o, \leq) \in [\![o]\!]_{\Sigma_o, \mathcal{A}}$. We denote by $ecp_{\Sigma_o, \mathcal{A}, o}$ the lpo $(E_o, \leq)$ where $e_1 \leq e_2$ if and only if $ECP(\Sigma_o, \mathcal{A}, o, e_1, e_2)$. The set of root causes of observation o is denoted by $rc_{\Sigma_o, \mathcal{A}, o}$ and is the collection of minimal events with respect to $ecp_{\Sigma_o, \mathcal{A}, o}$.*

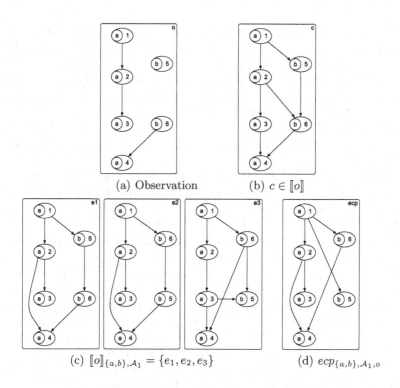

(a) Observation   (b) $c \in [\![o]\!]$

(c) $[\![o]\!]_{\{a,b\}, \mathcal{A}_1} = \{e_1, e_2, e_3\}$ (d) $ecp_{\{a,b\}, \mathcal{A}_1, o}$

Fig. 6. Observations, explanations and correlations

Intuitively, $ecp_{\Sigma_o, \mathcal{A}, o}$ contains all causal orderings that are certain according to the explanations of o provided by $\mathcal{A}$. Figure 6 illustrates these definitions. The graphical representation for lpos is similar to the representation adopted for pomsets, with the slight difference that we associate an unique number to each event to differentiate distinct occurrences of the same action. We consider in this figure that $\Sigma = \{a, b, c, d\}$ and $\Sigma_o = \{a, b\}$. Figure 6-a shows the observation called o. Figure 6-b shows a possible explanation of o called c. Let us suppose that the model of the systems behaviors is the $\mathbb{P}$-automaton $\mathcal{A}_1$ of Figure 4-a. For this automaton, c is not a model-based explanation of o, as c does not belong to $\pi_{\Sigma_o}(\mathcal{L}(\mathcal{A}_1))$. Lpo's e_1, e_2 and e_3 in Figure 6-c are possible members of $\pi_{\Sigma_o}(\mathcal{L}(\mathcal{A}))$ which embed the ordering given by o. As these different explanations do not agree on the respective ordering of events 3 and 4, 3 and 5, 4 and 5, nor 5 and 6, they shall not be ordered in $ecp_{\Sigma_o, \mathcal{A}_1, o}$, as depicted in Figure 6-d. For this case, the root cause of the observation o is event 1 which is labeled by a.

Theorem 3 shows that the ECP problem is hard, but fortunately, Theorem 4 identifies one case where this problem can be solved in polynomial time. Moreover, the constructive proof leads directly to an effective algorithm.

Theorem 3. *Let $\mathcal{A}$ be a $\mathbb{P}$-automaton whose events are labeled by Σ, $o = (E_o, \leq_o)$ be a lpo labeled by $\Sigma_o \subseteq \Sigma$ and (e, e') be in E_o^2. Then $ECP(\Sigma_o, \mathcal{A}, o, e, e')$ is CoNP-complete.*

Proof. We want to show that answering to the following question is NP-complete: Is there a lpo $l = (E_o, \leq) \in [\![o]\!]_{\Sigma_o, \mathcal{A}}$ such that $e \not\leq e'$? This can be proved with an extension of the proof of Th. 5 in Alur et al's paper [1]. First, let us show that ECP is in NP. A *solution* is a path ρ of $\mathcal{A}$, such that $\pi_{\Sigma_o}(\alpha_\odot(\rho)) = [E, \leq]$ is an isomorphism class that contains an explanation of o with $f(e) \not\leq f(e')$, where f is the map which assigns each event class of E to its instance in E_o. Let us consider the $\mathbb{B}$-automaton $\mathcal{A}' = \mathcal{M}_{\bar{\pi}_{\Sigma_o} \mathbb{B}}(\mathcal{A})$. Theorem 2 says that $\pi_{\Sigma_o}(\mathcal{L}(\mathcal{A})) = UL(\mathcal{A}')$. Thus, ρ is also a path in $\mathcal{A}'$ such that $U(\alpha_\boxdot(\rho)) = [E, \leq]$ is an isomorphism class that contains an explanation of o with $f(e) \not\leq f(e')$. Let us assume that the size of ρ is greater than $|o||\mathcal{A}||\Sigma|^2$. Then, as ρ should have at most $|o|$ transitions in $\mathcal{A}'$ with observable events, we can find a sequence of unobservable transitions in $\mathcal{A}'$ of size at least $|\mathcal{A}||\Sigma|^2$. That means that an unobservable transition t appears more than $|\Sigma|$ times in $\mathcal{A}'$. As, for any boxed pomset $b_i = [E_i^- \cup E_i^+, \leq_i]$ we have $b_i^{|\Sigma|} = b_i^{|\Sigma|+1}$ and $b_1 \boxdot b_2 = b_2 \boxdot b_1$, we can remove some occurrences of t to build a shorter path ρ' of size bounded by $|o||\mathcal{A}||\Sigma|^2$. Finally, we found ρ' in $\mathcal{A}'$, and thus in $\mathcal{A}$, such that $|\rho'| \leq |o||\mathcal{A}||\Sigma|^2$ and ρ' is a solution. This concludes the NP part.

Second, let us show that ECP is NP-hard. We provide a reduction from the NP-complete problem ONE-IN-THREE-3SAT : given a 3-CNF formula ϕ, is there a satisfying assignment to the variables such that each clause of ϕ gets exactly one literal assigned true ? From a 3-CNF formula $\phi = C_1 \wedge \ldots \wedge C_n$ over variables $x_1 \ldots x_m$, we define a $\mathbb{P}$-automaton $\mathcal{A}$ whose events are labeled by $\Sigma = \{a_i \mid 1 \leq i \leq n\} \cup \{b_j \mid 1 \leq j \leq m\}$. $\mathcal{A}$ has only one state, which is initial and final, and has $2m$ transitions labeled by p_{x_j} and $p_{\bar{x}_j}$, for $1 \leq j \leq m$.

Each p_{x_j} contains an event b_j and an event a_i for each clause C_i where variable x_j appears positively. Similarly, each $p_{\bar{x}_j}$ contains an event b_j and an event a_i for each clause C_i where variable x_j appears negatively. Now, consider the lpo $o = (E_o, \emptyset)$ which contains exactly one event for each possible label, and no causal ordering among these events, and a predicate ψ that returns false to any entry in Σ^2. Moreover, let us simply call e_σ the event of E_o labeled by σ. Thus, for any σ, σ' in Σ, deciding $not(ECP(\Sigma, \mathcal{A}, o, e_\sigma, e_{\sigma'}))$ is equivalent to knowing if there exists $l = (E_o, \leq) \in [\![o]\!]_{\Sigma_o, \mathcal{A}}$ such that $e_\sigma \not\leq e_{\sigma'}$. As all events of o are independent, and as labeling is bijective, solving ECP for o means that there exists a valuation which answers ONE-IN-THREE-3SAT. This concludes the proof. $\square$

Theorem 4. *Let $\mathcal{A}$ be a $\mathbb{P}$-automaton whose events are labeled by Σ and $o = (E_o, \leq_o)$ be a lpo labeled by $\Sigma_o \subseteq \Sigma$. If o has no auto-concurrency and Σ is fixed, then for every $(e, e') \in E_o^2$, $ECP(\Sigma_o, \mathcal{A}, o, e, e')$ is NLOGSPACE. More precisely, ECP can be solved in $O(|\mathcal{A}||o|^{|\Sigma||\Sigma_o|})$.*

Proof. Let us show that the ECP problem can be translated into finding accessible states of an automaton of size $O(|\mathcal{A}||o|^{|\Sigma||\Sigma_o|})$. We will use lpos instead of pomsets when we need to recall the identity of events, which is the case for ECP. Of course, the operations and mappings defined for pomsets and boxed pomsets extend to lpos and to boxed lpos.

To complete the proof, we need to define the notion of unfolding for boxes lpos. The *unfolding* of a boxed lpo b, denoted by $\mathcal{U}_b$, is a finite boxed lpo automaton, i.e. an automaton labeled by boxed lpos. $\mathcal{U}_b = (S, \rightarrow, \mathcal{B}, s_0, s_f)$, where:

- S is the set of prefixes of $B(l)$, i.e. the set of boxed lpos $\{b' \mid \exists b'', b = b' \boxdot b''\}$. Note that prefixes depend also on relation ψ used for composition;
- $\mathcal{B}$ is a set of boxed lpos that are used by the transition relation;
- $s_0 = \epsilon_{\mathbb{B}}$ is the initial state, and $s_f = b$ is the final state;
- $s_1 \xrightarrow{b'} s_2$ iff $s_1 \boxdot b'$ is an explanation of s_2, i.e. if they have the same event set and $\leq_{s_2} \subseteq \leq_{s_1 \boxdot b'}$.

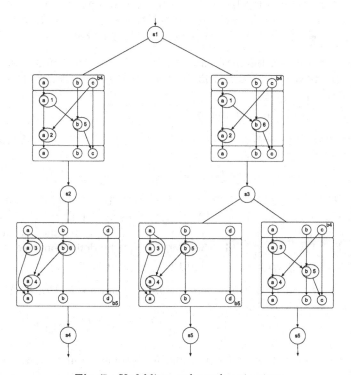

Fig. 7. Unfolding and synchronization

Note that for a boxed lpo in our unfolding, all labels in ports are not useful. For instance, consider boxed lpo b_5 in Figure 7: label d does not have to appear in the ports of this lpo as it is not connected to an event of the inside box of b_5. Hence, we can define a smaller set of labels $\mathcal{B}$ for our unfolding by considering only boxed lpo b whose ports are defined over labels that are connected to the inside box of b.

Lemma 1. *Let l be a lpo labeled by Σ_o. Then $U(\mathcal{L}(\mathcal{U}_{B(l)})) = [\![l]\!]$. If l has no auto-concurrency then the number of states of $\mathcal{U}_l$ is bounded by $|l|^{|\Sigma||\Sigma_o|}$.*

Proof. ($\Rightarrow$) If $l' \in U(\mathcal{L}(\mathcal{U}_{B(l)}))$ then there exists $b' = b'_1 \boxdot \ldots \boxdot b'_k$ such that $U(b') = l'$. Let us make an induction on k. First, let us assume that $k = 1$. Then, as b' is an explanation of $B(l)$, $U(b') = l'$ is an explanation of $UB(l) = l$ (Prop. 1). Let us then have $b'_1 \boxdot \ldots \boxdot b'_{k-1}$ an explanation of b_{k-1}, the state reached after reading $b'_1 \ldots b'_{k-1}$. By definition of $\mathcal{U}_{B(l)}$, $b_{k-1} \boxdot b'_k$ is an explanation of b_k. Let us remind that we manipulate only boxed lpos with minimal number of events in ports. Thus $E_{b_{k-1}} = E_{b'_1 \boxdot \ldots \boxdot b'_{k-1}}$ and $\leq_{b_{k-1}} \subseteq \leq_{b'_1 \boxdot \ldots \boxdot b'_{k-1}}$, and we obtain that $b'_1 \boxdot \ldots \boxdot b'_k$ is an explanation of b_k. ($\Leftarrow$) If $l' \in [\![l]\!]$ then l' is an explanation of l and $B(l')$ is a possible transition in $\mathcal{U}_{B(l)}$ from s_0 to s_f.

About the complexity statement : If we want to count the number of possible prefix of a boxed lpo, the simplest way is to consider that each event in output ports records a prefix of the boxed lpo. Moreover, if b has no auto-concurrency, it suffices to record only one event for each observable label - corresponding to the maximal observed event for this label - in order to record a prefix. □

The *product* of a boxed lpo automaton $\mathcal{A}_1$ and a $\mathbb{B}$-automaton $\mathcal{A}_2$, denoted by $\mathcal{A}_1 \times \mathcal{A}_2$ is the boxed lpo automaton resulting on the cartesian product of states of these automata and such that $(s_1, s_2) \xrightarrow{l} (s'_1, s'_2)$ iff $s_1 \xrightarrow{l} s'_1$ and $s_2 \xrightarrow{b} s'_2$, with l an instance of the boxed pomset b.

Lemma 2. *Let $\mathcal{A}$ be a $\mathbb{P}$-automaton whose events are labeled by Σ and l be a lpo labeled by $\Sigma_o \subseteq \Sigma$. Then $U(\mathcal{L}(\mathcal{U}_{B(l)} \times \mathcal{M}_{\bar{\pi}_{\Sigma_o} B}(\mathcal{A}))) = [\![l]\!]_{\Sigma_o, \mathcal{A}}$. If l has no auto-concurrency then the number of states is bounded by $|\mathcal{A}||l|^{|\Sigma||\Sigma_o|}$.*

Proof. $l' \in U(\mathcal{L}(\mathcal{U}_{B(l)} \times \mathcal{M}_{\bar{\pi}_{\Sigma_o} B}(\mathcal{A})))$ is equivalent to $l' \in U(\mathcal{L}(\mathcal{U}_{B(l)}))$ and l' is an instance of an element of $U(\mathcal{L}(\mathcal{M}_{\bar{\pi}_{\Sigma_o} B}(\mathcal{A})))$, using definition of $\times$. Moreover, this is also equivalent to $l' \in [\![l]\!]$ (Lemma 1) and l' is an instance of an element of $\pi_{\Sigma_o}(\mathcal{L}(\mathcal{A}))$ (Theorem 2). This is also equivalent, by definition, to $l' \in [\![l]\!]_{\Sigma_o, \mathcal{A}}$. Complexity comes from Lemma 1 and the definition of $\times$. □

Corollary 1. *Let $\mathcal{A}$ be a $\mathbb{P}$-automaton whose events are labeled by Σ and $o = (E_o, \leq_o)$ be a lpo labeled by $\Sigma_o \subseteq \Sigma$.*
*   Then $ecp_{\Sigma_o, \mathcal{A}, o} = (E_o, (\bigcap_{(E_o, \leq_l) \in L} \leq_l)^*)$, where $L = U(\mathcal{L}(\mathcal{U}_{B(l)} \times \mathcal{M}_{\bar{\pi}_{\Sigma_o} B}(\mathcal{A})))$.*

The constructive proof of Theorem 4 and its corollary immediately provide an algorithm to find $ecp_{\Sigma_o, \mathcal{A}, o}$ for a given observation o and a model $\mathcal{A}$. The first step is to compute $\mathcal{M}_{\bar{\pi}_{\Sigma_o} B}(\mathcal{A})$. The second step is to compute the product of the unfolding of $B(o)$ with $\mathcal{M}_{\bar{\pi}_{\Sigma_o}B}(\mathcal{A})$, and restrict this product to accessible states. Each accepting path of the product generates an explanation for o, and $ecp_{\Sigma_o,\mathcal{A},o}$ can then be obtained by intersecting the orders given by these explanations. Figure 7 shows an example of synchronization $\mathcal{U}_{B(o)} \times \mathcal{M}_{\bar{\pi}_{\Sigma_o}}(\mathcal{A}_2)$, where o is the lpo of Figure 6-a, and $\mathcal{A}_2$ is the automaton of Figure 4-b. States of this product are boxed lpos which are prefixes of $B(o)$. Path $\rho_1 = s_1 \xrightarrow{b_4} s_2 \xrightarrow{b_5} s_4$ corresponds to e_1 (as $U\alpha_{\boxminus}(\rho_1) = e_1$), path $\rho_2 = s_1 \xrightarrow{b_4} s_3 \xrightarrow{b_5} s_5$ corresponds to e_2 and path $\rho_2 = s_1 \xrightarrow{b_4} s_3 \xrightarrow{b_4} s_6$ corresponds to e_3, where e_1, e_2, and e_3 are the model-based explanations of o given in Figure 6-c.

Theorem 4 explicitly rules out observations with autoconcurrency. This restriction is only due to complexity reasons, as considering autoconcurrency would make our algorithm exponential in the size of the observation rather than in the size of the observed labels. This should not be considered as a severe limitation of the approach, as these requirements are naturally met in an observation framework where each sensor produces different observed labels (for instance by tagging an action name with a unique identity), and where local sequential ordering on each sensor is not lost during communication to the log system.

5   Conclusion

We have shown how to perform event correlation from an observation with a partial order model. This work opens two perspectives. The first one is to distribute computations as proposed previously [8]. Indeed, we know that the complexity of correlation is in $O(|\mathcal{A}||o|^{|\Sigma||\Sigma_o|})$. We can define distributed monitoring architectures, where local log systems observe only a subset of the network. Within this kind of architecture, Σ_o is partitioned into subsets of observable actions. Event correlation can be performed in parallel by each local log system with lower complexity. The main challenge is then to combine the local results to obtain a global view. The second perspective is to look at probabilistic models. So far, we can only answer whether a causal relation among some events is sure or not. It may be interesting to have a more qualitative answer, given as a probability.

References

1. Alur, R., Etessami, K., Yannakakis, M.: Realizability and verification of MSC graphs. In: Orejas, F., Spirakis, P.G., van Leeuwen, J. (eds.) ICALP 2001. LNCS, vol. 2076, pp. 797–808. Springer, Heidelberg (2001)
2. Benveniste, A., Fabre, E., Jard, C., Haar, S., Haar, S.: Diagnosis of asynchronous discrete event systems, a net unfolding approach. IEEE Transactions on Automatic Control 48(5), 714–727 (2003)
3. Dousson, C., Thang, V.D.: Discovering chronicles with numerical time constraints from alarm logs for monitoring dynamic systems. In: Proc. of IJCAI'99, pp. 620–626 (1999)
4. Fidge, C.: Logical time in distributed computing systems. IEEE Computer 24(8), 28–33 (1991)

5. Genest, B., Hélouët, L., Muscholl, A.: High-level message sequence charts projection. In: Amadio, R.M., Lugiez, D. (eds.) CONCUR 2003. LNCS, vol. 2761, pp. 308–322. Springer, Heidelberg (2003)
6. Gischer, J.L.: The equational theory of pomsets. TCS 61(2-3), 199–224 (1988)
7. IETF Network Working Group. A simple network management protocol (snmp). Technical report, IETF (1990)
8. Hélouët, L., Gazagnaire, T., Genest, B.: Diagnosis from scenarios. In: WODES'06 (2006)
9. ITU-TS. Recommendation Z.120: Message Sequence Chart (MSC) (2004)
10. Jéron, T., Marchand, H., Pinchinat, S., Cordier, M.O.: Supervision patterns in discrete event systems diagnosis. In: WODES'06 (2006)
11. Mattern, F.: Virtual time and global states of distributed systems. In: Workshop on Parallel and Distributed Algorithms (1989)
12. Nygate, Y.A.: Event correlation using rule and object based techniques. In: Proc. of the 4th Integrated network Management, pp. 278–289 (1995)
13. Pratt, V.: Modeling concurrency with partial orders. International Journal of Parallel Programming 15(1), 33–71 (1986)
14. Sampath, M., Sengupta, R., Lafortune, S., Sinnamohideen, K., Teneketzis, D.C: Failure diagnosis using discrete-event models. IEEE Transactions on Control Systems Technology 4(2), 105–124 (1996)

A Simple Positive Flows Computation Algorithm for a Large Subclass of Colored Nets

S. Evangelista, C. Pajault, and J.F. Pradat-Peyre

CEDRIC - CNAM Paris
292, rue St Martin, 75003 Paris
{evangeli,christophe.pajault,peyre}@cnam.fr

Abstract. Positive flows provide very useful informations that can be used to perform efficient analysis of a model. Although algorithms computing (a generative family of) positive flows in ordinary Petri nets are well known, computing a generative family of positive flows in colored net remains an open problem. We propose in this paper a pragmatic approach that allows us to define an algorithm that computes a generative family of particular but useful positive flows in a large subclass of colored nets: the simple well-formed nets.

1 Introduction

One of the principal reasons to use Petri nets to model distributed algorithms is that one can combine structural techniques (that use only the structure of the net) with model-checking techniques (that perform exhaustive simulations) in order to analyze a net and demonstrate properties. Among structural techniques, invariants computation can be viewed as the most fundamental one : invariants give immediate indication on the behavior of the model (i.e. without needing to "execute" it) ; invariants are needed to perform structural reductions (like the implicit place reduction [1], [14], or efficient transitions agglomeration [10,17]); places or transitions invariants can be used to define/classify kind of Petri nets with simplified liveness conditions (e.g. flexible manufacturing systems) [13], and so on. Among invariants, it is well known that positive flows (flows that use only positive weights) are the most useful ones and give accurate information on the net. In ordinary Petri nets, invariants are computed with the Gauss algorithm when no positive constraint is added or with the Farkas algorithm when a generative family of positive flows is needed (both algorithms are described in [4]).

However, in many cases one uses colored Petri nets for modeling algorithms. Indeed, they allow a more concise description of a problem than ordinary Petri nets. Furthermore, defining parameterized models permits to study a set of solutions with a unique model. So, computing invariants in a colored net is an interesting challenge. However, these calculus raise new problems : we have to manipulate color mapping instead of integer values, models may be parameterized and then algorithms must tackle with this additional difficulties. When dealing with flows computation, two main approaches are used : generalizing Gauss

J. Derrick and J. Vain (Eds.): FORTE 2007, LNCS 4574, pp. 177–195, 2007.

algorithm to take into account color mapping (in particular with the use of the notion of "generalized inverse") [15], [20], [25], [7]; this first approach permits to obtain a generative family (for the last citation) but requires to fix parameters and computed flows are not easily usable. The second approach consists in restricting color nets; this lead to different algorithms that compute parameterized and useful flows in regular nets [16] or ordered and associative nets [8].

Nevertheless, only one algorithm is known today in the case of colored positive flows computation [5], and this algorithm works only on very restricted models : unary regular nets or unary predicate/transitions nets.

We propose in this paper an algorithm that computes particular, but useful, positive flows in a high level model : the simple well-formed nets. This model is a restriction of the general well-formed nets [3], but sufficient enough to model Ada programs [2]. This paper is organized as follow : after some definitions we show, in section 3, how we can take advantage of both syntactic restrictions used to define nets and positive flows to obtain a particular "fractal" and "regular" equations system. Then we propose an algorithm that computes a generative family of *simple* positive flows (note that this family does not generate *all* positive flows). At last we conclude and propose future possible extensions of this algorithm.

2   Definitions

2.1   Colored Petri Nets

Petri nets form a well known formalism used to express and to analyze concurrent behaviours [21,23]. However, it is often difficult to model complex problems because of the "low level" expression power provided by Petri nets. In practice, one uses colored nets, that are an abbreviation of Petri nets. This abbreviation is based on the idea to associate to the classical Petri net token a type (also called a color) that gives it a high level semantic : instead saying "there are three tokens in place p" one can say for instance "there are the token 1, the token 4 and the token 13 in place p". In this way, one can model complex synchronization schemes involving data carried by processes.

Definition 1 (Multi-sets). *A multi-set over a finite and non empty set C is an application from C to $I\!N$. We denote by $Bag_{I\!N}(C)$ (or $Bag(C)$ for short) the set of multi-sets over C and we represent a multi-set by the formal sum $a = \sum_{y \in C} a(y).y$. If a and b are two multi-sets over C, then $a + b$ is the multi-set over C defined by $a + b = \sum_{y \in C}(a(y) + b(y)).y$ and if λ is a natural, then $\lambda.a$ is the multi-set over C defined by $\lambda.a = \sum_{y \in C}(\lambda.a(x)).x$. One say that a is greater or equal than b, denoted $a \geq b$ if and only if $\forall y \in C, a(y) \geq b(y)$.*

Definition 2. *A colored net is a 6-tuple $CN = \langle P, T, \mathcal{C}, G, W^+, W^- \rangle$ with :*

- *P is the non empty and finite set of places*
- *T is the non empty and finite set of transitions (disjoint with P);*
- *$\mathcal{C}$ is the color mapping from $P \bigcup T$ to ω where ω is a set including the finite and non empty sets. An item of $\mathcal{C}(s)$ is called a color of s and $\mathcal{C}(s)$ denotes the color domain of s.*

- G associates each transition t with a boolean application G_t on $C(t)$ called the guard of t.
- W^+ (resp. W^-) is the post (resp. pre) incidence mapping that associates to each transition t and to each place p a color mapping from $C(t)$ to $Bag(C(p))$ which defines the tokens that are needed, consumed or produced by the firing of a transition (see def. 3). We note $W = W^+ - W^-$ (note that $W(t,p)$ is a mapping from $C(t)$ to $Bag_{Z\!\!\!Z}(C(p))$).

We note $\epsilon = \{\bullet\}$ the color domain reduced to the unique value $\bullet$ (the token); this allows us to consider ordinary Petri nets as particular colored Petri nets (the unique and common color domain is ϵ).

Definition 3 (Marking and Firing rule). *A marking is a mapping that associates to each place p a value in $Bag(C(p))$. We note m_0 the initial marking of a net.*

A transition t is enabled for an instance $c_t \in C(t)$ from a marking m (denoted by $m[t, c_t\rangle$) if

$$G_t(c_t) = True \ and \ \forall p \in P, m(p) \geq W^-(t,p)(c_t)$$

The firing of t for $c_t \in C(t)$ from m leads to the marking m' ($m[t, c_t\rangle m'$) defined by

$$\forall p \in P, m'(p) = m(p) + W^+(t,p)(c_t) - W^-(t,p)(c_t)$$

A marking m' is reachable from a marking m if there exists a sequence $t_1, c_1, \ldots, t_k, c_k$ such that $m[t_1, c_1\rangle m_1, \ m_1[t_2, c_2\rangle m_2, \ \ldots, \ m_{k-1}[t_k, c_k\rangle m'$. We denote by $Acc(CN, m_0)$ the set of all reachable markings from m_0.

Consider the following colored net that models a solution to the dining philosophers paradigm. In this model, X denotes the identity mapping over the finite set D and !X denotes the "successor" mapping over D (i.e. the mapping that associates to an item x its successor in D that is supposed to be ordered). Semantics of this model is quite simple: a philosopher x who wants to eat must first take a chair by firing transition takeChair. Then it has to take in sequence its fork (transition $takeL$) and the fork of its right neightbour (transition $takeR$) to access state (place) Eating; the chair is released as soon as a philosopher gets its two forks (transition $takeR$). An eating philosopher can go back to the Thinking state by firing in sequence transitions giveL, giveR and end. Possible concurrent defects highlighted by this paradigm are the deadlock and the starvation problems.

Many analysis techniques have been adapted to colored nets, and in particular, automatic places invariants computation [19,24,20,25,26,16,7,6]. Indeed, places invariants give rich informations on the behavior of the model without needing its execution; their definition and their computation involve only the structure of the model. Within different places invariants, positive flows are those that give the most usable information; this can be explained by the fact that the positive constraint added on weights simplify interpretation of these invariants. We recall now the definition of these places invariants.

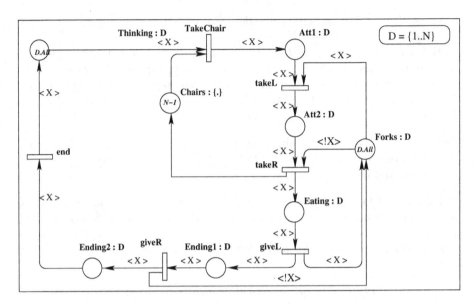

Fig. 1. A colored net for the dining philosophers paradigm

Definition 4 (Colored positive flow). *Let C_{inv} be a color domain. A positive flow $\mathcal{F}$, with color domain C_{inv} ($C(\mathcal{F}) = C_{inv}$), is a vector over P, noted as the formal sum $\mathcal{F} = \sum_{p \in P} \mathcal{F}_p.p$, such that $\forall p \in P, \mathcal{F}_p$ is a mapping from $Bag(C(p))$ to $Bag(C_{inv})$ and such that $\forall t \in T, \sum_{p \in P} \mathcal{F}_p \circ W(t, p) = 0$.*[1]

This definition implies that for any positive flow $\mathcal{F}$, and for any reachable marking m we have that $\sum_{p \in P} \mathcal{F}_p(m(p)) = \sum_{p \in P} \mathcal{F}_p(m_0(p))$. A flow can then be interpreted as an equations set linking the marking of a subset of places with the original marking of these places:

$$\forall m \in Acc(CN, m_0), \forall c \in C(\mathcal{F}), \sum_{p \in P} \sum_{c_p \in C(p)} [\mathcal{F}_p(c_p)(c)].m(p)(c_p) = cst(\in \mathbb{N})$$

Consider again the model of figure 1. In this net there are at least three positive flows on the color domain D:

- $\mathcal{F}_1 = \langle X \rangle.Thinking + \langle X \rangle.Att1 + \langle X \rangle.Att2 + \langle X \rangle.Eating + \langle X \rangle.Ending1 + \langle X \rangle.Ending2$
- $\mathcal{F}_2 = \langle !X \rangle.Forks + \langle !X \rangle.Att2 + \langle !X \rangle.Eating + \langle X \rangle.Eating + \langle X \rangle.Ending1$
- $\mathcal{F}_3 = \langle . \rangle.Att1 + \langle . \rangle.Att2 + \langle 1 \rangle Chairs$

where $\langle X \rangle$ denotes the identity mapping over $Bag(D)$, $\langle !X \rangle$ denotes the successor mapping over $Bag(D)$, $\langle 1 \rangle$ denotes the identity mapping over ϵ, and $\langle . \rangle$ the projection from D to *epsilon* defined by $\forall d \in D, .(d) = \bullet$. Note that by sake of simplicity we often do not note $\langle 1 \rangle$.

---

[1] 0 denotes here the null mapping from $C(t)$ to $Bag(C(\mathcal{F}))$.

The first one characterizes the sequential structure of philosophers that can be in one of the six states Thinking, Att1, Att2, Eating, Ending1, Ending2. Indeed, its interpretation is [2]: $\forall m \in Acc(CN, m_0), \forall x \in D, m(Thinking)(x) + m(Att1)(x) + m(Att2)(x) + m(Eating)(x) + m(Ending1)(x) + m(Ending2)(x) = 1$. The second one, $\mathcal{F}_2$, tells us that, given $x \in D$, the fork $!x$ is either free (place Forks is marked with $!x$) or is either owned by philosopher $!x$ that is in state Eating or Att2 or is used by philosopher x which is in state Eating or Ending.

At last, $\mathcal{F}_3$ highlights that chairs are either free (place Chairs is marked) or are shared by philosophers that are in state Att1 or Att2. Its interpretation is $\forall m \in Acc(CN, m_0), \sum_{x \in C} m(Att1)(x) + \sum_{x \in C} m(Att2)(x) + m(Chairs) = N - 1$ and, combined with $\mathcal{F}_2$, ensures that place Forks cannot become empty and then, that no deadlock is possible.

As we can note, positive flows give precious information of the behavior of a model using only its structure.

However, computing positive flows is a difficult task. Up to now, only one algorithm exists [5] and is restricted to regular net (a sub-class of colored nets) with an unique color domain. A possible explanation is that most researches focus on a generative family computation (a family that generate all positive invariants of the net). This leads to very complex equations systems even if algorithms are defined on strong restriction of colored nets. We do not propose here to focus on a generative family but on **useful** family of positive flows. For doing this we impose a syntactic restriction on positive flows definition and we associate this restriction to a similar restriction on colored net definition. We call this kind of net "Simple Well-Formed nets" and we designed our positive flow as "simple positive flows".

2.2 Simple Well-Formed Colored Nets and Simple Positive Flows

Modeling and verification are two strongly linked activities. A formalism has to define a good compromise between the simplicity provided for modeling and the richness of possible automatic tools or techniques that can be used to verify properties on the model.

In the Petri net domain, general formalisms have been proposed (like colored nets) but most of theoretical analysis results have been obtained on restrictions of general models. One can cite the regular nets [16], the ordered nets [8], and a formalism with a same modeling power as colored nets but with syntactic restrictions, the well-formed nets [3].

We propose here a slight restriction of this last formalism that we named simple well-formed nets (or SWF nets for short). This formalism remains sufficient for modeling large and complex problems; in particular we use it to model a large subset of Ada programs in order to validate them (see for instance models proposed in [12] or in [11]). As for the original model, we define our formalism by restricting the possible color mapping and the color domain construction.

Definition 5 (Basic color mapping). *Let C be a finite ordered set. The basic mapping are the* identity, *denoted by X_C, the* diffusion *(also called global*

---

[2] Remember that $\langle X \rangle(c)(c') = 1$ if $c = c'$ and $\langle X \rangle(c)(c') = 0$ otherwise.

synchronization), denoted by All_C, *the* successor, *denoted by* $!X_C$ *and all constant mappings,* $\lambda_C^c, c \in C$. *They are defined from* C *to* $Bag(C)$ *by:* $\forall x \in C$, $X_C(x) = x$, $All_C(x) = \sum_{c \in C} c$, $!X_C(x) = $ *successor of* x *in* C *and* $\lambda_C^c(x) = c$.

Remark 1. It is a common usage to use other literals, $X, Y, Z, Ph, \ldots$, to denote the identity or successor mapping, and when the context is clear, one often omits the domain on which operates the mapping (X instead of X_C). All classes are considered to be ordered (in a circular way). So each item has a unique successor in the class (the successor of the last item is the first one). All these mappings can be extended to mapping from $Bag(C)$ to $Bag(C)$. When $C = \epsilon$ all these mappings coincide.

Definition 6 (Simple color mappings). *Let* C *be a finite ordered set. A simple color mapping on* C *is a mapping from* C *to* $Bag(C)$ *if either it's a constant mapping or if it can be written as a additive composition* $\alpha.X_C + \beta.All_C + \gamma.!X_C$ *with* α, β, γ *integer values such that* $\beta \geq 0$, $\beta + \alpha \geq 0$ *and* $\beta + \gamma \geq 0$ *(and* $\beta + \alpha + \gamma \geq 0$ *in the very case where* $|C| = 1$*).*

Remark 2. The constraints on α, β and γ ensure that a color mapping defines a positive value for each color of C (and then belongs to $Bag(C)$). When $C = \epsilon$ all simple color mappings are reduced to a constant mapping (an integer value).

Definition 7 (Simple color functions). *Let* $C = C_1 \times C_2 \times \ldots \times C_k$ *be a finite product of finite and non empty sets. A mapping* f *from* C *To* $Bag(C)$ *is a* simple color function *if it can be written* $f = \langle f_1, f_2, \ldots, f_k \rangle$ *with* $\forall i$, f_i *a simple color mapping on* C_i *or an arbitrary unitary[3] application from* C_i *to* $Bag(C_i)$. *If* $\langle c_1, \ldots, c_k \rangle \in C$ *then* $f(c) = \langle f_1, f_2, \ldots, f_k \rangle(\langle c_1, \ldots, c_k \rangle)$ $= \langle f_1(c_1), f_2(c_2), \ldots, f_k(c_k) \rangle$.

When useful, we will note $\langle f_1, f_2, \ldots, f_k \rangle$ *as* $f_1.\langle f_2, \ldots, f_k \rangle$ *and extend by linearity this notation to weighted sums of tuples.*

We are in position to define nets we use to analyze Ada programs in our tool Quasar.

Definition 8 (Simple Well-Formed nets). *A colored net* $\langle P, T, \mathcal{C}, G, W^-, W^+ \rangle$ *is a* simple well-formed net *if* $\forall p \in P$, $\forall t \in T$,

- $W^+(t, p) \neq 0$ *or* $W^-(t, p) \neq 0$ *implies that* $\mathcal{C}(t) = \mathcal{C}(p) \times C_p'$ *(*$\mathcal{C}(t)$ *equals or includes* $\mathcal{C}(p)$*);*
- $W^+(t, p)$ *and* $W^-(t, p)$ *are a composition of a simple color function over* $\mathcal{C}(p)$ *with a projection from* $\mathcal{C}(t)$ *to* $\mathcal{C}(p)$ *(when color domain of* t *is "larger" than the color domain of* p*);*
- *if* $W^+(t, p)$ *uses a constant mapping on a class* C_i *then an arc between* p *and an other transition cannot use the mapping* All_{C_i}.

We say that the net is homogeneous *if all color domains are identical (i.e.* $\exists C_1$, $\ldots$, C_K *such that* $\forall s \in P \cup T$, $\mathcal{C}(s) = C_1 \times \ldots \times C_k$*), if all guards are always*

---

[3] f_i is an unitary application if $\forall c \in C_i, |f_i(c)| = 1$.

evaluated to True (there is no guards) and if all color mappings are only built with X, All and $!X$ basic mappings (no constants and no arbitrary mappings must appear on arcs).

Remark 3. The third point is used to ensure that we can always homogenize a simple well-formed net; i.e. construct an equivalent model (or that perform a weak simulation of the original one) but with a unique color domain for each place and each transition (see subsection 3.5).

SWF nets are a restriction of well-formed nets [3]. In particular, we do not allow guarded functions or additive composition of different instances of the same color class (e.g. $\langle X \rangle + \langle Y \rangle$ is forbidden). However, the expressiveness provided by this definition remains sufficient for modeling almost all problems. For instance, as said previously, we use this formalism to model precisely the behavioral semantics of Ada programs (with possible dynamics task creation) in order to analyze them.

We give now the definition of positive flows we will compute on SWF nets. This definition restricts the "functional" structure of the flow to a regular one.

Definition 9 (Simple positive flows). *A positive flow $\mathcal{F}$ on the color domain D is said to be a simple positive flow if $\forall p \in P$, $\mathcal{C}(p) = D \times \mathcal{C}'_p$ ($\mathcal{C}(p)$ "includes" D), $\mathcal{F}_p$ is a composition of a simple color function over $\mathcal{C}(p)$ using no constant with a projection from D to $\mathcal{C}(p)$.*

These restrictions are not very severe; indeed, the third last flows, presented with model of figure 1 are simple positive flows. Furthermore, this definition provides two advantages:

1. Their definition uses only simple color mapping, and then, these positive flows can be very easily interpreted or used by specific tools (like structural reductions): they can characterize critical section (like $\mathcal{F}3$ in the previous example), they can also characterize process structure ($\mathcal{F}1$) or the way resources are shared ($\mathcal{F}2$);
2. They can be computed in a systematic way as we will see in the next section.

For more clarity, we use in positive flow notation a dot . to highlight the projection from $\mathcal{C}(p)$ to the color domain of the flow. For instance, if the color domain of a flow is $D = C_1 \times C_3$ and the color domain of a place involved in the flow is $C = \mathcal{C}_1 \times \mathcal{C}_2 \times \mathcal{C}_1 \times \mathcal{C}_3$, we will note $\langle ., ., X', Z \rangle$ to denote the composition of the mapping $\langle X, Y, X', Z \rangle$ with the projection Π from C to D defined by $\Pi(x, y, x', z) = (x', z)$.

Given an homogeneous SWF net we can construct from its incidence matrix W the integer matrix $W^{n_1, \ldots, n_k}$, indexed by $(T \times C1 \times \ldots \times C_k) \times (P \times C1 \times \ldots \times C_k)$ and defined by:

$$W^{n_1, \ldots, n_k}(t, c'_1, \ldots, c'_k)(p, c_1, \ldots, c_k) = W(t, p)(\langle c'_1, \ldots, c'_k \rangle)(\langle c1, \ldots, c_k \rangle)$$

This construction consists only in "unfolding" color mapping that constitutes coefficients of the matrix W. In the same way, it is possible to "unfold" a positive flow $\mathcal{F}$ by building the set of integer vectors defined by all possible interpretations of the colored flow. Indeed, given a positive flow $\mathcal{F}$ and an interpretation c_{inv} we can define the integer vector $\overrightarrow{F}_{c_{inv}}$ indexed by $(C1 \times \ldots \times C_k \times P)$ and defined by:

$$\overrightarrow{F}_{c_{inv}}(c_1, \ldots, c_k, p) = \mathcal{F}_p(\langle c1, \ldots, c_k \rangle)(c_{inv})$$

Using these notations we have by definition:

Proposition 1. $\mathcal{F}$ is a positive flow if and only if $\forall c_{inv} \in C, W^{n_1, \ldots, n_k} . \overrightarrow{F}_{c_{inv}} = 0$.

So, computing positive flows of a homogeneous colored net consists in solving the system $W^{n_1, \ldots, n_k} . \overrightarrow{F}_{c_{inv}} = 0$ with, for instance, the Farkas algorithm described in [4]. However, this raises two main drawbacks:

1. this calculation requires to fix the parameters which is then equivalent to unfold the net and to compute positive flows in the unfolded net which is a very inefficient process;
2. as computed flows are integer vectors, it is very difficult to "recolor" them in the general case and leads to useless invariants.

We will prove that it is possible to solve this system in a **parametric way** without unfolding the net. For doing that we first prove that incidence matrix can be reordered in a "fractal" form.

3   Simple Positive Flows Computation for SWF Nets

In this section we propose to show how to compute a generative family of simple positive flows in a SWF net. Note that the computed set generates all simple positive flows **but not all** positive flows.

For this purpose, we first suppose that every considered net is homogeneous (we provide, in the last subsection, the mechanism used to transform a simple well-formed net into an homogeneous one). We show then that the constraints on SWF nets mappings and on simple positive flows definitions lead to a system with a "fractal" form which can be reduce to a set of nonparametric equations.

We adopt the following notations:

- $C = C_1 \times C_2 \times \ldots \times C_k$ denotes the common color domain of places and transitions;
- $n_1 = |C_1|, n_2 = |C_2|, \ldots, n_k = |C_k|,$
- $C_j = \{c_j^i\}_{i=1..n_j}$;
- $\forall p \in P, \forall t \in T, W(t,p) = \langle w_1(t,p), \ldots, w_k(t,p) \rangle$ with for all i in $[1..k]$, $w_i(t,p) = a_i(t,p).X_{C_i} + b_i(t,p).All_{C_i} + d_i(t,p).!X_{C_i}$
- we compute positive flow on domain C; so we fix $C_{inv} = C$.
- if $\mathcal{F} = \sum_p \mathcal{F}_p.p$ is a simple positive flow, we note $\mathcal{F}_p = \langle f_1^p, \ldots, f_k^p \rangle$ and $f_i^p = \alpha_i.X_i + \beta_i.All_i + \gamma_i.(!X_i)$;
- we note $E = (\mathbb{Q}^+)^P$;

3.1   Reordering Equations

The matrix of an homogeneous SWF net can be defined by a recursive construction, highlighting a "fractal" form that can be used to define an efficient algorithm for simple positive flow computation. In this construction, transitions are organized into lines (corresponding to the equations of the system) and places into columns (corresponding to the variables of the system). This construction is based on the notion of block matrix that we recall now.

Definition 10 (Square block matrix). *A matrix $A = (a_{i,j})$ in $I\!N^{K.n \times K.m}$ is an integer square block matrix if each $a_{i,j}$ is a $m \times n$ integer matrix or a square block matrix (in which case, $n = k'.n'$ and $m = k'.m'$). We note $A(i,j) = a_{i,j}$ the item on i^{th} line and j^{th} column.*

Definition 11 (Matrix fractal form). *A block matrix $W = (w_{i,j})$ in $I\!N^{K.n \times K.m}$ has a "Simple Well Formed Net Fractal form" (or has a fractal form for short) if there exist three matrices A, B, D with the same dimension such that:*

1. *matrices A, B, D are either three integer matrices or three block matrices with also a fractal form;*
2. *items of W satisfy:*

$$\forall i, j \in 1..K, w_{i,j} = \begin{cases} A + B & \text{if } i{=}j \\ D + B & \text{if } j{=}i{+}1 \text{ modulo } n \\ B & \text{in other cases} \end{cases}$$

For instance, if A, B, D are three integer matrices with the same dimension then the following $n \times n$ matrix has a fractal form.

$$W = \begin{bmatrix} (A+B) & (D+B) & B & \cdots & B \\ B & (A+B) & (D+B) & \cdots & B \\ \cdots & \cdots & \ddots & \ddots & \cdots \\ B & \cdots & B & (A+B) & (D+B) \\ (D+B) & B & \cdots & B & (A+B) \end{bmatrix}$$

Consider now an homogeneous SWF net (W is its incidence matrix). Remember that k denotes the number of classes of the net and then, the number of different parameters of the system and that $W(t,p) = \langle w_1(t,p), \ldots, w_k(t,p) \rangle$ with for all i in $[1..k]$, $w_i(t,p) = a_i(t,p).X_{C_i} + b_i(t,p).All_{C_i} + d_i(t,p).!X_{C_i}$.

Definition 12 (Extracting a fractal form of a homogeneous SWF net)
Given $v \in [1..k+1]$, and three sets $I_A, I_B, I_D \subseteq \{n_1, n_2, \ldots, n_k\}$ we define the integer or block matrix $W_v^{I_A, I_B, I_D}$ recursively by:

– *if $v = k+1$ then $W_{k+1}^{I_A, I_B, I_D} = (w_{t,p})$ is the $T \times P$ integer matrix*

$$w_{t,p} = \prod_{i \in I_A} a_i(t,p). \prod_{j \in I_D} d_j(t,p). \prod_{l \in I_B} b_l(t,p)^4$$

---

[4] In this product we use the convention that a product on the empty set equals 1 ($\prod_{i \in \emptyset} f(i) = 1$).

– if $v \leq k$, then $W_v^{I_A, I_B, I_D} = (w_{i,j})$ is the $n_v \times n_v$ square block matrix defined by

$$w_{i,j} = \begin{bmatrix} W_{v+1}^{I_A \cup \{v\}, I_B, I_D} + W_{v+1}^{I_A, I_B \cup \{v\}, I_D} & \text{if } i=j \\ W_{v+1}^{I_A, I_B, I_D \cup \{v\}} + W_{v+1}^{I_A, I_B \cup \{v\}, I_D} & \text{if } j=i+1 \text{ modulo } n_v \\ W_{v+1}^{I_A, I_B \cup \{v\}, I_D} & \text{in other cases} \end{bmatrix}$$

We note W' the square block matrix $W_1^{\emptyset, \emptyset, \emptyset}$ and when there is no ambiguity, we note $A = W_2^{\{1\}, \emptyset, \emptyset}$, $B = W_2^{\emptyset, \{1\}, \emptyset}$ and $D = W_2^{\emptyset, \emptyset, \{1\}}$.

Proposition 2. *We have the following results:*

1. *The two matrices W and W' are equivalent for defining a SWF homogenous net; i.e. $\forall p \in P, \forall t \in T, \forall c = \langle c_1, \ldots, c_k \rangle \in C, \forall c' = \langle c'_1, \ldots, c'_k \rangle \in C$, we have $W'(c_1, c'1)(c_2, c'2)\ldots(c_k, c'k)(t, p) = W(t, p)(c')(c)$.*
2. *The matrix W' has a fractal form (as soon as $k \geq 1$).*

Proof. Point 2 is a direct consequence of the definition of $W_1^{\emptyset, \emptyset, \emptyset}$. For proving point 1, it sufficient to note that $W(t, p)(\langle c_1, \ldots, c_k \rangle) = \langle w_1(t, p)(c_1), \ldots, w_k(t, p)(c_k) \rangle$ and that $w_i(t, p)(c_i)(c'_i) = b_i(t, p) + \delta_{c_i, c'_i}.a_i(t, p) + \delta_{c_i, !c'_i}.d_i(t, p)$ where δ is the Kronecker symbol defined by $\delta_{c_i, c'_i} = 0$ if $c_i \neq c'_i$ and $\delta_{c_i, c_i} = 1$; it comes that

$$W(t, p)(\langle c_1, \ldots, c_k \rangle)(\langle c'_1, \ldots, c'_k \rangle) = \Pi_{i=1..k}(b_i(t, p) + \delta_{c_i, c'_i}.a_i(t, p) + \delta_{c_i, !c'_i}.d_i(t, p))$$

Now remark that when $c_v = c'_v$ we have added v to the set I_A, when $c_v = !c'_v$ we have added v to the set I_D and that we use these sets to compute the integer values of the latest matrices and we obtain the result.   □

If we consider an homogeneous SWF net with two classes (two parameters), the incidence matrix can be written:

$$W = \begin{bmatrix} (A+B) & (D+B) & B & \ldots & B \\ B & (A+B) & (D+B) & \ldots & B \\ \ldots & \ldots & \ddots & \ddots & \ldots \\ B & \ldots & B & (A+B) & (D+B) \\ (D+B) & B & \ldots & B & (A+B) \end{bmatrix}$$

with

$$A = W_2^{\{1\}, \emptyset, \emptyset} = \begin{bmatrix} (AA+AB) & (AD+AB) & AB & \ldots & AB \\ AB & (AA+AB) & (AD+AB) & \ldots & AB \\ \ldots & \ldots & \ddots & \ddots & \ldots \\ AB & \ldots & AB & (AA+AB) & (AD+AB) \\ (AD+AB) & AB & \ldots & AB & (AA+AB) \end{bmatrix}$$

$$B = W_2^{\emptyset, \{1\}, \emptyset} = \begin{bmatrix} (BA+BB) & (BD+BB) & BB & \ldots & BB \\ BB & (BA+BB) & (BD+BB) & \ldots & BB \\ \ldots & \ldots & \ddots & \ddots & \ldots \\ BB & \ldots & BB & (BA+BB) & (BD+BB) \\ (BD+BB) & BB & \ldots & BB & (BA+BB) \end{bmatrix}$$

$$D = W_2^{\emptyset, \emptyset, \{1\}} = \begin{bmatrix} (DA+DB) & (DD+DB) & DB & \ldots & DB \\ DB & (DA+DB) & (DD+DB) & \ldots & DB \\ \ldots & \ldots & \ddots & \ddots & \ldots \\ DB & \ldots & DB & (DA+DB) & (DD+DB) \\ (DD+DB) & DB & \ldots & DB & (DA+DB) \end{bmatrix}$$

and with

- $AA(t,p) = a_1(t,p).a_2(t,p)$, $AB(t,p) = a_1(t,p).b_2(t,p)$, $AD(t,p) = a_1(t,p).d_2(t,p)$
- $BA(t,p) = b_1(t,p).a_2(t,p)$, $BB(t,p) = b_1(t,p).b_2(t,p)$, $BD(t,p) = b_1(t,p).d_2(t,p)$
- $DA(t,p) = d_1(t,p).a_2(t,p)$, $DB(t,p) = d_1(t,p).b_2(t,p)$, $DD(t,p) = d_1(t,p).d_2(t,p)$

3.2   Reordering Solutions and Simplifying Equations

First, note that any simple positive flow $\mathcal{F}$ can be written in a unique way as a sum $F_{<>} = \langle X_1, X_2, \ldots, X_k \rangle f_1 + \langle X_1, X_2, \ldots, !X_k \rangle f_2 + \langle X_1, X_2, \ldots, All_k \rangle f_3 + \ldots + \langle All_1, All_2, \ldots, All_k \rangle f_{3^k}$ with f_i integer vectors over P.

Second, remark that the reorganization performed on the incidence matrix can also be applied to the solutions of the studied system (and we need to do it).

Indeed, a positive flow $\mathcal{F}$ (in a functional form) defines for each value $c_{inv} \in C$ a developed vector $\overrightarrow{F}_{c_{inv}}$ in $E^{n_1 \times \cdots \times n_k}$. Remark also that this vector can be viewed as a vector of $(E^{n_2 \times \cdots \times n_k})^{n_1}$ i.e. a vector of size n_1 with each component in $E^{n_2 \times \cdots \times n_k}$.

$$
\overrightarrow{F}_{c_{inv}} = \begin{bmatrix} \overline{F[1]}_{c_{inv}} \\ \vdots \\ \overline{F[n_1]}_{c_{inv}} \end{bmatrix} \text{ with } \forall i \in 1..n_1, \overline{F[i]}_{c_{inv}}(c_2, \ldots, c_k, p) = \overrightarrow{F}_{c_{inv}}(c_1^i, c_2, \ldots, c_k, p)
$$

As we restrict positive flow computation to simple positive flow computation we can use the particular form of such vector and write them in a "parametric" form.

Proposition 3. *Given a* **simple** *positive flow $\mathcal{F}$ and a color interpretation c_{inv}, then $\overrightarrow{F}_{c_{inv}}$ has a unique decomposition:*

$$
\overrightarrow{F}_{c_{inv}} = \begin{bmatrix} 0 \\ \ldots \\ 0 \\ F_X \\ 0 \\ \ldots \\ 0 \end{bmatrix} + \begin{bmatrix} 0 \\ \ldots \\ 0 \\ 0 \\ F_{!X} \\ \ldots \\ 0 \end{bmatrix} + \begin{bmatrix} F_{All} \\ \ldots \\ F_{All} \\ F_{All} \\ F_{All} \\ \ldots \\ F_{All} \end{bmatrix}
$$

where F_X, $F_{!X}$ and F_{All} are three $E^{n_2 \times \cdots \times n_k}$ vectors depending on the value of $\{\alpha_i^p\}_p$ for F_X, of $\{\gamma_i^p\}_p$ for $F_{!X}$ and of $\{\alpha_i^p, \gamma_i^p, \beta_i^p\}_p$ for F_{All}, and such that if, $c_{inv} = \langle c_1^i, c_2, \ldots, c_k \rangle$, then F_X is on the ith row and $F_{!X}$ is on the $(i+1)^{th}$ row.

Proof. Let $c_{inv} = \langle c_1'^i, c_2', \ldots, c_k' \rangle$ and $j, j' \in 1..n_1$ both distinct of i and $i+1$. Suppose that $\overrightarrow{V}$ is the vector defined by $\overrightarrow{V} = \overline{F[j]}_{c_{inv}} - \overline{F[j']}_{c_{inv}}$. We have $\forall p, c_2, \ldots, c_k, \overrightarrow{V}(p, c_2, \ldots, c_k) = \overrightarrow{F}_{c_{inv}}(p, c_1^j, c_2, \ldots, c_k) - \overrightarrow{F}_{c_{inv}}(p, c_1^{j'}, c_2, \ldots, c_k)$.

So, $\overrightarrow{V}(p, c_2, \ldots, c_k) = \mathcal{F}_p(\langle c_1'^j, \ldots, c_k \rangle)(c_{inv}) - \mathcal{F}_p(\langle c_1^{j'}, \ldots, c_k \rangle)(c_{inv})$ that can be written $\langle f_1^p(c_1^j, c_1^i), f_2^p(c_2, c'2), \ldots, f_k^p(c_k, c'k) \rangle - f_1^p(c_1^{j'}, c_1^i), f_2^p(c_2, c'2), \ldots,$

$f_k^p(c_k, c'k)$. As j and j' are **both** distinct of i and $i+1$ it comes that $f_1^p(c_1^j, c_1^i) - f_1^p(c_1^{j'}, c_1^i) = 0$ and then $\overrightarrow{V} = \overrightarrow{0}$. We note F_{All} the vector $\overrightarrow{F[j]}_{c_{inv}}$.

Let then $\overrightarrow{V_X}$ the vector defined by $\overrightarrow{V_X} = \overrightarrow{F[i]}_{c_{inv}} - \overrightarrow{F[j]}_{c_{inv}}$. Using a same argumentation it comes that $\overrightarrow{V_X}(p, c_2, \ldots, c_k) = \langle f_1^p(c_1^i, c_1^i), f_2^p(c_2, c'2), \ldots, f_k^p(c_k, c'k) \rangle - \langle f_1^p(c_1^j, c_1^i), f_2^p(c_2, c'2), \ldots, f_k^p(c_k, c'k) \rangle$. As $f_1^p(c_1^i, c_1^i) - f_1^p(c_1^j, c_1^i) = \alpha_i^p$ we can note $F_X = V_X$. We can proceed also to the same construction for defining in an unique way $F_{!X} = V_{!X}$. $\square$

Now, if we combine the regular fractal form of a SWF homogeneous net with the particular form of simple positive flows, we can simplify the system that has to be solved.

Proposition 4. *Using previous notations we have that* $W_{n_1, \ldots, n_k} . \overrightarrow{F}_{c_{inv}} = 0$ *iff:*

$$B.F_{All} = A.F_{!X} = D.F_X = A.F_X + D.F_{!X} = B.(F_X + F_{!X}) + (A + D).F_{All} = 0$$

Proof. The system can be written

$$
\begin{bmatrix}
(A+B) & (D+B) & B & \cdots & & B \\
B & (A+B) & (D+B) & \cdots & & B \\
\cdots & \cdots & \ddots & \ddots & & \cdots \\
B & \cdots & B & (A+B) & (D+B) \\
(D+B) & B & \cdots & B & (A+B)
\end{bmatrix}
\cdot
\begin{bmatrix}
F_{All} \\
\cdots \\
F_{All} \\
F_X + F_{All} \\
F_{!X} + F_{All} \\
\cdots \\
F_{All}
\end{bmatrix}
= 0
$$

Since simple positive flows are defined only with integer vectors (they don't use n_1 as coefficient) and since a simple positive flow defines solutions for any value of n_1, it comes that $B.F_{All} = 0$. If we develop now equations (and using the fact that $B.F_{All} = 0$), we obtain only four distinct equations:

- $(A + D).F_{All} + B.(F_X + F_{!X}) = 0$;
- $(A + B).F_X + (B + D).F_{!X} + (A + D).F_{All} = 0$;
- $B.F_X + (A + B).F_{!X} + (A + D).F_{All} = 0$;
- $(B + D).F_X + B.F_{!X} + (A + D).F_{All} = 0$.

By subtracting the first one to the others we obtain the result. Now, if F_X, F_{All} and $F_{!X}$ fulfill the previous equation it is clear that the vector $\overrightarrow{F}_{c_{inv}}$ is solution of $\overrightarrow{F}_{c_{inv}} = 0$ (whatever the positive value of n_1 is). $\square$

3.3   Computing Simple Positive Flow in the Homogenous Case

We are now in position to propose an algorithm for computing simple positive flow for an homogeneous SWF net. For doing that we need to define two matrices operators: the first one, the "stacking" operator define how to stack matrices of the same dimension. The second one, the "juxtaposition" operator, define how to put side by side matrices of the same dimension. These two operators differ from classical ones in the sense that they keep the fractal structure of matrices when stacking or juxtaposing them.

Definition 13 (Stacking and juxtaposing matrices). *Let* $W^1 = [w^1_{i,j}]_{i\in[1..n],j\in[1..m]}, \ldots, W^q = [w^q_{i,j}]_{i\in[1..n],j\in[1..m]}$ *q matrices.*

1. *If* $W^1, \ldots, W^q$ *are all integer matrices then*
   - *the stacking of* $W^1, \ldots, W^q$, *noted* $[W^1/\ldots/W^q]$, *is the matrix* $[s_{i,j}]_{i\in[1..q.n],j\in[1..m]}$ *(m columns and q.n lines) with* $s_{(q.i)-r,j} = w^{q-r}_{i,j}$, $r \in 0..q-1$.
   - *the juxtaposition of* $W^1, \ldots, W^q$, *noted* $[W^1|\ldots|W^q]$, *is the matrix* $[s_{i,j}]_{i\in[1..n],j\in[1..q.m]}$ *(n lines and q.m columns) with* $s_{i,(q.j)-r} = w^{q-r}_{i,j}$, $r \in 0..q-1$.
2. *If* $W^1, \ldots, W^q$ *are all block matrices (their items are others matrices) then*
   - *the stacking of* $W^1, \ldots, W^q$, *noted* $[W^1/\ldots/W^q]$, *is the matrix* $[s_{i,j}]_{i,j\in[1..n]}$ *recursively defined by* $s_{i,j} = [w^1_{i,j}/\ldots/w^q_{i,j}]$
   - *the juxtaposition of* $W^1, \ldots, W^q$, *noted* $[W^1|\ldots|W^q]$, *is the matrix* $[s_{i,j}]_{i,j\in[1..n]}$ *recursively defined by* $s_{i,j} = [w^1_{i,j}|\ldots|w^q_{i,j}]$

Remark 4. As a vector can be seen as a single column matrix, these two operators can also be applied to vectors.

Proposition 5. *If* $W^1, \ldots, W^q$ *are fractal matrices of the same dimension then* $[W^1/\ldots/W^q]$ *and* $[W^1|\ldots|W^q]$ *are also fractal matrices.*

Using these operators, we can rewrite previous system.

Proposition 6. *Using previous notations, we have that* $W_{n1,\ldots,n_k}.\overrightarrow{F}_{c_{inv}} = 0$ *iff:*

$$\left[[0|0|B]/[0|A|0]/[D|0|0]/[A|D|0]/[B|B|A+D]\right].\left[F_X/F_{!X}/F_{All}\right] = 0$$

Proof. A direct consequence of the operators definition. $\qquad\square$

We propose now an algorithm that computes a generative family of simple positive flows. Input of this algorithm is either an integer matrix and a set Parameters reduced to the empty set (no parameterized system) or a fractal block matrix with a set Parameters compatible with W (the size of W has the size $n_1 \times n_1$ and each items is either an integer matrix or a fractal one with the size $n_2 \times n_2$ and so on). The output is either a set of integer vectors (when Parameters is reduced to the empty set) or a set of formal sums $F_{<>} = \langle X_1, X_2, \ldots, X_k \rangle f_1 + \langle X_1, X_2, \ldots, !X_k \rangle f_2 + \langle X_1, X_2, \ldots, All_k \rangle f_3 + \ldots + \langle All_1, All_2, \ldots, All_k \rangle f_{3^k}$ with f_i integer vectors over P that generate simple positive flows.

Algorithm 1: Simple_Positive_Solutions(W, Parameters = $\{n_1, \ldots, n_k\}$)

If (Parameters $= \emptyset$) Then

   + return $\{X|W.X = 0\}$ – *integer vectors computed with the Farkas algorithm*

Else

+ Construct the **fractal** matrix W' defined by[5]

$$W' = \big[\, [0|0|B] \,/\, [0|A|0] \,/\, [D|0|0] \,/\, [A|D|0] \,/\, [B|B|A+D] \,\big]$$

+ Compute the set SF of solutions of the system $W'. \big[F_X / F_{!X} / F_{All} \big] = 0$. with this algorithm: $SF := \text{Simple\_Positive\_Flows}(W', \{n_2, \ldots, n_k\})$[6]
+ Return the set of formal sums

$$\big\{ F = X_{C_1}.F_X + All_{C_1}.F_{All} + !X_{C_1}.F_{!X},\ \big[F_X / F_{!X} / F_{All} \big] \in SF \big\}$$

End if;

Proposition 7. *The set computed by the previous algorithm defines a generative family of simple positive flows (of a SWF net).*

Proof. By recurrence on the set Parameters:

1. if Parameters $= \emptyset$ then the set computed is a generative family since we use the Farkas algorithm;
2. Suppose that given any fractal matrix W' and a compatible set $\{n_2, \ldots, n_k\}$ the previous algorithm computes a generative family of simple positive flows.
   (a) formal sums computed by the algorithm define simple positive flows of net defined by W. Indeed, recurrence hypothesis combined with proposition 6 ensure that we effectively compute simple positive flows.
   (b) the set is generative. Indeed, let $\mathcal{F}0$ be a simple positive flow. Using proposition 3, any interpretation $\overrightarrow{F0}_{c_{inv}}$ of $\mathcal{F}0$ can be written with $F0_X$, $F0_{All}$ and $F0_{!X}$ as defined in this proposition. Using the proposition 6, we obtain that $W'. \big[F0_X / F0_{!X} / F0_{All} \big] = 0$. By recurrence hypothesis, as we compute a generative family of solutions of $W'. \big[F_X / F_{!X} / F_{All} \big] = 0$ then $\big[F0_X / F0_{!X} / F0_{All} \big]$ is generated by this set and then all interpretation of $\mathcal{F}0$ is generated by the set computed. So, formal sums computed by the previous algorithm generate all simple positive flows of the SWF net defining by the fractal matrix W.   □

If we note $K_{P \times T}$ the complexity of the Farkas algorithm for a net with P places and T transitions, then the complexity of the previous algorithm is $K_{3^k.P \times 5^k.T}$ with k the number of classes of the net. However, as matrices built by the algorithm are very sparce, first results we obtained seem to prove that the algorithm behaves as its complexity was $2^k.K_{P \times T}$ which is a good complexity since, even for very complex models, k remains lower than 5.

3.4   Dealing with Non Homogeneous SWF Nets

Suppose now that the net is not homogeneous. In order to use previous algorithm, we have to homogenize the net. Two different cases have to be considered:

---

[5] As previously, we note A, B and D the blocks of the fractal matrix W.
[6] If $k < 2$, then $\{n_2, \ldots, n_k\} = \emptyset$.

1) a transition has a color domain larger than its adjacent places (the contrary is not possible due to the definition of SWF nets); 2) a color mapping use a constant value or an arbitrary mapping. In order to make homogeneous the studied net we proceed in two steps:

1. As soon as a constant mapping (of a class C) or an arbitrary mapping appears on an arc valuation, we replace all mappings on this class by the mapping All_C; this replacement leads to a synchronization loosening and then the obtained net makes a weak simulation of the original one. So, all computed flows in this net are also flows of the original one [7]. Furthermore, as we forbid the mixing of constant and of the mapping All_C in the simple well-formed net definition, we have not to fix the parameter size of C (which would be necessary if we need to homogenize an arc with mapping All_C since it would be replaced by $|C|.All_C$).

2. Compute the lowest common multiple (C_{lcm}) of color domain (by extending classical multiplication and division to product of classes) and extend color domain of each place (and of each transition) such that their color domain equals C_{lcm}. Modify also accordingly the original marking. For instance, the lcm of $C_1 \times C_1 \times C_2$, $C_1 \times C_2 \times C_3$ and $C3 \times C_3$ is $C_1 \times C_1 \times C2 \times C_3 \times C_3$. Suppress in each flow computed the additive color part. As these transformations do not modify the behavior of the model it is clear that computed positive flows by this manner are those of the original model.

For instance, consider the simple well-formed net depicted in Figure 2 that models an atomic assignment **Free** := **f(Id, X)** where f is an arbitry Ada boolean function and where places **Write** models a read-write lock.

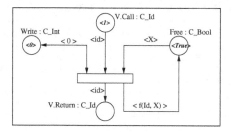

Fig. 2. A simple net

The first step (constant and arbitrary mapping homogenization) produces the model depicted in the left of Figure 3.

The lowest common multiple color domain is $C\_Id \times C\_Int \times C\_Bool$. After homogenization of the net we obtain the model depicted in the right of Figure 3.

On can remark that information concerning color domain C_Bool have been forgotten by the homogenization process (and that the model is quite less readable).

Once homogenization is done, one can compute positive flow: for instance the sum $\langle X, All, All \rangle.(V.Call + V.Return)$ defines a simple positive flow of the

---

[7] It is possible to treat cleverly constant mapping.

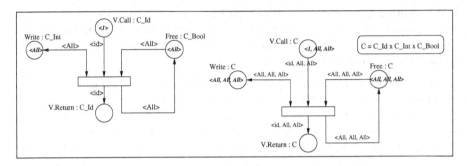

Fig. 3. The previous net homogenized (step 1 and 2)

latest model. In order to obtain positive flows of the original model it's sufficient to suppress carefully color part added for homogenization: for the previous invariant, we obtain the "correct" positive flow $\langle X \rangle.(V.Call + V.Return)$.

3.5 Example

Consider again the net of figure 1. Its incidence matrix after homogenization is:

$$
W = \begin{array}{c}
\\ TakeChairs \\ takeL \\ takeR \\ giveL \\ giveR \\ end
\end{array}
\begin{array}{ccccccccc}
Thinking & Att1 & Att2 & Eating & Ending1 & Ending2 & Forks & Chairs \\
-\langle X \rangle & \langle X \rangle & 0 & 0 & 0 & 0 & 0 & -\langle All \rangle \\
0 & -\langle X \rangle & \langle X \rangle & 0 & 0 & 0 & -\langle X \rangle & 0 \\
0 & 0 & -\langle X \rangle & \langle X \rangle & 0 & 0 & -\langle !X \rangle & \langle All \rangle \\
0 & 0 & 0 & -\langle X \rangle & \langle X \rangle & 0 & \langle X \rangle & 0 \\
0 & 0 & 0 & 0 & -\langle X \rangle & \langle X \rangle & \langle !X \rangle & 0 \\
\langle X \rangle & 0 & 0 & 0 & 0 & -\langle X \rangle & 0 & 0
\end{array}
$$

The corresponding matrices A, B and D are:

$$
A = \begin{array}{c}
\\ TakeChairs \\ takeL \\ takeR \\ giveL \\ giveR \\ end
\end{array}
\begin{array}{ccccccccc}
Thinking & Att1 & Att2 & Eating & Ending1 & Ending2 & Forks & Chairs \\
-1 & 1 & 0 & 0 & 0 & 0 & 0 & 0 \\
0 & -1 & 1 & 0 & 0 & 0 & -1 & 0 \\
0 & 0 & -1 & 1 & 0 & 0 & 0 & 0 \\
0 & 0 & 0 & -1 & 1 & 0 & 1 & 0 \\
0 & 0 & 0 & 0 & -1 & 1 & 0 & 0 \\
1 & 0 & 0 & 0 & 0 & -1 & 0 & 0
\end{array}
$$

$$
B = \begin{array}{c}
\\ TakeChairs \\ takeL \\ takeR \\ giveL \\ giveR \\ end
\end{array}
\begin{array}{ccccccccc}
Thinking & Att1 & Att2 & Eating & Ending1 & Ending2 & Forks & Chairs \\
0 & 0 & 0 & 0 & 0 & 0 & 0 & -1 \\
0 & 0 & 0 & 0 & 0 & 0 & 0 & 0 \\
0 & 0 & 0 & 0 & 0 & 0 & 0 & 1 \\
0 & 0 & 0 & 0 & 0 & 0 & 0 & 0 \\
0 & 0 & 0 & 0 & 0 & 0 & 0 & 0 \\
0 & 0 & 0 & 0 & 0 & 0 & 0 & 0
\end{array}
$$

$$
D = \begin{array}{c}
\\ TakeChairs \\ takeL \\ takeR \\ giveL \\ giveR \\ end
\end{array}
\begin{array}{ccccccccc}
Thinking & Att1 & Att2 & Eating & Ending1 & Ending2 & Forks & Chairs \\
0 & 0 & 0 & 0 & 0 & 0 & 0 & 0 \\
0 & 0 & 0 & 0 & 0 & 0 & 0 & 0 \\
0 & 0 & 0 & 0 & 0 & 0 & -1 & 0 \\
0 & 0 & 0 & 0 & 0 & 0 & 0 & 0 \\
0 & 0 & 0 & 0 & 0 & 0 & 1 & 0 \\
0 & 0 & 0 & 0 & 0 & 0 & 0 & 0
\end{array}
$$

Applying algorithm of page 189 leads to 6 flows:

- $\mathcal{F}_1 = \langle X \rangle.Thinking + \langle X \rangle.Att1 + \langle X \rangle.Att2 + \langle X \rangle.Eating + \langle X \rangle.Ending1 + \langle X \rangle.$
  $Ending2$
- $\mathcal{F}_1' = \langle !X \rangle.Thinking + \langle !X \rangle.Att1 + \langle !X \rangle.Att2 + \langle !X \rangle.Eating + \langle !X \rangle.Ending1 + \langle !X \rangle.Ending2$
- $\mathcal{F}_1'' = \langle All \rangle.Thinkin + \langle All \rangle.Att1 + \langle All \rangle.Att2 + \langle All \rangle.Eating + \langle All \rangle.Ending1 + \langle All \rangle.Ending2$
- $\mathcal{F}_2 = \langle !X \rangle.Forks + \langle !X \rangle.Att2 + \langle !X \rangle.Eating + \langle X \rangle.Eating + \langle X \rangle.Ending1$
- $\mathcal{F}_3 = \langle All \rangle.Att1 + \langle All \rangle.Att2 + \langle X \rangle Chairs$
- $\mathcal{F}_3' = \langle All \rangle.Att1 + \langle All \rangle.Att2 + \langle X! \rangle Chairs$

This example emphasizes that, in many cases, our algorithm computes a generative family of all positive flows. However, it underlines also two difficulties associated to our method. First we compute useless flows such as $\mathcal{F}_1'$, $\mathcal{F}_1''$ or $\mathcal{F}_3'$; indeed, as soon as $\langle X_C \rangle.F$ is a flow $\langle X!_C \rangle.F$ and $\langle All \rangle.F$ are also two flows and if $\langle X_C \rangle.F + \langle X!_C \rangle.F'$ is a flow then $\langle All \rangle.(F + F')$ is also a flow. Our first experimentations show that we compute in average one useless flow per flow and per color domain. As the complexity of the Farkas algorithm depends principally on the number of solutions, our method behaves as if we compute positive flows on a net two times bigger than the original one. We are studying algorithm heuristics to solve this slight problem. The second problem is that, by definition, some positive flows cannot be computed. For instance, a flow involving three different colors (X, $X!$ and $X!!$) or a flow using the cardinal of a class as weight ($n_1.\langle X \rangle.F$) are not simple positive flows and thus, are not computed. If we don't foresee now a solution to include parameters in flows definition, we can easily adapt the definition and the associated computation algorithm of simple positive flows to take into account more complex flows.

4 Conclusion

We have proposed an algorithm that computes a generative family of particular but useful positive flows of a slightly restricted subclass of colored nets. This algorithm is being implemented in our tool Helena [9] (http://helena.cnam.fr) and its distributed version Cyclades [22]. It will be used to enforce structural techniques, such as structural reductions, stubborn sets computation or distributed partitioning used in these tools to verify concurrent programs in the Quasar project (http://quasar.cnam.fr).

The way we define our algorithm allows its extension to other kinds of nets as soon as they provide some regularity. For instance, it can be immediately adapted to deal with all non guarded mappings used in normalized symmetric nets definitions[18].

References

1. Berthelot, G.: Checking properties of nets using transformations. In: Rozenberg, G. (ed.) Advances in Petri Nets 1985. LNCS, vol. 222, Springer, Heidelberg (1985)
2. Bruneton, E., Pradat-Peyre, J.F.: Automatic verification of concurrent ada programs. In: González Harbour, M., la de Puente, J.A. (eds.) Ada-Europe 1999. LNCS, vol. 1622, pp. 146–157. Springer, Heidelberg (1999)
3. Chiola, C., Dutheillet, C., Franceschinis, G., Haddad, S.: On well-formed colored nets and their symbolic reachability graph. In: ICATPN, Paris-France (June 1990)
4. Colom, J.M., Silva, M.: Convex geometry and semiflows in P/T nets. A comparative study of algorithms for computation of minimal P-semiflows. Lecture Notes in Computer Science. Advances in Petri Nets 1990, (NewsletterInfo: 33,390) vol. 483, pp. 79–112 (1991)
5. Couvreur, J.M., Haddad, S., Peyre, J.F.: Computation of generative families of positive semi-flows in two types of coloured nets. In: Proceedings of the 12th International Conference on Application and Theory of Petri Nets, Gjern, Denmark, pp. 122–144, NewsletterInfo: 39 (June 1991)
6. Couvreur, J.M., Haddad, S., Peyre, J.F.: Generative families of positive invariants in coloured nets sub-classes. In: Rozenberg, G. (ed.) Advances in Petri Nets 1993. LNCS, vol. 674, pp. 51–70. Springer, Heidelberg (1993)
7. Couvreur, J.M.: The general computation of flows for coloured nets. In: proc of the 11th International Conference on Application and Theory of Petri-Nets, Paris (June 1990)
8. Couvreur, J.M., Haddad, S.: Towards a general and powerful computation of flows for parameterized coloured nets. In: 9th European Workshop on Application and Theory of Petri Nets, vol. II, Venice (Italy) (June 1988)
9. Evangelista, S.: Helena, an efficient high level Petri nets analyser. Technical report, CEDRIC, CNAM, Paris (2004)
10. Evangelista, S., Haddad, S., Pradat-Peyre, J.F.: New coloured reductions for software validation. In: Workshop on Discrete Event Systems (2004)
11. Evangelista, S., Kaiser, C., Pajault, C., Pradat-Peyre, J.F., Rousseau, P.: Dynamic tasks verification with quasar. In: Vardanega, T., Wellings, A.J. (eds.) Ada-Europe 2005. LNCS, vol. 3555, Springer, Heidelberg (2005)
12. Evangelista, S., Kaiser, C., Pradat-Peyre, J.F., Rousseau, P.: Quasar: a new tool for analysing concurrent programs. In: Rosen, J.-P., Strohmeier, A. (eds.) Ada-Europe 2003. LNCS, vol. 2655, Springer, Heidelberg (2003)
13. Ezpeleta, J., García-Vallés, F., Colom, J.M.: A class of well structured petri nets for flexible manufacturing systems. In: Desel, J., Silva, M. (eds.) ICATPN 1998. LNCS, vol. 1420, pp. 64–83. Springer, Heidelberg (1998)
14. Garcia-Valles, F., Colom, J.M.: Implicit places in net systems. In: Proc. 8th Int. Workshop on Petri Net and Performance Models (PNPM'99), 8-10 October 1999, Zaragoza, Spain, pp. 104–113 (1999)
15. Genrich, H.J., Lautenbach, K.: S-invariance in predicate/transition nets. In: Pagnoni, A., Rozenberg, G. (eds.) Informatik-Fachberichte 66: Application and Theory of Petri Nets — Selected Papers from the Third European Workshop on Application and Theory of Petri Nets, Varenna, Italy, September 27–30, 1982, pp. 98–111. Springer-Verlag (1983)
16. Haddad, S., Girault, C.: Algebraic structure of flows of a regular coloured net. In: Rozenberg, G. (ed.) Advances in Petri Nets 1987. NewsletterInfo: 27, LNCS, vol. 266, pp. 73–88. Springer, Heidelberg (1987)

17. Haddad, S., Pradat-Peyre, J.-F.: New efficient petri nets reductions for parallel programs verification. Parallel Processing Letters 16(1), 101–116 (2006)
18. Hillah, L., Kordon, F., Petrucci-Dauchy, L., Trèves, N.: Pn standardisation: A survey. In: Najm, E., Pradat-Peyre, J.F., Donzeau-Gouge, V.V. (eds.) FORTE 2006. LNCS, vol. 4229, pp. 307–322. Springer, Heidelberg (2006)
19. Jensen, K.: Coloured Petri nets and the invariant method. T.C.S. 14, 317–336 (1981)
20. Memmi, G., Vautherin, J.: Computation of flows for unary-predicates/transition nets. In: Rozenberg, G. (ed.) Advances in Petri Nets 1984. LNCS, vol. 188, pp. 455–467. Springer, Heidelberg (1985)
21. Murata, T.: Petri nets: properties, analysis and applications. Proceedings of the IEEE 77(4), 39–50 (1989)
22. Pajault, C., Pradat-Peyre, J.F.: Distributed colored petri net model-checking with cyclades, LNCS vol. 4346. Springer-Verlag, Heidelberg (2006) (To appear 2007)
23. Reisig, W.: EATCS-An Introduction to Petri Nets. Springer-Verlag, Heidelberg (1983)
24. Reisig, W.: Petri nets and algebraic specifications. Theoretical Computer Science, NewsletterInfo: 38,39, vol. 80, pp.1–34 (1991)
25. Silva Suarez, M., Martinez, J., Ladet, P., Alla, H.: Generalized inverses and the calculation of symbolic invariants for colored petri nets. Technique et Science Informatiques, NewsletterInfo: 16,21,22, vol. 4(1), pp.113–126 (1985)
26. Vautherin, J.: Calculation of semi-flows for pr/T-systems. In: Int. Workshop on Petri Nets and Performance Models, Madison, Wisconsin, NewsletterInfo: 29, pp. 174–183. IEEE Computer Society Press, Washington (1987)

Improvements for the Symbolic Verification of Timed Automata[*]

Rongjie Yan[1,2], Guangyuan Li[1], Wenliang Zhang[1,2], and Yunquan Peng[1,2]

[1] State Key Laboratory of Computer Science
Institute of Software, Chinese Academy of Sciences,Beijing,100080,China
[2] Graduate School of the Chinese Academy of Sciences,Beijing,100039,China
{yrj,ligy}@ios.ac.cn

Abstract. Based on the equivalence relation for location based reachability between continuous and integer semantics of closed timed automata, Beyer et al. have implemented the verifier Rabbit, with the uniform representation of reachable configurations. However, the growth of maximal constant of clock variables will decline the performance of Rabbit. The paper proposes an improved symbolic method, using binary decision diagrams (BDDs) to store the symbolic representation of discretized states, for the verification of timed systems. Compared with Rabbit, experiments demonstrate that besides the memory reduction, our implementation is also less sensitive to the size of clock domain.

Keywords: verification, timed systems, symbolic method, BDD.

1 Introduction

Formal verification is one of the effective methods to ensure the correctness of real-time systems. Timed automata (TAs) [1] provide a formal framework for the automatic analysis and verification of real-time systems, and in the past few years several tools for the model checking of TAs have been developed and used, including Uppaal [13], Kronos [8], Red [16], Rabbit [6] and FPTA [17], which have implemented the computation for the set of all reachable configurations by reachability analysis. However, the exploding increase of time consumption for the computation and memory consumption for the representation of the reachable configurations is still a main problem.

Within the model checking community, many works were based on symbolic representations of the state space. The *region equivalence* of [1] is the precursor of the symbolic methods in which the state space is covered using regions with the same integer parts of clock values and the ordering of fractional parts. Currently, most of real-time verifiers apply abstractions based on *zones* (the constraint sets) in order to be coarser. Difference bound matrices (DBMs) [4] are a common data structure to describe zones. However, this structure cannot

---

[*] Supported by 973 Program of China under Grant No. 2002cb312200; and the National Natural Science Foundation of China under Grant Nos. 60673051, 60421001.

J. Derrick and J. Vain (Eds.): FORTE 2007, LNCS 4574, pp. 196–210, 2007.
© IFIP International Federation for Information Processing 2007

unify the representation of configurations which consist of locations and clock valuations.

Besides DBMs, clock difference diagrams (CDDs) [3] and their variants [16,15] were used to combine the representation of locations and clock valuations in zones. Their common disadvantage is that the lack of a unique canonical representation may hinder the containment relation detection.

The work in [9] introduced the BDD representation of reachable configurations based on the methods of time discretization [10]. The work in [2] proposed that closed timed automata (CTAs), whose clock constraints only contain $\geq, \leq$ relations, can just consider integer clock valuations for the reachability analysis. Based on the observation in [2], the work in [5] implemented BDD-based reachability analysis, which formally defined the integer semantics of closed automata and proved the equivalence between integer and continuous semantics for location based reachability. All these BDD-based verifiers share the same problem of BDD's: they are sensitive to the size of clock domain.

Based on the work of [5], we introduce symbolic structures for the representation of reachable configurations, in the integer semantics of closed timed automata, which is similar to the work of [17]. To reduce the memory consumption, BDD is applied to store the reachable symbolic sets. The combination not only reduces the sensitivity to the scale of clock constants, but also unifies the representation of locations and clock valuations.

The paper is organized as follows. In section 2, we briefly recall the definition of TAs, CTAs and their semantics. In section 3, we present the new symbolic data structures and the reachability analysis algorithm for the integer semantics. In section 4, we demonstrate the performance of our prototype implementation. Section 5 concludes and discusses future work.

2   Preliminaries

The section introduces the definition of TAs and their continuous and integer semantics.

A timed automaton (TA), proposed by Alur and Dill [1], is a finite state automaton extended with a finite set of real-valued clock variables.

Definition 1. *(Syntax of Timed Automata).*
Let X be a finite set of clocks, and $C(X)$ be the clock constraint set over X, given by the syntax:

$$\phi ::= (x \sim c) \mid \phi_1 \wedge \phi_2 \mid true$$

where $x \in X$, $\sim \in \{<, \leq, >, \geq\}$ and $c \in \mathbb{N}^+$ ($\mathbb{N}^+$ is the set of non-negative integers).

A timed automaton over X is a tuple $A = \langle L, l_0, \Sigma, X, I, E \rangle$, where

- *L is a finite set of locations, and $l_0 \in L$ is the initial location,*
- *I is a mapping that labels each location $l \in L$ with some constraint in $C(X)$, and $I(l)$ is called the invariant of l,*

- Σ is a finite set of synchronization labels, and
- $E \subseteq L \times C(X) \times \Sigma \times 2^X \times L$ is the set of transitions.

A transition $(l, g, \sigma, Y, l') \in E$ means that one can move from the location l to l' through a transition labelled with $\sigma \in \Sigma$. Moreover, g the guard must be satisfied by the current clock values, and all the clocks in Y ($Y \subseteq X$) are reset to 0.

Closed timed automata [2] restrict the clock constraints. The restricted constraints ϕ over X is:

$$\phi ::= x \leq c | x \geq c | \phi_1 \wedge \phi_2,$$

where $x \in X$, and $c \in \mathbb{N}^+$.

2.1 Continuous Semantics of TA

In continuous semantics, clock variables have non-negative real valuations. A clock valuation is a function $\mu : X \mapsto \mathbb{R}^+$, where $\mathbb{R}^+$ is the set of non-negative reals. μ_X denotes the set of all clock valuations over X. For $t \in \mathbb{R}^+$, $\mu + t$ denotes the clock valuation such that $\mu(x + t) = \mu(x) + t$, for all $x \in X$. For $Y \subseteq X$, $\mu[Y := 0]$ denotes the clock valuation such that $\mu[Y := 0](x) = 0$, for all $x \in Y$ and otherwise $\mu[Y := 0](x) = \mu(x)$. μ satisfies a constraint $\phi \in C(X)$, denoted by $\mu \models \phi$, if ϕ evaluates to *true* under the assignment given by μ.

The continuous semantics of a timed automaton $A = \langle L, l_0, \Sigma, X, I, E \rangle$ over X is defined as a transition system $\langle S, s_0, \Sigma \cup \mathbb{R}^+, \rightarrow \rangle$, where $S = L \times \mu_X$; $s_0 = (l_0, \mu_0)$ is the initial state where $\mu_0(x) = 0$ for all $x \in X$; and the transition relation $\rightarrow$ comprises two kinds of moves:

- delay transition: $(l, \mu) \xrightarrow{\delta} (l, \mu + \delta)$, if $\delta \in \mathbb{R}^+$ and $\mu \models I(l)$ and $\mu + \delta \models I(l)$;
- discrete transition: $(l, \mu) \xrightarrow{\sigma} (l', \mu[Y := 0])$, if $(l, g, \sigma, Y, l') \in E$ and $\mu \models g$ and $\mu[Y := 0] \models I(l')$.

Let A be a TA. For a state $s_k = (l, \mu)$ where $l \in L, \mu \in \mu_X$. If there is a finite state sequence such that $s_0 \xrightarrow{\alpha_0} s_1 \xrightarrow{\alpha_1} \cdots \xrightarrow{\alpha_{k-1}} s_k$, then s_k is called reachable and l the reachable location in the continuous semantics of A, where $\alpha_i \in \Sigma \cup \mathbb{R}^+$, $0 \leq i < k$.

2.2 Integer Semantics of TA

The differences between integer and continuous semantics are the definitions of clock valuations and transition relations. In integer semantics, clock variables have integer valuations. A clock valuation is a function $\nu : X \mapsto \mathbb{N}^+$, where $\mathbb{N}^+$ is the set of non-negative integers. ν_X denotes the set of all clock valuations over X.

The integer semantics of a timed automaton [5] $A = \langle L, l_0, \Sigma, X, I, E \rangle$ is defined as a transition system $\langle S, s_0, \Sigma \cup \mathbb{N}^+, \rightarrow_{\mathcal{I}} \rangle$, where $S = L \times \nu_X$, $s_0 = (l_0, \nu_0)$ is the initial state where $\nu_0(x) = 0$ for all $x \in X$, and the transition relation $\rightarrow_{\mathcal{I}}$ comprises two kinds of moves:

- delay transition: $(l, \nu) \xrightarrow{\delta} (l, \nu \oplus \delta)$, if $\delta \in \mathbb{N}^+$ and $\nu \models I(l)$, $\nu \oplus \delta \models I(l)$;
- discrete transition: $(l, \nu) \xrightarrow{\sigma} (l', \nu[Y := 0])$, if $(l, g, \sigma, Y, l') \in E$ and $\nu \models g$, $\nu[Y := 0] \models I(l')$.

where $(\nu \oplus \delta)(x) = \min\{\nu(x) + \delta, \ c_{\mathcal{A}}(x) + 1\}$, $c_{\mathcal{A}}(x)$ is the maximal constant compared with x in the clock constraints of A.

Let A be a TA. For a state $s_k = (l, \nu)$ where $l \in L, \nu \in \nu_X$. If there is a finite state sequence such that $s_0 \xrightarrow{\alpha_0} s_1 \xrightarrow{\alpha_1} \cdots \xrightarrow{\alpha_{k-1}} s_k$, then s_k is called reachable and l the reachable location in the integer semantics of A, where $\alpha_i \in \Sigma \cup \mathbb{N}^+$, $0 \leq i < k$.

The work in [5] proved the equivalence relation for the set of reachable locations between integer and continuous semantics of CTAs, which formed the basis of BDD-based reachability analysis.

3   Reachability Analysis for CTAs

In the integer semantics, the number of reachable configurations and the time consumption grow greatly with the increasing size of clock domain. Though BDD can reduce the memory consumption by data sharing, dealing with such enormous reachable sets will slow down the verification process.

Based on the symbolic representation for integer clock valuations in [17], we apply the symbolic method to record the reachable configurations of CTAs during the verification process. Meanwhile, we use BDD to record the symbolic sets to increase the data sharing and reduce the memory consumption.

3.1   Delay Sequence

Reachability is one of the most common properties being checked by verifiers. There are two kinds of search strategies for reachability analysis during state space exploration: forward and backward search. Currently our tool uses the forward search technique.

The forward analysis of the reachable configurations starts from the initial state (l_0, v_0). Whenever allowed by the invariant of l_0, time delays can form the sequence $(l_0, v_0 \oplus 0) \xrightarrow{1} (l_0, v_0 \oplus 1) \xrightarrow{1} \cdots$, where $v_0 \oplus i \models I(l_0)$. For example, given $A = \langle L, l_0, \Sigma, X, I, E \rangle$, let $l_0 \in L$ be the initial location with the invariant $x \leq 10^6$, where $x \in X$. Then there may be a sequence: $(l_0, 0) \xrightarrow{1} (l_0, 1) \xrightarrow{1} \cdots \xrightarrow{1} (l_0, 10^6)$. Even with BDD representation for the set of states in this sequence, the frequent operations with the increasing number of reachable configurations are burdensome. To relieve this problem, here we introduce a symbolic representation for this kind of sequence.

Definition 2. *(Symbolic Representation of Delay Sequence)*
Given location l and clock valuation v, let $< l, v >$ denote the set of states $\{(l, v') | v' = v \oplus i, \text{ where } i \geq 0, \text{ and } v' \models I(l)\}$. Based on the maximal constant abstraction, for every $x \in X$, all the clock valuations greater than $c_{\mathcal{A}}(x) + 1$ are

treated as $c_A(x) + 1$. *Therefore, though time can progress infinitely, the number of states in the delay sequence is finite.*

  Therefore, a delay sequence (DS) generated by delay transitions from the state $s = (l, v)$ *can be denoted by* $< l, v >$. *And the number of states in* $< l, v >$ *can be determined by* $I(l)$ *and clock valuation* v.

Let $A = \langle L, l_0, \Sigma, X, I, E \rangle$ be a timed automaton. For a state $s = (l, v)$ and a transition $e = (l, g, \sigma, Y, l') \in E$, where $l \in L$ and $v \in \nu_X$, $post(s, e)$ denotes the set of states $\{< l', v' > |$ if $\exists i \in \mathbb{N}^+$ such that $v \oplus i \models I(l) \wedge g, \ v' = v \oplus i[Y := 0]$ and $v' \models I(l')\}$.

  Given the symbolic representation of DS, the symbolic semantics can be defined as follows.

Definition 3. *(Symbolic Semantics)*
Let $A = \langle L, l_0, \Sigma, X, I, E \rangle$ *be a timed automaton. The symbolic semantics of A is based on the transition system* $\langle S, s_0, \leadsto \rangle$, *where* $S = L \times \nu_X$, $s_0 = < l_0, v_0 >$, *and* $\leadsto$ *is defined by the following rule:*
$< l, v > \leadsto < l', v' >$, *if there exist a transition* $(l, g, \sigma, Y, l') \in E$ *and an* $i \in \mathbb{N}^+$, *such that* $v \oplus i \models I(l) \wedge g, \ v' = v \oplus i[Y := 0]$ *and* $v' \models I(l')$.

Given a time automaton $A = \langle L, l_0, \Sigma, X, I, E \rangle$, and a state (l, v). l is reachable in the integer semantics of A, iff it is reachable in the symbolic semantics $\langle S, s_0, \leadsto \rangle$.

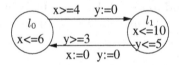

Fig. 1. A simple example

Example 1. The simple timed automaton in Figure 1 is to illustrate the application of DS during the reachability analysis. Every state is denoted by $(l_i, (v(x), v(y)))$, where $(v(x), v(y))$ are two clock valuations of the timed automaton.

  One of the runs in the example is: $(l_0, (0, 0)) \xrightarrow{1} (l_0, (1, 1)) \xrightarrow{1} (l_0, (2, 2)) \xrightarrow{1} (l_0, (3, 3)) \xrightarrow{1} (l_0, (4, 4)) \rightarrow (l_1, (4, 0)) \xrightarrow{1} (l_1, (5, 1)) \cdots$. We list the unfolded state space in Figure 2. The state sequence generated from $(l_0, (0, 0))$ by delay transitions can be represented by $< l_0, (0, 0) >$, and the sequence generated from $(l_1, (4, 0))$ by delay transitions can be represented by $< l_1, (4, 0) >$. Therefore, with DS representation, the size of state space can be reduced. Figure 3 shows the reduced state space.

3.2   Series of Delay Sequences

In a delay sequence, when some states satisfy the guard of a transition, the corresponding discrete transition can be taken, leading to the new states. From these

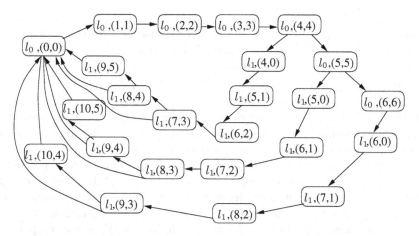

Fig. 2. Unfolded state space of the example

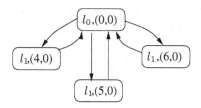

Fig. 3. State space represented by DS

new states, the execution of delay or discrete transitions will be continued. For instance, in the example of Figure 1, some states in delay sequence $< l_0, (0,0) >$ can trigger the discrete transition from l_0 to l_1. Then the corresponding successor states are $(l_1, (4,0)), (l_1, (5,0)), (l_1, (6,0))$. After the discrete transition, only valuations of reset clocks are different from their precursors. If we ignore the reset clocks, we will find that other clock valuations in these successors still obey the rule of "$\oplus$" operation.

Then given a state generated by the discrete transition, we can compute all other new successors from the states in the same delay sequence. Let v_r be the clock valuation after a discrete transition, where Y is the reset clock set. The clock valuaton of the ith state from v_r is $v_{ir} = v_r \circledast i$, where $(v_r \circledast i)(x) =$
$$\begin{cases} v_r(x) + i & x \notin Y \\ 0 & x \in Y \end{cases}.$$
Based on this observation, we can define a coarser data structure, which comprises more than one DS.

Definition 4. *(Series of Delay Sequences)*
*Let $((l,v), k, Y)$ be the symbolic representation for the set of states $\{< l, v' >$
$|v' = v \circledast i, 0 \le i < k\}$. We call this representation the series of delay sequence (SDS). Let $s_0 = (l,v)$ be the so-called start state, then the SDS is denoted by (s_0, k, Y). (s_0, k, Y) is denoted by $(s_0, 1, \emptyset)$ if $Y = \emptyset$.*

Then in Example 1, delay sequences $< l_1, (4,0) >$, $< l_1, (5,0) >$, $< l_1, (6,0) >$ computed from $< l_0, (0,0) >$ by the discrete transition can be represented by $((l_1, (4,0)), 3, \{y\})$. The state space is further reduced.

3.3   Reachability Analysis

During the forward search of the reachable configurations in integer semantics, we use DS to compute the successors and record the set of visited states. Given a DS t, the process for successor computation from t is: the delay sequence from t can trigger the discrete transition e when some states in the sequence satisfy its guard. Then the set of new configurations is computed. In other words, if t is not in P the set of visited configurations, then by the discrete transition e, the delay sequence from t can generate the set of configurations $T = post(s, e)$. And the new successors will be added to the waiting list W for the computation loop. The verification will stop when W is empty or the property is satisfied.

Because the structure of a DS is similar to that of a discrete state, to save the memory consumption during the verification process, we use BDD to represent the set of reachable DSs. The generalized algorithm for reachable analysis is as follows:

1: **Reachability()**
2: $W = \{< l_0, v_0 >\}$;
3: **while** $W \neq \emptyset$ **do**
4:     get $s =< l, v >$ from W;
5:     **if** $s \in P$ **then**
6:         *continue*
7:     **end if**
8:     **for all** $e \in \{(l, g, \sigma, Y, l')\}$ **do**
9:         $T = post(s, e)$;
10:        **if** $\exists t \in T, t \models \phi$ **then**
11:            return *true*
12:        **end if**
13:        **if** $T \not\subseteq W$ **then**
14:            $W = W \cup T$
15:        **end if**
16:        $P = P \cup \{s\}$;
17:    **end for**
18: **end while**
19: return *false*

3.4   The Application of SDS

Because the result of $post(s, e)$ is a set of interrelated DSs, we can use SDS to represent the set of DSs. Then W can be organized as the list of SDSs to reduce the occupied memory during the verification process. Meanwhile, time consumption for computing new reachable configurations from DSs in the same SDS can be saved for their interrelation.

To explain how to compute successors for a SDS, we firstly show the corresponding computation for a DS. Then we discuss the relation between two SDSs with the same locations. Finally we present the SDS-based reachability analysis algorithm.

3.4.1 Successor Computation for DS

Given a timed automaton $A = \langle L, l_0, \Sigma, X, I, E \rangle$, a state (l, v) and $e = (l, g, \sigma, Z, l') \in E$, where $l \in L$ and $v \in \nu_X$. To compute the successors, we need to consider the constraints involving $I(l)$ and g. That is, to trigger the discrete transition, the states should satisfy the constraint $I(l) \wedge g$.

For convenience, given a clock valuation $v \in \nu_X$, let $\theta_X^v = \max\{ c_A(x) - v(x)|x \in X\}$. Given a constraint ϕ, we define

- X_ϕ is the set of all clock variables occuring in ϕ.
- $\phi_l = \bigwedge\{x \le c|x \le c$ is in $\phi\}$.
- $\phi_g = \bigwedge\{x \ge c|x \ge c$ is in $\phi\}$.
- c_ϕ is the maximal constant occuring in ϕ.
- $c_\phi(x)$ be the maximal constant compared with x in ϕ.

In the following computation, for constraint $\varphi = I(l) \wedge g$, let

$$m = \max\{\{c_{\varphi_g}(x) - v(x)|x \in X_{\varphi_g}\}, 0\} \tag{1}$$

$$n = \min\{\{c_{\varphi_l}(x) - v(x)|x \in X_{\varphi_l}\}, \theta_X^v\} \tag{2}$$

Then in the delay sequence $< l, v >$, set of states $\{(l, v \oplus j)|j \in [m, n]\}$ can take the discrete transition $e = (l, g, \sigma, Z, l')$.

Example 2. For the timed automaton in Figure 1, given the initial state $(l_0, (0, 0))$ and the discrete transition from l_0 to l_1. Firstly, $\theta_X^v = 10$ and $\varphi = x \ge 4 \wedge x \le 6$. According to the definition, we get that $\varphi_l = x \le 6$, $c_{\varphi_l}(x) = 6$, $\varphi_g = x \ge 4$, and $c_{\varphi_g}(x) = 4$. Then $m = 4$ and $n = 6$, the set $\{(l_0, (4, 4)), (l_0, (5, 5)), (l_0, (6, 6))\}$ in $< l_0, (0, 0) >$ can take the discrete transition from l_0 to l_1.

Therefore, to get successors from a DS, we have to consider the computation and judgement between clock valuations and constraints.

3.4.2 Successor Computation for SDS

If all successors of DSs in a SDS can be computed according to the successors of one DS, the effort can be saved by avoiding the repeated computation between clock valuations and constraints.

Given a SDS $d = ((l, v), k, Y)$ and $e = (l, g, \sigma, Z, l')$, we have observed that $v(x) \oplus i = v(x) \otimes i$ for all $x \in X - Y$. So some states in the ith delay sequence $< l, v \otimes i >$ and the delay sequence $< l, v >$ may have same valuations except for the clocks in Y.

With this observation, we discuss the corresponding process for computing new configurations. We firstly determine the set of states that can trigger the discrete transition for the start state (l, v).

For the constraint φ and SDS d, let

$$a_1 = \max\{\{c_{\varphi_g}(x) - v(x) | x \in Y \cap X_{\varphi_g}\}, 0\} \tag{3}$$

$$b_1 = \min\{\{c_{\varphi_l}(x) - v(x) | x \in Y \cap X_{\varphi_l}\}, \theta_Y^v\} \tag{4}$$

$$a_2 = \max\{\{c_{\varphi_g}(x) - v(x) | x \in (X - Y) \cap X_{\varphi_g}\}, 0\} \tag{5}$$

$$b_2 = \min\{\{c_{\varphi_l}(x) - v(x) | x \in (X - Y) \cap X_{\varphi_l}\}, \theta_{(X-Y)}^v\} \tag{6}$$

Then $m = \max\{a_1, a_2\}$, and

$$n = \begin{cases} \max\{b_1, b_2\} & \text{if } X_{\varphi_l} = \emptyset \\ b_2 & \text{if } (X_{\varphi_l} \cap Y) = \emptyset \\ b_1 & \text{if } (X_{\varphi_l} \cap X - Y) = \emptyset \\ \min\{b_1, b_2\} & \text{if } (X_{\varphi_l} \cap Y) \neq \emptyset \wedge (X_{\varphi_l} \cap X - Y) \neq \emptyset \end{cases}.$$

Set of states $\{(l, v \oplus j) | j \in [m, n]\}$ in the delay sequence $< l, v >$ can trigger the discrete transition $e = (l, g, \sigma, Z, l')$.

Example 3. Now we use SDS $((l_1, (4, 0)), 3, \{y\})$ and the transition from l_1 to l_0 in Figure 1 as the example. For the start state $(l_1, (4, 0))$ and guard $y \geq 3$ in the transition, we get that $\varphi = x \leq 10 \wedge y \leq 5 \wedge y \geq 3$. According to the Equation 3 $\sim$ 6, $a_1 = 3$, $b_1 = 5$, $a_2 = 0$, and $b_2 = 6$ respectively. Because $X_{\varphi_l} = \{x, y\}$ and $Y = \{y\}$, neither $X_{\varphi_l} \cap Y$ nor $X_{\varphi_l} \cap X - Y$ is empty. Therefore $m = 3$, $n = 5$, the set of states $\{(l_1, (4, 0) \oplus j) | j \in [3, 5]\}$ in the delay sequence $< l_1, (4, 0) >$ can take the discrete transition.

After the computation for the successors of the start state in SDS, we can get the set of successors from other DSs in the same SDS according to the feature of SDS.

For the delay sequence of $< l, v \circledast i >$ where $0 \leq i < k$, $m = \max\{a_1, a_2 - i\}$, and

$$n = \begin{cases} \max\{b_1, b_2\} & \text{if } X_{\varphi_l} = \emptyset \\ \max\{b_2 - i, 0\} & \text{if } (X_{\varphi_l} \cap Y) = \emptyset \\ b_1 & \text{if } (X_{\varphi_l} \cap X - Y) = \emptyset \\ \min\{b_1, \max\{b_2 - i, 0\}\} & \text{if } (X_{\varphi_l} \cap Y) \neq \emptyset \wedge (X_{\varphi_l} \cap X - Y) \neq \emptyset \end{cases},$$

states that can trigger the discrete transition e are the set $\{(l, (v \circledast i) \oplus j) | j \in [m, n]\}$.

Example 4. For SDS $((l_1, (4, 0)), 3, \{y\})$, we have obtained that $a_1 = 3$, $b_1 = 5$, $a_2 = 0$, and $b_2 = 6$. Then

1. For the delay sequence $< l_1, (4,0) \circledast 1 >$, set of states $\{(l_1, (5,0) \oplus j) | j \in [3,5]\}$ can trigger the discrete transition.
2. For the delay sequence $< l_1, (4,0) \circledast 2 >$, set of states $\{(l_1, (6,0) \oplus j) | j \in [3,4]\}$ can trigger the discrete transition.

3.4.3 SDS-Based Reachability Analysis

The following is the reachability analysis algorithm by the application of SDS.

```
 1: ReachabilitySDS
 2: SDS d';
 3: stack of SDS W;
 4: W.push((l_0, v_0), 1, ∅);
 5: while W ≠ ∅ do
 6:    get d = (s_0, k, Y) from W;
 7:    for all e = (l, g, σ, Y', l') enabled at d do
 8:       SuccessorN(a_1, b_1, a_2, b_2, d, e);
 9:       for i = 0; i < k; i + + do
10:          s_i = s_0 ⊛ i;
11:          if s_i ∈ P then
12:             continue
13:          end if
14:          distance = getdistance(i, φ, a_1, b_1, a_2, b_2);
15:          if distance < 0 then
16:             break
17:          end if
18:          s' = (l', (s_i.v ⊕ max{a_1, a_2 − i})[Y' := 0]);
19:          d' = (s', distance + 1, Y');
20:          if ∃s ∈ d', s ⊨ φ then
21:             return true
22:          end if
23:          if d' ∉ W then
24:             W.push(d')
25:          end if
26:          P = P ∪ {s_i};
27:       end for
28:    end for
29: end while
30: return false
```

Line 8 $SuccessorN$ computes the related ranges for the start state according to the certain discrete transition. Line 9-27 compute all the successors of d, and Line 13 $getdistance$ is to get the number of states in every DS which is capable of taking the discrete transition (the number of successors for every DS). Then Line 18, 19 generate a new set of DSs.

3.5   Inclusion Relation of SDS

When we get a new set of reachable configurations, we need to judge its relation with those SDSs in W to avoid the repeated computation and ensure the termination of checking. The relation between the new set d' and $d \in W$ is:

- *equivalence*, if their start states, the number of DSs, and the set of reset clocks are equal, which is a special case of inclusion. Or
- *intersection*, if two sets of reset clocks are equal, and there exists $0 \leq i < k$, $0 \leq j < k'$, such that all the valuations of $s_0 \circledast i$ and $s'_0 \circledast j$ are the same state. Or
- *irrelevance*, neither with equivalence nor intersection relation.

The algorithm for judging SDS relations is as follows. The idea of the algorithm is: firstly we should judge whether the differences between two clock valuations are the same. If some clock differences are different from others, there is no equivalence or intersection relation. If all clock valuations except for reset ones have the same difference, two SDSs may intersect, or one is a subset of the other.

1: **SDSRelation**(d, d')
2: select an x which $x \notin Y \wedge s_0(x) < c_\mathcal{A}(x) \wedge s'_0(x) < c_\mathcal{A}(x)$;
3: diff$=s_0(x) - s'_0(x)$;
4: **for all** $x \in X - Y$ **do**
5:    **if** $s_0(x) - s'_0(x) \neq$ diff **then**
6:        **return** *irrelevance*
7:    **end if**
8: **end for**
9: **if** diff $\leq 0 \wedge$ diff $+ k \geq k'$ **then**
10:    **return** $d \supseteq d'$
11: **else**
12:    **if** diff $\geq 0 \wedge$ diff $+ k \leq k'$ **then**
13:        **return** $d \subseteq d'$
14:    **end if**
15: **end if**
16: **return** *intersection*

---

4   Experiments

Based on the symbolic data structure, we have implemented a prototype to support the verification of real-time systems with multi-processes, synchronizations, and broadcasts. The tool is available at http://lcs.ios.ac.cn/~ligy/tools/. We compare the experiment results with those of Rabbit. All experiments were performed on a 2.6GHz Pentium 4 with 512MB of memory. And experiments were limited to 30 minutes of CPU time.

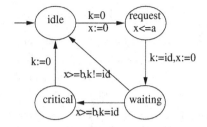

Fig. 4. Fischer's mutual exclusive protocol

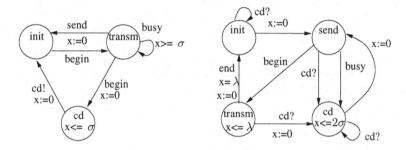

Fig. 5. CSMA/CD protocol

We use Fischer's mutual exclusive protocol(f) [12] (see Figure 4), CSMA/CD protocol(c) [7] (see Figure 5) and two industrial case studies (Gear Controller [14], and an Audio/Video Protocol [11]) as the examples. In the following tables, we list the time consumption(t) in seconds and the number of reachable configurations (*state* for Rabbit, and DS for our implementation). *BDD* is the number of nodes in the BDD representation for the whole reachable configuration when the verification finishes, which is in direct proportion to the memory consumption. "-" indicates that the result is unavailable.

To compare the sensitivity of tools to clock constants, we demonstrate experiment results for different valuations of a and b in Fischer's mutual exclusive protocol, λ and σ in CSMA/CD protocol. Here the complete state space was generated.

As we know, the greater the maximal constant, the more the number of reachable configurations will be. Table 1 and 2 list results of Rabbit and our prototype under different valuations for two protocols. Comparing results in two tables, the number of reachable configurations in Rabbit and the prototype increases rapidly, as well as the time consumption. However, w.r.t. the finial number of BDD nodes and the number of reachable configurations, the increase of our prototype are quite less than that of Rabbit. For both Fischer's protocol and CSMA/CD protocol, our prototype scales better with the growth of constants.

For the industrial examples, the complete state space of Gear Controller was explored in 177.22 seconds with 64872 BDD nodes recording all the reachable configurations; and the complete state space of Audio/Video protocol was

Table 1. Rabbit's results for Fischer's (f) and CSMA/CD (c)

No.	a=2,b=4			a=4,b=8			a=8,b=16			a=16,b=32		
	t	state	BDD	t	state	BDD	t	state	BDD	t	state	BDD
f2	0	193	133	0	467	216	0	1399	374	0	4799	684
f3	0	1893	605	0	7095	1318	0	36939	3385	0	234867	9998
f4	0	17577	1956	0	102291	5531	1	922479	19741	4	1.08322e+07	85485
f5	0	158449	4720	0	1.43358e+06	16218	3	2.2305e+07	75043	29	4.8236e+08	450942
f6	1	1.40518e+06	8751	2	1.97584e+07	34284	8	5.2812e+08	191567	-	-	-
f7	0	1.23492e+07	13821	2	2.69305e+08	58725	22	1.23136e+10	371250	-	-	-
f8	1	1.07952e+08	19897	5	3.63936e+09	88780	-	-	-	-	-	-
f9	1	9.40233e+08	26960	10	4.88237e+10	124248	-	-	-	-	-	-
f10	2	8.16454e+09	35014	17	6.50652e+11	165133	-	-	-	-	-	-
	$\lambda = 4, \sigma = 1$			$\lambda = 8, \sigma = 2$			$\lambda = 16, \sigma = 4$			$\lambda = 32, \sigma = 8$		
c2	0	157	213	0	358	459	0	982	994	1	3118	2195
c3	0	1446	620	0	4609	1614	2	19569	4308	2	105025	12579
c4	2	11225	1237	1	49645	3636	2	325631	11369	10	2.9609e+06	44015
c5	1	84140	2035	1	502835	7792	8	5.02002e+06	32181	-	-	-
c6	0	594174	2851	3	4.75103e+06	13836	19	7.22529e+07	70441	-	-	-
c7	1	4.01893e+06	3667	5	4.27544e+07	20989	-	-	-	-	-	-
c8	2	2.63267e+07	4483	9	3.71571e+08	28482	-	-	-	-	-	-

Table 2. Our results for Fischer's (f) and CSMA/CD (c)

No.	a=2,b=4			a=4,b=8			a=8,b=16			a=16,b=32		
	t	DS	BDD	t	DS	BDD	t	DS	BDD	t	DS	BDD
f2	0.05	22	62	0.05	22	72	0.05	22	82	0.05	22	92
f3	0.08	107	151	0.16	119	181	0.09	143	211	0.16	191	241
f4	0.14	476	273	0.19	588	333	0.33	812	393	0.80	1260	453
f5	0.44	1970	416	0.78	2620	512	1.95	3920	608	5.97	6520	704
f6	1.97	7679	583	4.13	10717	721	11.63	16793	859	38.59	28945	997
f7	9.95	28551	772	22.13	41123	958	63.48	66267	1144	222.56	116555	1330
f8	43.75	102382	987	102.95	150610	1227	313.00	247066	1467	1063.27	439978	1707
f9	190.83	357176	1222	466.16	533102	1522	1398.83	884954	1822	-	-	-
f10	932.52	1220153	1481	-	1839819	1847	-	3079151	2213	-	-	-
	$\lambda = 4, \sigma = 1$			$\lambda = 8, \sigma = 2$			$\lambda = 16, \sigma = 4$			$\lambda = 32, \sigma = 8$		
c2	0.08	31	86	0.08	46	106	0.09	78	149	0.09	142	226
c3	0.16	202	180	0.17	387	311	0.23	885	551	0.47	2385	2141
c4	0.34	1038	344	0.61	2123	787	2.25	5507	1965	18.06	16643	5730
c5	1.70	4479	619	3.84	9814	1578	31.59	28672	4381	659.59	101732	14177
c6	8.67	17786	910	28.66	41580	2441	455.17	139100	7046	-	634740	23636
c7	37.45	67046	1202	183.61	166701	3308	-	-	-	-	-	-
c8	179.45	243741	1494	1243.05	641407	4175	-	-	-	-	-	-

unfolded in 917.67 seconds with 2351 BDD nodes. However, Rabbit failed in the limited memory. The performance of our prototype is dramatic compared with Rabbit.

Therefore, our tool's sensitivity to constant valuations is lower than that of Rabbit. The reason is that BDD representation for DS is coarser than that for explicit states in integer semantics.

5   Conclusions and Further Work

In this paper we propose a new symbolic structure for the discrete states in the integer semantics of closed timed automata for the reachability analysis. Concluded from the experiment results, our structure is better than the pure BDD representation for explicit configurations w.r.t. the influence of the magnitude of clock constants. And the memory consumption is greatly reduced, benefited from the data sharing ability of BDD.

However, the prototype does not use BDD to represent the transition relations yet, which results in the transformation from DS to BDD frequently. The transformation and judgement between DS and BDD waste lots of time. So our time consumption is higher than that of Rabbit. For further work, we need to investigate the combination of BDD representation for transition relations and our symbolic data structure to improve the performance of our prototype.

References

1. Alur, R., Dill, D.L.: A theory of timed automata. Theoretical Computer Science 126(2), 183–235 (1994)
2. Asarin, E., Maler, O., Pnueli, A.: On discretization of delays in timed automata and digital circuits. In: Sangiorgi, D., de Simone, R. (eds.) CONCUR 1998. LNCS, vol. 1466, pp. 470–484. Springer, Heidelberg (1998)
3. Behrmann, G., Larsen, K.G., Pearson, J., Weise, C., Yi, W.: Efficient timed reachability analysis using clock difference diagrams. In: Computer Aided Verification, pp. 341–353 (1999)
4. Bellman, R.: Dynamic Programming. Princeton University Press, Princeton (1957)
5. Beyer, D.: Improvements in BDD-based reachability analysis of timed automata. In: Oliveira, J.N., Zave, P. (eds.) FME 2001. LNCS, vol. 2021, pp. 318–343. Springer, Heidelberg (2001)
6. Beyer, D., Lewerentz, C., Noack, A.: Rabbit: A tool for BDD-based verification of real-time systems. In: Hunt Jr., W.A., Somenzi, F. (eds.) CAV 2003. LNCS, vol. 2725, pp. 122–125. Springer, Heidelberg (2003)
7. Beyer, D., Noack, A.: Can decision diagrams overcome state space explosion in real-time verification? In: König, H., Heiner, M., Wolisz, A. (eds.) FORTE 2003. LNCS, vol. 2767, pp. 193–208. Springer, Heidelberg (2003)
8. Bozga, M., Daws, C., Maler, O., Olivero, A., Tripakis, S., Yovine, S.: Kronos: A model-checking tool for real-time systems. In: Hu, A.J., Vardi, M.Y. (eds.) CAV 1998. LNCS, vol. 1427, pp. 546–550. Springer, Heidelberg (1998)
9. Asarin, E., Bozga, M., Kerbrat, A., Maler, O., Pnueli, A., Rasse, A.: Data structures for the verification of timed automata. In: Maler, O. (ed.) Hybrid and Real-Time Systems, Grenoble, France. LNCS, pp. 346–360. Springer Verlag, Heidelberg (1997)
10. Gollü, A., Puri, A., Varaiya, P.: Discetization of timed automata. In: Proceedings of the 33rd IEEE conferene on decision and control, pp. 957–958 (1994)
11. Havelund, K., Skou, A., Larsen, K.G., Lund, K.: Formal modeling and analysis of an audio/video protocol: An industrial case study using UPPAAL. In: Proc. of the 18th IEEE Real-Time Systems Symposium, pp. 2–13. IEEE Computer Society Press, Los Alamitos (1997)

12. Lamport, L.: A fast mutual exclusion algorithm. ACM Trans. Comput. Syst. 5(1), 1–11 (1987)
13. Larsen, K.G., Pettersson, P., Yi, W.: UPPAAL in a nutshell. International Journal on Software Tools for Technology Transfer 1(1-2), 134–152 (1997)
14. Lindahl, M., Pettersson, P., Yi, W.: Formal design and analysis of a gear controller. In: Steffen, B. (ed.) ETAPS 1998 and TACAS 1998. LNCS, vol. 1384, pp. 281–297. Springer, Heidelberg (1998)
15. Møller, J., Lichtenberg, J., Andersen, H.R., Hulgaard, H.: Difference decision diagrams. In: Flum, J., Rodríguez-Artalejo, M. (eds.) CSL 1999. LNCS, vol. 1683, pp. 111–125. Springer, Heidelberg (1999)
16. Wang, F.: Efficient verification of timed automata with bdd-like data-structures. In: VMCAI 2003. Proceedings of the 4th International Conference on Verification, Model Checking, and Abstract Interpretation, London, UK, pp. 189–205. Springer-Verlag, Heidelberg (2003)
17. Yan, R., Li, G., Tang, Z.: Symbolic model checking of finite precision timed automata. In: Van Hung, D., Wirsing, M. (eds.) ICTAC 2005. LNCS, vol. 3722, pp. 272–287. Springer, Heidelberg (2005)

The DHCP Failover Protocol: A Formal Perspective

Rui Fan[1], Ralph Droms[2], Nancy Griffeth[3], and Nancy Lynch[1]

[1] MIT CSAIL
[2] Cisco Systems
[3] Lehman College, CUNY

Abstract. We present a formal specification and analysis of a fault-tolerant DHCP algorithm, used to automatically configure certain host parameters in an IP network. Our algorithm uses ideas from an algorithm presented in [5], but is considerably simpler and at the same time more structured and rigorous. We specify the assumptions and behavior of our algorithm as traces of Timed Input/Output Automata, and prove its correctness using this formalism. Our algorithm is based on a composition of independent subalgorithms solving variants of the classical leader election and shared register problems in distributed computing. The modularity of our algorithm facilitates its understanding and analysis, and can also aid in optimizing the algorithm or proving lower bounds. Our work demonstrates that formal methods can be feasibly applied to complex real-world problems to improve and simplify their solutions.

1 Introduction

The *Dynamic Host Configuration Protocol (DHCP)* [4] is a widely deployed mechanism allowing devices to automatically obtain a unique IP address and other configuration information needed for communication on an IP network such as the Internet. Current implementations of DHCP use a single DHCP *server* to assign addresses from a predefined address pool. If the server fails, then addresses from the pool can no longer be reassigned, and are in effect lost from the address space. DHCP has recently been supplemented by the *DHCP Failover (DHCPF)* protocol [5], which manages an address pool using multiple servers. DHCPF increases the fault tolerance of DHCP, and also allows greater performance through load-balancing.

The main difficulty encountered in managing addresses using multiple servers instead of one is the need to maintain a consistent view across all the servers of the currently assigned addresses. Most standard database consistency techniques cannot be used to solve the DHCPF problem because they are too slow. A key insight of the algorithm described in [5] is to use two mechanisms for assigning addresses. The first mechanism relies on *synchronized clocks*; it is fast, requiring no communication, but limits how long addresses can be assigned. The second mechanism is slower, using explicit acknowledgments between the servers, but avoids the limitations on assignments. This algorithm is currently described in

J. Derrick and J. Vain (Eds.): FORTE 2007, LNCS 4574, pp. 211–226, 2007.

an Internet Draft that is over 130 pages long. Part of the length of the Draft is due to the need to deal with many possible types of concurrent server failures. The algorithm represents different combinations of failures as states of a system, and defines a large number of transitions between the states as failures occur or are resolved.

In this paper, we look at the DHCPF problem from a more formal and theoretical perspective. First, we extract the essential behavior of the algorithm in [5] and precisely specify the behavior as traces of a set of interacting *Timed I/O Automata (TIOA)* [6]. In this formulation, DHCPF is a kind of timed mutual exclusion problem. As in mutex, the safety condition requires that any address is used by at most one client at a time. The liveness condition requires that, under certain favorable timing conditions that are likely to occur in practice, any client wanting an IP address is granted one, as long as some addresses are available.

Our second contribution is to *decompose* this mutual exclusion problem into several simpler and independent subproblems, each mimicking a standard problem in distributed computing. In particular, we view DHCPF as involving the following two steps. First, for each IP address, we choose a *leader* server to be the only server allowed to assign that address. The leader for an address can change as different servers fail and recover, but we guarantee that there is at most one leader at a time. Thus, the first part of the problem can be seen as a multi-shot leader election problem. The second part of the problem consists of the leader assigning its address in such a way that even if it fails, and a different server becomes leader, the subsequent leader preserves the safety and liveness properties on that address. This can be seen as implementing a single-writer, multi-reader shared register, where the writer can change over time. In particular, only the current leader of an address is allowed to write assignments for the address to the register, but any server that takes over for a failed leader can read the register to ensure it does not double-allocate the address, and also gains the privilege to write to the register. The main idea that we adopt from [5] is to write to the register in two ways, either by an *implicit*, fast write, requiring no communication but relying on synchronized clocks, or by an *explicit*, slow write, using server acknowledgments.

There are several benefits to our formal treatment of DHCPF. First, the precise specification of DHCPF helps end-users of the service, who may need a rigorous understanding of the behavior of DHCPF that is difficult to obtain from the Internet Draft. Second, implementing DHCPF as a composition of smaller subalgorithms helps to understand and analyze its behavior, and also makes the algorithm easier to improve or optimize. For example, we can study the effects of tuning network parameters, such as the amount of clock skew or the bound on message delay, on the performance of our algorithm by studying their effects on the individual subalgorithms. We can also isolate the effects of different types of failures on the algorithm to how they affect the subalgorithms. This isolation is the main reason that our algorithm is simpler than the algorithm in [5]. Lastly, our decomposition suggests that it may be possible to prove lower bounds for the DHCPF problem by proving lower bounds for the subproblems, which seems to be a considerably easier task.

Our treatment of DHCPF, while formal, was not mechanical. A considerable effort was involved in distilling the expansive description of DHCPF in the Internet Draft into a more concise formal specification. Nevertheless, parts of our specification are still more complicated than we would like. A second problem was finding a modular DHCPF algorithm, by matching parts of the specification against self-contained distributed computing problems. Systematizing this design process, indeed, formalizing the formalization process, would be a fascinating challenge.

The remainder of this paper is organized as follows. In Section 2, we describe the TIOA model. We give an overview of DHCPF and state the properties it satisfies in Section 3. We describe a DHCPF algorithm in Section 4, and prove its correctness and performance properties in Section 5. Finally, we conclude in Section 6.

2   Model and Notation

We model the clients, servers and communication network of our DHCPF algorithm as interacting Timed I/O Automata (*TIOA*). TIOA allows modeling of automata with continuous state spaces, whose executions evolve in real time. Our algorithm does not use the full power of this formalism. In what follows, we describe the TIOA model only to the extent necessary to understand our algorithm and its proof. Please see [6] for additional details. Each Timed I/O automaton has internal *state* variables, and discrete or continuous actions which change its state. We call discrete actions simply *actions*, and we call continuous actions *trajectories*. Actions always occur instantly, while a trajectory may have a positive time duration. As an example, we can model a mobile robot by a TIOA. The state represents the position of the robot. Trajectories are movements of the robot, and actions are changes in its destination (which we imagine as involving an instantaneous computations).

Several TIOAs can be *composed*. Roughly speaking, this forms a new automata whose state space is a Cartesian product of the state spaces of the constituent automata, and whose action space is the union of the constituent action spaces. However, certain states and actions become identified in the composition process; we describe this in more detail later. An *execution* is a sequence of the form $\alpha = \gamma_0 \sigma_1 \gamma_1 \sigma_2 \ldots \gamma_n \sigma_n$. Here, each γ_i represents a trajectory, and each σ_i represents a (discrete) action. We say a *state occurrence* (resp., *action occurrence*) is a *particular instance* of a state (resp., action) which occurs in an execution. Note that this is different from the state or action itself, which can occur multiple times in an execution. Let α be an execution, and let s, s' be state occurrences in α. We write $s \prec s'$ if s occurs before s' in α. We define $s \preceq s'$ in the obvious way; we also extend this notation to action occurrences σ, σ' in α. We write $s'' \in [s, s']$ if s'' is a state occurrence in α, and $s \preceq s'' \preceq s'$. Lastly, we say the *time* at which a state occurrence s occurs is the sum of the time durations of all the trajectories before s. We write this as $\zeta(s)$.

To model the clients in DHCPF, let C be an index set representing an arbitrary set of client processes. We use the notation i, i', i_1, etc. throughout the paper to denote clients. Similarly, let S be an index set representing server processes; we use j, j', j_1, etc. to denote servers. Each server can *fail* or *recover*. When a server fails, it stops performing any actions or trajectories. When it recovers, all its internal state variables are set to default values, and it begins executing from its initial state. We do not consider malicious server behaviors. Let Φ denote an arbitrary set of IP addresses; we write $\phi \in \Phi$ for a particular IP address. Servers will allocate addresses from Φ to clients. Each client and server is equipped with a real valued monotonically nondecreasing *clock* variable, which intuitively represents that process's perception of real time[1]. For the remainder of this paper, fix an arbitrary $\Delta \in \mathbb{R}^{\geq 0}$. We assume the *clock* of any process differs from real time by at most Δ. That is, we assume

Assumption 1. *Let $k \in C \cup S$. Then for any state occurrence s in any execution, we have $|s.clock_k - \zeta(s)| \leq \Delta$.*

Clients and servers communicate over a point-to-point message passing network. We assume that the network may lose, duplicate or reorder messages, but does not generate spurious messages. The network works as follows. Let $k, k' \in C \cup S$ be any two processes. When k wants to send a message m to k' during some action σ, we say that k *adds* (m, k') *to buffer*. If m is not lost by the network, then after a finite but nondeterministic time representing the message delay, the action $\mathsf{recv}_{k,k'}(m)$ occurs, causing k' to receive m; furthermore, k' knows that k sent the message. Note that these notational conventions are adopted from [6]. In describing our DHCPF algorithm in Section 4, we assume a network service exists which implements these communication actions.

3   A Formal Specification of DHCPF

In this section, we formally define the DHCPF problem. In particular, we define the interface between clients and servers in DHCPF. We also define the assumptions DHCPF makes about its operating environment. Finally, we define the properties DHCPF satisfies, given the environmental assumptions, in terms of the traces of a TIOA. In Section 4, we describe an algorithm satisfying this specification.

3.1   The DHCPF Interface

Figure 1 shows the client/server interface in DHCPF. It mimics, except for superficial differences, the client/server interface of the non-fault-tolerant DHCP. This is done to make the use of DHCPF instead of DHCP transparent to clients, in order to facilitate its deployment.

---

[1] Note that *clock* evolves according to a trajectory. In fact, *clock* is the only variable in our algorithm whose value follows a trajectory; the values of all other variables only change by (discrete) actions.

We will describe the interface of DHCPF by describing its typical modes of operation. DHCPF works by leasing IP addresses to clients. That is, a server tells a client that it can use a certain address up to some *lease* time, after which the client is supposed to release the address. There are two main types of interactions in DHCPF. When a client does not have a lease, it tries to *request* a lease. If the client already has a lease, it can try to *renew* the lease. Each type of interaction requires sending and receiving multiple messages. It is helpful to be able to identify all the messages in an interaction. We do this by labeling all the messages sent during the interaction by an *interaction instance* κ. Any two different interactions (even by the same client) are labeled with different κ. This labeling can be achieved using standard timestamping techniques [7,3]. We let K denote the set of all interaction instances.

We now describe the interaction for a client i to request a lease. Please also see Figure 1. Client i first broadcasts a discover message to all the servers, labeled by some interaction instance κ. A server j that receives the discover message sends an offer message to i for some address $\phi \in \Phi^2$. Note that j must offer i an address immediately (if any are available). That is, the DHCP (and hence DHCPF) specification does not give j time to first communicate with the other servers to find out the current lease times for all addresses, before deciding what address to offer to i. It is precisely this need for an immediate response by j that prevents most database algorithms from being used to implement DHCPF. i may get offers for several ϕ's from different servers. i chooses one such ϕ as its preferred IP address, and broadcasts a request to lease that ϕ until time τ. Some server then responds to i with an ack message, leasing ϕ to i until time τ', where τ' may be *different* from the lease time τ which i requested. i is supposed to release ϕ when i's *clock* variable equals τ'.

If i already has a lease for ϕ until time τ', then i can try to renew its lease. To do this, i broadcasts a renew message to all the servers, including in the message the values of ϕ, τ' and τ, where τ is the new lease time that i wants. The message is labeled by κ. Some server then responds to i with an ack message extending i's lease on ϕ to time τ'', where τ'' may be different from i's desired lease τ.

In this paper, we assume that clients behave *correctly*. In particular, we assume that clients follow the order of interaction described above to request or renew an address. We also assume that clients release an IP address after their lease for the address expires. In general however, the servers have little means to enforce, or sometimes to even detect such behaviors. We leave the task of dealing with faulty clients as interesting future work.

Lastly, for any $j \in S$, we model server j's (stop) failure and recovery via the fail$_j$ and recover$_j$ actions.

3.2 DHCPF Assumptions

In this section, we describe the assumptions that DHCPF makes about its environment. The safety and liveness properties of DHCPF rely on different assumptions.

---

[2] If all the addresses in Φ are already offered or leased to other clients, then the server does not send offer.

$\mathsf{bcast}_i(\langle \mathsf{discover}, \kappa \rangle)$	i looks for an IP address; κ is the interaction instance.
$\mathsf{recv}_{i,j}(\langle \mathsf{discover}, \kappa \rangle)$	j receives i's discover message.
$\mathsf{send}_{j,i}(\langle \mathsf{offer}, \kappa, \phi \rangle)$	j offers ϕ to i.
$\mathsf{recv}_{j,i}(\langle \mathsf{offer}, \kappa, \phi \rangle)$	i receives j's offer.
$\mathsf{bcast}_i(\langle \mathsf{request}, \kappa, \phi, \tau \rangle)$	i requests ϕ till time τ.
$\mathsf{recv}_{i,j}(\langle \mathsf{request}, \kappa, \phi, \tau \rangle)$	j receives i's lease request.
$\mathsf{bcast}_i(\langle \mathsf{renew}, \kappa, \phi, \tau, \tau' \rangle)$	i wants to renew ϕ till time τ; τ' is i's last lease time for ϕ.
$\mathsf{recv}_{i,j}(\langle \mathsf{renew}, \kappa, \phi, \tau, \tau' \rangle)$	j receives i's renew message.
$\mathsf{send}_{j,i}(\langle \mathsf{ack}, \kappa, \phi, \tau \rangle)$	j gives i address ϕ till time τ.
$\mathsf{recv}_{j,i}(\langle \mathsf{ack}, \kappa, \phi, \tau \rangle)$	i receives j's acknowledgment.
$\mathsf{fail}_j, \mathsf{recover}_j$	j fails or recovers.

Fig. 1. The DHCPF protocol interface, for $i \in C, j \in S$

The DHCPF safety property roughly says that any IP address is leased to at most one client at a time. To satisfy this property, DHCPF requires a *failure detector*, which is a service telling every server which other servers have failed. The DHCPF liveness properties says that when a client requests or tries to renew an address, it will get an address within a few message round trips' time, as long as some addresses are available. This property is only satisfied in "nice" periods of an execution. These assumptions are described in the proceeding sections.

An effort was made to "minimize" the assumptions that DHCPF relies upon. Indeed, at an intuitive level, it seems unlikely that any DHCPF algorithm can work correctly if servers have no idea about each others' status, if servers continuously fail and recover, or if the network delays messages for very long times. Furthermore, we believe that the assumptions we make are sufficiently weak that they are likely to be satisfied, at least typically, in practice. Finally, while we do not study questions related to minimality or impossibility in this paper, we believe that these may be interesting future work.

In the remainder of this section, let α be an arbitrary execution. All state and action occurrences are assumed to occur in α.

A Failure Detector Service. Recall that each server can fail, and then subsequently recover. We define the following.

Definition 3.1. *Let $j \in S$ and let s be a state occurrence. We say j is* alive *in s if there exists an action occurrence $\sigma = \mathsf{recover}_j$ such that $\sigma \prec s$, and for all action occurrences σ' such that $\sigma \prec \sigma' \prec s$, we have $\sigma' \neq \mathsf{fail}_j$. If j is not alive in s, we say j is* dead *in s.*

We assume that all servers are initially alive.

Definition 3.2. *Let s and s' be state occurrences, with $s \prec s'$. We let $\Lambda(s, s') = \{j \mid (j \in S) \land (\forall s'' \in [s, s'] : j \text{ is alive in } s'')\}$ be the set of servers that are alive throughout the interval $[s, s']$.*

A *failure detector* service Υ informs each server which other servers are alive or dead. In practice, Υ might represent a system administrator who manually informs servers about failures and recoveries. Formally, we assume that for each $j \in S$, in addition to j's actions shown in Figure 1, j also has the following two sets of actions, which we call *FD-actions*.

1. $\forall j' \in S : \mathsf{recv}_{\Upsilon,j}(\langle dead, j' \rangle)$. Υ informs j that j' is dead.
2. $\forall j' \in S : \mathsf{recv}_{\Upsilon,j}(\langle alive, j' \rangle)$. Υ informs j that j' is alive.

In order to be useful, Υ is required to be *accurate* and *timely*. In particular, let λ be some nonnegative constant. The accuracy property says that if a server j' has been alive or dead for λ or more time before the current time, then any information Υ gives to a server j about j' is correct. The timeliness property says that if j is alive for at least λ time, then j will receive failure information from Υ about every server $j' \in S$. These are captured in the following definition.

Definition 3.3. *Let $\lambda \in \mathbb{R}^{\geq 0}$. We say a failure detector Υ is λ-perfect if the following hold for any state occurrences s and s' such that $\zeta(s') - \zeta(s) \geq \lambda$.*

1. *(Accuracy) Let $j, j' \in S$, and suppose the action occurrence $\mathsf{recv}_{\Upsilon,j}(\langle dead, j' \rangle)$ (resp., $\mathsf{recv}_{\Upsilon,j}(\langle alive, j' \rangle)$) immediately precedes s'. Then j' is dead (resp., alive) in some state during $[s, s']$.*
2. *(Timeliness) Suppose $j \in \Lambda(s, s')$. Then for every $j' \in S$, either $\mathsf{recv}_{\Upsilon,j}(\langle fail, j' \rangle) \in [s, s']$ or $\mathsf{recv}_{\Upsilon,j}(\langle recover, j' \rangle) \in [s, s']$.*

In order to guarantee correct behavior, the DHCPF algorithm we describe in Section 4 requires that a λ-perfect Υ, for some finite λ. In [5], a weaker failure detector is used which can sometimes give incorrect information. However, in such cases, the algorithm of [5] can actually allocate the same IP address to more than one client. We believe that this limitation is inherent. That is, we believe (though we do not prove) that any fault-tolerant algorithm implementing a reasonable form of DHCP requires the use of a server failure detector satisfying similar safety and liveness properties to those we define above. Indeed, failure detectors are a widely adopted notion in distributed computing, and are provably necessary to solve many problems, especially *agreement problems* of the type similar to DHCPF; see e.g. [1,2].

Stable and Timely Periods. We now describe the assumptions DHCPF makes in order to satisfy its liveness properties. As mentioned earlier, these properties only hold during "nice" periods of an execution. A nice period roughly corresponds to a sufficiently long time interval in which no servers fail or recover, and in which messages are delivered quickly. More precisely, we define the following.

Definition 3.4. *Let $\lambda \in \mathbb{R}^{\geq 0}$, and let s and s' be state occurrences with $s \prec s'$. We say that $[s, s']$ is λ-stable if we have the following*

1. *There exists $j \in S$ such that j is alive in state occurrence s'', $\forall s'' : \zeta(s) - \lambda \leq \zeta(s'') \leq \zeta(s')$.*
2. *For all action occurrences σ such that $\zeta(s) - \lambda \leq \zeta(\sigma) \leq \zeta(s')$, we have $\sigma \notin \{fail_*, recover_*\}$.*

Thus, $[s, s']$ is λ-stable if in the entire time duration $[\zeta(s) - \lambda, \zeta(s')]$, no servers fail or recover, and there is at least one live server.

Definition 3.5. *Let s and s' be state occurrences such that $s \prec s'$, and let $\lambda \in \mathbb{R}^{\geq 0}$ be such that $\lambda \leq \zeta(s') - \zeta(s)$. We say $[s, s']$ is λ-timely if for any message m, for any $k, k' \in C \cup S$, and for any action occurrence σ adding (m, k') to buffer, such that $\zeta(s) \leq \zeta(\sigma) \leq \zeta(s') - \lambda$, there exists action occurrence $\sigma' = recv_{k,k'}(m)$, such that $\sigma \prec \sigma' \preceq s'$.*

Thus, $[s, s']$ is λ timely if the interval is at least λ in duration, and any message sent during the interval at least λ time before s' is received during $[s, s']$.

3.3   DHCPF Properties

In this section, we state the properties that DHCPF guarantees, under the assumptions of Section 3.2. We first define the following.

Definition 3.6. *Let $i \in C$, $\phi \in \Phi$, and let s be a state occurrence.*

1. *We say i owns ϕ in s if there exists an action occurrence*
   $\sigma = send_{*,i}(\langle ack, *, \phi, \tau \rangle)$ *such that $\sigma \prec s$, and $\zeta(s) \leq \tau + \Delta$.*
2. *We let $\omega(s, \phi) = \{ i \mid (i \in C) \wedge (i \text{ owns } \phi \text{ in } s) \}$.*

Thus, i owns ϕ in s if i has been sent an acknowledgment before state s to lease ϕ until time τ, and s happens at or before time $\tau + \Delta$. Intuitively, the Δ in the definition is to account for the fact that, when i is given a lease on ϕ for time τ, i may not release ϕ until real time $\tau + \Delta$, due to i's clock skew.

The following definition describes the properties satisfied by the DHCPF protocol. The safety property states that at most one client owns any IP address at a time. The request and renew liveness properties are complicated to state. But intuitively, they simply say that in nice time periods in which servers do not fail or recover, messages are delivered quickly, and not all IP addresses have already been allocated, a client always succeeds in quickly requesting or renewing an address. The liveness properties are described in more detail following Definition 3.7.

Definition 3.7. *Let $\nu, \delta \in \mathbb{R}^{\geq 0}$. Suppose Υ is a ν-perfect failure detector. Then an algorithm $\mathcal{A}$ satisfies the DHCPF protocol if $\mathcal{A}$'s external actions includes the actions shown in Figure 1, and for every execution α of $\mathcal{A}$, the following properties hold.*

1. **Safety:** *For any $\phi \in \Phi$ and any state occurrence s, we have $|\omega(s, \phi)| \leq 1$.*
2. **Request Liveness:** *Let $i \in C$, $\kappa \in K$, and let s and s' be state occurrences, with $s \prec s'$. Let $\sigma = bcast_i(\langle discover, \kappa, * \rangle)$. Let $\sigma_j = recv_{j,i}(\langle discover, \kappa, *, \rangle)$, $\forall j \in S$. Let $\sigma_\phi = send_{*,i}(\langle offer, \kappa, \phi, * \rangle)$, $\forall \phi \in \Phi$. Suppose that $[s, s']$ is $(4\nu + 4\Delta)$-stable and δ-timely, and $\zeta(s') - \zeta(s) \geq 4\delta$. Also suppose that $\sigma \in [s, s']$, and $\zeta(\sigma) \leq \zeta(s') - 4\delta$. Then there exists $\xi_1, \xi_2 \in \mathbb{R}^{\geq 0}$ such that the following hold.*

(a) For every $j \in \Lambda(s, s')$, we have $\sigma_j \in [s, s']$, and $\zeta(\sigma_j) \leq \zeta(\sigma) + \delta$. Let s_j
   be the state occurrence immediately following σ_j, $\forall j \in \Lambda(s, s')$.
(b) Either there exists $\phi \in \Phi$ such that $\sigma_\phi \in [s, s']$ and $\zeta(\sigma_\phi) \leq \zeta(\sigma) + 2\delta$, or
   for every $\phi \in \Phi$, there exists $j_\phi \in S$ such that one of the following holds.

    i. Let $\sigma_\phi^1 = \mathsf{send}_{j_\phi, *}(\langle \mathsf{offer}, *, \phi, *, \rangle)$ and $\sigma_\phi^2 = \mathsf{recv}_{*, j_\phi}(\langle \mathsf{request}, *, \phi, * \rangle)$.
       We have $\sigma_\phi^1 \prec \sigma_{j_\phi}$, $\zeta(\sigma_\phi^1) \geq \zeta(\sigma_{j_\phi}) - \xi_1 - 2\Delta$, and $\sigma_\phi^2 \not\prec \sigma_{j_\phi}$.
    ii. Let $\sigma_\phi^3 = \mathsf{recv}_{*, *}(\langle \mathsf{request}, *, \phi, \tau_\phi \rangle)$. We have $\sigma_\phi^3 \prec \sigma_{j_\phi}$, and $\zeta(\sigma_{j_\phi}) \leq$
       $\max(\tau_\phi + 3\Delta, \zeta(\sigma_\phi^3) + \xi_2 + 3\Delta)$.
    iii. Let $\sigma_\phi^4 = \mathsf{recv}_{*, *}(\langle \mathsf{renew}, *, \phi, \tau_\phi', * \rangle)$. We have $\sigma_\phi^4 \prec \sigma_{j_\phi}$, and $\zeta(\sigma_{j_\phi}) \leq$
       $\max(\tau_\phi' + 3\Delta, \zeta(\sigma_\phi^4) + \xi_2 + 3\Delta)$.
(c) Let $\Phi' \subseteq \Phi$, and suppose $\forall \phi \in \Phi' : \sigma_\phi \in [s, s']$. Let
   $\sigma_\phi' = \mathsf{recv}_{*, i}(\mathsf{ack}, \kappa, \phi, *)), \forall \phi \in \Phi$. Then there exists $\phi \in \Phi'$ such that
   $\sigma_\phi' \in [s, s']$ and $\zeta(\sigma_\phi') \leq \zeta(\sigma) + 4\delta$.
3. **Renew Liveness:** Let $i \in C$, $\kappa \in K$, $\tau, \tau' \in \mathbb{R}^+$, $\phi \in \Phi$, and let s and
   s' be state occurrences with $s \prec s'$. Let $\sigma = \mathsf{send}_{*, i}(\langle \mathsf{ack}, *, \phi, \tau' \rangle)$, $\sigma' = \mathsf{bcast}_i(\langle \mathsf{renew}, \kappa, \phi, \tau, \tau' \rangle)$, and $\sigma'' = \mathsf{recv}_{*, i}(\langle \mathsf{ack}, \kappa, \phi, * \rangle)$. Suppose $[s, s']$ is
   $(4\nu + 4\Delta)$-stable and δ-timely, and $\zeta(s') - \zeta(s) \geq 2\delta$. Also, suppose $\sigma \in [s, s']$,
   with $\sigma \prec \sigma'$, $\zeta(\sigma') \leq \zeta(s') - 2\delta$ and $\zeta(\sigma') \leq \tau' - \delta - \Delta$. Then $\sigma'' \in [s, s']$ and
   $\zeta(\sigma'') \leq \zeta(\sigma') + 2\delta$.

We now describe conditions 2 and 3 in more detail. Intuitively, the request
liveness property says that a client that requests an IP address will get one
quickly, unless there is some "excuse" not to give it one. Specifically, let $[s, s']$
be an interval that is at least 4δ time long, and is stable and timely. Then if a
client i broadcasts a discover message at time $t = \zeta(\sigma)$, its message is received
by all live servers no later than time $t + \delta$. Condition 2.b states that either i
receives an offer for some IP address ϕ, or the servers have an excuse not to offer
i any address; conditions $2.b.i - 2.b.iii$ list various excuses not to offer i address
ϕ. In condition $2.b.i$, ϕ has recently been offered to some client, but has not been
requested. Thus, ϕ is reserved for the other client. In $2.b.ii$, some client requested
ϕ for time τ_ϕ in action occurrence σ_ϕ^3. The quantity $\max(\tau_\phi + 3\Delta, \zeta(\sigma_\phi^3) + \xi_2 + 3\Delta)$
represents a lease for ϕ that was potentially given out to that client[3]. If $\zeta(\sigma_{j_\phi}) \leq$
$\max(\tau_\phi + 3\Delta, \zeta(\sigma_\phi^3) + \xi_2 + 3\Delta)$, then i's discover message arrived at server j_ϕ
before the last (potential) lease for ϕ has expired, which justifies i not being
offered ϕ. Condition $2.b.iii$ is similar to $2.b.ii$, but deals with a renew on ϕ by
another client. Lastly, condition $2.c$ says that if i is offered some IP addresses,
then i will also be given a lease for some such address no later than time $t + 4\delta$.
The renew liveness condition says that in a stable and timely interval, if client
i tries to renew ϕ sufficiently long before its previous lease τ' on ϕ expires, then
i will be granted a new lease on ϕ. Finally, note that despite their complicated
statement, the excuses in the liveness property are in some ways inherent to the
DHCPF problem. Nevertheless, it would be desirable to find a more succinct
way of expressing them.

---

[3] The ξ_2 and Δ terms represent some "slack" in the estimate for the potential lease.

4   A DHCPF Algorithm

In this section, we describe an algorithm satisfying the DHCPF specification in Definition 3.7. Our algorithm uses ideas described in [5], and also introduces several new ones. Compared to [5], our algorithm is more structured, and is considerably simpler to understand and analyze. The algorithm is based on a decomposition of the DHCPF protocol into two subproblems, with the goal to base the subproblems on well-studied problems in distributed computing, and to maximize the amount of "independence" between the subproblems. In the first problem, we find, for each address $\phi \in \Phi$, a server which we call the *leader* for ϕ. The leader for ϕ is the only server that is allowed to lease ϕ to the clients. The leader for ϕ may change during an execution, as servers fail and recover. However, we will ensure that at all times, there is at most one leader for ϕ. We call this the *leader election* problem. Given a leader for ϕ, say $j \in S$, the second problem involves j leasing ϕ to the clients in a way such that even if j fails, and another server j' takes over as leader for ϕ, the leases given out by j' for ϕ will not conflict with leases given out by j. We call this the *lease* problem. In the remainder of this section, we first describe an algorithm to solve the leader election problem, then give an algorithm which uses the leader election algorithm to solve the lease problem. Our DHCPF algorithm, satisfying the properties in Definition 3.7, is the (formal) composition of these two algorithms.

4.1   Leader Election Algorithm

We now present the *Elect* algorithm for solving the leader election problem. We first describe the algorithm, then prove the properties it satisfies in Theorems 4.2 and 4.3. For the remainder of this section, fix an arbitrary $\nu \in \mathbb{R}^{\geq 0}$. *Elect* uses a ν-perfect failure detector Υ. Recall that Δ is a bound on the maximum clock skew of any server (or client).

The pseudocode for server j running the $Elect_j$ algorithm is shown in Figure 2. For each $\phi \in \Phi$, let $<_\phi$ be a total ordering on the set S. If $S' \subseteq S$, then $\min_\phi S'$ denotes the minimum server in S', with respect to ordering $<_\phi$. The

```
input recvϒ,j(⟨dead, j'⟩)            input recvϒ,j(⟨alive, j'⟩)
Effect:                              Effect:
    live ← live\{j'}                     live ← live ∪ {j'}
    for every φ ∈ Φ do                   for every φ ∈ Φ do
      if ((j = minφ live)∧                 if (j ≠ minφ live) then
         (clock ≥ rec-time + 2ν + 2Δ)) then      leader ← leader \ {φ}
        leader ← leader ∪ {φ}
        lead-time[φ] ← clock          output leadj(φ)
        lead[φ] ← true                Precondition:
                                          lead[φ] = true
input alivej                         Effect:
Effect:                                  lead[φ] ← false
    rec-time ← clock
```

Fig. 2. The $Elect_j$ algorithm, for $j \in S$

idea of *Elect* is to let the $\min_\phi$ *live server* be the leader for ϕ[4]. Information about which servers are alive is provided to j by Υ; j keeps track of the servers it thinks are alive in the set *live*, which initially equals S. j keeps track of the IP addresses for which it is the leader in the set *leader*[5]; *leader* initially equals $\emptyset$. *lead*[ϕ] is a helper variable to flag when j becomes the leader for ϕ. When j recovers from a failure, it stores the time of its recovery in *rec-time*. Whenever j receives an alive message about server j' from Υ, j adds j' to *live*. After this, if for any $\phi \in \Phi$, j is no longer the $\min_\phi$ live server, it removes ϕ from *leader*. When j receives a dead message for j' from Υ, j removes j' from *fail*. Then, if j becomes the $\min_\phi$ server for ϕ, and if j's current time is sufficiently larger than j's last recovery time, j becomes leader for ϕ, by adding ϕ to *leader*. j also records the time it becomes leader in *lead-time*[ϕ].

Correctness of *Elect*. Before stating the correctness properties *Elect* satisfies, we first define the following.

Definition 4.1. *Let $\phi \in \Phi$, and let s be any state occurrence. We say $\Omega(s, \phi) = \{j \mid (j \in S) \wedge (\phi \in s.leader_j)\}$ is the set of* leaders *for ϕ in s.*

Recall that for state occurrences $s \prec s'$, $\Lambda(s, s')$ is the set of servers that are alive throughout the interval $[s, s']$, and $\zeta(s)$ is the real time at which s occurs.. The following safety property states that for any address ϕ, there is at most one server that is the leader for ϕ at any time. Due to lack of space, we omit the full proof of the theorem; it appears in the full version of this paper.

Theorem 4.2 (Safety). *For any execution α of* Elect, *any state occurrence s in α, and any $\phi \in \Phi$, we have $|\Omega(s, \phi)| \leq 1$.*

Proof. The basic idea is that each server waits for a period of time after it recovers before trying to become leader. During that time, because Υ is timely, the server will be able to hear about any other live servers which might be competing to become leader. Thus, all candidates to become leader will know about each other, and so only the minimum one will be elected leader.   □

The following liveness property says that in any sufficiently stable state occurrence, for any $\phi \in \Phi$, the $\min_\phi$ live server is the leader for ϕ. The proof appears in the full paper. The basic idea is that in a stable execution, all the live servers know about each other, and so the minimum live server is elected leader.

Theorem 4.3 (Liveness). *Let α be any execution, and let s be any state occurrence such that s is $(4\nu + 4\Delta)$-stable. Then for all $\phi \in \Phi$, we have $\phi \in s.leader_{\min_\phi \Lambda(s,s)}$.*

---

[4] Note that the reason we use a (possibly) different ordering $<_\phi$ for each ϕ is for load-balancing. Indeed, we can define a canonical ordering $<$ on S and let the minimum (w.r.t. $<$) live server be the leader for every IP address; but this may overload the minimum live server while the other servers do nothing.

[5] Note that j can be the leader for several addresses at the same time.

4.2 Lease Algorithm

In this section, we describe the lease algorithm, uncreatively named *Lease*. *Lease* uses *Elect*; in particular, every server $j \in S$ running *Lease* needs to know *lead-time*$[\phi]_j$, for all $\phi \in \Phi$, and also needs to know *leader*$_j$. That is, j needs to know when it last became the leader for ϕ (if ever), and what addresses it is leader for. The *Lease* algorithm is shown in Figure 3. We first describe the algorithm, then prove the properties it satisfies in the next section.

Consider any $\phi \in \Phi$, and suppose j is the current leader for ϕ. The main thing *Lease* needs to ensure is that when j gives out a lease for ϕ, the other servers know about this lease in some way, so that if j later fails, the next leader for ϕ will not give out a conflicting lease. To let other servers know about its leases, j gives out *two types* of leases: an (intuitively, short)*Minimum Client Lead Time (MCLT) lease*, and an (intuitively, long) *acknowledged lease*. For the remainder of this paper, we fix a constant $\mu \in \mathbb{R}^+$ which we call the *MCLT value*. Roughly speaking, when a client i sends j a **request** message to lease ϕ until time τ, j first gives i a lease equal to j's current clock value plus μ. This is the MCLT lease; note that it may be less than τ. Immediately after acknowledging the client, j broadcasts a **potlease-write** message to all the servers containing ϕ and τ. When a server j' receives this message, it sets *potlease*$[\phi]_{j'} \leftarrow \tau$; now, j' knows that some client has requested a lease of τ on ϕ. j' also acknowledges j with a **potlease-write-ack** message. When j receives acks about ϕ and τ from *every server* in S, j sets *acklease*$[\phi]_j \leftarrow \tau$. Now, if i sends a **renew** message for ϕ for time τ', j will give i a lease for time τ; this is an acknowledged lease. Thus intuitively, j begins by giving i a "temporary" MCLT lease, intended to tide i over while j negotiates a "real" acknowledged lease for i with the other servers.

We now describe the *Lease* algorithm for a server j in more detail, keeping in mind the above schema. In j's initial state, we set *reserved*$_j = \emptyset$, *potlease*$[\phi]_j =$

```
input leadⱼ(φ)
Effect:
    potlease[φ] ← max(lead-time[φ]+
        μ + 2Δ, potlease[φ])


input recvᵢ,ⱼ(⟨discover, κ, τ⟩)
Effect:
    S ← {φ | (φ ∈ leader) ∧ ((*, φ, *) ∉ reserved)∧
        (potlease[φ] + 2Δ < clock)}
    if S ≠ ∅ then
        choose φ ∈ S
        reserved ← reserved ∪ {(κ, φ, clock)}
        add ((offer, κ, φ, 0), i) to buffer


input recvᵢ,ⱼ(⟨request, κ, φ, τ⟩)
Effect:
    reserved ← reserved\(κ, *, *)
    if (φ ∈ leader) ∧ (potlease[φ] + 2Δ < clock) then
        acklease[φ] ← clock + μ
        τ ← max(τ, acklease[φ])
        potlease[φ] ← acklease[φ]
        add ((ack, κ, φ, acklease[φ]), i) to buffer
        for every j' ∈ S do
            add ((potlease-write, φ, κ, τ), j') to buffer
```

```
input recvᵢ,ⱼ(⟨renew, κ, φ, τ, τ'⟩)
Effect:
    if (φ ∈ leader) ∧ (τ' ≥ clock) then
        acklease[φ] ← max(clock + μ, acklease[φ])
        τ ← max(τ, acklease[φ])
        potlease[φ] ← max(acklease[φ], potlease[φ])
        add ((ack, κ, φ, acklease[φ]), i) to buffer
        for every j' ∈ S do
            add ((potlease-write, φ, κ, τ), j') to buffer


input recvⱼ',ⱼ(⟨potlease-write, φ, κ, τ⟩)
Effect:
    potlease[φ] ← max(τ, potlease[φ])
    add ((potlease-write-ack, φ, κ, τ), j') to buffer


input recvⱼ',ⱼ(⟨potlease-write-ack, φ, κ, τ⟩)
Effect:
    write-acks[κ] ← write-acks[κ] ∪ {j'}
    if write-acks[κ] = S then
        acklease[φ] ← max(τ, acklease[φ])


input cleanupⱼ()
Effect:
    S ← {(κ, φ, t) | ((κ, φ, t) ∈ reserved)∧
        (t < clock − θ)}
    reserved ← reserved \ S
```

Fig. 3. The *Lease*$_j$ algorithm

$acklease[\phi]_j = 0, \forall \phi \in \Phi$, and $write\text{-}acks[\kappa]_j = \emptyset, \forall \kappa \in K$. To request a lease, a client i broadcasts a discover message. When j receives this message, it checks three things. First, j checks that it is the leader for ϕ, i.e. $\phi \in leader_j$. Then j checks that $\phi \notin reserved_j$; that is, no other client asked j for ϕ before i. Lastly, j checks that $potlease[\phi]_j + 2\Delta < clock_j$. $potlease[\phi]_j$ represents the j's estimate of the highest lease which could possibly have been given out for ϕ, by any server (e.g., by previous leaders for ϕ). If $potlease[\phi]_j + 2\Delta < clock_j$, then j knows that any previous leases for ϕ have definitely expired. If all three conditions hold, then j sends an offer for ϕ to i. j also adds i's interaction instance κ, along with ϕ and the current time, to $reserved_j$. Having received offers from possibly multiple servers, i sends a request message for its preferred address. If j receives a request message from i for ϕ with lease time τ, it again checks the above conditions. If they hold, then j sends i an MCLT lease, i.e., a lease equal to $clock_j + \mu$. j also sends potlease-write for ϕ and τ to all the servers. If j' receives j's potlease-write, it sets $potlease[\phi]_{j'} \leftarrow \max(\tau, potlease[\phi]_{j'})$, and acknowledges j with potlease-write-ack. j keeps track of which servers have acknowledged it in $write\text{-}acks[\kappa]_j$. When $write\text{-}acks[\kappa]_j = S$, j sets $acklease[\phi]_j \leftarrow \max(\tau, acklease[\phi]_j)$.

When a client i which currently has a lease time τ' for ϕ asks j to renew ϕ for time τ, j first checks that it is the owner for ϕ, and then that $\tau' \geq clock_j$. The latter condition checks that the current lease τ' has not yet expired, giving i the right to renew ϕ. If both conditions hold, j sets $acklease[\phi]_j \leftarrow \max(clock_j + \mu, acklease[\phi]_j)$, and sends i a lease for ϕ until time $acklease[\phi]_j$; thus, j gives i an acknowledged lease. j also broadcasts potlease-write for ϕ and τ to the other servers.

For the remainder of this paper, fix a constant $\theta \in \mathbb{R}^+$. The cleanup$_j$ action removes addresses from $reserved_j$ that were offered at least θ time ago to some clients, but have not been requested. This is to reclaim addresses offered to clients that fail (or are slow) after being offered an address.

4.3 The Composed DHCPF Algorithm

We define our DHCPF algorithm to be the formal composition $\prod_j Elect_j \times Lease_j$. We refer to [6] for a full description of the composition operator $\times$. Briefly, $\times$ works by sharing the variables that the composed automata have in common, and identifying the output actions of one automaton with the input actions of the same name of another automaton. In our case, this means that for all $j \in S$, $Elect_j$ and $Lease_j$ both have access to the variables $leader_j$, and $lead\text{-}time[\phi]_j$, $\forall \phi \in \Phi$. $Elect_j$ and $Lease_j$ have only one type of action in common, $lead_j(\phi)$, $\forall \phi \in \Phi$. By composing the algorithms, the input action $lead_j(\phi)$ of $Lease_j$ is triggered whenever the output action $lead_j(\phi)$ of $Elect_j$ occurs. Thus, $Elect_j$ notifies $Lease_j$ whenever j becomes the leader for ϕ. We will call $\prod_j Elect_j \times Lease_j$ the algorithm $\mathcal{C}$, for "composed".

5 Properties of $\mathcal{C}$

In this section, we show that the execution traces of $\mathcal{C}$ satisfy the DHCPF specification in Definition 3.7. In the remainder of this section, fix $\alpha = \gamma_0 \sigma_1 \gamma_1 \ldots \sigma_n \gamma_n$

to be an arbitrary execution of $\mathcal{C}$. Define s_k to be the state of $\mathcal{C}$ immediately before γ_k, for $k \in 0..n$. We first consider the safety properties.

5.1   Safety Properties of $\mathcal{C}$

The basic idea for showing that $\mathcal{C}$ never allocates the same IP address to more than one client is to show that the $potlease[\phi]$ value of the leader for ϕ is always an overestimate of the actual lease given out for ϕ. For example, suppose the last lease for ϕ was given out by server $j' \neq j$, at real time t. Then, if j' gave out an MCLT lease, the value of the lease is approximately $t + \mu$. If j becomes the leader for ϕ, at a time $t' > t$, its first step is to set its $potlease[\phi]$ value to at least $t' + \mu + 2\Delta$, which overestimates the real lease time. Otherwise, if the lease given out by j' was an acknowledged lease, then j received a potlease-write message for the lease from j', and thus also set its $potlease[\phi]$ value to be at least the value of j''s lease. Now, because the leader's $potlease[\phi]$ value is at least as large as the highest lease given out for ϕ, and because the leader checks that the current time on its clock (plus some slack) is larger than $potlease[\phi]$ before giving out a new lease for ϕ, then ϕ will never be double allocated. We now state a series of lemmas to formalize this idea. Due to lack of space, the complete proofs appear in the full paper. The proof method in most cases is an induction on the execution length. That is, we show a lemma holds in the initial state of the execution, and check that every step of the execution preserves the lemma. The lemmas were chosen so that these checks are typically quite straightforward. In fact, most of the proofs seem to be checkable by interactive theorem prover tools.

The first lemma states that $potlease[\phi]_j$ never decreases during α, for any j and ϕ.

Lemma 5.1. *Let $j \in S, \phi \in \Phi$, and let s and s' be state occurrences such that $s \prec s'$. Then $s.potlease[\phi]_j \leq s'.potlease[\phi]_j$.*

We define the following.

Definition 5.2. *Let $i \in C$, $\kappa \in K$, $\phi \in \Phi$, $\tau, \tau' \in \mathbb{R}^{\geq 0}$, and suppose there exists an action occurrence $\sigma = bcast_i(\langle request, \kappa, \phi, \tau \rangle)$ or $\sigma' = bcast_i(\langle renew, \kappa, \phi, \tau, \tau' \rangle)$ in α. Then we define $i_\kappa = i$, $\phi_\kappa = \phi$, and $\tau_\kappa = \tau$.*

Thus, i_κ, ϕ_κ, and τ_κ are the client, IP address and desired lease time associated with a request or renew interaction instance κ. Note that these are well defined because every interaction in α uses a different κ, so that at most one of σ or σ' can occur in α. The following lemma says that given an interaction instance κ and its associated ϕ_κ and τ_κ, if one server is contained in the $write\text{-}acks[\kappa]$ variable of another server, then the former server's $potlease[\phi_\kappa]$ is at least τ_κ.

Lemma 5.3. *Let $\kappa \in K$, $j, j' \in S$, and let s be a state occurrence. Suppose $j \in s.write\text{-}acks[\kappa]_{j'}$. Then $s.potlease[\phi_\kappa]_j \geq \tau_\kappa$.*

The next lemma compares the values of $potlease[\phi]$, $acklease[\phi]$ and $clock$ at different servers, for any ϕ. The basic proof idea is that j can estimate $acklease[\phi]_{j'}$

either through a potlease-write message from j' when j' gives out an acknowledged lease, or by adding μ to j's own clock, when j' gives out an MCLT lease. The 2Δ term accounts for the possible skew between j and j''s clocks.

Lemma 5.4. *Let $\phi \in \Phi$, $j, j' \in S$, and let s be a state occurrence. Then we have* $\max(s.potlease[\phi]_j, s.clock_j + \mu + 2\Delta) \geq s.acklease[\phi]_{j'}$.

The next lemma states that the $potlease[\phi]$ value of the leader for ϕ is at least as large as any $acklease[\phi]$ value. The proof uses Lemma 5.4, the fact that there is at most one leader for ϕ at a time (by Theorem 4.2), and the fact that j sets $potlease[\phi]_j$ to $\max(lead\text{-}time[\phi]_j + \mu + 2\Delta, potlease[\phi]_j)$ upon becoming leader for ϕ.

Lemma 5.5. *Let $\phi \in \Phi$, $j \in S$, and let s be a state occurrence. Then if $\Omega(s, \phi) \neq \emptyset$, we have $s.potlease[\phi]_{\Omega(s,\phi)} \geq s.acklease[\phi]_j$.*

The next lemma states that $acklease[\phi]$ never decreases, for any j and ϕ.

Lemma 5.6. *Let $j \in S, \phi \in \Phi$, and let s and s' be state occurrences such that $s \prec s'$. Then $s.acklease[\phi]_j \leq s'.acklease[\phi]_j$.*

Combining the above lemmas, the following theorem states that at most one client is assigned any IP address at any time. Intuitively, the theorem holds because the leader for ϕ has a good estimate of the maximum possible lease given out for ϕ using $potlease[\phi]$, and checks that this lease has expired before giving out a new lease for ϕ.

Theorem 5.7. *Any execution of $\mathcal{C}$ satisfies the safety property in Definition 3.7.*

5.2   Liveness Properties of $\mathcal{C}$

The next two theorems state that $\mathcal{C}$ satisfies the request and renew liveness conditions of the DHCPF specification. Recall that θ is the amount of time a server reserves an IP address for a client after receiving its discover message. Complete proofs appear in the full paper.

Theorem 5.8. *Let $\xi_1 = \theta$, and $\xi_2 = \mu$. Then any execution of $\mathcal{C}$ satisfies the request liveness property in Definition 3.7.*

Proof. Despite the complicated statements of the request and renew liveness properties, it is in fact straightforward to show that $\mathcal{C}$ satisfies them. This is because the properties are basically a list of all the problems which might occur to prevent liveness. Thus, the liveness proof consists of showing that when all such problems are ruled out, $\mathcal{C}$ is live. $\square$

Theorem 5.9. *Any execution of $\mathcal{C}$ satisfies the renew liveness property in Definition 3.7.*

Combining Theorems 5.7, 5.8 and 5.9, we have shown that $\mathcal{C}$ satisfies all the properties of a DHCPF protocol.

6   Conclusions

In this paper, we presented a formal specification of a fault-tolerant DHCP algorithm for unique IP address assignment. The algorithm is implemented as a composition of two algorithms, modeling dynamic versions of the leader election and shared register problems. This structure facilitated the proof of correctness of the algorithm. Its simplicity also lends well to practical implementations and deployment.

There are several directions for extending our work. While we feel that DHCPF is naturally modeled as a timed mutual exclusion problem, as in our Definition 3.7, there seems to be substantial freedom in choosing the various parameters and assumptions making up this definition. For example, is a failure detector really necessary to implement DHCPF? Do we need stable and timely periods to ensure liveness? If so, can these periods be made smaller than in our definition? Can we find other natural ways to characterize liveness properties, perhaps avoiding the complexity of the request liveness definition? In another vein, having specified DHCPF in a particular way, is the decomposition of the problem into leader election and shared register abstractions the best one? For example, does this decomposition ensure the most independence between the subproblems, so that each problem can be solved in isolation and later composed? Does decomposing DHCPF into subproblems lead to a less efficient, if also less complex solution than solving the problem as a monolithic whole? Some of these questions can be expressed as formal questions of lower bounds. For others, especially the design issues, we currently lack a proper theory to rigorously address them. We hope that our abstract model and analysis contributes to understanding these interesting and important problems.

References

1. Chandra, T.D., Hadzilacos, V., Toueg, S.: The weakest failure detector for solving consensus. J. ACM 43(4), 685–722 (1996)
2. Chandra, T.D., Toueg, S.: Unreliable failure detectors for reliable distributed systems. J. ACM 43(2), 225–267 (1996)
3. Dolev, D., Shavit, N.: Bounded concurrent time-stamping. SIAM J. Comput. 26(2), 418–455 (1997)
4. Droms, R.: Dynamic Host Configuration Protocol. RFC 2131 (Draft Standard) Updated by RFCs 3396, 4361 (March 1997)
5. Droms, R., Kinnear, K., Stapp, M., et al.: DHCP Failover Protocol (March 2003) http://www3.ietf.org/proceedings/03mar/I-D/draft-ietf-dhc-failover-12.txt
6. Kaynar, D.K., Lynch, N.A., Segala, R., Vaandrager, F.W.: The Theory of Timed I/O Automata. Morgan and Claypool (2005)
7. Lamport, L.: Time, clocks, and the ordering of events in a distributed system. Commun. ACM 21(7), 558–565 (1978)

Verifying Erlang/OTP Components in μCRL

Qiang Guo

Department of Computer Science,
The University of Sheffield,
Regent Court, 211 Portobello Street, S1 4DP, UK
Q.Guo@dcs.shef.ac.uk

Abstract. Erlang is a concurrent functional programming language with explicit support for real-time and fault-tolerant distributed systems. Generic components encapsulated as design patterns are provided by the Open Telecom Platform (OTP) library. Although Erlang has many high-level features, verification is still non-trivial. One (existing) approach is to perform an abstraction of an Erlang program into the process algebra μCRL, upon which standard verification tools can be applied. In this paper we extend this work and propose a model that supports the translation of an OTP finite state machine design pattern into a μCRL specification. Then a standard toolset such as CADP can be applied in order to check properties that should hold for the system under development. Two small examples are presented, which experimentally show how the proposed model assists in model checking Erlang OTP components in μCRL.

Keywords: Erlang, OTP, process algebra, μCRL, Verification.

1 Introduction

Model checking [8] has been widely used in system design and verification. The advantage of using model checking based techniques for system verification is that, when a fault is detected, model checker can generate a counter example given as a trace. These traces are useful since they help the system designer to understand the reasons that cause the occurrence of failures and provide clues for fixing the problem.

Model checking can be applied in two ways. One way, in combination with a model checker, is to use a formal specification language such as a process algebra [15], to obtain a correct specification. The specification is then used to develop an implementation in a programming language such as Erlang [1]. The other way uses the program code as a starting point and abstracts it into a form suitable for use by a model checker, and this requires an interpretation mechanism to support the translation of the programming language into the formal specification language used by the model checker.

Recently this second approach has been applied to the verification of Erlang programs and OTP components [2,3,6,10]. Here the process algebra μCRL [13] has been used as the formal language upon which verification is carried out. A

J. Derrick and J. Vain (Eds.): FORTE 2007, LNCS 4574, pp. 227–246, 2007.
© IFIP International Federation for Information Processing 2007

toolset, *etomcrl*, has been developed to automate the process of translation of an Erlang program into a μCRL specification. The translation from Erlang to μCRL is performed in two stages, where in the first, a source to source transformation is applied, resulting in Erlang code that is optimised for the verification, but has identical behaviour. Then second, this output is translated to μCRL.

Erlang/OTP software is usually written according to strict design patterns that make extensive use of software components. Encapsulated in the extensive OTP library are a variety of design patterns, each of which is intended to solve a particular class of problem. Solutions to each such problem come in two parts. The generic part is provided by OTP as a library module and the specific part is implemented by the programmer in Erlang. Typically these specific callback functions embody algorithmic features of the system, whilst the generic components provide for fault tolerance, fault isolation and so forth. The *etomcrl* translation tool currently produces translations of the callback modules of the OTP generic servers and supervisors.

In addition to generic servers and supervisors, OTP provides further generic components including finite state machines, event handlers, and applications. These considerably simplify the building of systems. In this paper we extend the above approach to develop a model that supports the translation of OTP finite state machines (FSMs) into μCRL.

To do so, the Erlang state function in the FSM is translated into two parts in μCRL, one of which defines a μCRL state-process that can be called or synchronized by some other processes, while, the other consists of a series of μCRL state functions. The set of sequences of actions defined in an Erlang state function are translated into a set of pre-defined action sets in μCRL, each of which is uniquely indexed by an integer. A μCRL state-process starts by calling its μCRL state function. The function returns an index number that determines which pre-defined action set needs to be performed. we use a simple stack to simulate the management of FSM states and data. In order to define the correct translation we use techniques proposed in [16] which are needed to deal with the presence of overlapping patterns in pattern matching.

The rest of this paper is organized as follows: Section 2 introduces the Erlang programming language; Section 3 describes the process algebra μCRL; Section 4 reviews the related work for the translation of Erlang programs into μCRL; Section 5 investigates the translation of Erlang FSM programs into μCRL; Section 6 evaluates the proposed model with two case studies; conclusions are finally drawn in Section 7.

2   Erlang and OTP

The programming language Erlang [1] is a concurrent functional programming language with explicit support for real-time and fault-tolerant distributed systems. Since being developed, it has been used to implement some substantial business critical applications such as the Ericsson AXD 301 high capacity ATM switch [4]. Erlang is available under an Open Source licence from Ericsson, and its use has spread to a variety of sectors. Applications include TCP/IP programming (HTTP, SSL, Email, Instant messaging, etc), web-servers, databases, advanced call control services, banking, 3D-modelling.

Erlang is a *functional* programming language, and as such an Erlang program consists of a set of modules, each of which define a number of functions. Functions that are accessible from other modules need to be explicitly declared as *export*. A function named *f_name* in the module *module* and with arity N is often denoted as *module:f_name/N*.

Erlang is a *concurrent* programming language, and as such provides a lightweight process model. Several concurrent processes can run in the same virtual machine, each of which being called a *node*. Each process has a unique identifier to address the process and a message queue to store the incoming messages. Erlang has an asynchronous communication mechanism where any process can send (using the ! operator) a message to any other process of which it happens to know the *process identifier*. Sending is always possible and non-blocking; the message arrives in the unbounded mailbox of the specified process. The latter process can inspect its mailbox by the `receive` statement. A sequence of patterns can be specified to read specific messages from the mailbox. When reading a message, a process is suspended until a matching message arrives or timeout occurs. A distributed system can be constructed by connecting a number of virtual machines.

A unique feature of Erlang is the OTP architecture, which is designed to support the construction of fault-tolerant systems containing soft real-time requirements. Its use has been very successful since Erlang/OTP software is usually written according to strict design patterns that make extensive use of software components. Each design patterns solves a particular class of problem, and solutions to each such problem come in two parts: the generic part is provided as a library module and the specific part is implemented by the programmer. The specific callback functions implement the necessary algorithm, and fault tolerance, fault isolation etc is provided by the generic component. The following briefly reviews generic servers, supervisors and finite state machines - the three key components which account for around 80% of OTP compliant code.

Generic servers and supervisors. The Erlang/OTP supports a generic implementation of a server by providing the *gen_server* module which provides a standard set of interface functions for synchronous and asynchronous communication, debugging support, error and timeout handling, and other administrative tasks. A generic server is implemented by providing a *callback module* where (*callback*) functions are defined specifying the concrete actions of the server such as server state handling and response to messages. When a client wants to synchronously communicate with the server, it calls the standard *gen_server:call* function with a certain message as an argument. If an asynchronous communication is required, the *gen_server:cast* is invoked where no response is expected after a request is sent to the server. A *terminate* function is also defined in the call back module. This function is called by the server when it is about to terminate, which allows the server to do any necessary cleaning up.

When developing concurrent and distributed systems, a commonly accepted assumption is that any Erlang process may unexpectedly terminate due to some failures. Erlang/OTP supports fault-tolerance by using the *supervision tree*, which is a structure where the processes in the internal nodes (supervisors) monitor the processes in the external leaves (children). A supervisor is a process that starts a number of child processes, monitors them, handles termination and stops them on request. The children themselves can also be supervisors, supervising their children in turn.

Finite state machines. The Erlang/OTP architecture supports the implementation of finite state machines by providing the *gen_fsm* module, and these are used extensively in a variety of contexts.

A (deterministic) FSM M can be described as a set of relations of the form $State(S) \times Event(E) \rightarrow (Action(A), State(S))$ where S, E and A are finite and nonempty sets of states, events and actions respectively. If M is in state $s \in S$ and receives event $e \in E$, action $a \in A$ is performed, moving M to a state $s' \in S$. For an implementation using the *gen_fsm* module, *gen_fsm* is started by calling *start_link(Code)*:

$$start\_link(Code) \rightarrow$$
$$gen\_fsm : start\_link(\{local, fsm\_name\},$$
$$callback\_module\_name, Code, [\,]).$$

$\{local, fsm\_name\}$ implies that the FSM is locally registered as *fsm_name*; *callback_ module_name* is the name of the callback module where the callback functions are located; *Code* is a term that is passed to the callback function *init*; the last argument, [ ], is a list of options. If the registration succeeds, the new *gen_fsm* process calls the callback function *callback_module_name:init(Code)*. This function is expected to return $\{ok, StateName, StateData\}$ where *StateName* saves the name of initial state and *StateData* the corresponding state data.

The state transition rules are written as a number of state functions that conform to the following convention:

StateName(Event, StateData) →
... code for actions ...;
{next_state,StateName′,StateData′,Timer}.

Having performed all pre-defined actions, the state function returns a tuple that contains the name of the next state, *StateName′*, and an updated state data, *StateData′*. *StateName′* is updated as the new current state by the *gen_fsm* module. *Timer* is an optional element, if it is set to a value, a timer is instantiated, and a *timeout* event will be generated when the time-up occurs.

The function *send_event* is defined to trigger a transition. When *send_event* is executed, the *gen_fsm* module automatically calls the *current state* function.

Example - a door with code lock. The initial design for a door with a code lock is illustrated in Figure 1, and consists of two states, *locked* and *open*, and a

Fig. 1. FSM - door with code lock

-module(fsm_door).
-export([start_link/1, button/1, init/ 1]).
-export([locked/2, open/ 2]).

    start_link(Code) →
        gen_fsm:start_link(local, fsm_door,
             fsm_door, Code,[]).

    init(Code) →
        {ok, locked, Code}.

    button(Password) →
        gen_fsm:send_event(fsm_door,
           {button, Password}).

locked({button, Password}, Code) →
   case Password of
      Code →
         action:do_unlock(),
         {next_state, open, Code};
      _Wrong →
         action:display_message(),
         {next_state, locked, Code}.

open({button, Password}, Code) →
   action:do_lock(),
   {next_state, locked,Code};

Fig. 2. The Erlang code for a door with code lock

system code for opening the door. Initially, the door is set to *locked* while the code
is set to a word. The door switches between states, driven by an external event.

The Erlang/OTP implementation of the system is shown in Figure 2 where
the function *button* is defined to simulate the receiving of a password. The action
send_event triggers a state transition where a state function is executed, in this
example either *locked* or *open*. A password generated from an external action
is evaluated, and if the door is in the state *locked* and the received password is
correct, the door will be opened through action *send_event*. Otherwise, if the
password is not correct, the door remains locked. When the door is in the state
open and action *send_event* is performed, the door will be locked, regardless of
the password received.

3   The Process Algebra μCRL

The process algebra μCRL (micro Common Representation Language) [13] is an
extension of the process algebra ACP [14], where equational *abstract data types*
have been integrated into the process specification to enable the specification of
both data and process behaviour (in a way similar to LOTOS).

A μCRL specification comprises two parts: the data types and the processes.
Processes are declared using the keyword *proc*, and contains actions representing

atomic events that can be performed. These actions must be explicitly declared using the keyword *act*. Data types used in μCRL are specified as the standard abstract data types, using sorts, functions and axioms. Sorts are declared using the keyword *sort*, functions are declared using the keywords *func* and *map*. Axioms are declared using the keyword *rew*, referring to the possibility to use rewriting technology for the evaluation of terms.

A number of process-algebraic operators are defined in μCRL, these being: sequential composition ($\cdot$), non-deterministic choice ($+$), parallelism ($\parallel$) and communication ($\mid$), encapsulation (∂), hiding (τ), renaming (ρ) and recursive declarations. A conditional expression $true \triangleleft condition \triangleright false$ allows data elements to influence the flow of control in a process, and the operator ($\sum$) provides the possibly infinite choice over some sorts.

In μCRL, parallel processes communicate via the synchronization of actions. The communication in a process definition is described by its communication specification, denoted by the keyword *comm*. This describes which actions may synchronize on the level of the labels of actions. For example, in *comm in|out*, each action $in(t_1, ..., t_k)$ can communicate with $out(t'_1, ..., t'_k)$ provided $k = m$ and t_1, t'_1 denote the same element for $i = 1, ..., k$.

As an example, consider the specification of a stack in μCRL given in Figure 3. The stack, initially defined in [3] for coping with side-effect functions, defines six actions, these being *rcallvalue*, *wcallresult*, *push_callstack*, *rcallresult*, *wcallvalue* and *pop_callstack*; *rcallvalue* | *wcallresult* = *push_callstack* and *rcallresult* | *wcallvalue* = *pop_callstack*. The action *rcallvalue* pushes a value to stack, while, the action *rcallresult* pops up the top value from stack.

sort
  TermStack
func
  empty: $\rightarrow$ TermStack
  push: Term # TermStack $\rightarrow$
      TermStack
map
  is_top: Term # TermStack $\rightarrow$ Bool
  is_empty: TermStack $\rightarrow$ Bool
  pop: TermStack $\rightarrow$ TermStack
  top: TermStack $\rightarrow$ Term
  eq: TermStack # TermStack $\rightarrow$ Bool
var
  S_1, S_2: TermStack
  T_1, T_2: Term
rew
  is_top(T_1,empty) = F
  is_top(T_1,push(T_2,S_1))= eq(T_1,T_2)
  is_empty(empty) = T

is_empty(push(T_1,S_1)) = F
pop(push(T_1,S_1)) = S_1
top(push(T_1,S_1)) = T_1
eq(empty,S_2) = is_empty(S_2)
eq(push(T_1,S_1),S_2)
  = and(is_top(T_1,S_2),eq(S_1,pop(S_2)))

act
  rcallvalue,wcallresult,push_callstack: Term
  rcallresult,wcallvalue,pop_callstack: Term
comm
  rcallvalue | wcallresult = push_callstack
  rcallresult | wcallvalue = pop_callstack
proc
  CallStack(S TermStack) =
    sum(Value:Term,rcallvalue(Value).
      CallStack(push(Value,S))) +
    (delta $\triangleleft$ is_empty(S)$\triangleright$ wcallvalue(top(S)).
      CallStack(pop(S)))

Fig. 3. The syntax of μCRL stack

An interleave relation with the process *CallStack* needs to be defined for those processes that will exchange data with the stack. To save a *Value*, a process needs to perform *wcallresult(Value)* first, which leads to the synchronization between this process and process *CallStack*. The action *sum(Value : Term, rcallresult(Value))* is consequently performed, which pushes the value into the stack. To read a value, a process needs to perform *sum(Value : Term, rcallresult(Value))* where *wcallvalue* is performed to pop up the top value from stack and assign it to *Value*.

4   Related Work

As discussed in the introduction, Benac Earle *et al.* [2,3,6,10] have studied the translation of Erlang programs into μCRL and developed a toolset, *etomcrl*, for automating the process of translation.

4.1   Translating Erlang Programs into μCRL

The translation from Erlang to μCRL is performed in two stages. First, a source to source transformation is applied, resulting in Erlang code that is optimized for the verification, but has identical behaviour. Second, this code is translated to μCRL.

The actual translation is quite involved due to particular language features in Erlang. For example, Erlang makes use of higher-order functions, whereas μCRL is 1st order; Erlang is dynamically typed, but μCRL is statically typed; in Erlang communication can take place in a computation, in μCRL it cannot. However, μCRL is sufficiently close that such a translation is feasible, and model checking on it computationally tractable even if the translation is involved.

Because Erlang is dynamically typed it is necessary to define in μCRL a data type *Term* where all data types defined in Erlang are embedded. The translation of the Erlang data types to μCRL is then basically a syntactic conversion of constructors as shown in Figure 4.

sort
    Term
func
        pid: Natural $\rightarrow$ Term
        int: Natural $\rightarrow$ Term
        nil: $\rightarrow$ Term
        cons: Term # Term $\rightarrow$ Term
        tuplenil: Term $\rightarrow$ Term
        tuple: Term # Term $\rightarrow$ Term
        true: $\rightarrow$ Term
        false: $\rightarrow$ Term

Fig. 4. The translation scheme for Erlang data types

Atoms in Erlang are translated to μCRL constructors; *true* and *false* represent the Erlang booleans; *int* is defined for integers; *nil* for the empty list; *cons* for a list with an element (the head) and a rest (the tail); *tuplenil* for a tuple with one element; *tuple* for a tuple with more than one element; and *pid* for process identifiers. For example, a list $[E_1, E_2, ..., E_n]$ is translated to μCRL as $cons(E_1, cons(E_2, cons(..., cons(E_n, nil))))$. A tuple $\{E_1, E_2, ..., E_n\}$ is translated to μCRL as $tuple(E_1, tuple(E_2, ..., tuplenil(E_n)))$.

Variables in Erlang are mapped directly to variables in μCRL. Operators are also translated directly, specified in a μCRL library. For example, $A + B$ is mapped to *mcrl_plus(A,B)*, where *mcrl_plus(A,B) = int(plus(term_to_nat(A), term_to_nat(B)))*. Higher-order functions in an Erlang programs are flattened into first-order alternatives. These first-order alternatives are then translated into rewrite rules.

Program transformation is defined to cope with side-effect functions. With a source-to-source transformation, a function with side-effects is either determined as a pure computation or a call to another function with side-effects. *Stacks* are defined in μCRL where *push* and *pop* operations are defined as communication actions. The value of a pure computation is pushed into a stack and is popped when it is called by the function.

Communication between two Erlang processes, which can be asynchronous, is translated via defining two process algebra processes, one of which is a buffer, while the other implements the logic. The synchronous communication is modelled by the synchronizing actions of process algebra. One action pair is defined to synchronize the sender with the buffer of the receiver, while another action pair to synchronize the active receive in the logic part with the buffer. In this way the asynchronous communication and the Erlang message queue is simulated directly in the μCRL abstraction.

4.2   Overlapping in Pattern Matching

Erlang makes extensive use of pattern matching in its function definitions. The toolset *etomcrl* translates pattern matching in a way where overlapping patterns are not considered. This might induce faults in the μCRL specification in our translation, and we need to use techniques to cope with the occurrence of overlapping patterns.

In Erlang, evaluation of pattern matching works from top to bottom and from left to right. When the first pattern is matched, evaluation terminates after the corresponding clauses are executed. However, the μCRL toolset instantiator does not evaluate rewriting rules in a fixed order. If there exists overlapping between patterns, the problem of overlapping in pattern matching occurs, which could lead to the system being represented by a faulty model.

The problem of overlapping in pattern matching was studied in [16]. An approach was proposed where an Erlang program with overlapping patterns is transformed into a counterpart program without overlapping patterns. The rewriting operation rewrites all pattern matching clauses in the original code into some calling functions. A calling function is activated by a guard that is determined by the function *patterns_match*. Function *patterns_match* takes the predicate of the pattern matching clauses and one pattern as arguments and is *true* iff the predicate matches the pattern.

A data structure called the Structure Splitting Tree (SST) is defined and applied for pattern evaluation, and its use guarantees that no overlapping patterns will be introduced to the transformed program. The evaluation of an SST is equivalent to the searching of nodes in a tree, and thus is of linear complexity.

After an Erlang program has been translated into a μCRL specification, one can check the system properties by using some existing tools such as CADP [7]. The toolset CADP provides a number of tools for system behaviour checking. It includes an interactive graphical simulator, a tool for the visualization of labelled transition systems (LTSs), several tools for computing bisimulations and a model checker.

Properties one wishes to check with the CADP model checker are formalized in the regular alternation-free μ-calculus (a fragment of the modal μ-calculus), a first-order logic with modalities, and least and greatest fixed point operators [9]. Automation for property checking can be achieved by using the Script Verification Language (SVL). SVL provides a high-level interface to all CADP tools, which enables an easy description and execution of complex performance studies. We very briefly illustrate the approach in Section 6 where a few simple properties are defined for our running examples.

5   Translating Erlang/OTP FSMs into μCRL

This section investigates the translation of the OTP FSM design pattern into μCRL.

5.1   Simulating State Management

When translating an Erlang FSM program into μCRL, the first thing one needs to consider is how to maintain the FSM states and data. In particular, a scheme needs to be defined to store and update the *current state* and the *state data* in μCRL. Normally a global variable would be used to perform such a task, however, μCRL does not support the use of global variables. Thus we use a (one place) stack for simulating the management of states and data as it has well been defined in μCRL. Alternatively, one might define some other mechanics such as data buffer for state and datum management.

The translation rules are defined in Figure 5, where three actions, *s_event*, *r_event* and *send_event*, are defined respectively. A command, generated from an external action is sent out to some other processes by action *s_event*. This command is received through action *r_event* and is used for further processing; *s_event* : *r_event* = *send_event*.

An Erlang FSM state is assigned a μCRL state name ("s_" plus the state name) and a state process ("fsm_" plus the state name). For example, state S_1 is given a μCRL state name s_S_1 and a state process fsm_S_1. The *current state* and the *state data* are coded in a tuple with the form of *tuple*(*state*,

act
  s_event, r_event, send_event: Term

comm
  s_event | r_event = send_event

proc
  write(Val:Term) =
    wcallresult (Val)

  read(Cmd:Term)=
    sum(Val:Term, recallresult(Val).
     fsm_S₁(Cmd,element (2,Val))
      ◁ is_s_S₁(element(1,Val)) ▷
      fsm_S₂(Cmd,element (2,Val))
       ◁ is_s_S₂(element(1,Val)) ▷
         ...
      fsm_Sₙ(Cmd,element(2,Val))
       ◁ is_s_Sₙ(element(1,Val))▷
         delta)

fsm_change_state =
  sum(Cmd:Term,
      r_event(Cmd).read(Cmd))

fsm_init(S:Term,Data:Term) =
  fsm_next_state(S,Data)

fsm_next_state(S:Term,Data:Term) =
  wcallresult(tuple(S,tuplenil(Data))).
  sum(Cmd:Term,r_command(Cmd).
     s_event(Cmd).fsm_change_state)

fsm_S₁(Cmd:Term, Data:Term) =
  pre_defined actions ...
  fsm_next_state(nex_State, new_data)
  ....
fsm_Sₙ(Cmd:Term, Data:Term) =
  pre_defined actions ...
  fsm_next_state(next_State,new_data)

Fig. 5. Rules for translating state processes

tuplenil($state\_data$)) and saved in the stack. The stack used for managing states and data is defined in a way where only one element can be read/written. This ensures that only one *current state* is available.

The process *write* is defined to push the *current state* and the *state data* onto the stack while a process called *read* is used to pop the *current state* and the *state data* from the stack. The process *fsm_init*($State:Term, Data:Term$) is defined to initially push *tuple*($Init\_State, tuplenil(State\_Data)$) onto the stack. The process *fsm_next_state*($State:Term, Data:Term$) updates the *current state* and the *state data* in the stack.

The process *fsm_next_state* will receive commands through the action *r_command*. The action *r_command* communicates with the action *s_command* which is externally performed. When a command is received, the process *fsm_state_change*, guarded by the action *s_event*, is enabled. It passes the command to the process *read* where the *current state* and the *state data* are read from stack. The *current state* determines which state process is about to be activated.

A state process *fsm_Sᵢ* starts by calling its μCRL state function S_i(Command : Term, Data : Term). Function S_i returns a tuple with the form of *tuple* ($next\_state, tuple(new\_data, tuplenil(index))$) where *next_state* shows the next state; *new_data* the updated state data. The *index* saves an index number for the sequence of actions to be selected. Rules for the translation of Erlang state functions are discussed in Section 5.2.

Having performed all actions, a state process ends up by calling the process *fsm_next_state*($next\_state, new\_data$), updating the *current state* and the *state data* in stack. The process *CommandList*($CmdList : Term$) is defined to simulate the behaviour of the external actions. A list of commands is initialized in *CmdList*, where commands in the list define the logic for verification. The process *fsm_next_state* will synchronize with *CommandList* through the actions *r_command* and *s_command*, *r_command* | *s_command* = *cmd*. Each time, *fsm_next_state* reads the head of *CmdList*, and communication terminates when *CmdList* is empty.

5.2 Translating the State Functions

An Erlang state function may consist a list of branches, each of which defines a sequence of actions to be performed. A branch is usually guarded by a pattern, and only when the function arguments match the pattern of its guards, can a branch be selected for execution. Thus in the door locking example above, the state function *locked* defines a number of actions (*do_unlock, display_message*) which are selected depending on the value of the password inputted.

$$S_i(N) \rightarrow$$

case N of	$S_i(N)$ when N is of $P_1 \rightarrow$
$P_1 \rightarrow$	actions(1);
actions(1);	$S_i(N)$ when N is of $P_2 \rightarrow$
$P_2 \rightarrow$	actions(2);
actions(2);	...
...	$S_i(N)$ when N is of $P_n \rightarrow$
$P_n \rightarrow$	actions(n).
actions(n).	
A: Matching.	B: Guards.

Fig. 6. Guarded Erlang programs

In general there are two ways in which such pattern matching can be defined, and Figure 6 illustrates an example where the program in Figure 6-A is written using pattern matching, while, in Figure 6-B, with a set of guards. When N matches P_i, the action sequence *action(i)* is enabled. In general, overlapping might exist between patterns P_i and P_j, and only the first matched action sequence *action(i)* will be performed.

The translation of an Erlang state function into μCRL starts by splitting the function into two parts, one of which defines a series of μCRL state functions while the other a set of action sequences. Every set of action sequences is translated into a pre-defined action set in μCRL. According to the order that patterns and guards occur in the function, the pre-defined action sets are uniquely indexed with a set of integers. For example, in Figure 6, the set of action sequences {*actions*(1), ..., *actions*(n)} is indexed with an integer set {1, ..., n} where integer i identifies the pre-defined action set *actions(i)*.

The selection of a μCRL state function for execution is determined by the pattern of function arguments. By the end, the function returns a tuple with the form of *tuple(next_state, tuple(new_data, tuplenil(index)))* where *next_state* returns the next state, *new_data* the updated state data and *index* the index of the action sequence that needs to be performed.

To eliminate any potential overlapping between patterns, techniques proposed in [16] are applied. Specifically, pattern matching clauses in the program are replaced by a series of case functions. These case functions are guarded by the *patterns_match* function that takes the predicate of pattern matching clauses and one pattern as arguments, then if the predicate matches the pattern, function *patterns_match* returns *true*; otherwise, *false*, and this eliminates the overlapping between patterns and ensures that the index returned by the μCRL state function is deterministic and unique. Figure 7 illustrates an example for the state functions shown in Figure 6.

```
rew
  S_i(Args) =
    S_i_case_0(patterns_match(Args,P_1),Args)
  S_i_case_0(true,Args) =
    tuple(S_j,tuple(Data,tuplenil(1)))
  S_i_case_0(false,Args) =
    S_i_case_1(patterns_match(Args,P_2),Args)
  S_i_case_1(true,Args) =
    tuple(S_k,tuple(Data,tuplenil(2)))
    ...
  S_i_case_(n-1)(true,Args) =
    tuple(S_u,tuple(Data,tuplenil(n-1)))
  S_i_case_(n-1)(false,Args) =
    S_i_case_n(patterns_match(Args,P_n),Args)
  S_i_case_n(true,Args) =
    tuple(S_v,tuple(Data,tuplenil(n)))
```

```
proc
  fsm_S_i(Cmd:Term,Data:Term) =
    actions(1).
    fsm_next_state(element(1,S_i(Cmd,Data)),
      element(2,S_i(Cmd,Data)))
    ◁ element(3,S_i(Cmd,Data))=1 ▷
    (actions(2).
    fsm_next_state(element(1,S_i(Cmd,
      Data)),element(2,S_i(Cmd,Data)))
      ◁ element(3,S_i(Cmd,Data))=2 ▷
    ...
    (actions(n).
    fsm_next_state(element(1,S_i(Cmd,
      Data)),element(2,S_i(Cmd,Data)))
    ◁ element(3,S_i(Cmd,Data))=n ▷
      delta)...)
```

Fig. 7. Translation rules for Erlang state function

When the state process *fsm_S_i* starts, it first calls the μCRL state function $S_i(Cmd, Data)$. S_i returns an index number i that determines which action sequence *action(i)* is about to be performed. The process *fsm_S_i* ends up by calling process *fsm_next_state*, updating the *current state* and the *state data* in the stack.

6   Case Studies

To illustrate the approach we present two case studies, one of which is a door with code lock system, while, the other a coffee machine system. As discussed in Section 2, *gen_fsm:send_event* is often called through some external actions. Therefore, before starting a simulation process, a sequence of actions needs to be initialized in the process *CommandList* to simulate the external behaviour.

6.1   A Door with Code Lock

Consider the example given in Section 2. In the simulation, the system code is set to *abc*. The function *button* is defined to input a password.

Following the rules defined in Section 5, the OTP component is translated into μCRL, and the resultant μCRL specification is listed in the appendix. A sequence of external actions $[\{abb\}, \{abc\}]$ is initialized in the μCRL specification, stating that two passwords, *abb* and *abc*, are consecutively inputted. The LTSs derived from CADP are shown in Figure 8 where Figure 8-A lists all actions, while, Figure 8-B hides the actions *push_callstack* and *pop_callstack* as internal actions.

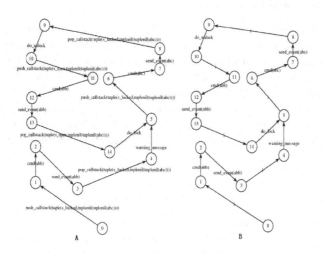

Fig. 8. LTSs derived from the door with code lock system

From the LTSs it can be seen that, initially, the system pushes the state *s_locked* and the code *abc* onto the stack. This simulates the *start_link* function in the Erlang program where the initial state and the system code are set to *s_locked* and *abc* respectively. When the action *send_event* is performed, the state *s_locked*, saved in the stack, is read out. The state *s_locked* determines process *fsm_locked* is about to be activated. This simulates the process that the current state function is executed when *gen_fsm* : *send_event* is invoked. Since the first password is not correct, $abb \neq abc$, a warning message is given and the door remains locked. After *abc* is received, the door is opened and the state *s_open* is pushed onto the stack.

We can then use a toolset such as CADP to verifying design properties of the system. For instance, to check "without receiving a correct password "*abc*", the door cannot be opened", the property can be formulated as:

$$[\text{not (``cmd(abc)'')}* . \text{``do\_unlock''}]\ \text{false},$$

Another property one might wish to check can be formulated as:

<true*. "cmd(abb)" . ("pop_calls(tuple(s_locked,tuplenil (tuplenil(abc))))")* . "warning_message"> true,

stating that when an incorrect password *"abb"* is received and the current state is *s_lokced*, the action *warning_message* will be fairly performed. Thus once we have a specification in μCRL, applying model-checking approaches is standard.

However, the example given in this section is simple and the system is comparatively easy to be verified. In the next sub-section, a more complicated system is designed to further evaluate the proposed model.

6.2   Coffee Machine

A coffee machine has three states, these being, *selection*, *payment* and *remove*. State *selection* allows a buyer to choose the type of drink, while, state *payment* displays the price of a selected drink and requires payment for the drink; after enough coins being paid, the machine goes to the state *remove* where the drink is prepared and the change is returned.

Four types of drink are sold: *tea, cappuccino, americano* and *espresso*. A buyer can select a type of drink at a machine, pays for it and takes a cup after the drink is ready. A buyer can also cancel the current transaction where the pre-paid coins will be returned.

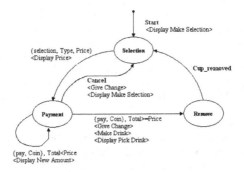

Fig. 9. FSM - coffee machine

Figure 9 illustrates the FSM design of the coffee machine. The program initially sets the current state to *selection*.

The OTP component is then translated into μCRL, and four actions *display_price, pay_coin, return_coin* and *remove_cup* are defined in the μCRL specification where *display_price* displays the price for a selected drink; *pay_coin* requires a buyer to pay coins for the drink; *return_coin* returns the change if more coins have been paid for the drink, or gives back the pre-paid coins if the transaction is cancelled.

Before verifying the system's properties, a set of verification tasks is required, each of which consists of a set of commands to simulates the process on buying a drink. Two sequences of external actions are constructed. The first simulates "selecting *cappuccino* (£5 for a cup), paying £4 and then trying to take the drink away", while, the second simulates "selecting *tea* (£4 for a cup), paying £5 and then taking the drink away". The sequences are coded in the lists

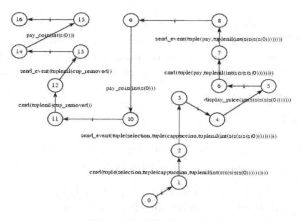

A: Cappuccino with the payment less than the price

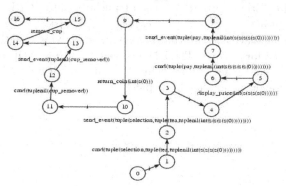

B: Tea with the payment greater than the price

Fig. 10. LTSs derived from the coffee_machine system

[{selection, cappuccino, 5}, {pay, 4}, {cup_remove}] and [{selection, tea, 4}, {pay, 5}, {cup_remove}]. They are then initialized in the process *CommandList* respectively.

The LTSs, derived from the CADP, are shown in Figure 10. Figure 10-A shows that the system initially pushes *s_selection* onto the stack. Once *cappuccino* is selected, its price is displayed. When a buyer pays less coins (£4) than the price (£5), the machine stays in *payment*, asking for the rest of payment (£1). Figure 10-B shows that, after *tea* (£4 for a cup) is selected and more coins (£5) are paid, the machine will prepare the drink and returns the change (£1). When the drink is taken away, the machine moves back to *selection*.

System properties can then be verified by the CADP model checker. For example, to check the property "After *cappuccino* is selected, its price will be displayed.", the property can be formulated as:

[true*. "cmd(tuple(selection,tuple(cappuccino,tuplenil (5))))" . (not "display_price(5)")*]
<true* . "display_price(5)"> true

Similarly, to check the properties "When *cappuccino* is selected and £4 has been paid, if the rest of payment £1 is not paid, the drink cannot be taken away.", and "When *tea* is selected and £5 has been paid, before the drink being taken away, change must be returned.", we formulated them as (respectively):

[true* . ('cmd(tuple(selection,tuple(cappuccino,tuplenil (5)))) . *' and 'cmd(tuple(pay, tuplenil(4))). *'). (not "pay_coin(1)")* . "cmd(tuplenil(cup_removed))"] false

[true* . ('cmd(tuple(selection,tuple(tea,tuplenil(4)))) . *' and 'cmd(tuple(pay, tuplenil(5))). *'). (not "return_coin(1)")* . "cmd(tuplenil(cup_removed))"] false

We applied the translation approach to a faulty implementation to evaluate the model's capability for fault detection. In stead of using *payment ≥ price*, the faulty Erlang program implements the logic *payment > price* for selling a drink. The faulty Erlang program is then translated into μCRL.

A sequence of actions, [{*selection, cappuccino*, 5}, {*pay*, 5}, {*cup_remove*}] is constructed to simulate the external behaviour of "paying exactly £5 for a cup of cappuccino (£5 for a cup)". The LTS derived from the CADP toolset is shown in Figure 11. It can be seen the machine requires additional £0 for the drink, even though enough money has been paid.

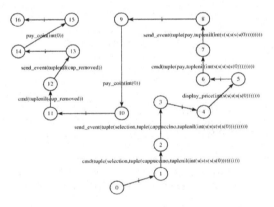

Fig. 11. LTSs derived from the faulty Erlang program

We then checked the derived model against the property:

["cmd(tuple(selection,tuple(cappuccino,tuplenil(5))))"* . "cmd(tuple(pay,tuplenil(5)))"* . (not "remove_cup")*] <true* . "remove_cup"> true

stating that, when cappuccino is selected and after £5 has been paid, the drink will be prepared. Using this property the CADP model checker can correctly distinguish the correct and faulty implementations based upon the design we wish to check against.

7   Conclusions and Future Work

In this paper we have extended work on model checking Erlang in μCRL. The principal aim of the work is to define rules that will translate Erlang/OTP programs (assumed to be correctly implemented) into a μCRL specification, and then to verify properties that the system should hold with standard toolsets such as CADP. We have extended previous work by investigated the model checking of Erlang/OTP Finite State Machine components in the process algebra μCRL. Specifically, a model was proposed to support the translation of an Erlang FSM design pattern into a μCRL specification, where a stack is defined in μCRL to simulate the management of the FSM states and the up-to-date state data.

The particular challenge is not the writing of a FSM in a process algebra, which is, of course, trivial, but the correct translation of how Erlang treats and defines FSMs, and the parameters with which it can be invoked. Furthermore, the translation needs to be faithful to the translation of other OTP components, that is, maintain the same design philosophy, and specifically the level of abstraction of the mapping from Erlang to μCRL.

Here, the state function defined in the Erlang FSM is translated into two parts in μCRL, one of which defines a μCRL state-process that can be called or synchronised by some other μCRL processes, while, the other defines a series of μCRL state functions determined by the patterns defined in the Erlang state function. A sequence of actions defined in an Erlang state function and guarded by a pattern is translated into a pre-defined action set in μCRL indexed with a unique integer number. A μCRL state-process will receive an index number from a μCRL state function that determines which pre-defined action set will be triggered.

Two small examples illustrate the proposed model, one of which looked at a door with code lock system while the other studied a coffee machine system. Both systems were modelled by Erlang/OTP *gen_fsm* design pattern first, and then translated into a μCRL specification. By using a model checker such as CADP, properties can be verified which represent an abstraction over the original Erlang code.

The algorithm presented performs an abstraction of the Erlang code, and is currently being implemented and integrated into the *etomcrl* toolset so that complex OTP designs involving generic servers, FSMs etc can be translated. There are a number of issues that we have not had space to discuss here. One is correctness of the translation, which is involved as it depends on verification against a semantics of Erlang. Such issues of correctness of the approach are discussed in [5]. The other issue is that the model discussed in this paper does not define rules for the translation of *timeout* events. However, in some real applications, *timeout* events in a FSM play a significant role in the OTP design, and there are two approaches to extending the work we have presented here. The first is to use a timed extension to μCRL (which exist, but have limited tool support), the second is to incorporate explicit *tick* events in the untimed μCRL. We have recently experimented successfully with the second approach, and again the translation produces tractable μCRL specifications.

Acknowledgements

This work is supported by the UK Engineering and Physical Sciences Research Council (EPSRC) grant EP/C525000/1. We would like to thank the developers of the tool sets of μCRL and CADP for permitting the use of tools for system verification. Thanks also go to my supervisor, John Derrick, for his help with this work.

References

1. Armstrong, J., Virding, R., Wikström, C., Williams, M.: Concurrent Programming in Erlang, 2nd edn. Prentice-Hall, Englewood Cliffs (1996)
2. Arts, T., Benac, C.: Verifying Erlang code: a resource locker case-study. In: Eriksson, L.-H., Lindsay, P.A. (eds.) FME 2002. LNCS, vol. 2391, pp. 184–203. Springer, Heidelberg (2002)
3. Arts, T., Benac Earle, C., Penas, J.J.S.: Translating Erlang to μCRL. In: Proceedings of the Fourth International Conference on Application of Concurrency to System Design (ACSD'04), pp. 135–144 (2004)
4. Blau, J., Rooth, J., Axell, J., Hellstrand, F., Buhrgard, M., Westin, T., Wicklund, G.: AXD 301: A new generation ATM switching system. Computer Networks 31, 559–582 (1999)
5. Benac Earle, C.: Model check the interaction of Erlang components. PhD thesis, The University of Kent, Canterbury, Department of Computer Science (2006)
6. Fredlund, L.-A., Benac Earle, C., Derrick, J.: Verifying fault-tolerant Erlang programs. In: Sagonas, K., Armstrong, J. (eds.) 2005, pp. 26–34. ACM Press, New York (2005)
7. CADP. http://www.inrialpes.fr/vasy/cadp/
8. Clarke, E., Grumberg, O., Long, D.: Model Checking. MIT Press, Cambridge (1999)
9. Kozen, D.: Results on the propositional μ-calculus. TCS 27, 333–354 (1983)
10. Benac Earle, C., Fredlund, L.-A.: Verification of Language Based Fault-Tolerance. In: EUROCAST, pp. 140–149 (2005)
11. Huch, F.: Verification of Erlang programs using abstract interpretation and model checking. ACM SIGPLAN Notices 34(9), 261–272 (1999)
12. Fredlund, L.-A., Gurov, D., Noll, T., Dam, M., Arts, T., Chugunov, G.: A verification tool for Erlang. International Journal on Software Tools for Technology Transfer 4, 405–420 (2003)
13. Groote, J.F., Ponse, A.: The syntax and sematics of μCRL. In: Algebra of Communicating Processes 1994, Workshop in Computing, pp. 26–62 (1995)
14. Baeten, J.C.M., Bergstra, J.A.: Process algebra with signals and conditions. Report P9008, University of Amsterdam (1990)
15. Baeten, J.C.M., Weijland, W.P.: Process Algebra. Cambridge University Press, Cambridge (1990)
16. Guo, Q., Derrick, J.: Eliminating overlapping of pattern matching when verifying Erlang programs in μCRL. In: The 12th International Erlang User Conference (EUC'06), Stockholm, Sweden (2006)

Appendix: The μCRL Specification for Code Lock Door

sort
  Term
func
  s_locked, s_open, abc, abb: -> Term
act
  s_event, r_event, send_event, s_command, r_command, cmd: Term
  do_lock, do_unlock, warning_message
comm
  s_event | r_event = send_event
  s_command | r_command = cmd
map
  patterns_matching: Term # Term -> Term
  locked: Term # Term -> Term
  open: Term # Term -> Term
  locked_case_0_0: Term # Term # Term -> Term
  locked_case_0_1: Term # Term # Term -> Term
var
  Command, LoopData: Term
  Pattern1, Pattern2: Term
rew
  locked(Command, LoopData) =
    locked_case_0_0(patterns_matching(Command, element(int (1),LoopData)),
Command, LoopData)
  locked_case_0_0(true, Command, LoopData) =
    tuple(s_open, tuple(LoopData, tuplenil(tuplenil(int(1)))))
  locked_case_0_0(false, Command, LoopData) =
    locked_case_0_1(patterns_matching(Command, do_not _care), Command,
LoopData)
  locked_case_0_1(true, Command, LoopData) =
    tuple(s_locked, tuple(LoopData,tuplenil(tuplenil(int(2)))))
  open(Command, LoopData) =
    tuple(s_locked, tuple(LoopData,tuplenil(tuplenil(int(1)))))
  patterns_matching(Pattern1, Pattern2) = equal (Pattern1,Pattern2)
proc
  write(Val:Term) =
    wcallresult(Val)

  read(Command:Term) =
    sum(Val:Term, rcallresult(Val).
    (fsm_locked(Command,element(int(2),Val))
          $\lhd$ is_s_locked(element(int(1),Val)) $\rhd$
              (fsm_open(Command,element(int(2),Val))
                    $\lhd$is_s_open(element(int(1),Val)) $\rhd$ delta)))
  fsm_locked(Command:Term,LoopData:Term) =

(do_unlock.
fsm_next_state(element(int(1),locked(Command,LoopData)),
element(int(2),locked (Command,LoopData))))
◁term_to_bool(equal(element(int(1),element(int(3),
locked(Command,LoopData))),int(1)))▷
(warning_message.
fsm_next_state(element(int (1),locked(Command,LoopData)),
element(int (2),locked(Command,LoopData)))
◁ term_to_bool(equal (element(int(1),element(int(3),
locked (Command,LoopData))),int(2)))
▷ delta)
fsm_open(Command:Term,LoopData:Term) =
do_lock.
fsm_next_state(element(int(1),open(Command,LoopData)),
element(int(2),open (Command,LoopData)))
◁ term_to_bool(equal(element(int(1),element (int(3),
open(Command,LoopData))),int(1))) ▷ delta
fsm_change_state =
sum(Command:Term,r_event(Command).read(Command))

fsm_init(S:Term, LoopData:Term) =
fsm_next_state(S,LoopData)

fsm_next_state(S:Term, LoopData:Term) =
wcallresult(tuple(S,tuplenil(LoopData))).
sum(Command:Term, r_command(Command).
s_event(Command).fsm_change_state)
fsm_command(Command:Term, CmdSet:Term) =
s_command(hd(CmdSet)).
fsm_command(tl(CmdSet), CmdSet)
◁ is_nil(Command) ▷
s_command(hd(Command)).fsm _command(tl(Command),
CmdSet)
init
encap({s_command,r_command},fsm_command(nil,cons(abb, cons(abc,
nil))) ||
hide({push_callstack,pop_callstack},
encap (rcallvalue,wcallvalue,rcallresult,wcallresult,s_event,
r_event,
CallStack(empty) || fsm_init(s_locked, tuplenil(abc))||
fsm_change_state)))

Formal Analysis of Publish-Subscribe Systems by Probabilistic Timed Automata

Fei He[1], Luciano Baresi[2], Carlo Ghezzi[2], and Paola Spoletini[2]

[1] Department of Computer Science & Technology, Tsinghua University
Beijing, China, 100084
`hef02@mails.tsinghua.edu.cn`
[2] Dipartimento di Elettronica e Informazione, Politecnico di Milano
Milano, Italy, 20133
{`baresi,ghezzi,spoleti`}`@elet.polimi.it`

Abstract. The publish-subscribe architectural style has recently emerged as a promising approach to tackle the dynamism of modern distributed applications. The correctness of these applications does not only depend on the behavior of each component in isolation, but the interactions among components and the delivery infrastructure play key roles. This paper presents the first results on considering the validation of these applications in a probabilistic setting. We use probabilistic model checking techniques on stochastic models to tackle the uncertainty that is embedded in these systems. The communication infrastructure (i.e., the transmission channels and the publish-subscribe middleware) are modeled directly by means of probabilistic timed automata. Application components are modeled by using statechart diagrams and then translated into probabilistic timed automata. The main elements of the approach are described through an example.

1 Introduction

The publish-subscribe architectural style [1, 2, 3] has recently emerged as a promising approach to tackle the dynamism and flexibility of modern distributed applications. Components do not communicate directly, but their interactions are mediated by a dedicated element called *dispatcher*. Components dynamically *subscribe* to the messages they are interested in, and the dispatcher *notifies* them as soon as a message that matches their subscriptions is *published* by one of the other components. The dispatcher is the only element that knows how to route the messages in the system, and thus the sender of a message does not know its receivers. This peculiarity allows components to join and leave an application seamlessly without any need to restructure the whole system.

The correctness of these applications does not only depend on the correct behavior of each component in isolation. We also need the right intertwining among subscriptions, publications, and notifications, to allow components to receive the messages they need, and an infrastructure that actually delivers all the messages exchanged within the system. Therefore, the formal analysis of

J. Derrick and J. Vain (Eds.): FORTE 2007, LNCS 4574, pp. 247–262, 2007.

publish and subscribe systems must consider two orthogonal aspects: (a) the subscriptions and unsubscriptions that can dynamically change the topology of the system, and its interaction paths, and (b) the underlying infrastructure that cannot always guarantee that all messages, along with subscriptions and unsubscriptions, be delivered to all interested parties.

Among the many attempts [4, 5, 6, 7, 8, 9, 10] to model and validate publish-subscribe systems, model checking has been considered as an attractive solution. However, all these works assume deterministic systems and neglect the uncertainty that characterize practical publish-subscribe applications. Differently from these works, in this paper we do not discuss the fine-grained analysis of subscriptions and notifications, but we present the first results on extending these approaches by considering the problem in a probabilistic setting. We use probabilistic model checking techniques on stochastic models to tackle the uncertainty that is intrinsic in these systems. Even if we assume that application components are correct, stochastic models help us reason on the reliability of the infrastructure, that is, the probability with which messages can be lost during the transmission. Moreover, since probabilistic model checking involves the exhaustive exploration of all possible paths, it can also supply important information about the model: for example, the optimal size of buffers, average delays, and so on.

In our approach, we provide independent models for the communication infrastructure, which includes the transmission channels and the middleware, and for application components. The transmission channels provide the mechanisms for message delivery. The middleware supports subscriptions, unsubscriptions, and message routing. Both are problem-independent, and their models are reusable in different systems. Application components are problem-specific and are not usually reused. In this paper, the communication infrastructure is modeled by means of probabilistic timed automata directly. Application components are modeled with statechart diagrams, and we provide some easy clues for translating these diagrams to probabilistic timed automata. An example helps us validate the effectiveness of our approach by means of the probabilistic model checker PRISM.

The rest of the paper is organized as follows. Section 2 briefly surveys some related works. Section 3 introduces an abstract model of publish-subscribe systems. Section 4 provides some background definitions about probabilistic timed automata. Section 5 presents our proposal, while Section 6 exemplifies it on a simple case study. Section 7 concludes this paper.

2   Related Work

This paper builds on the previous efforts of some of the authors [4,5,6] by extending the formal analysis of publish-subscribe systems in a probabilistic setting. In [4], application components are modeled as UML statechart diagrams while the communication infrastructure is supplied as a configurable predefined component. UML statechart diagrams are translated into Promela and validated through the SPIN model checker. While this approach builds on top of an existing model checker, [5, 6] extend the Bogor model checker and the communication mechanisms of publish-subscribe infrastructures are embedded in it. Some domain-specific knowledge is used to reduce the state space.

In [7,8], the authors present a generic framework for automatically analyzing publish-subscribe systems and also provide a translation tool to automatically generate analysis models. Although the ideas presented in these papers are similar to those described here, there are some differences. We extend this work by adding the probabilistic environment and we also allow components to change their subscriptions at run-time. These proposals are also extended in [9], which improves the representation of events, event delivery policies, and event-method bindings. Finally, [10] presents a transformation framework for the approach.

In [11], the authors present a compositional reasoning framework for verifying publish-subscribe systems. A system specification is decomposed into the properties of its components, which are then model checked separately under several environmental assumptions. The main drawback of this approach is the difficulty in decomposing the specification and providing appropriate assumptions.

3   Abstract Publish-Subscribe Architecture

The common denominator of the many variants proposed for the publish-subscribe paradigm is the decoupling in time and space of application components [2, 1, 3].

Fig. 1 illustrates the abstract model of a publish-subscribe infrastructure that we use for analysis via model checking. It comprises a dispatcher, the components, and a number of buffers that describe the transmission channels. Each buffer buf is characterized by a maximum size, MAX_buf; n_buf denotes the current number of elements stored in buffer buf. All buffers adopt a FIFO policy.

Components send their messages (i.e., publications, subscriptions, and unsubscriptions) to the dispatcher, by inserting them into buffer bpi. The message is tagged with the component that delivered the message. Messages are eventually transferred into buffer bpo, which models the input buffer to the dispatcher. Moving a message from bpi to bpo reflects the physical operation of message transmission. Since the message is tagged with the name of the originating component[1], it is possible to associate different probabilities with the delivery of messages from different components to the dispatcher. The messages delivered from the dispatcher are inserted into buffer bni. Each component Ci has an input buffer $bno[i]$ in which it receives the notifications. The transfer of a message from bni to a buffer $bno[i]$ reflects the physical operation of message transmission from the dispatcher to the notified component. The messages are transferred from bni into all the buffers of the target components to which it has to be delivered, based on the routing information stored in the subscription table. Again, a probability can be associated with the transfer of a message from bni to its target buffer in order to model unreliable channels.

---

[1] Tags are then removed when the messages are dispatched to their subscribers.

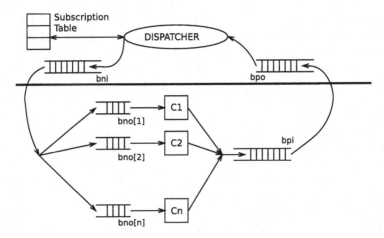

Fig. 1. Publish-subscribe infrastructure

We make the following assumptions, under which systems are analyzed via model checking: (a) transmission channels preserve the order of messages delivered through them, (b) messages are dropped in case of buffer overflow, and (c) transmission channels are unreliable. Messages may be lost during transmission according to a certain probability, which varies from component to component. We denote by p_i the probability of message loss for the i-th component[2]. We also introduce some timed parameters that are relevant to represent time-related properties of the system: TPL and TPH are the minimal and maximal time delay for the dispatcher to process a message, TDL and TDH are the minimal and maximal time delay for the dispatcher to process a subscription/unsubscription, and TRL and TRH are the minimal and maximal transmission delays of a message through the communication channels.

The thorough analysis of these parameters might lead to the explosion of the state space. If we consider all the combinations among the possible values for these parameters, we would easily obtain an unmanageable finite state model. Some *domain-specific* abstractions can help us constrain the problem and obtain a model more suitable for analysis. For example, if we consider an embedded system whose components are distributed over a local area network, we can easily assume that $TRL = TRH = 0$ since transmission delay can be ignored, and thus the number of possible different states (combination of parameter values) decreases.

4   Probabilistic Timed Automata

Probabilistic timed automata provide a modeling framework for time-related systems with probability. Our definition is derived from timed automata [12,13], and we also follow the definitions in [14,15,16] with minor modifications.

---

[2] Notice that, since we model subscriptions and messages delivery with different buffers, our model allows to assign different probabilities to each component depending on the direction of the communication.

A finite **discrete probability distribution** over a set S is a mapping $p : S \rightarrow [0,1]$ such that $\sum_{s \in S} p(s) = 1$ and the set $\{s | s \in S \text{ and } p(s) > 0\}$ is finite. The set of all finite discrete probability distributions over S is denoted by $\mu(S)$.

A **Markov decision process** is a discrete time stochastic process characterized by a set of states; in each state there are several actions from which the decision maker can choose. For a state s and an action a, a state transition function $p(s')$ determines the transition probabilities to the next state s'. A Markov decision process can be represented as a tuple $(Q, Steps)$, where Q is a set of states, and $Steps : Q \rightarrow 2^{\mu(Q)}$ is a function assigning a set of probability distributions to each state.

A **clock** is a real-valued variable which increases at a given rate. Let X be a set of clock variables, ranging over the nonnegative real numbers R^+. A valuation of X assigns a nonnegative real value to every clock in set X. We denote the set of all clock valuations of X with R^X.

A clock constraint is an inequality of the form $x \sim c$ or $x_i - x_j \sim c$, where $\sim$ is an operator in $\{<, \leq, >, \geq\}$ and c is a nonnegative integer number or infinity. A **clock zone** is a convex subset of the valuation space R^X described by a conjunction of constraints. Let $Z(X)$ be the set of all zones of X.

Given a clock zone $\lambda \in Z(X)$ and a valuation $v \in R^X$, $\lambda(v)$ is the boolean value obtained by replacing each occurrence of a clock $x \in X$ with $v(x)$. If $\lambda(v) = true$, we say that v satisfies λ, denoted as $v \triangleright \lambda$.

Definition 1. *Let AP be a fixed, finite set of atomic propositions. A probabilistic timed automaton is a 7-tuple $M = (S, S_0, L, X, inv, prob, \langle \tau_s \rangle_{s \in S})$, where*

- *S is a finite set of locations.*
- *s_0 is the initial location.*
- *$L : S \rightarrow 2^{AP}$ is a labeling function that associates each location $s \in S$ with the set $L(s)$ of atomic propositions that are valid in s.*
- *X is a finite set of clocks.*
- *$inv : S \rightarrow Z(X)$ is a mapping that associates each location with an invariant condition.*
- *$prob : S \rightarrow P_{fn}(\mu(S \times 2^X))$ is a mapping function that associates each location with a finite and non-empty set of discrete probability distributions on $S \times 2^X$.*
- *$\langle \tau_s \rangle_{s \in S}$ is a family of functions where for any $s \in S$, $\tau_s : prob(s) \rightarrow Z(X)$ associates each $p \in prob(s)$ with an enabling condition.*

A state of a probabilistic timed automaton is a pair $\langle s, v \rangle$, where $s \in S$, $v \in R^X$, and $v \triangleright inv(s)$. The system starts in location s_0, with all clocks initialized to 0. The values of all the clocks increase uniformly as time passes.

If we assume that the present state is $\langle s, v \rangle$, a probabilistic timed automaton has two basic types of transitions:

- *Delay transition*: the system can remain in the current location s and lets time pass, provided that the invariant condition in s can continuously be satisfied while time passes.

– *Action transition*: the system can make a discrete transition according to any probability distribution in $Prob(s)$ whose enabling condition is satisfied by the current time valuation v.

These concepts are exemplified by the automaton of Fig. 2. It consists of: two locations s_0 and s_1, two clocks x_0 and x_1, and two probabilistic distributions, a and b, associated with s_0 and s_1, respectively. The first distribution (a) defines a discrete transition from s_0 to s_1 with probability 1. The second distribution (b) defines a discrete transition from s_1 to s_0 again with probability 1. s_0 is the initial location, and the automaton starts with state $(s_0, x_0 = 0, x_1 = 0)$. Before the clock x_0 reaches the value 4, the automaton may remain in the location s_0 (delay transition). After 2 time units, the enabling condition for the discrete transition from s_0 to s_1 is satisfied, and the automaton can either move to the location s_1 (action transition) or remain in location s_0 (delay transition).

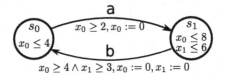

Fig. 2. An example of probabilistic timed automaton

5   Implementation

In this section, we explain how publish-subscribe systems can be formally specified and verified by means of probabilistic timed automata.

As discussed earlier, a model for a publish-subscribe system can be separated into two parts: the reusable part, consisting of the dispatcher and the transmission channels, and the problem-specific components. Following the model illustrated in Fig. 1, we start the presentation with the probabilistic timed automata that model the dispatcher and transmission channels, respectively, and then we continue with the application-specific components.

5.1   Dispatcher

Fig. 3 shows the probabilistic timed automaton that models the dispatcher. The automaton starts in location 0. The enabling conditions and actions are attached to the transitions as follows:

$$cond_1 \wedge cond_2 \wedge \cdots \wedge cond_m, act_1, act_2, \ldots, act_n$$

The semantics of labels is that if the conjunction of the conditions in the first part of the label holds, the sequence of actions that follows is performed atomically before the transition terminates.

The dispatcher monitors the receiving buffer bpo. If it is not empty, the dispatcher fetches the first message in the buffer. If the message is a subscription,

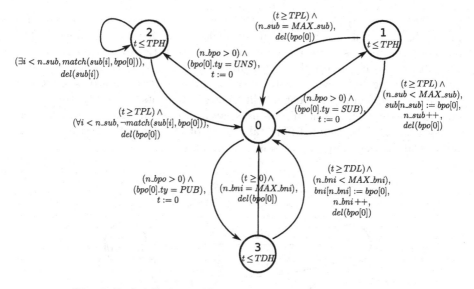

Fig. 3. Probabilistic timed automaton modeling the dispatcher

the dispatcher moves to location 1 by resetting timer t. The invariant in location 1 means that the dispatcher may process the message for at most TPH time units. Before t reaches the timeout, the dispatcher leaves location 1 and goes back to location 0 by either recording this subscription in the table (if the table is not full), or by dropping this subscription (if the table is full).

If the message is an unsubscription, the dispatcher moves to location 2 by resetting timer t. Then the dispatcher searches all the entries in the subscription table and removes those that match this unsubscription. Finally, it returns back to location 0 after at least a time delay. If the message is a publication, the dispatcher moves to location 3 by resetting timer t. Note that if the buffer bni is full, the dispatcher does not transfer the message and moves back to location 0. Otherwise the dispatcher transfers the message to buffer bni after a time delay. Operation match, which labels some of the transitions, performs the matching of a message against a subscription, and evaluates to true if its arguments match. The function encapsulates the details of the specific linguistic mechanisms supported by the publish-subscribe middleware to specify the matching. Operation del removes an element from a buffer (or subscription table).

5.2   Channels

The probabilistic timed automaton of Fig. 4 models the transmission of messages from components to the dispatcher. It commences in location 0. If buffer bpi is not empty, the automaton moves to location 1 by resetting timer t. The transitions exiting location 1 describe the fact that the channel may drop the message if the receiving buffer is full, or perform the probabilistic transmission otherwise. The probabilistic transition is drawn in the Fig. 4 as two directed shared edges

connected by an arc. For readability reasons, we only show one example of a
probabilistic transition, although there should be one for each component. The
enabling condition is attached to the arc, and the actions are attached to the
two edges. The message is lost with probability $p[i]$, and the message arrives
at the receiving buffer with probability $1 - p[i]$. Notice that the message loss
probability $p[i]$ can be different for different components. Moreover, this model
does not distinguish if transmitted messages are subscriptions, unsubscriptions,
or notifications; the channel only takes care of queueing the messages in the
buffer and then the dispatcher deals with them.

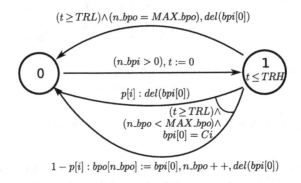

Fig. 4. Probabilistic timed automaton modeling message transmission to the dispatcher

The probabilistic timed automaton of Fig. 5 models the notifications, i.e., the
delivery of messages to the registered components. It starts in location 0 and if
buffer bni is not empty, the channel moves to location 1 by initializing variable j
to 0. The sequence of transitions from location 1 to locations 2 and 3, to end in
location 1, models the notification of a message to a component. The transition
from location 1 to location 2 models the match of the message with the j-th
subscription. Variable $tmp1$ is used to record the identifier of the component that
delivered the subscription, and variable $tmp2$ is used to record the number of
elements currently stored in buffer $bno[tmp1]$. The self-loop transition in location
1 describes the mismatch of the j-th subscription with the message; the value of
j is also incremented by 1.

5.3   Application Components

This section describes how to model application-specific components. The infrastructure provides the following operations to the designers of application
components to let them communicate:

- subscribe(pid,t): component pid subscribes to messages that match pattern
  t.
- unsubscribe(pid,t): component pid withdraws its former subscriptions that
  match pattern t.

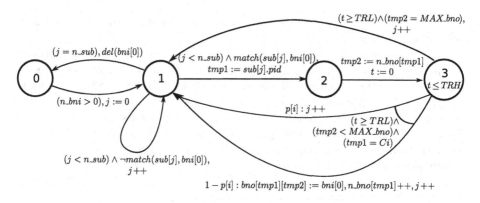

Fig. 5. Probabilistic timed automaton modeling notification

- `publish(k)`: a component publishes message k.
- `consume(k)`: a component removes message k from its receiving buffer bno.

As defined in Section 3, we assume that operation `consume` takes at least TCL and at most TCH time units. Probabilistic timed automata allow us to model the above operations as shown in Fig. 6. Component designers specify the behavior of components by means of statechart diagrams, and use the above operations to model the interaction among components. They can then translate the statechart diagrams to probabilistic timed automata according to the translation rules defined in Fig. 6.

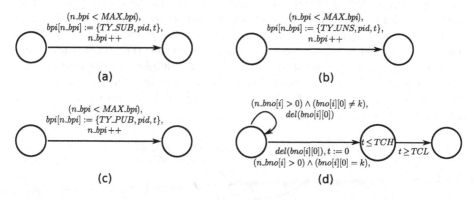

Fig. 6. Probabilistic timed automata modeling communication operations: (a) `subscribe(pid,t)`, (b) `unsubscribe(pid,t)`, (c) `publish(k)`, and (d) `consume(k)`

6   Example Application

This section applies our approach to a simple example taken in the domain of embedded control systems. The example consists of two sensors, a main processor, and an actuator. The main processor reads the responses from the sensors, and then feeds the actuator. This system can be implemented by using a publish-subscribe architecture as shown in Fig. 7.

First, the main processor publishes events to request data from the sensors. Then, the main processor, which receives responses from the sensors, publishes a message to feed the actuator[3]. The sensors take from $TSDL$ to $TSDH$ time units to give their responses, and the actuator uses from $TADL$ to $TADH$ time units to be fed. Since the message may be lost during the transmission, we assume an upper bound TMW for the main processor to wait for data. We start a timer as soon as the main process begins to work. If a time-out occurs, the main process terminates and reports a failure.

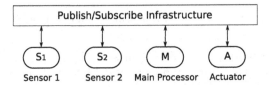

Fig. 7. Publish-subscribe architecture of the embedded control system

Fig. 8 and Fig. 9 show the statechart diagrams for the sensors and the main processor, respectively. The statechart diagram for the actuator is not illustrated here since it is similar to the one for the sensors. The corresponding probabilistic timed automata can be obtained from the statechart diagrams by applying the translation rules of Fig. 6. For example, the probabilistic timed automaton obtained from the statechart diagram for sensors is shown in Fig. 10. The probabilistic timed automaton of the main processor can be obtained similarly. In this example, subscriptions cannot change dynamically (i.e., while the system executes); they are defined statically. Hence the complete model contains the above described components and the dispatcher presented in Section 5, where subscription and unsubscription messages are ignored. Accordingly, the model in Fig. 4 only handles publication messages.

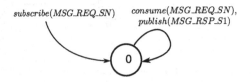

Fig. 8. Statechart diagram for a sensor

The choice of only considering static subscriptions is not due to limitations of the proposed approach, but to the nature of the example application, since embedded systems are often statically configured. However, should we need to

---

[3] Notice that all the messages are mediated through the dispatcher.

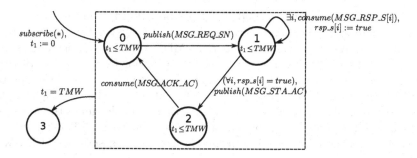

Fig. 9. Statechart diagram for the main processor

add dynamic subscriptions, the components ought to be modified by adding two new outgoing transitions from location 0 to model subscription and unsubscription requests, respectively. These transitions are taken with a given probability to simulate the success of these operations and thus how the scenario changes[4]. If one of these transitions is taken, the automaton moves to a new location, from which we model the subscription (or unsubscription) request.

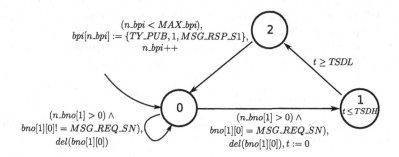

Fig. 10. Probabilistic timed automata for a sensor

6.1   PRISM Model

PRISM [17,18,19] is the model checker we selected to verify our models. PRISM is a probabilistic model checker developed at the University of Birmingham and is a tool for the design and analysis of systems that exhibit probabilistic behaviors. It supports three types of probabilistic models: Discrete-Time Markov Chains (DTMCs), Markov Decision Process (MDPs), and Continuous-Time Markov Chains (CTMCs). Models are specified in a simple, high-level modeling language, which is a variant of the Reactive Modules formalism of Alur and Henzinger [20]. Properties are described by the PRISM property specification language, which is based on the two probabilistic temporal logics called Probabilistic Computation Tree Logic (PCTL) [21, 22] and Continuous Stochastic Logic (CSL) [23, 24].

---

[4] Notice that in this example, this probability is 0, since with do not permit dynamic subscriptions and unsubscriptions and thus the arcs are skipped.

Since we are interested in modeling both probabilistic (unreliable channels with message loss) and non-deterministic (time delays) behaviors of publish-subscribe systems, we decided to adopt the MDP formalism, which allows us to mix the two different types of behaviors. The translation from probabilistic timed automata to PRISM models is easy. Each automaton in the publish-subscribe system corresponds to a PRISM module. The buffers and the subscription table are rendered as global variables. Since all the timers should run at the same rate, it is required that all the time passing actions be synchronized. For example, the dispatcher staying in location 1 with time progressing is described in PRISM as:

```
[time] s_dp=1 & t_dp<TPH -> t_dp'=min(t_dp+1,TPH);
```

Similarly, sensor 1 staying in location 2 with time progressing can be described in PRISM as:

```
[time] s_s1=1 & t_s1<TSDH -> t_s1'=min(t_s1+1,TSDH);
```

Notice that these two commands are labeled with the same action time to mean that these two commands need to be synchronized.

PRISM models can be augmented with *rewards structures*[5], which associate real values with certain states or transitions of the model. With reward structures, PRISM can be used to reason about the properties related to the expected values of these rewards. In our model, we assign a reward of 1 to all the transitions labeled with action *time*. All the others maintain 0 as default value. This way we can verify the properties related to expected time.

6.2   Experimental Results

This section presents some results obtained by using the PRISM model checker to verify the example system.

Service provision. The first concern is to understand if the task finishes successfully. This means that the automaton of the main processor must end in location 0 without generating a time-out. This can be expressed in PRISM as:

```
label "succeed" = s_mn=0 & t_mn>0;
Pmax=?[true U "succeed"], Pmin=?[true U "succeed"]
```

Notice that the probabilities for an MDP can only be computed after nondeterminism is resolved. Here we have two types of probabilities: P_{max} and P_{min} correspond to the resolutions that all the delays take the minimum or maximum values. We checked the effect of p_0 (message loss probability for the main processor) on the two probabilities and Fig. 11 shows the results. Notice that the two probabilities behave the same way, so we use the term *probability* in Fig. 11 to refer to both the probabilities. Similar results can be obtained for other message loss probabilities. It is easy to understand that probability P_{max} (or P_{min}) decreases as the message loss probability increases.

---

[5] Interested readers can refer to [25, 26] for a detailed presentation.

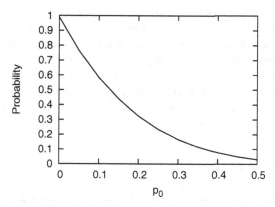

Fig. 11. Effect of p_0 on the probability (P_{max}, P_{min})

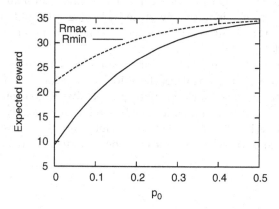

Fig. 12. The effect of TDL on $Rmin$

Average time. Our second concern is about the average time the system takes to complete the task. It can be expressed in PRISM as:

```
label "terminate" = (s_mn=0 & t_mn>0) | (s_mn=3);
Rmax=?[F "terminate"], Rmin=?[F "terminate"]
```

where R=? [F prop] is a reward-based property. It accumulates rewards along each path until `prop` is satisfied, and then returns the expected value [26].

We have tested the effect of p_0 on both R_{max} and R_{min}. Since we assign a reward of 1 to all the transitions labeled with action *time*, the values of R_{max} and R_{min} just give the average times in the case of maximum and minimum delays, respectively. The results are plotted in Fig. 12 and show that when p_0 increases, the probability of the task to successfully finish decreases, as a result the average time increases accordingly. Needless to say, the system takes more time if the sub-tasks fail. There is also an upper bound for the two expected values.

Effect of buffer size. If we consider the probabilities computed in the first experiment, the values of P_{max} and P_{min} are the same. However, if we reduce the size of the corresponding buffers, the value of P_{min} may become 0. To understand this result, we need to consider the scenario in which all the sensors send their responses to the dispatcher at (almost) the same time. If the size of the receiving buffer is not large enough, or if the dispatcher cannot process existing messages quickly enough, there is a buffer overflow and the arrival of a new message would be dropped directly. The same situation can happen to the other buffers. Our experiments show that probabilistic model checking help optimize the appropriate size of buffers of the system model.

7   Conclusions and Future Work

This paper presented an approach to modeling and validating publish-subscribe systems by using probabilistic model checking. The infrastructure (transmission channels, dispatcher) is modeled by probabilistic timed automata. Application-specific components are modeled by statechart diagrams and then translated into probabilistic timed automata. The actual validation is carried out by using the PRISM model checker.

This paper presented some preliminary results we obtained so far, which are motivating us to keep investigating these ideas. Our long-term goal is to design an integrated tool-set for the multi-perspective validation of the highly dynamic software architectures, which are becoming increasingly important and widespread in practice. Publish-subscribe architecture are a first notable class of such architectures, on which we initially focused our research.

References

1. Carzaniga, A., Rosenblum, D.S., Wolf, A.L.: Design and evaluation of a wide-area event notification service. ACM Transactions on Computer Systems 19(3), 332–383 (2001)
2. Eugster, P.T., Felber, P.A., Guerraoui, R., Kermarrec, A.M.: The many faces of publish/subscribe. ACM Comput. Surv. 35(2), 114–131 (2003)
3. Cugola, G., Picco, G.P.: Reds: a reconfigurable dispatching system. In: SEM '06: Proceedings of the 6th international workshop on Software engineering and middleware, pp. 9–16. ACM Press, New York, NY, USA (2006)
4. Zanolin, L., Ghezzi, C., Baresi, L.: An approach to model and validate publish/subscribe architectures. In: Proceedings of the SAVCBS'03 Workshop, Helsinki, Finland (2003)
5. Baresi, L., Ghezzi, C., Mottola, L.: Towards fine-grained automated verification of publish-subscribe architectures. In: Najm, E., Pradat-Peyre, J.F., Donzeau-Gouge, V.V. (eds.) FORTE 2006. LNCS, vol. 4229, pp. 131–135. Springer, Heidelberg (2006)
6. Baresi, L., Ghezzi, C., Mottola, L.: On accurate automatic verification of publish-subscribe architectures. In: (To appear) Proceedings of the 29th International Conference on Software Engineering (ICSE07), Minneapolis (MN, USA) (2007)

7. Garlan, D., Khersonsky, S.: Model checking implicit-invocation systems. In: Proc. of the 10th Int'l Workshop on Software Specification and Design, pp. 23–30 (2000)

8. Garlan, D., Khersonsky, S., Kim, J.S.: Model checking publish-subscribe systems. In: Proc. of the 10th Int'l SPIN Workshop on Model Checking of Software (2003)

9. Bradbury, J.S., Dingel, J.: Evaluating and improving the automatic analysis of implicit invocation systems. In: FSE (2003)

10. Zhang, H., Bradbury, J.S., Cordy, J.R., Dingel, J.: A transformational framework for testing and model checking implicit invocation systems. In: Proc. Int. Work. on Distr. Event-Based Systems (DEBS'04) (2004)

11. Caporuscio, M., Inverardi, P., Pelliccione, P.: Compositional verification of middleware-based software architecture descriptions. In: ICSE '04: Proceedings of the 26th International Conference on Software Engineering, pp. 221–230. IEEE Computer Society Press, Los Alamitos (2004)

12. Alur, R., Courcoubetis, C., Dill, D.: Model-checking for real-time systems. In: Proceedings of Fifth Annual IEEE Symposium on Logic in Computer Science, pp. 414–425 (1990)

13. Alur, R., Dill, D.L.: A theory of timed automata. Theor. Comput. Sci. 126(2), 183–235 (1994)

14. Kwiatkowska, M., Norman, G., Segala, R., Sproston, J.: Automatic verification of real-time systems with discrete probability distributions. Theoretical Computer Science 282, 101–150 (2002)

15. Kwiatkowska, M., Norman, G., Sproston, J., Wang, F.: Symbolic model checking for probabilistic timed automata. In: Lakhnech, Y., Yovine, S. (eds.) FORMATS 2004 and FTRTFT 2004. LNCS, vol. 3253, pp. 293–308. Springer, Heidelberg (2004)

16. Kwiatkowska, M., Norman, G., Parker, D., Sproston, J.: Performance analysis of probabilistic timed automata using digital clocks. Formal Methods in System Design 29, 33–78 (2006)

17. Kwiatkowska, M., Norman, G., Parker, D.: Probabilistic symbolic model checking with PRISM: A hybrid approach. International Journal on Software Tools for Technology Transfer (STTT) 6(2), 128–142 (2004)

18. Kwiatkowska, M., Norman, G., Parker, D.: Quantitative analysis with the probabilistic model checker PRISM. Electronic Notes in Theoretical Computer Science 153(2), 5–31 (2005)

19. Hinton, A., Kwiatkowska, M., Norman, G., Parker, D.: PRISM: A tool for automatic verification of probabilistic systems. In: Hermanns, H., Palsberg, J. (eds.) TACAS 2006 and ETAPS 2006. LNCS, vol. 3920, pp. 441–444. Springer, Heidelberg (2006)

20. Alur, R., Henzinger, T.A.: Reactive modules. Formal Methods in System Design: An. International Journal 15(1), 7–48 (1999)

21. Hansson, H., Jonsson, B.: A logic for reasoning about time and reliability. Formal Aspects of Computing 6(5), 512–535 (1994)

22. Bianco, A., de Alfaro, L.: Model checking of probabilistic and nondeterministic systems. In: Thiagarajan, P.S. (ed.) Foundations of Software Technology and Theoretical Computer Science. LNCS, vol. 1026, pp. 499–513. Springer, Heidelberg (1995)

23. Aziz, A., Sanwal, K., Singhal, V., Brayton, R.K.: Verifying continuous time markov chains. In: Alur, R., Henzinger, T.A. (eds.) CAV 1996. LNCS, vol. 1102, pp. 269–276. Springer, Heidelberg (1996)

24. Baier, C., Katoen, J.P., Hermanns, H.: Approximate symbolic model checking of continuous-time markov chains. In: Baeten, J.C.M., Mauw, S. (eds.) CONCUR 1999. LNCS, vol. 1664, pp. 146–161. Springer, Heidelberg (1999)
25. Kwiatkowska, M., Norman, G., Pacheco, A.: Model checking expected time and expected reward formulae with random time bounds. In: Proc. 2nd Euro-Japanese Workshop on Stochastic Risk Modelling for Finance, Insurance, Production and Reliability (2002)
26. Prism user manual, http://www.cs.bham.ac.uk/~dxp/prism/manual/

Testing Distributed Systems Through Symbolic Model Checking

Gabriel Kalyon*, Thierry Massart**, Cédric Meuter,
and Laurent Van Begin***

Université Libre de Bruxelles (U.L.B.),
Boulevard du Triomphe, CP-212, 1050 Bruxelles, Belgium
{gkalyon,tmassart,cmeuter,lvbegin}@ulb.ac.be

Abstract. The observation of a distributed system's finite execution can be abstracted as a partial ordered set of events generally called finite (partial order) trace. In practice, this trace can be obtained through a standard code instrumentation, which takes advantage of existing communications between processes to partially order events of different processes. We show that testing that such a distributed execution satisfies some global property amounts therefore to model check the corresponding trace. This work can be time consuming; we therefore provide an efficient symbolic CTL model-checking algorithm for traces. This method is based on a symbolic data structure, called Interval Sharing Trees, allowing to efficiently represent and manipulate sets of k-uples of naturals. Efficient symbolic operations are defined on this data structure in order to deal with all CTL modalities. We show that in practice this data structure is well adapted for CTL model checking of traces.

Keywords: testing, asynchronous distributed systems, global property, model checking of traces, trace checking.

1 Introduction

A distributed system is typically a set of distributed hardware equipments which run concurrent processes, communicating through some network. The design of such system is known to be a difficult task. When the purpose of such a system is to perform some control of critical equipment like an industrial plant, a plane, or a satellite, its correctness is extremely important. The designer can ease her work by various techniques [1, 2, 3] including validation and debugging. In particular, traditional model-based approaches abstract the action the system can do into *events* which change the system's *global state*. Validation works therefore on a labelled directed graph called a Kripke structure which describes the possible

* Supported by the Belgian National Science Foundation (FNRS) under a FRIA grant.
** Supported by the Belgian Science Policy IAP-Phase VI: MoVES and Centre Fédéré en Vérification (FNRS-FRFC n 2.4530.02).
*** Research fellow supported by the Belgian National Science Foundation (FNRS).

J. Derrick and J. Vain (Eds.): FORTE 2007, LNCS 4574, pp. 263–279, 2007.

system's behaviours. *Verification* tools (e.g. [4, 5, 6]) can be used to validate parts of models. For instance, such tools can be used to check that, in the system, every time the system goes in a state where a condition p holds, it is followed by a state where q and r holds. p can for instance be an abstraction for some alarm detected through some given sensor, while q and r, may correspond to, possibly distributed, values assignment on some actuators.

Unfortunately in practice, even with this abstraction, the *state-explosion problem* generally prevents the designer from exhaustively verifying the whole system, even with efficient exploration techniques such as partial order reduction [7, 8] or symbolic model checking [9, 10, 11]. In such cases, the designer generally falls back to *testing* which cannot guarantee that a system is completely bug-free, but if achieved on a large number of test-cases (e.g. covering all the functionalities of the system), can give a *reasonable* confidence that the system is correct. In this context, a test-case *defines* the model of the part of the system which corresponds to a particular execution. Testing may therefore be seen as the validation of this smaller model. To extract this smaller model from a system, the implementation is instrumented to record only relevant events. A special process, called the *monitor*, records this model (the events of the system), that we can just call *execution* here, and then checks that it satisfies some desired property. Notice that an execution can also be extracted from a design model. In particular *scenarios* of executions, modelled as MSC (Message Sequence Charts) is a particular form of such execution and can also be validated. Hence, at both the design and implementation levels, it is an important activity for which efficient methods must be provided.

In the centralized case, an execution of the system is a *sequence of events*. Determining if such an execution satisfies a property is in general simple. In the distributed case, if the system to control is slow enough, one can assume that all processes of the system are synchronized using a global discrete clock. This so-called *synchrony hypothesis* allows to see such distributed execution as a *sequence of set of events* where all events in a set are seen as simultaneous. This hypothesis allows a relatively simple validation of such a distributed execution. Unfortunately, if the system to control is too fast compared to the synchronization mechanism offered by the implementation, the synchrony hypothesis cannot be made and the asynchronism between distributed processes must be taken into account in the analysis. In this case, the exact order in which two concurrent events occur in the execution is, in general, not always known or guaranteed. By taking into account the communications between processes, only a partial order on the events of the execution can be obtained. In practice, this partial order relation, often called the *happened-before* relation [12], can be obtained through correct code instrumentation using, for instance, vector clocks [12, 13].

Hence in this case, an execution is a partially ordered set of events often called *partial order trace* or simply *trace*. Since the order in which the events of this *(partial order) trace* are interleaved is generally relevant to the safety of the system, testing that a distributed execution satisfies a *global property* ϕ amounts to verifying that every sequential execution, *compatible* with the partial order, satisfies ϕ or, in other terms, model checking ϕ on the corresponding *trace*. Unfortunately, this problem is hard [14], since the number of compatible sequential executions and the size of the Kripke structure which models an execution may be exponential in the number of concurrent processes. Therefore, to tackle this complexity, instead of working on the underlying Kripke structure, efficient techniques have been developed to work directly on the partial order itself, which is, in general, exponentially more compact. In this line, in [15], A. Sen and Garg present the temporal logic RCTL (for *regular*-CTL), which is a subset of the branching time temporal logic CTL [16] and shows that the compact symbolic data structure called *computation slice* [17], can be used to efficiently compute all global states which satisfy a RCTL formula. However, RCTL does not include such simple CTL property as $\mathsf{AG}(p \implies \mathsf{AF}(q \wedge r))$, i.e. every p is eventually followed by a state where q and r hold true; formula that may be very useful during validation. In general, a computation slice is too restrictive to represent any arbitrary set of global states of a finite trace.

This motivates our work; in this paper, we introduce an efficient symbolic method using *Interval Sharing Trees* (IST) [18, 19]. This data structure allows to represent any set of global states of a finite trace. We define how to use IST to provide a full CTL model checking of finite traces. We show that *intervals* of naturals can be used, in practice, to have a compact representation for sets of global states of the trace satisfying the desired formula and hence, to provide an efficient algorithm for CTL model checking of finite traces. Moreover, we show that our algorithms perform very well compared to standard symbolic model checking using BDDs [11] and implemented in the tool NuSMV [6].

This paper is organized as follows. In Sec. 2, we detail related works. In Sec. 3, we introduce our model for traces and define the CTL over this model. In Sec. 4, we explain how sets of configurations can be represented compactly using intervals and interval sharing trees. In Sec. 5, we show how CTL model checking on traces can be solved using this symbolic representation. Next, in Sec. 6, we experimentally validate our method on various examples compared to CTL model-checking with the NuSMV tool. Finally, conclusion and future works are given in Sec. 7.

2 Related Works

Testing and monitoring the global behaviours of distributed systems can be categorized in two classes: *trace model-checking* and *global predicate detection*.

Trace model checking has been studied mainly theoretically through the definition of several linear temporal logic for Mazurkiewicz traces. A Mazurkiewicz trace [20], over an alphabet Σ with a independence relation I, can be defined as a Σ-labelled partial order set of events with special properties not explained here. For Mazurkiewicz traces, *local* [21, 22] and *global* [23, 24, 25] trace logics have been defined. However, in our case, the *trace*[1] is an abstraction of a distributed execution (or of a scenario) and models a set of possible interleavings of events

---

[1] Our trace can be seen as a prime event structure with an empty conflict relation [26].

the distributed system may have had. Since we do not suppose to have information about independence between actions, none of these actions are independent a priori; testing must then check that all these possible orderings of events are correct. Since the independence relation is not a data that *trace temporal logics* may exploit, we do not use these logics to model-check our executions and stick to simple sequence (interleaving) semantics.

Global predicate detection initially aims at answering reachability questions, i.e. does there exist a possible global configuration of the system, that satisfies a given global predicate ϕ. Garg and Chase showed in [14] that this problem is NP-complete for an arbitrary predicate, even when there is no inter-process communication. Efficient (polynomial) methods have been proposed for various classes of predicates, such as *stable* predicates proposed by Chandy and Lamport [27], *independent* predicates by Charron-Bost *et al* [28], *conjunctive* predicates by Garg and Waldecker [29, 30], *linear* and *semi-linear* predicates by Chase and Garg [14], *regular* predicates by Garg and Mittal [31] and predicates expressed by a finite automata that can be checked online by Jard *et al* [32]. Garg and Mittal implicitly use a symbolic data structure called *computation slice*, to compute efficiently all global states, compatible with a given execution satisfying a given regular predicate [17]. This structure in used by A. Sen and Garg in their work on the temporal logic RCTL [15]. In [33, 34] K. Sen *et al.* use an automaton to specify the system's monitor. The authors provide an explicit exploration of the state space and to limit this exploration a *window* is used. In a previous work [35], we have used this technique to provide an efficient LTL tester of distributed executions.

3   Framework

In this section, we detail our framework. We start by formally introducing our model for traces of distributed systems, i.e. finite *partial order trace*. Then, we define the branching time temporal logic CTL over such finite traces.

Partial Order Trace. Our executions are obtained by a fixed numbers of concurrent processes, each executing a finite sequence of assignments. Moreover, due to inter-process communications, other causal dependencies are added. These communications will usually be done by message passing, but if some processes are not distributed, can be done by other means such as shared variable. An execution is modeled as a finite partial order trace, i.e. a finite partially ordered set of events, where each event belongs to some process and is labeled by the assignment which took place during this event.

Definition 1 (Partial order trace). *A partial order trace of k processes and over a set of variables $\mathbb{V}$ is a tuple $\mathbf{T} = \langle E, \alpha, \preceq \rangle$ where:*

- *$E = P_1 \cup P_2 \cup ... \cup P_k$ is a finite set of events partitioned into k disjoint non empty subsets P_i, called processes; $\mathsf{pid}(e)$ denotes the process of event e belongs to ($\mathsf{pid}(e) = i$ iff $e \in P_i$);*

$$P_1 \quad \text{w:=1} \longrightarrow \text{y:=3} \longrightarrow \text{x:=0}$$

$$P_2 \quad \text{x:=4} \longrightarrow \text{w:=0}$$

Fig. 1. Example of partial order trace

- $\alpha : E \mapsto \mathbb{V} \times \mathbb{Q}$ *is a labeling function mapping each event to an assignment,*
  i.e. $\alpha(e) = (x, v)$ *associates the assignment* $x := v$ *to* e; *if* $\alpha(e) = (x := v)$,
  var(e) *denotes* x *and* val(e) *denotes* v;
- $\preceq \subseteq E \times E$ *is a partial order relation on* E *such that* $\forall e, e' \in E$:
  (i) pid$(e) = $ pid$(e') \Rightarrow (e \preceq e') \vee (e' \preceq e)$
  (ii) var$(e) = $ var$(e') \Rightarrow (e \preceq e') \vee (e' \preceq e)$.

Condition (i) on $\preceq$ ensures that all events from the same process are ordered and condition (ii) enforces that all events assigning the same variable are ordered. Given an event $e \in E$, we define $\downarrow e = \{e' \in E \mid e' \preceq e\}$, the past of e (including itself), and pos$(e) = |\downarrow e \cap P_{\text{pid}(e)}|$ (where $|\cdot|$ denotes the size of sets), the position of e in its process. A *cut* is a subset $C \subseteq E$ such that $\forall e \in C : \downarrow e \subseteq C$. cuts$(\mathbf{T}) = \{C \subseteq E \mid \forall e \in C : \downarrow e \subseteq C\}$ is the set of all cuts in $\mathbf{T}$. In the remainder of this paper, we always consider the set of variables $\mathbb{V}$ and the partial order trace of k processes $\mathbf{T} = \langle E, \alpha, \preceq \rangle$.

Given a cut $C \in$ cuts$(\mathbf{T})$, we define enabled$(C) = \{e \in E \setminus C \mid (\downarrow e \setminus \{e\}) \subseteq C\}$ the set of events enabled in C. If e is enabled in the cut C, then it can be fired from C leading to $C \cup \{e\}$, the successor of C for e. Note that if $C \in$ cuts$(\mathbf{T})$, so is $C \cup \{e\}$ for all $e \in$ enabled(C). Given a set of cuts $X \subseteq$ cuts$(\mathbf{T})$, pre$^{\exists}(X) = \{C \in$ cuts$(\mathbf{T}) \mid \exists e \in$ enabled$(C) : C \cup \{e\} \in X\}$ is the set of existential predecessors of X, i.e. the set of cuts having at least one successor in X, and pre$^{\forall}(X) = \{C \in$ cuts$(\mathbf{T}) \mid \forall e \in$ enabled$(C) : C \cup \{e\} \in X\}$ is the set of universal predecessors of X, i.e. the set of cuts having all their successors in X. Additionally, given a sequence of cuts $\sigma = C_0, C_1, ..., C_n$, σ_i denotes C_i, the ith element of σ, and $|\sigma| = n$ denotes the size of σ. A *run from a cut* C is a sequence $\sigma \in$ cuts$(\mathbf{T})^*$ such that *(i)* $\sigma_0 = C$, *(ii)* $\sigma_{|\sigma|} = E$, and *(iii)* $\forall 0 \leq i < |\sigma| : \sigma_i \in$ pre$^{\exists}(\{\sigma_{i+1}\})$, i.e. a sequence of cuts *(i)* starting in C, *(ii)* ending in E, and *(iii)* σ_{i+1} is a successor of σ_i for any i. The set of runs starting in $C \in$ cuts$(\mathbf{T})$ is denoted by runs(C). Finally, runs$(\emptyset)$ is the set of runs of the trace $\mathbf{T}$.

A trace $\mathbf{T} = \langle E, \alpha, \preceq \rangle$ can be represented using a directed acyclic graph $(E, \rightarrow)$ called Hasse diagram. In this graph, there is an edge from event e to event e' if and only if they are ordered, i.e. $e \preceq e'$, and if their order is not imposed by transitivity, i.e. $\neg \exists e'' \in E : e \prec e'' \prec e'$ where $e_1 \prec e_2$ denotes $e_1 \preceq e_2$ and $e_1 \neq e_2$. As an example, Fig. 1 depicts such a graph for a partial order trace with two processes. That trace describes an execution of a distributed system with two concurrent sub-system. During that execution, the first process makes three assignments to variables w, y, x and the second one makes two assignments to x and w. An edge between two events e and e' in the Hasse graph such that pid$(e) \neq$ pid(e') models a communication between processes (noted $e \rightarrow_c e'$). Communication edges model either message passing between processes or the fact that the event e assigns a value to a shared variable used in e'. Note that v in event $x := v$ can be obtained by evaluating an expression involving the variable appearing in e. For instance, the arrow between w:=0 and y:=3 in Fig. 1 can model that value 3 is obtained at run time by evaluating an expression where w appears and its value is given by the first assignment. In the following, we always consider that we have the Hasse diagram corresponding to $\mathbf{T}$.

CTL **over Finite Partial Order Trace.** A predicate p is a constraint $x \bullet c$ where c is a rational constant, $x \in \mathbb{V}$ and where $\bullet \in \{<, \leq, >, \geq, =, \neq\}$. A formula in the CTL logic is built on predicates using classical boolean operators, and temporal modalities. If p denotes a predicate and ϕ, ϕ_1, ϕ_2 denote CTL formulae, then the set of CTL formulae is defined as follows:

$$\phi ::= \top \mid p \mid \neg\phi \mid \phi_1 \vee \phi_2 \mid \phi_1 \wedge \phi_2 \mid \mathsf{EX}\phi \mid \mathsf{AX}\phi \mid \mathsf{EG}\phi \mid \mathsf{AG}\phi \mid \mathsf{E}[\phi_1\mathsf{U}\phi_2] \mid \mathsf{A}[\phi_1\mathsf{U}\phi_2]$$

where A stands for *for all runs*, E for *exists a run*, X for *next*, G for *globally* and U for *until*. Two other temporal modalities, EF and AF, where F stands for *finally*, are derived syntactically as follows: $\mathsf{EF}\phi \equiv \mathsf{E}[\top\mathsf{U}\phi]$ and $\mathsf{AF}\phi \equiv \mathsf{A}[\top\mathsf{U}\phi]$.

Basic formulae are constraints over one variables in $\mathbb{V}$. Since all assignments to a particular variable are ordered, each cut $C \in \mathsf{cuts}(\mathbf{T})$ induces a unique valuation on the variables in $\mathbb{V}$ no matter the order in which the events are executed. Formally, given a cut C, we can define inductively the valuation induced by C, noted v_C, as follows:

- if $C = \emptyset$ then $\forall x \in \mathbb{V}$, $v_C(x) = 0$,
- if $C = C' \cup \{e\}$ with $C' \in \mathsf{cuts}(\mathbf{T})$ then $\forall x \in \mathbb{V} : v_C = \begin{cases} \mathsf{val}(e) & \text{if } \mathsf{var}(e) = x \\ v_{C'}(x) & \text{otherwise} \end{cases}$

Hence, we forget variables in $\mathbb{V}$ and only consider cuts of $\mathbf{T}$ when defining the semantics of CTL formula. More precisely, the semantics of a CTL formula is given by the satisfaction relation $\models$ defined hereafter.

$$
\begin{aligned}
&C \models \top \\
&C \models p && \text{iff } v_C(p) \text{ is true} \\
&C \models \neg\phi && \text{iff } C \not\models \phi \\
&C \models \phi_1 \vee \phi_2 && \text{iff } (C \models \phi_1) \vee (C \models \phi_2) \\
&C \models \phi_1 \wedge \phi_2 && \text{iff } (C \models \phi_1) \wedge (C \models \phi_2) \\
&C \models \mathsf{EX}\phi && \text{iff } \exists e \in \mathsf{enabled}(C) : C \cup \{e\} \models \phi \\
&C \models \mathsf{AX}\phi && \text{iff } \forall e \in \mathsf{enabled}(C) : C \cup \{e\} \models \phi \\
&C \models \mathsf{EG}\phi && \text{iff } \exists \sigma \in \mathsf{runs}(C), \forall i \in [0, |\sigma|] : \sigma_i \models \phi \\
&C \models \mathsf{AG}\phi && \text{iff } \forall \sigma \in \mathsf{runs}(C), \forall i \in [0, |\sigma|] : \sigma_i \models \phi \\
&C \models \mathsf{E}[\phi_1\mathsf{U}\phi_2] && \text{iff } \exists \sigma \in \mathsf{runs}(C), \exists i \in [0, |\sigma|] : \\
& && \quad (\sigma_i \models \phi_2) \wedge (\forall j \in [0, i) : \sigma_j \models \phi_1) \\
&C \models \mathsf{A}[\phi_1\mathsf{U}\phi_2] && \text{iff } \forall \sigma \in \mathsf{runs}(C), \exists i \in [0, |\sigma|] : \\
& && \quad (\sigma_i \models \phi_2) \wedge (\forall j \in [0, i) : \sigma_j \models \phi_1)
\end{aligned}
$$

Note that according to this semantics, when the execution of $\mathbf{T}$ is finished (when the cut E is reached), for any CTL formula ϕ, we have that $E \not\models \mathsf{EX}\phi$ and $E \models \mathsf{AX}\phi$. We note $[\![\phi]\!]$ the set $\{C \in \mathsf{cuts}(\mathbf{T}) \mid C \models \phi\}$ of cuts that satisfy formula ϕ.

4   Symbolic Representation for Sets of Cuts

The number of cuts, i.e. the size of $\mathsf{cuts}(\mathbf{T})$, is in general exponential in the size of $\mathbf{T}$. Hence, efficient representations for large sets of cuts are needed. Our proposal is based on the following observation: a cut can be represented by a k-uple $\overrightarrow{x}$ of naturals where the ith component of $\overrightarrow{x}$ gives the number of events of the ith process that already occured. For example, if a trace $\mathbf{T}$ is composed of 3 processes, the 3-uple $\langle 1, 2, 0 \rangle$ represents the cut where process P_0 has executed its first event, i.e. $e \in P_1$ with $\mathsf{pos}(e) = 1$, process P_2 has executed its first 2 events, i.e. $e_1, e_2 \in P_2$ with $\mathsf{pos}(e_i) = i$ ($i \in \{1, 2\}$), and process P_3 has executed no events. The successor (predecessor) relation between cuts can be lifted to their vector representation: an event $e \in P_i$ is enabled in $\overrightarrow{x} = \langle x_1, \ldots, x_k \rangle$ if $x_{\mathsf{pid}(e)} < \mathsf{pos}(e) \wedge \forall e' \in \downarrow e \setminus \{e\} : \mathsf{pos}(e') \leq x_{\mathsf{pid}(e)}$ and the successor of $\overrightarrow{x}$ for e is $\langle x_1, \ldots, x_i + 1, \ldots, x_k \rangle$. Note that a vector $\overrightarrow{x}$ is not necessarily a representation for a cut. Indeed, if $\exists i \neq j \in [1, k], \exists e \in P_i, \exists e' \in \downarrow e \cap P_j : (\mathsf{pos}(e) \leq x_i) \wedge (\mathsf{pos}(e') > x_j)$ then $\overrightarrow{x}$ does not represent a cut, otherwise it does. Given a subset $X \subseteq \mathbb{N}^k$, we note $\mathsf{sets}(X) = \{C \subseteq E \mid \exists \overrightarrow{x} \in X, \forall 1 \leq i \leq k : |C \cap P_i| = x_i\}$ the set of subsets of events represented by the set X. Moreover, $\overrightarrow{x} \leq \overrightarrow{x}'$ denotes that $\forall i \in [1..k] : x_i \leq x_i'$ which in terms of cuts corresponds to inclusion. In conclusion, in order to represent sets of cuts, we show how to efficiently represent large set of tuples of naturals.

Multi-rectangles. A k-multi-rectangle M is a tuple of intervals over natural values of dimension k. M defines the set of k-uples $\langle x_1, \ldots, x_k \rangle$ over naturals such that $\forall 1 \leq i \leq k : x_i$ is in the interval corresponding to the ith dimension of M. Assuming that each interval contains n values, M represents a set of n^k k-uples. Hence, it is a compact representation for the set it represents. Moreover, k-multi-rectangles correspond to a natural class of sets of cuts. Indeed, suppose $k = 2$ and the events $e_{i,1}, e_{i,2} \ldots, e_{i,m_i}$ of P_i ($i \in \{1, 2\}$) occurring sequentially without any restrictions on the events of P_{3-i} and such that $\forall j \in [1, m_i] : \mathsf{pos}(e_{i,j}) = j$. Then, the set of cuts where P_1 and P_2 have executed some of those events corresponds to the multi-rectangle $\langle [1, m_1], [1, m_2] \rangle$. This multi-rectangle represents succinctly the result of all possible interleavings of P_1, P_2. However, due to communications between processes, sets of cuts are not represented in general by one k-multi-rectangle, but a set thereof. Hence, to prevent a *symbolic* state explosion, we use a data structure, called *Interval Sharing Tree* (IST), to represent efficiently large sets of k-multi-rectangles.

Interval Sharing Tree. *Interval Sharing Trees* [19] is a compact data structure for representing sets of k-uples. An IST is basically a sharing tree [36], i.e. a directed acyclic graph, where each node is labelled with an interval of integers. Each path in such a graph represents a k-multi-rectangle. The sharing of common prefixes and suffixes of k-multi rectangles allows to obtain a compact representation for sets of k-multi-rectangles. Interval sharing tree are defined as follows.

Definition 2 (Interval Sharing Tree (IST)). *An interval sharing tree $\mathcal{I}$, is a labelled directed acyclic graph $\langle N, \iota, \mathsf{succ} \rangle$ where:*

- $N = N_0 \cup N_1 \cup N_2 \cup \ldots \cup N_k \cup N_{k+1}$ *is the finite set of nodes, partitioned into* $k+2$ *disjoint subsets* N_i *called layers with* $N_0 = \{root\}$ *and* $N_{k+1} = \{end\}$*;*
- $\iota : N \mapsto \mathbb{Z} \times \mathbb{Z} \cup \{\top, \bot\}$ *is the labelling function such that* $\iota(n) = \top$ *(resp.* $\bot$*) if and only if* $n = root$ *(resp. end);*
- $\mathsf{succ} : N \mapsto 2^N$ *is the successor function such that:*
  (i) $\mathsf{succ}(end) = \emptyset$*;*
  (ii) $\forall i \in [0, k], \forall n \in N_i : \mathsf{succ}(n_i) \subseteq N_{i+1} \wedge \mathsf{succ}(n_i) \neq \emptyset$*;*
  (iii) $\forall n \in N, \forall n_1, n_2 \in \mathsf{succ}(n) : (n_1 \neq n_2) \Rightarrow (\iota(n_1) \neq \iota(n_2))$*;*
  (iv) $\forall i \in [0, k], \forall n_1 \neq n_2 \in N_i : (\iota(n_1) = \iota(n_2)) \Rightarrow (\mathsf{succ}(n_1) \neq \mathsf{succ}(n_2))$*.*

In other words, an IST is a directed acyclic graph where each nodes are labelled with couples of integers except for two special nodes (*root* and *end*), such that (i) the *end* node has no successors, (ii) all nodes from layer i have their successors in layer $i + 1$, (iii) a node cannot have two successors with the same label, (iv) two nodes with the same label in the same layer do not have the same successors. For a node n (except *root* and *end*), $\iota(n)$ is interpreted as an interval of integers. We note $x \in \iota(n)$ if an integer value x belongs to that interval. Figure 2 illustrates some IST. A path of an IST $\mathcal{I}$ is a sequence of node $root, n_1, n_2, \ldots, n_k, end$ such that $n_1 \in \mathsf{succ}(root), end \in \mathsf{succ}(n_k)$ and $\forall i \in [1, k) : n_{i+1} \in \mathsf{succ}(n_i)$. A k-uple $\overrightarrow{x} = \langle x_1, x_2, \ldots, x_k \rangle$ is accepted by an IST $\mathcal{I}$ if and only if there exists a path $root, n_1, n_2, \ldots, n_k, end$ in $\mathcal{I}$ such that $\forall i \in [1, k] : x_i \in \iota(n_i)$. The set of k-uples accepted by $\mathcal{I}$ is denoted by $\mathsf{tuple}(\mathcal{I})$ and if $\mathsf{tuple}(\mathcal{I}) \subseteq \mathbb{N}^k$, then $\mathsf{sets}(\mathcal{I}) = \mathsf{sets}(\mathsf{tuple}(\mathcal{I}))$. In practice, sharing of prefixes (iii) and suffixes (iv) in IST allow a non-negligible memory saving, which can be exponential in the best cases (there exists IST whose number of nodes and edges is logarithmic in the number of k-multi rectangles it represents).

Standard set operations have been defined symbolically over IST's, namely, union, noted $\mathcal{I}_1 \cup \mathcal{I}_2$, intersection, noted $\mathcal{I}_1 \cap \mathcal{I}_2$, set difference, noted $\mathcal{I}_1 \setminus \mathcal{I}_2$ and complementation, noted $\overline{\mathcal{I}}$. Other operations have been defined like downward closure, noted $\downarrow\mathcal{I}$, such that $\mathsf{tuple}(\downarrow\mathcal{I}) = \{\overrightarrow{x} \in \mathbb{N}^k \mid \exists \overrightarrow{x}' \in \mathsf{tuple}(\mathcal{I}) : \overrightarrow{x} \leq \overrightarrow{x}'\}$, and shift of a variable, i.e. replace x_i by $x_i + \delta$ for $i \in [1, k]$ and $\delta \in \mathbb{Z}$, noted $\mathcal{I}^{[x_i \leftarrow x_i + \delta]}$. Formally, $\mathsf{tuple}(\mathcal{I}^{[x_i \leftarrow x_i + \delta]}) = \{\langle x_1, \ldots, x_i + \delta, \ldots, x_k \rangle \mid \overrightarrow{x} \in \mathsf{tuple}(\mathcal{I})\}$. Symbolic algorithm, i.e. algorithms that do not enumerate all the paths of IST, for those operations have been defined. Since the number of paths is in general larger than the size of the IST, symbolic algorithms allow efficient manipulation of k-multi-rectangles sets taking into account their prefix and suffix sharing. Note that the counter-part of the compactness of IST is that most of their operations cannot be computed in polynomial time in general. Hence, (most of) the symbolic algorithms to manipulate IST are exponential in their worst case (see [18] for more details). However, those algorithms are in general far from their worst case in practice and IST have been shown to be more efficient than other known data-structure (to represent subsets of $\mathbb{N}^k$) both in execution time and memory saving [37].

5   Using IST for CTL Model Checking

A basic approach to solve the CTL model checking problem over partial order traces consists in flattening the trace by building a graph where nodes are cuts and edge corresponds to the successor relation and then solve the classical CTL model checking on Kripke structures. Unfortunately, that method is not practicable since the resulting graph is in general exponential in the size of the trace. To overcome that problem, we propose to build $[\![\phi]\!]$ without flattening the partial order trace but working directly on it. Our method builds $[\![\phi]\!]$ inductively on the structure of ϕ. Since $[\![\phi]\!]$ can be large, we use IST to efficiently represent and manipulate sets of cuts. We now present in details the construction. The proofs of all lemmata and theorems of this section can be found in [38].

Tautology. If $\phi \equiv \top$, $\mathcal{I}_\top$ is an IST representing all possible cuts of the trace **T**. The principle to build $\mathcal{I}_\top$ is to start from the very simple IST $\mathcal{I}_0$ where sets($\mathcal{I}_0$) is the set of cuts if we do not consider communication edges of the Hasse diagram. Then, we consider communication edges one by one, i.e. we build the IST $\mathcal{I}_0, \mathcal{I}_1, \mathcal{I}_2, \ldots$ where $\mathcal{I}_i$ is built from $\mathcal{I}_{i-1}$ ($i > 0$) by taking into account one more communication edge until we have considered all of them. To take into account a communication edge, we remove from sets($\mathcal{I}_{i-1}$) the sets of events that do not satisfy the definition of cuts because of that edge. Hence, assuming the Hasse diagram has v communication edges, sets($\mathcal{I}_0$) $\supseteq$ sets($\mathcal{I}_1$) $\supseteq$ $\ldots \supseteq$ sets($\mathcal{I}_v$) = $[\![\top]\!]$. $\mathcal{I}_0$ is defined as follows:

- $N = \{root\} \cup \{n_1\} \cup \{n_2\} \cup \ldots \cup \{n_k\} \cup \{end\}$
- $\forall i \in [1, k] : \iota(n_i) = [0, |P_i|]$
- succ($root$) = $\{n_1\}$, succ(n_k) = $\{end\}$, and $\forall i \in [1, k) :$ succ(n_i) = $\{n_{i+1}\}$,

To take into account a communication $e \rightarrow_c e'$, we need to remove from sets($\mathcal{I}_i$) all the sets of events that do not satisfy the definition of cuts, i.e. the sets that contain e' but not e. To achieve that goals, we first build an IST $\mathcal{B}(e)$ representing all the sets of events that do not contain e (and have a vector representation). In other words, $\mathcal{B}(e)$ is the same as $\mathcal{I}_0$ except for the layer pid(e) where $\iota(n_{\text{pid}(e)}) = [0, \text{pos}(e) - 1]$. Then, we build an IST $\mathcal{A}(e')$ representing all the sets of events that contain e' (having a vector representation), i.e. $\mathcal{A}(e')$ is the same as $\mathcal{I}_0$ except for $\iota(n_{\text{pid}(e')}) = [\text{pos}(e'), |P_{\text{pid}(e')}|]$. The events to remove from sets($\mathcal{I}_i$) are in the intersection of sets($\mathcal{A}(e')$) and sets($\mathcal{B}(e)$). Hence, to remove them we compute $\mathcal{I}_i = \mathcal{I}_{i-1} \setminus (\mathcal{A}(e') \cap \mathcal{B}(e))$. We iterate this construct until all communication edges are taken into account. Figure 2 illustrates the method by computing the IST corresponding to the set of cuts satisfying $\top$ in the trace from Fig. 1.

Lemma 1. *Given a trace* **T** $= \langle E, \alpha, \preceq \rangle$, *we have that* sets($\mathcal{I}_\top$) = $[\![\top]\!]$

Predicates. If $\phi \equiv p$, where p is a predicate $x \bullet c$, we proceed as follows. First, we collect all events that can potentially modify the truth value of p. Let $E_p = \{e \in E \mid \text{var}(e) = x\}$ be the set of those events. All events in E_p

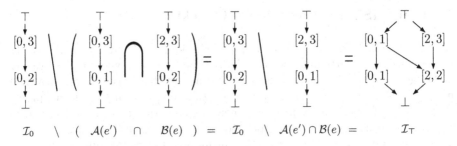

Fig. 2. Computation of $\mathcal{I}_\top$

assign the same variable, and by condition (ii) of definition 1, they are totally ordered. Let $\rho = e_1, e_2, ..., e_m$ be the linearization of E_p, i.e. $\forall i \in [1, m] : e_i \in E_p$, $|E_p| = m$ and $\forall i \in [1, m) : e_i \prec e_{i+1}$. This sequence can be used to determine *slices* of **T** where p is true. Indeed, let $s_1, s_2, ..., s_\ell$ be the sequence of indices splitting ρ into $\ell - 1$ contiguous blocks $e_{s_1}, ..., e_{s_2-1}, e_{s_2}, ..., e_{s_3-1}, ..., e_{s_\ell}, ..., e_m$ such that the value of p remains the same inside each block and changes in the following block. Formally, this is the sequence satisfying the following constraints $(m = s_{\ell+1} - 1)$:

(i) $1 = s_1 < s_2 < ... < s_\ell$
(ii) $\forall i \in [1, \ell], \forall j_1, j_2 \in [s_i, s_{i+1}) : (\downarrow e_{j_1} \models p) \iff (\downarrow e_{j_2} \models p)$
(iii) $\forall i \in [1, \ell) : (\downarrow e_{s_i} \models p) \iff (\downarrow e_{s_{i+1}} \not\models p)$

Note that, given a block $i \in [1, \ell]$, the value of p in any cuts between e_{s_i} and $e_{s_{i+1}-1}$ is determined by e_{s_i}. This set of cuts can be represented using $\mathcal{A}(e_{s_i}) \cap \mathcal{B}(e_{s_{i+1}})$, as described above. Thus, for all block $i \in [1, \ell]$ such that $\downarrow e_{s_i} \models p$, we add $\mathcal{A}(e_{s_i}) \cap \mathcal{B}(e_{s_{i+1}})$ to $\mathcal{I}_p$ initially empty. Additionally, we must take into account the cuts at the beginning and at the end of **T**. If p is satisfied at the beginning of **T** $(\emptyset \models p)$, we must add $\mathcal{B}(e_{s_1})$ to $\mathcal{I}_p$, and similarly, if p is true at the end of **T** $(E \models p)$, we add $\mathcal{A}(e_{s_m})$ to $\mathcal{I}_p$. Finally, in order to keep only cuts, we take the intersection with $\mathcal{I}_\top$.

Lemma 2. *Given a trace* **T** $= \langle E, \alpha, \preceq \rangle$ *and a predicate* p, *we have that* $\mathsf{sets}(\mathcal{I}_p) = [\![p]\!]$.

Boolean Operators. In order to deal with boolean operators $\phi_1 \vee \phi_2$ (resp. $\phi_1 \wedge \phi_2$, $\neg\phi_1$), we can use standard operation on IST [18] and compute $\mathcal{I}_\phi = \mathcal{I}_{\phi_1} \cup \mathcal{I}_{\phi_2}$ (resp. $\mathcal{I}_\phi = \mathcal{I}_{\phi_1} \cap \mathcal{I}_{\phi_2}$, $\mathcal{I}_\phi = \overline{\mathcal{I}_{\phi_1}} \cap \mathcal{I}_\top$).

Lemma 3. *Given a trace* **T** $= \langle E, \alpha, \preceq \rangle$ *and* CTL *formulae* ϕ, ϕ_1 *and* ϕ_2, *we have that* $\mathsf{sets}(\mathcal{I}_{\phi_1 \vee \phi_2}) = [\![\phi_1 \cup \phi_2]\!]$, $\mathsf{sets}(\mathcal{I}_{\phi_1 \wedge \phi_2}) = [\![\phi_1 \cap \phi_2]\!]$ *and* $\mathsf{sets}(\mathcal{I}_{\neg\phi}) = [\![\neg\phi]\!]$.

Existential Modalities. The treatment of existential modalities can be computed through the use of the $\mathsf{pre}^\exists(\cdot)$ operator, greatest and least fixed point (as explained e.g. in [9]):

$$\llbracket \mathsf{EX}\phi \rrbracket = \mathsf{pre}^{\exists}(\llbracket \phi \rrbracket)$$
$$\llbracket \mathsf{EG}\phi \rrbracket = \mathbf{gfp}\ \lambda X \cdot \llbracket \phi \rrbracket \cap \mathsf{pre}^{\exists}(X)$$
$$\llbracket \mathsf{E}[\phi_1 \mathsf{U}\phi_2] \rrbracket = \mathbf{lfp}\ \lambda X \cdot \llbracket \phi_2 \rrbracket \cup (\llbracket \phi_1 \rrbracket \cap \mathsf{pre}^{\exists}(X))$$

In order to compute ISTs corresponding to those temporal formulae, we only need an algorithm for computing symbolically the $\mathsf{pre}^{\exists}(\cdot)$ operation. For that, we decompose $\mathsf{pre}^{\exists}(\cdot)$ into a function of $\mathsf{pre}_i^{\exists}(\cdot)$, where $\mathsf{pre}_i^{\exists}(X) = \{C \in \mathsf{cuts}(\mathbf{T}) \mid \exists e \in \mathsf{enabled}(C) \cap P_i : C \cup \{e\} \in X\}$ denotes the set of existential predecessors of X only for process P_i. This decomposition is provided by the following lemma.

Lemma 4. *Given a trace* $\mathbf{T} = \langle E, \alpha, \preceq \rangle$ *and a subset* $X \subseteq \mathsf{cuts}(\mathbf{T})$, *we have that* $\mathsf{pre}^{\exists}(X) = \bigcup_{i \in [1,k]} \mathsf{pre}_i^{\exists}(X)$.

The only remaining step is to characterize symbolically $\mathsf{pre}_i^{\exists}(X)$. This characterization is given by the following lemma.

Lemma 5. *Given a trace* $\mathbf{T} = \langle E, \alpha, \preceq \rangle$, *and an IST* $\mathcal{I}$ *such that* $\mathsf{sets}(\mathcal{I}) \subseteq \mathsf{cuts}(\mathbf{T})$, *we have that* $\mathsf{pre}_i^{\exists}(\mathsf{sets}(\mathcal{I})) = \mathsf{sets}(\mathcal{I}^{[x_i \leftarrow x_i - 1]} \cap \mathcal{I}_\top)$.

Finally, we can define the symbolic existential predecessors on IST.

Definition 3 (Symbolic existential predecessors). *Given a trace* $\mathbf{T} = \langle E, \alpha, \preceq \rangle$ *and an IST* $\mathcal{I}$ *such that* $\mathsf{sets}(\mathcal{I}) \subseteq \mathsf{cuts}(\mathbf{T})$, *the symbolic existential predecessors of* $\mathcal{I}$, *noted* $\mathsf{spre}^{\exists}(\mathcal{I})$, *is defined as follows:*

$$\mathsf{spre}^{\exists}(\mathcal{I}) = \bigcup_{i \in [1,k]} \left(\mathcal{I}^{[x_i \leftarrow x_i - 1]} \cap \mathcal{I}_\top \right)$$

As a direct consequence of lem. 4 and lem. 5, we get the next theorem.

Theorem 1 (Correctness $\mathsf{spre}^{\exists}(\cdot)$). *Given a trace* $\mathbf{T} = \langle E, \alpha, \preceq \rangle$, *and an IST* $\mathcal{I}$ *such that* $\mathsf{sets}(\mathcal{I}) \subseteq \mathsf{cuts}(\mathbf{T})$, *we have that* $\mathsf{pre}^{\exists}(\mathsf{sets}(\mathcal{I})) = \mathsf{sets}(\mathsf{spre}^{\exists}(\mathcal{I}))$.

Universal modalities. Universal modalities are treated in a similar way then existential ones. For these, we can use the following equivalence (taken from [10, sec. 2.4]):

$$\llbracket \mathsf{AX}\phi \rrbracket = \mathsf{pre}^{\forall}(\llbracket \phi \rrbracket)$$
$$\llbracket \mathsf{AG}\phi \rrbracket = \mathbf{gfp}\ \lambda X \cdot \llbracket \phi \rrbracket \cap \mathsf{pre}^{\forall}(X)$$
$$\llbracket \mathsf{A}[\phi_1 \mathsf{U}\phi_2] \rrbracket = \mathbf{lfp}\ \lambda X \cdot \llbracket \phi_2 \rrbracket \cup (\llbracket \phi_1 \rrbracket \cap \mathsf{pre}^{\forall}(X))$$

Computing ISTs corresponding to universal formulae amounts to defining a symbolical version of the $\mathsf{pre}^{\forall}(\cdot)$ operator on sets of cuts. The $\mathsf{pre}^{\forall}(\cdot)$ operation can be computed through the equivalence $\mathsf{pre}^{\forall}(\llbracket \phi \rrbracket) = \llbracket \mathsf{AX}\phi \rrbracket = \llbracket \neg\mathsf{EX}\neg\phi \rrbracket = \mathsf{cuts}(\mathbf{T}) \setminus \mathsf{pre}^{\exists}(\llbracket \neg\phi \rrbracket)$. On the other hand, we may compute $\mathsf{pre}^{\forall}(\cdot)$ in an alternate way, similarly to what we did for the $\mathsf{pre}^{\exists}(\cdot)$. We can decompose $\mathsf{pre}^{\forall}(\cdot)$ as a function of $\mathsf{pre}_i^{\forall}(\cdot)$, where $\mathsf{pre}_i^{\forall}(X) = \{C \in \mathsf{cuts}(\mathbf{T}) \mid \forall e \in \mathsf{enabled}(C) \cap P_i : C \cup \{e\} \in X\}$ denotes the set of universal predecessors of X only for process P_i. This decomposition is given by the following lemma.

Lemma 6. *Given a trace* $\mathbf{T} = \langle E, \alpha, \preceq \rangle$, *and an subset* $X \subseteq \mathsf{cuts}(\mathbf{T})$, *we have that* $\mathsf{pre}^\forall(X) = \bigcap_{i \in [1,k]} \mathsf{pre}_i^\forall(X)$.

To compute symbolically $\mathsf{pre}_i^\forall(\cdot)$, we need to characterize exactly which cuts are in $\mathsf{pre}_i^\forall(X)$. By definition, $\mathsf{pre}_i^\forall(X)$ denotes the set of cuts from which all enabled events of process P_i lead to a cut in X. $\mathsf{pre}_i^\forall(X)$ is composed of two classes of cuts: (i) $\mathsf{blocked}_i = \{C \in \mathsf{cuts}(\mathbf{T}) \mid \mathsf{enabled}(C) \cap P_i = \emptyset\}$, the class of cuts in X where process P_i is blocked; and (ii) the class of cuts where the next event of P_i is enabled and leads to a cut in X, i.e. $\mathsf{pre}_i^\exists(X)$.

Lemma 7. *Given a trace* $\mathbf{T} = \langle E, \alpha, \preceq \rangle$, *and an subset* $X \subseteq \mathsf{cuts}(\mathbf{T})$, *we have that* $\mathsf{pre}_i^\forall(X) = \mathsf{pre}_i^\exists(X) \cup \mathsf{blocked}_i$.

We already have a way to compute $\mathsf{pre}_i^\exists(X)$ symbolically (see lem.5). The following lemma characterized $\mathsf{blocked}_i$.

Lemma 8. *Given a trace* $\mathbf{T} = \langle E, \alpha, \preceq \rangle$ *and a process* $P_i \subseteq E$, *we have that* $C \in \mathsf{blocked}_i$ *holds if and only if* $\forall e \in E \cap P_i : (\mathsf{pos}(e) = |C \cap P_i| + 1) \implies (\exists e' \in E \setminus C : e' \to_c e)$.

This result can be used to define an IST $\mathcal{I}_{\mathsf{blocked}_i}$ for $\mathsf{blocked}_i$. Indeed, from Lemma 8, we can see that $\mathsf{blocked}_i$ is composed of the set of all the cuts including all events of P_i and the set of all the cuts where the next event to be triggered by P_i is waiting for an incoming communication. Therefore, the computation of $\mathcal{I}_{\mathsf{blocked}_i}$ starts with an IST $\mathcal{I}_F$ representing the set of sets C of events where process P_i has finished its execution, i.e. where $|C \cap P_i| = |P_i|$. $\mathcal{I}_F$ is the same as $\mathcal{I}_0$ except for layer i, where $\iota(n_i) = [|P_i|, |P_i|]$. Then, for each incoming communication $e \to_c e'$ with $e' \in P_i$, we build an IST where process P_i is ready to execute e' and where process $P_{\mathsf{pid}(e)}$ has not executed e yet. This IST is the same as $\mathcal{I}_0$, except for layer i, where $\iota(n_i) = [\mathsf{pos}(e') - 1, \mathsf{pos}(e') - 1]$ and for layer $\mathsf{pid}(e)$, where $\iota(n_{\mathsf{pid}(e)}) = [0, \mathsf{pos}(e) - 1]$. The IST representing the sets of events where P_i is blocked is obtained by making the union between $\mathcal{I}_F$ and all the IST built for the communication edges. Finally, in order to keep only valid cuts, we simply take the intersection of the resulting IST with $\mathcal{I}_\top$. It is then easy to see, that $\mathcal{I}_{\mathsf{blocked}_i}$ contains exactly those cuts satisfying the condition of lem. 8. This leads us to the following symbolic characterization of $\mathsf{pre}_i^\forall(\cdot)$.

Lemma 9. *Given a trace* $\mathbf{T} = \langle E, \alpha, \preceq \rangle$, *and an IST* $\mathcal{I}$ *such that* $\mathsf{sets}(\mathcal{I}) \subseteq \mathsf{cuts}(\mathbf{T})$, *we have that* $\mathsf{pre}_i^\forall(\mathsf{sets}(\mathcal{I})) = \mathsf{sets}((\mathcal{I}^{[x_i \leftarrow x_i - 1]} \cap \mathcal{I}_\top) \cup \mathcal{I}_{\mathsf{blocked}_i})$.

We can now define the symbolic universal predecessors.

Definition 4 (Symbolic universal predecessor). *Given a trace* $\mathbf{T} = \langle E, \alpha, \preceq \rangle$ *and an IST* $\mathcal{I}$ *such that* $\mathsf{sets}(\mathcal{I}) \subseteq \mathsf{cuts}(\mathbf{T})$, *the symbolic universal predecessors of* $\mathcal{I}$, *noted* $\mathsf{spre}^\forall(\mathcal{I})$, *is defined as follows:*

$$\mathsf{spre}^\forall(\mathcal{I}) = \bigcap_{i \in [1,k]} \left((\mathcal{I}^{[x_i \leftarrow x_i - 1]} \cap \mathcal{I}_\top) \cup \mathcal{I}_{\mathsf{blocked}_i} \right)$$

As a direct consequence of lem. 6 and 9, we get the next theorem.

Theorem 2 (Correctness $\mathsf{spre}^\forall(\cdot)$). *Given a trace* $\mathbf{T} = \langle E, \alpha, \preceq \rangle$, *and an IST* $\mathcal{I}$ *such that* $\mathsf{sets}(\mathcal{I}) \subseteq \mathsf{cuts}(\mathbf{T})$, *we have that* $\mathsf{pre}^\forall(\mathsf{sets}(\mathcal{I})) = \mathsf{sets}(\mathsf{spre}^\forall(\mathcal{I}))$

Note that it is possible to reduce an *always until* formula to an *exist until* formulae. However, using this translation might explode the size of the formula, and is therefore rejected in favor of a fixed point computation using $\mathsf{pre}^\forall(\cdot)$.

Improving the computation of $[\![\mathsf{EF}\phi]\!]$ and $[\![\mathsf{AG}\phi]\!]$. To compute $\mathcal{I}_{\mathsf{EF}\phi}$, one can simply use the equivalence $[\![\mathsf{EF}\phi]\!] = [\![\mathsf{E}[\top \mathsf{U}\phi]]\!] = \mathbf{lfp}\ \lambda X \cdot [\![\phi]\!] \cup ([\![\top]\!] \cap \mathsf{pre}^\exists(X))$, and compute the fix point using the $\mathsf{spre}^\exists(\cdot)$ operator. But, in this particular case, since $\mathsf{pre}^\exists(X) \subseteq [\![\top]\!]$, this fix point can be reduced to $\mathbf{lfp}\ \lambda X \cdot [\![\phi]\!] \cup \mathsf{pre}^\exists(X)$. Using IST, we can directly obtain the result of this fix point symbolically, in one operation using the downward closure. Indeed, we have that $\mathcal{I}_{\mathsf{EF}\phi} = \downarrow\mathcal{I}_\phi \cap \mathcal{I}_\mathsf{T}$.

Lemma 10. *Given a trace* $\mathbf{T} = \langle E, \alpha, \preceq \rangle$ *of k processes and a* CTL *formula ϕ, we have that* $\mathsf{sets}(\downarrow\mathcal{I}_\phi \cap \mathcal{I}_\mathsf{T}) = [\![\mathsf{EF}\phi]\!]$.

Moreover, the quickest way to compute $[\![\mathsf{AG}\phi]\!]$ is generally through the translation $\mathsf{AG}\phi \equiv \neg\mathsf{EF}\neg\phi$ which avoids the fixpoint computation.

6   Experimental Results

In this section, we experimentally validate our method. We compare our symbolic approach using IST with a state-of-the-art symbolic model checking (of the trace) using the tool NuSMV [6]. We considered several classical academic examples and compared the running time of our early prototype against NuSMV. Running time was limited to 10 minutes. This seems to be a reasonable assumption considering that the testing should be achieved on a large number of traces. On all the examples we considered, memory consumption was not an issue. The IST manipulated in these examples contains no more than 7000 nodes. Those results are presented in table 1. The first example we considered was the *Peterson* mutual exclusion protocol with two processes (*Pet*), where communication is done through shared variables. We used a monitor to check mutual exclusion: $\mathsf{AG}(\mathtt{ncrit} < 2)$. On this property, we experimented two ways of computing AG. The first using the downward closure on IST, and the second using the fixed point on the $\mathsf{spre}^\forall(\cdot)$ operator, as explained in sec. 5. As expected the downward closure method is quicker (with the fixpoint methods the results recorded for 2000, 5000 and 15000 events were 1.45 sec, 15.2 sec and 323.59 sec). We therefore decided to keep only the downward closure method for the remaining experiments. Even on this relatively small example, we can already see a big difference in running time: NuSMV runs out of time after 2000 events, whereas out tool can handle 15000 events in the allotted time. We also considered a generalization of this protocol for n processes (*PetN*) using the same mutual exclusion property. We experimented on 2, 5 and 10 processes. Again, we can see that our approach using IST outperforms the traditional symbolic

Table 1. Experimental results; ↑↑ indicates (> 10 min.)

Model	#proc	#events	IST (in sec.)	NuSMV (in sec.)	Model	#proc	#events	IST (in sec.)	NuSMV (in sec.)
Pet	2	2000	0.46	349.57	ABP	2	1000	13.60	297.28
	2	5000	7.53	↑↑		2	2000	27.56	↑↑
	2	15000	189.65	↑↑		2	5000	257.29	↑↑
PetN	2	2000	0.20	294.46	Phil	3	100	0.15	6.36
	2	5000	6.44	↑↑		3	200	1.11	↑↑
	2	20000	390.90	↑↑		3	2000	366.22	↑↑
	5	1000	2.04	13.74		5	100	0.25	↑↑
	5	1500	6.82	↑↑		5	200	27.05	↑↑
	5	5000	176.62	↑↑		5	500	125.56	↑↑
	10	1500	7.53	150.23		10	100	1.67	↑↑
	10	2000	27.01	↑↑		10	200	26.94	↑↑
	10	5000	147.89	↑↑		10	500	↑↑	↑↑

approach using BDD. The third model we considered was the *alternating-bit protocol* between two process *ABP*, i.e. a sender and a receiver. This time the communication is achieved using asynchronous channel. We verified that every message tagged with a 0 is followed by one with the same tag, which translates in CTL as follows: $AG((\text{sent\_msg} = 0) \implies AF(\text{received\_msg} = 0))$. This formula is a bit more complicated. Nonetheless, our method is still scalable up to 5000 events, whereas NuSMV stops after 1000. The last example we considered was the *Dining Philosopher* problem (*Phil*). We considered 3, 5 and 10 philosophers. We verified that whenever philosopher 1 is eating, either he keeps eating until the end of the trace or his left neighbour cannot eat until he stops. In CTL, this property is expressed as $AG((\text{state1} = eat) \implies (AG(\text{state1} = eat) \;||\; A[(\text{state0} \neq eat) \; U \; (\text{state1} \neq eat)]))$. We deliberately chose a complex formula to test the robustness of our approach. On this example, NuSMV can only handle 3 philosophers with 100 events, with the (too complex) property in the allotted time whereas we can still manage to terminate the analysis on some instances of respectable size. This can be explained by the fact that, in this models, the processes are more independant, thus leading to more interleavings. For each example, we have computed the size of the lattice of cuts. In the 10 minutes of allotted times, our prototype is capable of handling instances of up to 10^{10} cuts, whereas NuSMV stops at 10^5. This leads us to conclude that our approach is more scalable for this problem.

7   Conclusion and Future Works

In this paper, we have presented a new symbolic technique for the testing of distributed systems, that seems to work well in practice. We still need to validate our approach on more realistic examples. For that purpose, our method will be integrated shortly in our tool TraX and fully interfaced with our distributed controllers design environment $_d$SL [1, 2] to allow efficient testing of real industrial distributed controllers. We will also continue to investiguate possible further improvements of our technique, as the one inspired on the RCTL model checking with computation slicing described in [15]. We also intend to investigate the use of our method in different frameworks. A first candidate is the validation of Message Sequence Charts (MSC). We must study how our method can improve the efficiency of existing MSC validation methods.

Finally, from a theoretical point of view, the exact complexity class of CTL over partial order trace is not known. We plan to determine that full CTL and some interesting fragments (like RCTL).

References

1. De Wachter, B., Massart, T., Meuter, C.: dSL: An Environment with Automatic Code Distribution for Industrial Control Systems. In: Papatriantafilou, M., Hunel, P. (eds.) OPODIS 2003. LNCS, vol. 3144, pp. 132–145. Springer, Heidelberg (2004)
2. De Wachter, B., Genon, A., Massart, T., Meuter, C.: The Formal Design of Distributed Controllers with dSL and Spin. Formal Aspects of Computing 17(2), 177–200 (2005)
3. Massart, T.: A Calculus to Define Correct Tranformations of LOTOS Specifications. In: FORTE '91, North-Holland Publishing Co, pp. 281–296 (1992)
4. Holzmann, G.J.: The Model Checker SPIN. IEEE Trans. Software Eng. 23(5), 279–295 (1997)
5. McMillan, K.: The SMV System. Technical Report CMU-CS-92-131, Carnegie Mellon University (1992)
6. Cimatti, A., Clarke, E.M., Giunchiglia, E., Giunchiglia, F., Pistore, M., Roveri, M., Sebastiani, R., Tacchella, A.: NuSMV 2: An OpenSource Tool for Symbolic Model Checking. In: Brinksma, E., Larsen, K.G. (eds.) CAV 2002. LNCS, vol. 2404, pp. 359–364. Springer, Heidelberg (2002)
7. Godefroid, P.: Partial-Order Methods for the Verification of Concurrent Systems - An Approach to the State-Explosion Problem. In: Godefroid, P. (ed.) Partial-Order Methods for the Verification of Concurrent Systems. LNCS, vol. 1032, Springer, Heidelberg (1996)
8. Valmari, A.: On-the-fly verification with stubborn sets. In: Courcoubetis, C. (ed.) CAV 1993. LNCS, vol. 697, pp. 397–408. Springer, Heidelberg (1993)
9. Clarke, E., Grumberg, O., Peled, D.: Model Checking. The MIT Press, Cambridge (1999)
10. McMillan, K.L.: Symbolic model checking: an approach to the state explosion problem. Carnegie Mellon University (1992)
11. Bryant, R.E.: Symbolic boolean manipulation with ordered binary-decision diagrams. ACM Comput. Surv. 24(3), 293–318 (1992)
12. Lamport, L.: Time, clocks, and the ordering of events in a distributed system. Commun. ACM 21(7), 558–565 (1978)
13. Mattern, F.: Virtual time and global states of distributed systems. In: Proc. Workshop on Parallel and Distributed Algorithms, North-Holland / Elsevier, pp. 215–226 (1989)

14. Chase, C.M., Garg, V.K.: Detection of global predicates: Techniques and their limitations. Distributed Computing 11(4), 191–201 (1998)
15. Sen, A., Garg, V.K.: Detecting temporal logic predicates in distributed programs using computation slicing. In: OPODIS, pp. 171–183 (2003)
16. Clarke, E.M., Emerson, E.A.: Design and synthesis of synchronization skeletons using branching-time temporal logic. In: Logic of Programs, pp. 52–71 (1981)
17. Mittal, N., Garg, V.K.: Computation slicing: Techniques and theory. In: DISC, pp. 78–92 (2001)
18. Ganty, P., Meuter, C., Begin, L.V., Kalyon, G., Raskin, J.F., Delzanno, G.: Symbolic data structure for sets of k-uples of integers. Technical Report 570, Département d'Informatique - Université Libre de Bruxelles (2006)
19. Ganty, P.: Algorithmes et structures de données efficaces pour la manipulation de contraintes sur les intervalles. Master's thesis, Université Libre de Bruxelles (2002)
20. Mazurkiewicz, A.W.: Trace theory. In: Advances in Petri Nets, pp. 279–324 (1986)
21. Thiagarajan, P.S.: A trace based extension of linear time temporal logic. In: Abramsky, S. (ed.) Proceedings of the Ninth Annual IEEE Symp. on Logic in Computer Science, LICS 1994, pp. 438–447. IEEE Computer Society Press, Los Alamitos (1994)
22. Alur, R., Peled, D., Penczek, W.: Model checking of causality properties. In: Proceedings of the 10th Annual IEEE Symposium on Logic in Computer Science (LICS'95), San Diego, California, pp. 90–100 (1995)
23. Niebert, P., Peled, D.: Efficient model checking for ltl with partial order snapshots. In: Hermanns, H., Palsberg, J. (eds.) TACAS 2006 and ETAPS 2006. LNCS, vol. 3920, pp. 272–286. Springer, Heidelberg (2006)
24. Thiagarajan, P.S., Walukiewicz, I.: An expressively complete linear time temporal logic for mazurkiewicz traces. Inf. Comput. 179(2), 230–249 (2002)
25. Diekert, V., Gastin, P.: LTL is expressively complete for Mazurkiewicz traces. Journal of Computer and System Sciences 64(2), 396–418 (2002)
26. Nielsen, M., Plotkin, G.D., Winskel, G.: Petri nets, event structures and domains, part i. Theor. Comput. Sci. 13, 85–108 (1981)
27. Chandy, K.M., Lamport, L.: Distributed snapshots: Determining global states of distributed systems. ACM Trans. Comput. Syst. 3(1), 63–75 (1985)
28. Charron-Bost, B., Delporte-Gallet, C., Fauconnier, H.: Local and temporal predicates in distributed systems. ACM Trans. Program. Lang. Syst., vol. 17(1) (1995)
29. Garg, V.K., Waldecker, B.: Detection of weak unstable predicates in distributed programs. IEEE Trans. Parallel Distrib. Syst. 5(3), 299–307 (1994)
30. Garg, V.K., Waldecker, B.: Detection of strong unstable predicates in distributed programs. IEEE Trans. Parallel Distrib. Syst. 7(12), 1323–1333 (1996)
31. Garg, V.K., Mittal, N.: On slicing a distributed computation. In: ICDCS, pp. 322–329 (2001)
32. Jard, C., Jéron, T., Jourdan, G.V., Rampon, J.X.: A general approach to trace-checking in distributed computing systems. In: ICDCS, pp. 396–403 (1994)
33. Sen, K., Rosu, G., Agha, G.: Online efficient predictive safety analysis of multithreaded programs. In: Jensen, K., Podelski, A. (eds.) TACAS 2004. LNCS, vol. 2988, pp. 123–138. Springer, Heidelberg (2004)
34. Sen, K., Rosu, G., Agha, G.: Detecting errors in multithreaded programs by generalized predictive analysis of executions. In: Steffen, M., Zavattaro, G. (eds.) FMOODS 2005. LNCS, vol. 3535, pp. 211–226. Springer, Heidelberg (2005)

35. Genon, A., Massart, T., Meuter, C.: Monitoring distributed controllers: When an efficient ltl algorithm on sequences is needed to model-check traces. In: Misra, J., Nipkow, T., Sekerinski, E. (eds.) FM 2006. LNCS, vol. 4085, pp. 557–572. Springer, Heidelberg (2006)
36. Zampunieris, D., Le Charlier, B.: Efficient handling of large sets of tuples with sharing trees. In: Proceedings of the 5th Data Compression Conference (DCC'95), p. 428. IEEE Computer Society Press, Los Alamitos (1995)
37. Ammirati, P., Delzanno, G., Ganty, P., Geeraerts, G., Raskin, J.F., Van Begin, L.: Babylon: An integrated toolkit for the specification and verification of parameterized systems. In: 2nd workshop on Specification, Analysis and Validation for Emerging technologies (SAVE02) (2002)
38. Kalyon, G., Massart, T., Meuter, C., Van Begin, L.: Testing Distributed System through Symbolic Model Checking. Technical Report 571, Département d'Informatique - Université Libre de Bruxelles (2007)

An Incremental and Modular Technique for Checking LTL\X Properties of Petri Nets

Kais Klai[1], Laure Petrucci[1], and Michel Reniers[2]

[1] LIPN, CNRS UMR 7030
Université Paris 13
99 avenue Jean-Baptiste Clément
F-93430 Villetaneuse, France
{kais.klai,laure.petrucci}@lipn.univ-paris13.fr
[2] Design and Analysis of Systems (OAS)
Department of Mathematics and Computer Science
Technical University Eindhoven (TU/e)
P.O. Box 513, NL-5600 MB Eindhoven, The Netherlands
M.A.Reniers@tue.nl

Abstract. Model-checking is a powerful and widespread technique for the verification of finite state concurrent systems. However, the main hindrance for wider application of this technique is the well-known state explosion problem. Modular verification is a promising natural approach to tackle this problem. It is based on the "divide and conquer" principle and aims at deducing the properties of the system from those of its components analysed in isolation. Unfortunately, several issues make the use of modular verification techniques difficult in practice. First, deciding how to partition the system into components is not trivial and can have a significant impact on the resources needed for verification. Second, when model-checking a component in isolation, how should the environment of this component be described? In this paper, we address these problems in the framework of model-checking LTL\X action-based properties on Petri nets. We propose an incremental and modular verification approach where the system model is partitioned according to the actions occurring in the property to be verified and where the environment of a component is taken into account using the linear place invariants of the system.

1 Introduction

Model-checking is a powerful and widespread technique for the verification of finite state concurrent systems. Given a property and a model of the system, the model-checker performs an exhaustive exploration of the state space of the system to check the validity of the property. When the property is proved unsatisfied by the system, the model-checker supplies a *counterexample*, i.e., an execution scenario illustrating the violation of the property. However, the main hindrance for wider application of the model-checking approach to verify concurrent and distributed systems is the well-known state explosion problem. In fact, the size of the state space of systems grows exponentially with the number of

J. Derrick and J. Vain (Eds.): FORTE 2007, LNCS 4574, pp. 280–295, 2007.

their components. Numerous techniques have been proposed to tackle the state explosion problem in order to get a manageable state space. Among them, *on-the-fly* model-checking (e.g., [10,5]) allows for generating only the "interesting" part of the model; *partial order reduction* (e.g., [1,19]) is a reduction technique exploiting independence of some transitions in the system to discard unnecessary parts; *symbolic model-checking* (e.g., [7,9,6]) aims at checking the property on a compact representation of the system by using BDD (Binary Decision Diagram) techniques [2]. More related to this paper, *modular verification* (e.g., [20,3,13,12]) is a promising natural approach which takes advantage of the modular design of concurrent and distributed systems. Using the "divide and conquer" principle, the system is broken down into components and each of these is analysed separately. Thus, the verification of the global system is downsized to the analysis of its individual components. This could reduce dramatically the complexity of the analysis. However, several issues make using modular verification difficult. First, deciding how to partition the system into components is not trivial and can have a significant impact on the resources needed for verification [4]. Second, when model-checking a component in isolation, a model of the environment interacting with the component often has to be introduced, so that the component is not completely free in its interaction with the environment. In [15], Mc Millan calls this problem *the environment problem*. Finally, once each component is specified with the abstraction of its environment, it is of utmost importance to prove that the decomposition characterises completely the properties of the whole system.

   In this paper, we address these problems by supplying some heuristical but formal solutions. First, the global net N is viewed as the composition of n components $\langle N_1, \ldots, N_n \rangle$ where N_1 is a subnet containing all the actions occurring in the property to be checked, and $\forall i, j = 1, \ldots, n$, $i \neq j$, N_i and N_j are two subnets with disjoint sets of places. The choice of places and transitions within the components follows a particular scheme (see Section 3). Then, each subnet N_i is augmented with some additional places in order to abstract the environment i.e. $\{N_j \mid j = 1, \ldots, n, j \neq i\}$ (see Section 4). The set of the abstraction places is formally determined by using the linear invariants of the global system. Based on these decomposition and abstraction steps, our modular verification approach of a LTL\X formula φ on the global net N can be summarised as follows: We first prove that once φ holds in all components (completed by their environment abstraction) analysed separately, one can check it on a reduced synchronised product of the components built in an incremental way. Then, if φ is unsatisfied by one component, a *non-constraining relation* is defined as a property allowing, when satisfied, to deduce that it is unsatisfied by the global net as well. The non-constraining relation is asymmetric and should be checked between two components. Its satisfaction makes the analysis of modules separately equivalent to a global analysis. In this paper, we present a modular algorithm to check this relation. When the non-constraining relation is unsatisfied, the partition $\langle N_1, \ldots, N_n \rangle$ is refined by composing its first elements (N_1 and N_2) leading to a smaller partition which will be processed in the same way. In the worst case the property will be checked on a partition of size 1 (i.e. the whole net).

After recalling basic notions and notations related to Petri nets and the LTL logic in Section 2, Section 3 presents our decomposition scheme. Based on this decomposition, Section 4 shows how linear invariants can be used to complete a module with an abstraction of its environment. Section 5 discusses how a local counterexample is allowed by the environment of the corresponding component. This is achieved using the *non-constraining* relation which is checked in a modular way. Section 6 is dedicated to our incremental and modular verification approach. Section 7 is devoted to final discussion and comparison with related works on modular verification. Finally, concluding remarks and perspectives are presented in Section 8.

2   Preliminaries and Notations

In this section, we recall some basic notions of Petri net theory and introduce some notations. We also recall the syntax and semantics of the LTL logic.

Vectors and matrices. Let v be a vector or a matrix, then v^T denotes its transpose. So, if v, v' are two vectors then $v^T.v'$ corresponds to their scalar product. Let v be a vector of $\mathbb{N}^P$. The support of v is $||v|| = \{p \in P \mid v(p) > 0\}$.

Petri nets. A Petri net is a tuple $N = \langle P, T, Pre, Post \rangle$ with disjoint sets P and T of places and transitions, and the backward and forward incidence matrices $Pre : P \times T \longrightarrow \mathbb{N}$ and $Post : P \times T \longrightarrow \mathbb{N}$. Given a transition t, $Pre(t)$ and $Post(t)$ denote the t-column of Pre and $Post$ respectively. The preset of a place p (resp. a transition t) is defined as ${}^\bullet p = \{t \in T \mid Post(p, t) > 0\}$ (resp. ${}^\bullet t = \{p \in P \mid Pre(p, t) > 0\}$), and its postset as $p^\bullet = \{t \in T \mid Pre(p, t) > 0\}$ (resp. $t^\bullet = \{p \in P \mid Post(p, t) > 0\}$). The preset (resp. postset) of a set X of nodes is given by the union of the presets (resp. postsets) of all nodes in X. ${}^\bullet X^\bullet$ denotes the union of the preset and the postset of X. Given a place p, 1_p denotes the vector of $\mathbb{N}^P$ where each element is zero except the element indexed by place p, which has value 1.

A marking of a net is a mapping $m : P \longrightarrow \mathbb{N}$. We call $\langle N, m_0 \rangle$ a net with initial marking m_0. A marking m enables the transition t ($m \xrightarrow{t}$) iff $m(p) \geq Pre(p, t), \forall p \in P$. In this case the transition can occur, leading to the new marking m', given by: $m'(p) = m(p) - Pre(p, t) + Post(p, t), \forall p \in P$. This occurrence is denoted by $m \xrightarrow{t} m'$. If there exists a chain $(m_0 \xrightarrow{t_1} m_1 \ldots \xrightarrow{t_n} m_n)$, denoted by $m_0 \xrightarrow{\sigma} m_n$, the sequence $\sigma = t_1 \ldots t_n$ is also called a computation or a firing sequence. We denote by T^* (resp. T^∞) the set of finite (resp. infinite) sequences of T. $T^\omega = T^* \cup T^\infty$ denotes the set of all sequences of T. The finite (resp. infinite) language of (N, m_0) is the set $L^*(\langle N, m_0 \rangle) = \{\sigma \in T^* \mid m_0 \xrightarrow{\sigma}\}$ (resp. $L^\infty(\langle N, m_0 \rangle) = \{\sigma \in T^\infty \mid m_0 \xrightarrow{\sigma}\}$) and $L^\omega(\langle N, m_0 \rangle) = L^*(\langle N, m_0 \rangle) \cup L^\infty(\langle N, m_0 \rangle)$.

Subnets. Let $N = \langle P, T, Pre, Post \rangle$ be a Petri net. $N' = \langle P', T', Pre', Post' \rangle$ is a subnet of N induced by (P', T'), $P' \subseteq P$ and $T' \subseteq T$, iff $\forall (p, t) \in P' \times T'$, $Pre'(p, t) = Pre(p, t)$ and $Post'(p, t) = Post(p, t)$. If m is a marking of N then its projection on the places of N', denoted by $m_{\lfloor P'}$, is defined by $m'(p) = m(p), \forall p \in P'$. If σ is a computation of N, the projection of σ on a set of transitions $X \subseteq T$, denoted by $\sigma_{\lfloor X}$, is the sequence obtained by removing from σ all transitions not in X. The projection function is extended to sets of sequences (i.e., languages) as follows: $\forall \Gamma \subseteq T^\omega$, $\Gamma_{\lfloor X} = \{\sigma_{\lfloor X} \;\text{—}\; \sigma \in \Gamma\}$. Given a subnet N' of N, we also use the projection notations to denote by $m_{\lfloor N'}$ (resp $\sigma_{\lfloor N'}$) the restriction of marking m (resp. sequence σ) to places (resp. transitions) of N'.

Linear invariants. Let v be a vector of $\mathbb{N}^P$, v is a positive linear invariant iff $v.W = 0$, where $W = Post - Pre$. If v is a positive linear invariant and $m \xrightarrow{\sigma} m'$ is a firing sequence, then $v^T.m' = v^T.m$.

Linear-time Temporal Logic (LTL). LTL formulae are defined by: $\varphi ::= a \mid \neg\varphi \mid \varphi \wedge \varphi \mid \mathbf{G}\,\varphi \mid \mathbf{F}\,\varphi \mid \varphi\,\mathbf{U}\,\varphi \mid \mathbf{X}\,\varphi$, where a is an action label, $\mathbf{G}$, $\mathbf{F}$, $\mathbf{U}$ and $\mathbf{X}$ denote the *always*, *eventually*, *until* and *next* operators respectively. A LTL formula is generally interpreted over labelled transition systems (e.g. a Petri net reachability graph). For a detailed description of LTL, refer to [16]. In this paper we deal with LTL\X (LTL minus the next operator) properties.

3 Decomposition Scheme

In this section, we present a decomposition of a Petri net N according to some LTL\X formula φ and discuss its properties. Before giving a formal definition of the retained decomposition, we first define a more general decomposition. Here, we require that the composition of the components using transition fusion results in the original net, and that the components have no place in common.

Definition 1 (Decomposition). *Let $N = \langle P, T, Pre, Post \rangle$ and, for $1 \leq i \leq n$, $N_i = \langle P_i, T_i, Pre_i, Post_i \rangle$ be nets. Then $\langle N_1, \ldots, N_n \rangle$ is a decomposition of N iff the following criteria hold:*

- $P = \bigcup_{i=1}^n P_i$ *and* $P_i \cap P_j = \emptyset$, *for* $1 \leq i < j \leq n$;
- $T = \bigcup_{i=1}^n T_i$;
- $\forall i \in [1..n], \forall p \in P_i, \forall t \in T_i : Pre(p,t) = Pre_i(p,t)$;
- $\forall i \in [1..n], \forall p \in P_i, \forall t \in T_i : Post(p,t) = Post_i(p,t)$;
- $\forall i \in [1..n], \forall p \in P_i, {}^\bullet p(N_i) = {}^\bullet p(N)$.

Given a partition $\langle N_1, \ldots, N_n \rangle$ of a given Petri net N and two elements N_k and N_l of this partition, with $k \leq l$, we denote by $N_{(k,l)}$ the subnet obtained by the composition of all subnets $N_k, N_{k+1}, \ldots, N_l$. Such a composition leads to a new partition $\langle N_1, \ldots, N_{(k,l)}, \ldots, N_n \rangle$ which involves $n - l + k$ components. The following definition introduces the structure of the subnet $N_{(k,l)}$ for $1 \leq k \leq l$.

Definition 2. *Let $\langle N_1, \ldots, N_n \rangle$ be a decomposition of a net $N = \langle P, T, Pre, Post \rangle$. $\forall 1 \leq k \leq l \leq n$, $N_{(k,l)} = \langle P_{(k,l)}, T_{(k,l)}, Pre_{(k,l)}, Post_{(k,l)} \rangle$ is defined as follows:*

- $P_{(k,l)} = \bigcup_{i=k}^l P_i$;
- $T_{(k,l)} = \bigcup_{i=k}^l T_i$;

- $Pre_{(k,l)}(p,t) = Pre(p,t)$, for all $p \in P_{(k,l)}$ and $t \in T_{(k,l)}$;
- $Post_{(k,l)}(p,t) = Post(p,t)$, for all $p \in P_{(k,l)}$ and $t \in T_{(k,l)}$.

From now on, we denote by $\langle N_1, I, N_2 \rangle$ the decomposition of a Petri net N into two subnets N_1 and N_2 with disjoint sets of places and that share the set of interface transitions I. For any subnet $N_{(k,l)}$ of N, the language of $N_{(k,l)}$ contains the language of N restricted to the transitions of $N_{(k,l)}$:

Proposition 1. *Let $\langle N_1, \ldots, N_n \rangle$ be a decomposition of a net N. $\forall 1 \leq k \leq l \leq n$ and for all markings m of N:*

$$L^{\omega}(\langle N_{(k,l)}, m_{\lfloor N_{(k,l)}}\rangle) \supseteq L^{\omega}(\langle N, m \rangle)_{\lfloor N_{(k,l)}}$$

Definition 1 allows for many different decompositions of a Petri net into n components. In the following, we define a specific decomposition which is guided by the knowledge of the transitions occurring in the formula φ to be checked on N.

Definition 3 (Decomposition according to a formula φ)
Let $N = \langle P, T, Pre, Post \rangle$ be a Petri net and let φ be a LTL$\backslash X$ formula involving a non-empty subset of transitions T_{φ}. Then $N_{T_{\varphi}} = \langle N_1, \ldots, N_n \rangle$ is the decomposition of N according to φ iff $N_{T_{\varphi}}$ is a decomposition of N such that for all $1 \leq i < n$, the nets $N_i = \langle P_i, T_i, Pre_i, Post_i \rangle$ satisfy the following criteria:

- $P_1 = {}^{\bullet}T_{\varphi}{}^{\bullet}$ and $P_{i+1} = {}^{\bullet}T_i{}^{\bullet} \setminus \bigcup_{j=1}^{i} P_j$;
- $T_i = {}^{\bullet}P_i{}^{\bullet}$.

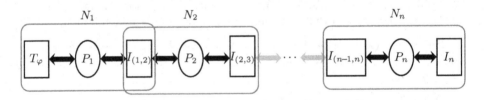

Fig. 1. Iterative decomposition scheme

Figure 1 illustrates the decomposition scheme of Definition 3. Note that this decomposition is such that each component interacts with at most two other ones (i.e. they are positioned linearly) and that the leftmost component in this scheme contains the transitions T_{φ} that occur in the formula φ to be checked. One could consider the subnet containing T_{φ} only as the first leftmost subnet. However, such a choice would allow all possible sequences on T_{φ} (i.e., T_{φ}^{ω}) and hence needs to be restricted further. This is ensured by completing the subnet with the places connected to T_{φ} in the original net. Then, the transitions connected to these places are also added so that the subnet obtained still satisfies Definition 1. Subnets N_i and N_{i+1} share a subset of transitions which we call $I_{(i,i+1)}$.

Example 1. Figure 2 illustrates an example of a decomposable Petri net model of a simplified *client-server* system. The server switches between states Passive

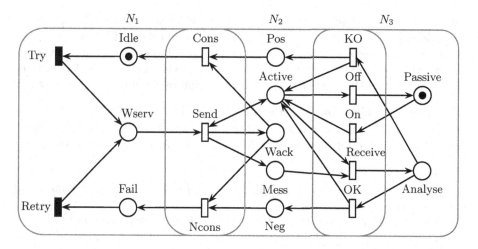

Fig. 2. A decomposable Petri net

and Active on reception of On and Off signals respectively. The client is initially Idle. When it wants to send a message, it waits for the server to be active (place Wserv). Then, it sends its message and waits for an acknowledgement (place Wack). In case of a positive acknowledgement, it becomes Idle again. Otherwise, it tries to retransmit the message (place Fail). On reception of a message, the server analyses it and sends an acknowledgement (place Analyse).

The considered set of transitions T_φ is {Try, Retry} (the black transitions in Figure 2). Using these two transitions, one can express several properties characterising the communication between the client and the server. For instance the formula $\mathbf{G}(Retry \Rightarrow ((\neg Retry)\mathbf{U}Try))$ states that each message sent can be retransmitted at most once. In this decomposition of the client-server model, subnet N_1 is unbounded since transition Cons can be executed infinitely often, thus flooding place Idle with tokens. A correct modular approach should analyse a component of the system completed by an abstraction of its environment. In the next subsection, we show how to exploit the system invariants in order to automatically construct such an abstraction.

4 Abstraction of the Environment Using Linear Invariants

Linear invariants of a Petri net correspond to a safety property of the system (see e.g. [8,11]). They are computed by finding a generative family of positive solutions of a linear equation system. Even though the worst case time complexity of this computation is not polynomial, in practice the algorithm behaves efficiently w.r.t. the reachability graph construction.

Here, we propose to use linear invariants as a witness of the synchronisation between the two subnets of the net N with decomposition $\langle N_1, I, N_2 \rangle$. Let V_N be the set of positive linear invariants of net N; these are called the global invariants. With an invariant $v \in V_N$, we associate two places $a_1^{(v)}, a_2^{(v)}$ which are added to N_1 and N_2 respectively. The current marking of the added places summarises the information given by the corresponding positive linear invariant v. The net obtained by adding an abstraction place for each invariant from a set $V \subseteq V_N$ is called the *component subnet* for V and denoted from now on by $\widehat{N}_j$.

Definition 4 (*Component subnet*). *Let $\langle N_1, I, N_2 \rangle$ be a decomposition of a net N and let $V \subseteq V_N$. The component subnet related to $N_i = \langle P_i, T_i, Pre_i, Post_i \rangle$ generated from the set of invariants V is $\widehat{N}_i = \langle \widehat{P}_i, \widehat{T}_i, \widehat{Pre}_i, \widehat{Post}_i \rangle$ such that:*

- $\widehat{T}_i = T_i$;
- $\widehat{P}_i = P_i \cup A_j$ *(where $i \in \{1, 2\}$ and $j \neq i$), with $A_j = \{a_j^{(v)} | v \in V\}$ the set of abstraction places;*
- *for all $p \in \widehat{P}_i$ and $t \in \widehat{T}_i$, $\widehat{Pre}_i(p, t) = Pre(t)^T.\Phi(p)$ and $\widehat{Post}_i(p, t) = Post(t)^T.\Phi(p)$, where the mapping Φ from $P \cup A_1 \cup A_2$ to $\mathbb{N}^{P \cup A_1 \cup A_2}$ is defined by $\Phi(p) = 1_p$, for $p \in P$, and $\Phi(a_j^{(v)}) = \sum_{p \in P_j} v(p).1_p$ for $a_j^{(v)} \in A_j$.*

The mapping from a *global* marking to markings of the component subnets is now defined to determine the initial marking of places representing the invariants.

Definition 5. *Let $\langle N_1, I, N_2 \rangle$ be the decomposition of a net N and let $\widehat{N}_i$ ($i = 1, 2$) be the induced component subnets. For each marking m of N, Φ_i the projection mapping on $\widehat{N}_i$ is defined by: $\Phi_i(m)(p) = m^T.\Phi(p)$ for all $p \in \widehat{P}_i$.*

For transitions of the component subnet, all computations of the original marked net are also computations of the component subnet.

Proposition 2. *Let $\langle N_1, T_I, N_2 \rangle$ be a decomposition of a net N. Then, for all markings m of N, $L^\omega(\langle \widehat{N}_i, \Phi_i(m) \rangle) \supseteq L^\omega(\langle N, m \rangle)_{\lfloor \widehat{N}_i}$.*

Note that it is also the case that $L^\omega(\langle N_i, m_{\lfloor N_i} \rangle) \supseteq L^\omega(\langle \widehat{N}_i, \Phi_i(m) \rangle)$: the addition of the places representing the invariant(s) is restricting the computations. The more invariants, the more precise the approximation of the global net behaviour.

As a consequence of proposition 2, we can use the invariants of the original net to obtain component subnets that hopefully disallow all counterexamples. Which set of invariants should be used for constructing the component subnets is a difficult question which will not be answered in this paper. However, we note that considering invariants that only have a support in one of the components is useless since they typically lead to a disconnected place in the other component. As a heuristic we propose to use all invariants that have support in both components, thus providing most information about the environment. Hence, we compute the component subnets for the decomposition $\langle N_{(1,i)}, I_{(i,i+1)}, N_{(i+1,n)} \rangle$ using *all* invariants that have support in both $N_{(1,i)}$ and $N_{(i+1,n)}$.

Example 2. The generative family of invariants of the model of Figure 2 is:

1. $v = Idle + Fail + Wserv + Wack$
2. $v' = Idle + Fail + Wserv + Mess + Analyse + Pos + Neg$
3. $v'' = Active + Passive + Analyse$

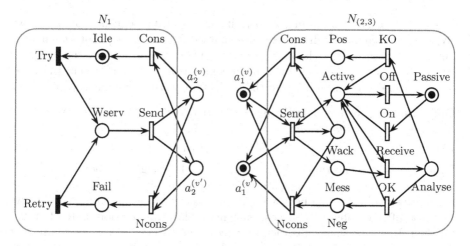

Fig. 3. The component subnets $\widehat{N}_1$ and $\widehat{N}_{(2,3)}$

The first two invariants cover both subnets while the third one is local to subnet $N_{(2,3)}$. Figure 3 illustrates the client *component subnet* obtained by using the first two invariants. The *component subnet* corresponding to the server can be obtained in a similar way. Note that the original client subnet has been enlarged with abstraction places $a_2^{(v)}$ and $a_2^{(v')}$. Let us explain for instance the underlying meaning of the abstraction place $a_2^{(v')}$. Since $\Phi(a_2^{(v')}) = 1_{\text{Mess}} + 1_{\text{Analyse}} + 1_{\text{Pos}} + 1_{\text{Neg}}$, this place contains the sum of tokens of these four places (i.e., 0). As Mess is an output place of the transition Send and the three other ones are not, $Post(a_2^{(v')}, \text{Send}) = 1$. The other arcs are obtained in a similar way.

Up to now, we have proposed a decomposition scheme based on the LTL\X formula to be checked and exploited the place invariants in order to abstract the environment of a given component while keeping some information about the interaction around the interface between two parts of the system. This scheme will be used in the following to deal with model-checking. Given a component of the system completed with an abstraction of its environment (a component subnet) how useful is a separate analysis of this component w.r.t. a global analysis of the whole net? The next section is devoted to characterising and checking whether a counterexample found locally in a component is allowed by its environment.

5   Checking the Validity of Local Counterexamples

In order to check the validity of a counterexample found locally for a component, we introduce a sufficient condition, namely the *non-constraining relation*.

5.1   The Non-constraining Relation

The *non-constraining relation* is an asymmetric property to be checked between two given marked *component subnets* obtained from a net decomposition:

$\langle N_2, m_2 \rangle$ does not constrain $\langle N_1, m_1 \rangle$ if for any firing sequence enabled from $\langle N_1, m_1 \rangle$, there exists a firing sequence enabled from $\langle N_2, m_2 \rangle$, both having the same projection on the shared transitions. Then, we prove that the firing sequences enabled in the non-constrained component exactly represent the firing sequences of the global net, up to the projection on the component transitions.

Definition 6 (Non-constraining relation). *Let $\langle N_1, m_1 \rangle$ and $\langle N_2, m_2 \rangle$ be two marked nets with disjoint sets of places. Then, $\langle N_2, m_2 \rangle$ does not constrain $\langle N_1, m_1 \rangle$ iff $L^\omega(\langle N_1, m_1 \rangle)_{\lfloor N_2} \subseteq L^\omega(\langle N_2, m_2 \rangle)_{\lfloor N_1}$.*

Expressed as an inclusion between two projected languages, the non-constraining relation can be considered as a strong condition characterising a complete freeness of the involved component w.r.t. its interface with the environment. A naive partition of the global net into components makes this relation quite often unsatisfied. However, using abstraction places, the freeness of a given component on the interface transitions is reduced and its communication behaviour is finely approximated. For instance, in Figure 3 both component subnets have the same projected language on the interface transitions, i.e. $Send.(Cons + Ncons)^\omega$.

Proposition 3. *Let $\langle N_1, I, N_2 \rangle$ be a decomposition of a net N and let m be a marking of N. If $\langle \widehat{N}_2, \Phi_2(m) \rangle$ does not constrain $\langle \widehat{N}_1, \Phi_1(m) \rangle$ then the following assertion holds: $L^\omega(\langle \widehat{N}_1, \Phi_1(m) \rangle) \subseteq L^\omega(\langle N, m \rangle)_{\lfloor \widehat{N}_1}$.*

Note that the non-constraining relation is a sufficient but not necessary condition for deducing the validity of a counterexample. It ensures that all possible local counterexamples are valid. This approach could be refined so that each representative of a set of counterexamples is checked separately.

A direct consequence of Proposition 3 is that, if $\langle \widehat{N}_2, \Phi_2(m) \rangle$ does not constrain $\langle \widehat{N}_1, \Phi_1(m) \rangle$, one can deduce that a given LTL\X formula φ does not hold in the global net N as soon as it is proved unsatisfied by $\langle \widehat{N}_1, \Phi_1(m) \rangle$.

Proposition 4. *Let $\langle N_1, I, N_2 \rangle$ be a decomposition of a net N and m a marking of N. Let φ be an LTL\X formula such that the involved actions belong to N_1. If $\langle \widehat{N}_2, \Phi_2(m) \rangle$ does not constrain $\langle \widehat{N}_1, \Phi_1(m) \rangle$ then the following assertion holds:*

$$\langle \widehat{N}_1, \Phi_1(m) \rangle \not\models \varphi \implies \langle N, m \rangle \not\models \varphi$$

The non-constraining relation is defined as an inclusion between languages. Checking such a property represents the main difficulty of our approach. A naive test of this relation would result in building the synchronised product of the reachability graphs of the component subnets, which could drastically limit the applicability of our method. Thus, the remaining part of this section will be devoted to reducing the complexity of checking the non-constraining relation.

5.2   Reduction of the Non-constraining Relation Test

Given two nets $\langle N_1, m_1 \rangle$ and $\langle N_2, m_2 \rangle$ with disjoint sets of places, the idea is to insert a new net $\langle N_3, m_3 \rangle$ in the non-constraining relation checking process so that the following implication holds: if $\langle N_2, m_2 \rangle$ does not constrain $\langle N_3, m_3 \rangle$, then $\langle N_2, m_2 \rangle$ does not constrain $\langle N_1, m_1 \rangle$.

Obviously, from the point of view of efficiency, this would reduce the complexity of the non-constraining relation check if and only if checking whether $\langle N_2, m_2 \rangle$ does not constrain $\langle N_3, m_3 \rangle$ is less expensive than checking whether it does not constrain $\langle N_1, m_1 \rangle$. In the following proposition, we first present the general context of this reduction by giving the minimal conditions for N_3 so that the above implication holds. Then, based on our decomposition scheme, we define the component subnet that will play the role of N_3 and which guarantees the reduction of the complexity of the non-constraining relation check.

Proposition 5. *Let N_1, N_2 and N_3 be nets with sets of transitions T_1, T_2 and T_3 respectively, such that $T_1 \cap T_2 \subseteq T_3$. Let m_1, m_2 and m_3 be markings for N_1, N_2 and N_3, respectively. If $L^\omega(\langle N_3, m_3 \rangle)_{\downarrow N_1} \supseteq L^\omega(\langle N_1, m_1 \rangle)_{\downarrow N_3}$, then $\langle N_2, m_2 \rangle$ is non-constraining for $\langle N_3, m_3 \rangle \Rightarrow \langle N_2, m_2 \rangle$ is non-constraining for $\langle N_1, m_1 \rangle$.*

Now, using the same abstraction principle, one can abstract both component subnets. This leads to what we call the *interface component subnet*, which allows for representing the language of the global net compactly, up to a projection on the interface. It is obtained by connecting the interface transitions to the abstraction places of both components. This structure is used in the next section in order to check efficiently the non-constraining relation.

Definition 7 (Interface component subnet). *Let $\langle N_1, I, N_2 \rangle$ be the decomposition of a net N and let $\widehat{N}_i$ $(i = 1, 2)$ be the induced component subnets for a set of invariants $V \subseteq V_N$. The interface component subnet related to this decomposition is $\widehat{I} = \langle \widehat{P}, \widehat{T}, \widehat{Pre}, \widehat{Post} \rangle$ such that, for $i, j \in \{1, 2\}$, $i \neq j$:*

- $\widehat{T} = I$;
- $\widehat{P} = A_1 \cup A_2$, *with $A_i = \{a_i^{(v)} | v \in V\}$ the set of abstraction places of $\widehat{N}_i$;*
- *for all $a \in A_i$ and $t \in \widehat{T}$, $\widehat{Pre}(a, t) = \widehat{Pre}_j(a, t)$ and $\widehat{Post}(a, t) = \widehat{Post}_j(a, t)$.*

For a marking m of N, $\widehat{m}(p) = \Phi_1(m)(p) + \Phi_2(m)(p)$ for all $p \in \widehat{P}$.

Example 3. Figure 4 represents the interface component subnets involved in the decomposition of the net in Figure 2 associated with their initial markings.

Proposition 6. *Let $\langle N_1, I, N_2 \rangle$ be a decomposition of a net N. Let $\widehat{N}_i$ $(i = 1, 2)$ and $\widehat{I}$ be the induced (interface) component subnets for a set of invariants $V \subseteq V_N$. Let m be a marking of N. Then: $\langle \widehat{N}_2, \Phi_2(m) \rangle$ is non-constraining for $\langle \widehat{I}, \widehat{m} \rangle \Rightarrow \langle \widehat{N}_2, \Phi_2(m) \rangle$ is non-constraining for $\langle \widehat{N}_1, \Phi_1(m) \rangle$.*

This proposition is exploited in order to restrain the test of the non-constraining relation of $\widehat{N}_{(i+1,n)}$ w.r.t. $\widehat{N}_{(1,i)}$, to a lighter relation between $\widehat{N}_{(i+1,n)}$ and the interface component subnet $\widehat{I}_{(i,i+1)}$. One can apply the same principle in an iterative way to deduce the following implication: if $\widehat{N}_{(j,n)}$ is non-constraining for $\widehat{I}_{(j-1,j)}$ for all $i + 1 \leq j \leq n$, then $\widehat{N}_{(i+1,n)}$ is non-constraining for $\widehat{N}_{(1,i)}$.

This can drastically reduce the complexity of checking the non-constraining relation, since it is modularly checked on very small components, one at a time.

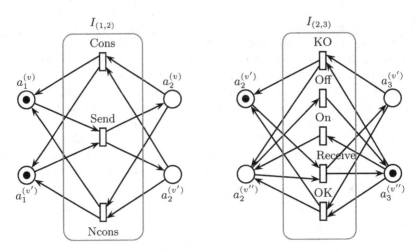

Fig. 4. The Client-Server interface component subnets

6   An Incremental and Modular Model-Checker

In this section, we use the decomposition and abstraction techniques presented in the previous sections to give an incremental modular technique for establishing the validity of a formula φ on a net N. Algorithm 1 illustrates the technique. The net is supposed to be decomposed as described in Definition 3: $N = \langle N_1, \ldots, N_n \rangle$. The algorithm verifies the validity of formula φ on the component subnet $\widehat{N}_{(1,j)}$ starting from $j = 1$ (first loop). To establish $\widehat{N}_{(1,j)} \models \varphi$, one can use any standard model checker for LTL\X formulas on Petri nets. In case the formula φ holds in this component subnet (line 4), the validity of φ w.r.t. the other component subnet $N_{(j+1,n)}$ is checked. This is done modularly on $\widehat{N}_i$ for all $i, j < i \le n$ (lines 6–8). Since the component subnets $\widehat{N}_i$ do not contain any transition of T_φ, $\widehat{N}_i \models \varphi$ can be established only using reachability, deadlock and divergence information; for example using symbolic observation graphs as in [9]. When the property φ is proved satisfied by $\widehat{N}_{(1,j)}$ and all $\widehat{N}_i$ (for $i > j$), analysed separately, the property is checked on a reduced synchronised product (lines 9–10) using algorithm 2. This task is discussed and detailed in section 6.1.

If one of the verifications of φ fails, the next phase of the algorithm consists in checking whether the component subnets not involved in the previous verification process allow the counterexample to occur. This step is ensured by checking the non-constraining relation between the component in which φ is unsatisfied and these components considered as its environment. Algorithm 3 performs this task in a modular way, as described in section 6.2.

At this point of the algorithm, we know that the property does not hold either in $\widehat{N}_{(1,j)}$ nor in $\widehat{N}_k$ for some $j < k \le n$. In the first case, the environment is the right-hand side partition $\langle \widehat{N}_{j+1}, \ldots, \widehat{N}_n \rangle$ and the non-constraining relation step is invoked once (line 19). While, in the second case, the environment is the

---

Algorithm 1. Checking φ on the components of a decomposition

Require: $\varphi, \langle N_1, \ldots, N_n \rangle$
Ensure: Check φ on $\langle N_1, \ldots, N_n \rangle$
1: **int** i,j;
2: j=1;
3: **while** j¡n **do**
4:   **if** $\widehat{N}_{1,j}$ satisfies φ **then**
5:     i=j+1;
6:     **while** $\widehat{N}_i$ satisfies φ **do**
7:       i=i+1;
8:     **end while**
9:     **if** i ¿ n **then**
10:       Check property φ on a
        reduced synchronised product
11:     **else**
12:       **if** $\neg(\langle \widehat{N}_{i-1}, \ldots, \widehat{N}_1 \rangle$ constrains
        $\widehat{I}_{(i-1,i)})$ **and** $\neg(\langle \widehat{N}_{i+1}, \ldots, \widehat{N}_n \rangle$
        constrains $\widehat{I}_{(i,i+1)})$ **then**
13:         **return** false; // $N \not\models \varphi$
14:       **else**
15:         j=j+1;
16:       **end if**
17:     **end if**
18:   **else**
19:     **if** $\neg(\langle \widehat{N}_{j+1}, \ldots, \widehat{N}_n \rangle$ constrains
        $\widehat{I}_{(j,j+1)})$ **then**
20:       **return** false; // $N \not\models \varphi$
21:     **else**
22:       j=j+1;
23:     **end if**
24:   **end if**
25: **end while**
26: **return** true; // $N \models \varphi$

---

left-hand side partition $\langle \widehat{N}_1, \ldots, \widehat{N}_{i-1} \rangle$ and the right-hand side one $\langle \widehat{N}_{i+1}, \ldots, \widehat{N}_n \rangle$, and both have to be non-constraining for $\widehat{N}_i$. Thus the non-constraining relation is checked at most twice, once for each part of the environment (line 12). If the non-constraining relation step is successful, the counterexample is allowed by the corresponding environment and it is also allowed by the net as a whole. Thus, the invalidity of φ can be deduced: $N \not\models \varphi$. If the counterexample turns out not to be allowed by these component subnets, the verification process is started again, but a larger component subnet $\widehat{N}_{(1,j+1)}$ is then used (lines 15 and 22).

Two parts of algorithm 1 are not described yet: how to check the property on a reduced synchronised product (line 10) and how to check the non-constraining relation (lines 12 and 19). This is the issue of the following subsection.

6.1 Checking a Property on a Reduced Synchronised Product

Given a Petri net N and its decomposition in n component subnets $\langle \widehat{N}_1, \ldots, \widehat{N}_n \rangle$, the fact that an LTL\X property φ holds in each component $\widehat{N}_i$ (for $i = 1 \ldots n$) is not sufficient to deduce that φ holds in N as well. However, it helps to deduce that the possible invalidity of φ in N comes necessarily from the interaction between the different components. Hence we need to focus on the behaviour of these components around the interface and abstract the local behaviours since they have been proved satisfying the property. The symbolic observation graph (SOG) technique [9] is particularly well-suited for that purpose. Indeed, a SOG is a graph, built according to a subset of observed actions *Obs* where nodes are sets of states connected to one another by unobserved actions and arcs are exclusively labeled with action from *Obs*. Checking a LTL\X property on this graph is equivalent to checking the property over the original reachability graph.

The size of the SOG is as small as the number of actions involved in the formula to be checked. In general its size is negligible w.r.t. the size of the original graph.

Algorithm 2. Checking φ on a reduced synchronised product

Require: $\langle N_1, \ldots, N_n \rangle, \varphi$
Ensure: check φ over $N = \langle N_1, \ldots, N_n \rangle$
1: **int** k;
2: j=2
3: **while** j¡n **do**
4:    Build SOG, the symbolic observation graph of $\widehat{N}_{(1,j)}$
5:    **if** $SOG \not\models \varphi$ **then**

6:    **if** $\neg(\langle \widehat{N}_{j+1}, \ldots, \widehat{N}_n \rangle$ constrains $\widehat{I}_{(j,j+1)})$ **then**
7:        **return** false; // $N \not\models \varphi$
8:    **end if**
9:    **end if**
10:    j=j+1
11: **end while**
12: **return** true; // $N \models \varphi$

Algorithm 2 uses this technique in an incremental way to check the property by exploiting our decomposition and abstraction schemes. Starting from the first component $\widehat{N}_{(1,1)}$, the property is checked iteratively on the SOG of $\widehat{N}_{(1,j)}$, for $j = 2, \ldots, n$, obtained by composing the component subnets $\widehat{N}_{(1,j-1)}$ and $\widehat{N}_j$ (lines 4–5). The model checking is performed on an incremented component subnet (line 10) and the associated SOG in two cases: the property holds in all the previous iterations, the property does not hold and the non-constraining property is unsatisfied. In the worst case, the property will be checked on the whole net. As soon as the non-constraining relation is proved satisfied, the algorithm returns *false* (the property does not hold in the global net).

6.2   The Non-constraining Checking Algorithm

In [9], the authors propose an algorithm for checking the non-constraining relation between two subnets based on the synchronisation of their symbolic observation graphs. Here, we follow the same principle and propose a modular way for checking such a relation so that the global result is deduced from several tests performed on reduced subnets. Checking the non-constraining relation between

---

Algorithm 3. Checking the non-constraining relation

Require: $\langle N_1, \ldots, N_n \rangle, I$
Ensure: check whether$\langle N_1, \ldots, N_n \rangle$ is nont constraining for I
1: **int** k;
2: $I_{(0,1)} = I$;
3: k=n;
4: **while** k¿1 **do**
5:    **if** N_k is constraining for $\widehat{I}_{(k-1,k)}$ **then**

6:        **return** false; //the non-constraining relation is unsatisfied
7:    **end if**
8:    k=k-1;
9: **end while**
10: **return** true; //the non-constraining relation holds

---

two decomposed Petri nets is, in turn, done iteratively as described in Algorithm 3. The parameters of this step are a partition $\langle N_1, \ldots, N_n \rangle$ and a subnet

I which is supposed to be adjacent to N_1. This hypothesis explains the fact that the partition $\langle \widehat{N}_{i-1}, \ldots, \widehat{N}_1 \rangle$ at line 12 of Algorithm 1 is used instead of $\langle \widehat{N}_1, \ldots, \widehat{N}_{i-1} \rangle$. Hence, the goal is to check whether the subnet induced by the partition constrains I. This task is done iteratively (lines 4–9) starting from the right-hand side of the partition and going left building towards the non-constraining of I. The correctness of this algorithm follows from Proposition 6.

7 Discussion and Related Work

Several techniques have been proposed to push further the use of modularity in model-checking concurrent systems. As far as the verification is concerned, taking benefit from the structural composition of Petri nets is known to be a hard problem. Mainly, structural approaches aim at preserving some basic properties, such as liveness and boundedness, by composition of Petri nets (e.g. [12,18,17]). More general or behavioural approaches like [3,13] deal with the minimisation of the reachable state space of each module by hiding the internal moves, before the synchronisation of modules. Reachability analysis has been proved to be effective on the resulting structure in [14] and the method has been extended to operate the model-checking of LTL\X formulae. However, experimental results show that this technique is efficient for some models, but for others the combinatorial explosion still occurs.

A common limit of existing modular approaches is that the components of the system are supposed to be known *a priori*. Even though the decomposition presented here is rather simple, having an adequate structuration into components is essential for the applicability of modular verification techniques.

In structural approaches, rather restrictive conditions are forced, thus reducing drastically the applicability to concrete systems while the synchronised product between components state graphs is quite often unavoidable in behavioral modular approaches.

Regarding the existing modular verification approaches, the contribution of this paper can be summarised in three points. First, our decomposition scheme is general and no restriction on the structure of the model is imposed. Second, we present an original formal way to combine decomposition and invariant-based abstraction of the system. Finally, we propose a modular algorithm for checking the equivalence between local and global verification. The approach we present here improves and generalises the work presented in [12]. The main improvements can be summarised in the three following points: First, contrary to [12], the decomposition scheme is not supposed to be known *a priori*. Indeed, even if the system can be decomposed intuitively into components, the decomposition obtained is not guaranteed to be suitable for the model-checking process. In this paper, we proposed to take advantage of the knowledge of the actions involved in the property to be verified in order to define a set of possible decompositions and combine such decompositions with the invariant-based abstraction. Second, in [12] the class of properties that can be handled by the method is not clearly identified. The authors speak about infinite observed sequences but it is not easy to say whether a given property depends on this kind of sequences only. Here, we extend the approach to LTL\X properties. Finally, we proposed a complete and self-contained modular verification approach for the LTL\X logic.

8   Conclusion

In this paper we addressed the modular verification of LTL\X properties over finite systems described as Petri nets. Our algorithm for such a modular verification aims at verifying a formula on a part of the system only. To achieve this, a subnet containing actions occurring in the property is completed by an abstraction of its environment and incrementally refined by including more and more details from the original system until the property can be proved either true or false. We exploit the structure of the system to both decompose the model w.r.t. the property to be checked and to compute the abstraction of the obtained components. The *non-constraining* relation is used to establish whether or not the counterexamples that might result from the local verification are globally allowed by the system. Some of the non-constraining relations that need to be established can themselves be checked iteratively.A tool implementing these algorithms is currently under development. It will provide experimental data fro testing on the efficiency of our algorithm and on some of the heuristics incorporated in it such as the decision to use all place invariants of the system. An interesting perspective of this work would be the refinement of the non-constraining relation. In fact, instead of checking the inclusion of two components projected languages, one could check whether the projection of a specific counterexample on the interface transitions is allowed by the environment component.

References

1. Bhat, G., Peled, D.: Adding partial orders to linear temporal logic. In: Mazurkiewicz, A., Winkowski, J. (eds.) CONCUR 1997. LNCS, vol. 1243, pp. 119–134. Springer, Heidelberg (1997)
2. Bryant, R.E.: Symbolic Boolean manipulation with ordered binary-decision diagrams. ACM Computing Surveys 24(3), 293–318 (1992)
3. Christensen, S., Petrucci, L.: Søren Christensen and Laure Petrucci. Computer Journal 43(3), 224–242 (2000)
4. Cobleigh, J., Giannakopoulou, D., Pasareanu, C.: Learning assumptions for compositional verification. In: Garavel, H., Hatcliff, J. (eds.) ETAPS 2003 and TACAS 2003. LNCS, vol. 2619, Springer, Heidelberg (2003)
5. Couvreur, J.-M.: On-the-fly verification of linear temporal logic. In: Woodcock, J.C.P., Davies, J., Wing, J.M. (eds.) FM 1999. LNCS, vol. 1709, pp. 253–271. Springer, Heidelberg (1999)
6. Couvreur, J.-M.: A bdd-like implementation of an automata package. In: CIAA 2004. LNCS, vol. 3317, pp. 310–311. Springer, Heidelberg (2004)
7. Geldenhuys, J., Valmari, A.: Techniques for smaller intermediary bdds. In: Larsen, K.G., Nielsen, M. (eds.) CONCUR 2001. LNCS, vol. 2154, pp. 233–247. Springer, Heidelberg (2001)

8. Girault, C., Valk, R.: Petri Nets for Systems Engineering — A Guide to Modeling, Verification, and Applications. Springer, Heidelberg (2003)
9. Haddad, S., Ilié, J.-M., Klai, K.: Design and evaluation of a symbolic and abstraction-based model checker. In: Wang, F. (ed.) ATVA 2004. LNCS, vol. 3299, Springer, Heidelberg (2004)
10. Henzinger, T.A., Kupferman, O., Vardi, M.Y.: A space-efficient on-the-fly algorithm for real-time model checking. In: Sassone, V., Montanari, U. (eds.) CONCUR 1996. LNCS, vol. 1119, pp. 514–529. Springer, Heidelberg (1996)
11. Jensen, K.: Coloured Petri Nets. Basic Concepts, Analysis Methods and Practical Use. Springer, Three Volumes (1997)
12. Klai, K., Haddad, S., Ilié, J.-M.: Modular verification of Petri nets properties: A structure-based approach. In: Wang, F. (ed.) FORTE 2005. LNCS, vol. 3731, pp. 189–203. Springer, Heidelberg (2005)
13. Lakos, C., Petrucci, L.: Modular analysis of systems composed of semiautonomous subsystems. In: Int.Conf. on Application of Concurrency to System Design (ACSD), pp. 185–194. IEEE Comp. Soc. Press, Los Alamitos (2004)
14. Latvala, T., Mäkelä, M.: LTL model-checking for modular Petri nets. In: Cortadella, J., Reisig, W. (eds.) ICATPN 2004. LNCS, vol. 3099, pp. 298–311. Springer, Heidelberg (2004)
15. McMillan, K.L., Qadeer, S., Saxe, J.B.: Induction in compositional model checking. In: Emerson, E.A., Sistla, A.P. (eds.) CAV 2000. LNCS, vol. 1855, pp. 312–327. Springer, Heidelberg (2000)
16. Pnueli, A.: Applications of temporal logic to the specification and verification of reactive systems: A survey of current trends. In: Rozenberg, G., de Bakker, J.W., de Roever, W.-P. (eds.) Current Trends in Concurrency. LNCS, vol. 224, pp. 510–584. Springer, Heidelberg (1986)
17. Sibertin-Blanc, C.: A client-server protocol for composition of Petri nets. In: Ajmone Marsan, M. (ed.) Application and Theory of Petri Nets 1993. LNCS, vol. 691, Springer, Heidelberg (1993)
18. Souissi, Y., Memmi, G.: Compositions of nets via a communication medium. In: Rozenberg, G. (ed.) Advances in Petri Nets 1990. LNCS, vol. 483, pp. 457–470. Springer, Heidelberg (1991)
19. Valmari, A.: A stubborn attack on state explosion. Formal Methods in System Design 1(4), 297–322 (1992)
20. Valmari, A.: Composition and abstraction. In: Valmari, A. (ed.) MOVEP. LNCS, vol. 2067, pp. 58–98. Springer, Heidelberg (2000)

Identifying Acceptable Common Proposals for Handling Inconsistent Software Requirements

Kedian Mu[1] and Zhi Jin[2]

[1] School of Mathematical Sciences
Peking University, Beijing 100871, P.R. China
[2] Academy of Mathematics and System Sciences
Chinese Academy of Sciences, Beijing 100080, P.R. China

Abstract. The requirements specifications of complex systems are increasingly developed in a distributed fashion. It makes inconsistency management necessary during the requirements stage. However, identifying appropriate inconsistency handling proposals is still an important challenge. In particular, for inconsistencies involving many different stakeholders with different concerns, it is difficult to reach an agreement on inconsistency handling. To address this, this paper presents a vote-based approach to choosing acceptable common proposals for handling inconsistency. This approach focuses on the inconsistency in requirements that results from conflicting intentions of stakeholders. Informally speaking, we consider each distinct stakeholder (or a distributed artifact) involved in the inconsistency as a voter. Then we transform identification of an acceptable common proposal into a problem of combinatorial vote. Based on each stakeholder's preferences on the set of proposals, an acceptable common proposal is identified in an automated way according to a given social vote rule.

1 Introduction

It is widely recognized that inconsistency management is one of the important issues in requirements engineering. For any complex software system, the development of requirements typically involves many different stakeholders with different concerns. Then the requirements specifications are increasingly developed in a distributed fashion, Viewpoints-based approaches [1,2,3] being a notable example. It makes inconsistency management necessary during the requirements stage. Generally speaking, inconsistency management may be divided into two parts, i.e. consistency checking and inconsistency handling. Consistency checking is a pervasive issue in requirements validation and verification. It focuses on techniques for detecting inconsistencies in a collection of requirements, including logic-based approaches [4,5,6] and consistency rule-based approaches [7,8]. In contrast, inconsistency handling focuses on how to identify an appropriate proposal for handling given inconsistencies and to evaluate the impact it has on other aspects of requirements stage [7,8].

Identifying appropriate inconsistency handling actions is still a difficult, but important challenge [5]. Generally, the choice of an inconsistency-handling action

J. Derrick and J. Vain (Eds.): FORTE 2007, LNCS 4574, pp. 296–308, 2007.

should depend on the nature and context of these inconsistencies [9,10]. But the context of the inconsistencies in requirements is always rather complex. Many factors such as misunderstanding between customers and analysts, inappropriate statements of requirements, and conflicting intentions of stakeholders can cause inconsistencies during requirements stage. It is not easy to provide a universal methodology to handle all the inconsistencies in requirements engineering.

In this paper, we concentrate on a particular kind of inconsistency that results from conflicting intentions of stakedholers. We would assume that there is no shortcoming in the ways that developers elicit and restate the requirements. That is, the inconsistent requirements are correctly elicited, stated, and represented from the perspective of corresponding stakeholders. There is no cause other than conflicting intentions of different stakeholders for the inconsistency. When an inconsistency resulting from conflicting intentions of stakeholders are detected, the different stakeholders involved in the inconsistency often present different proposals for handling the inconsistency from their own perspectives. These proposals reflect different concerns and intentions, and it is difficult to reach agreement on choice of proposals. Then the final proposal for handling the inconsistency is often an unsuccessful compromise among these different stakeholders. However, for this kind of inconsistency handling , there are two key problems associated with the identification of acceptable common proposals. One is how to evaluate an individual proposal from the perspective of each distinct stakeholder. That is, each stakeholder involved in the inconsistency needs to express his/her preferences on a set of proposals. It will provide a basis for identifying an acceptable common proposal. Another one is how to identify an acceptable common proposal from the set of these different proposals. Clearly, the latter problem is concerned with the mechanism of choosing the proposals such as negotiation and vote.

To address this, we present a combinatorial vote-based approach to identifying an acceptable common proposal for handling the inconsistency resulting from conflicting intentions of stakeholders in Viewpoints framework [1] in this paper. Combinatorial vote is located within the larger class of group decision making problems. Each one of a set of voters initially expresses his/her preferences on a set of candidates, these preferences are then aggregated so as to identify an acceptable common candidate in an automated way [11]. Informally speaking, for the inconsistency resulting from conflicting intentions of viewpoints (or stakeholders), we transform a set of proposals into a set of candidates with combinatorial structure. Then we consider each distinct viewpoint (or stakeholder) as a voter with different preferences on the set of candidates. Then an acceptable common proposal will be identified according some social vote rules in an automated way.

The rest of this paper is organized as follows. Section 2 gives some preliminaries about inconsistency handling in Viewpoints framework. Section 3 presents the combinatorial vote-based approach to identifying an acceptable common proposal for handling inconsistency. Section 4 gives some comparison and discussion about the vote-based approach. Finally, we conclude this paper in section 5.

2   Preliminaries

2.1   Viewpoints

The *Viewpoints* approach [1] has been developed to provide a framework in which the different perspectives and their relationships could be represented and analyzed. Viewpoint-oriented approaches to requirements engineering have been used for requirements elicitation [2], modeling [3], validation[12], and elaboration [13]. In the Viewpoints framework, a viewpoint is a description of system-to-be from the perspective of a particular stakeholder, or a group of stakeholders. It reflects the concerns of a particular stakeholder. The requirements specification of the system-to-be comprises a structured collection of loosely coupled, locally managed, distributable viewpoints, with explicit relationships between them to represent their overlaps [14].

The Viewpoints may allow different viewpoints use different notations and tools to represent their requirements during the requirements stage. However, the first order predicate calculus is appealing for formal representation of requirements statements since most tools and notations for representing requirements could be translated into formulas of the first order predicate calculus [5]. That is, predicate calculus may be considered as a promising tool to represent requirements from multiple sources. Moreover, we focus on the inconsistency handling rather than inconsistency checking in this paper. Then we need not consider reasoning with inconsistency in this paper.[1] For these reasons, we use the predicate calculus to illustrate our approach in this paper.

Let $\mathcal{L}$ be a first order language and let $\vdash$ be the consequence relation in the predicate calculus. Let $\alpha \in \mathcal{L}$ be a well-formed formula and $\Delta \subseteq \mathcal{L}$ a set of formulas in $\mathcal{L}$. In this paper, we call Δ a *set of requirements statements* or *a partial requirements specification* while each formula $\alpha \in \Delta$ represents a requirements statement.

As mentioned earlier, in this paper, we are concerned with the problem of handling inconsistency that involves multiple viewpoints. We would assume that $V = \{v_1, \cdots, v_n\}(n \geq 2)$ is the set of distinct viewpoints. Let Δ_i be the set of requirements of viewpoint v_i. Then the partial requirements specification is represented by a n tuple $< \Delta_1, \cdots, \Delta_n >$. For any $\Gamma_i \subseteq \Delta_i (1 \leq i \leq n)$, we call $\bigcup_i \Gamma_i$ an integrated requirements collection, which could be viewed as a combination of requirements of multiple viewpoints. For example $\Gamma_1 \cup \Gamma_2$ and $\Gamma_1 \cup \Gamma_3 \cup \Gamma_n$ are two integrated requirements collections.

Further, for each $i(1 \leq i \leq n)$, G_i denotes the goal of viewpoint v_i. Intuitively, for each i, if the set of requirements Δ_i is sound with regard to v_i, then $\Delta_i \vdash G_i$. Generally, we call $< G_1, \cdots, G_n >$ a goal base.

2.2   Inconsistency in Viewpoints

The term of *inconsistency* has different definitions in requirements engineering [6]. In this paper we will be concerned with the logical contradiction: any

---

[1] This assumption is just for convenience. If not, we may use a paraconsistent adaptation of predicate calculus, such as Annotated Predicate Calculus [15], to represent requirements statements [16].

situation in which some fact α and its negation $\neg\alpha$ can be simultaneously derived from the same requirements collection [4]. Moreover, we focus on the inconsistency arising from multiple viewpoints.

Definition 1 (Inconsistency). *Let $< \Delta_1, \cdots, \Delta_n >$ be the requirements specification comprising n viewpoints. Let Δ be an integrated requirements collection. If there exists a formula α such that $\Delta \vdash \alpha$ and $\Delta \vdash \neg\alpha$, then Δ is inconsistent; otherwise, Δ is consistent. We abbreviate $\alpha \wedge \neg\alpha$ by $\bot$, which we read as "inconsistency". Further, if $\Delta = \bigcup_{j=1}^{k} \Gamma_{i_j} (1 \leq i_j \leq n)$, then we say that viewpoints $v_{i_1}, \cdots, v_{i_k}$ are involved in the inconsistency.*

If Δ is inconsistent, then Δ may be partitioned into two collections. One is the set of requirements statements being free from inconsistency, and another is the set of requirements statements involved in inconsistency. Actions for handling inconsistencies are always concerned with the set of requirements statements involved in inconsistency. Let

$$\mathsf{INC}(\Delta) = \{\Gamma \subseteq \Delta | \Gamma \vdash \bot\},$$
$$\mathsf{MI}(\Delta) = \{\Phi \in \mathsf{INC}(\Delta) | \forall\Psi \in \mathsf{INC}(\Delta), \Psi \not\subset \Phi\},$$
$$\mathsf{CORE}(\Delta) = \bigcup_{\Phi \in \mathsf{MI}(\Delta)} \Phi,$$
$$\mathsf{FREE}(\Delta) = \Delta - \mathsf{CORE}(\Delta).$$

Essentially, $\mathsf{INC}(\Delta)$ is the set of inconsistent subsets of Δ; $\mathsf{MI}(\Delta)$ is the set of minimal inconsistent subsets of Δ; $\mathsf{CORE}(\Delta)$ is the union of all minimal subsets of Δ; and $\mathsf{FREE}(\Delta)$ is the set of requirements that don't appear in any minimal inconsistent subset of Δ, that is, it is a set of requirements statements being free from inconsistency. In contrast, $\mathsf{CORE}(\Delta)$ could be considered as a collection of all the requirements statements involved in inconsistency of Δ. It is this set that is of concern in the inconsistency handling.

Now we give an example to illustrate these concepts.

Example 1. Consider the following setting in development of residential area management system, which deals with the maintenance of fixed garages for vehicles. *Alice*, a manager who is in charge of maintenance, supplies the following demands:

- *The damaged garages should be maintained;*
- *An individual free garage, Garage 1 is damaged.*

Alice's goal is

- *Garage 1 should be maintained.*

Bob, a manager who is in charge of distribution of garages, gives the following demands:

- *Each garage on the expiration of utilization should be routinely maintained;*
- *All the free garages should not be maintained;*
- *Another individual garage, Garage 2 is on the expiration.*

Bob's goal is

- *Garage 2 should be maintained.*

Then the requirements of viewpoint v_A, denoted Δ_A, is

$$\Delta_A = \{ \ (\forall x)(Damaged(x) \rightarrow Maintain(x)),$$
$$Damaged(Garage\ 1) \wedge Free(Garage\ 1)\}.$$

The requirements of viewpoint v_B, denoted Δ_B, is

$$\Delta_B = \{(\forall x)(Expire(x) \rightarrow Maintain(x)),$$
$$(\forall x)(Free(x) \rightarrow \neg Maintain(x)),$$
$$Expire(Garage\ 2)\}.$$

The goal base $< G_A, G_B >$ is

$$< \{Maintain(Garage\ 1)\}, \{Maintain(Garage\ 2)\} > .$$

Let $\Delta = \Delta_A \cup \Delta_B$. We can conclude that

$$\Delta_A \vdash G_A,$$
$$\Delta_B \vdash G_B,$$
$$\Delta \vdash Maintain(Garage\ 1) \wedge \neg Maintain(Garage\ 1).$$

Then Δ is inconsistent. In this case,

$$\mathsf{MI}(\Delta) = \{\Phi_1\}$$
$$\mathsf{FREE}(\Delta) = \{(\forall x)(Expire(x) \rightarrow Maintain(x)),$$
$$Expire(Garage\ 2)\},$$
$$\mathsf{CORE}(\Delta) = \Phi_1, \text{ where}$$
$$\Phi_1 = \{(\forall x)(Damaged(x) \rightarrow Maintain(x)),$$
$$(\forall x)(Free(x) \rightarrow \neg Maintain(x)),$$
$$Damaged(Garage\ 1) \wedge Free(Garage\ 1)\}.$$

As mentioned above, the repair actions should be performed on $\mathsf{CORE}(\Delta)$. Generally, just for the simplicity of reasoning, the requirements set Δ_i contains both preliminary requirements statements and relevant facts. For example, *Damaged* (*Garage* 1) $\wedge$ *Free(Garage* 1) and *Expire(Garage* 2) are facts in Δ_A and Δ_B, respectively. These facts are used to model the certain scenario associated with each viewpoint's goal. This paper focuses on how to elect an acceptable common proposal for modifying the preliminary requirements specification , then we will view the facts as being correct and not subject to the modification of preliminary requirements. This will allow us to focus our attention on choice of actions performed for modifying the preliminary requirements. Thus, we are concerned with proposals for modifying a set of problematical preliminary requirements, denoted $\mathsf{CORE}(\Delta)_P$, which is a subset of $\mathsf{CORE}(\Delta)$. In the example above,

$$\mathsf{CORE}(\Delta)_P = \{(\forall x)(Damaged(x) \rightarrow Maintain(x)),$$
$$(\forall x)(Free(x) \rightarrow \neg Maintain(x))\}.$$

2.3   Combinatorial Vote

Combinatorial vote has been presented by Lang in [11], where a group of voters (or agents) is supposed to express their preferences and come to a common decision concerning a set of non-independent variables to assign. Of course, the set of candidates $\mathcal{X}$ has combinatorial structure [11]. A combinatorial vote problem consists of two steps:

(1) the voters express their preference on a set of candidates within a fixed representation language;
(2) one or several optimal candidate(s) is (are) determined automatically, using a fixed vote rule.

A preference profile consists of a preference structure for each of the voters. A relational preference structure consists of a binary relationship $\geq$ on $\mathcal{X}$. A vote rule V is defined as a function mapping every preference profile P to an elected candidate, or a subset of candidates. Given a preference profile P and a vote rule V, the set of elected candidates is denoted by $Select_V(P)$. Scoring rules consists in translating the preference relation $\geq_i$ of voters into scoring function $s_i(\mathbf{x})$, such that the score $s_i(\mathbf{x})$ of a candidate $\mathbf{x}$ with respect to voter i is a function of its position in the relation $\geq_i$. The plurality and the veto rules are appropriate for combinatorial vote [11]. In this paper, we adopt the plurality rule as the vote rule to illustrate our approach. Actually, the choice of social vote rules used in the practice should depend on the specific circumstances.

The plurality rule is the scoring rule obtained by taking $s_i(\mathbf{x}) = 1$ if and only if $\mathbf{x}$ is non-dominated for $\geq_i$, i.e., iff there is no $\mathbf{y}$ such that $\mathbf{y} >_i \mathbf{x}$. $Select_{plurality}(P)$ is the set of candidates maximizing the number of voters for whom $\mathbf{x}$ is non-dominated.

3   Identifying an Acceptable Common Proposal of Inconsistency Handling

In this section, we will transform the problem of identifying an appropriate proposal for handling inconsistency into combinatorial vote. It consists of four key steps:

(1) We define a 1-1 mapping from the set of proposals to a set of candidates that has combinatorial structure;

(2) We transform the evaluation of proposals from the perspective of an individual viewpoint into a voter's preference representation on the set of candidates;
(3) Given a social vote rule, the set of elected candidates is identified automatically.
(4) The set of elected candidates is transformed into the set of acceptable common proposals.

3.1   Proposals of Inconsistency Handling

Generally, handling inconsistency in an integrated requirements collection Δ means that stakeholders or viewpoints involved in the inconsistency are trying to reach an agreement on the modification of $CORE(\Delta)_P$.

Informally, proposal for handling inconsistency should be a series of actions performed to modify $CORE(\Delta)_P$. For each requirements $\alpha \in CORE(\Delta)_P$, an individual proposal for handling the inconsistency will delete it from $CORE(\Delta)_P$ or retain it.

Now we try to transform the problem of identifying appropriate proposals for inconsistency handling into a problem of combinatorial vote. Let $|CORE(\Delta)_P|$ be the number of requirements in $CORE(\Delta)_P$. Suppose that $|CORE(\Delta)_P| = m$ and $A = \{a_1, \cdots, a_m\}$ be a set of propositional variables that don't appear in Δ. Then we can define a 1-1 mapping f from $CORE(\Delta)_P$ to A. Further, let Π be a set of possible proposals for handling the inconsistency in $CORE(\Delta)_P$, then $|\Pi| = 2^m$.

Definition 2 (Transformation Mapping). *Let* $\mathcal{X} = \{a_1, \neg a_1\} \times \cdots \times \{a_m, \neg a_m\}$. *Let* Π *be the set of possible proposals for handling inconsistency. Transformation mapping* t *is a 1-1 mapping from* Π *to* $\mathcal{X}$ *such that for every* $\pi \in \Pi$, $t(\pi) = (t_1, \cdots, t_n)$, *where for each* i *(* $1 \leq i \leq n$ *)*

- $t_i = a_i$, *if* π *retains requirements* $f^{-1}(a_i)$ *in* $CORE(\Delta)_P$;
- $t_i = \neg a_i$, *if* π *deletes requirements* $f^{-1}(a_i)$ *from* $CORE(\Delta)_P$;

Essentially, by transformation mapping t, we transform the set of possible proposals into a set of candidates with combinatorial structure. Suppose that $v_{i_1}, \cdots, v_{i_k}$ involved in the inconsistency of Δ, the the problem of identifying appropriate proposal is transformed into the following problem:

- *Voters* $v_{i_1}, \cdots, v_{i_k}$ *to elect a winner in* $\mathcal{X}$.

Since $\mathcal{X}$ has combinatorial structure, then the latter is a problem of combinatorial vote [11]. Now we give an example to illustrate this transformation.

Example 2. Consider *Example 1.* again. *Alice* and *Bob* are involved in the inconsistency and

$$CORE(\Delta)_P = \{(\forall x)(Damaged(x) \rightarrow Maintain(x)),$$
$$(\forall x)(Free(x) \rightarrow \neg Maintain(x))\}.$$

Now we define mapping f from $\mathsf{CORE}(\Delta)_P$ to $\{a_1, a_2\}$ as follows:

$$f((\forall x)(Damaged(x) \rightarrow Maintain(x))) = a_1,$$
$$f((\forall x)(Free(x) \rightarrow \neg Maintain(x))) = a_2.$$

There are 4 possible proposals for handling inconsistency:

- π_1: to delete $(\forall x)(Damaged(x) \rightarrow Maintain(x))$ from $\mathsf{CORE}(\Delta)_P$;
- π_2: to delete $(\forall x)(Free(x) \rightarrow \neg Maintain(x))$ from $\mathsf{CORE}(\Delta)_P$;
- π_3: to delete all the requirements in $\mathsf{CORE}(\Delta)_P$;
- π_4: to retain all the requirements in $\mathsf{CORE}(\Delta)_P$.

Then $\Pi = \{\pi_1, \pi_2, \pi_3, \pi_4\}$ and

$$t(\pi_1) = (\neg a_1, a_2);$$
$$t(\pi_2) = (a_1, \neg a_2);$$
$$t(\pi_3) = (\neg a_1, \neg a_2);$$
$$t(\pi_4) = (a_1, a_2).$$

Now we transform inconsistency handling problem into a combinatorial vote problem:

- Two voters (stand for Alice and Bob, respectively) to elect a winner in $\{(\neg a_1, a_2), (a_1, \neg a_2), (\neg a_1, \neg a_2), (a_1, a_2)\}$.

3.2   Voting for a Common Proposal

As mentioned earlier, voters' preferences on the set of candidates play an important role in combinatorial vote. In this paper, for a particular voter, we focus on the relational preference structure on $\mathcal{X}$. It should be associated with the viewpoint's preference on the set of proposals.

Intuitively, the viewpoint's preferences on the set of proposals are always associated with the degree of satisfaction of his/her goal by performing each proposal. For each proposal $\pi_i \in \Pi$, let $\pi_i(\Delta)$ denote the modification of Δ by performing the proposal π_i. Let $\lfloor G^i_j \rfloor$ denote the number of formulas of goal G_j that can be derived from $\pi_i(\Delta_j)$ consistently. Then $\lfloor G^i_j \rfloor$ may be viewed as a measure of the degree of satisfaction of the goal.

Definition 3 (Preference on Π). *Let Π be the set of possible proposals. For each i ($1 \leq i \leq n$), a binary relationship with regard to viewpoint v_i on Π, denoted $\geq_i$, is defined as follows:*

$$\forall\, \pi_l, \pi_j \in \Pi, \pi_l \geq_i \pi_j \text{ if and only if } \lfloor G^l_i \rfloor \geq \lfloor G^j_i \rfloor.$$

Note that $\pi_l >_i \pi_j$ if and only if $\pi_l \geq_i \pi_j$ and $\pi_j \not\geq_i \pi_l$.

Definition 4 (Preference on $\mathcal{X}$). *Let Π be the set of possible proposals. For each i ($1 \leq i \leq n$), $\geq_i$ is a binary relationship with regard to viewpoint v_i on Π. Let t is a transformation mapping from Π to $\mathcal{X}$. Then $\forall\, t(\pi_l), t(\pi_j) \in \mathcal{X}$,*

$$t(\pi_l) \geq_i t(\pi_j) \ \textit{if and only if} \ \pi_l \geq_i \pi_j.$$

Now we give an example to illustrate the preferences of voters.

Example 3. Consider the proposals mentioned in *Example 2.* For viewpoint v_A,

$$\lfloor G_A^1 \rfloor = 0;$$
$$\lfloor G_A^2 \rfloor = 1;$$
$$\lfloor G_A^3 \rfloor = 0;$$
$$\lfloor G_A^4 \rfloor = 0.$$

And for v_B,

$$\lfloor G_B^1 \rfloor = 1;$$
$$\lfloor G_B^2 \rfloor = 1;$$
$$\lfloor G_B^3 \rfloor = 1;$$
$$\lfloor G_A^4 \rfloor = 0.$$

Then

$$\pi_2 \geq_A \pi_1, \pi_3, \pi_4$$
$$\pi_1, \pi_2, \pi_3 \geq_B \pi_4.$$

and

$$(a_1, \neg a_2)$$
$$\geq_A (\neg a_1, a_2), (\neg a_1, \neg a_2), (a_1, a_2);$$
$$(\neg a_1, a_2), (a_1, \neg a_2), (\neg a_1, \neg a_2)$$
$$\geq_B (a_1, a_2).$$

Note that candidates written on a same line are equally preferred.

In this paper, we adopt the plurality rule as the vote rule. As mentioned earlier, the plurality rule is the scoring rule obtained by taking $s_i(\mathbf{x}) = 1$ if and only if $\mathbf{x} \in \mathcal{X}$ is non-dominated for $\geq_i$, i.e., iff there is no $\mathbf{y}$ such that $\mathbf{y} >_i \mathbf{x}$. Given preferences profile P, the set of acceptable common candidates, denoted $Select_{plurality}(P)$, is the set of candidates maximizing the number of voters for whom $\mathbf{x}$ is non-dominated.

Example 4. Consider the example above again. In this case, there are two voters v_A and v_B. The preference ordering $\geq_A$, and $\geq_B$ are:

$$(a_1, \neg a_2)$$
$$\geq_A (\neg a_1, a_2), (\neg a_1, \neg a_2), (a_1, a_2);$$
$$(\neg a_1, a_2), (a_1, \neg a_2), (\neg a_1, \neg a_2)$$
$$\geq_B (a_1, a_2).$$

The plurality rule is used as the vote rule. Then the scores of candidates are:

$$s_A((\neg a_1, a_2)) = 0;$$
$$s_A((a_1, \neg a_2)) = 1;$$
$$s_A((\neg a_1, \neg a_2)) = 0;$$
$$s_A((a_1, a_2)) = 0;$$
$$s_B((a_1, \neg a_2)) = 1;$$
$$s_B((\neg a_1, a_2)) = 1;$$
$$s_B((\neg a_1, \neg a_2)) = 1;$$
$$s_B((a_1, a_2)) = 0;$$

Clearly, $Select_{plurality}(P) = \{(a_1, \neg a_2)\}$. That is, $(a_1, \neg a_2)$ is the winner in $\mathcal{X}$. Since $t^{-1}((a_1, \neg a_2)) = \pi_2$, π_2 is the acceptable common proposal for handling the inconsistency in $\Delta_A \cup \Delta_B$. Therefore, by voting, $(\forall x)(Free(x) \to \neg Maintain(x))$ should be deleted from Δ_B for maintaining consistency.

The combinatorial vote-based approach to identifying the acceptable common proposals presented above may be illustrated as follows:

$$(\Pi, \geq_i) \xrightarrow{t} (\mathcal{X}, \geq_i) \xrightarrow{plurality\ rule} Selet_{plurality}(\geq_i, \ 1 \leq i \leq n) \xrightarrow{t^{-1}} \pi_i(winner).$$

4   Discussion and Comparison

For the combinatorial vote, the computational complexity of the different problems obtained from the choice of a given representation language (propositional logic) and a give vote rule (plurality rule) has been studied by Lang in [11]. However, there are other vote rules such as the veto rule also appropriate for combinatorial vote mentioned in [11]. The veto rule is obtained by letting $s_i(\mathbf{x}) = 1$ if and only if there is at least a candidate $\mathbf{y}$ such that $\mathbf{x} >_i \mathbf{y}$. If the veto rule is used as the vote rule in *Example 4.*, then

$$s_A((\neg a_1, a_2)) = 0;$$
$$s_A((a_1, \neg a_2)) = 1;$$
$$s_A((\neg a_1, \neg a_2)) = 0;$$
$$s_A((a_1, a_2)) = 0;$$
$$s_B((a_1, \neg a_2)) = 1;$$
$$s_B((\neg a_1, a_2)) = 1;$$
$$s_B((\neg a_1, \neg a_2)) = 1;$$
$$s_B((a_1, a_2)) = 0;$$

And $Selet_{veto}(P) = \{(a_1, \neg a_2)\}$. The winner is also $(a_1, \neg a_2)$ under the veto rule. Of course, it is possible to get the different winners under different vote rules.

On the other hand, inconsistency handling in requirements engineering is a rather complex issue. Most works focus on the inconsistencies that result from misunderstand customer's demands or incorrect statement of requirements [17,18,5]. In contrast, the combinatorial vote-based approach is more appropriate to handling inconsistencies that result from conflictive goals or intentions of stakeholders. This kind of inconsistency handling is always associated with many social activities such as vote and negotiation. It is not just a technical issue. The vote-based approach may be viewed as a first attempt to provide appropriate mechanism for handling inconsistencies result from conflict goals or intentions.

The preferences on the set of possible proposals of each individual viewpoints play an important role in electing the acceptable common proposals in the vote-based approach. In this paper, we just use $\lfloor G_i^l \rfloor$ to evaluate the relative importance of proposal π_l from the perspective of viewpoint v_i. However, different goals (formulas) in G_i may have different relative importance. So the relative importance of each formula of G_i that can be derived from $\pi_l(\Delta_i)$ should be also taken into consideration in representing preferences on Π of v_i. This would be a direction of future work.

5   Conclusions

We have presented a combinatorial vote-based approach for identifying the acceptable common proposals for handling inconsistency in Viewpoints framework.

Identifying appropriate inconsistency handling actions is still a difficult, but important challenge. The vote-based approach presented in this paper focuses on the inconsistency that results from conflicting intentions of different stakeholders. The main contribution of this paper is to transform identifying appropriate proposals for handling inconsistency into a problem of combinatorial vote. It consists of four key steps:

(1) we define a 1-1 mapping from the set of proposals to a set of candidates that has combinatorial structure;
(2) we transform the evaluation of proposals from the perspective of an individual viewpoint into a voter's preference representation on the set of candidates;
(3) Given a social vote rule, the set of elected candidates is identified automatically.
(4) The set of elected candidates is transformed into the set of acceptable common proposals.

However, inconsistency handling in requirements engineering is a rather complex issue. For the vote-based approach presented in this paper, the choice of social vote rules used in the combinatorial vote and the approaches to evaluating each proposal should be considered further in the future work.

Acknowledgements

This work was partly supported by the National Natural Science Fund for Distinguished Young Scholars of China under Grant No.60625204, the Key Project of

National Natural Science Foundation of China under Grant No.60496324, the National Key Research and Development Program of China under Grant No. 2002CB312004, the National 863 High-tech Project of China under Grant No. 2006AA01Z155, the Knowledge Innovation Program of the Chinese Academy of Sciences, and the NSFC and the British Royal Society China-UK Joint Project.

References

1. Finkelsetin, A., Kramer, J., Nuseibeh, B., Finkelstein, L., Goedicke, M.: Viewpoints: A Framework for Integrating Multiple Perspectives in System Development. International Journal of Software Engineering and Knowledge Engineering 2(1), 31–58 (1992)
2. Kotonya, G.I.: Sommerville: Viewpoints for requirements definition. IEE Software Eng.Journal 7, 375–387 (1992)
3. Andrade, J., Ares, J., Garcia, R., Pazos, J., Rodriguez, S., Silva, A.: A methodolog ical framework for viewpoint-oriented conceptual modeling. IEEE Trans. Softw. Eng. 30, 282–294 (2004)
4. Gervasi, V.D.: Zowghi: Reasoning about inconsistencies in natural language re quirements. ACM Transaction on Software Engineering and Methodologies 14, 277–330 (2005)
5. Hunter, A.B.: Nuseibeh: Managing inconsistent specification. ACM Transactions on Software Engineering and Methodology 7, 335–367 (1998)
6. Zowghi, D., Gervasi, V.: On the interplay between consistency, completeness, and correctness in requirements evolution. Information and Software Technology 45, 993–1009 (2003)
7. Nuseibeh, B., Easterbrook, S., Russo, A.: Leveraging inconsistency in software development. IEEE Computer 33, 24–29 (2000)
8. Nuseibeh, B.S., Easterbrook, A.: Russo: Making inconsistency respectable in software development. Journal of Systems and Software 58, 171–180 (2001)
9. Gabbay, D., Hunter, A.: Making inconsistency respectable 2:meta-level handling of inconsistent data. In: Moral, S., Kruse, R., Clarke, E. (eds.) ECSQARU 1993. LNCS, vol. 747, pp. 129–136. Springer, Heidelberg (1993)
10. Finkelstein, A., Gabbay, D., Hunter, A., Kramer, J., Nuseibeh, B.: Inconsistency handling in multiperspective speci?cations. IEEE Trans. on Software Engineering 20, 569–578 (1994)
11. Lang, J.: From logical preference representation to combinatorial vote. In: Proceedings of 8th International Conference on Principles of Knowledge Representation and Reasoning, pp. 277–288. Morgan Kaufmann, San Francisco (2002)
12. Leite, J.P.A.: Freeman: Requirements validation through viewpoint resolution. IEEE Trans. on Soft. Eng. 17, 1253–1269 (1991)
13. Robinson, W.N.: Integrating multiple specifications using domain goals. In: IWSSD '89: Proceedings of the 5th international workshop on Software specification and design, pp. 219–226. ACM Press, New York, NY, USA (1989)
14. Nuseibeh, B., Kramer, J., Finkelstein, A.: Viewpoints: meaningful relationships are difficult? In: Proceedings of the 25th International Conference on Software Engineering, pp. 676–681. IEEE Computer Society Press, Los Alamitos (2003)

15. Kifer, M., Lozinskii, E.L.: A logic for reasoning with inconsistency. Journal of Automated Reasoning 9, 179–215 (1992)
16. Mu, K., Jin, Z., Lu, R.: Inconsistency-based strategy for clarifying vague software requirements. In: Zhang, S., Jarvis, R. (eds.) AI 2005. LNCS (LNAI), vol. 3809, pp. 39–48. Springer, Heidelberg (2005)
17. Easterbrook, S., Nuseibeh, B.: Managing inconsistencies in an evolving specification. In: Proceedings of the Second International Symposium on Requirements Engineering (RE95), pp. 48–55 (1995)
18. Easterbrook, S.M., Chechik, A.: framework for multi-valued reasoning over inconsistent viewpoints. In: Proceedings of International Conference on Software Engineering (ICSE'01), Toronto, Canada, pp. 411–420 (2001)

Formalization of Network Quality-of-Service Requirements

Christian Webel and Reinhard Gotzhein

Computer Science Department, University of Kaiserslautern, Kaiserslautern,
Germany
{webel,gotzhein}@informatik.uni-kl.de

Abstract. The provision of *network Quality-of-Service* (network QoS)
is a major challenge in the development of future communication systems. Before designing and implementing these systems, the network
QoS requirements are to be specified. Existing approaches to the specification of network QoS requirements are mainly focused on specific
domains or individual system layers. In this paper, we present a holistic,
comprehensive formalization of network QoS requirements, across layers.
QoS requirements are specified on each layer by defining QoS domain,
consisting of QoS performance, reliability, and guarantee, and QoS scalability, with utility and cost functions. Furthermore, we derive preorders
on multi-dimensional QoS domains, and present criteria to reduce these
domains, leading to a manageable subset of QoS values that is sufficient
for system design and implementation. The relationship between layers is formalized by two kinds of QoS mappings. QoS domain mappings
associate QoS domains of two abstraction levels. QoS scalability mappings associate utility and cost functions of two abstraction levels. We
illustrate our approach by examples from the case study *Wireless Video
Transmission*.

1 Introduction

One of the major challenges in communication networks is the provision of *network quality of service* (network QoS). By network QoS, we refer to the degree of
well-definedness and controllability of the behaviour of a communication system
with respect to quantitative parameters [1]. The need for network QoS arises
from the fact that, for state-of-the-art distributed applications, it is essential
that they offer their functionality with specified performance, reliability, and
guarantee. In addition, communication systems and applications have to adapt
to varying traffic and channel quality. The realization of such adaptive behaviour
can in fact be seen as one of the key challenges in the development of communication systems supporting *network quality of service*. It requires a cross-layer
approach with suitable abstractions and mappings between resource views of
different layers.

Our current work aims at establishing a holistic engineering approach for communication systems, including network QoS provision. In this context, we are

J. Derrick and J. Vain (Eds.): FORTE 2007, LNCS 4574, pp. 309–324, 2007.
© IFIP International Federation for Information Processing 2007

investigating techniques for the formal specification of QoS requirements on different system levels. Existing techniques are mainly focused on specific domains or system layers. In this paper, we present a formalization of network QoS requirements across layers. The formal relationship between layers is established by QoS domain mappings. To formalize scalability, we define utility and cost functions on each layer, which are used to derive preorders on QoS domains. Utility and cost functions of different layers are related by QoS scalability mappings. To achieve consistency between these functions of different layers, QoS scalability mappings are derived from QoS domain mappings.

The remaining part of the paper is organized as follows: In Section 2, we survey related work. In Section 3, we present our formalization and specification of network QoS requirements. Section 4 describes the different abstraction levels in communication systems supporting QoS and the mappings between these levels. Section 5 illustrates the approach by a case study. Last, Section 6 presents conclusions and future work.

2 Related Work

To cope with various requirements of system designs, user preferences, middleware, hardware, networks, operating systems, and applications, several QoS specification techniques have been proposed (see [2] for a classification):

- QML (Quality Modelling Language) [3] is focused on the specification of application layer QoS requirements. QoS requirements of lower layers, QoS scaling, and QoS mappings are not addressed.
- CQML [4] adopts some of the fundamental concepts of QML, and also addresses dynamic QoS scaling. As QML, it is focused on the application layer.
- QDL (Quality Description Language) has been proposed as a part of the QuO (Quality Objects) framework [5] that supports QoS on the CORBA object layer. With QDL, it is possible to specify QoS requirements on application layer and on resource layer, and to define QoS scaling.
- The Quality Assurance Language (QuAL) is part of QoSME [6]. With QuAL, QoS requirements are specified in a process-oriented way. The Quality-of-Service Architecture (QoS-A) [7] uses a parameter-based specification approach.
- In [8], an approach for specifying and mapping QoS in distributed multimedia systems is presented. Based on the specification, fuzzy-control is used for QoS scaling.
- Formal QoS mappings have not been studied thoroughly so far. Some partial results can be found in [9] and [10].

In summary, it can be stated that previous formal treatments of QoS address only some aspects of QoS requirement specification, focusing, for instance, on a subset of abstraction layers, or leaving out QoS mappings. Our work comprises the aforementioned issues and therefore provides a holistic, comprehensive formalization of network QoS requirements, across layers.

3   Formalization of Network Quality of Service

The need for *formalization* of network quality of service arises from the fact that a *precise* description of network QoS between service user and service provider is needed to police, control, and maintain the data flow a user emits to the communication system. Further on, the mechanisms realizing these functionalities require a *precise* QoS description. These mechanisms are typically integrated across layers; therefore, more than one viewpoint on the network QoS requirements is needed. To rigorously relate these viewpoints, formal QoS mappings are to be defined. In this section, we start to formalize network QoS by defining *QoS domain*, *QoS scalability* and *QoS specification*. The formal definition of QoS mappings will be addressed in Sect. 4.

3.1   QoS Domain

The *QoS domain* captures the QoS characteristics of a class of data flows, i.e. performance, reliability, and guarantee:

Definition 1 (QoS Domain). *The QoS domain Q is defined as $Q = P \times R \times G$, where P is the performance domain, R is the reliability domain, and G is the guarantee domain. $q = (p, r, g)$ denotes an element of Q, called QoS value.*

QoS performance describes efficiency aspects characterizing the required amount of resources and the timeliness of the service (e.g., peak and average throughput, delay, jitter, burst characteristics). The relevant aspects are included in the *QoS performance domain P*, which we formalize as follows:

Definition 2 (QoS Performance). *A QoS performance domain P is defined as $P = P_1 \times \ldots \times P_n = \prod_{i=1}^{n} P_i$, where $P_1, \ldots, P_n$ are performance subdomains.*

QoS reliability describes the *safety-of-operation* aspects characterizing the fault behaviour (e.g., loss rate and distribution, corruption rate and distribution, error burstiness). It can significantly impact the overall throughput and functionality on lower system layers, since it requires redundancy (e.g., retransmission, forward error control). The relevant aspects are included in the *QoS reliability domain R*:

Definition 3 (QoS Reliability). *The QoS reliability domain R is defined as $R = Loss \times Period \times Burstiness \times Corruption$, with $Loss = \mathbb{N}_0$, $Period = \mathbb{R}_+$, $Burstiness = \mathbb{R}_+$, and $Corruption = \{r \in \mathbb{R} \mid 0 \leq r < 100\}$.*

Reliability addresses *loss* corresponding to a layer-specific data unit (e.g. picture frames or lower system layer PDUs), the *period* in which data loss occurs, and the *burstiness*, i.e. the duration of a successional appearance of data loss. As a fourth parameter, the permitted *corruption rate* for a layer specific data unit in percent is given.

QoS guarantee describes the degree of commitment characterizing the binding character of the service. Four degrees of commitment are distinguished. *Best-effort* denotes the minimal degree, meaning that no guarantees are given. *Deterministic* refers to the highest degree, meaning that hard guarantees are provided.

Statistical expresses that guarantees are given with a specified probability. Finally, *enhanced best-effort* denotes better-than-best-effort guarantees: in periods of sufficient resources, statistical or deterministic guarantees are provided; otherwise, a priority-based best-effort scheme is used. QoS guarantee is formalized by the *QoS guarantee* domain:

Definition 4 (QoS Guarantee). *The domain of QoS guarantee G is defined as* $G = DoC \times Stat \times Prio$, *where* $Stat = \{p \in \mathbb{R} \mid 0 < p \leq 1\}$, $Prio = \mathbb{N}$, *and* $DoC = \{bestEffort, enhancedBestEffort, statistical, deterministic\}$.

The guarantee consists of a degree of commitment *DoC*, a corresponding value *Stat* in case of statistical guarantees, and a *priority*. The priority determines the relative importance between two or more QoS requirements (traffic contracts).

3.2   QoS Scalability

Varying communication resources require adaptive mechanisms to avoid network overload, and to scale the application service. The *QoS scalability S* describes the control aspects characterizing the scope for a dynamic adaptation of the QoS aspects of a data flow (described by a QoS domain) to a certain granted network quality of service:

Definition 5 (QoS Scalability). *Let Q be a QoS domain. The domain of QoS scalability S is defined as* $S = Util \times Cost \times Up \times Down$, *where* $Util = \{u \mid u : Q \to [0,1]\}$, $Cost = \{c \mid c : Q \to \mathbb{R}_+\}$, *and* $Up, Down \in \{x \in \mathbb{R}_+ \mid 0 \leq x \leq 1\}$.

The elements of *Util* and *Cost* are called *utility functions* and *cost functions*, respectively. A utility function determines the usefulness of QoS values $q \in Q$. This information is crucial for upscaling and downscaling, and has to be provided on all system layers. The utility of QoS values depends on the application scenario, but not necessarily on the amount of needed resources. The latter is expressed by the cost function, which can be tailored to the actual resource situation, associating higher costs with scarcer resources. In other words, given two QoS values q and q' with $u(q) > u(q')$, it is possible that $c(q) < c(q')$, i.e., q consumes less resources than q'. We will have to take this into account when defining QoS scalability mappings (see Sect. 4.3). Related to the utility function, two values $up \in Up$ and $down \in Down$ are used to define thresholds for up- and downscaling, i.e. a scaling is only performed, if the benefit for the user increases/decreases more than $up/down$ percent.

According to [8], the utility function u can be defined using functions on P, R and G:

$$u_P : P \to [0,1], \quad u_R : R \to [0,1], \quad u_G : G \to [0,1] \tag{1}$$

A possible definition u for a QoS value $q = (p, r, g)$ is:

$$u(q) = \min\{u_P(p) \cdot w_P, u_R(r) \cdot w_R, u_G(g) \cdot w_G\} \tag{2}$$

This definition emphasizes that usually, a minimum benefit of each of the QoS value constituents is required. Other definitions can be given by introducing weights w_P, w_R, and w_G, reflecting the relative importance of performance, reliability, and guarantee, respectively, in the current application scenario, with $u(q)$ being the sum of the weighted constituents of q. In both cases, the result of (2) has to be normalized into the interval $[0, 1]$ (see Definition 5).

The utility function u (the cost function c) induces an *equivalence relation* $\sim_u$ ($\sim_c$) and a preorder $\lesssim_u$ ($\lesssim_c$) on the QoS domain Q:

$$\sim_u =_{\text{DF}} \{(q_1, q_2) \in Q \times Q \mid u(q_1) = u(q_2)\} \tag{3}$$

$$\lesssim_u =_{\text{DF}} \{(q_1, q_2) \in Q \times Q \mid u(q_1) \leq u(q_2)\} \tag{4}$$

In certain scenarios, several QoS values may have the same usefulness according to the utility function u. For instance, a user may not be able to distinguish between 25 and 26 picture frames per second, and therefore assigns the same utility value to both QoS values. For this reason, $\lesssim_u$ is a preorder on Q in general. Based on $\sim_u$ ($\sim_c$), we define u-equivalence (c-equivalence) classes of Q:

$$[x]_u = \{q \in Q \mid q \sim_u x\} \tag{5}$$

These definitions form the basis for consistency criteria of QoS mappings introduced in Sect. 4.

Apart from defining the utility of QoS values, the actual costs are required in order to provide the scope for dynamic adaptation. For instance, it is possible that for QoS values q, q', and q'', $u(q) > u(q') > u(q'')$, while the costs in terms of resources are $c(q') > c(q) > c(q'')$. Assume that q'' is currently provided, and the resource situation improves. In this case, it is certainly better to directly scale to q, omitting q'. This means that although q' has a utility in-between q and q'', it should not be used. This observation can be exploited such that for a given utility, the QoS value with minimum cost is selected. For each u-equivalence class, we keep one representative value with minimum cost (Step 1). Next, we observe that in general, while the utility increases, the cost may decrease. Therefore, some u-equivalence classes become obsolete, as it would be better to skip some QoS values to get even better utility for less cost (Step 2). These ideas are formalized in the following definitions.

To formalize Step 1 (keeping one representative per u-equivalence class with minimum cost), we define the *reduced* QoS domain Q^u by selecting the best element of each u-equivalence class of Q regarding c. Let m be the cardinality of $Q/\sim_u$, the quotient set of Q w.r.t. $\sim_u$, and let $[x]_u^i$ denote the ith element of $Q/\sim_u$ regarding $\lesssim_u$ (ith u-equivalence class). Then,

$$Q^u = \{q_1, \ldots, q_m\} \cap Q', \quad q_i = q \in [x]_u^i \mid \forall y \in [x]_u^i . q \lesssim_c y, \quad 1 \leq i \leq m \tag{6}$$

Q^u contains elements in the specified subset Q' of a QoS domain Q (see Sect. 3.3, (8)) and is totally ordered by $\lesssim_u$.

To formalize Step 2 (discarding of QoS values with higher cost, but less utility), we define the derived QoS domain $Q^{u,c}$ as follows:

$$Q^{u,c} = \{q \in Q^u \mid \forall y \in Q^u . c(q) > c(y) \Rightarrow u(q) > u(y)\} \tag{7}$$

3.3   Specification of Network QoS Requirements

A *QoS requirements specification* captures the concrete QoS requirements on one system layer by defining the set of valid QoS domain values and a QoS scalability value. The specification is used to configure, manage and maintain QoS mechanisms located on each system layer.

Definition 6 (QoS Requirements Specification). *Let Q be a QoS domain and S be a QoS scalability domain. A QoS requirements specification qosReq is defined as a triple (q_{min}, q_{opt}, s), where $q_{min}, q_{opt} \in Q$ and $s \in S$.*

The QoS values q_{min} and q_{opt} specify the set $Q' \subseteq Q$ of valid QoS domain values. To obtain Q' from q_{min} and q_{opt}, the preorder $\precsim_u$ induced by the utility function (see (4)) is applied:

$$Q' = \{q \in Q \mid q_{min} \precsim_u q \precsim_u q_{opt}\} \tag{8}$$

4   QoS Mappings

So far, we have introduced the formalization and specification of network QoS requirements. Such requirements can be specified from different viewpoints, on different levels of abstraction. To relate QoS requirements of different levels, QoS mappings are needed. The reason for that is that QoS management tasks are typically embedded in the communications system, prevalent across layers, hiding complex tasks from the application. This leads to simple QoS specifications on higher system layers, whereas on lower system layers, the complexity increases.

In this section, we will start by identifying several levels of abstraction, and will then formally define mappings between QoS domains and QoS scalability.

4.1   QoS Abstraction Levels

To implement network QoS requirements, QoS mechanisms on several system layers are needed, each with its own viewpoint describing the data flow traversing the (communication) system. We call these different viewpoints *QoS Abstraction Levels*:

1. *User Level:* From the user's point of view, the application is characterized in terms of scenarios, e.g., *surveillance* or *panorama*.
2. *Application Level:* From the user scenarios, the system developer derives the network QoS requirements of the application level. QoS parameters are application-specific, e.g., picture frame rate, or JPEG quality.
3. *Communication Level:* QoS parameters of the communication level characterize the data flow in terms of, e.g., transmission units, transmission periods, transmission delay, delay jitter. On this level, the QoS requirements are still platform-independent.

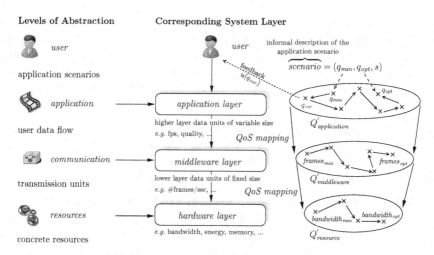

Fig. 1. Abstraction Levels and QoS Mappings

4. *Resource Level:* On resource level, the QoS requirements are specified in terms of concrete hardware parameters, e.g., bandwidth, energy, cpu cycles, memory. This specification is platform-specific.

The abstraction levels are shown in Fig. 1 (left), and associated with a specific system layer (middle). Network QoS requirements are specified on all abstraction layers, expressing the particular viewpoint. To implement the requirements, these viewpoints have to be related. For instance, QoS performance of the video application – stated in terms of resolution, JPEG quality, and picture frames per second – must be related to QoS performance of the communication level – stated in terms of number of data frames per picture frame and period. We introduce two kinds of QoS mappings to formalize this relationship, the QoS domain mapping, and the QoS scalability mapping.

4.2 QoS Domain Mapping

To relate QoS requirements of different abstraction levels, QoS mappings are needed. In this section, we introduce *QoS domain mappings* between a higher layer QoS domain Q_h and a lower layer domain Q_l. This is illustrated in Fig. 1 (right).

Definition 7 (QoS Domain Mapping). *Let Q_h, Q_l be QoS domains on different system layers. A QoS domain mapping $dm : Q_h \rightarrow Q_l$ is a function from a (higher layer) QoS domain Q_h to a (lower layer) QoS domain Q_l. The domain mapping dm may be defined using auxiliary functions as follows:*

$$dm_P : Q_h \rightarrow P_l \ \ (performance \ mapping)$$
$$dm_R : Q_h \rightarrow R_l \ \ (reliability \ mapping)$$
$$dm_G : Q_h \rightarrow G_l \ \ (guarantee \ mapping)$$

In general, QoS mappings are neither injective nor surjective. This means that two different QoS values $q_1, q_2 \in Q_h$ could be mapped to the same $q_l \in Q_l$, and that the values of dm do not span the whole codomain Q_l. For these reasons, the mapping of the scalability requirements specification, especially the utility function, is nontrivial. In the following, we elaborate on the three auxiliary functions.

QoS Performance Mapping. The QoS performance mapping dm_P translates the performance parameters into each other. The performance parameters are system layer and hardware dependent, i.e. parameters like the maximum transfer unit (MTU), the path MTU, or the frame format have to be considered.

Definition 8 (QoS Performance Mapping). *Let P_h, P_l be performance domains on different system layers. A QoS performance mapping $dm : P_h \to P_l$ is a function translating performance values $p_h \in P_h$ into new values $p_l \in P_l = P_{l_1} \times \cdots \times P_{l_n}$. To define dm_P, auxiliary functions $dm_{P_i}(p_h) = p_{l_i}$, $\forall i \leq l_n$ can be used.*

QoS Reliabiliy Mapping. Higher layer transmission units (e.g., picture frames) can be larger than lower layer units and therefore have to be fragmented and reassembled. This, however, complicates the definition of the QoS reliability mapping (see [11]). To illustrate this, consider the example in Fig. 2. On application layer, the variable-size picture frames are fragmented into maximum-size middleware packets. On middleware layer, we assume a loss ratio of 30%. The loss can be caused by packet loss, corrupted, dropped, or late-delivered PDUs. Further, we assume that a loss of even one lower layer packet results in the loss of the entire picture frame. In Figure 2.a, the loss ratio results in a picture frame loss of 33%. If the loss is uniformly distributed (as shown in Fig. 2.b), the same ratio leads to a loss on application layer of 100%.

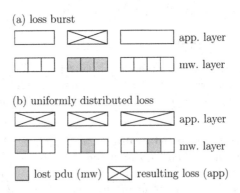

Fig. 2. Upper layer PDUs vs. lower layer PDUs

Notice that a simple description of the lower layer loss or corruption probability is not sufficient for deriving the expected upper layer reliability parameters.

Moreover, uniformly distributed losses may be more adverse than bursty losses. To define the QoS reliability mapping, a segmentation model of the user data is needed. In our case study, this model would introduce probability distributions of picture frame sizes and resulting probability mass functions of the number of needed middleware packets. Further, an error models characterizing the loss and/or corruption process is needed. This error model strongly depends on the chosen base technology. The definition of segmentation and error model are out of the scope of this paper. A treatment of these aspects can be found in [11].

QoS Guarantee Mapping. The function dm_G maps the guarantees specified on one system layer to corresponding guarantees on another. Ideally the guarantees should stay the same during a mapping process. But in exceptional cases, e.g., if the underlying base technology does not support required degree of commitment, an upgrade is permitted. For example, a mapping from *statistical* to *deterministic* guarantees is always feasible, whereas a mapping vice versa could result in a violation of the traffic contract.

4.3   QoS Scalability Mapping

QoS scalability describes the control aspects characterizing the scope for dynamic adaptation of QoS parameters. To apply scaling on different levels of abstraction, a QoS scalability mapping is needed. For consistency, this mapping has to ensure that the utility of QoS values of different abstraction levels that are related by the QoS domain mapping dm is the same. To enforce this consistency condition, we will now define a scalability mapping such that, given a utility function u_h, yields the corresponding utility function u_l. Next, we will introduce a *cost function* that associates costs with QoS values. Based on this cost function, we will finally arrive at a reduced set of QoS values characterizing the actual scope for dynamic adaptation.

In the following definition, let $Q_l^* = \{q_l \in Q_l \mid \exists q_h \in Q_h . dm(q_h) = q_l\}$ denote the set of mapped QoS values, and let $[q_h]_{dm} = \{x \in Q_h \mid x \sim_{dm} q_h\}$, $\sim_{dm} = \{(q_h, q_h') \in Q_h \times Q_h \mid dm(q_h) = dm(q_h')\}$, denote the equivalence classes containing those QoS values q_h that are mapped to the same q_l.

Definition 9 (QoS Scalability Mapping). *Let S_h, S_l be scalability domains on different system layers. A QoS scalability mapping is a set of four mapping functions sm_{Util}, sm_{Cost}, sm_{Up} and sm_{Down}, translating the different scalability domains into each other (see Fig. 3):*

$$sm_{Util} : Util_h \to Util_l; \; \forall u_h \in Util_h . \forall q_l \in Q_l^* . u_l(q_l) =_{DF} u_h(q_h) \mid$$
$$q_h \in Q_h \wedge dm(q_h) = q_l \wedge \forall x \in [q_h]_{dm} . u_h(q_h) \geq u_h(x)$$
$$sm_{Cost} : Cost_l \to Cost_h; \; \forall c_l \in Cost_l . \forall q_h \in Q_h . c_h(q_h) =_{DF} c_l(dm(q_h))$$
$$sm_{Up} : Down_h \to Up_l; \forall x \in Up_h . sm_{Up}(x) =_{DF} x$$
$$sm_{Down} : Down_h \to Down_l; \forall x \in Down_h . sm_{Down}(x) =_{DF} x$$

Some explanations are in order. Let $q_h, q_h' \in Q_h$, $u_h(q_h) > u_h(q_h')$, $dm(q_h) = dm(q_h')$. In other words, although the utility of q_h is higher than that of q_h', they

$$higher\ layer: \quad S_h = Util_h \times Cost_h \times Up_h \times Down_h$$

$$\downarrow sm_{Util} \quad \uparrow sm_{Cost} \quad \downarrow sm_{Up} \quad \downarrow sm_{Down}$$

$$lower\ layer: \quad S_l = Util_l \times Cost_l \times Up_l \times Down_l$$

Fig. 3. Scalability mapping

consume the same amount of resources $q_l = dm(q_h)$. In this case, the utility of q_l is chosen as $u_l(q_l) =_{DF} u_h(q_h)$, i.e. the better value. This means, that when the resources q_l are available, they are exploited as best as possible. This idea is generalized in the definition of the mapping function sm_{Util}, where to each value of $q_l \in Q_l^*$, the maximum utility of all corresponding values $q_h \in Q_h$ is assigned. Note that costs are mapped from lower to higher system layer and that the thresholds for upscaling and downscaling remain unmodified by the QoS scalability mapping.

With the QoS mappings dm, sm and the reduced QoS domain (see (7)), it is possible to define a *scaling function* to be used in system design and implementation. A scaling function $scal_{u,c_l} : Q_l \rightarrow Q^{u,c_h} \cup \{0\}$ maps a lower layer QoS values describing the currently granted network QoS to a higher layer *cost-optimal* QoS value. The function selects the best possible, i.e. the *optimum* QoS value $q \in Q^{u,c_h}$ regarding the utility function u in compliance with the currently granted QoS resources $q_{granted} \in Q_l$, if such an element exists, otherwise 0. For this reason, the cost function c_l has to be mapped to a corresponding higher layer cost function c_h in order to properly reduce Q. The scaling function is defined as follows:

$$scal_{u,c_l}(q_{granted}) = \max{}_u\{q \in Q^{u,sm_{Cost}(c_l)} \mid c_l(dm(q)) \leq c_l(q_{granted})\} \quad (9)$$

whereas the maximum operator max_f for a given set X defines x as an f-maximal element of X iff $x \in X$ and $\forall y \in X : (f(x) \leq f(y) \Rightarrow x = y)$, short $\max_f\{X\}$. The maximum of an empty set is defined as zero, i.e. $\max_f \varnothing = 0$.

5   Case Study *Wireless Video Transmission*

We illustrate the formalization of network QoS by the application *Wireless Video Transmission*, which is used in our remotely controlled airship [12]. The quality of video transmission as perceived by the user depends on picture frame resolution, JPEG compression rate, and picture frame rate. On communication layer, this translates to the number of messages per picture frame, message rate and delay, and finally to channel bandwidth and delay.

In this application (see Fig. 4), we distinguish two usage scenarios, *surveillance* for movement detection and *panorama* for landscape recording. Given the QoS domain Q_{video}, the network QoS requirements $qosReq_{sur}$ and $qosReq_{pan}$ are defined by triples, consisting of optimal and minimal QoS values, and a QoS scalability value. From these triples, the subsets *surveillance* and *panorama* of Q_{video} are determined, applying the preorder $\lesssim_u$ induced by the utility function.

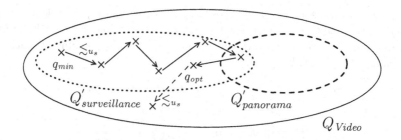

Fig. 4. QoS Requirements Specification

5.1   QoS Domain

A QoS domain Q is specified by defining concrete subdomains performance P, reliability R, and guarantee G. As an example, we define subdomains for the QoS domain Q_{video}, and concrete QoS requirement specifications $qosReq_{sur}$ and $qosReq_{pan}$.

The quality of video transmission depends on picture frame resolution, JPEG compression rate, and picture frame rate. Further QoS parameters are transmission delay and delay jitter, which we omit in the following. For our case study, the concrete domains on application layer are $P_1 = Resolution$, $P_2 = Quality$, $P_3 = FrameRate$, yielding P_{video}.

$$P_{video} = Resolution \times Quality \times FrameRate$$
$$Resolution = \{(320, 240), (480, 360), (640, 480)\}$$
$$Quality = \{25, 50, 75\}$$
$$FrameRate = \{f \in \mathbb{N} \mid 1 \leq f \leq 25\} \tag{10}$$

Typical element of P_{video} is $p = (\, (res_x, res_y), qual, fps\,)$. An appropriate specification of the required performance for surveillance purposes is given by

$$p_{minSur} = ((320, 240), 25, 10), \quad p_{optSur} = ((640, 480), 75, 20)\,. \tag{11}$$

The reliability specification identifies concrete values for loss, period, burstiness, and corruption (see Definition 3). For the video transmission, we define $r_{minSur} = r_{optSur} = (3, 1, 2, 0)$, specifying a permitted data loss of *three* picture frames per *one* second, loss bursts of up to *two* picture frames, and a corruption rate of *zero* percent.

A guarantee specification is given by $g_{minSur} = g_{optSur} = (enhancedBestEffort, 0.8, 8)$. If due to the current resource situation only priority best-effort guarantees can be provided, the priority of 8 enables the wireless video transmission to gain privilege over other applications with lower priorities (< 8). If adequate statistical guarantees are offered, a minimum of 80 percent is required.

5.2   QoS Scalability

To specify QoS scalability, concrete utility functions u_P, u_R, u_G, cost function c, and two thresholds up and $down$ are to be defined. Due to limitations of space, we omit the specification of cost functions, which in principle are similar in style to the utility functions. For the video transmission, we start by defining auxiliary functions for each performance subdomain, normalizing the utility of each parameter to a value in $[0, 1]$:

$$u_{res} : Resolution \rightarrow [0,1], \quad u_{res}(res) \quad = \frac{res_x - 160}{480}$$

$$u_{qual} : Quality \quad \rightarrow [0,1], \quad u_{qual}(qual) = \frac{qual}{75}$$

$$u_{fps} : FrameRate \rightarrow [0,1], \quad u_{fps}(fps) \quad = \frac{fps}{25} \tag{12}$$

Next, we define weights reflecting the relative importance of each subdomain corresponding to the current application scenario. For instance, picture frame rate is the decisive video parameter in case of surveillance, while resolution and quality are of particular importance in the panorama scenario. With the weights $\omega_{res} = 0.1$, $\omega_{qual} = 0.1$, $\omega_{fps} = 0.8$ for surveillance and $\upsilon_{res} = 0.4$, $\upsilon_{qual} = 0.4$, $\upsilon_{fps} = 0.2$ for panorama, we obtain the following performance utility functions:

$$u_{P_{sur}} : P_{video} \rightarrow [0,1], \quad u_{P_{sur}} = 0.1 \cdot u_{res} + 0.1 \cdot u_{qual} + 0.8 \cdot u_{fps}$$

$$u_{P_{pan}} : P_{video} \rightarrow [0,1], \quad u_{P_{pan}} = 0.4 \cdot u_{res} + 0.4 \cdot u_{qual} + 0.2 \cdot u_{fps} \tag{13}$$

Since $r_{min} = r_{opt}$ and $g_{min} = g_{opt}$ in both QoS requirement specifications, the utility subfunctions operating on R and G can be defined as follows:

$$u_G(x) = \begin{cases} 0 & \text{if } x < g_{min} \\ 1 & \text{otherwise} \end{cases}, \quad u_R(x) = \begin{cases} 0 & \text{if } \frac{l}{p} > \frac{l_{min}}{p_{min}} \vee b > b_{min} \vee c > c_{min} \\ 1 & \text{otherwise} \end{cases}$$

$$\tag{14}$$

u_G implies an order on the guarantee domain that can be intuitively given by arranging the values (1) according to their degree of commitment (*bestEffort* to *deterministic*), then (2) according to the statistical component and last (3) according to their priority. The parameters l, p, b, and c in the definition of u_R refer to loss, period, burstiness, and corruption, respectively.

Inserting into (2) yields the following utility functions on Q_{video}:

$$u_{sur}(q) = \min\{u_{P_{sur}}(p), u_R(r), u_G(g)\}, \quad u_{pan}(q) = \min\{u_{P_{pan}}(p), u_R(r), u_G(g)\}$$
$$\tag{15}$$

In both cases, downscaling should be performed if the benefit decreases by 10 percent and upscaling should only be done if the benefit increases by 20 resp. 10 percent, leading to the following complete specification of the scalability requirements:

$$s_{sur} = (u_{sur}, c_{sur}, 0.2, 0.1), \quad s_{pan} = (u_{pan}, c_{pan}, 0.1, 0.1) \tag{16}$$

Based on the utility functions, the QoS values are divided into equivalence classes. Table 1 lists some $u_{P_{sur}}$-equivalence classes of P_{video}. In order to minimize the overall number of classes, the utility has been rounded to two decimal places, resulting in a reduction from 125 to 44 classes.

In Figure 5, the QoS domain is reduced, applying Steps 1 and 2 as defined in Sect. 3.2. The utility function u_{sur} partitions Q_{video} into 45 u_{sur}-equivalence

Table 1. $u_{P_{sur}}$-equivalence classes of P_{Video}

utility	$u_{P_{sur}}$-equivalence class
0.1	((320,240),25,1)
0.13	((480,360),25,1) ((320,240),25,2) ((320,240),50,1)
...	...
0.39	((320,240),25,10) ((640,480),75,6) ... ((480,360),25,9) ((480,360),50,8)
0.42	((640,480),25,9) ((480,360),25,10) ... ((320,240),25,11) ((480,360),75,8)
...	...
0.84	((640,480),25,22) ((640,480),75,20) ... ((480,360),25,23) ((320,240),75,22)
...	...
1.0	((640,480),75,25)

classes (rounded to two decimal places). Since the result of u_R resp. u_G could be 0, the overall number of equivalence classes increases by one (cf. $u_{P_{sur}}$-equivalence classes). If all values of the QoS domain Q are arranged along the x-axis, respecting the preorder $\lesssim_u$, then the resulting graph is a monotonically increasing step function. In addition, a cost function c is depicted in Fig. 5, describing the needed resources on lower system layer. Note that the costs basically increase with the utility, however, within a given u_{sur}-equivalence class, different costs may be associated with QoS values having the same utility. The reduced domain Q^u is formed by selecting the cost-optimal QoS values out of each u_{sur}-equivalence class (see Table 2) and intersecting this selection with Q', leading to $Q^u = \{q_{16}^u, \ldots, q_{39}^u\}$. Step 2 (cf. (7)) induces a further reduction of the overall number of QoS values, since for example q_{37}^u can be omitted due to the higher cost but less utility compared to q_{38}^u. This leads to $Q^{u,c}$ with a total number of 16 QoS values.

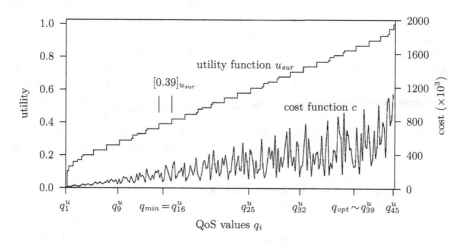

Fig. 5. Reduction of Q

Table 2. Cost-optimal QoS values

utility	QoS value		cost
0.0	q_1^u	$(\,((320, 240), 25, 1),\ r_{minSur},\ < g_{minSur}\,)$	7000
0.1	q_2^u	$(\,((320, 240), 25, 1),\ r_{optSur},\ g_{optSur}\,)$	7000
0.13	q_3^u	$(\,((320, 240), 50, 1),\ r_{optSur},\ g_{optSur}\,)$	11000
...	...	...	...
0.39	$q_{min} = q_{16}^u$	$(\,((320, 240), 25, 10),\ r_{optSur},\ g_{optSur}\,)$	70000
0.42	q_{17}^u	$(\,((320, 240), 25, 11),\ r_{optSur},\ g_{optSur}\,)$	77000
...	...	...	...
0.81	q_{37}^u	$(\,((320, 240), 75, 21),\ r_{optSur},\ g_{optSur}\,)$	315000
0.83	q_{38}^u	$(\,((320, 240), 25, 24),\ r_{optSur},\ g_{optSur}\,)$	168000
0.84	$q_{opt} \sim q_{39}^u$	$(\,((320, 240), 50, 23),\ r_{optSur},\ g_{optSur}\,)$	253000
...	...	...	...
1.0	q_{45}^u	$(\,((640, 480), 75, 25),\ r_{optSur},\ g_{optSur}\,)$	1125000

5.3   QoS Mapping

The QoS performance mapping from the application layer performance domain P_{video} to an underlying middleware layer with $P_{mw} = \#Frames \times Period$ is formally defined as follows:

$$dm_P : P_{video} \to P_{mw}$$
$$dm_P((res_x, res_y), fps, quality) = (\#frames, period), \text{ with}$$
$$dm_{P_1}((res_x, res_y), fps, quality) = \#frames = \left\lceil \frac{(160 \cdot quality + 3000) \cdot (res_x - 160)/160}{payload\ bytes\ per\ frame} \right\rceil$$
$$dm_{P_2}((res_x, res_y), fps, quality) = period = \frac{1}{fps}$$

On application layer, QoS performance is defined by resolution, picture frames per second, and quality. On middleware layer, we have the number of data frames required for the transmission of one picture frame, and the period between two picture frames, i.e. a burst of data frames.

The QoS reliability mapping is to be based on segmentation and error models, which are outside the scope of this paper, and therefore omitted. For the QoS guarantee mapping, we assume that the guarantees specified on higher levels are supported by the base technology, so that the guarantees can be maintained across layers.

The QoS scalability mapping is universally defined in Definition 9, independent from application, system, and hardware. Therefore, no specific mapping is needed.

6   Conclusion and Future Work

In this paper, we have presented a holistic, comprehensive formalization of network QoS requirements, across layers. QoS requirements are specified on each layer by defining a multi-dimensional QoS domain and QoS scalability. Based on these definitions, we have derived preorders on multi-dimensional QoS domains, and have presented criteria to reduce these domains to manageable subsets, sufficient as a starting point for system design and implementation. To formally relate layers, we have introduced two kinds of QoS mappings, called QoS domain mappings and QoS scalability mappings.

All formalizations so far are based on mathematics. For better usability, we intend to define a formal QoS requirement specification language, with intuitive keywords and structuring capabilities. This language should be powerful enough to host the concepts and criteria we have introduced in this paper. Also, the language should be supported by tools that can, for instance, construct QoS mappings as far as they have been defined in this work.

Another step is to specify designs that satisfy given QoS requirement specifications. In particular, there is need for defining a network QoS system architecture, with QoS functionalities such as QoS provision, QoS control, and QoS management on each abstraction layer. We expect that this requires extensions to existing design languages such as UML or SDL. Finally, implementations are to be generated from design models. In our group, we have a complete development process and tool chain for model-driven development. It is a challenging task to extend them to QoS-aware system development.

Acknowledgments. The work presented in this paper was (partially) carried out in the BelAmI (Bilateral German-Hungarian Research Collaboration on Ambient Intelligence Systems) project, funded by German Federal Ministry of Education and Research (BMBF), Fraunhofer-Gesellschaft and the Ministry for Science, Education, Research and Culture (MWWFK) of Rheinland-Pfalz.

References

1. Schmitt, J.: Heterogeneous Network Quality of Service Systems. Kluwer Academic Publishers, Boston (2003) ISBN: 07937410X
2. Jin, J., Nahrstedt, K.: QoS Specification Languages for Distributed Multimedia Applications: A Survey and Taxonomy. IEEE MultiMedia 11(3), 74–87 (2004)
3. Frølund, S., Koistinen, J.: QML: A Language for Quality of Service Specification. Technical Report HPL-98-10, pp. 63, Software Technology Laboratory, Hewlett-Packard Company (1998)
4. Aagedal, J.Ø.: Quality of Service Support in Development of Distributed Systems. PhD thesis, University of Oslo, Oslo, Norway (2001)
5. Vanegas, R., Zinky, J.A., Loyall, J.P., Karr, D., Schantz, R.E., Bakken, D.E.: QuO's Runtime Support for Quality of Service in Distributed Objects. In: Proceedings of the IFIP International Conference on Distributed Systems Platforms and Open Distributed Processing (Middleware'98), The Lake District, UK, pp. 207–222 (1998)
6. Florissi, P.G.S.: QoSME: QoS Management Environment. PhD thesis, Columbia University (1996)
7. Campbell, A.T.: A Quality of Service Architecture. PhD thesis, Computing Department, Lancaster University (1996)
8. Koliver, C., Nahrstedt, K., Farines, J.M., Fraga, J.D.S., Sandri, S.A.: Specification, Mapping and Control for QoS Adaptation. Real.-Time. Systems 23(1-2), 143–174 (2002)

9. Huard, J.F., Lazar, A.A.: On QoS Mapping in Multimedia Networks. In: 21th IEEE Annual International Computer Software and Application Conference (COMPSAC'97), IEEE Computer Society Press, Los Alamitos (1997)

10. Fukuda, K., Wakamiya, N., Murata, M., Miyahara, H.: QoS Mapping between User's Preference and Bandwidth Control for Video Transport. In: 5th International Workshop on Quality of Service (IWQoS'97), Kluwer Academic Publishers, Dordrecht (1997)

11. DaSilva, L.A.: QoS Mapping Along the Protocol Stack: Discussion and Preliminary Results. In: Proceedings of IEEE International Conference on Communications (ICC'00). vol. 2. New Orleans, LA, pp. 713–717 (2000)

12. Webel, C., Fliege, I., Geraldy, A., Gotzhein, R., Krämer, M., Kuhn, T.: Cross-Layer Integration in Ad-Hoc Networks with Enhanced Best-Effort Quality-of-Service Guarantees. In: Proceedings of World Telecommunications Congress (WTC 2006), Budapest, Hungary (2006)

Robustness in Interaction Systems

Mila Majster-Cederbaum and Moritz Martens

University of Mannheim
Mannheim, Germany
mcb@informatik.uni-mannheim.de
mmartens@informatik.uni-mannheim.de

Abstract. We treat the effect of absence/failure of ports or components on properties of component-based systems. We do so in the framework of *interaction systems*, a formalism for component-based systems that strictly separates the issues of local behavior and interaction, for which ideas to establish properties of systems were developed. We propose how to adapt these ideas to analyze how the properties behave under absence or failure of certain components or merely some ports of components. We demonstrate our approach for the properties local and global deadlock-freedom as well as liveness and local progress.

1 Introduction

Component-based design techniques are an important paradigm for mastering design complexity and enhancing reusability. In the object-oriented approach subsystems interact by invoking in their code operations or methods of other subsystems and hence rely on the availability of these subsystems. In contrast to this, components are designed independently from their context of use. They are put together by some kind of gluing mechanism. This view has lead some authors, e.g. [1,2,3], to consider a component as a black box and to concentrate on the combination of components using a syntactic interface description of the components. However, if we want to make assertions about the behavior of a component system, be it functional, temporal or quantitative, knowledge about the components has to be provided.

There have been approaches using different techniques to model the behavior of a component, e.g. Petri-nets [4], process algebra [5,6] or channel-based methods [7]. Except for model-checking, where the complete global state space has to be analyzed, there are not many approaches that investigate generic properties of systems as deadlock-freedom, liveness, etc. In some previous work [5,8] the question of deadlock-freedom is addressed for special cases.

We build here on *interaction systems*, a model for component-based systems that was proposed and discussed by Sifakis et al. in [9,10,11,12] and has been implemented in the PROMETHEUS [13] as well as the BIP tool [14].

The model strictly separates the description of the components from the way they are glued together. Each component i has a *static* description that gives the information about its interface, which is here modeled by a set A_i *of ports*. The

J. Derrick and J. Vain (Eds.): FORTE 2007, LNCS 4574, pp. 325–340, 2007.

dynamics of a component is given by a transition system where the edges are labeled with elements from A_i. Components are glued together via *connectors*. A connector is a set of ports which contains at most one port for every component. The connectors give the information how components cooperate. When each component is ready to perform its port in a connector c then all ports in c can be performed conjointly. The same set of components can be glued together differently (i.e. with other connectors) for different applications. The behavior of the global system *Sys*, i.e. the component system, is fully determined by the static and dynamic description of each component and by the connectors. The model is suitable to investigate important properties of component-based systems, as e.g. local/global deadlock-freedom, local progress and liveness. In [15,16,17] it is shown that deciding deadlock-freedom is PSPACE-hard and deciding liveness is NP-hard for interaction systems. However, as the information about the individual components is maintained in the model it can be exploited to develop sufficient conditions for the desired properties that can be tested in polynomial time [18,19,17]. As violations of safety properties can be expressed as deadlocks broad classes of properties can be handled in this approach.

Here we deal with the question of robustness in interaction systems in the following sense. Consider e.g. an interaction system *Sys* that is deadlock-free, i.e. the system may proceed in every state. Let us now assume that the system has been running for a certain amount of time when a subset A' of the set of all ports becomes unavailable (out of service). This might be because the ports in A' suffer some kind of failure or malfunction but it is also possible to model a situation where certain ports or components are switched off. Can the system *Sys* still proceed in every state? How are other properties affected? Can a component that could previously make progress in the system still make progress? How do we know if a component is live in *Sys* when some ports are out of service, etc?

In a first attempt one might try to solve these problems by simply removing the ports in A' from the description of *Sys* and by then investigating the resulting construct. However, this is not feasible as will be shown later. What we propose to do is to adapt the sufficient conditions and derived algorithms for the desired properties appropriately so that they can be used to answer the questions posed.

Not much work has been done that theoretically investigates the question what effect the failure/absence of parts of a component system has on interesting properties of the system. This is also due to the fact that there is not much work on the theoretical analysis of properties of component-based systems. In [20] component systems are modeled in a way such that they are fault tolerant to a certain extent. This is achieved by requesting that local faulty behavior in a component is detected and handled within the affected component itself. A particular question concerning the classification of safety and liveness in the context of failures has been investigated in [21].

The paper is structured as follows. In Sect. 2 we give a summary of the model of interaction systems. In Sect. 3 we present properties of interaction systems. In Sect. 4 we explain how the sufficient conditions for a desired property can be adapted to the situation where A' is not available. We do so in detail at the hand of global deadlock-freedom of a system and liveness of a set of components. Finally we sketch how local progress and local deadlock-freedom can be treated in a similar way. The paper is summarized by a short conclusion in Sect. 5.

2   Components, Connectors and Interaction Systems

In this section we present the basic definitions for interaction systems that were first introduced in [9]. An interaction system models the behavior of a component-based system for a set K of components. It is the superposition of a static model, called interaction model, that considers a component as a black box with interface description and specifies the "glue code", and the dynamic model, which gives the description of the local behavior of the components. For every component $i \in K$, a set A_i of actions or ports is specified and constitutes the interface. Gluing of components is achieved via so-called connectors. A connector c is a finite nonempty set of ports that contains at most one port for every component in K. It describes a cooperation of those components which have a port in c. When each component is ready to perform its port in c then all ports in c can be performed conjointly. A subset of a connector is called an interaction. We may declare certain interactions to be complete. If an interaction is declared complete it can be performed independently of the environment. It is a design decision which interactions are chosen to be complete. Connectors may be of different sizes and one port may be contained in two or more connectors of different sizes. Thus the model allows for a very flexible way of gluing and consequently of cooperation among components.

Definition 1 (Interaction Model). *Let K be the set of components and A_i be a port set for component $i \in K$ where any two port sets are disjoint. Ports are also referred to as actions. A finite nonempty subset c of $A = \bigcup_{i \in K} A_i$ is called a connector, if it contains at most one port of each component $i \in K$, that is $|c \cap A_i| \leq 1$ for all $i \in K$. A connector set is a set C of connectors that covers all ports and contains only maximal elements:*

$$\text{1. } \bigcup_{c \in C} c = A \qquad \text{2. } c \subseteq c' \Rightarrow c = c' \text{ for all } c, c' \in C.$$

$I(c)$ denotes the set of all nonempty subsets of connector c and is called the set of interactions of c and $I(C) = \bigcup_{c \in C} I(c)$ is the set of interactions of the connector set C. For component i and interaction $\alpha \in I(C)$, we put $i(\alpha) = A_i \cap \alpha$. We say that component i participates in α, if $i(\alpha) \neq \emptyset$. Let $Comp \subseteq I(C)$. We call

$$IM := (C, Comp)$$

an interaction model. The elements of C are also called maximal interactions and those of $Comp$ are called complete interactions.

If not otherwise stated we always assume that $K = \{1, \ldots, n\}$ for some $n \in \mathbb{N}$ or that K is countably infinite. We take up an example from [22].

Example 1. We consider a set of tasks i ($i \in K = \{1, ..., n\}$) that compete for some resource in mutual exclusion. Task i is represented by the component i with port set $A_i = \{activate_i, start_i, resume_i, preempt_i, finish_i, reset_i\}$. The connector set is chosen as $C_{tasks} = \{conn_1^i, conn_2^{ij}, conn_3^{ij}, conn_g | i, j \in K, i \neq j\}$, where

$$conn_1^i := \{activate_i\}$$
$$conn_2^{ij} := \{preempt_i, start_j\}$$
$$conn_3^{ij} := \{resume_i, finish_j\}$$
$$conn_g := \{reset_1, \ldots, reset_n\}$$

and the complete interactions are given by

$$Comp_{tasks} = \{\{start_j\}, \{finish_j\} | i, j \in K \wedge i \neq j\},$$

and $IM_{tasks} := (C_{tasks}, Comp_{tasks})$.

So far we have only described components as black boxes with ports and have specified the possible structure of cooperation in between them. A further level of description of a component characterizes its local behavior. Basically this can be understood as a control of the way in which a component offers its ports. We assume here that this local behavior of every component $i \in K$ is given by a labeled transition system T_i. From the local transition systems and the interaction model we obtain the global behavior of the component-based system.

Definition 2 (Interaction System). *Let K be a set of components with associated port sets $\{A_i\}_{i \in K}$ and $IM = (C, Comp)$ an interaction model for it. Let for each component $i \in K$ a transition system $T_i = (Q_i, A_i, \rightarrow_i, Q_i^0)$ be given where $\rightarrow_i \subseteq Q_i \times A_i \times Q_i$ and $Q_i^0 \subseteq Q_i$ is a non-empty set of initial states. We write $q_i \xrightarrow{a_i}_i q_i'$ instead of $(q_i, a_i, q_i') \in \rightarrow_i$.*

The induced interaction system *is given by $Sys := (IM, \{T_i\}_{i \in K})$ where the global behavior $T = (Q, C \cup Comp, \rightarrow, Q^0)$ is obtained from the local transition systems of the individual components in a straightforward manner:*

1. *The global state space $Q := \prod_{i \in K} Q_i$ is the Cartesian product of the Q_i which we consider to be order independent. We denote states by tuples $q := (q_1, \ldots, q_j, \ldots)$ and call them* (global) states. *Elements of Q_i are called* local states *of component i.*
2. *$Q^0 := \prod_{i \in K} Q_i^0$, the Cartesian product of the local initial states. We call the elements of Q^0* (global) initial states.
3. *$\rightarrow \subseteq Q \times (C \cup Comp) \times Q$, the labeled transition relation for Sys defined by*

$$\forall \alpha \in C \cup Comp \; \forall q, q' \in Q : q = (q_1, \ldots, q_j, \ldots) \xrightarrow{\alpha} q' = (q_1', \ldots, q_j', \ldots) \Leftrightarrow$$

$$\forall i \in K : q_i \xrightarrow{i(\alpha)}_i q_i' \text{ if } i \text{ participates in } \alpha \text{ and } q_i' = q_i \text{ otherwise.}$$

A state $q_i \in Q_i$ is called complete *if there is some interaction $\alpha \in C \cup Comp$ and some q_i' such that $q_i \xrightarrow{\alpha}_i q_i'$. Otherwise it is called* incomplete.

Note that a system may proceed in a global state q if q_i is complete for some $i \in K$. The converse does not hold.

Definition 3 (Enabled). *Let Sys be an interaction system and let $i \in K$ be a component. For $a_i \in A_i$ we set $en(a_i) := \left\{ q_i \in Q_i | \exists q_i' : q_i \xrightarrow{a_i}_i q_i' \right\}$. For $\alpha \in C \cup Comp$ we set $en(\alpha) := \left\{ q \in Q | \exists q' : q \xrightarrow{\alpha} q' \right\}$.*

If $q_i \in en(a_i)$ we say that a_i is enabled in q_i or that q_i offers a_i and analogously for q and α. Given a set of components, an interaction model $IM = (C, Comp)$ and a transition system T_i for each component i the induced interaction system describes the behavior of the composed system. In particular, in a given global state $q = (q_1, \ldots, q_j, \ldots)$ an interaction $\alpha \in C \cup Comp$ may take place provided that each component j participating in α offers $j(\alpha)$ in q_j.

Example 1 continued. The transition system T_i for task i is given in Fig. 1 where every local state is a starting state.

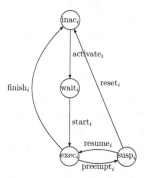

Fig. 1. Transition system of task i

We put $Sys_{tasks} := (IM_{tasks}, \{T_i\}_{i \in K})$.

Remark 1. In what follows, we often mention $Sys = \left(IM, \{T_i\}_{i \in K} \right)$. It is understood that $IM = (C, Comp)$ is an interaction model for the set K of components with port sets A_i and $T_i = \left(Q_i, A_i, \to_i, Q_i^0 \right)$ for $i \in K$ and T are given as above.

3   Properties of Interaction Systems

Properties of systems have been classified into safety- and liveness-properties in [23] and have been investigated in various settings, see for example [24,25]. In Sect. 3.1 we define the properties that we consider here w.r.t. absence/failure of ports. The properties are local/global deadlock-freedom, local progress of a set of components and liveness. These properties of interaction systems have been studied in detail in [22,18,19,17,15]. In Sect. 3.2 we define what we mean by robustness.

Remark 2. From now on we will assume that the local transition systems have the property that every local state offers at least one action. We also identify singleton sets with their element if it is convenient to do so.

3.1   Properties

Definition 4 (Reachable). *Let Sys be an interaction system, $q \in Q$. q is reachable in Sys if there is a sequence $q^0 \overset{\alpha_0}{\to} q^1 \overset{\alpha_1}{\to} \ldots \overset{\alpha_{n-1}}{\to} q$ such that $q^0 \in Q^0$.*

First we take up the notion of local and global deadlock-freedom for interaction systems from [18,22].

Definition 5 (Local/Global Deadlock-Freedom). *Let Sys be an interaction system. Sys is called* globally deadlock-free *if for every reachable state $q \in Q$ there exists $\alpha \in C \cup Comp$ such that $q \in en(\alpha)$.*

A nonempty set $K' \subseteq K$ is in local deadlock *in the reachable global state q if for all $i \in K', a_i \in A_i, \alpha \in C \cup Comp$: $(q_i \in en(a_i) \wedge a_i \in \alpha)$ implies that there is some $j \in K'$ with $j(\alpha) \neq \emptyset \wedge q_j \notin en(j(\alpha))$. We say that Sys is* locally deadlock-free *if there is no reachable state q for which some subset $K' \subseteq K$ is in local deadlock in q.*

A subset K' of components is in local deadlock in a reachable global state q if every component $i \in K'$ needs for each of the actions enabled in q_i the cooperation of some component in $j \in K'$ to proceed which in q_j does not offer the action needed. If $K' = K$ we speak of a global deadlock in q. In such a state the system is not able to proceed. A system that is globally deadlock-free may still contain local deadlocks. As violations of safety properties can be expressed as deadlocks, the investigation of deadlock-freedom deserves particular attention.

Definition 6 (Run). *Let Sys be a globally deadlock-free interaction system, $q \in Q$ a reachable state. A* run *of Sys is an infinite sequence $\sigma = q \overset{\alpha_0}{\to} q^1 \overset{\alpha_1}{\to} q^2 \ldots$ with $q^l \in Q$ for all $l \in \mathbb{N}$.*

Let $i \in K$ be a component and let σ be a run of Sys. If there exists l such that i participates in α_l we say that i participates in σ.

The notions of local progress and liveness of a component have been defined for interaction systems in [22,19].

Definition 7 (Local Progress and Liveness). *Let Sys be a globally deadlock-free interaction system and let $K' \subseteq K$ be a nonempty set of components.*

1. *K' can make* local progress *in Sys if for every reachable state $q \in Q$ there exists a run $\sigma = q \overset{\alpha_0}{\to} q^1 \overset{\alpha_1}{\to} \ldots$ starting in q such that some $i \in K'$ participates in σ.*
2. *K' is* live *in Sys if for every run σ of Sys there is some $i \in K'$ that participates in σ.*

Example 1 continued. In [22] this example was discussed in detail. In particular it was shown that Sys_{tasks} is globally deadlock-free and that every component can make local progress. It was explained that mutual exclusion is achieved under a rule of maximal progress defined in [22].

3.2   Robustness of Properties

Let us now assume a situation where a set $A' \subsetneq A$ of ports may become unavailable in a running system. This might be because the ports in A' suffer some kind of failure or malfunction at a certain point of time but it is also possible to model a situation where certain actions or components are switched off for performance reasons for example. We want to formulate what it means that a property is present when A' becomes unavailable. For this we partition $C \cup Comp$ to separate those interactions that involve A' from those that don't.

Definition 8 (EXCL and WITH). *Let Sys be an interaction system as above and let $A' \subsetneq A$. We define $EXCL(A') := \{\alpha \in C \cup Comp | \alpha \cap A' = \emptyset\}$ and $WITH(A') := \{\alpha \in C \cup Comp | \alpha \cap A' \neq \emptyset\}$*

$EXCL(A')$ denotes the set of all maximal and complete interactions that do not involve any action from A'. Analogously $WITH(A')$ is the set of all maximal and complete interactions that involve some action from A'.

We consider each of the above properties separately w.r.t. absence of A'. Note that it is not possible to just delete the ports of A' from the interaction-system and then check if the definition of a certain property is satisfied by the resulting "system" for two reasons. Firstly, this construct may fail to be an interaction system according to the definition (see Sect. 4), and secondly, the failure of A' may occur at a point of a run where actions from A' may have been previously executed in this run. We discuss deadlock-freedom in terms of robustness which means that we consider a system that is deadlock-free and remains so under failure of A'.

Definition 9 (Robustness of Deadlock-Freedom). *Let Sys be a globally deadlock-free interaction system and let $A' \subsetneq A$ be a non-empty subset of ports. In Sys global deadlock-freedom is robust w.r.t. absence of A' if for every reachable state $q \in Q$ there exists $\alpha \in EXCL(A')$ with $q \in en(\alpha)$.*

Let Sys be locally deadlock-free. In Sys local deadlock-freedom is not robust w.r.t. absence of A', if there is some reachable state q and K' such that for any $i \in K'$, for any a_i which is enabled in q_i and for any $\alpha \in EXCL(A')$ with $a_i \in \alpha$ there is some $j \in K'$ with $j(\alpha) \neq \emptyset$ and $q_j \notin en(j(\alpha))$. Otherwise local deadlock-freedom is said to be robust w.r.t. absence of A'.

Remark 3. In a globally deadlock-free system Sys where $K' \subseteq K$ is live it is not possible that global deadlock-freedom is robust w.r.t. absence of $A' := \bigcup_{i \in K'} A_i$.

If this was the case it would be possible to construct a run not letting any component from K' participate which is not possible. The converse does not hold.

We now consider local progress and liveness of a set of components in a system where global deadlock-freedom is robust w.r.t. absence of A'. First we need to adapt the notion of a run.

Definition 10 (Run without A'). *Let Sys be a globally deadlock-free interaction system and $A' \subsetneq A$. Let global deadlock-freedom in Sys be robust with respect to absence of A'. Let q be a reachable state.*

A run without A' is an infinite sequence $\sigma = q \xrightarrow{\alpha_0} q^1 \xrightarrow{\alpha_1} \dots$ with $q^l \in Q, l \geq 1$, and $\alpha_l \in EXCL(A'), l \geq 0$.

In a system where global deadlock-freedom is robust w.r.t. absence of $A' \subsetneq A$ such runs always exist by a simple induction argument.

Definition 11 (Local Progress and Liveness without A'). *Let Sys be a globally deadlock-free interaction system and let $A' \subsetneq A$. Let global deadlock-freedom in Sys be robust w.r.t. absence of A' and let $K' \subseteq K$ be a nonempty set of components.*

1. *K' can make local progress without participation of A' if for every reachable state $q \in Q$ there exists a run without A' $\sigma = q \xrightarrow{\alpha_0} q^1 \xrightarrow{\alpha_1} \dots$ such that some $i \in K'$ participates in σ.*
2. *K' is live without participation of A' if for every run without A' $\sigma = q \xrightarrow{\alpha_0} q^1 \xrightarrow{\alpha_1} \dots$ there is some $i \in K'$ that participates in σ.*

Note that, in analogy to deadlock-freedom, we could formulate a notion of robustness of the property of local progress. In a system where component i can make local progress we could say that this property is robust w.r.t. absence of $A' \subsetneq A$ if i can make local progress without participation of A'. By contrast it does not make sense to consider robustness of liveness. If a set K' of components is live in a system, then for every run σ there is a component $i \in K'$ that participates in σ. This is true in particular for all runs without A'. Therefore liveness of K' without A' follows from liveness of K' and robustness of deadlock-freedom w.r.t. A'. Nonetheless it is interesting to investigate liveness of K' without participation of $A' \subsetneq A$ because it is possible that certain runs in which K' does not participate infinitely many often are no longer present when the ports from A' are not available any more.

4 Testing Robustness

From our results about the PSPACE-hardness of deciding deadlock-freedom [16] and NP-hardness of deciding liveness of a set of components [15,17] it is clear that deciding robustness of deadlock-freedom w.r.t. $A' \subsetneq A$ respectively liveness without $A' \subsetneq A$ is at least as hard. One way to deal with the complexity issue for properties is to establish conditions that ensure a desired property and can be tested more easily, see for example [22,18,19,26]. In this paper we want to explain how one can systematically use such conditions to obtain results in the case of failure of A'. One could raise the question why we study robustness instead of applying the definitions and results of [22,18,19] to a suitably modified "interaction system". One could try to do so by simply removing the ports in A' from the components of the interaction system under consideration. This approach does not work for two reasons. Firstly, a thus modified construct is in general no longer an interaction system according to our definition. One of the problems that arise can be seen as follows. Consider e.g. the removal of a port a_j of component j. It could be the case that every $c \in C$ containing a_k for some $k \in K$ also contains a_j. On removal of a_j the connectors containing a_j have to be removed as well. But then the condition in Definition 1 that every port of k is contained in some connector $c \in C$ is violated. This condition is however crucial in various places and in particular for correctness of the criterion presented in [22]. Secondly, the failure of A' may occur at a point of a run such that actions from A' may have been previously executed in this run. It would not be possible to model this situation in a system with alphabet $A \backslash A'$.

4.1 Robustness of Deadlock-Freedom

Definition 12 (Incomplete States). *Let Sys be an interaction system and let $i \in K$ be a component. We denote by $inc(i) := \{q_i \in Q_i | q_i \text{ is incomplete}\}$ the set of incomplete states of component i.*

We obtain a criterion for robustness of global deadlock-freedom by adapting the condition of [22] for global deadlock-freedom of an interaction system. This condition involves a graph G_{Sys}. The nonexistence of certain cycles in G_{Sys} guarantees deadlock-freedom. G_{Sys} can be built in time polynomial in $|C \cup Comp|$ and the sum of the sizes of the local transition systems for finite interaction systems.

Definition 13 (Dependency Graph). *Let Sys be an interaction system. The dependency graph for Sys is a labeled directed graph $G_{Sys} := (K, E)$ where the set of nodes is given by the components of Sys, the set of labels is given by $L := L_1 \cup L_2$ with*

$$L_1 := \{c \in C | \nexists \alpha \in Comp : \alpha \subsetneq c\}$$

$$L_2 := \{(c, \alpha) \, | c \in C, \alpha \in Comp \text{ such that } \alpha \subseteq c \wedge \nexists \beta \in Comp : \beta \subsetneq \alpha\},$$

and the set of edges $E \subseteq V \times L \times V$ is defined as follows:

1. *For $c \in L_1 :$ $(i, c, j) \in E \Leftrightarrow j(c) \neq \emptyset \wedge \exists q_i \in en(i(c)) \cap inc(i)$.*
2. *For $(c, \alpha) \in L_2 :$ $(i, (c, \alpha), j) \in E \Leftrightarrow j(\alpha) \neq \emptyset \wedge \exists q_i \in en(i(c)) \cap inc(i)$.*

Further we define the snapshot of G_{Sys} w.r.t. state $q = (q_1, q_2, \ldots)$ as $G_{Sys}(q) := (K, E(q))$ where $E(q) \subseteq E$ such that

1. *For $c \in L_1 :$ $(i, c, j) \in E(q) \Leftrightarrow j(c) \neq \emptyset \wedge q_i \in en(i(c)) \cap inc(i)$.*
2. *For $(c, \alpha) \in L_2 :$ $(i, (c, \alpha), j) \in E(q) \Leftrightarrow j(\alpha) \neq \emptyset \wedge q_i \in en(i(c)) \cap inc(i)$.*

Let $G_f = (K_f, E_f)$ be a subgraph of G_{Sys}. G_f is successor-closed if $K_f \neq \emptyset$ and for all $i \in K_f$ and all edges $e = (i, l, j) \in E$ where $l \in L$ and $j \in K$ we have $e \in E_f$ and $j \in K_f$.

The intuitive meaning of the graph is as follows. An edge (i, c, j) means that i and j participate in c and that there is an incomplete local state $q_i \in Q_i$ such $i(c)$ is enabled in q_i. This means that there could be a global state where i is waiting for j due to the connector c.

Example 1 continued. The dependency graph $G_{Sys_{tasks}}$ is given in Fig. 2 for $n = 3$. For better readability we define $l_{ij} := \left(conn_3^{ij}, \{finish_j\} \right)$ where $conn_3^{ij} = \{resume_i, finish_j\}$. Moreover we omit the label $conn_g$. Therefore all edges without label in Fig. 2 carry the label $conn_g$.

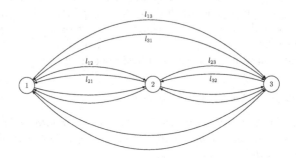

Fig. 2. $G_{Sys_{tasks}}$

Next we define predicates that are evaluated on Q.

Definition 14. *Let Sys be an interaction system.*

1. *For $e = (i, c, j)$ we set $cond(e) := en(i(c)) \wedge \exists x \in c : \neg en(x)$.*
2. *For $e = (i, (c, \alpha), j)$ we set $cond(e) := en(i(c)) \wedge \exists x \in \alpha : \neg en(x)$.*
3. *For a path $p = e_1, \ldots, e_r$ in G_{Sys} we set $cond(p) := \bigwedge_{l=1}^{r} cond(e_l)$.*

For an edge $e = (i, c, j)$, $cond(e)$ is satisfied in state $q = (q_1, \ldots, q_i, \ldots) \in Q$ if $i(c)$ is enabled in q_i but c is not enabled in q because at least one component does not provide the necessary action.

Definition 15. *Let Sys be an interaction system.*

1. *A path p in G_{Sys} is called* critical *if $\left(cond(p) \wedge \bigwedge_{i \in p} inc(i) \right) \not\equiv false$. A path p in $G_{Sys}(q)$ is called* critical *if $\left(cond(p) \wedge \bigwedge_{i \in p} inc(i) \right)(q) = true$. A path that is not critical is called* non-critical.
2. *Let p be a critical cycle in a successor-closed subgraph $G_f = (K_f, E_f)$ of G_{Sys}. p is refutable, if, whenever p lies in $G_f(q)$ where $q_i \in inc(i)$ for all i, there is a non-critical path $\hat{p}$ in $G_f(q)$.*

A path is critical if there is some $q = (q_1, \ldots, q_i, \ldots) \in Q$ such that q_i is incomplete for all components i on the path and $cond(e)$ is satisfied in q for every edge e on the path. If a cycle in G_{Sys} is critical it describes a potential circular waiting relation among components.

Theorem 1. *Let Sys be a globally deadlock-free interaction system as above and let $A' \subsetneq A$ be a set of ports. Global deadlock-freedom is robust in Sys w.r.t. absence of A' if the following conditions hold.*

1. *There is no $a \in A'$ such that $\{a\} \in C \cup Comp$.*
2. *G_{Sys} contains a finite successor-closed subgraph $G_f = (K_f, E_f)$ such that*
   (a) *For all $e = (i, c, j) \in E_f$ we have $c \in EXCL(A')$.*
   (b) *For all $e = (i, (c, \alpha), j) \in E_f$ we have $\alpha \in EXCL(A')$.*
   (c) *Every critical cycle in G_f is refutable.*

The proof can be found in the technical report [27]. Basically, if G_{Sys} contains a successor-closed subgraph G_f as above, for every state $q \in Q$ this subgraph yields $\alpha \in C \cup Comp$ that can be executed in q.

Example 1 continued. It is not hard to see that the conditions of Theorem 1 are satisfied for any $A' \subseteq \{resume_1, \ldots, resume_n\}$ and robustness of global deadlock-freedom w.r.t. absence of A' follows. A situation where $resume_i$ fails for some i can be understood in such a way that the system may function as usual without this action as long as component i does not allow any other component to enter the critical region before it has finished its task. In case it performs a $preempt_i$ action together with some other component, the component i will be excluded from any further participation while the global system continues operating.

4.2   Liveness Without A'

Here we transform the criterion of [19] that ensures liveness of a set of components K' to handle the case of failure of A'.

We define $excl(A', K')$ the set of maximal and complete interactions that neither involve any action from A' nor any component from K'.

Definition 16. *Let $K' \subseteq K$ be a subset of components. Let $excl(A', K') := \{\alpha \in EXCL(A') \mid \forall i \in K' : i(\alpha) = \emptyset\}$.*

Definition 17. *Let Sys be an interaction system as above and let $j \in K$ be a component.*

1. *We define $need_j(A') := \{a_j \in A_j \mid a_j \in \alpha \Rightarrow \alpha \in WITH(A')\}$ the set of ports of j that only occur in maximal or complete interactions also involving A'.*
2. *Let $B_j \subseteq A_j$ be a subset of actions of j. B_j is weakly inevitable w.r.t. A' in T_j if the following two conditions hold:*

   (a) *There is an infinite path in the transition system obtained by canceling all transitions in T_j that are labeled with an action from $need_j(A')$.*
   (b) *On every infinite path in the transition system obtained this way only finitely many transitions labeled with $a_j \in A_j \backslash B_j$ can be performed before some action from B_j must be performed.*

3. *Let $\Lambda \subseteq I(C)$ be a nonempty set of interactions and let $j \in K$ be a compo-*
   nent. We define $\Lambda[j] := A_j \cap \bigcup_{\alpha \in \Lambda} \alpha$ the set of ports of j that participate in
   one of the interactions of Λ.

The set $need_j(A')$ contains exactly those actions of j that can only be performed in the global system if an action from A' is also performed at the same time. Note that it is clear that $(A' \cap A_j) \subseteq need_j(A')$. Further a subset of actions of component j is weakly inevitable w.r.t. A' in T_j if it is possible in T_j to choose an infinite path that does not contain a transition labeled with an action from $need_j(A')$ and if for all such paths there are infinitely many transitions that are labeled with some action from the set in question. The last part of the definition introduces a sort of a projection-operator that yields those actions of component j that participate in one of the interactions in Λ.

In the following we define a graph $G := (K, E)$ for an interaction system with a finite set K of components and finite port sets which is a modification of the graph introduced [19] to establish liveness. Informally, an edge $e = (i, j) \in E$ has the meaning that component j can only participate in finitely many global steps before i has to participate as well.

Definition 18. *Let $G := (K, E)$ with $E := \bigcup_{m=0}^{\infty} E_m$, where:*

$$E_0 := \{(i, j) \,|\, A_j \backslash excl(A', i)[j] \text{ is weakly inevitable w.r.t. } A' \text{ in } T_j\}$$

$$E_{n+1} := \{(i, j) \,|\, A_j \backslash excl(A', R^n(i))[j] \text{ is weakly inevitable w. r. t. } A' \text{ in } T_j\}$$

$$R^n(i) := \{j \,|\, j \text{ is reachable from } i \text{ in } (K, \cup_{m=0}^n E_m)\}$$

Theorem 2. *Let Sys be a globally deadlock-free finite interaction system such that global deadlock-freedom is robust w.r.t. absence of $A' \subsetneq A$. Let $K' \subseteq K$ be a set of components. K' is live without participation of A' in Sys if all components i in $K \backslash K'$ such that T_i contains an infinite path that is only labeled with actions that are not in $need_i(A')$ are reachable from K' in G. The construction of the graph and the reachability analysis can be performed in time polynomial in $|C \cup Comp|$ and the sum of the sizes of the local transition systems.*

The proof can be found in the technical report [27].

Example 2. We model a system consisting of a user u, two service components s_1 and s_2 and two maintenance components m_1 and m_2. The local transition systems of these components are given in Fig. 3. It is understood that the port sets are given implicitly by the transition systems. The initial states are marked by ingoing arrows.

The following connector set defines the allowed cooperations:

$$C := \{\{internal_i\}, \{req_i, service_i\}, \{maint_i, m_j^i\} \,|\, i, j = 1, 2\}$$

Further we define $Comp := \emptyset$. In the global system a state where a global deadlock occurs cannot be reached. It is clear that global deadlock-freedom is robust w.r.t. absence of A_{m_2}.

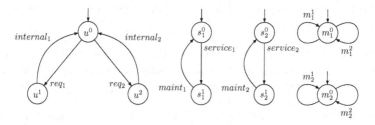

Fig. 3. A system of one user and two servers

Figure 4 depicts part of the graph G for this system. It is clear that the condition of Theorem 2 is satisfied yielding liveness of m_1 without A_{m_2}. This property guarantees, that after each use a service component will undergo maintenance even if the second maintenance component fails.

Fig. 4. G for the user/server example

4.3   Treating Local Progress and Local Deadlock

Here we want to outline the ideas how the criteria for local progress of a component [22] and local deadlock-freedom [18] can be adapted such that they can be used to test whether a component $i \in K$ can make local progress without $A' \subsetneq A$ respectively whether local deadlock-freedom is robust w.r.t. absence of $A' \subsetneq A$.

In [22] a criterion for local progress of a component i was presented. This criterion is based on the dependency graph from Definition 13. The criterion demands the existence of a successor-closed subgraph $G_{f,i}$ as in Theorem 1 such that $i \in G_{f,i}$. Moreover every subset of nodes of $G_{f,i}$ has to be controllable for the notion of controllability defined for subsets $K' \subseteq K$ of components in [22]. Controllability of K' basically ensures that, whenever a global interaction needs participation of components from K', a certain path ending in a state that provides the needed interaction can be chosen in the subsystem defined by K'. This idea can be adapted to test whether a component can make local progress without $A' \subsetneq A$. Again it must be possible to choose $G_{f,i}$ such that no label contains any action from A'. Furthermore the definition of controllability has to be changed such that the path eventually providing the needed interaction can be chosen such that it does not involve any port from A'.

Finally we discuss robustness of local deadlock-freedom. We informally explain how our algorithm from [18] can be adapted such that it can be used to ensure that local deadlock-freedom is robust with respect to absence of $A' \subsetneq A$.

First we will sketch the idea of the algorithm from [18]: in a first step for every three-element subset $\{i, j, k\} \subseteq K$ this algorithm calculates the states q_{ijk} that are reachable in the system consisting of these three components under the assumption that for every connector the actions belonging to components from $K \setminus \{i, j, k\}$ are always available[1]. This amounts to an over-approximation of the projection of the set of the globally reachable states to $\{i, j, k\}$. Then for each of these triple-states the algorithm checks the following necessary condition for a local deadlock. If there is a global state q and a set $D \subseteq K$ such that D is in local deadlock in q there must be $i, j, k \in D$ with $i \neq j \neq k$ such that i is blocked by j and j is blocked by k where a component j blocks a component i in q if i offers an action that occurs in a maximal or complete interaction c that j participates in, but $j(c)$ is not enabled in q_j. If this condition is violated for every such subsystem the algorithm affirms local deadlock-freedom. This idea only needs to be slightly adapted in order to ensure that local deadlock-freedom is robust w.r.t. absence of $A' \subsetneq A$ in a system. The first step of the algorithm is identical to the original algorithm. This reflects our assumption that A' may fail at any point of time which means that to begin with all states that can be reached in the original system can also be reached in the system where A' may fail. The necessary condition for a local deadlock has to be adapted. First it is possible that because of the absence of A' there might be a local state q_i of component i for which all actions that are offered in this state only occur in $\alpha \in WITH(A')$. Such a state should be detected as a locally deadlocked state. The existence of such a state can be checked by investigating all local transition systems and the set $C \cup Comp$. If no such state exists a local deadlock can only occur if there is a set $D \subseteq K$ and a reachable state q such that for every component $i \in D$ the fact that a_i is enabled in q_i and $a_i \in \alpha$ for $\alpha \in EXCL(A')$ implies that there is at least one $j \in D$ such that $j(\alpha)$ is not enabled in q_j. From the second step of the algorithm it follows that there is at least one such α for every $i \in D$. Moreover there must be at least one $i \in D$ such that a_i is enabled in q_i that occurs in $\alpha \in WITH(A')$. If this was not the case then the local deadlock would have been there before the failure of A' which is a contradiction to the assumption. Therefore the necessary condition for a local deadlock amounts to checking whether there are $i, j, k \in K$ and a reachable sub-global state such that k blocks j and j blocks i (this time only interactions from $EXCL(A')$ are considered for possible blockings) and at least one of the three components is affected by the loss of A' in the sense described above. If this condition is never fulfilled the system at hand does not contain any local deadlocks even if the actions from A' are not available any more.

5   Conclusion and Future Work

This work investigates a notion of robustness in interaction systems. The contributions are as follows. 1) We presented notions of robustness of global and local deadlock-freedom w.r.t. failure of a set $A' \subsetneq A$ of ports. Further we introduced

---

[1] We can increase accuracy by considering subsystems of fixed size d.

notions of local progress and liveness without participation of a set $A' \subsetneq A$ of ports. 2) We explained how sufficient conditions for desired properties can be adapted to handle a situation where a set $A' \subsetneq A$ of ports becomes unavailable. We did so in detail for robustness of global deadlock-freedom and for liveness without $A' \subsetneq A$. 3) We informally explained how a similar adaptation is possible for local progress and local deadlock-freedom.

Work is in progress towards treating malfunction of components or ports by introducing probabilities into the framework of interaction systems. In every local state we assign each enabled action a probability that it might fail such that we can make statements such as "with probability p no deadlock will arise" about properties of components. It is clear that this quantitative approach is different from the approach taken here were we want to make assertive statements about the properties in situation where services may fail.

References

1. Arbab, F.: Abstract Behavior Types: A Foundation Model for Components and Their Composition. In: de Boer, F.S., Bonsangue, M.M., Graf, S., de Roever, W.-P. (eds.) FMCO 2002. LNCS, vol. 2852, pp. 33–70. Springer, Heidelberg (2002)
2. Chouali, S., Heisel, M., Souquières, J.: Proving Component Interoperability with B Refinement. In: Proceedings of FACS'05. vol. 160. ENTCS, pp. 157–172 (2006)
3. Moschoyiannis, S., Shields, M.W.: Component-Based Design: Towards Guided Composition. In: Proceedings of ACSD'03, pp. 122–131. IEEE Computer Society, Los Alamitos (2003)
4. Bastide, R., Barboni, E.: Software Components: A Formal Semantics Based on Coloured Petri Nets. In: Proceedings of FACS'05. vol. 160, ENTCS, pp. 57–73 (2006)
5. Allen, R., Garlan, D.: A Formal Basis for Architectural Connection. ACM Trans. Softw. Eng. Methodol. 6(3), 213–249 (1997)
6. Nierstrasz, O., Achermann, F.: A Calculus for Modeling Software Components. In: de Boer, F.S., Bonsangue, M.M., Graf, S., de Roever, W.-P. (eds.) FMCO 2002. LNCS, vol. 2852, pp. 339–360. Springer, Heidelberg (2003)
7. Broy, M.: Towards a Logical Basis of Software Engineering. In: Broy, M., Steinbrüggen, R. (eds.) Calculational System Design, IOS. NATO ASI Series, Series F: Computer and System Sciences, vol. 158, pp. 101–131. Springer, Heidelberg (1999)
8. Baumeister, H., Hacklinger, F., Hennicker, R., Knapp, A., Wirsing, M.: A Component Model for Architectural Programming. In: Proceedings of FACS'05. ENTCS, vol. 160, pp. 75–96. Elsevier, Amsterdam (2006)
9. Gössler, G., Sifakis, J.: Composition for Component-Based Modeling. Sci. Comput. Program. 55(1-3), 161–183 (2005)
10. Sifakis, J.: A Framework for Component-based Construction, SEFM 2005, pp. 293–300 (2005)
11. Gössler, G., Sifakis, J.: Component-Based Construction of Deadlock-Free Systems. In: Pandya, P.K., Radhakrishnan, J. (eds.) FST TCS 2003: Foundations of Software Technology and Theoretical Computer Science. LNCS, vol. 2914, pp. 420–433. Springer, Heidelberg (2003)

12. Gössler, G., Sifakis, J.: Composition for Component-Based Modeling. In: de Boer, F.S., Bonsangue, M.M., Graf, S., de Roever, W.-P. (eds.) FMCO 2002. LNCS, vol. 2852, pp. 443–466. Springer, Heidelberg (2002)

13. Gössler, G.: Prometheus — A Compositional Modeling Tool for Real-Time Systems. In: Proceedings of RT-TOOLS 2001, Technical report 2001-014, Uppsala University, Department of Information Technology (2001)

14. Basu, A., Bozga, M., Sifakis, J.: Modeling Heterogeneous Real-Time Components in BIP. In: Proceedings of SEFM'06, pp. 3–12. IEEE Computer Society Press, Los Alamitos (2006)

15. Martens, M., Minnameier, C., Majster-Cederbaum, M.: Deciding Liveness in Component-Based Systems is NP-hard. Technical report TR-2006-017, Universität Mannheim (2006)

16. Majster-Cederbaum, M., Minnameier, C.: Deriving Complexity Results for Interaction Systems from 1-Safe Petrinets (2007) (Submitted for publication)

17. Majster-Cederbaum, M., Martens, M., Minnameier, C.: Liveness in Interaction Systems (2007) (Submitted for publication)

18. Majster-Cederbaum, M., Martens, M., Minnameier, C.: A Polynomial-Time-Checkable Sufficient Condition for Deadlock-freeness of Component Based Systems. In: van Leeuwen, J., Italiano, G.F., van der Hoek, W., Meinel, C., Sack, H., Plášil, F. (eds.) SOFSEM 2007. LNCS, vol. 4362, pp. 888–899. Springer, Heidelberg (2007)

19. Gössler, G., Graf, S., Majster-Cederbaum, M., Martens, M., Sifakis, J.: An Approach to Modelling and Verification of Component Based Systems. In: van Leeuwen, J., Italiano, G.F., van der Hoek, W., Meinel, C., Sack, H., Plášil, F. (eds.) SOFSEM 2007. LNCS, vol. 4362, pp. 295–308. Springer, Heidelberg (2007)

20. Troubitsyna, E.: Developing Fault-Tolerant Control Systems Composed of Self-Checking Components in the Action Systems Formalism. In: Van, H.D., Liu, Z. (eds.) Proceeding of FACS'03, TR 284, UNU/IIST, pp. 167–186 (2003)

21. Charron-Bost, B., Toueg, S., Basu, A.: Revisiting Safety and Liveness in the Context of Failures. In: Palamidessi, C. (ed.) CONCUR 2000. LNCS, vol. 1877, pp. 552–565. Springer, Heidelberg (2000)

22. Gössler, G., Graf, S., Majster-Cederbaum, M., Martens, M., Sifakis, J.: Ensuring Properties of Interaction Systems. In: Program Analysis and Compilation. LNCS, vol. 4444, pp. 201–224. Springer, Heidelberg (2007)

23. Lamport, L.: Proving the Correctness of Multiprocess Programs. IEEE Trans. Software Eng. 3(2), 125–143 (1977)

24. Berard, B., et al.: Systems and Software Verification. Springer, Heidelberg (1999)

25. Cheng, A., Esparza, J., Palsberg, J.: Complexity Results for 1-Safe Nets. Theoretical Computer Science 147(1-2), 117–136 (1995)

26. Attie, P.C., Chockler, H.: Efficiently Verifiable Conditions for Deadlock-Freedom of Large Concurrent Programs. In: Cousot, R. (ed.) VMCAI 2005. LNCS, vol. 3385, pp. 465–481. Springer, Heidelberg (2005)

27. Majster-Cederbaum, M., Martens, M.: Robustness in Interaction Systems. Technical report TR-2007-004, Universität Mannheim (2007)

Transactional Reduction of Component Compositions

Serge Haddad[1] and Pascal Poizat[2,3]

[1] LAMSADE UMR 7024 CNRS, Université Paris Dauphine, France
`Serge.Haddad@lamsade.dauphine.fr`
[2] IBISC FRE 2873 CNRS, Université d'Évry Val d'Essonne, France
[3] ARLES Project, INRIA Rocquencourt, France
`Pascal.Poizat@inria.fr`

Abstract. Behavioural protocols are beneficial to Component-Based Software Engineering and Service-Oriented Computing as they foster automatic procedures for discovery, composition, composition correctness checking and adaptation. However, resulting composition models (*e.g.*, orchestrations or adaptors) often contain redundant or useless parts yielding the state explosion problem. Mechanisms to reduce the state space of behavioural composition models are therefore required. While reduction techniques are numerous, *e.g.*, in the process algebraic framework, none is suited to compositions where provided/required services correspond to transactions of lower-level individual event based communications. In this article we address this issue through the definition of a dedicated model and reduction techniques. They support transactions and are therefore applicable to service architectures.

1 Introduction

Component-Based Software Engineering (CBSE) postulates that components should be reusable from their interfaces [27]. Usual Interface Description Languages (IDL) address composition issues at the signature (operations) level. However, compositions made up of components compatible at the signature level may still present problems, such as deadlock, due to incompatible protocols [13]. In the last years, the need for taking into account protocol descriptions within component interfaces through the use of *Behavioural IDLs* has emerged as a solution to this issue. BIDLs yield more precise descriptions of components. They support component discovery, composability and substitutability checking (see, *e.g.*, [6,24,3,15]) and, if mismatch is detected, its automatic solving thanks to adaptor generation (see, *e.g.*, [28,26,18,9,14]). With the emergence of Service Oriented Architectures (SOA) [22], behavioural techniques are also valuable, *e.g.*, to discover and compose services [10,4], to verify service orchestrations and choreographies [25,7,17] or to build adaptors [11]. BIDLs usually rely on Labelled Transition Systems (LTS), *i.e.*, finite automata-like models where transition labels correspond to the events exchanged between communicating components or

J. Derrick and J. Vain (Eds.): FORTE 2007, LNCS 4574, pp. 341–357, 2007.
© IFIP International Federation for Information Processing 2007

services. Several works rather use process algebras such as the π-calculus in order to ensure conciseness of behavioural descriptions, yet verification techniques rely on the process algebras operational semantics to obtain LTSs.

These behavioural techniques, grounding on operations such as LTS products, often yield big global (system-level) models for compositions or adaptations, *i.e.*, coordinators or adaptors, which also contain redundant or useless parts. This occurs even when all the basic component models are optimal with respect to some standard criterium, *e.g.*, their number of states. This problem limits the applicability of composition and adaptation techniques, especially in domains where they are to be applied at run-time on low-resources devices, *e.g.*, pervasive computing or ambient intelligence. *Reduction techniques supporting component and service[1] composition and adaptation are therefore required.*

Transactions are important in component composition, *e.g.*, for Web Services [19]. Here, we address transactions from an applicative point of view: to ensure a given high-level service (the transaction), components usually proceed by exchanging several lower-level events. For example, to book a tourism package, service bookTour, a client should give in sequence elements about the country, the hotel requirements, and eventually price constraints. At the same time, to achieve this, the service may itself communicate with external services such as bookHotel, bookPlane and rentACar. The overall complexity of the bookTour service is adequately encapsulated into the (application-level) transaction concept. Transactions are also important in adaptation where they correspond to long-run sets of exchanges one wants to ensure using adaptors. Deadlock-freedom adaptation [14] is closely related to component final states, which in turn enable the definition of transactions in component protocols. *This makes the support for transaction a mandatory feature of behavioural reduction techniques* since in order to consider behaviours equivalent, and thereafter remove duplicates, complete transactions should to be taken into account.

Related Work. The usual techniques to deal with complexity problems are abstraction, on-the-fly, compositional and equivalence techniques. *Abstraction*, *e.g.*, [8], is used to achieve behavioural descriptions at a high level, avoiding details. A problem with abstraction is that it can be difficult to relate abstract results (*e.g.*, a composition scenario or an adaptor) and lower-level models (*e.g.*, a Web Service orchestration in BPEL4WS). *On-the-fly techniques*, *e.g.*, [20], compute global LTSs not before but during a given process. Branches can be discarded if not relevant or not consistent with reference to the process issue. *Compositional techniques* rely on the fact that some properties can lift from the local level (in a component) to the global one (in a composite). However, many interesting properties such as deadlock freedom are not compositional [2]. Various *equivalences or reductions techniques* have been developed in the field of process algebras and reused afterwards for component models (see, *e.g.*, [24,25]). They are based on the hiding of internal or synchronized events (using τ transitions). A first problem is that the ability of two components to synchronize

---

[1] In the sequel, we use *component* as a general term covering both software components and services, *i.e.*, mainly an entity to be composed.

is an important element for the usefulness of a composition. Synchronizations also yield a structuring information supporting the implementation of coordinators or adaptors: to which subcomponent event they do correspond. Hence, they cannot just be hidden and removed.

Moreover, abstraction, on-the-fly, compositional and reduction techniques do not support transactions. Action refinement and related equivalences [5] should do. Yet, action refinement is not suited to component composition or adaptation. This is first because the relations between two connected components cannot be always seen as an unidirectional refinement. Moreover, action refinement relates two components while composition or adaptation may apply on a wider scale. In [15] an approach based on component interaction automata with generic (over a set of events) equivalence and substitutability notions is proposed. However, its absence of specific treatment for component final states may prevent its support for transactions and deadlock-freedom adaptation.

Contribution. The contributions of this article are twofold. First we propose a hierarchical component model with behavioural descriptions and expressive binding mechanisms combining different degrees of synchronization and encapsulation. These binding mechanisms enable one to define composition and adaptation contracts that would not be expressible in other component models such as the Fractal ADL [12] or UML 2.0 component diagrams [21] due to consistency constraints between component interface or port names. Our model supports open systems and enables one to achieve compositionality (composites are components). As discussed in related work, almost all reduction techniques forget the structure of composites and are thus inappropriate when *one does not want to (or cannot) re-design the subcomponents.* So our second contribution are reduction techniques which, on the one hand, take into account the transactional nature of communications between components and, on the other hand, do not modify the internal behaviour of the subcomponents. As a side effect, they also enforce deadlock-freedom adaptation between components that was previously handled by specific algorithms.

Organization. The article is organised as follows. In Section 2, we motivate the need for specific features in hierarchical component models and we informally introduce ours. It is then formalized in Section 3. Section 4 defines transaction-based reductions and corresponding algorithms are given. Finally, we conclude and present perspectives in Section 5.

2   Informal Presentation of the Model

Behaviours. As advocated in the introduction, component models should take into account means to define the behavioural interfaces of components through BIDLs. Let us introduce this part of our model using a simple example. Two components, an email server (SERVER) and an email composer (GUI) are interacting altogether and with the user. Their behavioural interfaces are described by LTSs (Fig. 1) where transition labels denote events that take place at the level of the component, either receptions or emissions. Receptions correspond to provided services and emissions to required ones. LTSs can be obtained either at design-time as a form of behavioural contract for components, but may also be obtained by reverse engineering code.

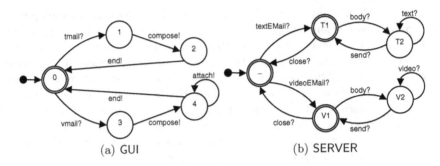

(a) GUI   (b) SERVER

Fig. 1. Mail System – Components (LTS)

At the composer level, one begins with a user opening a new window for a simple email (tmail?) or a video email (vmail?), which requires a special authentication not modelled here for conciseness. Afterwards, different user actions can be performed on the window. To keep concise, we only represent the corresponding triggered emissions in GUI. A text input (triggering compose!) is possibly followed by attachments (triggering attach!) for video email, and the mail is asked to be send (triggering end!). The server works on a session mode and allows, again with authentication, two kind of sessions: one dedicated to emails with text file attachments (textEMail?) and one dedicated to emails with video attachments (videoEMail?). Content is received using body?, attachments with either text? or video?, and the sending request with send?. Sessions are closed with close?. The usual notations are used for initial (black bullet) and final (hollow circles) states.

Architectural descriptions and hierarchical models. Simple components may be either the starting point of an architectural design process or the result of a discovery procedure [4]. In both cases, their composition has then to be described. This can take different forms, it can be directly given by the designer, or it can be computed from a high-level service or property description using conversation integration [4], service aggregation [10] or component adaptation [14]. However, in both cases, what one ends up with is an architectural description where correspondences between required and provided services are given. We advocate that, in order to deal with complexity, a composition model has to be hierarchical and to yield composites that can be related to components, and therefore, once defined, be reused in other higher-level composites. UML 2.0 component diagrams and Fractal ADL are such models and we refer to these for more details on the interests of hierarchical notations.

Expressive inter-component bindings. Even if components are meant to be reused, one may not expect all the components in an architecture have been designed to match perfectly, neither at the signature, nor at the behavioural level [13]. Therefore, it is important to be able to describe *composition/ adaptation mapping contracts* where correspondences between required and provided services may not correspond to name identity (*e.g.*, the end! required service in GUI corresponds to the send? provided service in SERVER), or could even be non one-to-one mappings (*e.g.*, the services related to the opening and closing of sessions provided by SERVER have no counterpart in GUI which is not session-oriented). These are current limitations of the UML 2.0 and Fractal ADL models which impose restrictions on bindings between components interfaces.

The role of transactions and their support. One may expect from a correct adaptation of the SERVER and GUI components that, of course they are able to communicate in spite of their incompatible interfaces, but also that the adaptor ensures the system eventually ends up in a global state where both SERVER and GUI are in a stable (final) state, namely _, T1 or V1, and 0. We base our approach on *implicit transactions* that correspond to this notion, and are sequences of transitions begining in an initial or a final state and ending in a final state. Explicit transactions are a complementary approach that could be supported with additional definitions (sequences of events) to be given for components. In GUI transactions are the sending of a text email and the sending of a video email. In SERVER, transactions correspond to the opening and the closing of sessions, to the creation of a text email and the creation of a video email. LTSs models provide the support for implicit transactions for free, however, to perform reduction more elements are to be taken into account.

The reduction of a composition model is a process that results in removing behaviours from it, mainly removing transitions. One expects from such a process that, in every context, replacing a component by one of its reductions can be achieved without hurt, *e.g.*, without introducing new deadlocks. This corresponds to the substitutability concept, *i.e.*, that all *useful* behaviours are still available for further composition. There is therefore a need for means to define the utility of transitions and sequences of transitions with reference to the available transactions in components. Reduction is usually enabled in composites by hiding and then removing synchronized events, we have seen in the introduction the problems with this. Here for example, this would apply to the synchronizing between end! and send?. Not only this synchronizing is an important information as it ends a global-level transaction (the sending of an email) hence it is a witness of it, but its removal also makes it impossible to implement it afterwards as a communication between end! in GUI and send? in SERVER.

Composition = synchronization + encapsulation. Using the basic components behavioural models and architectural descriptions one may obtain the behaviour of the global system using formal semantics (and hence, tools). However, as we have seen above, the correspondence between services is often confused with the encapsulation level of these services, *i.e.*, synchronized correspondences in-between the subcomponents of a composite are internal (hidden) while ports remaining free may eventually be exported so that the composite interface is defined in terms of its subcomponents ones. This misses distinction in nature between *synchronization* (related to communication) and *encapsulation* (related to observability). We advocate that architectural composition should provide means to describe separately synchronization and encapsulation. We define *binding connectors* (or connectors for short) as an architectural level concept supporting the definition of both synchronization and encapsulation. Synchronization is defined thanks to *internal bindings* which relate a binding connector with at least one subcomponent port. Encapsulation is defined thanks to *external bindings* which relate a binding connector with at most one port of the composite. A component port can be either *synchronizable*, and in such a case it can be synchronized or not, or *observable*. Four different encaspulation levels are possible: inhibition, hiding, observability and synchronizability. Component ports not bound to some connector are inhibited. Connectors not bound to composite ports corresponds to the internal level and events which may be removed by reduction. Connectors bound to synchronizable ports of composites are synchronizable (support for n-ary synchronisation). In between, observability acts as an intermediate encapsulation level and is used to denote internal, yet useful, information for transactions. Binding connectors are a solution to the issues related to transactions and reductions presented above. They propose a good balance between the possible hiding of synchronizations (to enable reduction, yet stressing their possible utility thanks to the observability notion) and the possible retrieval of synchronized events (thanks to the internal bindings information).

Table 1. Architectural Notations

	observable	synchronizable	
		not synchronized	synchronized
inhibited			not applicable
internal			
observable			
synchronizable	forbidden		

In Table 1 we present the graphical notation for our architectural concepts. Binding connectors are denoted with black bullets, observable component ports with white bullets and synchronizable ports with Ts as in Fractal ADL.

The architecture corresponding to the composition/adaptation contract for our example is given in Figure 2. Two ports of GUI are connected to the composite synchronizable ports in order to model the possible action of the user

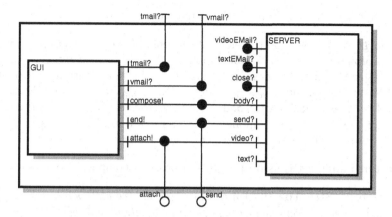

Fig. 2. Mail System – System Architecture

on this component. There are three connectors for internal synchronization between components: one for the body of emails (compose! with body?), one for video attachments (attach! with video?) and one for the sending requests (end! with send?). In order to denote that the two latter ones should not be taken into account when reducing the composite behaviour (*i.e.*, should not be removed), they are made observable (using respectively observable ports attach and send in the composite interface). Three ports of SERVER are synchronizable but not synchronized. This means that in the composition corresponding events may be generated by an adaptor when needed (see [14] for more details on such adaptation contracts). Yet, they are hidden which means that the corresponding events are not observable and may be removed when reduction is performed. To end, one port of SERVER, namely text? is inhibited (not used in the composition/adaptation contract).

3   Formalization of the Model

We focus on events triggered by (basic or composite) components. There are two possible related views of such events: (i) the external view (encapsulation) which distinguishes events depending on the ability to observe them and to synchronize with them, and (ii) the internal view (synchronization) which additionally includes in case of a composite event, the activities of subcomponents and synchronizations between them that have produced the external event. The external view leads to *elementary alphabets* while the internal view leads to *structured alphabets*. Given an event of the latter kind we will obtain an event of the former one by abstraction. The next definitions formalize these concepts.

Definition 1 (Elementary Alphabet). *An elementary alphabet Σ is given by the partition $\Sigma = \Sigma^s \uplus \Sigma^o \uplus \{\tau\}$ where Σ^s represents the synchronizable events, Σ^o represents the observable (and non synchronizable) events and τ represents an internal action. Furthermore, Σ does not include $\bot$ (do-nothing event).*

In the sequel, we use the letter Σ for elementary alphabets.

Example 1. Let us describe the elementary alphabets of our example. The elementary alphabet of the GUI subcomponent, Σ_{GUI} is defined by $\Sigma^o_{\text{GUI}} = \emptyset$ and $\Sigma^s_{\text{GUI}} = \{\text{tmail?}, \text{vmail?}, \text{compose?}, \text{end!}, \text{attach!}\}$. The elementary alphabet of the SERVER subcomponent, Σ_{SERVER} is defined by $\Sigma^o_{\text{SERVER}} = \emptyset$ and $\Sigma^s_{\text{SERVER}} = \{\text{videoEMail?}, \text{textEMail?}, \text{close?}, \text{body?}, \text{send?}, \text{video?}, \text{text?}\}$. The elementary alphabet of the composite component (*i.e.*, its external view), Σ is defined by $\Sigma^s = \{\text{tmail?}, \text{vmail?}\}$ and $\Sigma^o = \{\text{attach}, \text{send}\}$.

A structured alphabet is associated with a possibly composite component.

Definition 2 (Structured Alphabet). *A structured alphabet $A = \Sigma \times \prod_{i \in Id} (A_i \cup \{\bot\})$ is recursively defined by: Σ an elementary alphabet, Id a (possibly empty) finite totally ordered set, and A_i a structured alphabet for every $i \in Id$. To denote an item of A, we use the tuple notation $v = v_0 : \langle v_1, \ldots, v_n \rangle$ with $Id = \{id_1, \ldots, id_n\}$, $v_0 \in \Sigma$ and $\forall 1 \leq i \leq n, v_i \in A_i \cup \{\bot\}$.*

Id represents the set of subcomponent identifiers and the occurrence of $\bot$ in v_i, where v belongs to the structured alphabet, means that subcomponent id_i does not participate to the synchronization denoted by v. Obviously Id is isomorphic to $\{1, \ldots, n\}$. However in the component-based framework, component identifiers are more appropriate. Note that every elementary alphabet can be viewed as a structured one with $Id = \emptyset$. The mapping $v \mapsto v_0$ corresponds to the abstraction related to the external view. Hence, in $v = v_0 : \langle v_1, \ldots, v_n \rangle$, v_0 plays a special role. We therefore introduce $root(v) = v_0$. Similarly, we note $root(A) = \Sigma$. The alphabets A_i are called subalphabets of A. We denote the empty word by ε. Let A be a structured alphabet and $w \in A^*$, the *observable part* of w, denoted $\lceil w \rceil$ is recursively defined by $\lceil \varepsilon \rceil = \varepsilon$, $\forall a \in A$, if $root(a) = \tau$ then $\lceil a \rceil = \varepsilon$ else $\lceil a \rceil = root(a)$ and finally $\lceil ww' \rceil = \lceil w \rceil \lceil w' \rceil$.

In our framework, component behaviours are described with *Labelled Transition Systems*.

Definition 3 (Labelled Transition System). *A Labelled Transition System (LTS) $\mathcal{C} = \langle A, Q, I, F, \rightarrow \rangle$ is defined by: A, a structured alphabet, Q, a finite set of states, $I \subseteq Q$, the subset of initial states, $F \subseteq Q$, the subset of final states, and $\rightarrow \subseteq Q \times A \times Q$ the transition relation. As usual, $(q, a, q') \in \rightarrow$ is also denoted by $q \xrightarrow{a} q'$. The observable language of $\mathcal{C}$, $\mathcal{L}(\mathcal{C})$, is defined as $\mathcal{L}(\mathcal{C}) = \{w \mid \exists \sigma = q_0 \xrightarrow{a_1} q_1 \ldots \xrightarrow{a_m} q_m \text{ s.t. } q_0 \in I, q_m \in F, w = \lceil a_1 \ldots a_m \rceil\}$.*

We now introduce *mapping vectors* and *mapping contracts* which express component bindings in order to build a composite component. Mapping vectors are items of a specific structured alphabet whose root alphabet Σ corresponds to the interface of the composite and whose subalphabet indexed by i corresponds to the interface of component id_i which is (generally) different from the alphabet of this component. A mapping contract is a subset of mapping vectors representing all the possible "local" or "synchronized" events of the composite.

Definition 4 (Mapping Vectors and Mapping Contracts). *Let Id be a set of component identifiers, $\mathcal{S} = \{\mathcal{C}_i\}_{i \in Id}$ be a finite family of LTS, for $i \in Id$, let A_i denote the alphabet of $\mathcal{C}_i$ and let Σ be an alphabet. Then a mapping vector v relative to $\mathcal{S}$ and Σ is an item of the structured alphabet $\Sigma \times \prod_{i \in Id} (root(A_i) \cup \{\bot\})$. Furthermore a mapping vector $v = v_0 : \langle v_1, \ldots, v_n \rangle$ fulfills the following requirements:*

- *$\exists i \neq 0, v_i \notin \Sigma_i^s \cup \{\bot\} \Rightarrow v_0 \notin \Sigma^s \wedge \forall j \notin \{0, i\}, v_j = \bot$;*
- *$\exists i \neq 0, v_i = \tau \Rightarrow v_0 = \tau$.*

A mapping contract $\mathcal{V}$ relative to $\mathcal{S}$ and Σ, is a set of mapping vectors such that every mapping vector v with some $v_i = \tau$ belongs to $\mathcal{V}$.

The requirements on mapping vectors and mapping contracts are consistent with our assumptions about the model (Tab. 1). Non synchronizable events of a subcomponent cannot be synchronized or transformed into a synchronizable event in the composite and internal events of a subcomponent cannot be made observable in the composite. The requirement about mapping contracts means that an internal event in a subcomponent cannot be inhibited in the composite.

The translation from the graphical notation to the formal model is straightforward. There is a mapping vector for each binding connector of the graphic, its root is either given by the composite port bound to this connector when it is present or τ. Each component of the mapping vector is either given by the corresponding component port bound to this connector when it is present or $\bot$.

Example 2. The mapping contract in Figure 2 is defined by: tmail? : $\langle$tmail?, $\bot\rangle$, vmail? : $\langle$vmail?, $\bot\rangle$, τ : $\langle\bot$, videoEMail?$\rangle$, τ : $\langle\bot$, textEMail?$\rangle$, τ : $\langle\bot$, close?$\rangle$, τ : $\langle$compose!, body?$\rangle$, send : $\langle$end!, send?$\rangle$, attach : $\langle$attach!, video?$\rangle$ and the vectors relative to internal events of the subcomponents.

Synchronous product is used to give a formal semantics to composites.

Definition 5 (Synchronized Product of LTS). *Let $\mathcal{S} = \{\mathcal{C}_i\}_{i \in Id}$ be a finite family of LTS, Σ be an alphabet and $\mathcal{V}$ be a mapping contract relative to $\mathcal{S}$ and Σ, then the synchronized product of $\mathcal{S}$ w.r.t. $\mathcal{V}$ is the LTS $\Pi(\mathcal{S}, \mathcal{V}) = \langle A, Q, I, F, \rightarrow \rangle$ where:*

- *$A = \Sigma \times \prod_{i \in Id}(A_i \cup \{\bot\})$, $Q = \prod_{i \in Id} Q_i$, $I = \prod_{i \in Id} I_i$, $F = \prod_{i \in Id} F_i$,*
- *$(q_1, \ldots, q_n) \xrightarrow{v_0 : \langle a_1, \ldots, a_n \rangle} (q'_1, \ldots, q'_n)$ iff $\exists v_0 : \langle v_1, \ldots, v_n \rangle \in \mathcal{V}$ and $\forall i \in Id$,*
  - *$v_i = \bot \Rightarrow a_i = \bot \wedge q'_i = q_i$,*
  - *$v_i \neq \bot \Rightarrow root(a_i) = v_i \wedge q_i \xrightarrow{a_i}_i q'_i$.*

This semantics is supported by the ETS plugin [23]. It can be obtained in an *on-the-fly* way to be more efficient. Thus in practice, we reduce Q to be the set of reachable states from I.

Example 3. The synchronized product of the GUI LTS and the SERVER one is described in Figure 3. For sake of readability, for each (structured) event

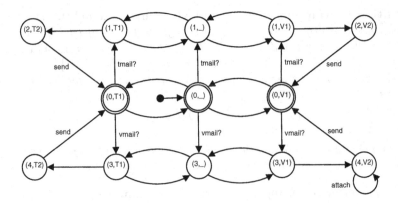

Fig. 3. Mail System – Resulting Adaptor/Coordinator ([13; 27] LTS)

occurring in this LTS, we have only represented its root and when this root is τ we have not represented it. For instance, the arc from $(2, T2)$ to $(0, T1)$ should be labelled send : $\langle$end!, send?$\rangle$ instead of send. The size of this LTS is $[13; 27]$ where 13 is the number of states and 27 is the number of transitions.

4   Transaction-Based Reductions

The goal of this section is the design of algorithms which reduce the LTSs associated with compositions. Due to our assumptions about components, two requirements must be fulfilled by such algorithms: the reduction only proceeds by transition removals (and as a side effect possibly by state removals) and the reduction must preserve the capabilities of the composite w.r.t. its transactions. We introduce first the transaction concept.

Definition 6 (Transactions of an LTS). *Let* $C = \langle A, Q, I, F, \rightarrow \rangle$ *be an LTS, a transaction* $tr = (s, w, s')$ *of* C *is such that* $s \in I \cup F$, $s' \in F$, $w \in (root(A))^*$ *and there exists a witnessing sequence* $\sigma = q_0 \xrightarrow{a_1} q_1 \ldots \xrightarrow{a_m} q_m$ *with* $s = q_0$, $s' = q_m$, $\forall 0 < i < m, q_i \notin F$ *and* $\lceil a_1 \ldots a_m \rceil = w$. *We denote by* $Seq(tr)$ *the set of witnessing sequences of transaction* tr *and by* $\mathcal{L}(s, s') = \{w \mid (s, w, s') \text{ is a transaction}\}$, *the language generated by transactions from* s *to* s'.

Example 4. Below, we exhibit the regular expresssions associated with every transaction language of the Figure 3 LTS:

$$\mathcal{L}((0, \_), (0, \_)) = \mathcal{L}((0, T1), (0, \_)) = \mathcal{L}((0, V1), (0, \_)) = \{\varepsilon\}$$

$$\mathcal{L}((0, \_), (0, T1)) = \mathcal{L}((0, T1), (0, T1)) = \mathcal{L}((0, V1), (0, T1)) = \text{tmail?} \cdot \text{send} + \text{vmail?} \cdot \text{send}$$

$$\mathcal{L}((0, \_), (0, V1)) = \mathcal{L}((0, T1), (0, V1)) = \mathcal{L}((0, V1), (0, V1)) = \text{tmail?} \cdot \text{send} + \text{vmail?} \cdot \text{attach}^* \cdot \text{send}$$

Since we want to preserve the transaction capabilities, we introduce a specific notion of simulation between states, where only initial and final states are considered and the transactions are viewed as atomic transitions.

Algorithm 1. transSimulation

computes the transaction simulation relation between states of C
inputs LTS $C = \langle A, Q, I, F, \rightarrow \rangle$
outputs Relation $\mathcal{R} \subseteq (I \cup F) \times (I \cup F)$
 1: **for all** $(i, j) \in (I \cup F) \times (I \cup F)$ **do** $\mathcal{R}[i, j] :=$ **true end for**
 2: **repeat** // *fixed point algorithm for* $i \sqsubseteq j$
 3:     *end* := **true**
 4:     **for all** $(i, j) \in (I \cup F) \times (I \cup F)$ s.t. $i \neq j \wedge \mathcal{R}[i, j] =$ **true do**
 5:         **for all** $k \in F$ **do**
 6:             // *is* $\mathcal{L}(i, k) \subseteq \bigcup_{k' \ s.t. \ \mathcal{R}[k, k']} \mathcal{L}(j, k')$?
 7:             $K' := \{k' \in F \mid \mathcal{R}[k, k'] = $ **true**$\}$
 8:             $\mathcal{R}[i, j] :=$lgInclusion(transLTS$(C, i, \{k\})$,transLTS(C, j, K'))
 9:             *end* := *end* $\wedge \, \mathcal{R}[i, j]$
10:         **end for**
11:     **end for**
12: **until** *end*
13: **return** $\mathcal{R}$

Definition 7 (Transaction Simulation Relation between States). *Let C and C' be two LTS and let $\mathcal{R}$ be a relation, $\mathcal{R} \subseteq (I \cup F) \times (I' \cup F')$. $\mathcal{R}$ is a transaction simulation relation iff for every pair (q_1, q_1') of $\mathcal{R}$ and every transaction $tr = (q_1, w, q_2)$ of C, there is a transaction $tr' = (q_1', w, q_2')$ of C' with $(q_2, q_2') \in \mathcal{R}$.*

We define $\sqsubseteq$ by $\sqsubseteq = \bigcup \{\mathcal{R} \mid \mathcal{R}$ is a transaction simulation relation$\}$.

In the Figure 3 LTS, any final state simulates the other ones:

$$\forall s, s' \in \{(0, \_), (0, \mathsf{T}1), (0, \mathsf{V}1)\}, s \sqsubseteq s'$$

Based on state simulation, the simulation of an LTS C by an LTS C' is defined. We require that every initial state of C is simulated by an initial state of C'.

Definition 8 (Transaction Simulation between LTS). *Given two LTS C and C', C' simulates C denoted by $C \sqsubseteq C'$ iff $\forall i \in I, \exists i' \in I', i \sqsubseteq i'$.*

We are now a position to define when an LTS C_{red} is a reduction of an LTS C: it is obtained from C by removal of transitions and states and still simulates it.

Definition 9 (Reduction of a LTS). *Given two LTS C and C_{red}, C_{red} is a reduction of C iff: $Q' \subseteq Q$, $I' \subseteq I$, $F' \subseteq F$, $\rightarrow' \subseteq \rightarrow$, and $C \sqsubseteq C_{red}$.*

Let us describe the principles of our reduction algorithm for an LTS C:

1. Algorithm 1 computes the simulation relation between initial and final states of C. It proceeds by iterative refinements of a relation until a fixed point has been reached. The number of iterations of this algorithm is polynomial w.r.t. the size of the LTS and every iteration involves a polynomial number of calls to the language inclusion procedure applied to simple transformations of C.

Algorithm 2. `stateReduction`

---

state-based reduction, constructs reduced LTS C' from LTS C with $C \sqsubseteq C'$
inputs LTS $C = \langle A, Q, I, F, \rightarrow \rangle$
outputs reduced LTS $C' = \langle A', Q', I', F', \rightarrow' \rangle$

1: $\mathcal{R} :=$ `transSimulation`(C)
2: $heap :=$ `getAMaximal`$(\mathcal{R}, I)$
3: $front := heap$
4: **repeat**
5:    extract some s from $front$
6:    $candidates := F \cap$ `reach`(`transLTS`$(C, s, F), \{s\})$
7:    **for all** $f \in candidates \setminus heap$ **do**
8:       $dom := \{f' \in candidates \setminus \{f\} \mid \mathcal{R}(f, f')\}$
9:       **if** `lgInclusion`(`transLTS`$(C, s, \{f\})$,`transLTS`(C, s, dom)) **then**
10:          remove f from $candidates$
11:       **end if**
12:    **end for**
13:    $front := front \cup (candidates \setminus heap)$
14:    $heap := heap \cup candidates$
15: **until** $front = \emptyset$
16: $I' := I \cap heap$; $F' := F \cap heap$
17: $Q' :=$ `reach`$(C, I') \cap$ `coreach`(C, F')
18: $I' := I' \cap Q'$; $F' := F' \cap Q'$; $\rightarrow' := \rightarrow \cap Q' \times A \times Q'$
19: **return** $\langle A, Q', I', F', \rightarrow' \rangle$

---

2. Then, based on the simulation relation between states, Algorithm 2 computes a subset of initial states and a subset of final states such that the LTS, obtained by deleting the other initial and final states, simulates the original one.
3. At last Algorithm 3 examines every transition of the step 2 LTS whose label $\tau : \langle v_1, \ldots, v_n \rangle$ is such that $\exists i, v_i \in \Sigma_i^s$ and removes it if the resulting LTS simulates the current one. The condition on labels ensures the approach is compatible with a grey-box vision of components where components are composed and/or adapted externally *without* modifying the way they internally work (*i.e.*, without removing internal or observable events).

The different steps of our reduction involve calls to `transLTS`. Given an LTS C, an arbitrary state s of C and a subset of final states S, this function produces an LTS C' whose observable language is the set of suffixes of transactions in C, starting from s and ending in S. After every reduction, we "clean" (in linear time) the LTS by eliminating the states that are not reachable from the initial states using the **reach** function and the ones that cannot reach a final state using the **coreach** function. This ensures deadlock-freedom adaptation. The (observable) language inclusion check between two LTS is performed by the `lgInclusion` function. It is the main factor of complexity as language inclusion is a PSPACE-complete problem. However the design of (empirically) efficient procedures is still an active topic of research with significant recent advances [16]. The procedure includes some non deterministic features (for instance the examination order of "τ transitions"). Thus it could be enlarged with heuristics in order to empirically improve its complexity but this is out of the scope of the current paper.

Algorithm 1 is based on a standard refinement procedure for checking simulation or bisimulation. Its specific feature is that it checks inclusion of languages rather than inclusion of set of labels (which entails an increasing of complexity).

Algorithm 2 starts with a maximal set of initial states given by function getAMaximal (line 2). The *heap* variable contains the current set of initial and final states that should be in the reduced LTS whereas the *front* variable contains the subset of *heap* whose "future" has not yet been examined. The main loop (lines 4–15) analyzes the transactions initiated from a state s extracted from *front*. In line 6, it computes the final states reached by such a transaction and stores them in variable *candidates*. For every f, *candidate* not already present in *heap*, it looks whether the language of transactions $\mathcal{L}(s, f)$ is included in the union of the languages of transactions $\mathcal{L}(s, f')$ with f' a candidate simulating f. In the positive case, it removes f from *candidates* (lines 7–12). At the end of loop, the remaining *candidates* not already present in *heap* are added to *heap* and *front*. For the Figure 3 LTS, the algorithm starts with $front = heap = \{(0, \_)\}$. During the first loop, *candidates* is set to $\{(0, \_), (0, \mathsf{T}1), (0, \mathsf{V}1)\}$, and then $(0, \mathsf{T}1)$ is removed. Therefore, at the beginning of the second loop, $front = \{(0, \mathsf{V}1)\}, heap = \{(0, \_), (0, \mathsf{V}1)\}$. During the second loop, *candidates* is set to $\{(0, \_), (0, \mathsf{T}1), (0, \mathsf{V}1)\}$, again $(0, \mathsf{T}1)$ is removed and at the end of second loop, $front = \emptyset, heap = \{(0, \_), (0, \mathsf{V}1)\}$. The resulting LTS is represented on the left-hand side of Figure 4.

Algorithm 3 main loop tries to remove (one by one) transitions which are unobservable at the composite level but are observable at the component level (lines 2–18). When the state reached s' from some state s by such a transition is a final state, then the subset of transaction suffixes that reach s' from s is reduced to the singleton $\{\varepsilon\}$. So, in order to remove the transition, the algorithm checks whether the empty word may be the suffix of a transaction starting in s, ending in a final state simulating s' without using this transition (lines 4–7). Otherwise it performs a similar test for every final state f reached from s (inner loop 10–15) comparing the languages of transaction suffixes. Starting from the LTS on the left-hand side of Figure 4, Algorithm 3 produces the right-hand side LTS. Note that even for such a small example, the reduction is significant w.r.t. the original LTS (*i.e.*, the size is approximatively divided by two).

A comparison with the usual reduction techniques (Fig. 5) demonstrates their inadequacy in our context: they are based on equivalences which are either too strong – bisimulation treats τs as regular transitions hence only removes few of them – or too weak – too many τ transitions are removed (*e.g.*, τ : $\langle$compose!, body?$\rangle$ between states $(1, \mathsf{V}1)$ and $(2, \mathsf{V}2)$) which makes it impossible

Algorithm 3. transReduction

---

transaction reduction, constructs reduced LTS C' from LTS C with $C \sqsubseteq C'$

inputs LTS $C = \langle A, Q, I, F, \rightarrow \rangle$

outputs reduced LTS $C' = \langle A', Q', I', F', \rightarrow' \rangle$

1: $C' := C$
2: **for all** $t = s \xrightarrow{\tau : \langle v_1, \ldots, v_n \rangle} s'$ s.t. $\exists i, v_i \in \Sigma_i^s$ **do**
3:    **if** $s' \in F'$ **then**
4:       $dom := \{f \in F' \mid \mathcal{R}(s', f)\}$; $C'' := C'$; $\rightarrow'' := \rightarrow'' \setminus \{t\}$
5:       **if** lgInclusion(emptyWordLTS(),transLTS(C'', s, dom)) **then**
6:          $\rightarrow' := \rightarrow' \setminus \{t\}$
7:       **end if**
8:    **else**
9:       $del :=$ **true**
10:      **for all** $f' \in F' \cap$ **reach**(transLTS(C', s, F'), $\{s\}$) **do**
11:         $dom := \{d \in F' \mid \mathcal{R}(f', d)\}$; $C'' := C'$; $\rightarrow'' := \rightarrow'' \setminus \{t\}$
12:         **if not** lgInclusion(transLTS($C', s', \{f'\}$),transLTS(C'', s, dom)) **then**
13:            $del :=$ **false**; **break**
14:         **end if**
15:      **end for**
16:      **if** del **then** $\rightarrow' := \rightarrow' \setminus \{t\}$ **endif**
17:   **end if**
18: **end for**
19: $Q' :=$ **reach**(C', I') $\cap$ **coreach**(C', F')
20: $I' := I' \cap Q'$; $F' := F' \cap Q'$; $\rightarrow' := \rightarrow \cap Q' \times A \times Q'$
21: **return** C'

---

afterwards to implement the composition between components. Moreover, acting only at the composition level, these reduction techniques may make it necessary to change the subcomponent protocols in order to implement compositions, while we want to support a non intrusive approach for composition and adaptation.

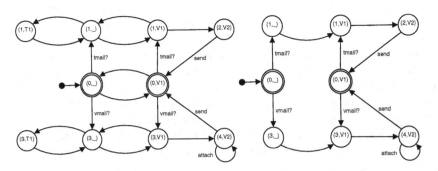

Fig. 4. Mail System – Reduced Adaptor/Coordinator (left: state reduction, [10; 19] LTS; right: transition reduction, [8; 11] LTS])

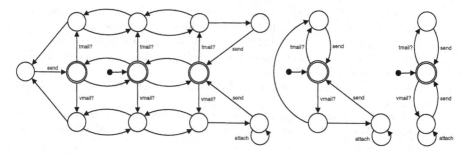

Fig. 5. Mail System – Reduced Adaptor/Coordinator (left: strong bisimulation reduction, [12; 26] LTS; center: weak bisimulation or branching reduction, [4; 7] LTS; right: trace or $\tau * a$ reduction, [3; 5] LTS)

5 Conclusion

In order to build efficient composite components, one needs both efficient basic components (which can be expected from, *e.g.*, Commercial-Off-The-Shelf) and efficient composition or adaptation techniques. This last constraint is related to the basic techniques which underpin the composition or adaptation process, *e.g.*, [10,4,14], but also to efficient reduction procedures for the resulting behavioural models. We have addressed this issue with techniques that take into account the transactional nature of communications between components. Reduction is supported by a component model with expressive binding mechanisms and different levels of synchronization and encapsulation.

A first perspective of this work concerns the integration of our reduction algorithms in a model-based adaptation tool [1] we have developed and assessment on real size case studies from the pervasive computing area. A second perspective is to relate our model-based reduction technique with adaptor implementation issues, mainly taking into account the controllability of events (*e.g.*, viewing emissions as non controllable events). Other perspectives are related to the enhancement of our reduction technique, addressing on-the-fly reduction (reduction while building the compositions or adaptors) and optimizing algorithms thanks to recent developments on language inclusion [16].

References

1. Adaptor, January 2007 distribution (LGPL licence) (2007)
   http://www.ibisc.univ-evry.fr/Members/Poizat/Adaptor
2. Achermann, F., Nierstrasz, O.: A calculus for reasoning about software composition. Theoretical Computer Science 331(2–3), 367–396 (2005)
3. Attiogbé, C., André, P., Ardourel, G.: Checking Component Composability. In: Löwe, W., Südholt, M. (eds.) SC 2006. LNCS, vol. 4089, pp. 18–33. Springer, Heidelberg (2006)

4. Ben Mokhtar, S., Georgantas, N., Issarny, V.: Ad Hoc Composition of User Tasks in Pervasive Computing Environments. In: Gschwind, T., Aßmann, U., Nierstrasz, O. (eds.) SC 2005. LNCS, vol. 3628, pp. 31–46. Springer, Heidelberg (2005)
5. Bergstra, J.A., Ponse, A., Smolka, S.A. (eds.): Handbook of Process Algebra. North-Holland, Elsevier (2001)
6. Bernardo, M., Inverardi, P. (eds.): SFM 2003. LNCS, vol. 2804. Springer, Heidelberg (2003)
7. Betin-Can, A., Bultan, T., Fu, X.: Design for Verification for Asynchronously Communicating Web Services. In: International Conference on World Wide Web, pp. 750–759 (2005)
8. Beyer, D., Henzinger, T., Jhala, R., Majumdar, R.: Checking Memory Safety with Blast. In: Cerioli, M. (ed.) FASE 2005. LNCS, vol. 3442, pp. 2–18. Springer, Heidelberg (2005)
9. Bracciali, A., Brogi, A., Canal, C.: A Formal Approach to Component Adaptation. Journal of Systems and Software 74(1), 45–54 (2005)
10. Brogi, A., Corfini, S., Popescu, R.: Composition-Oriented Service Discovery. In: Gschwind, T., Aßmann, U., Nierstrasz, O. (eds.) SC 2005. LNCS, vol. 3628, pp. 15–30. Springer, Heidelberg (2005)
11. Brogi, A., Popescu, R.: Automated Generation of BPEL Adapters. In: Dan, A., Lamersdorf, W. (eds.) ICSOC 2006. LNCS, vol. 4294, pp. 27–39. Springer, Heidelberg (2006)
12. Bruneton, E., Coupaye, T., Leclercq, M., Quéma, V., Stefani, J.-B.: The Fractal Component Model and Its Support in Java. Software Practice and Experience 36(11-12), 1257–1284 (2006)
13. Canal, C., Murillo, J.M., Poizat, P.: Software Adaptation. L'Object. Special Issue on Coordination and Adaptation Techniques for Software Entities 12(1), 9–31 (2006)
14. Canal, C., Poizat, P., Salaün, G.: Synchronizing Behavioural Mismatch in Software Composition. In: Gorrieri, R., Wehrheim, H. (eds.) FMOODS 2006. LNCS, vol. 4037, pp. 63–77. Springer, Heidelberg (2006)
15. Cerná, I., Vareková, P., Zimmerova, B.: Component Substitutability via Equivalencies of Component-Interaction Automata. In: International Workshop on Formal Aspects of Component Software, Elsevier, Amsterdam (2006)
16. De Wulf, M., Doyen, L., Henzinger, T., Raskin, J.-F.: Antichains: A new algorithm for checking universality of finite automata. In: Ball, T., Jones, R.B. (eds.) CAV 2006. LNCS, vol. 4144, pp. 17–30. Springer, Heidelberg (2006)
17. Foster, H., Uchitel, S., Magee, J., Kramer, J.: LTSA-WS: a tool for Model-Based Verification of Web Service Compositions and Choreography. In: ICSE, pp. 771–774. ACM Press, New York (2006)
18. Inverardi, P., Tivoli, M.: Deadlock Free Software Architectures for COM/DCOM Applications. Journal of Systems and Software 65(3), 173–183 (2003)
19. Little, M.: Transactions and Web Services. Communications of the ACM 46(10), 49–54 (2003)
20. Mateescu, R., Sighireanu, M.: Efficient On-the-Fly Model-Checking for Regular Alternation-Free Mu-Calculus. Science of Computer Programming 46(3), 255–281 (2003)
21. Objet Management Group. Unified Modeling Language: Superstructure. version 2.0, formal/05-07-04 (August 2005)
22. Papazoglou, M.P., Georgakopoulos, D.: Service-Oriented Computing. Communications of the ACM 46(10), 25–28 (2003)

23. Poizat, P.: Eclipse Transition Systems. French National Network for Telecommunications Research (RNRT) STACS Deliverable (2005)
24. Poizat, P., Royer, J.-C., Salaün, G.: Formal Methods for Component Description, Coordination and Adaptation. In: International Workshop on Coordination and Adaptation Techniques for Software Entities at ECOOP, pp. 89–100 (2004)
25. Salaün, G., Bordeaux, L., Schaerf, M.: Describing and Reasoning on Web Services using Process Algebra. International Journal of Business Process Integration and Management 1(2), 116–128 (2006)
26. Schmidt, H.W., Reussner, R.H.: Generating Adapters for Concurrent Component Protocol Synchronization. In: FMOODS, pp. 213–229 (2002)
27. Szyperski, C.: Component Software: Beyond Object-Oriented Programming. Addison-Wesley, Reading (1998)
28. Yellin, D.M., Strom, R.E.: Protocol Specifications and Components Adaptors. ACM Transactions on Programming Languages and Systems 19(2), 292–333 (1997)

Specifying and Composing Interaction Protocols for Service-Oriented System Modelling*

João Abreu[1], Laura Bocchi[1], José Luiz Fiadeiro[1], and Antónia Lopes[2]

[1] Department of Computer Science, University of Leicester
University Road, Leicester LE1 7RH, UK
{abreu,bocchi,jose}@mcs.le.ac.uk
[2] Department of Informatics, Faculty of Sciences, University of Lisbon
Campo Grande, 1749-016 Lisboa, Portugal
mal@di.fc.ul.pt

Abstract. We present and discuss a formal, high-level approach to the specification and composition of interaction protocols for service-oriented systems. This work is being developed within the SENSORIA project as part of a language and formal framework supporting the modelling of complex services at the business level, i.e. independent of the underlying platform and the languages in which services are programmed and deployed. Our approach is based on a novel language and logic of interactions, and a mathematical semantics of composition based on graphs. We illustrate our approach using a case study provided by Telecom Italia, one of our industrial partners in the project.

1 Introduction

SENSORIA – an IST-FET Integrated Project on *Software Engineering for Service-Oriented Overlay Computers* – is defining a formal framework for modelling service-oriented systems in a broad sense that encompasses and generalises the methods and techniques that are either available or envisioned for Web Services [1], as well as other platforms such as Grid Computing [9]. One of the strands of the project is the definition of a reference modelling language – SRML – that can address the higher levels of abstraction of "business modelling" by providing modelling primitives that are independent of the languages and the middleware infrastructure over which services are programmed. This includes a mathematical semantics that can support different kinds of analysis and in relation to which techniques for the deployment, publication, discovery and binding of services can be defined and proved to be correct.

In [6], we presented a preliminary account of our approach and the way it relates to the Service Component Architecture (SCA) [13], namely the notion of module that we adopt for describing complex services and support service discovery and composition. An algebraic semantics of SRML modules and module composition can be

---

* This work was partially supported through the IST-2005-16004 Integrated Project *SENSORIA: Software Engineering for Service-Oriented Overlay Computers,* and the Marie-Curie TOK-IAP MTK1-CT-2004-003169 *Leg2Net: From Legacy Systems to Services in the Net.*

J. Derrick and J. Vain (Eds.): FORTE 2007, LNCS 4574, pp. 358–373, 2007.

found in [7]. In this paper, we report in more detail on one of the key ingredients of service description and composition: the interaction protocols that are responsible for interconnecting the different parties that are involved in a composite service. The challenge here is twofold. On the one hand, to provide a formal model that is rich enough to capture the characteristics of interactions that are typical of service-oriented systems. This includes interactions that are 'conversational', i.e. that cannot be characterised by a transition involving only initial and final states. On the other hand, to make the interaction protocols independent of the way the parties involved in them engage in the interactions, for instance the workflows that determine when the parties actually interact. This is important for dynamic, run-time service discovery and binding, and also for reuse.

In Section 2, we discuss and justify the role that, in our approach, we assign to interaction protocols. In Section 3, we present the language that we use for describing and using interaction protocols in the connectors that establish wires between parties of a complex service. Finally, in Section 4, we present an algebraic semantics for interaction protocols. Throughout the paper, we use examples from a case study developed with Telecom Italia, one of our industrial partners in SENSORIA: the "Call and Pay Taxi through SMS" scenario.

2 Modelling Complex Services in SRML

From the more abstract point of view of systems modelling, i.e. once we abstract from the nature of the languages and platforms over which services are deployed, the main challenge raised by service-oriented systems is in the number of autonomic entities involved and the complexity of the interactions within them. That is, the complexity that matters is not so much in the "size" of the code through which such entities are programmed (size is a design time issue) but on the number, intricacy and dynamicity of the interactions in which they will be involved, what in [4] we have called *social complexity*.

This is why it is so important to put the notion of interaction at the centre of research in service-oriented system modelling. This is also why new methods and formal techniques become necessary. For instance, from an algebraic point of view, social complexity raises new challenges in that it does not make sense to see service-oriented systems as being compositions, in an algebraic sense, of simpler components: there is not a notion of whole to which the parts contribute but, rather, a number of autonomic entities that interact with each other through "interaction protocols" that are external to and independent from those entities.

2.1 The Module Structure

In what concerns the definition of a modelling language that can tackle these new challenges, our approach within SENSORIA is based on a notion of module through which we specify complex services and break the complexity of running systems by recognising larger chunks (sub-configurations) that have a meaning in the application domain, i.e. correspond to "business activities". This notion of module, which is inspired by recent work of *Service Component Architecture (SCA)* [13], supports the modelling of composite services as entities whose business logic involves a number of interactions among more elementary service components as well as the invocation of services provided by other parties. As in SCA, interactions are supported on the basis of service interfaces defined in a way that is "independent of the hardware platform, the operating system, hosting middleware and the programming language used to implement the service".

In order to illustrate our approach, we are going to use the *Call and Pay Taxi* service scenario used by Telecom Italia, one of the partners of SENSORIA, within its R&D activities on Parlay X telecommunications web services [1]. This is a complex service that involves different telecommunication services provided by mobile networks and other external parties in order to provide users the ability to call a taxi and pay for the ride by sending SMS's to a specified number (4777 in [1]). The business process enacted by the service consists of the following steps:

- The user sends an SMS to 4777 to ask for a taxi at his/her current location.
- The service retrieves information about the user from *User Profiler*, and its location from *User Locator Service*.
- The service selects a taxi company at the user's location.
- The service uses a *Call Agent* to set up a voice call between the user and the taxi company.
- The service sends the user and taxi driver an SMS with the taxi number and a "call-code" identifying the transaction.
- After the taxi ride, and in order to authorise the payment, the user sends an SMS with the information previously received and the amount to be paid.
- The service sends a charging request to a *Payment Service*.
- The taxi driver and the user receive a notification of the outcome of the payment via another SMS.

In order to model the *Call&PayTaxi* service through a module in SRML, we need to decide which entities of the scenario description are to be represented as internal components – in the sense that they are deployed when the module is instantiated – and which correspond to parties that need to be procured externally at run-time, in which case they are modelled by what we call *external interfaces*.

The module that we propose has the following structure:

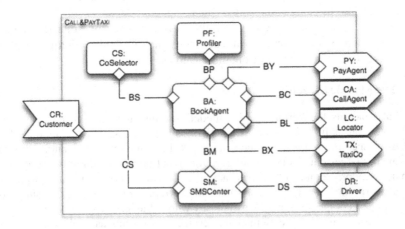

2.2 The Provides-Interface

Every service module in SRML has one distinguished external interface, what we call a *provides*-interface or EX-P for short. The EX-P declares the interactions and protocol that are supported between the service and any service requester. The EX-P of *Call&PayTaxi* is declared to be *CR* of type *Customer* – a business protocol that consists of a set of interactions and a specification of the dependencies that exist between them, including the order in which they are expected to occur. This subsumes what, in [2], are called external specifications i.e., the specification of which message exchange sequences are supported by the service, for example expressed in terms of constraints on the order in which service operations should be invoked.

This is how we specify a business protocol in SRML:

```
BUSINESS PROTOCOL Customer(myNumber:phoneNum) is
INTERACTIONS
    snd callTaxiOUT
    rcv callTaxiIN
        ⌂ text:string
    snd payTaxiOUT
        ⌂ text:string
    rcv payTaxiIN
        ⌂ text:string
BEHAVIOUR
    initiallyEnabled callTaxiOUT⌂?
    P_callTaxiOUT⌂? ensures callTaxiIN⌂!
    P_callTaxiIN⌂! ∧ callTaxiIN.text≠'NA' enables payTaxiOUT⌂?
    P_payTaxiOUT⌂? ensures payTaxiIN⌂!
```

A business protocol declares the interactions maintained by the service under what we call an *interaction signature* (or *signature*, for short). In the example above, we use one-way asynchronous interactions that correspond to the SMS's sent (*OUT*) and received (*IN*) by the customer. Notice that there is no declaration of which components inside the service are co-parties in these interactions; co-parties are identified through wires as discussed below, which also specify the protocol that coordinates the interaction between the two parties.

One-way interactions may have parameters, which are declared under ⌂. In the example above, these correspond to the text of the SMS. The business protocol itself has a parameter: *myNum* of type *phoneNum*. This parameter is instantiated with the phone number of the customer when the actual customer is bound to the *Call&PayTaxi* service.

Further to a signature, a business specification includes the properties of the conversation that any customer can have with the service. The first property declares that, initially (i.e. when the service is bound to the customer), the co-party is ready to accept a call for *callTaxiOUT*. The second property declares that the fact that the co-party has received a call for *callTaxiOUT* ensures that the service will issue a *callTaxiIN*. The third property declares that, if the *callTaxiIN* has been issued with a text other than 'No taxi available', the service is ready to receive a payment *payTaxiOUT*. Finally, the fourth property ensures that, having received a *payTaxiOUT*, the service will issue an acknowledgment *payTaxiIN*. The language in which these properties are expressed uses abbreviations of a temporal logic that we briefly discuss in Section 3.

2.3 Requires-Interfaces

The service provided through *CR* results from a business process that involves a number of internal components that may need to invoke external services specified in the module through what we call *requires*-interfaces (EX-R's for short). The discovery process for any given EX-R takes place at run-time when given declared triggers occur, and returns a service that implements a module whose EX-P matches the EX-R. Through the binding mechanisms of the underlying middleware, the components through which the discovered service is implemented become connected to those of the client service through the interaction protocols specified in the wires. The system thus assembled executes according to the orchestration that results from the assembly.

The external parties defined in our example are:

- The user locator *LC*.
- The call agent *CA* responsible for establishing phone calls.
- The payment agent *PY*.
- The taxi driver *DR*.
- The taxi company *TX*.

The specification of an EX-R is given by a business protocol much in the same way as for the provides-interface. As an example, consider the conversation with the taxi company *TX*:

```
BUSINESS PROTOCOL TaxiCo is

   INTERACTIONS
      r&s contactCompany
         ⌂ userNum:phoneNum, language:lang
         ⊠ taxiNum:reference, callCode:reference,
            driverNum:phoneNum
      snd requestCall
         ⌂ operatorNum

   BEHAVIOUR
      initiallyEnabled contactCompany⌂?
      P_contactCompany⌂? ensures requestCall⌂!
```

We use a two-way interaction – *contactCompany* of type **r&s** – which means that the taxi company is required to be able to engage in an interaction that is initiated by the co-party and issues a reply. The parameters of the reply event are declared under ⊠; in our case, they consist of the taxi number, a code, and the phone number of the driver. The signature of this business protocol also includes a one-way interaction of type **snd**: the taxi company is required to request a phone call with the customer.

The properties required of the taxi company are as follows: when bound to the module, this external service should be ready to accept the event *contactCompany⌂?*, after which it is required to issue a *requestCall*.

2.4 Service Components

A component in SRML corresponds to a resource that is used internally in the sense that it is not visible to whatever client becomes bound through the EX-P. Such resources are tightly bound inside the implementations of the module; they can be web-services, Java components, interfaces to databases, legacy systems, and so on.

The internal components that we decided to include are:

- A user profiler *PF*, which can be seen to correspond to a database of users owned and managed by the company providing the *Call&PayTaxi* service.
- The SMS centre *SM*, which is made available via a fixed phone number – 4777 in the case at hand.
- A component *BA* of type *BookAgent* that is responsible for orchestrating the interactions between all the elements of the module.
- The company selector *CS* that is used by *BA* to choose the most suitable taxi company for a given location and language.

Notice that, in SRML, the orchestration of the module is not necessarily delegated to a single internal component. The overall workflow of the business process emerges from the interconnections between the components of the module as captured through the interaction protocols of the wires that connect them.

Service components are specified through what we call *business roles*. These include a signature as for business protocols but, instead of a set of properties, we specify a transition system that captures the execution pattern of the component; we refer to this pattern as the *orchestration* of the component. For instance, consider the business role that models the SMS centre:

```
BUSINESS ROLE SMSCentre(serviceNum:phoneNum) is
    INTERACTIONS
        snd sendSMS[k:int]
            ⌂ origin:phoneNum, destination:phoneNum, text:string
        rcv receiveSMS[k:int]
            ⌂ origin:phoneNum, destination:phoneNum, text:string
        snd forwardIN[k:int]
            ⌂ origin:phoneNum, text:string
        rcv forwardOUT[k:int]
            ⌂ destination:phoneNum, text:string
    ORCHESTRATION
        transition inForward
          | triggeredBy receiveSMS[i]⌂?
          | guardedBy receiveSMS[i].destination=serviceNum
          | sends forwardIN[i]⌂!
          |   ∧ forwardIN[i].origin=receiveSMS[i].origin
          |   ∧ forwardIN[i].text=receiveSMS[i].text
        transition outForward
          | triggeredBy forwardOUT[i]⌂?
          | sends sendSMS[i]⌂!
          |   ∧ sendSMS[i].origin=forwardOUT[i].origin
          |   ∧ sendSMS[i].destination=serviceNum
          |   ∧ sendSMS[i].text=forwardOUT[i].text
```

In this example, interactions have *key*-parameters in addition to the normal ones. This allows us to handle occurrences of multiple interactions of the same type; in this case, sending and receiving SMS's. The wires that connect the SMS centre to other parties are responsible for deciding which key parameter is used for handling the relevant interactions. This is discussed in Section 3.

The business role has itself a parameter – *serviceNum* of type *phoneNum*. The idea is to define not one but a family of business roles, each modelling a component that operates a particular SMS service. Because SMS centres handle interactions in a way that is independent of the service number, it makes sense to parameterise their specification. Such parameters are fixed when we need a specific business role in a module; for instance, in *Call&PayTaxi*, we declare *SM:SMSCentre(4777)*, i.e. the component *SM* is of type *SMSCentre(4777)*.

Notice that no relative ordering is specified on the transitions; the orchestration of business roles can be much more complex, precisely to capture the richness of workflows that arise in business modelling [6].

3   The Role of Interaction Protocols in SRML

As mentioned several times in the previous section, we rely on what we call *wires* to establish and coordinate interactions between parties. More concretely, we have seen how components and external parties are modelled without any direct reference to the co-parties involved in the interactions. This is because, on the one hand, we want the interconnections between components and external parties to be established at run-time as a result of service discovery and binding and, on the other hand, we want to promote reuse at design time. Therefore, we treat all names as being local and rely on explicit name bindings to establish which are the peers involved in each interaction.

3.1   The Logic of Interactions

Before explaining how wires are specified in SRML, it is important to make a few remarks about the logic that is being developed for interactions. Our logic is based on $\mu UCTL$, a formalism being developed within SENSORIA for qualitative analysis [11]. This formalism is based on doubly-labelled transition systems which consist of:

- a set Q of states;
- an initial state q_0;
- a set Act of observable events;
- a transition relation $q \xrightarrow{\alpha} q'$ where α is a subset of $Act! \cup Act?$ with $Act! = \{e! \mid e \in Act\}$ and $Act? = \{e? \mid e \in Act\}$;
- a labelling function assigning to every atomic proposition p the set of states in which p is true.

By *e!* we denote the action of the initiating party sending the event *e* and by *e?* the action of its co-party processing it. In SRML, the set *Act* has more structure in that the events are generated from asynchronous interactions according to their type as shown in the figure below. We also allow synchronous interactions but, for simplicity, we do not discuss them in the paper. See [6] instead.

Interactions involve two parties and can be in both directions, i.e. they can be conversational. Interactions are described from the point of view of the party in which they are declared, i.e. "receive" means invocations received by the party and sent by the co-party, and "send" means invocations made by the party. We distinguish several events that can occur during such interactions:

interaction⏁	The event of initiating *interaction*
interaction⊠	The reply-event of *interaction* (**r&s** and **s&r** only)
interaction✓	The commit-event of *interaction* (**r&s** and **s&r** only)
interaction✗	The cancel-event of *interaction* (**r&s** and **s&r** only)
interaction✞	The revoke-event of *interaction* (**r&s** and **s&r** only)

The reply, commit, cancel and revoke events capture the conversational aspects of interactions. They are discussed in more detail in [6] together with the handling of deadlines, pledges and compensations. Being asynchronous, interactions do not require the party that initiates an event to block until the co-party receives it. As discussed in the next sub-section, there is a delay between sending and receiving an event that depends on the wire that connects the two parties. Notice that by *e?* we do not denote the act of *receiving* but of *processing* the event. This is because the co-party may not be in a state in which it can process the event *e*; if that is the case, *e!* occurs but *e?* does not. For instance, in the orchestration of the SMS centre we specified that events *receiveSMS[i]⏁* are only processed when their destination is the number of the SMS service.

Because interactions are asynchronous, the sender never blocks; however, there is no guarantee that the co-party will process an event. This is why it is important to state in the business protocols when the co-party is ready to process the events initiated by the party. For instance, in *Customer* we declared that the service is ready to process *callTaxiOUT⏁*, and that it is ready to process *payTaxiOUT⏁* after sending *callTaxiIN⏁* with a positive reply. If the customer calls these events in other circumstances, there is not guarantee that the service will process them.

The logic *μUCTL* uses the typical minimal fixed point operator based on a strong next operator [11]. In support of modelling, we tend to use abbreviations, as illustrated in the business protocols of Section 2, which can be defined as in [6].

3.2 Connectors

Wires bind the names of the interactions and specify the protocols that coordinate the interactions between two parties. For instance, this is how we declare the wire *CS* that connects the customer *CR* and the SMS centre *SM*:

WIRES

CR Customer(my)		CS		SM SMSCentre(4777)
snd callTaxiOUT	S_1	SendEmptySMS (my,4777)	R_1 i_1 i_2 i_3	rcv receiveSMS[1] origin destination text
rcv callTaxiIN text	R_1 i_1	SendSMS (my,4777)	S_1 i_1 i_2 i_3	snd sendSMS[1] origin destination text
snd payTaxiOUT text	S_1 i_1	SendSMS (my,4777)	R_1 i_1 i_2 i_3	rcv receiveSMS[2] origin destination text
rcv payTaxiIN text	R_1 i_1	SendSMS (my,4777)	S_1 i_1 i_2 i_3	snd sendSMS[2] origin destination text

Every wire is composed of one or more *connectors* each of which corresponds to a row of the table above. In SRML, connectors are specified independently of each other so as to increase reusability at design time. Every connector consists of an interaction protocol and two bindings. As an example, consider the connector:

CR Customer(my)		CS		SM SMSCentre(4777)
snd callTaxiOUT	S_1	SendEmptySMS (my,4777)	R_1 i_1 i_2 i_3	rcv receiveSMS[1] origin destination text

The interaction protocol of this connector is specified as follows:

```
INTERACTION PROTOCOL SendEmptySMS(cn,sn:phoneNum) is
    ROLE A
        snd S₁
    ROLE B
        rcv R₁
            △  i₁:phoneNum
               i₂:phoneNum
               i₃:string
    COORDINATION
        R₁ ≡ S₁
        R₁.i₁=cn
        R₁.i₂=sn
        R₁.i₃=''
```

Just like business roles and protocols, an interaction protocol is specified in terms of a number of interactions. Because interaction protocols establish a relationship between two parties, the interactions in which they are involved are divided in two subsets called *roles* – A and B. The "semantics" of the protocol is provided through a collection of properties – what we call the *interaction glue* – that establish how the interactions are coordinated. This may include routing events and transforming sent data to the format expected by the receiver.

For instance, in the example above, the roles are quite simple: each consists of a single interaction. The properties established by the glue are as follows:

- The first declares that the interactions declared in both roles are identical, i.e. that their corresponding events are the same. More precisely, this is an abbreviation for $R_1! \equiv S_1! \wedge R_1? \equiv S_1?$.

- The other three properties identify the parameters of the interaction of role B: they are all fixed by the parameters of the protocol and the fact that the text message is empty.

In addition, every wire W has an attribute $W.delay$ that determines the maximum delay that can take place in the transmission of events between the parties, i.e. between sending and receiving.

The interaction protocol used in the remaining connectors is quite straightforward:

INTERACTION PROTOCOL SendSMS(cn,sn:phoneNum) **is**

   ROLE A
      snd S_1
          i_1:string
   ROLE B
      rcv R_1
          i_1:phoneNum
             i_2:phoneNum
             i_3:string
   COORDINATION
      $R_1 \equiv S_1$
      $R_1.i_1 = cn$
      $R_1.i_2 = sn$
      $R_1.i_3 = S_1.i_1$

That is, the protocol just copies the text of the message.

In a connector, the interaction protocol is bound to the parties via mappings from its roles to the signatures of the parties, which is indicated in the rows of the table. The advantage of separating the definition of the interaction protocols from their use in the wires is that it promotes reuse.

As another example, consider the following connectors that are part of the wire that connects the booking agent *BA* and the SMS centre *SM*:

BA BookAgent		BM		SM SMSCentre(4777)

snd informCustomer
   driverPhone
   taxiNum
   callCode
   location
	S_1
	i_1
	i_2
	i_3
	i_4
		Internal2SMS	R_1
			i_1
			i_2
				rcv forwardOUT[1]
				   destination
				   text

rcv payTaxi
   amount
   taxiNum
   callCode
	R_2
	i_1
	i_2
	i_3
		SMS2Internal	S_1
			i_1
			i_2
				snd forwardIN[2]
				   origin
				   text

The first connector concerns the SMS that the booking agent needs to send to the customer with information about the taxi. According to the business role *SMSCentre*, *forwardOUT[1]△?* triggers *sendsSMS[1]△!* which we have just seen is the event *callTaxiIN△!* of the customer *CR*. The corresponding business protocol needs to convert the data received from *BA* into a text message that can then be sent to *CR*:

```
INTERACTION PROTOCOL Internal2SMS is
    ROLE A
        snd S₁
            △  i₁:phoneNum
               i₂:reference
               i₃:string
               i₄:geoData
    ROLE B
        rcv R₁
            △  i₁:phoneNum
               i₂:string
    LOCAL
        textify:reference,string,geoData→string
    COORDINATION
        S₁ ≡ R₁
        S₁.i₁=R₁.i₁
        R₁.i₂=textify(S₁.i₂,S₁.i₃,S₁.i₄)
```

The conversion is performed by an operation *textify* that is internal to the interaction protocol in the sense that the implementation of the interaction protocol needs to provide a method call to an object that can perform the operation.

The other connector performs a dual operation: it forwards the SMS received from the customer via *payTaxiIN△!* to the booking agent, for which it needs to parse the text message received from *CR*:

```
INTERACTION PROTOCOL SMS2Internal is
    ROLE A
        snd S₁
            △  i₁:phoneNum
               i₂:text
    ROLE B
        rcv R₁
            △  i₁:moneyValue
               i₂:reference
               i₃:string
    LOCAL
        parseMV:string→moneyValue
        parseRF:string→reference
        parseST:string→string
    COORDINATION
        S₁ ≡ R₁
        R₁.i₁=parseMV(S₁.i₂)
        R₁.i₂=parseRF(S₁.i₂)
        R₁.i₃=parseSR(S₁.i₂)
```

All these examples specify very simple interaction protocols but the formalism is expressive enough to handle more complex connectors, especially through the use of state variables. This is particularly relevant when we are reusing existing component to define the module and we need to interconnect them without changing their code.

3.3 Algebraic Semantics of Connectors

An algebraic formalisation of this notion of module and module composition has been given in [7] from the point of view of a notion of correctness defined based on the theory of institutions [12]. In this section, we explore the algebraic structure of connectors in more detail and in a more general setting that does not require the level of detail that we used in [7].

As motivated in Section 2, interactions constitute the core and the unifying element of the proposed approach to systems modelling: all the models that we work with – business roles, business protocols and interaction protocols – are based on structures of interactions. These structures are organised in a category **SIGN** (of signatures) whose morphisms capture "part-of" relationships, i.e. a morphism $\sigma:S_1 \rightarrow S_2$ formalises the way a signature (structure of interactions) S_1 is part of S_2 up to a possible renaming of the interactions and corresponding parameters. **SIGN** can be proved to be finitely co-complete, which allows us to use colimits to express composition.

The other structure that is important for interaction protocols is that of the glues; because we are working with an institution [12], glues can themselves be organised in a category **IGLU** and a functor **sign:IGLU→SIGN** returns, for every glue, the structure of interactions (signature) that are being coordinated by the protocol. As a consequence, a morphism $\sigma:G_1 \rightarrow G_2$ of glues captures the way G_1 is a sub-protocol of G_2, again up to a possible renaming of the interactions and corresponding parameters. That is, σ identifies the glue that, within G_2, captures the way G_1 coordinates the interactions **sign(G_1)** as a part of **sign(G_2)**. **IGLU** is also a finitely co-complete category, meaning that we can use colimits to compose interaction protocols. Basically, colimits compute unions of specifications. We also know that **sign$_{IGLU}$** is a functor that makes **IGLU** coordinated over **SIGN** in the sense of [3]. We denote by **iglu** its left-adjoint, which returns an "empty" glue, i.e. one that does not introduce any requirements on the way interactions need to be coordinated.

In this formal setting, every interaction protocol P consists of an interaction glue G and two signature morphisms $\pi_A:roleA \rightarrow sign_{IGLU}(G)$ and $\pi_B:roleB \rightarrow sign_{IGLU}(G)$. That is, an interaction protocol is a structured co-span in the sense of [8]:

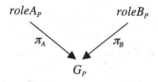

Because a wire interconnects two parties of the module, we need some means of relating the interaction protocols used by the wire with the specifications (business roles or protocols) of the parties. The connection for a given party n and interaction protocol P is characterised by a morphism μ_n that connects one of the roles (A or B) of P and the signature **sign(n)** associated with the node. These morphisms correspond to the mappings defined by the rows of the tables that define the connector, as discussed in Section 3.2.

In this formal setting, a *connector* for a wire $n \leftrightarrow m$ between entities n and m in a module, is a structure $<\mu_n, \pi_A, G, \pi_B, \mu_m>$ where $<\pi_A, G, \pi_B>$ is an interaction protocol P and $<\mu_n, \mu_m>$ are the morphisms that connect the roles of P to the entities n and m. Such a connector defines the following diagram in **SIGN**:

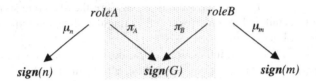

The interaction protocol $<\pi_A, G, \pi_B>$ corresponds to the shadowed part of the diagram. Given this, we take a module M to consist of:

- A graph, i.e. a set *nodes(M)* and a set *wires(M)* of pairs $n \leftrightarrow m$ of nodes
- A distinguished subset of nodes *requires(M)$\subseteq$nodes(M)*.
- At most one distinguished node *provides(M)$\in$nodes(M)\requires(M)*.
- A labelling function $\mathcal{L}$ such that:

  o $\mathcal{L}$*(provides(M))* is a business protocol if *provides(M)* is defined
  o $\mathcal{L}$*(n)* is a business protocol for every $n \in$*requires(M)*
  o $\mathcal{L}$*(n)* is a business role for every other node $n \in$*nodes(M)*
  o $\mathcal{L}$*(n$\leftrightarrow$m)* is a connector $<\mu_n, \pi_A, G, \pi_B, \mu_m>$.

An advantage of this algebraic characterisation is that we can easily explain how interaction protocols can be composed in support for run-time service discovery and binding. If we consider two interaction protocols with a common role:

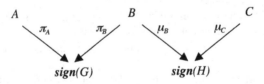

we compute the following pushout in **IGLU**:

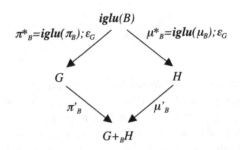

We define the composition of $<\pi_A, G, \pi_B>$ and $<\mu_B, H, \mu_C>$ to be $<\pi_A; sign(\pi'_B), G + {}_B H, \mu_C; sign(\mu'_B)>$.

Consider now module composition. A binding between modules M_n and M_k consists of:

- A node $r \in requires(M_n)$, i.e. one of the requires-interfaces of M_n. Let this node be labelled with a business protocol S_r.
- A morphism $\rho: sign(S_r) \twoheadrightarrow sign(S_p)$ where S_p is the business protocol of *provides(M_k)*, i.e. of the provides-interface of M_k, such that all the properties required by S_r are entailed by those provided by S_r.

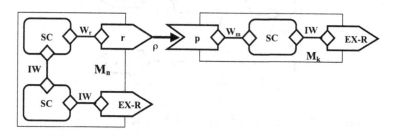

The module M that results from this process is defined by composing the wires W_r and W_k through the morphism ρ. This is achieved through the composition of the three co-spans that correspond to the interaction protocols of the wires W_r and W_k and, between them, the "external wire" established by the morphism ρ. Formally, the glue of this external wire, which is returned by the free functor *iglu*, is "empty" in the sense that the protocol reduces to the syntactic binding established by the morphism.

This composition is defined by the following diagram:

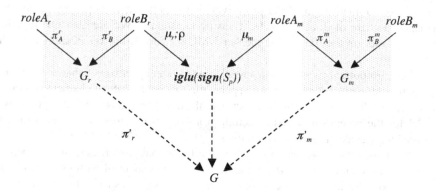

A new connector is defined by the composition of the morphisms that connect the roles to the new interaction glue:

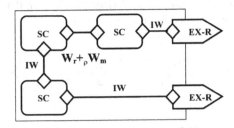

This connector is now used for the wire that results from the composition:

4 Concluding Remarks and Further Work

In this paper, we presented the approach that we are developing within the SENSORIA project for modelling complex services. More precisely, we focused on the way we specify the protocols that are used for coordinating the interactions among the different parties that compose a service. This includes a logic adapted from $\mu UCTL$, a formalism being developed within SENSORIA for supporting qualitative analysis [11]. Our version of the logic uses a richer language of events that results from a conversation model of interactions: interactions are not specified in terms of pre and post-conditions but, rather, on properties that concern transactional behaviour, including pledges, deadlines and compensations. We are currently working on the axiomatisation of the primitives that capture such properties based on a semantic domain of doubly-labelled transition systems. We are also investigating the use of the 'on the fly' model checker UMC for supporting verification and validation [10].

Another important aspect of our model is an algebraic semantics that accounts for interaction protocols as structured co-spans, the full mathematical characterisation of which can be found in [8]. In the paper, we illustrated how this semantics provides a model for the composition of interaction protocols, connectors and wires, which is required for service discovery and binding.

In this paper, we addressed almost only the functional properties of service behaviour. The exception was the *delay* parameter that is associated with every wire. In fact, the composition of wires involves non-functional properties: for instance, we have $(W_r +_\rho W_m).delay = W_r.delay + W_m.delay$ because the external wire corresponding to ρ has no delay – it just binds names. Other non-functional properties are addressed in another report [5], including a constraint-based approach to SLAs.

References

1. Alonso, G., Casati, F., Kuno, H., Machiraju, V.: Web Services. Springer, New York (2004)
2. Baïna, K., Benatallah, B., Casati, F., Toumani, F.: Model-driven web service development. In: Persson, A., Stirna, J. (eds.) CAiSE 2004. LNCS, vol. 3084, pp. 290–306. Springer, Heidelberg (2004)
3. Fiadeiro, J.L.: Categories for Software Engineering. Springer, New York (2004)
4. Fiadeiro, J.L.: Designing for software's social complexity. IEEE Computer 40(1), 34–39 (2007)
5. Fiadeiro, J.L., Lopes, A., Bocchi, L.: The SENSORIA Reference Modelling Language: Primitives for Configuration Management (2006) Available from www.sensoria-ist.eu
6. Fiadeiro, J.L., Lopes, A., Bocchi, L.: A formal approach to service-oriented architecture. In: Bravetti, M., Núñez, M., Zavattaro, G. (eds.) WS-FM 2006. LNCS, vol. 4184, pp. 193–213. Springer, Heidelberg (2006)
7. Fiadeiro, J.L., Lopes, A., Bocchi, L.: Algebraic semantics of service component modules. In: Fiadeiro, J.L., Schobbens, P.Y. (eds.) Algebraic Development Techniques, pp. 37–55. Springer, Heidelberg (2007)
8. Fiadeiro, J.L., Schmitt, V.: Structured co-spans: an algebra of interaction protocols. In: CALCO'07. LNCS. Springer, Berlin, Heidelberg, New York (In print 2007)
9. Foster, I., Kesselman, C. (eds.): The Grid 2: Blueprint for a New Computing Infrastructure. Morgan Kaufmann, San Francisco, CA (2004)
10. Gnesi, S., Mazzanti, F.: On the fly model checking of communicating UML state machines. In: Second ACIS International Conference on Software Engineering Research, Management and Applications (SERA2004), pp. 331–338 (2004)
11. Gnesi, S., Mazzanti, F.: A model checking verification environment for UML Statecharts. In: Proceedings of XLIII Congresso Annuale AICA Comunita' Virtuale dalla Ricerca all'Impresa dalla Formazione al Cittadino. University of Udine – AICA (2005) (paper available from fmt.isti.cnr.it)
12. Goguen, J., Burstall, R.: Institutions: abstract model theory for specification and programming. Journal ACM 39(1), 95–146 (1992)
13. SCA Consortium (2005) Building Systems using a Service Oriented Architecture. Whitepaper available from www-128.ibm.com/developerworks/library/specification/ws-sca/

Author Index

Abreu, João   358

Baresi, Luciano   247
Batth, S.S.   50
Bocchi, Laura   358

Campbell, Colin   112, 128
Cavalli, A.   50
Chae, Junghwa   97
Chao, Cai   81
Counsell, Steve   19

Dan, Haitao   19
Droms, Ralph   211

Ernits, Juhan   112
Evangelista, S.   177

Fan, Rui   211
Ferrari, Gianluigi   66
Fiadeiro, José Luiz   358
Frutos-Escrig, David de   143

Gazagnaire, Thomas   160
Ghezzi, Carlo   247
Gotzhein, Reinhard   309
Graf, Susanne   1
Gregorio-Rodríguez, Carlos   143
Griffeth, Nancy   211
Guanciale, Roberto   66
Guo, Qiang   227

Haddad, Serge   341
He, Fei   247
Hélouët, Loïc   160
Hierons, Robert M.   19
Hongli, Yang   81

Jin, Zhi   296
Jourdan, Guy-Vincent   35

Kalyon, Gabriel   263
Klai, Kais   280

Li, Guangyuan   196
Lopes, Antónia   358
Lynch, Nancy   211

Majster-Cederbaum, Mila   325
Martens, Moritz   325
Massart, Thierry   263
Meuter, Cédric   263
Mu, Kedian   296

Pajault, C.   177
Peng, Yunquan   196
Petrucci, Laure   280
Poizat, Pascal   341
Pradat-Peyre, J.F.   177

Quinton, Sophie   1

Reniers, Michel   280
Rosa-Velardo, Fernando   143

Schulte, Wolfram   128
Spoletini, Paola   247
Strollo, Daniele   66

Tuosto, Emilio   66

Ural, Hasan   35
Uyar, M.Ü.   50

Van Begin, Laurent   263
Veanes, Margus   112, 128
Vieira, E.R.   50

Wang, Shen   35
Webel, Christian   309

Xiangpeng, Zhao   81

Yan, Rongjie   196
Yenigün, Hüsnü   35

Zhang, Wenliang   196
Zongyan, Qiu   81

Lecture Notes in Computer Science

For information about Vols. 1–4453

please contact your bookseller or Springer

Vol. 4600: H. Comon-Lundh, C. Kirchner, H. Kirchner (Eds.), Rewriting, Computation and Proof. XVIII, 273 pages. 2007.

Vol. 4581: A. Petrenko, M. Veanes, J. Tretmans, W. Grieskamp (Eds.), Testing of Software and Communicating Systems. XII, 379 pages. 2007.

Vol. 4574: J. Derrick, J. Vain (Eds.), Formal Techniques for Networked and Distributed Systems – FORTE 2007. XI, 375 pages. 2007.

Vol. 4573: M. Kauers, M. Kerber, R. Miner, W. Windsteiger (Eds.), Towards Mechanized Mathematical Assistants. XIII, 407 pages. 2007. (Sublibrary LNAI).

Vol. 4549: J. Aspnes, C. Scheideler, A. Arora, S. Madden (Eds.), Distributed Computing in Sensor Systems. XIII, 417 pages. 2007.

Vol. 4547: C. Carlet, B. Sunar (Eds.), Arithmetic of Finite Fields. XI, 355 pages. 2007.

Vol. 4543: A.K. Bandara, M. Burgess (Eds.), Inter-Domain Management. XII, 237 pages. 2007.

Vol. 4542: P. Sawyer, B. Paech, P. Heymans (Eds.), Requirements Engineering: Foundation for Software Quality. IX, 384 pages. 2007.

Vol. 4541: T. Okadome, T. Yamazaki, M. Makhtari (Eds.), Pervasive Computing for Quality of Life Enhancement. IX, 248 pages. 2007.

Vol. 4539: N.H. Bshouty, C. Gentile (Eds.), Learning Theory. XII, 634 pages. 2007. (Sublibrary LNAI).

Vol. 4538: F. Escolano, M. Vento (Eds.), Graph-Based Representations in Pattern Recognition. XII, 416 pages. 2007.

Vol. 4537: K.C.-C. Chang, W. Wang, L. Chen, C.A. Ellis, C.-H. Hsu, A.C. Tsoi, H. Wang (Eds.), Advances in Web and Network Technologies, and Information Management. XXIII, 707 pages. 2007.

Vol. 4534: I. Tomkos, F. Neri, J. Solé Pareta, X. Masip Bruin, S. Sánchez Lopez (Eds.), Optical Network Design and Modeling. XI, 460 pages. 2007.

Vol. 4531: J. Indulska, K. Raymond (Eds.), Distributed Applications and Interoperable Systems. XI, 337 pages. 2007.

Vol. 4530: D.H. Akehurst, R. Vogel, R.F. Paige (Eds.), Model Driven Architecture- Foundations and Applications. X, 219 pages. 2007.

Vol. 4529: P. Melin, O. Castillo, L.T. Aguilar, J. Kacprzyk, W. Pedrycz (Eds.), Foundations of Fuzzy Logic and Soft Computing. XIX, 830 pages. 2007. (Sublibrary LNAI).

Vol. 4528: J. Mira, J.R. Álvarez (Eds.), Nature Inspired Problem-Solving Methods in Knowledge Engineering, Part II. XXII, 650 pages. 2007.

Vol. 4527: J. Mira, J.R. Álvarez (Eds.), Bio-inspired Modeling of Cognitive Tasks, Part I. XXII, 630 pages. 2007.

Vol. 4526: M. Malek, M. Reitenspieß, A. van Moorsel (Eds.), Service Availability. X, 155 pages. 2007.

Vol. 4525: C. Demetrescu (Ed.), Experimental Algorithms. XIII, 448 pages. 2007.

Vol. 4524: M. Marchiori, J.Z. Pan, C.d.S. Marie (Eds.), Web Reasoning and Rule Systems. XI, 382 pages. 2007.

Vol. 4523: Y.-H. Lee, H.-N. Kim, J. Kim, Y. Park, L.T. Yang, S.W. Kim (Eds.), Embedded Software and Systems. XIX, 829 pages. 2007.

Vol. 4522: B.K. Ersbøll, K.S. Pedersen (Eds.), Image Analysis. XVIII, 989 pages. 2007.

Vol. 4521: J. Katz, M. Yung (Eds.), Applied Cryptography and Network Security. XIII, 498 pages. 2007.

Vol. 4519: E. Franconi, M. Kifer, W. May (Eds.), The Semantic Web: Research and Applications. XVIII, 830 pages. 2007.

Vol. 4517: F. Boavida, E. Monteiro, S. Mascolo, Y. Koucheryavy (Eds.), Wired/Wireless Internet Communications. XIV, 382 pages. 2007.

Vol. 4516: L. Mason, T. Drwiega, J. Yan (Eds.), Managing Traffic Performance in Converged Networks. XXIII, 1191 pages. 2007.

Vol. 4515: M. Naor (Ed.), Advances in Cryptology - EUROCRYPT 2007. XIII, 591 pages. 2007.

Vol. 4514: S.N. Artemov, A. Nerode (Eds.), Logical Foundations of Computer Science. XI, 513 pages. 2007.

Vol. 4513: M. Fischetti, D.P. Williamson (Eds.), Integer Programming and Combinatorial Optimization. IX, 500 pages. 2007.

Vol. 4510: P. Van Hentenryck, L. Wolsey (Eds.), Integration of AI and OR Techniques in Constraint Programming for Combinatorial Optimization Problems. X, 391 pages. 2007.

Vol. 4509: Z. Kobti, D. Wu (Eds.), Advances in Artificial Intelligence. XII, 552 pages. 2007. (Sublibrary LNAI).

Vol. 4508: M.-Y. Kao, X.-Y. Li (Eds.), Algorithmic Aspects in Information and Management. VIII, 428 pages. 2007.

Vol. 4507: F. Sandoval, A. Prieto, J. Cabestany, M. Graña (Eds.), Computational and Ambient Intelligence. XXVI, 1167 pages. 2007.

Vol. 4506: D. Zeng, I. Gotham, K. Komatsu, C. Lynch, M. Thurmond, D. Madigan, B. Lober, J. Kvach, H. Chen (Eds.), Intelligence and Security Informatics: Biosurveillance. XI, 234 pages. 2007.

Vol. 4505: G. Dong, X. Lin, W. Wang, Y. Yang, J.X. Yu (Eds.), Advances in Data and Web Management. XXII, 896 pages. 2007.

Vol. 4504: J. Huang, R. Kowalczyk, Z. Maamar, D. Martin, I. Müller, S. Stoutenburg, K.P. Sycara (Eds.), Service-Oriented Computing: Agents, Semantics, and Engineering. X, 175 pages. 2007.

Vol. 4501: J. Marques-Silva, K.A. Sakallah (Eds.), Theory and Applications of Satisfiability Testing – SAT 2007. XI, 384 pages. 2007.

Vol. 4500: N. Streitz, A. Kameas, I. Mavrommati (Eds.), The Disappearing Computer. XVIII, 304 pages. 2007.

Vol. 4499: Y.Q. Shi (Ed.), Transactions on Data Hiding and Multimedia Security II. IX, 117 pages. 2007.

Vol. 4497: S.B. Cooper, B. Löwe, A. Sorbi (Eds.), Computation and Logic in the Real World. XVIII, 826 pages. 2007.

Vol. 4496: N.T. Nguyen, A. Grzech, R.J. Howlett, L.C. Jain (Eds.), Agent and Multi-Agent Systems: Technologies and Applications. XXI, 1046 pages. 2007. (Sublibrary LNAI).

Vol. 4495: J. Krogstie, A. Opdahl, G. Sindre (Eds.), Advanced Information Systems Engineering. XVI, 606 pages. 2007.

Vol. 4494: H. Jin, O.F. Rana, Y. Pan, V.K. Prasanna (Eds.), Algorithms and Architectures for Parallel Processing. XIV, 508 pages. 2007.

Vol. 4493: D. Liu, S. Fei, Z. Hou, H. Zhang, C. Sun (Eds.), Advances in Neural Networks – ISNN 2007, Part III. XXVI, 1215 pages. 2007.

Vol. 4492: D. Liu, S. Fei, Z. Hou, H. Zhang, C. Sun (Eds.), Advances in Neural Networks – ISNN 2007, Part II. XXVII, 1321 pages. 2007.

Vol. 4491: D. Liu, S. Fei, Z.-G. Hou, H. Zhang, C. Sun (Eds.), Advances in Neural Networks – ISNN 2007, Part I. LIV, 1365 pages. 2007.

Vol. 4490: Y. Shi, G.D. van Albada, J. Dongarra, P.M.A. Sloot (Eds.), Computational Science – ICCS 2007, Part IV. XXXVII, 1211 pages. 2007.

Vol. 4489: Y. Shi, G.D. van Albada, J. Dongarra, P.M.A. Sloot (Eds.), Computational Science – ICCS 2007, Part III. XXXVII, 1257 pages. 2007.

Vol. 4488: Y. Shi, G.D. van Albada, J. Dongarra, P.M.A. Sloot (Eds.), Computational Science – ICCS 2007, Part II. XXXV, 1251 pages. 2007.

Vol. 4487: Y. Shi, G.D. van Albada, J. Dongarra, P.M.A. Sloot (Eds.), Computational Science – ICCS 2007, Part I. LXXXI, 1275 pages. 2007.

Vol. 4486: M. Bernardo, J. Hillston (Eds.), Formal Methods for Performance Evaluation. VII, 469 pages. 2007.

Vol. 4485: F. Sgallari, A. Murli, N. Paragios (Eds.), Scale Space and Variational Methods in Computer Vision. XV, 931 pages. 2007.

Vol. 4484: J.-Y. Cai, S.B. Cooper, H. Zhu (Eds.), Theory and Applications of Models of Computation. XIII, 772 pages. 2007.

Vol. 4483: C. Baral, G. Brewka, J. Schlipf (Eds.), Logic Programming and Nonmonotonic Reasoning. IX, 327 pages. 2007. (Sublibrary LNAI).

Vol. 4482: A. An, J. Stefanowski, S. Ramanna, C.J. Butz, W. Pedrycz, G. Wang (Eds.), Rough Sets, Fuzzy Sets, Data Mining and Granular Computing. XIV, 585 pages. 2007. (Sublibrary LNAI).

Vol. 4481: J. Yao, P. Lingras, W.-Z. Wu, M. Szczuka, N.J. Cercone, D. Ślęzak (Eds.), Rough Sets and Knowledge Technology. XIV, 576 pages. 2007. (Sublibrary LNAI).

Vol. 4480: A. LaMarca, M. Langheinrich, K.N. Truong (Eds.), Pervasive Computing. XIII, 369 pages. 2007.

Vol. 4479: I.F. Akyildiz, R. Sivakumar, E. Ekici, J.C.d. Oliveira, J. McNair (Eds.), NETWORKING 2007. Ad Hoc and Sensor Networks, Wireless Networks, Next Generation Internet. XXVII, 1252 pages. 2007.

Vol. 4478: J. Martí, J.M. Benedí, A.M. Mendonça, J. Serrat (Eds.), Pattern Recognition and Image Analysis, Part II. XXVII, 657 pages. 2007.

Vol. 4477: J. Martí, J.M. Benedí, A.M. Mendonça, J. Serrat (Eds.), Pattern Recognition and Image Analysis, Part I. XXVII, 625 pages. 2007.

Vol. 4476: V. Gorodetsky, C. Zhang, V.A. Skormin, L. Cao (Eds.), Autonomous Intelligent Systems: Multi-Agents and Data Mining. XIII, 323 pages. 2007. (Sublibrary LNAI).

Vol. 4475: P. Crescenzi, G. Prencipe, G. Pucci (Eds.), Fun with Algorithms. X, 273 pages. 2007.

Vol. 4474: G. Prencipe, S. Zaks (Eds.), Structural Information and Communication Complexity. XI, 342 pages. 2007.

Vol. 4472: M. Haindl, J. Kittler, F. Roli (Eds.), Multiple Classifier Systems. XI, 524 pages. 2007.

Vol. 4471: P. Cesar, K. Chorianopoulos, J.F. Jensen (Eds.), Interactive TV: a Shared Experience. XIII, 236 pages. 2007.

Vol. 4470: Q. Wang, D. Pfahl, D.M. Raffo (Eds.), Software Process Dynamics and Agility. XI, 346 pages. 2007.

Vol. 4469: K.-C. Hui, Z. Pan, R.C.-k. Chung, C.C.L. Wang, X. Jin, S. Göbel, E.C.-L. Li (Eds.), Technologies for E-Learning and Digital Entertainment. XVIII, 974 pages. 2007.

Vol. 4468: M.M. Bonsangue, E.B. Johnsen (Eds.), Formal Methods for Open Object-Based Distributed Systems. X, 317 pages. 2007.

Vol. 4467: A.L. Murphy, J. Vitek (Eds.), Coordination Models and Languages. X, 325 pages. 2007.

Vol. 4466: F.B. Sachse, G. Seemann (Eds.), Functional Imaging and Modeling of the Heart. XV, 486 pages. 2007.

Vol. 4465: T. Chahed, B. Tuffin (Eds.), Network Control and Optimization. XIII, 305 pages. 2007.

Vol. 4464: E. Dawson, D.S. Wong (Eds.), Information Security Practice and Experience. XIII, 361 pages. 2007.

Vol. 4463: I. Măndoiu, A. Zelikovsky (Eds.), Bioinformatics Research and Applications. XV, 653 pages. 2007. (Sublibrary LNBI).

Vol. 4462: D. Sauveron, K. Markantonakis, A. Bilas, J.-J. Quisquater (Eds.), Information Security Theory and Practices. XII, 255 pages. 2007.

Vol. 4459: C. Cérin, K.-C. Li (Eds.), Advances in Grid and Pervasive Computing. XVI, 759 pages. 2007.